# COBOL

## Structured Programming Techniques for Solving Problems

## Other fine titles available from boyd & fraser

Introduction to Computers and Microcomputer Applications
Microcomputer Applications: Using Small Systems Software, Second Edition
Microcomputer Productivity Tools
Microcomputer Applications: A Practical Approach
Microcomputer Systems Management and Applications
Mastering Lotus 1-2-3®
Using Enable®: An Introduction to Integrated Software
PC-DOS®/MS-DOS® Simplified

## Computer Information Systems

Database Systems: Management and Design
Microcomputer Database Management Using dBASE III PLUS®
Microcomputer Database Management Using R:BASE System V®
dBASE III PLUS® Programming
A Guide to SQL
Applications Software Programming with Fourth-Generation Languages
Fundamentals of Systems Analysis with Application Design
Office Automation: An Information Systems Approach
Data Communications for Business
Learning Computer Programming: Structured Logic Algorithms, and Flowcharting
COBOL: Structured Programming Techniques for Solving Problems
Comprehensive Structured COBOL
Fundamentals of Structured COBOL
Advanced Structured COBOL: Batch and Interactive
BASIC Fundamentals and Style
Structured BASIC Fundamentals and Style for the IBM® PC and Compatibles
Applesoft BASIC Fundamentals and Style
Complete BASIC for the Short Course
Structuring Programs in Microsoft BASIC

## Shelly and Cashman Titles

Computer Concepts with Microcomputer Applications (Lotus 1-2-3®
  and VP-Planner Plus® versions)
Computer Concepts
Learning to Use WordPerfect®, Lotus 1-2-3®, and dBASE III PLUS®
Learning to Use WordPerfect®, VP-Planner Plus®, and dBASE III PLUS®
Learning to Use WordPerfect®
Learning to Use Lotus 1-2-3®
Learning to Use VP-Planner Plus®
Learning to Use dBASE III PLUS®
Computer Fundamentals with Application Software
Learning to Use SuperCalc®3, dBASE III®, and WordStar® 3.3: An Introduction
Learning to Use SuperCalc®3: An Introduction
Learning to Use dBASE III®: An Introduction
Learning to Use WordStar® 3.3: An Introduction
BASIC Programming for the IBM Personal Computer
Structured COBOL: Pseudocode Edition
Structured COBOL: Flowchart Edition

# COBOL

## Structured Programming Techniques for Solving Problems

**George C. Fowler**

Texas A&M University

COPYRIGHT 1990
BOYD & FRASER PUBLISHING COMPANY
BOSTON

**CREDITS:**

**Publisher:** Thomas Walker
**Editor:** Sarah Grover
**Production Editor:** Donna Villanucci
**Director of Production:** Becky Herrington
**Director of Manufacturing:** Dean Sherman
**Interior Design:** Becky Herrington
**Cover Design/Computer-Generated Art:** Ken Russo
**Typesetting:** UNICOMP
**Cover Photography:** Jon Goell
**Text Illustration:** Anne Craig

Manufactured in the United States of America

**Library of Congress Cataloging-in-Publication Data**

```
Fowler, George C., 1943-
    COBOL : structured programming techniques for solving problems /
  George C. Fowler.
        p.   cm.
    Includes index.
    ISBN 0-87835-329-1
    1. COBOL (Computer program language)  2. Structured programming.
  I. Title.
  QA76.73.C25F69   1989
  005.13'3--dc19                                      88-38171
                                                          CIP
```

34567H543210

## Dedication

To my wife, Tia,
my son, Michael,
and my former students.

# Brief Contents

## THE FUNDAMENTALS OF COBOL

## THE REAL WORLD OF COBOL

## PROJECT SETS

## DATA FILES

## APPENDICES

# Contents

## THE FUNDAMENTALS OF COBOL

### CHAPTER 1
### INTRODUCTION TO COBOL: THE COMMON BUSINESS-ORIENTED LANGUAGE

### CHAPTER 2
### STRUCTURED PROGRAMMING

## CHAPTER 3
# IDENTIFICATION AND ENVIRONMENT DIVISIONS

## CHAPTER 4
# DATA DIVISION

## CHAPTER 5
# PROCEDURE DIVISION

## CHAPTER 6
# PROCESSING A SEQUENTIAL FILE—DETAIL AND TOTAL TIMES

# THE REAL WORLD OF COBOL

## CHAPTER 10
### COPY LIBRARIES AND THE REAL WORLD OF COBOL

## CHAPTER 11
### TABLES

## CHAPTER 12
### SORTING

## CHAPTER 16
## SUBPROGRAMMING

# PROJECT SETS

## PROJECT A
## THE PROJECT MANAGEMENT SYSTEM

## PROJECT B
## THE EMPLOYEE SYSTEM

# DATA FILES

# APPENDICES

## APPENDIX A
## FLOWCHARTING  623

## APPENDIX B
## RESERVED WORDS  625

## APPENDIX C
## SAMPLE DOCUMENTATION PACKAGE—CIRCLE CLUB PROGRAM

## APPENDIX D
## CODING AND DOCUMENTATION STANDARDS

## APPENDIX E
## REPORT WRITER

## APPENDIX F
## INTERACTIVE PROGRAMMING

## APPENDIX G
## ANSWERS TO EVEN-NUMBERED CHAPTER REVIEW QUESTIONS  693

# PREFACE

This textbook can be used in a one-semester introductory COBOL programming course, or a two-semester course covering both introductory and advanced COBOL programming. It is also appropriate for independent study at any level. The educational environment may include technical or corporate training, 2-year colleges, and 4-year institutions of higher learning. The objectives of this textbook are:

- To provide students with comprehensive instruction in structured COBOL programming techniques.
- To encourage students to use COBOL in order to solve the kind of problems they are likely to encounter in today's corporate and industrial environments.
- To familiarize students with many "real world" features of COBOL programming including libraries, JCL, coding standards, documentation standards, and system utilities.

## WHY ANOTHER COBOL BOOK?

Granted, there are many COBOL books on the market today. So, why another? Many existing textbooks are lacking in the real-world flavor that adequately equips students to use COBOL in order to solve problems. A textbook that incorporates some of the new COBOL elements, such as COBOL '85 and interactive/PC COBOL, is needed. Also needed is a book that allows students to make an easy transition from classroom to the corporate world.

## A COMPREHENSIVE BOOK

COBOL provides both introductory and advanced material. The book is divided into two parts. "The Fundamentals of COBOL," (Chapters 1 through 9) and "The Real World of COBOL," (Chapters 10 through 16). In general, these parts correspond to the material likely to be covered in a one-semester, introductory COBOL programming course, or in a comprehensive, two-semester course sequence covering both introductory and advanced programming. A section called "Data Files" provides students with all of the data sets used in the programming assignments at the end of most chapters.

The "Project Sets" section of the text contains two complete programming project sets for ongoing use throughout the semester. Chapters in this text conclude with Programming Project Assignments that require students to test their programming skills using these Project Sets to build a complete system. Instructors may select one of the two projects for team or individual use throughout the semester. Instructors may use these projects either as regular assignments or in conjunction with the Copy Library Topic. The projects are provided on diskette as ASCII files which can be modified, offering the instructor complete flexibility.

Regardless of whether this book is used for one or two semesters, it is designed to outlive the student's classroom experience and to serve as a valuable reference text for the student's future use as a business programming professional.

## MAXIMUM FLEXIBILITY

COBOL allows instructors the maximum flexibility when preparing their course outline. For example, in the introductory course, instructors may elect to cover Chapters 1 through 9, "The Fundamentals of COBOL," and that part of Chapter 11 (Tables) that is appropriate for their course. Chapter 10 (Libraries) could be introduced in the first course, as well.

The advanced course could also be handled in one of several ways. Chapter 11 (Tables) might be used to begin the advanced course, since part of the chapter is review. Then the remainder of the chapters, 12 through 16, could be covered. If an instructor wishes to use the Project Sets, Chapter 10 could be the first chapter for the advanced course. However, Chapter 10 may be omitted without loss of continuity.

Two other features offer additional flexibility. They are Appendix E "Report Writer," and Appendix F "Interactive Programming on the PC." These appendices are self-contained and may be incorporated in a course as best suits the needs of students. For instance, interactive COBOL and the use of the Screen Section is introduced in Chapter 4 with the other Data Division entries. If an instructor is inclined to make the course more PC-oriented, he or she might cover the appendix material at this point, thereby allowing the assignments to be interactive.

If an instructor wants to use the Report Writer feature of COBOL, he or she might introduce it with Chapter 5 or 6 for writing simple reports, or might wait and introduce it as a powerful way of handling control-break logic in Chapter 9.

## DISTINGUISHING FEATURES

### Real-World Approach

This text takes a real-world approach to COBOL. This is particularly evident with the copy library topics introduced in Chapter 10. This chapter stresses the use of libraries for system development. The use of libraries and subprogramming is also discussed from the real-world view of enhancing system development and maintenance. Another aspect of the real world for those using the MVS operating system on an IBM main-frame is the incorporation of JCL and system utilities. These topics enhance the student's ability to make a successful transition from the classroom to the business world.

### Copy Libraries

This topic is essential in today's business environment. System development with project teams is greatly enhanced with the use of copy libraries.

In the real world, system development fully utilizes copy libraries. Project leaders develop the library elements, files, records, procedures, and the data dictionary for use by the programmers. This environment may be simulated by use of the two complete project sets included in the text.

### Complete COBOL Environment on Diskette

For convenience, the Project Sets and the Data Files found at the end of the book are available on diskette from Boyd & Fraser Publishing Company. For each project, the diskette contains the copy library elements, the corresponding data dictionaries, data sets, and programming assignments. These may be uploaded to the mainframe or PC library to allow the students to use the copy library feature throughout the advanced course. However, even if the copy libraries are not used, the projects may still be used. Students would simply key the library elements themselves.

### Complete Sample Documentation Package

The Circle Club Program, contained in Appendix C, is a complete sample documentation package that provides students with an example for class as well as a real-world example. This package includes the problem statement, hierarchy chart, IPO chart, flowchart, program listing, and results.

The Circle Club Program is referenced throughout the text. Primarily it is used as an illustration of many of the fundamental COBOL features. This program is also available from Boyd & Fraser Publishing Company on diskette, thus allowing an instructor the ability to tailor the sample program to fit his or her course.

### Problem-Solving Approach

Where possible in the chapters, problems are posed that lead to the examination of certain COBOL features (tools). This is a more productive approach than introducing a new COBOL tool and then trying to find a problem to solve. Using a problem to drive the discussion of each COBOL tool provides students with a reason for studying the feature and greatly enhances the overall learning process.

### Readability

The text is written in an informal conversational style. Students will find that this communicative tone enhances readability and comprehension of the material.

### End-of-Chapter Programs

As an aid to the student, complete running programs are provided at the end of appropriate chapters. These actual running programs are identified for the student by appearing on "computer paper" at the end of the chapter. These programs and their data sets are also available on diskette. Again, this allows instructors to use these programs in class as they are or to change them as desired.

### Maintenance

One of the areas graduates become involved in when they go to work is program maintenance. Taking existing programs and making changes is an entirely different experience than writing programs. The end-of-chapter programs may be used to expose students to program maintenance.

These programs are available to the instructor on diskette and may be uploaded onto the main system. Students may then be given modification specifications as assignments.

### COBOL '85

Throughout this textbook many of the COBOL '85 features such as scope indicators and EVALUATE are presented. Particular topics are also introduced to show the enhancements in COBOL. For instance, the in-line PERFORM is shown to demonstrate how more readable/maintainable code is produced using this '85 enhancement.

### Interactive COBOL/PC COBOL

The interactive features of COBOL are discussed with a primary focus on the PC. A full appendix is included that discusses many of the screen features of two popular PC COBOL compilers. While the topic is in an appendix, it is not ignored in the main text. In fact, the topic of interactive programming and the screen section of COBOL are introduced with the Data Division in Chapter 4. If an instructor wants to teach COBOL on a PC, then the appendix can be required at this point in the course. The rest of the course material using the text can be covered with few modifications. In fact, with most PC COBOL compilers, the ability to incorporate the copy library feature of the text is also possible.

### Programming Standards

In an attempt to further acquaint students with a real-world programming environment, a set of documentation and coding are provided in Appendix D.

## ANCILLARY MATERIALS

A comprehensive offering of instructor's resource materials are available to accompany *COBOL: Structured Programming Techniques for Solving Problems.* Information concerning how you may receive the valuable teaching aids listed here can be obtained by writing or calling Boyd & Fraser Publishing Company, 20 Park Plaza, Boston, MA 02116, (toll free) 1–800–225–3782.

### Instructor's Diskettes

Two instructor's diskettes are available for use with this textbook. Each diskette is provided for optional classroom use and may be uploaded onto a mainframe.

The first diskette contains all of the material for the Project Sets section of this book, including the data dictionary, library elements, data sets, and programming assignments for each of the two major projects. It also includes the Data Files for all end-of-chapter programming assignments. Finally, it includes The Circle Club Program, the complete sample documentation package used as an example throughout the text.

The second diskette contains all of the complete, running programs included at the end of most chapters. These programs may be used as examples "as is" or may be modified to suit the instructor's specific needs.

### Instructor's Manual

This valuable supplement contains chapter objectives and summaries; suggested teaching approaches and teaching tips; test questions; transparency masters; and answers to even-numbered questions.

### ProTest

Boyd & Fraser's state-of-the-art text-generating software, ProTest, has been designed specifically for this book. ProTest is an easy-to-use, menu-driven system that is supplied on an IBM-PC compatible diskette. ProTest allows instructors to create a customized test on the PC in a matter of minutes. ProTest provides true/false, multiple choice, and fill-in questions. Users may also enter their own questions into the test bank. It runs on any IBM PS/2, or compatible system with two floppy disk drives or a hard disk.

## ACKNOWLEDGMENTS

Many people deserve credit for their input, insights, and guidance in helping to develop this book. My thanks go to the following people who reviewed the book: Joseph Adamski, Grand Valley State University; Victor Barlow, Purdue University; Mark D'Cunha, University of Texas–Arlington; Thomas Dillon, Salisbury State College; Richard Discenza, University of Colorado; John Haney, South Western Oregon Community College; Cary Hughes, North Texas State University; Alden Lorents, Northern Arizona University; Ed Mooney, Quinnipiac College; Joan Pierson, James Madison University; Jerry Sitek, Southern Illinois University; and Pat Vacca, El Camino College.

Many keystrokes (approximately two million) are represented on the pages of this book. This book would never have been completed without the word processing help of Lica Hoekstra, Susan Edmisson, and Tia Fowler. I also wish to thank two of my graduate students, Roy Dejoie and Kevin McKenzie, who helped with the end-of-chapter programs; these programs are an important part of the book.

Without the support, understanding, and guidance of the Boyd & Fraser professionals, this project would not have been the wonderful experience it has been. Thanks to Tom Walker, Sarah Grover, Donna Villanucci and all the others at Boyd & Fraser.

My thanks go out to all of my students at Texas A&M University and Northern Arizona University. This textbook represents the many years I have taught COBOL with their help, input, patience and criticism.

My wife, Tia, showed patience and loving support; without her this textbook would still be a dream and not a reality. To my son, Michael, I promise that I will be as understanding of your needs as you were of mine during my writing.

George C. Fowler
College Station
January, 1989

# THE FUNDAMENTALS

# OF COBOL

# INTRODUCTION TO COBOL: THE COMMON BUSINESS-ORIENTED LANGUAGE

**OBJECTIVES**    In this chapter you will discover many of the factors that led to the development of the COBOL language. You will trace COBOL's life beginning with the original committee and going through the new COBOL '85 compiler.

You will also see that COBOL had several predecessors. These included compilers from UNIVAC and IBM.

After studying this chapter you will understand why COBOL's popularity grew rapidly. This popularity is evident even today with the newly released '85 compiler and with the increasing interest for COBOL on the personal computer.

In this chapter we will examine COBOL's language structure, its English-like syntax and punctuation and its use of files, records, fields and characters. I will also establish a standard notation so that you may study the command syntax more easily.

## TOPICS

- **COBOL's history**
- **the CODASYL committee**
- **design criteria in COBOL**
- **business data processing vs. scientific data processing**
- **COBOL's structure, syntax, and punctuation**

## KEY WORDS

- **COBOL '68, '74, '85**
- **FACT**
- **COMTRAN**
- **AIMACO**
- **Flowmatic**
- **ANSI COBOL**
- **Grace Hopper**
- **Common Business-Oriented Language (COBOL)**

## THE BEGINNING

Prior to the birth of COBOL, programming languages were highly machine dependent. They were, in fact, machine languages, or they were designed for scientific/mathematical problem solving (for example, FORTRAN). Some were both machine dependent and formula related. However, a need had developed for a programming language that was not machine dependent and that could handle large amounts of data. Picture the situation that our armed forces were in when they wanted to automate their payrolls. Uncle Sam was the largest user of computers at the time, and because of the bid process, the federal government had installed different kinds of computers at bases throughout the world. Systems were being developed at these various locations to be used by all units of the armed forces. You can see the problem: A payroll system developed with hundreds of man hours and thousands of dollars on one manufacturer's computer would not run when sent to another base with a different computer. More hundreds of man hours and thousands of dollars later, the modified system would run on the second computer. Obviously, this was not the right way to automate a payroll system.

The Department of Defense decided that a computer language that was common to all manufacturers' computers was needed. This would be a language that would allow systems developed on an IBM to run on a Honeywell or a Burroughs, and so on.

The first meeting aimed at laying the foundation for a common language was held in Philadelphia in April, 1959. This meeting led to the CODASYL Committee (*Co*nference on *Da*ta *Sy*stem *L*anguages). The executive committee was made up of representatives from government and industry.

### COBOL Compilers

Grace Hopper is the most widely recognized participant among the COBOL pioneers. She is known as the Mother of COBOL for all her contributions to the development of the language and to the establishment of the standards for COBOL. In fact, the whole idea of compilers is attributed to Grace Hopper.

Grace Hopper during a visit to Texas A&M University

However, contrary to common belief, COBOL was not the first business language. The first language endorsed by a CODASYL subcommittee was FACT. Both

FACT and COBOL were preceded by Flowmatic (from UNIVAC), COMTRAN (from IBM), and AIMACO (from Air Materials Command).

**'68 Compiler.**     All these efforts finally led to the first COBOL compiler. . . commonly known as COBOL '68. In truth, COBOL '68 had several predecessors, COBOL '60, COBOL '61, COBOL '61 Extended, and COBOL '65. However, COBOL '68 was the first American National Standards Institute (ANSI) standard compiler. Hence the common belief that COBOL '68 was the first.

COBOL's popularity as a business language grew by leaps and bounds. You can imagine why industry and business embraced COBOL. A single compiler meant only one language for systems people to keep up with. One compiler meant that systems would run on all their computers, no matter the manufacturer, as long as a COBOL compiler was available. This translated into savings and increased profits; therefore, business eagerly committed to COBOL.

**'74 Compiler.**     The next major step after COBOL '68 was the adoption of the COBOL '74 compiler. While COBOL was doing so well, operating systems were also growing up. Some operating system changes led to patchwork changes in the '68 compiler. Of significance was indexed file handling, in particular, ISAM (Indexed Sequential Access Method). The '74 compiler allowed for a slightly easier, more direct use of ISAM files.

**'85 Compiler.**     The latest compiler, COBOL '85, marks a major change in COBOL. It reflects efforts to make COBOL and structured programming more compatible. It includes the use of the END IF, END PERFORM, END READ, a direct case structure and other enhancements which will be covered throughout the text.

**COBOL'S Future.**     A new compiler with these enhancements speaks to the future role of COBOL. Much is being said about other languages and, in particular, the fourth generation languages (4GLs). While they are growing in popularity, business has too large an investment in COBOL to make wholesale conversion, and 4GLs have a hard time in an environment that may process five million transactions daily. Both of these facts say that COBOL will continue to be very popular. In fact, it is estimated that 70% of all business systems are written in COBOL. A recent survey in a PC oriented publication showed that 7% of all PC systems are written in COBOL. This shows the continued popularity of COBOL even in an environment that just recently included production quality COBOL compilers.

### The Making of COBOL. . .Design Criteria

The creation of COBOL didn't just happen. Much thought and work went into it. Certain criteria were established for the design of COBOL. These included:

1. A common language
2. Documentation
3. Ease of reading
4. Business orientation
5. Ease of update and revision

**Common Language.**     Let's take a closer look at these criteria. The need for a common language has already been shown. But don't misunderstand the meaning of common language. This does not mean all computers have to be the same. Instead, each manufacturer has to have a COBOL compiler that will take a COBOL source program and convert it to the manufacture's particular machine language. So the key was to have a standard language for which manufacturers could develop compilers. Figure 1.1 shows this environment.

**FIGURE 1.1**
Relationship of COBOL
Compiler to Source Program
and Computer

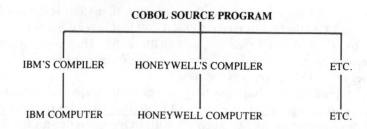

The common element is the COBOL language. I should mention that each manufacturer enhances its compilers with special nonstandard features called extensions. This should not surprise you. We live in a competitive world, and each manufacturer wants to be better than the next, so they all try to enhance their compilers. However, using extensions has both good and bad points. The good: They usually take advantage of the manufacturer's architecture. This will make coding some algorithms easier and more efficient. The bad: The extensions are usually machine-dependent. Therefore, they will not run on another manufacturer's machine. That's not a problem unless you want to change manufacturers.

## TIP

**Using extensions should be the exception to the rule. I have seen conversion problems grow in complexity just because of extensions.**

**Self-documenting.** The second criterion for a self-documenting language was met with great enthusiasm by all. Finally, a language that documented itself! Well, not really. Using the features of COBOL allows the programmer to document as he or she codes. At the time BASIC allowed one-character variable names and FORTRAN allowed for seven. COBOL allows for up to thirty (30) characters. No longer would we need to say:

$$G = R * H \qquad \text{(early BASIC)}$$

or

$$GP = WAGE * HOURS \qquad \text{(FORTRAN)}$$

We could say:

```
COMPUTE GROSS-PAY = RATE-OF-PAY * HOURS-WORKED
```

See what the designers meant about self-documenting?

**English-like.** I think the example above also illustrates the criterion that the language be English-like and therefore easy to read. However, that's not the only way COBOL is easy to read. You will soon see that COBOL's structure includes such English structures as paragraphs, sentences and statements. COBOL's sentences also have a familiar structure. They contain verbs like ADD, SUBTRACT, MOVE, READ, and

COMPUTE, and punctuation including periods, commas and more. Look at this example:

        C = C + 1            (BASIC)

vs.

        ADD 1 TO KOUNT       (COBOL)

Which is easier to read and understand? I think we would all agree the COBOL example is. (You might be asking why count is spelled with a "K". Well, COUNT spelled with a "C" is a reserved word in COBOL, a word that has a predefined meaning and use in COBOL and cannot be used as a variable name. We will see many other such examples throughout the text.)

**Business-oriented.**    When the designers established the criterion that COBOL be business-oriented, they had in mind a certain type of data processing problem. Up to the 1950s and 1960s, the most popular high-level language was FORTRAN. FORTRAN was considered a scientific language. It still is. So what is a scientific language as opposed to a business language? It probably would help to examine Figure 1.2.

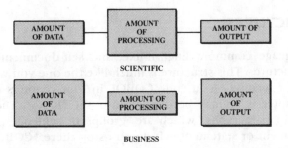

**FIGURE 1.2**
Business vs. Scientific Computing

Interpreting Figure 1.2, we could say that scientific data processing is characterized by relatively small amounts of input and output, with a comparatively larger amount of processing. On the other hand, business data processing has a relatively large amount of input/output compared to the amount of processing. Therefore, COBOL had to be able to handle large data files for both input and output, but the processing abilities did not have to be as extensive as those of FORTRAN. COBOL could do all math and logic, but a library of math routines was not included. FORTRAN has such a library which includes routines for sin, cos, and tan for instance.

Although COBOL '85 still does not include such a library, one of the revisions of COBOL '85 will probably include the addition of a scientific subroutine library.

**Easily-changed.**    The last criterion, ease of updating and revision, applies more to the COBOL language as a whole. The other criteria dealt directly with components of the language, but this criterion applies to the problem-solving tools the language provides to its users, and to their effectiveness. I think I can argue both sides of whether this criterion has been achieved for COBOL.

We have had three ANSI compilers, COBOL '68, '74, and '85, in nearly 20 years. It might seem either that the committees did a fantastic job of design, or it takes a long time to make changes. Come to think of it, both might be true. The design of COBOL has stood the test of time, and it still does. Changes were made to the language along the way. There were changes to allow for index (ISAM) file use, for instance. This was done easily and did not require a full new compiler. That was the design criterion in action.

On the other hand, a major upgrade like COBOL '85 might have been needed because the design criterion was not met previously. The trials and tribulations of COBOL '85's development make interesting reading. Garfunkel, in *The COBOL '85 Example Book* , calls the experience "the Caesarean Birth of COBOL '85." In fact, COBOL '85 was known as COBOL '8X for several years because we did not know when the final version would be accepted and would become the new ANSI COBOL standard.

Even in spite of development problems with COBOL '85, most in the profession agree that the five design criteria were met. As you learn COBOL, I hope you will also agree that the criteria were achieved. Since like most students, if not all, you have probably cut your teeth on another language, probably BASIC, you will from time to time question the completeness of the list of criteria, or at least question Criteria 2 and 3. In order to make COBOL English-like *and* self-documenting, the designers made it almost necessary that all COBOL programs be long or at least longer than what you could code in BASIC. That's true; however, our role in the information industry is not finished with a running program. Someone will probably have to maintain that program, and a well-written, documented, English-like program will be easier to maintain.

## COBOL'S STRUCTURES

To make the language common, English-like, and self-documenting, the designers gave COBOL a structure. This structure is much like the one you would use to organize a paper you are writing. You code COBOL in four chapters called DIVISIONS. Each program chapter is or may be divided into SECTIONS. These SECTIONS are then organized into paragraphs, which are groups of sentences, each of which is made up of a statement or statements. It doesn't stop there. COBOL has its own format and punctuation rules: commas, periods, margins, name formation. It even has verbs.

I guess by now you're saying that COBOL sounds very much like English. You're right! But it should. COBOL is a language, and all languages have their structures, which include punctuation and syntax. Wasn't one of the design criteria that COBOL be English-like?

Well, I suppose the good news is that it is English-like, and the bad news is that it is English-like. Remember my saying that students feel that at least one criterion may be missing from the criteria list? That missing criterion is: The program must be long. However, long is not necessarily bad. If it is long and the programmer did not use the design elements of COBOL that make it English-like and self-documenting, then that's bad. But that's not COBOL's fault, that's the programmer's fault. Probably there are no standards for the programmer to follow in such cases.

## COBOL'S FOUR DIVISIONS

Let's turn our attention more fully to COBOL's structure and syntax. As we saw earlier, COBOL has four DIVISIONS: the IDENTIFICATION, ENVIRONMENT, DATA and PROCEDURE.

**IDENTIFICATION DIVISION.** The IDENTIFICATION DIVISION must be the first division. Its purpose is to allow the programmer to name the program and identify the programmer.

**ENVIRONMENT DIVISION.** The ENVIRONMENT DIVISION, which must be second, has its major function tied to the computer environment. Within this DIVISION, we identify the computers, hardware, and files we will need in the program.

**DATA DIVISION.** The third DIVISION is the DATA DIVISION. It contains the description of every data element to be used in the solution of the problem. We must provide a description of every data element. The only exceptions to this rule are literals—both numeric and non-numeric. COBOL not only wants the definitions, but expects us to provide information about the data relationships as well. For that reason we work with a particular data hierarchy in COBOL as illustrated below:

> Files
>> Records
>>> Fields
>>>> Characters

As you probably learned in your introductory data processing course, computer languages expect us to define our data files. COBOL is no different, and since files are collections of records, it expects us to define the records and in turn the fields that make up these records. Lastly we must specify the types of fields—numeric, alphabetic or alphanumeric.

**PROCEDURE DIVISION.** Finally, we arrive at the PROCEDURE DIVISION. In this division, we provide all the logic for the solution to the problem. This is where we show how all the data is to be manipulated to provide the desired results. This division is almost a one-for-one match between the flowchart entries and the statements in the PROCEDURE DIVISION. We will see the relationship in the next chapter when we look at flowcharting and other problem-solving tools.

**SECTIONS.** SECTIONS, or groups of paragraphs, are the next level of organization of the COBOL program. Unlike DIVISIONS, SECTIONS are not always required. In some cases they are required, and in other cases they may or may not be used at our discretion. Look at the CIRCLE CLUB PROGRAM (Appendix C), and you will notice that only the ENVIRONMENT and DATA DIVISIONS have SECTIONS. We could have used them in the PROCEDURE DIVISION for readability but they were not required, and I thought it was readable as it stood. We will see, however, in the chapter on sorting that we will be required to use SECTIONS in the PROCEDURE DIVISION.

**Paragraphs.** A group of related sentences make up a paragraph in English. A COBOL paragraph is also a group of sentences. You will notice that a COBOL paragraph has a label. It starts with a paragraph name. Look again at the CIRCLE CLUB program. You can easily find the DIVISION and SECTIONS because they have the labels of DIVISION and SECTION. This makes it easy for us to find the sections, but, what is more important, it makes it easy for the compiler. You will also notice that both are coded in the same margin. But, they are not alone. Notice the other item in the same margin that is not labeled DIVISION or SECTION: That's a paragraph name. If you will glance at the PROCEDURE DIVISION, you will see that I tend to use paragraph names that include the abbreviation PARA. That's just my way, and it is not required by the compiler. I just find it handy and nice.

**Sentences and Statements.**     So much for the paragraph name; what about the paragraph's contents? One or more sentences make up a paragraph's contents. (A side note here. COBOL requires at least one sentence in a paragraph; no empty paragraphs are allowed.)

A COBOL sentence is made of one or more statements and, in COBOL '74, it ends with a period. So,

```
ADD 1 TO KOUNT.
```

is a COBOL sentence made up of one statement, while

```
IF MAJOR  =  'ACCOUNTING'
      ADD  1  TO  ACCT-COUNT
      ADD GRADE-POINTS  TO  ACCT-GRADE-POINTS.
```

is also a COBOL sentence, but it's made up of three statements: one conditional statement and two ADDs.

We can find many other good examples in the CIRCLE CLUB program (Appendix C). Let's look at the PROGRAM-ID. Do you recognize "*BILLING*" as a sentence? Probably not, but it is. Most sentences in COBOL, however, start with some action word or what we call a verb—IF, READ, SELECT, PERFORM for example, and are easy to recognize. Take a look at Figure 1.3. It visually summarizes all the above.

**FIGURE 1.3**
**COBOL Example of PROCEDURE DIVISION Structure**

```
IDENTIFICATION DIVISION.
paragraph.
paragraph.
```
An example of a division with paragraphs and no sections.

```
ENVIRONMENT DIVISION.
SECTION.
paragraph.
SECTION.
paragraph.
```
An example of multiple sections in a division. These sections are made up of paragraphs.

```
DATA DIVISION.
SECTION.

SECTION.
```
If you look at the CIRCLE CLUB PROGRAM, you see there are two sections, but the other entries don't look like paragraphs. I'll explain that later, OK?

```
PROCEDURE DIVISION.

paragraph.

paragraph.
      sentence.
      sentence.
      statement
      statement.
```
This is the best English—like example of paragraphs, sentences and statements.

## PUNCTUATION AND SYNTAX

Now that we have looked at COBOL's overall structure of DIVISIONS, SECTIONS, paragraphs, sentences, and statements, let's consider how the COBOL compiler recognizes these and other elements of a COBOL program. As you do when you read other languages including English, the compiler expects certain word formations and sentence formations, and it also expects certain of these to be presented in appropriate margins with appropriate punctuation. (This continues to sound like a language class! In a way it is.)

### Forming Data Names

Like any language, COBOL has certain rules for making up or forming words. These COBOL words are known as data names. If this sounds different from your introduction to data processing class where you talked about variables, it's not really. A COBOL data name is functionally the same as a variable. Both are the names of locations in memory that contain data. Since sentences and statements are made up of words, this seems like a good place to start our discussion on how these words are written and punctuated.

A COBOL data name must be formed using the following rules:

- up to thirty (30) characters may be used
- all alphabetic characters, the numbers 0–9 and the hyphen may be used
- no special characters may be used
- no blanks may be embedded in the name
- the hyphen may not be the first or last character

Data names are not the only COBOL names. We have procedure names (also known as section and paragraph names), condition names, reserved words and figurative constants (names with predefined values). Furthermore, we also have the use of numeric and non-numeric literals in COBOL.

### A Data Name by Any Other Name is a . . .

Don't let this array of names, words and literals bother you. Their use comes naturally, and you must remember just a few rules. Even if you don't remember the rules to start with, the compiler will let you know. Section names, paragraph names and condition names all follow the rules of data name formation. They are not known as data names simply because they may not describe data, and we prefer to refer to them by their functional names. If we want a label for a set of sentences (a paragraph), we form this paragraph name by using the rules for data name formation.

Let's take this a little further. You remember our discussion of the data hierarchy COBOL expects—files, records, fields, characters. When you name your files, records and fields, these names also follow the rules for data name formation. However, like paragraph names they are also known by their functional names: file name, record name and field name.

**Reserved Words.**    As you would expect, COBOL has a set of words that it reserves for use in specific ways. These are called, appropriately, reserved words (Appendix B). Look at the list and you will get a better feel for what a reserved word is. A good example might be the word DIVISION or the math words ADD, SUBTRACT, etc. Normally one does not try to use these for data names—but look further. See the word "count." It is a reserved word. Remember that, because you will understand why I spell count with a "K" in my programs and why I spelled it that way earlier in this chapter.

**Figurative Constants.**    COBOL also has reserved words that have preassigned values. These are called figurative constants. Some of these are:

- SPACE(S)
- ZERO(S)
- QUOTE

**Condition Names.**    The only items we haven't discussed yet are condition names and literals. Condition names are different from what we have talked about so far, except that they follow the same rules for formation and they are known by their function names. I will delay further discussion until we look at COBOL's condition statements in Chapter 8.

**Literals.**    As programmers we sometimes need to use literals. That is:

```
ADD 1 TO KOUNT
```

or

```
IF  MAJOR = 'ACCOUNTING'
```

The number 1 and the character string 'ACCOUNTING' are both literals. The 1 is a numeric literal, while 'ACCOUNTING' is a non-numeric literal. A numeric literal is any number. It is not presented within quotes. On the other hand, a non-numeric literal is any character or characters including numbers enclosed in quotes. The rules are below:

| Numeric Literals | Non-numeric Literals |
|---|---|
| - not enclosed in quotes | - enclosed in quotes |
| - up to 18 digits | - up to 120 characters |
| - may contain only numbers, a sign and a decimal | - may contain any character in the computer's character set |

According to these rules, the following are examples of numeric and non-numeric literals:

| Numeric | | Non-numeric | |
|---|---|---|---|
| Valid | Invalid | Valid | Invalid |
| 1234 | '1234' | '1234' | 1234 |
| 1.5 | 12AB | 'ABCD' | ABCD |
| 0.5 | 'ABC1' | '12AB' | 12AB |

You now know how to make up all kinds of names, literals, and such. But we are not finished.

### Delimiters

Let me ask you two questions. First, why are we not allowed to use the blank in forming a data name? Second, how does COBOL know where one name ends and another begins? Both questions are really the same question. COBOL uses the blank to know where one name or word stops and the other begins. Therefore, if we used an embedded blank the compiler would think, figuratively speaking, of course, that it had two successive words.

Look at the following COBOL statement with me:

```
ADD GROSS PAY TO TOTAL GROSS PAY
```

When the compiler tries to understand the statement, it thinks we want to ADD something called GROSS and something called PAY to TOTAL. That's probably not what we intended. Furthermore, even if it were, the compiler would choke on TOTAL GROSS PAY because it is not expecting the words GROSS or PAY after the word TOTAL. TOTAL GROSS PAY violates the syntax for an ADD statement. Let's rewrite the statement two ways:

```
ADD GROSSPAY TO TOTALGROSSPAY
```

and

```
ADD GROSS-PAY TO TOTAL-GROSS-PAY
```

Since the compiler uses the blank (at least one) as a delimiter between two successive words, we cannot use the blank to form a word. We then have the two choices above. In the first we simply remove the blanks while in the second one we replace the blanks with hyphens. Which do you find easier to read? The second one? Most of us do, and that's the form I will use in this text.

### Periods, Commas and More

We now know how the compiler recognizes a word and a sentence (the period). Are there any other rules? You bet there are. How does the compiler recognize a period (.), comma (,), semicolon(;), parentheses( () ), all the math operators (+, -, /, *, **, = ), and all the relational operators (<, >, =, etc.)?

In order for a period to be recognized as a period (and not a decimal point), it must not be preceded by a blank, but it must be followed by at least one blank. The same is true for the comma and semicolon. On the other hand, a decimal point may not be preceded or followed by a blank.

All math and relational operators must be preceded and followed by at least one blank in order to be recognized by the compiler. Let's look at the following two examples and notice that there are blanks before and after the operators.

```
IF  GROSS-PAY > 1000 . . .
```

and

```
COMPUTE GROSS-PAY = HOURS-WORKED * RATE-OF-PAY
```

### Parentheses

The parentheses are a little different. A leftmost parenthesis must be preceded by a space, and a rightmost parenthesis must be followed by a space. You do not use a space to the right of a left parenthesis or to the left of a right parenthesis. Get that? Sounds strange, but it's what you normally do anyway, so don't let it confuse you. Look at these examples:

```
COMPUTE ANSWER = (A + B) * (D - C)
COMPUTE ANSWER = ((A + B) * (D - C)) / (A - D + E)
```

See, it's not really strange to do; it just sounds strange.

### Margins

All the rules are nice because they allow us to communicate correctly with the COBOL compiler. The compiler not only expects certain punctuation and syntax; it also expects certain elements in certain columns or margins. In COBOL we work with two margins, the A margin and the B margin. The A margin is made up of columns 8 through 11, while the B margin is made up of columns 12 through 72. You will notice as we continue our discussion that while COBOL just uses these two margins we do use others for readability.

As I noted earlier, COBOL expects certain of its allowable statements to be in certain margins. For instance, remember our data organization? Well, look at this:

| Margin | Data type |
| --- | --- |
| A | File |
| A | Record |
| B | Field |

All files and records must be defined by starting the description in one of the columns making up the A margin (8 through 11). All data fields must be described within the B margin, columns 12 through 72.

You will also remember our discussion of COBOL's overall structure. Certain elements of this structure must begin in the A margin while others must be in the B margin.

| Margin | COBOL Entry |
| --- | --- |
| A | DIVISION |
| A | SECTION |
| A | PARAGRAPH |
| B | SENTENCE |
| B | STATEMENT |

Notice how all DIVISIONs, SECTIONs, and paragraphs must start in the A margin, while sentences and statements start in the B margin. When we get to the PROCEDURE DIVISION, you will also note that every statement starts with a verb—ADD, SUBTRACT, IF, READ, etc. Therefore, we may say that all COBOL verbs must be in the B margin. But that's what we should expect from our general rule about sentences and statements.

## STANDARD NOTATION

Since all COBOL entries have elements that are required, optional, programmer supplied, or that require a selection among several options, we need a standard notation for this text. It just makes it easier for us to see how to code a particular COBOL element. So here goes:

■ all required key words will be CAPITALIZED, **boldfaced**, and <u>underlined</u>

<u>**READ**</u>

■ all optional key words will be CAPITALIZED and **boldfaced** but not under-lined

**ELSE**

■ all lowercase words must be supplied by the programmer as needed

data-name

■ all words enclosed in brackets [ ] are optional depending on the program's needs

$$\begin{bmatrix} \textbf{ELSE} \\ \textbf{OTHERWISE} \end{bmatrix}$$

■ words enclosed in braces { } require a choice by the programmer

$$\begin{Bmatrix} \text{SEQUENTIAL} \\ \text{RANDOM} \\ \text{DYNAMIC} \end{Bmatrix}$$

■ ellipses, . . . , mean the words may be repeated

. . . data-name$_1$, data-name$_2$, . . .

Let's look at the COBOL WRITE verb with our notation rules in mind.

<u>**WRITE**</u> record-name [ <u>**FROM**</u> detail-record-name ]

$$\begin{bmatrix} \begin{Bmatrix} \textbf{BEFORE} \\ \textbf{AFTER} \end{Bmatrix} \textbf{ADVANCING} \begin{Bmatrix} \text{data-name } \textbf{LINES} \\ \text{integer } \textbf{LINES} \\ \text{mnemonic} \end{Bmatrix} \end{bmatrix}$$

Examining the parts together we find:

<u>**WRITE**</u>    Required reserved word. You can see why we have these. The com-piler needs to know what statement to expect, and the key word does that for us.

record-name    A name that must be supplied by the programmer.

[ <u>**FROM**</u> detail-record-name ]

    Since it is in brackets, this statement is optional. But if it is used, the FROM is required, and the programmer must supply the detail-record-name.

Finally notice that if we use the last optional part shown (in [ ]), we must choose (in { }) between the required keywords BEFORE and AFTER. See how that works? Since the whole thing is in brackets, [ ] we know it's optional depending on our needs. However, if we use it, we must now choose (indicated by the braces { }) between the required key words, boldfaced and underlined, **BEFORE** or **AFTER**.

On the other hand, the word **ADVANCING** is a key word (boldfaced), but not required since it is not underlined. Lastly we must make a choice among three possible entries, two of which have the optional reserved word **LINES**.

Look at the CIRCLE CLUB PROGRAM in Appendix C. You will see several examples. (See, it's not that hard. It just seems that way at first.) For instance, I could code a WRITE statement either of the two ways below and the compiler would be happy:

```
WRITE    REPORT-LINE    FROM  STUDENT-RECORD
         AFTER ADVANCING  2 LINES.
```

or

```
WRITE    REPORT-LINE    FROM  STUDENT-RECORD
         AFTER 2.
```

While the first is probably more English-like, I tend to use the second form just out of habit.

## SUMMARY

COBOL's development was an interesting one. It had a troubled beginning that seemed to surface again with the latest compiler, COBOL '85. However troubled in its beginning, COBOL has grown in popularity, mainly because it was, and still is, a common language.

COBOL was designed with several criteria in mind; particularly that it be easy to read and English-like. We have seen how this is so, and we will continue to see it throughout the text. While COBOL's structure of DIVISIONS, SECTIONS, paragraphs, sentences, statements and its syntax and punctuation tend to make it English-like, these also tend to make COBOL programs lengthy. I established a standard notation to help you study COBOL syntax. With this notation you know when a key word is required or optional; when you must make a choice between options; where to supply data names and so on.

We looked at the rules for formation of data names. We also saw that many of the data items in COBOL are defined with a data name but are known by their functional name—file names, record names, and paragraph names, for examples.

Hopefully, after reading this chapter, you should have a good idea about COBOL's history and its future. You should also have a good understanding of the elements that make up the language. Figure 1.4 is a short COBOL program that illustrates what a complete COBOL program looks like. I've noted many of the COBOL elements and features discussed in the Chapter. In future chapters we will spend our time studying all the elements and features thoroughly.

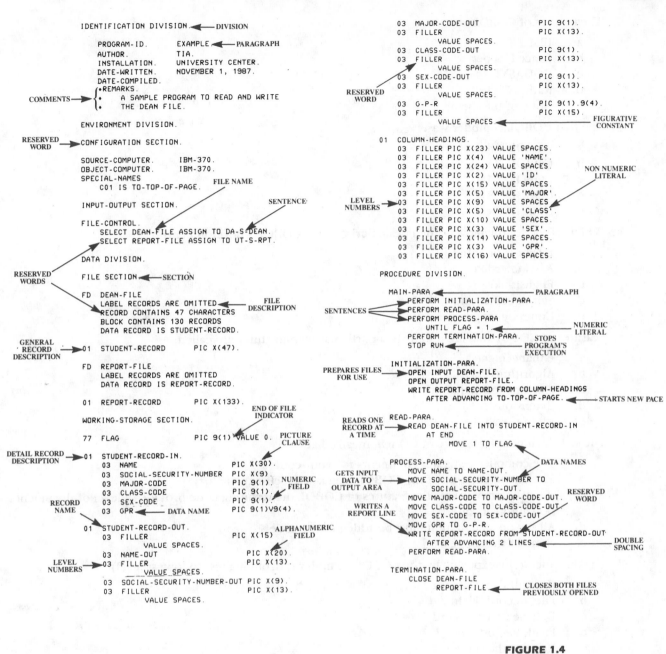

**FIGURE 1.4**
**Sample COBOL program Illustrating Language Features**

---

# EXERCISES

## Chapter Review Questions

1. The acronym COBOL stands for:

    a. Common Business-Operational Language

    b. Computerized Business-Oriented Language

    c. Common Business-Oriented Language

    d. Conference on Business-Oriented Language

    e. None of the above

2. The mother of COBOL is:
   a.   IBM
   b.   Grace Hopper
   c.   CODASYL
   d.   Kathy White
   e.   None of the above

3. The first COBOL compiler was:
   a.   COBOL '68
   b.   COBOL '74
   c.   COBOL '85
   d.   COBOL '58
   e.   None of the above

4. Which of the following was not a design criteria for COBOL's development?
   a.   Business-oriented
   b.   Assembler-like
   c.   English-like
   d.   Self-documenting
   e.   Common language

5. Features of COBOL that are unique to a particular manufacturer are called:
   a.   Enhancements
   b.   Algorithms
   c.   Machine independent
   d.   Extensions
   e.   All of the above

6. The self-documenting feature of COBOL means that:
   a.   The compiler generates comments for your code
   b.   The documentation of the COBOL language is self-explanatory
   c.   If a programmer uses the features of COBOL the resulting code provides a level of documentation automatically
   d.   All the documentation must be added to the code
   e.   None of the above

7. The data hierarchy expected by the COBOL compiler is (from highest to lowest level):
   a.   Record, File, Data Set
   b.   File, Record, Field
   c.   Data Set, File, Record
   d.   Field, Record, File
   e.   None of the above

8. Which of the following is not a COBOL Division?
   a.   DATA
   b.   FILE
   c.   IDENTIFICATION
   d.   PROCEDURE
   e.   ENVIRONMENT

9. The character used by the compiler as a delimiter is the:

    a.   Comma
    b.   Period
    c.   Space
    d.   Hyphen
    e.   All may be used

10. An example of a figurative constant in COBOL is:

    a.   SPACES
    b.   QUOTE
    c.   ZERO
    d.   ZEROS
    e.   All of the above

11. Which of the following is not a rule for data-name formation?

    a.   1–7 characters in length
    b.   A–Z, 0–9 and hyphen may be used
    c.   No blanks
    d.   No spacing characters
    e.   Hyphen may not be first on last character

12. Which of the following is true about COBOL margins?

    a.   The A margin includes columns 8–12
    b.   The C margin includes columns 72–80
    c.   Columns 1–6 are referred to as the continuation margin
    d.   Column 12–72 is the B margin
    e.   Column 8–11 is the B margin

13. Which of the following relations is true?

    a.   All divisions start in the A margin
    b.   All sentences start in the B margin
    c.   All sections start in the A margin
    d.   All paragraphs start in the A margin
    e.   All are true statements

14. A file name is:

    a.   A data name used to describe a record in a file
    b.   A data name used to reference a file
    c.   A special COBOL reserved word
    d.   A figurative constant
    e.   None of the above

15. Using our standard notation, words included in braces { }:

    a.   Require a choice by the programmer
    b.   Are optional
    c.   Are required if underlined only
    d.   Are data names
    e.   None of the above

## Discussion Questions

1. Briefly contrast the COBOL '68, COBOL '74 and COBOL '85 compilers.
2. What role did Grace Hopper play in the development of of COBOL?
3. Briefly explain the design criteria, Business-Oriented.
4. Briefly contrast a numeric literal and a non-numeric literal.
5. Briefly explain COBOL's language structure.

## Practice Problems

1. Which of the following are valid numeric literals:

```
12345
'12345'
AB12
'12A3'
ZERO
'SPACES'
10340
```

2. Which of the following are valid non-numeric literals:

```
'12345'
'ABCDE'
ABCDE
12345
ZERO
SPACES
```

3. Which of the following are valid data names:

```
TOTAL PAY
COUNT
KOUNT
AVERAGE-EMPLOYEE-PAY-BY-WAREHOUSE
```

## Programming Assignments

1. Using the computer system at your school, enter the sample program in Figure 1.4. Run the program using the Dean File data set, Data Set A form 1.
2. Run the CIRCLE CLUB program in Appendix C on your system. You may have to enter the program or your professor may make it available to you on the system. In either case make up a set of 20 records using the same format shown in the program.

# STRUCTURED PROGRAMMING

**OBJECTIVES** This chapter will provide us a means for reviewing structured programming. You will see how it has developed over the years and how it has come to be accepted as a standard. In the chapter we will look at the three programming eras: spaghetti bowl, modular programming, and structured programming. We will examine the three logic constructs as well: sequence, selection, and iteration. Two associated constructs that have evolved over the years will also be studied.

A major part of the chapter is devoted to the review of problem solving tools. In particular, we will study hierarchy charts, input-process-output charts, flowcharts and pseudocode. These tools are covered so that you may understand each, but also so that you may understand how they work together in helping us solve problems.

## TOPICS

- structured programming
- using hierarchy charts
- using IPO charts
- flowcharting
- pseudocoding
- relationships of problem-solving tools
- system development
- system maintenance
- spaghetti bowl era
- modular programming era
- structured programming era
- programmer vs. CPU cost
- top-down design
- cohesion
- coupling

## KEY WORDS

- structured programming constructs
- sequence
- iteration: DO WHILE and DO UNTIL
- selection: IF. . .THEN. . .ELSE
- case: nested IF. . .THEN. . .ELSEs
- pseudocode
- maintenance
- functional cohesion
- sequence cohesion
- data cohesion

- hierarchy
- IPO
- HIPO
- module/task/function
- flowchart
- top down

- procedural cohesion
- time-related cohesion
- logic-related cohesion
- coincidental cohesion
- content coupling
- control coupling

## STRUCTURED PROGRAMMING DEVELOPMENT

Tracing the development of COBOL and establishing some basic understanding of COBOL's design and structure are well and good. However, COBOL did not evolve in a vacuum. As you have heard in your introductory course, and in Chapter 1, the development of structured programming has played a major role in our profession. Since structured programming has had such a major influence on programming, we should take a moment and look at its development and role. We should also look at how structured programming and COBOL live together.

Most of you are probably too young to remember pre-structured programming. I have to admit, I not only remember it, I used to teach unstructured techniques. Back when I went to school (1960s), we had not heard of structured code. All we worried about was number of lines of code and execution time. In those days getting a programmer to spend more time on a working program to reduce the number of lines of code was not only acceptable, but expected. Look at Figure 2.1 to get an understanding of where we have been and where we are today.

**FIGURE 2.1**
**Graph of CPU Cost and Programmer Cost**

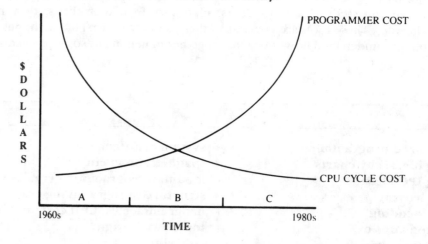

### The Spaghetti Bowl Era

The Spaghetti Bowl Era is the time period I just mentioned. CPU cost relative to manpower cost was much higher. Therefore, it made sense to spend more manpower dollars to reduce execution time and thereby execution cost. If a program was executed daily, it would not take long to pay back the additional manpower cost needed. So we wrote code that led to other code, and so on like strands of spaghetti, in a constant effort to get the most work out of programs. We used GO TOs all the time.

See where we get the name "Spaghetti Bowl"! But don't judge it too harshly. It was the best at the time, given cost and technology.

A related issue in this era was our bottoms-up approach to program development. During the spaghetti bowl period we loved programming so much we used to start solving problems by writing code. We could not wait to start coding. We developed solutions using the bottom-up technique. That is, we started with the detail coding and worked our way up to a full solution. We were all artists and loved doing it this way, and since manpower costs were relatively small, it seemed OK.

SPAGHETTI BOWL

**FIGURE 2.2**
Spaghetti Bowl Code

### Modular Programming Era

As CPU speeds increased and as people costs increased, new approaches were sought. It took longer and longer to break-even on additional programmer cost spent on making a program run faster. In the early part of the period labeled 'B', the marginal benefit was much less than it had been. What developed was a technique called modular programming. Instead of trying to write slick programs that had seemingly endless branching, we decided to break the problem down into parts or modules.

Modular programming evolved because of the changing cost relationship. With faster CPUs and more costly programmers, a new direction was needed. Data Processing managers could no longer afford the spaghetti bowl approach. They needed better control of program development. The modular approach afforded them this improved control. Before coding started, a problem's solution was broken down into related parts. Then each of these parts or modules was coded. This did at least two things for management: It provided better benchmarks for program development, and it broke down the spaghetti bowl into smaller, more manageable spaghetti bowls as shown in Figure 2.3.

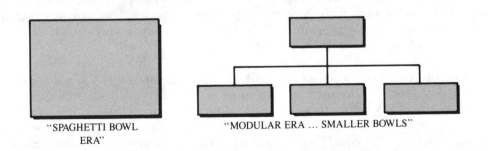

"SPAGHETTI BOWL
ERA"

"MODULAR ERA ... SMALLER BOWLS"

**FIGURE 2.3**
Modular Charts for the
Spaghetti Bowl and
Modular Programming Eras

### Structured Programming Era

With the continuing increase in programmer cost and the decreasing cost of CPU cycles, the evolution continued. But a new factor came into consideration: program maintenance. During the first two periods, many programs were put into production. These programs had to be modified to meet new user needs or changes in laws or both. Have you ever seen a spaghetti bowl program? Get your professor to show you one. See all the GO TOs? Can you imagine modifying it? And don't bother to ask for the flowchart or program specs. They usually don't exist, or they have long since been lost. Artists didn't like documentation then, and they still don't.

All this led to what we now call structured programming. We had to control both development and maintenance cost. We no longer could afford to spend more manpower just to save lines of code. We had to establish standards for development. These standards would also help down the road with maintenance. As with most things, need is the mother of invention. Dijkstra, in a paper in Communications of the ACM, proposed "Go To-less" programming. This was part of the result of the discovery that all program logic could be expressed with only three constructs. Can you imagine how that was accepted? The artists refused to accept the idea, and surprisingly, at first Data Processing managers did not fall in line either.

### Structured Programming Constructs

The three constructs that were put forth in the literature were those shown in Figure 2.4.

**FIGURE 2.4**
**The Logic Constructs**

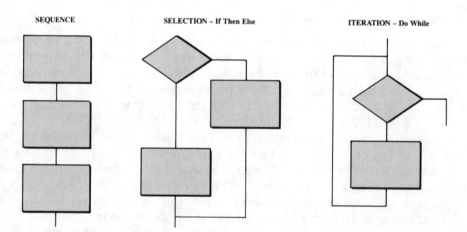

All logic could be expressed using these three constructs or combinations of the three. Can you imagine the impact of that revelation? The millions of lines of slick code could all be done with three standard constructs. What we did was take the artist's brush out of the programmer's hand and give him a set of rules. You can imagine how happy the programmers were.

However, let's not oversimplify the complex logic that may be handled with these constructs. Their discovery did not say that complex logic was a thing of the past. It just revealed that there was an order of things to our logic structures. For instance, Figure 2.5 shows that each part of the selection construct may itself be a sequence construct. It also shows the case of a selection path being an iteration. So, complex logic is still around. We represent it with combinations of our constructs.

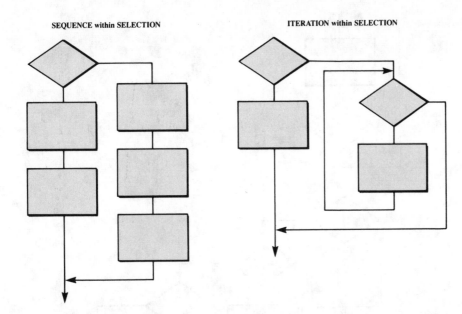

SEQUENCE within SELECTION            ITERATION within SELECTION

**FIGURE 2.5**
Logic Construct
Combinations

**Structured Programming Rules.**    So now we have not only gone to a top-down approach with smaller bowls of spaghetti, but also we have established the use of three standard logic constructs that reflect GO TO-Less programming philosophy. We did not stop there. We went further and established some structure programming rules dealing with program development.

- Each module should have one entry and one exit point.
- A module should be approximately 50 lines of code.
- Each module should contain related code (be cohesive).

Note: We also have rules that apply to COBOL and we will look at those a little later.

**The Constructs Cousins.**    As you can imagine, after the initial revelation of the three constructs and many years of use, other constructs have been added to the list of the original three. I call these the first cousins. The two first cousins are shown in Figure 2.6.

The second form of iteration, DO UNTIL, is a first cousin to the DO WHILE. The basic difference occurs when the test is performed. With the DO WHILE, the test is done first to see if the process should be done at all. In other words, the process could be skipped under the right condition. The DO UNTIL, however, allows the process to be done at least once and checks to see if it should be done some more. Notice that after the initial execution of the process, the DO WHILE and DO UNTIL are the same.

The case construct is simply a set of selection constructs. I sometimes refer to them as nested IF THEN ELSEs. You can see why I call it the first cousin to the IF THEN ELSE construct. COBOL '74 has an instruction that fits this construct to an extent. It is the GO TO. . .DEPENDING. It is a set of GO TOs; it therefore violates the rule of minimizing GO TOs. COBOL '85 has a new verb, EVALUATE, that allows for implementing the case construct directly.

**FIGURE 2.6**
The DO UNTIL and CASE
Constructs

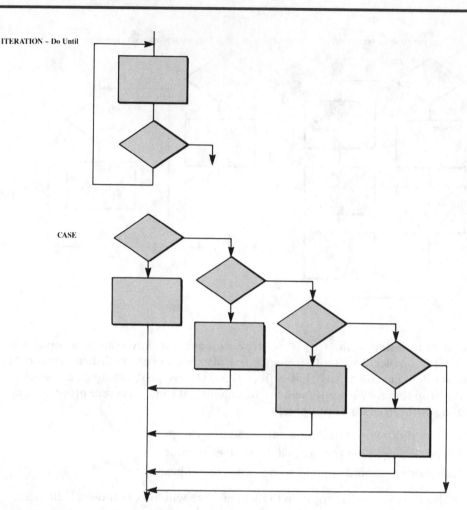

ITERATION – Do Until

CASE

## STANDARDS AND MANAGEMENT

We have already noted that with the changing relationship of CPU costs and people costs and the vastly increasing number of production programs, management needed programming standards. If you look at CPU time as a resource to be managed and you also look at programmer time as a resource, then being a Data Processing manager involves managing these resources. The manager is never at a loss for new projects. Whether the new projects consist of creating new systems or maintaining existing ones, the manager needs to plan resource allocation to these projects. In the spaghetti bowl days, when the manager inquired of the artist assigned to a system development, "How far along are you?", one very popular answer was, "About 90% done." In fact, most projects were about 90% done for 90% of the project life. (That last 10% of the project must have been a *bear*!) You can see the dilemma the manager was in. How could he or she schedule resources under those circumstances?

When we evolved to modular programming, the manager was given some benchmarks. How many modules were finished? "Well, mine is 90% finished," said one programmer. "Ditto," said another. So while the top-down and modular approaches helped, it wasn't until we added structured techniques and standards that things improved drastically. By approaching problems from a top-down approach *and* breaking the problem into modules *and* using structured techniques, managers could actually see test results of these modules and have a better idea of how far along projects were in their development.

As we examine some features of COBOL, we will see how and why features like making modules subprograms for individual testing has become popular. Such features and their application—by project teams, for instance—we have allowed structured concepts and approaches to enhance managers' abilities to do project management.

## RELATION TO COBOL—A BRIEF LOOK

How does modular, top-down programming using the structured programming constructs fit in with COBOL programming? Actually it fits very well, and even better with COBOL '85. Can you imagine programming with the bottom-up approach? That would be like starting to code before the overall problem is visualized and its major task and their relationships are understood. It would be much like trying to teach someone how to bowl by first talking about how to place the ball over a mark on the floor to get a strike. The person being taught doesn't even know the object of the game. What is a strike? Is it good or bad? Is each turn independent of another? Do you want to achieve a high score or a low score? We obviously would confuse the person if we didn't start with an overall view of bowling first.

That example is much like our bottom-up approach to programming. We didn't understand the full picture. We didn't know how everything fits together. Compounding that ignorance was our lack of modularity. Remember, our modular chart at this point in history looked like:

One module with hundreds of lines, possibly thousands of lines of code. This code was all intertwined with GO TOs to minimize lines of code. It was a mess!

Now we have modular charts, called hierarchy charts, and we approach problems from the top, not the bottom. COBOL handles these nicely (Figure 2.7).

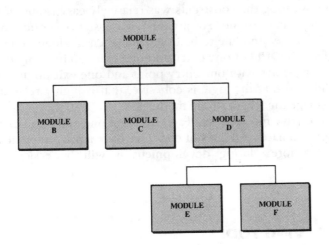

**FIGURE 2.7**
**Example Hierarchy Chart**

Given the hierarchy chart above, we can apply our standards with COBOL as follows:

```
MODULE-A.
    PERFORM MODULE-B.
    PERFORM MODULE-C.                                SEQUENCE
    PERFORM MODULE-D.

MODULE-B.
    :
    IF  GPR > 3.00
        ADD 1 TO TOP-STUDENT-COUNT                   SELECTION
    ELSE
        ADD 1 TO OTHER-COUNT.

MODULE-C.
    :
    :

MODULE-D.
    PERFORM MODULE-E.
    PERFORM MODULE-F                                 ITERATION
        10 TIMES.

MODULE-E.
    :
    :

MODULE F.
    :
    :
```

MODULE-A contains three PERFORMs, which are the control statements in COBOL that says, "Go do the named procedure (module) and come back." Therefore, the three PERFORMs constitute an example of the sequence construct. In MODULE-B we make a choice between ADDing 1 TO one of two counts. This is a good example of the selection construct. Finally, "PERFORM MODULE-F 10 TIMES" causes MODULE-F to be executed 10 times. Unlike the other modules that are done once, this logic causes a loop or iteration of MODULE-F.

While demonstrating the constructs was relatively easy, some of the other structured programming rules are not so obvious. For instance, notice that I said a PERFORM caused the named module to be done, and then the logic returned to the PERFORM. This gives MODULE-B one entry and one exit. So by using the PERFORM we can easily design modules with one entry point and one exit point. Furthermore, by designing modules so that the logic is cohesive, that is highly related to a particular function, we manage the length of the modules.

Now with cohesive modules that each have but one entry and exit point and that each contain approximately 50 lines of code, we have a program that will be easier to maintain. Furthermore, during development it will be easier to monitor the developer's progress.

## PROBLEM-SOLVING TOOLS

We have already looked at one of the tools we will use to help solve problems, the hierarchy chart. We will use others as well:

- IPO chart
- Program flowchart
- Pseudocode

I will use program flowcharts at first because they fit so well with COBOL that for the beginning COBOL programmer it is easy to see how everything goes together. Your professor may decide to use pseudocode or some other tool. That's fine. They all are used to help solve the problems.

---

## TIP

**Once you become comfortable with the tools, use the one you like. But use one!**

---

### Hierarchy Charts

A hierarchy chart is a module chart that shows all the major tasks or functions that need to be done to solve a problem. Each module is placed in the chart to show its relationship to other modules. Some modules are control modules, others are detail modules. Still others are both. Consider the chart in Figure 2.8.

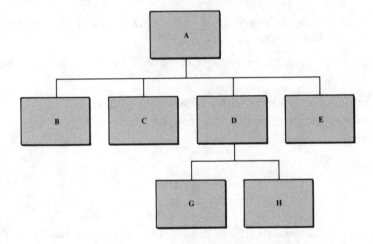

**FIGURE 2.8**
**A Simple Hierarchy Chart with Lettered Modules**

MODULE-A would be considered a control module because it causes Modules B, C, D, and E to be done. Also notice that in this chart Modules B, C, D, and E are executed only by MODULE-A. Look at Modules C, G, H, and E. Are they control or detail modules? If you said, "Detail," you were correct. They do not cause any other modules to be executed, so they have no control function. All they contain is detail logic: ADDs, IFs, MOVEs, but no PERFORMs.

What about Module D? MODULE-D is controlled by MODULE-A, and in turn it controls MODULE-G and MODULE-H. Therefore, we know that MODULE-D contains two PERFORMS, but it may also contain detail logic.

Let's redraw the chart, Figure 2.9, showing the control/detail relationship more explicitly.

I hope Figure 2.9 helps you visualize the control/detail relationship. Have you noticed how the hierarchy chart follows the top-down approach? We don't worry about the detail modules until the bottom, while we start with overall control at the top. Therefore, the amount of detail increases from top down.

**FIGURE 2.9**
Hierarchy Chart Showing
Control/Detail Relationships

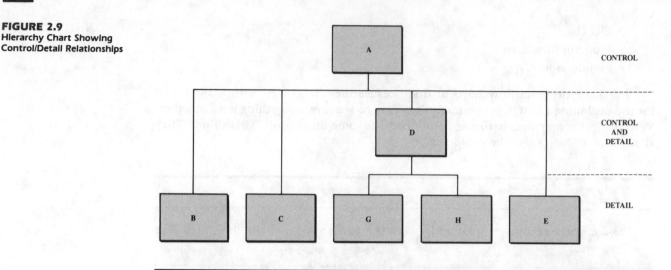

> ## TIP
>
> When you break down a module, decompose it into at least two modules. For instance, MODULE-B might be decomposed into B-1 and B-2. It would not help much to decompose B only into B-1.

How about looking at a very simple problem? I picked the problem not to task your mind, but to demonstrate the hierarchy chart.

**Problem:** The dean of the college of business wants a program that will produce:

1. A listing of all students with a GPR below 2.00, and
2. A count of students in the following GPR ranges:

$$= 4.0$$
$$> = 3.0 \text{ and } < 4.0$$
$$> = 2.0 \text{ and } < 3.0$$
$$< 2.0$$

Given these requirements I have designed the following hierarchy chart (Figure 2.10).

If you envisioned a different chart don't worry about it. Mine is just one solution not necessarily the best solution. But let's use mine to discuss the modules. I just used the standard of labeling the highest module (main module) to reflect the particular problem. Then I tried to identify the major tasks.

| | |
|---|---|
| **Initialization** | I will need to set variables to 0 for counting. |
| **Headlines for Detail Listing** | This is the logic to write headings for detail report. |
| **Read Student Record** | This causes the first student's record to be executed. Notice (How could you miss it?) the dog ear. This means it is a common module and has more than one module that causes it to be executed. We will look at this in a moment. |

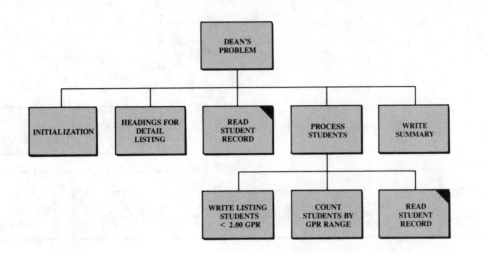

**FIGURE 2.10**
Hierarchy Chart for the
Dean's List and Count

**Process Students**

This is my *detail processing* (or detail time). I could have just left this module intact, but I broke it down into three logical modules:

- Writing of the detail listing
- Counting the students by GPR range
- Reading the rest of the students' records

These are three cohesive modules that probably would not total fifty lines of code altogether. I broke them down not because of length but because writing, counting, and reading of the students is just not as cohesive as the individual modules. In fact, leaving them all together would cause the module to be referred to as "coincidentally cohesive" (they all work with students).

**Write summary**

This module will write the counts. Notice that it is outside of the processing loop. Once all students are processed, then the counts are written. This is called *total time*.

Since I said this is not the only possible solution, let's look at another one. I've shown this in Figure 2.11.

This example appeals to me. The second level includes the major tasks—initialization, processing, summary. Then, as needed, these are broken down into the detail modules. While I like both ways, either is OK, and they are both correct.

Are we finished? No! We must take this to the dean and sit down and talk through our solution with him. Only if he agrees with our understanding of the problem and the direction we are taking with the solution will we take the next step. Otherwise we will have to start over.

**FIGURE 2.11**
**Modified Hierarchy Chart**
**for Dean's List and Count**

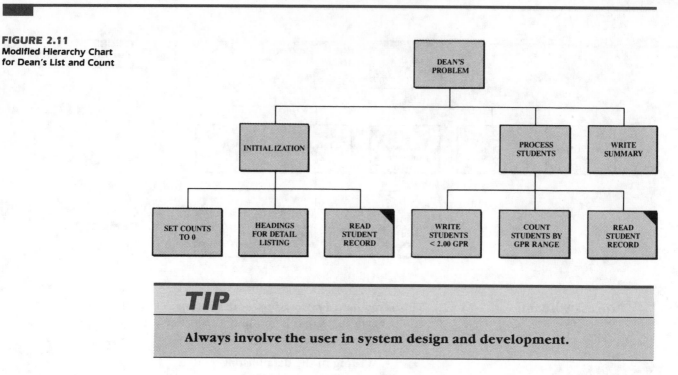

**TIP**

**Always involve the user in system design and development.**

Have you noticed that we haven't looked at any detail logic yet? We haven't even written a line of code. You're seeing top-down design in action. We start with the big picture and all the parts before we write code. It hasn't always been this way, but most of us are glad it has changed.

### Input-Process-Output (IPO) Charts

Having received the dean's approval on the hierarchy chart, we take the next step in the development of the solution: the IPO chart. The IPO chart is used to show the input and output requirements and the processing needed to provide the output, given the input. Figure 2.12 shows the form of the IPO chart that we will use.

**FIGURE 2.12**
**The IPO Chart Form**

| SYSTEM/PROGRAM: _____ | | |
|---|---|---|
| AUTHOR: _____ | | DATE: _____ |
| INPUT | PROCESS | OUTPUT |
| | | |

**An IPO for Each Module.**    Technically, we should provide an IPO for each module of the hierarchy chart. That is, we should have an IPO for the DEAN'S PROBLEM module and every other module including the COUNT STUDENTS BY GPR RANGE module. What we normally find in a classroom environment is one IPO for a problem, since the problems tend to be small compared with industry problems.

**Developing the IPO.**    How do you develop the IPO charts? Well different people do different things, especially with the process part of the chart. I'll try to show you an example of a couple of acceptable ways, but your professor may like yet another way. That's OK, since our objective is to have a good problem solution.

In the dean's problem, Figure 2.10, we have an acceptable hierarchy chart. Now our task is to get a little more detail with the modules, that is, to develop an IPO for each. That would be technically what we should do with a much larger problem, but with this small problem let's just develop one IPO for the whole problem.

Where do we start? If we don't know what we want to end up with, how do we know what to do to get there? Therefore, we will also start with the output in developing our IPO Chart.

The dean wants two reports. The first report is a listing of all students that are below a 2.0 GPR and a summary report to include the count of students in the four GPR ranges requested. What does the dean want on these reports? Ask the user! Let's assume he or she tells us and we show the request in Figure 2.13.

**FIGURE 2.13**
IPO Showing Output Requirements for the Dean's List and Count Problem

| INPUT | PROCESS | OUTPUT |
|---|---|---|
| | | **List of Students**<br><br>(Report 1)<br>    name<br>    major<br>    classification<br>    GPR<br><br>**Summary Report**<br><br>(Report 2)<br>    count of students:<br>      with GPR = 4.0<br>      $> = 3.0$ and $< 4.0$<br>      $> = 2.0$ and $< 3.0$<br>      $< 2.0$ |

SYSTEM/PROGRAM: _____

AUTHOR: _____    DATE: _____

Given the output request, we would next look at our data source. Let's for now assume we have a sequential file that contains a record of data for each student in the college. The contents are listed in the input column in Figure 2.14.

Once we have the output requirements and we know the input that is available, we can determine our processing needs. How? By looking at our list of items required in our output and seeing if we have corresponding items in input or if we need to develop them during processing.

A few things can happen at this point in development. First, you may find that *all* the required output is either provided from input or can be developed from the input data. Or, you may discover that *more input data* is needed to allow for the required output. This would probably require a change in the dean file. Finally, no matter if either or both of the first two things happen, the dean may see your design and realize he or she needs something else. The dean might like the parents' address on Report 1. He or she may also want a count of these students and a count of all students might also be nice on the summary report. You had better get used to requested changes. They are not unusual.

**FIGURE 2.14**
IPO Chart Showing Input and Output Requirements for the Dean's List and Count Problem

| | | | |
|---|---|---|---|
| SYSTEM/PROGRAM: _____ | | | |
| AUTHOR: _____ | | DATE: _____ | |

| INPUT | PROCESS | OUTPUT |
|---|---|---|
| **Dean File**<br><br>name<br>id<br>major<br>classification<br>sex code<br>parent's address<br>GPR | | **List of Students**<br>(Report 1)<br>name<br>major<br>classification<br>GPR<br><br>**Summary Report**<br>(Report 2)<br>count of students<br>with GPR = 4.0<br>> = 3.0 and < 4.0<br>> = 2.0 and < 3.0<br>< 2.0 |

You see that a pencil with a good eraser is a required tool for this part of the development. We would have to go back to the hierarchy chart to reflect the changes described above and then change the IPO chart as well. But let's be optimistic and assume the dean was happy and didn't request any changes. So we can check off each item in our output to see what, if anything, we need to do to provide it on the report(s).

The name, major, classification and GPR all come from the input. All we need to do is read and write. Remember though: we don't list all students. We list only those below a 2.0 GPR. Therefore, we need to show this process. Now look at the summary report. Obviously the counts do not come from the input. They must be generated. So they need to be shown as part of the processing. What does the process part of the IPO look like so far? Something like it is shown in Figure 2.15.

**FIGURE 2.15**
A First Look at the Process Needed for the Dean's List and Count Problem

| INPUT | PROCESS | OUTPUT |
|---|---|---|
| | If GPR < 2.0<br>　　Write student on list<br><br>If GPR = 4.0<br>　　Add 1 to Count A<br>If GPR > = 3.0 and < 4.0<br>　　Add 1 to Count B<br>If GPR > = 2.0 and < 3.0<br>　　Add 1 to Count C<br>If GPR < 2.0<br>　　Add 1 to Count D | |

See why we need th
not come directly from
data, writing the headin
ideally we would do ar
look back at our chart
done this for you. Figu
on Report 2 to include t

SYST
AUTHOR:

INPUT

**Dean File**
name
id
major
classificatior
sex code
parent's add
GPR

**Understanding the I**
is OK. That is, it does
output for the proble
at it. Study all the ele
Remember that v
these two and the hi
the naming of the ite
problem? Everything
classification, and GI
put. What if on inpu
you know these wei
names to the output.
very similar if not ex
This naming con
say we are to write
from? Input? No, th
used the same names
A big question i
process column of t
people like what I h
in theirs. I have red
this IPO takes on a
If Else.

**FIGURE 2.17**
Modified IPO for the Dean's
List and Count Problem

| SYSTEM/PROGRAM: | DEAN'S REPORT | |
| --- | --- | --- |
| AUTHOR: George Fowler | | DATE: 11/17/87 |

| INPUT | PROCESS | OUTPUT |
| --- | --- | --- |
| **Dean File**<br><br>name<br>id<br>major<br>classification<br>sex code<br>parent's address<br>GPR | Write Report 1 heading<br>Set counts to 0<br>Read first student record<br>Do while more records<br>  If GPR < 2.0<br>    Write student on list<br>  If GPR = 4.0<br>    Add 1 to Count A<br>  Else<br>    If GPR > = 3.0 and < 4.0<br>      Add 1 to Count B<br>    Else<br>      If GPR > = 2.0 and < 3.0<br>        Add 1 to Count C<br>      Else<br>        Add 1 to Count D<br>  Read next student record<br>End Do<br>Write summary headings<br>Write counts on summary | **List of Students**<br><br>(Report 1)<br>  name<br>  major<br>  classification<br>  GPR<br><br>**Summary Report**<br><br>(Report 2)<br>  count of students:<br>    COUNT A<br>    COUNT B<br>    COUNT C<br>    COUNT D |

Whatever your preference, always remember that on the front end of the project development you are using tools to help you understand the problem and communicate this understanding to the user. You will then give these to the programmer to be used during development. Ultimately, at the end of the project, the HIPO will be part of the documentation package that will play a very important part in system maintenance.

## Flowcharting

Assuming we have received the dean's go ahead to this point, we now need to design the detailed solution to the problem. Up until now we have looked at major functions (hierarchy chart) and the input, processing and output requirements (IPO chart). We now have to put all this down into enough detail and establish a sequence to the processing to allow for the coding of the solution. I realize that the dean's problem is small and that with your experience you could start coding at this point. However, not all problems are this small. Let's use the dean's problem as a vehicle for reviewing flowcharting, and let's not be concerned with the lack of complexity. I say that because I assume you have seen flowcharts in your introduction to data processing class and therefore simply need to review flowcharting. It will, however, be a detailed review.

**What is a Flowchart?** The function of a flowchart is two-fold. On one hand it is used to help in the development of the solution. Once the program or system is put into production it becomes a very important part of the documentation package.

A flowchart is a semi-graphical representation of the solution to a problem. It not only shows the steps needed for the solution; it also shows the sequence required. We will use a standard set of symbols (Appendix A) to represent our solution, and we will develop a flowchart for each module in the hierarchy chart. But first let's look at some rules.

- Logic should flow from top to bottom and left to right.
- Logic should generally be shown in columns.
- Use one equation/process per process block except for initialization of variables.
- In an input/output process, use READ: or WRITE: to indicate which is to be done.
- Try to keep your decisions answerable by YES/NO or TRUE/FALSE.
- Each block should have only one flow arrow entering and one flow arrow exiting (except for decisions).
- For the beginning terminal, use the name of the module used in the hierarchy chart.
- For the ending terminal, use the term RETURN. In the main module use STOP or STOP RUN.
- Until you get to be an expert, you should use arrowheads on all flow lines. But at some point you may need to use them only when the standard flow is not used.

Let's take a look at a flowchart using symbols only (Figure 2.18).

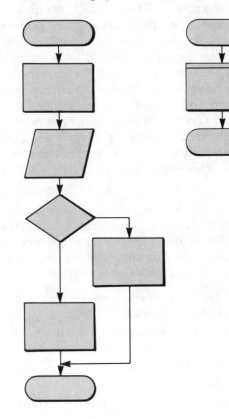

**FIGURE 2.18**
**Flowchart Using Symbols only**

**Interpreting the Symbols.**    What does this symbolic flowchart say to us? Well, it should be saying something like the following:

   1st    The terminal identifies the beginning of the module.

   2nd    A process is done.

3rd    An input or output operation is done.

4th    A decision is made.

5th    One of two paths (but not both) is followed and the process is done.

6th    A connector that contains a label, 1, that shows where to connect. That is, a 1 connects to a 1.

7th    A predefined process: An external set of logic is executed.

8th    Another predefined process is used.

9th    The ending terminal identifies the end of the module.

Amazing, isn't it? We didn't even know what the module or problem was, but we can look at the symbols and tell what type of process is to be done. Not only that, but we can also see when the processes are to be done. That's one of the beauties of flowcharts: They communicate.

**Developing a Flowchart.**    We now have a hierarchy chart and an IPO. Now we are ready to develop the flowcharts. We develop one for each module in the hierarchy chart. Technically, we will have several flowcharts, but we usually refer only to it as the problem flowchart. With the HIPO in hand, we should truly understand the problem and have a solution to the problem as well. What would the flowchart look like for the dean's problem? Let's build it, Figure 2.19, using the hierarchy chart shown in Figure 2.10.

**Understanding the Main Module.**    Let's take a minute here to digest what we have done. In the dean's module we have a predefined process for each module it controls. We also establish a sequence of execution for these modules. I know, they are in the same order as in the hierarchy chart. That's only coincidence. Since we tend to do things from left to right, our hierarchy charts tend to be developed that way. However, there is no rule that says a hierarchy chart needs to show order from left to right. You should also notice something really nice. Read the flowchart that we have developed so far. It says we do some initialization, then we write headings for our detail report. Next we read a record, process it and continue to process students until *End Of File*. Finally we write the summary report. Sounds like the big picture or the top of a top-down design. It is! Now let's see the rest of the flowchart in Figure 2.20.

**"Executing" the Flowchart.**    Are you amazed at the length? That's the cost we absorb for the clarity and the one-to-one relationship between a detailed flowchart and the COBOL program. Please don't let the length bother you. The benefits far outweigh the costs. Let's look at the flowchart and execute it ourselves. You need to know how it works if you are to build flowcharts yourself.

1st    The INITIALIZATION predefined process is executed. This causes the Initialization module to be executed.

2nd    The initialization module is executed, which sets the counts to zero and initializes the EOF flag. Then the logic returns to the predefined process.

3rd    The HEADINGS FOR DETAIL REPORT predefined process is executed. This causes the headings to be done.

4th    The page and column headings are written. Control returns to the predefined process.

5th    The READ A STUDENT RECORD predefined process is executed.

6th    A record is read from the DEAN FILE. If the read is successful, we simply return to the predefined process. If the read is not successful, we set the EOF flag to 1 and then return to the predefined process.

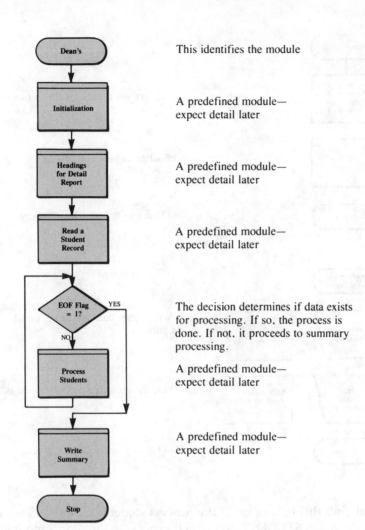

This identifies the module

A predefined module—
expect detail later

A predefined module—
expect detail later

A predefined module—
expect detail later

The decision determines if data exists
for processing. If so, the process is
done. If not, it proceeds to summary
processing.

A predefined module—
expect detail later

A predefined module—
expect detail later

**FIGURE 2.19**
Flowchart for the Main
Module of the Dean's List
and Count Problem

7th   Check EOF flag. If it's not = 1, we received a record from the dean's file on the last read and we need to process the student. So we do the PRO-CESS STUDENT predefined process. (Steps 8 through 15 are repeated.) If we had not received a record on the last read, the EOF flag would have been set to 1 and that would stop our looping and cause us to go to the SUMMARY predefined process (step 16).

8th   The PROCESS STUDENT predefined process is done.

9th   Now the WRITE STUDENTS BELOW 2.0 predefined process is executed.

10th   The GPR is checked, and if it is below 2.0, the student is written to the report.

11th   The COUNT STUDENTS BY GPR RANGE predefined process is executed.

12th   The module is executed. It checks the ranges and counts the student appropriately.

13th   READ A STUDENT RECORD predefined process is executed again.

14th   A record is read. If the read is successful, we return to the predefined process in the PROCESS STUDENT module. (You always go back to the predefined process that got you where you are.)

**FIGURE 2.20a**
**The Rest of the Flowchart for the Dean's List and Count Problem**

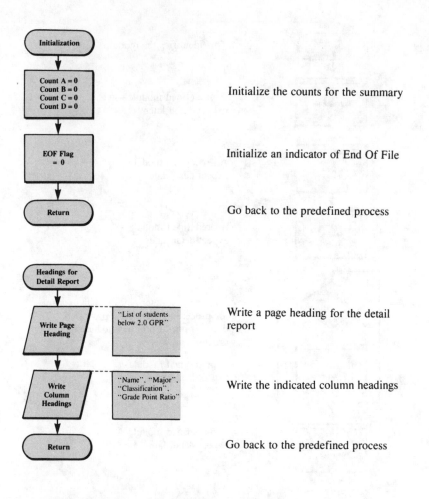

Initialize the counts for the summary

Initialize an indicator of End Of File

Go back to the predefined process

Write a page heading for the detail report

Write the indicated column headings

Go back to the predefined process

15th   That ends this pass through the process students module, so we go back to the PROCESS STUDENT predefined process in the dean's module.

16th   The WRITE SUMMARY predefined process is executed.

17th   Write the summary report heading.

18th   through 21st
Write the Counts with line descriptions.

22nd   STOP RUN (finally!).

Well, we are not finished with looking at flowcharts. You should have at least a couple of questions. What about the common module that reads students? Why do we cause records to be read from two separate places, the DEAN'S module and the PROCESS STUDENTS module? The answer to both these questions has to do with structured programming. It is a technique that eliminates the need for using GO TOs in our read logic.

---

## TIP

**Use flowcharting to help you visualize solutions to problems.**

FIGURE 2.20b

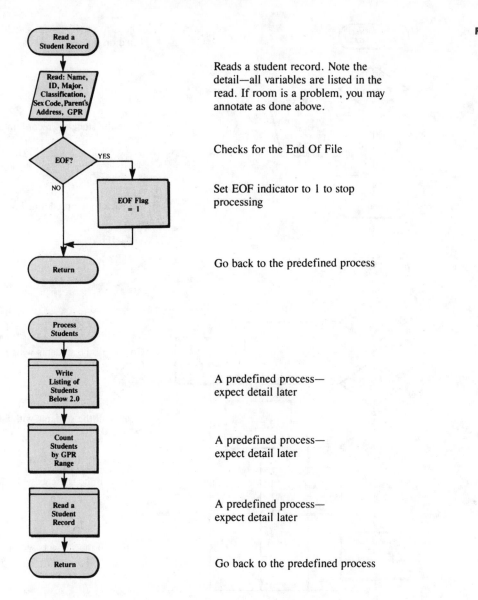

Reads a student record. Note the detail—all variables are listed in the read. If room is a problem, you may annotate as done above.

Checks for the End Of File

Set EOF indicator to 1 to stop processing

Go back to the predefined process

A predefined process—expect detail later

A predefined process—expect detail later

A predefined process—expect detail later

Go back to the predefined process

Notice how this module looks like a "main module" in that it contains all control and no detail.

## THE LEAD READ

The common read module reflected in the hierarchy chart and used in the flowchart is known as the lead read, initial read, or priming read technique. I prefer the name lead read, but they all describe the same process. That process, as mentioned before, is a way to minimize GO TOs in a program. I guess the best way to show you how it works is to show you the GO TO way. Let's modify the dean module and the process student module as an example (Figure 2.21).

Notice the lead read is no longer in the DEAN'S module. Therefore, the PROCESS STUDENTS module must start by reading a student's record. Do you see the GO TO problem? Look at the loop back. How do we skip everything when we reach

**FIGURE 2.20c**

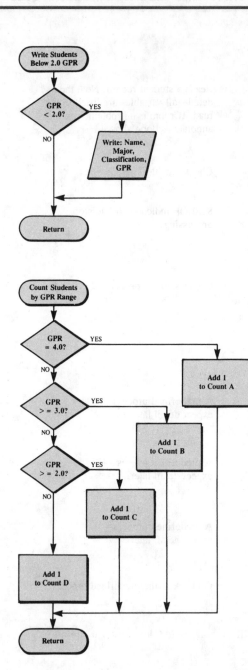

Check to see if student should be listed on the report.

Write the student's record on the report.

Go back to the predefined process.

Counts all the students with a 4.0 GPR

Counts all the students with a GPR >= 3.0.

Counts all the students with a GPR >= 2.0.

Counts all the students with a GPR < 2.0.

Go back to the predefined process.

Note: Once a student is classified, one is added to the appropriate count and then the logic skips to the Return which allows for the simple decisions and reduces the number of decisions by one. I don't have to ask if GPR < 2.0 since that's the only possibility if all the NO branch's are followed.

end of file? Branch around . . . that's a GO TO in each case. By placing the read first, we need to have the two branches. That will require GO TOs in COBOL. However, by having the initial read external to the process module, the branching is eliminated. At least the branch at EOF is eliminated. Look back at our original dean's module. See the loop back there also? In COBOL that loop can be controlled without a GO TO. In fact, I usually draw that part of the dean's module as I've shown in Figure 2.22.

FIGURE 2.20d

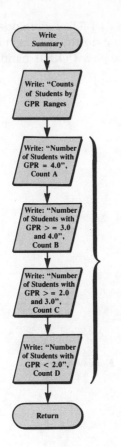

Write the report heading.

Write the four counts with an appropriate line descriptor (not column heading). Notice how we write a literal, enclosed in quotes, and a variable, the counts, as one record each.

Go back to the predefined process.

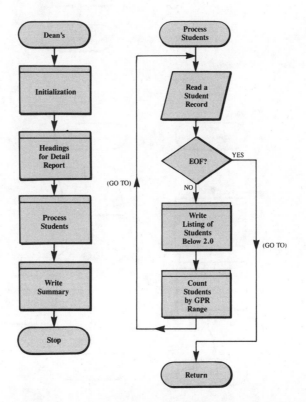

**FIGURE 2.21**
**The Modified Dean and Process Modules**

Figure 2.23 shows the lead read structure. This is one technique that lends itself to the removal of GO TOs in the read logic. COBOL handles the lead read nicely. In fact, the lead read is an implementation of the DO UNTIL logic construct, isn't it? Figure 2.23 shows that the read is done, and then we do the process until something (in this case, EOF) happens. In a little bit we will see how COBOL handles this. So be patient with me for a while.

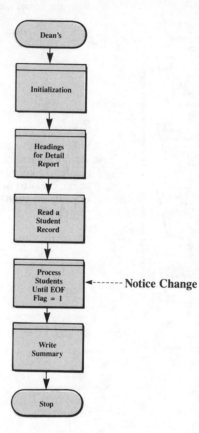

**FIGURE 2.22**
Revised Dean's Module
Showing EOF within
Predefined Module

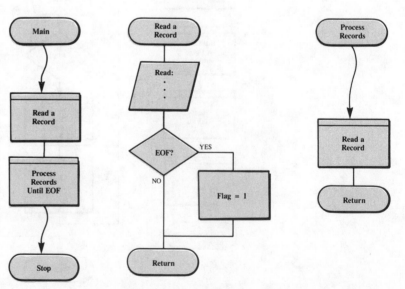

**FIGURE 2.23**
Flowchart Showing the
Lead Read

*Pseudocode*

Flowcharting is not the only tool we can use for setting out the sequence of events required for the solution to a problem. Pseudocode has become very popular as a problem-solving tool. While it tends to lose the one-to-one relationship with the modules and the COBOL program, it is more concise and definitely not as long as a flowchart. That's the part most of us like. The thing I don't like, at least at the beginning of your journey through COBOL, is that it doesn't have that clear one-to-one relationship I've talked about. It also may not provide as much detail as a flowchart. And probably the biggest problem is not a pseudocode problem at all, but it's people's problem. Do you recognize the pseudocode in Figure 2.24? Compare it with the process in Figure 2.17. Do they look similar? Look at the process. Looks like pseudocode, doesn't it? It is! So I think we lose something. I have no problem using pseudocode, but if we use it in the IPO, what do we use to code from? How do we structure the program? Flowcharting is a good tool to start with because it is a visual aid and matches the program so well. Once we become comfortable with the task at hand we can go to pseudocode.

```
Set variables to 0
Write page heading
Write column headings
Read student record
Do until EOF
    If GPR < 2.0
        Write student on report
    If GPR = 4.0
        Add 1 to count A
    Else
        If GPR >= 3.0
            Add 1 to count B
        Else
            If GPR >= 2.0
                Add 1 to count C
            Else
                Add 1 to count D
    Read student record
End Do
Write summary headings
Write counts and descriptions
```

**FIGURE 2.24**
**Pseudocode for Dean's List and Count Problem**

## HOW DO YOU USE THE TOOLS TOGETHER?

In this chapter we have looked at hierarchy charts, IPO charts and flowcharts. How do they work together and how do they work with COBOL? Well, let's take a brief look.

The hierarchy chart is a tool that lets us show all the major tasks/functions for the solution to a problem. We also identify and show the relationships between modules. Once we saw the hierarchy chart, we progressed to the IPO chart. We saw how to design it. We also said that in reality we would design an IPO for each module. Finally we developed the detailed program flowchart. Actually it was a set of flowcharts, one for each module. So far they all seem to work together.

**Numbering the Modules.**     At this point let's introduce a segment from our standards, Appendix D.  This standard says that to best show the hierarchical relationships in our charts and in our COBOL code, we should use a module numbering system. The main or highest level should be number 0000 and subordinate modules at the next level would be 1000, 2000, etc., for as many modules as we have.  Subsequent modules subordinate to 1000 would be 1100, 1200, etc.  We can depict this graphically as shown in Figure 2.25.

**FIGURE 2.25**
Hierarchy Chart Showing
Numbering System

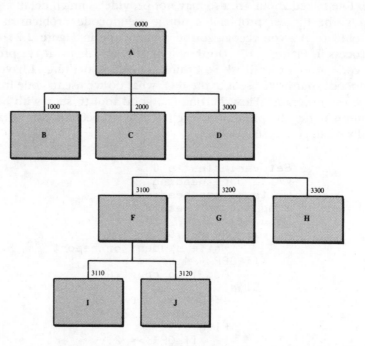

Given the numbering scheme, even if the labels within the modules are not exactly the same, the numbering system should leave little doubt as to which module is being referenced.

If we developed an IPO for each module, then on the form's heading we would also include the module number.  Then each flowchart module via the starting terminal block would also contain the module number.  Nice, isn't it?  They all fit together and now there is no doubt as to the relationships.

But what about COBOL?  Well, it's a little early, but you should remember the structure of a COBOL program we discussed in Chapter 1, in particular the PROCEDURE DIVISION, since that is where all logic is coded.  Here is a PROCEDURE DIVISION for the hierarchy chart in Figure 2.25.

Notice how each paragraph (-PARA) in the PROCEDURE DIVISION matches a module in the hierarchy chart and flowchart.  They do work well together, don't they?

**FIGURE 2.26**
COBOL Code Showing
Corresponding Numbering
System

```
PROCEDURE DIVISION.

0000-A-PARA.
      PERFORM 1000-B-PARA.
      PERFORM 2000-C-PARA.
      PERFORM 3000-D-PARA.
      STOP RUN.

1000-B-PARA
            :
            :

2000-C-PARA
      :
      :

3000-D-PARA.
      PERFORM 3100-F-PARA.
      PERFORM 3200-G-PARA.
      PERFORM 3300-H-PARA.
                :
3100-F-PARA.
      PERFORM 3110-I-PARA.
                :
      PERFORM 3120-J-PARA.
                :
3110-I-PARA.
      :
      :

3120-J-PARA.
      :
      :

3200-G-PARA.
      :
      :

3300-H-PARA.
      :
      :
```

## THE THEORY OF COHESION AND COUPLING

### Module Cohesion

Cohesion is also part of structured programming thought, along with coupling. Both are very important to our understanding of structured programming. Cohesion refers to how well code sticks together. The code within a module is cohesive if the logic fits together or is logically related so as to adhere into a logical unit.

There are several types of cohesion, with varying levels of desirability.  Following is a list of the types from best to worst.

Types of Cohesion

Functional
Sequential
Data
Procedural
Time Related
Logical
Coincidental

**Functional Cohesion.**     Modules are said to exhibit this most desirable type of cohesion if they perform a well-defined task.  Notice that I said task, singular.  That's critical to a module's being functionally cohesive.

Looking back at our hierarchy chart, Figure 2.10, and corresponding flowchart for the dean's list and count problem, which modules would we assign as examples of functional cohesion?  How about the following ones?

- Read student record
- Headings for detail report listing
- Count students by GPR range

I use these as examples because it is easy to see they all perform one set of related tasks: reading, writing headings and counting by GPR.  One very nice thing about functionally cohesive modules is that they are easy to maintain because each is devoted to one task.

**Sequential Cohesion.**     Typical of this type of cohesion are modules that require that the elements within the module be executed in a particular sequence.  Examples of these from our problem would be:

- Write summary
- Write students below 2.00 GPR

Both of these contain elements that must be executed in a particular sequence.  In write summary module we do write the counts but we also close the files, since we are finished with the program.  In writing the students we first have a series of moves that have to be executed.

In the first case maybe we should have related the write summary module with a control module called termination.  It would then control two modules, write summary and closing.  By doing this we would have made a sequentially cohesive module into three functionally cohesive modules.

However, in the second example I think I would be satisfied with the level of cohesion since without those moves it is functionally cohesive.  COBOL requires the moves, however.  This is a case where sequential fades into functional.

Think of these levels of cohesions as you might think about a baseball player's batting average.  An average of 1.000 is perfect, but we would all be happy with .400.  Willie Mays didn't hit that average, but he was said to have held the Giants together.  Was he functionally cohesive?  You bet he was!  But my point is, there is nothing wrong with a module being less than perfectly cohesive.

**Data Cohesion.**     All modules that manipulate the same data item are said to be data cohesive. Our Dean's List Solution doesn't have any that clearly fall into this type. However, if we looked at a program that validates data records, modules that usually carry a paragraph name like VALIDATION-PARA or VALIDATION-DATA-RECORD-PARA are expected to be data-cohesive.

**Procedural Cohesion.**     This type of cohesion relates to the control structures we use to solve our problem. One of the best examples of this is the case where we want to add up the contents of an array. In a flowchart we might show this addition as in Figure 2.27.

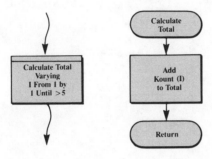

FIGURE 2.27
An Example of Procedural Cohesion

**Time-Related Cohesion.**     The classic examples of this type of cohesion are initialization and termination. Both must be executed at a particular time in the program. However, in COBOL we cannot avoid this type of module. Even though it is low in rank we still must do both these tasks.

**Logical Cohesion.**     A module exhibits logical cohesion if it performs several tasks that are in some way related but that still could be functionally decomposed. For instance, some people might have questioned my reasons for not including the write logic for those students below a 2.00 with the logic counting those same students. Both deal with the student's GPR, but they are two separate tasks, and even though they are logically cohesive I prefer functional decomposition.

**Coincidental Cohesion.**     This type of module has several tasks, and the only thing they have in common is that they are in the same module. Remember our write summary module. It could be said to be coincidentally cohesive because we put all the tasks in that one module just because it was all that we had left to do, and the module would not be too long anyway.

On a closing note, you probably noticed that while I ranked the different types of cohesion, in practice things are not black and white, there are some gray areas. Some modules may be typed in a couple of ways, and the classification would be correct. We should strive for that 1.000 batting average, but in reality we should be satisfied with something less.

### Module Coupling

The more one module needs to know about the other to which it is coupled, in order to execute, the more coupled they are said to be. If very little needs to be known, the modules are said to be loosely coupled. This is the type of module we want. If it is very independent, then maintenance to that module is made easier, since we don't have to worry about possible effects on the other module in the couple.

Three types of coupling exist:

- Content
- Control
- Data

**Content Coupling.**    This is the strongest form of coupling and the least desirable. It should be avoided.  By following our guideline of GO TO-less programming we can generally avoid content coupling because content coupling occurs when one module refers to the contents of another in this manner:

```
A-PARA.
  .
  .
  GO TO X-PARA.
  .
  .
  X-PARA.
  .
  .
  .
```

**Control Coupling.**    One of the best examples of this type of coupling is the EOF FLAG.  The PERFORM. . . UNTIL. . .FLAG = 1 is dependent on the read module's setting FLAG to 1 before returning to the PERFORM.  One module is dependent on the contents of another.

We don't necessarily want to eliminate this type of coupling.

**Data Coupling.**    This is the weakest form and therefore the most desired type of coupling.  Modules are connected because of their access to common data items.  Using this definition, the module to write the students and the module to count the students are data coupled, since they both refer to the student data.

## SUMMARY

Structured Programming has become a standard today.  While it wasn't received with open arms at first, its value was soon recognized by Data Processing managers and other Data Processing professionals.  Its acceptance can also be attributed to the changing cost relationship between programmers and CPU.  As programmers became more expensive, goals for program development changed.  No longer was it cost effective to try to reduce lines of code at the expense of programmer time.  This realization did not take place overnight.  We saw how programming evolved from spaghetti bowl-like code through modular programming to structured programming.  Our study of structured programming took us through a discussion of the logic constructs.  We saw the first three constructs that were identified; sequence, selection, iteration.  We took a look at the two constructs that have developed over the years: Another form of the iteration and the case.  We saw that the discovery of these innocent looking constructs did not mean that complex code was eliminated.  It just meant that our understanding of logic structures had matured and our code still represents complex algorithms.

These changes also had an impact on COBOL and on the common problem-solving tools.  The impact on COBOL is evidenced by the new '85 compiler.  The changes in the tools can be seen through the top-down approach to problem solving and the use of hierarchy charts, IPO charts, flowcharts and pseudocode. We saw how the solution to a problem evolves by using these tools. And we saw how the tools work together toward the problem solution and that they eventually become part of the system documentation to help with system maintenance.

We also took a look at the ideas of cohesion and coupling. Both result from our study of structured programming. In both cases we also rated the various types. We found that functional cohesion was to be encouraged while coincidental was to be avoided. Furthermore, we said that of the three types of coupling (content, control, data), content was to be avoided while data coupling was our goal.

## EXERCISES

### Chapter Review Questions

1. The relationship of CPU cost to manpower cost during the spaghetti bowl era is best described as:

    a. Higher manpower cost
    b. Higher CPU cost
    c. About equal
    d. Depended on CPU manufacturer
    e. None of the above

2. One of the objectives of structured programming is:

    a. Eliminating all GO TOs
    b. To increase the use of GO TOs
    c. Minimize the use of GO TOs
    d. To only use GO (BACK) TOs
    e. All the above

3. The early stages of modular programming can be depicted as:

    a. Single module programs
    b. Smaller bowls of spaghetti
    c. Larger bowls of spaghetti
    d. Smaller bowls of ravioli
    e. None of the above

4. Which of the following is not one of the original structured programming constructs:

    a. DO WHILE
    b. DO UNTIL
    c. IF THEN ELSE
    d. SEQUENCE
    e. All were original constructs

5. The Top-down approach to programming says:

    a. Start with the overall picture of the problem
    b. Start with the detail
    c. Start with the lowest module and code
    d. Develop the solution starting with the big picture and working down to the detail
    e. Both a and d are true

6. The DO WHILE
    a. Test before
    b. Test after
    c. Test both before and after
    d. Test during
    e. None of the above

7. HIPO stands for:
    a. A large water animal
    b. Hierarchy chart
    c. Hierarchy and INPUT-PROCESS-OUTPUT CHART
    d. A type of code
    e. None of the above

8. The rectangle indicates what activity in a flowchart:
    a. Decision
    b. I/O
    c. Process
    d. Predefined process
    e. None of the above

9. The highest level of a hierarchy chart would most likely contain:
    a. Control statements and detail statements
    b. Detail only
    c. Control only
    d. All of the above
    e. None of the above

10. The control statement in COBOL that is used to show the control relationship in a hierarchy chart is the:
    a. GO TO
    b. PERFORM
    c. DO WHILE
    d. DO UNTIL
    e. None of the above

11. The IPO chart is normally developed starting with the:
    a. INPUT
    b. PROCESS
    c. OUTPUT
    d. Either INPUT or PROCESS
    e. None of the above

12. In the real world, for each module in a hierarchy chart you would have:
    a. One IPO per module
    b. Only one IPO for the chart
    c. One or more IPOs per module depending on module complexity
    d. No set relation exists
    e. None of the above

13. The PROCESS part of the IPO shows:

    a. The detail logic needed

    b. All processes needed

    c. All processes needed including sequencing

    d. Pseudocode for processes needed

    e. Either a or d

14. What problem-solving tool is said to be: A semi-graphical representation of the solution to a problem?

    a. Hierarchy chart

    b. IPO

    c. Module chart

    d. Flowchart

    e. All of the above

15. Using our module numbering system, module 3400 would be controlled by module:

    a. 3300

    b. 3410

    c. 3000

    d. 3000 and module 400

    e. None of the above

16. "How well code sticks together" is known as:

    a. Coupling

    b. Pseudocoding

    c. Cohesion

    d. Flowcharting

    e. Top-down design

17. The most desirable type of coupling is:

    a. Content

    b. Control

    c. Logical

    d. Data

    e. None of the above

18. The most desirable type of cohesion is:

    a. Sequential

    b. Coincidental

    c. Time-related

    d. Procedural

    e. None of the above

19. The relationship between ease of maintenance and module independence is:

    a. Direct; more independent, easier to maintain

    b. Indirect; more independent, harder to maintain

    c. No relation exists

    d. Best exhibited with cohesive modules

    e. None of the above

20. Module decomposition refers to the need to break a module into:
    a.    Two new modules
    b.    One new module
    c.    Three new modules
    d.    One additional control module
    e.    Both a and c are true

## Discussion Questions

1. Briefly explain the lead read technique.
2. Explain the relationship of the hierarchy chart, IPO chart, flowchart and COBOL program.
3. Briefly contrast cohesion and coupling.
4. Briefly contrast the DO WHILE and DO UNTIL constructs.
5. Briefly explain the benefits afforded to a DP manager by modular programming.
6. Briefly explain how an IPO is developed.

## Practice Problems

1. Draw a hierarchy chart with at least three levels.  Indicate which modules are detail, control or both.
2. Modify the Dean's List Flowchart in order to provide the average GPR for all students.
3. Assume you have the Personnel File whose RECORD CONTENTS are given in Data File B, develop the HIPO and Detail Program Flowchart to list all employees.  On a summary report provide the following:
    a.    Count of the number of employees in each store
    b.    Count of the number of employees in each department
    c.    Total year to date earnings
    d.    Average year to date earnings by store
4. For Problem 3, develop the pseudocode instead of the flowchart.

# IDENTIFICATION AND ENVIRONMENT DIVISIONS

_**OBJECTIVES**_   In this chapter we will study the first two divisions of a COBOL program: IDENTIFICATION DIVISION and ENVIRONMENT DIVISION. We will see that the function of the IDENTIFICATION DIVISION is primarily documentation.

The ENVIRONMENT DIVISION, on the other hand, contains more than just documentation. The two parts of the ENVIRONMENT DIVISION, CONFIGURATION SECTION and INPUT-OUTPUT SECTION, are contrasted. While the first is mostly documentation, the second is our first chance at programming.

In CONFIGURATION SECTION we will look at the concepts associated with source and object computers. Production and development environments are presented.

Finally, we look at the SELECT clause in the INPUT-OUTPUT SECTION. This will open discussions of JCL (Job Control Language) and how file names in a COBOL program are associated with data sets on a system's disk pack somewhere in the confines of the data center.

## _TOPICS_

- development environment
- production environment
- source/object programs
- subprogramming
- internal file name
- external file name
- european notation
- system flowchart
- JCL
- JCL-less systems

## _KEY WORDS_

- IDENTIFICATION DIVISION
- ENVIRONMENT DIVISION
- PROGRAM-ID
- DATE-WRITTEN
- OBJECT COMPUTER
- SELECT
- ASSIGN
- device type

- DATE-COMPILED
- AUTHOR
- SECURITY
- CONFIGURATION SECTION
- INPUT-OUTPUT SECTION
- SOURCE COMPUTER

- device organization
- JCL
- DD
- data set
- DSN
- data set name

## INTRODUCTION

Every COBOL program is made up of four DIVISIONs: IDENTIFICATION, ENVIRON-MENT, DATA, and PROCEDURE. Not only must it contain these four DIVISIONs; they must also be presented in that order. Therefore, since this chapter covers two of the four DIVISIONs, when we finish this chapter, we will be halfway through COBOL. Well, not really. As you can tell by looking at the table of contents, this chapter cannot possibly cover half of COBOL. In fact, you will see that the IDENTI-FICATION and ENVIRONMENT DIVISIONs are mostly documentation. It isn't until INPUT-OUTPUT SECTION of the ENVIRONMENT DIVISION that we become pro-grammers, so to speak.

## PURPOSE

The IDENTIFICATION DIVISION's purpose is two-fold. First, it is used to identify both the programmer and the program. This is accomplished by two of the para-graphs available for our use.

## IDENTIFICATION DIVISION

Let's take a closer look at the IDENTIFICATION DIVISION's elements and related entries.

IDENTIFICATION DIVISION.

    PROGRAM-ID. program-name.
    [ AUTHOR. programmer's name. ]
    [ INSTALLATION. name of computer installation. ]
    [ DATE-WRITTEN. date program was written. ]
    [ DATE-COMPILED.[ date program was last compiled ] ]
    [ SECURITY. comment on special security procedures. ]
    [ REMARKS. comments describing program. ]

Notice that all entries in the **IDENTIFICATION DIVISION** are Paragraphs. How do we know that? Remember that all divisions or sections contain the key word "DIVISION" or "SECTION" respectively. Therefore, these entries in

**IDENTIFICATION DIVISION** must be paragraphs since they do not include the word DIVISION or SECTION, and they start in the A-margin.

PROGRAM-ID is required, while COBOL makes all other entries optional. I require my students to use them all except for security! You should be certain what your professor wants you to use. In any case, let's discuss all the entries anyway.

## PROGRAM-ID

As previously noted, this paragraph is the only one required. The entry, program-name, is not just commentary (as are all other entries in the optional paragraphs). The program-name must follow certain rules for formation:

- It must be unique.
- It must be 1–8 characters in length.
- It may use only 0–9 and/or A–Z.
- It may not use special characters, including blanks and hyphens.
- It may not use reserved words.

## AUTHOR

This paragraph allows you to enter your name or your team members' names. In the real world, this helps when modifications are going to be made.

## INSTALLATION

The name of the computer installation is the entry in this optional paragraph. This is useful in the event that systems are developed at different locations.

## DATE-WRITTEN

As you would expect, this is where you enter the date the program is written. What date is that? Unless you write the whole program on the same day, you must make a choice. You might just enter the month and year, such as JULY 1987. In the academic environment, let me suggest the date you use is the day the program is assigned. Doing this will help you keep track of your time. In the business world, use whatever is appropriate for you or your organization.

## DATE-COMPILED

This paragraph is a little different. You have the option of supplying the actual date or leaving it blank.

## TIP

I suggest that you leave the date entry blank. Then when the program is compiled, the compiler will supply the system date for you. This is for keeping a development log. It also is useful as a reference during maintenance of the programs.

## SECURITY

Within this paragraph, you might specify procedures that the program will go through for security purposes: password use, label records on files and the like.

## REMARKS

This paragraph allows us to include a brief description of the program. If you look at Appendix C, the CIRCLE CLUB PROGRAM, you will see how I used it. I used it to give you a description of the problem. Don't do it that way! I was insuring that when you had the program you would also have the problem statement. What you should use is a much briefer statement.

In COBOL '74, the actual use of REMARKS was eliminated. I still like to use it. When you use REMARKS, you must make it a comment entry by placing an asterisk in column 7.

By now you probably have noticed that not only are all the paragraphs, except PROGRAM-ID, optional, but also the entries within the paragraphs are treated as comments. For example, for INSTALLATION, I could say MARS. For AUTHOR, I could say HEMINGWAY or even WILLIE NELSON. While both are authors, I doubt that either had/has a knowledge of COBOL. Figure 3.2 is a full example.

```
IDENTIFICATION DIVISION.

PROGRAM-ID.      EXAMPLE.
AUTHOR.          GEORGE FOWLER.
INSTALLATION.    TEXAS A&M.
DATE-WRITTEN.    FEBRUARY 29, 1988.
DATE-COMPILED.
*REMARKS.         THIS IS AN EXAMPLE.
```

## ENVIRONMENT DIVISION

As the name implies, this division describes the environment in which the program will run. It also allows—in fact, requires—the programmer to specify all input and output files that will be used. Given these two purposes, the division is made of two sections, CONFIGURATION SECTION and INPUT-OUTPUT SECTION.

A quick look at the entries that make up **ENVIRONMENT DIVISION** shows these two sections. It also provides us with a look at the entries within these sections—the paragraphs.

<u>ENVIRONMENT DIVISION</u>.

<u>CONFIGURATION SECTION</u>.

[ <u>SOURCE-COMPUTER</u>. computer name. ]
[ <u>OBJECT-COMPUTER</u>. computer name. ]
[ <u>SPECIAL-NAMES</u>. ]

<u>INPUT-OUTPUT SECTION</u>

[ <u>FILE-CONTROL</u>.
       <u>SELECT</u> clause(s). ]
[ <u>I-O-CONTROL</u>. ]

### CONFIGURATION SECTION

The entries in **CONFIGURATION SECTION** specify information about the computer(s) and their characteristics. This is accomplished with three optional paragraphs—SOURCE-COMPUTER, OBJECT-COMPUTER, and SPECIAL-NAMES.

**SOURCE-COMPUTER and OBJECT-COMPUTER.**     Let me ask you a question—since this is a text, it must be rhetorical! What is a **SOURCE-COMPUTER**? What is an **OBJECT-COMPUTER**? If I were walking down the hall would I recognize either if I passed it? Does a source computer have a maroon cape and a large "S" on it's chest as shown in Figure 3.1?

**FIGURE 3.1**
Source Computer?

No, that's not what we mean by **SOURCE-COMPUTER** or **OBJECT-COMPUTER**. **SOURCE-COMPUTER** is the computer where the compiler lives. In other words, it's where your source program will be compiled.

Then what is the **OBJECT-COMPUTER**? It is the computer that will execute your object program. I know that it is best not to define something by using the term I'm defining. So let's also look at it this way:

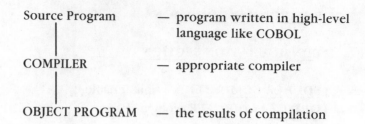

Source Program    — program written in high-level
                    language like COBOL

COMPILER          — appropriate compiler

OBJECT PROGRAM    — the results of compilation

Are these computers necessarily different computers?  No, they are not.  In fact, in most academic environments, they are one and the same.  But they *may* be different.  Why?  The answer has to do with the real world.

Imagine that you are developing a new program for your boss.  Your work environment would be one that requires you to compile, correct, compile, correct, etc., until you get the syntax right and get a complete object program.  You would then execute the program using test data and check your answers.  More than likely you would need to make revisions to the source and you would start the process again.  This process is shown in Figure 3.2.

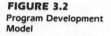
**FIGURE 3.2**
**Program Development
Model**

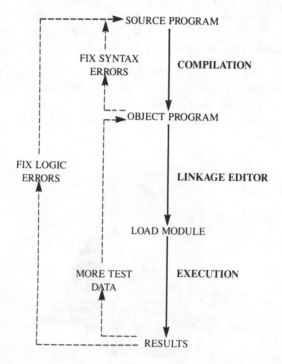

From Figure 3.2 you can see the development environment.  While this is the environment in which you operate in school, it is not the full picture of the real world.  When you get the correct answers (results) you turn in your lab assignment, get your gold star and start your next assignment.  In the business world you get your gold star from your boss, but your program is then put into production.  It is made available to the user(s) to use daily, weekly, or whatever it was intended for.  At this point does the program need to be compiled every time it is used?  No, it doesn't.  In fact, that would be a waste of valuable resources.  Furthermore, we probably don't want the user(s) to re-compile the program without some control over when and where it is done.  Therefore, production programs are executed on computers that *do not* have access to compilers and programs in development do not interfere with production programs.

So once all testing is done the object code is placed into a production environment. If changes need to be made, then they are done within the development environment. Once finished, the revised object program replaces the old object program in the production environment.

**SPECIAL-NAMES.**    This is a very interesting paragraph. In the vast number of cases it is used to define a data-name that will be used for report spacing with the WRITE verb. We will look at this feature when we study the WRITE verb. However, **SPECIAL-NAMES** may also be used to change the comma and decimal and to specify a different currency symbol like the English pound sign "£" for the American dollar sign "$".

For instance, in some European countries, our use of the decimal and comma are reversed, and the $ sign is not the currency designation. For example,

$76,593.10  would be 76.593,10

and to cause this to happen, we would code the following:

```
SPECIAL-NAMES
    CURRENCY SIGN IS "£"
    DECIMAL-POINT IS COMMA.
```

The general syntax is:

**SPECIAL-NAMES**

[ function name **IS** mnemonic-name ]

[ <u>**CURRENCY SIGN**</u> **IS** literal ]

[ <u>**DECIMAL-POINT**</u> **IS** <u>**COMMA**</u> ].


## *INPUT-OUTPUT SECTION*

All programs that require input or output files require this section's FILE-CONTROL paragraph. On the other hand, the I-O-CONTROL paragraph may be specified with the paragraph, but most analysts find they don't need these features for the systems they are designing.

**The FILE-CONTROL Paragraph and the SELECT.**    The entries in these paragraphs are the SELECT clauses. For each file that is used in the program, a SELECT clause will be needed. It is at this point in coding the program that the programmer truly becomes a programmer.

The format of the SELECT clause is:

<u>**SELECT**</u> filename <u>**ASSIGN TO**</u> system specifications.

Look at the Circle Club Program in Appendix C and also look at the system flowchart in Figure 3.3.

In the Circle Club Program, we needed the customer file as input and we needed a report file to allow us to write the required physical report. The system flowchart also shows the same needs: an input file and an output file. But it says more. The input file is a disk file while the output file is a printed file. Do we use this information? You can bet on it. With the ASSIGN clause, we specify the type of file, its organization and a data-name that is used to associate our internal file-name, SELECT filename, to our actual file on the computer system. This data-name is called the external file name.

**FIGURE 3.3**
Example System Flowchart

The general format of the ASSIGN clause is:

. . . . . . <u>**ASSIGN TO**</u> system-name.

where file-name is a data-name that we as programmers make up. The rules of data-name formulation still apply. Our standards also require the suffix of FILE to be used. Therefore, SELECT MEMBERSHIP-FILE might be appropriate for the Circle Club or SELECT CUSTOMER-FILE might be used for an accounts receivable data file.

The file name we choose is the one we must use to reference the file in our COBOL program. That's why I call it the internal file name. I call the system name the external file name because it is used for reference outside of (external to) our source code.

The form of the system-name varies from installation to installation and from system to system. In an IBM environment it takes the form:

**ASSIGN** TO device-type-organization-file-name

device-type is    UR  for unit record like card reader, printer, punch
                  UT  for utility like tape, disk, etc.
                  DA  for direct access devices like disk, drums, etc.

organization is   S   specifies a physical sequential file
                 I    specifies an indexed file
                 R   specifies a relative file

file name is       a data-name of no more than eight characters. It is the link between our internal file name and the actual name of our data set on the system's storage device. This is the name referred to earlier as the external file name.

**More on SELECT.**     I should tell you at this point that the full form of SELECT includes many other options. Most of these are used only for random files.

<u>SELECT</u> internal-name <u>ASSIGN</u> TO device-org-external-filename

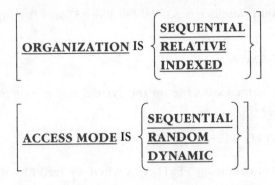

[ <u>RECORD KEY</u> IS data-name ]

[ <u>FILE STATUS</u> IS data-name ]

**ORGANIZATION.**    As the programmer, you may specify that the file is organized in a manner that is sequential, relative or indexed. If you don't specify an organization, it is assumed to be sequential. That's why I didn't use the clause earlier, since our files are physically organized sequentially. If we have random files, we may choose either relative or indexed. Both of those file organizations will be discussed fully in later chapters. So for now just know they exist.

**ACCESS MODE.**    This clause lets us specify how we will use the file. With sequentially-organized files, the access must be sequential. However, with random files, both relative and indexed, we may access the file all three ways.

**RECORD KEY.**    With random files we must specify which field will be used to address the file. Randomly organized files allow us to access records directly by specifying a RECORD KEY value and then issuing an input/output command.

You can see that this clause and the access mode clause are used for randomly organized files—relative and indexed.

**FILE STATUS.**    This clause is used to communicate with the system. That is to say, when we try to read or write a record from a file, the system will put a standard two digit code into the data name specified with FILE STATUS. We can then check the code to see what happened (to find the status). For instance a code of 00 usually means a successful operation, while a FILE STATUS code of 22 means a duplicate key was used.

We will also look closer at this feature when we use random files.

## A WORD ABOUT JCL

It is necessary to take a brief look at JCL (Job Control Language) statements here. (The JCL used in this text is for IBM MVS Systems.) Let's say that we want to run and test a COBOL program using a data file that has been created by using some available method like a system editor. We type in the data and save it with the name TESTDATA. At that time the system assigns a full name called a data set name (DSN for short) to your file. It might look something like

```
DSN = account-number.TESTDATA
```

so that if your LOGON account-number is something like S573 (S for student) then the DSN would be:

```
DSN=S573.TESTDATA
```

So now we have a uniquely named data file on the system and in our program we have the following SELECT clause:

```
SELECT EXAMPLE-FILE ASSIGN TO DA-S-TEST.
```

How do we get a record of data from TESTDATA when we read EXAMPLE-FILE?

| **COBOL Program** | | **DSN** |
|---|---|---|
| EXAMPLE-FILE | → ??????????? → | TESTDATA |

We need something to link the two. We use JCL and the external name on the ASSIGN.

```
//TEST      DD  DSN=S573.TESTDATA
```

With this JCL statement, called a DD (data definition) statement, we link our internal file name to the data set on the system via the external file name. Here is our complete graphic:

| **COBOL Program** | **JCL** | **DSN** |
|---|---|---|
| EXAMPLE-FILE | → TEST → | TESTDATA |
| (internal name) | (external name) | (data set name) |

Compare this graphic with Figure 3.4.

**FIGURE 3.4**
**An Illustration of the Relationship among the External, Internal File Names and the DD Statement**

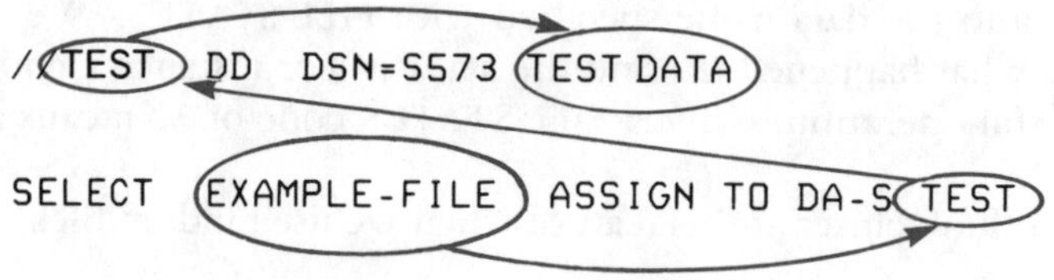

Do you see how a reference to EXAMPLE-FILE gets us to TESTDATA? (I will explain JCL syntax later in this text.)

I'm sure you're asking why you can't just reference the data set directly? Well, remember that COBOL was designed to be portable. The SELECT clause goes a long way in doing that. If we were able to reference the DSN directly with, say, "READ TESTDATA" and we had many such references, what would happen if we went to a different environment that used different DSN conventions? Each reference would have to be changed. But with the buffer that the SELECT/ASSIGN provides, we would have to change the external name just once along with the corresponding DD statement. All internal references do not need changing.

### JCLess Systems

On some systems we simply make the association via EXEC files, and yet on others we make the association via the File Description, which I describe later in this text.

Some of you may have access to COBOL on a micro. You will notice that on RMCOBOL the SELECT/ASSIGN simply references the file as follows:

```
SELECT EXAMPLE-FILE ASSIGN TO "B:TESTDATA".
```

The bottom line is that the SELECT is our link to the data sets. That linkage is accomplished in various ways on various systems. You should check to see how it will be done on your system.

**I-O CONTROL Paragraph.**    This is rarely used any more. However, special techniques such as reserving more I/O buffer areas, and sharing file and/or record areas, may be specified in this paragraph. As an application warrants, I will show these throughout the text.

## AN EXAMPLE

If we were going to write a COBOL program for the Dean of the College of Business, what would the IDENTIFICATION and ENVIRONMENT DIVISIONs look like?

Let's say we have a sequential data file with a DSN of STUDENTS and the dean wants a report listing all students to include all data fields shown in Data File A. Figure 3.5 illustrates the request.

**FIGURE 3.5**
**System Flowchart for
Dean's Listing Problem**

Given this problem, the Identification and Environment divisions would be:

```
IDENTIFICATION DIVISION.

PROGRAM-ID.     EXAMPLE.
AUTHOR.         G.C. FOWLER
INSTALLATION.   TEXAS A&M.
DATE-WRITTEN.   JULY 7, 1989
DATE-COMPILED.
SECURITY.       NONE.
*REMARKS.
*     PROGRAM LISTS STUDENTS IN THE
*     COLLEGE OF BUSINESS.
```

```
ENVIRONMENT DIVISION.

CONFIGURATION SECTION.

SOURCE-COMPUTER.     IBM-470.
OBJECT-COMPUTER.     IBM-470.
SPECIAL-NAMES.
    C01 IS  TOP-OF-PAGE.              <--- I'll get to this
                                           soon.
INPUT-OUTPUT SECTION.

FILE-CONTROL.
    SELECT  STUDENT-FILE   ASSIGN TO  DA-S-STUDENT.
    SELECT  REPORT-FILE    ASSIGN TO  UT-S-REPORT.
```

## SUMMARY

So now you know half of COBOL's divisions. The fun stuff is yet to come. However, some very important items and concepts were discussed in this chapter.

We learned that IDENTIFICATION DIVISION is mostly comment. The PROGRAM-ID is required (I require most paragraphs) because it actually has a functional reason for being—it is used in subprogramming.

In the ENVIRONMENT DIVISION, we examined two sections: CONFIGURATION and INPUT-OUTPUT SECTIONs. We had some fun here. Remember our discussion on SOURCE and OBJECT computers? The concept of two environments is very important. You should understand what they are and why they exist. In the real world, we don't want development efforts to compete for computer resources with production efforts and vice versa. Therefore, all maintenance and development is done in the source computer environment and all "running" programs are executed in the object computer environment.

Probably the most important discussion we had was about the SELECT clause. You probably picked up that I consider the SELECT clause as one of the most important clauses in COBOL. It helps make COBOL portable and is our means of associating our program file names with the actual data sets on the system.

Using the SELECT clause, we define the internal file name and associate it via the ASSIGN with an external file name. Along with the external file name we specify the device type and file organization. The external file name is in turn used on a DD statement that links it to the data set (DSN).

## EXERCISES

### Chapter Review Questions

1. Which of the following is the purpose of the IDENTIFICATION DIVISION?
    a.   Identify the hardware
    b.   Identify the programmer
    c.   Identify the files
    d.   Identify the program
    e.   Both b and d are true

2. The DATE-COMPILED:

    a.    May be supplied by operating system

    b.    May be supplied by programmer

    c.    Must be coded

    d.    Is not part of the IDENTIFICATION DIVISION

    e.    Either a or b

3. The REMARKS Paragraph:

    a.    Is no longer part of COBOL '74

    b.    Is still part of COBOL '74

    c.    Is an enhancement of COBOL '85

    d.    Must always be included

    e.    None of the above

4. Which paragraph must always be included in the IDENTIFICATION DIVISION?

    a.    DATE-WRITTEN

    b.    PROGRAM-ID

    c.    AUTHOR

    d.    REMARKS

    e.    SECURITY

5. The source computer is the computer where the program is:

    a.    Written

    b.    Compiled

    c.    Executed (run)

    d.    Put into production

    e.    None of the above

6. During development, testing a program with a new data set would include:

    a.    Compiling the program again

    b.    Just running the object program

    c.    Placing the program into production first

    d.    Running the source program

    e.    None of the above

7. Syntax errors are found during:

    a.    Execution

    b.    Compilation

    c.    During linkage editing

    d.    Within the object program

    e.    None of the above

8. For each file used in a program a SELECT CLAUSE is needed.

    a.    True

    b.    False

9. Which of the following is an allowable device type specification of the ASSIGN Clause?

    a.    UR

    b.    UT

    c.    DA

    d.    DP

    e.    All but d are allowable

10. An organization specification of I says:

    a. Individual File
    b. Indexed File
    c. Item File
    d. Information File
    e. None of the above

11. The access mode options available with a random file are:

    a. Dynamic
    b. Indexed
    c. Relative
    d. Sequential
    e. Both a and d are correct

12. DSN stands for:

    a. Detail System Network
    b. Data Starting Number
    c. Data Set Number
    d. Data Set Name
    e. None of the above

13. The internal file name is linked to the data set on the system via the:

    a. External file name on the DD statement
    b. External file name on the ASSIGN statement
    c. Data set name
    d. SELECT file name statement
    e. None of the above

14. JCL stands for:

    a. Jumbo COBOL Language
    b. Just COBOL Linkage
    c. Job Control Language
    d. Job Control Linkage
    e. None of the above

15. Which of the following is a type of FILE ORGANIZATION available in COBOL?

    a. DIRECT
    b. SEQUENTIAL
    c. RANDOM
    d. RELATIVE
    e. Both b and d

## Discussion Questions

1. Briefly explain the function of the select clause.
2. Briefly show the relationship of the select clause and the DD JCL statement.
3. Explain how you might use the SPECIAL-NAMES clause in a program.
4. Write a complete SELECT clause to match the following:

```
//MASTER DD DSN=N007.JB.DATA
```

    where   data is an index file
    and     you need to access it sequentially
    and     the key field is INVENTORY-NUMBER

*Practice Problems*

1. Code the IDENTIFICATION and ENVIRONMENT DIVISIONS for a program that will READ and WRITE the Personnel File in Data File B.

2. Code the IDENTIFICATION and ENVIRONMENT DIVISIONS for a program that will READ and WRITE the Inventory File in Data File C.

# DATA DIVISION

**OBJECTIVES**   In the DATA DIVISION we describe all data that will be used in the program. Files, records, and data fields must all be described. While this chapter introduces five sections of the DATA DIVISION, we spend most of our time with the FILE SECTION where we describe all data files, and the WORKING-STORAGE SECTION where we describe our records. The LINKAGE, REPORT, and SCREEN SECTIONs are more appropriate for later topics.

This chapter guides you in studying two major topics, file descriptions and record descriptions. We will look at all the features and techniques of file descriptions (FDs), including blocking (grouping of records), buffers (input/output areas) and general record descriptions (G-R-Ds).

In the WORKING-STORAGE SECTION, we look at detail record descriptions (D-R-Ds). We will see how the use of level numbers for D-R-Ds is functionally the same as Roman numerals for doing an outline of a chapter. Discussion of the techniques for doing D-R-Ds then leads us into the discussion of edit characters and their use.

Finally, we will look at a variety of record descriptions according to function. You will be shown D-R-Ds used for describing input data, the body of reports (detail lines), page and column headings and total lines.

## TOPICS

- **general record description (G-R-D)**
- **detail record description (D-R-D)**
- **blocking**
- **buffers, I/O work areas**
- **system flowcharts**
- **file description**
- **data hierarchy and level numbers**
- **logical vs. physical record length**
- **types of data—A, 9, X**
- **group items**
- **elementary items**
- **editing**
- **interactive COBOL**
- **input record description**
- **output or detail or report body record description**
- **page heading**
- **column headings**
- **total lines**
- **printer layout forms**
- **data flow concept**
- **data names**
- **requirement of unique references**

## PURPOSE

The third division in a COBOL program is the DATA DIVISION. In this division we will describe every item of data that we will use in the PROCEDURE DIVISION. We must describe files, records associated with the files, independent and work records, data fields within the records and the size and type of data associated with each field.

You can see that our job in the DATA DIVISION is both important and large. In fact, much of the coding time is spent on this division. Once all input and output files, including reports, have been designed by the systems analyst and approved by the user, the coding can start.

In the DATA DIVISION we will use five sections to accomplish our description of data:

1. FILE SECTION
2. WORKING-STORAGE SECTION
3. LINKAGE SECTION
4. REPORT SECTION
5. SCREEN SECTION

The FILE SECTION, as the name implies, is where the characteristics of all the files used in the program will be specified. In the WORKING-STORAGE SECTION we will give detailed descriptions of all the records and fields we plan to use. This will include more than just input and output records, but also temporary work areas needed for mathematical results, status indicators (flags) and other items like condition names. Beyond just describing each record and its associated fields, we also establish a data relationship or hierarchy. This hierarchy makes data handling in COBOL a very powerful, unique feature.

I mentioned subprogramming in Chapter 2 in relation to the PROGRAM-ID. Well, guess what? The LINKAGE SECTION is also used for subprogramming. Therefore, I'll discuss it later in the text.

The REPORT SECTION is used with the REPORT WRITER feature. It is also a very powerful feature of COBOL, and we will look at it later in Appendix G. Finally, we look at the SCREEN SECTION. This section is dedicated to interactive COBOL on micros. The section *is not* a COBOL standard, but it is found in some COBOL compilers for microcomputers. And, even if the section is not included in a particular compiler, many of the screen-handling features are included. Since micros are so popular, we will look at some common features in this chapter and show some common procedures in Appendix F.

## DATA LEVEL INDICATION

COBOL requires us to describe all files, records and fields. We must also say what types of characters make up the fields and give the size of those fields. How do we communicate all this to the compiler? How does the compiler know a file description from a record description from a field description? With level indicators!

In describing our data we use the following indicators:

| Indicators | Element |
|---:|---|
| FD | files |
| 01 | records |
| 02–49 | fields |
| 77 | independent items |
| 88 | condition names |

The FD stands for File Description. We must have one for each file selected in the INPUT-OUTPUT SECTION of the ENVIRONMENT DIVISION. Within the FD we specify the characteristics of the file being described.

Records are described with level number (indicator) 01. Don't let me confuse you here. We tell the compiler that we are going to describe a record by starting our description with an 01. However, a record may be made up of several fields and, therefore, would be followed by several entries in the 02–49 level number range.

So all fields making up a record are designated by 02–49 level numbers. The sum of all these within an 01 makes up the record description. The 01 entry alone does not necessarily comprise the entire record description—although it might.

## FILE SECTION

As I have said before, in the FILE SECTION we will define all the files we will use in the program. These files have already been identified in the ENVIRONMENT DIVISION with the SELECT clause. Therefore, the compiler now expects an FD for each of the SELECTs.

I think the best way to go about this is to look at the FD and its options:

FD filename

LABEL RECORDS ARE $\left\{ \begin{array}{l} \text{OMITTED} \\ \text{STANDARD} \end{array} \right\}$

[ RECORD CONTAINS # CHARACTERS ]

[ BLOCK CONTAINS # RECORDS ]

DATA $\left\{ \begin{array}{l} \text{RECORD IS} \\ \text{RECORDS ARE} \end{array} \right\}$ record-name.

### FD

The **FD** file name specifies that this is a file description for the file name listed. Consider, for instance, if we had used the following SELECT clause:

SELECT example-file ASSIGN TO DA-S-EXAMPLE
ORGANIZATION IS SEQUENTIAL.

The compiler would then expect:

FD EXAMPLE-FILE

Once we had established that link between SELECT and **FD**, then we would continue the file description.

---

## TIP

You must have one FD for each SELECT clause.

---

### The LABEL RECORDS Clause

The **LABEL RECORDS** clause is the only one required by the '74 compiler. (I tend to use all the options anyway). With this clause, we specify that, on tape files and disk files, a record containing information about the file, which would insure the correct file has been mounted for processing, may be written as the first and last record on the file as shown in Figure 4.1.

**FIGURE 4.1**
File Showing Use of LABEL
RECORD Clause

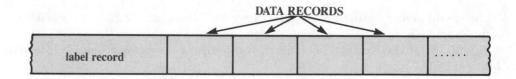

If we specify **LABEL RECORDS** ARE STANDARD, then a standard label for that file is written. However, we may specify that labels are not used with the OMITTED option. For instance, printer and card files would not use labels, but we have the option when using tape and disk files.

### The RECORD CONTAINS Clause

This clause allows us to specify the number of characters in the record. If our data record contains 100 bytes, we can code:

```
RECORD CONTAINS 100 CHARACTERS
```

I say we can code that entry because all clauses are optional except for LABEL RECORDS.

### The BLOCK CONTAINS Clause

At this point we have specified the presence or absence of labels and the size in characters of the records making up the file. Now we may specify a blocking factor.

A blocking factor is simply a means for specifying a group of records that should be grouped together and then written to the physical file. Or when we read, we get not one record but a group (block) of records. An individual record, say 100 characters, is known as a logical record. In other words, that's what we logically designed for our data needs. The block/group is called a physical record. It is associated with how we physically store the data on a tape or disk.

Let's look at an example. Assume we have 1,000 records of 100 characters each to store on a tape. Remember (from your intro class) that for you to store data on a tape it must be brought up to speed, the data is written, and then it must stop. This process causes unused spaces called gaps between records. For our example let's assume a gap is 1″. (That's large, but it works nicely for our example.) So, how much tape would be required to store the data on a tape rated at 1,000 BPI (bytes per inch)?

$$
\begin{array}{r}
1{,}000 \ \text{records} \\
\underline{100} \ \text{char/record} \\
100{,}000 \ \text{total characters @ 1,000 BPI} = 100″ \text{ for data}
\end{array}
$$

Now, if we don't block the file, every time we write, we start, write, and stop the tape. Therefore, we will have a 1 to 1 ratio of gaps to records.

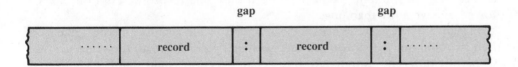

**FIGURE 4.2**
Layout of Records in an Unblocked File

This gives us 1,000 gaps, which converts to 1,000″. The total inches required would then be:

$$
\begin{array}{r}
100″ \ \text{data} \\
+ \ 1{,}000″ \ \text{gaps} \\
\hline
1{,}100″ \ \text{Total}
\end{array}
$$

What if we used a blocking factor of 100 records? We would still need the 100″ for data. After all, we still need to record the information. However, we don't physically write a record for each write command. The operating system keeps all the records we write until it has a block to write. In other words, we now have a 1 to 100 gap to record ratio, depicted as shown in Figure 4.3. Therefore, only 10 writes to the tape are required, causing 10 gaps. That requires 10″ of tape, giving us a total for our blocked file of:

$$100'' \text{ data}$$
$$\underline{10'' \text{ gaps}}$$
$$110'' \text{ Total}$$

While this is a loaded example, it does show one benefit of blocking. . .saving storage spaces.   But blocking does more.   How many physical or actual writes are done for the unblocked example? How many for the blocked example?

unblocked 1,000 writes. . . .one per record
blocked 10 writes. . . . . . .one per block

**FIGURE 4.3**
**Layout of Records in a Blocked File**

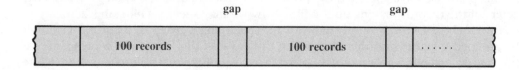

Ten writes vs. 1,000 writes!  What's the benefit?  Which is faster, main memory or disk I/O speed?  You're right! Memory speeds are now measured in MIPS.  So, you have not only saved space on disk or tape, but you have also enhanced execution time of your program.  Now how can you beat that by simply saying, **BLOCK CONTAINS** 100 RECORDS?

Well, it's not all gravy!  The system needs to use memory space during execution to contain your requested block size.  While that's a cost, it's minimal.  However, it does bring to mind that different computer systems set up optimal/maximum block sizes.  You should check to see what your computer system uses.

### The DATA RECORD Clause

The **DATA RECORD** clause is for documentation only; it too is optional and in fact is no longer part of the '85 compiler.  However, it does add to the readability of the FD, and I suggest you use it.  All we are saying with it is that the record(s) making up the file are called record-name(s).  We then follow with the 01 record description(s) for the file.  Most of the time we have or need only one record description, but we are allowed to have more than one.

For instance, if we were processing a transaction file against a master inventory file, then it would not be hard to see that while all records are all the same size, the formats may be different.  A transaction to delete a record would simply have to have one field, the item number, so that we could identify the corresponding record in the master file.  However, adding a new inventory item would require more than just the item number.  We might need a description, quantity on hand, cost per item.  See my point?  The file may contain more than one record format, and COBOL accommodates our needs.

DATA RECORD IS EXAMPLE-RECORD.

01 EXAMPLE-RECORD PICTURE IS X(100).

or

```
            DATA RECORDS ARE DELETE-RECORD
                            ADD-RECORD.

      01  DELETE-RECORD.
            :
      01  ADD-RECORD.
            :
```

What does the completed FD look like for our continuing example? Well, here it is!

```
      FD    EXAMPLE-FILE
            LABEL RECORDS ARE OMITTED
            RECORD CONTAINS 100 CHARACTERS
            BLOCK CONTAINS 100 RECORDS
            DATA RECORD IS EXAMPLE-RECORD.
      01    EXAMPLE-RECORD PICTURE IS X(100).
```

Why is the 01 shown, since it says the same thing as the RECORD CONTAINS clause? Because COBOL requires us to have at least one 01 associated with an FD. In fact, if we used the **DATA RECORDS** clause, we would need an 01 for each record listed. So, this 01 is required! Since the RECORD CONTAINS clause is optional, we specify the size and name of the record with the 01. It also establishes the I/O work area used by the system. This area is used by the system for all I/O operations with the file. It is also called the buffer.

## A PROBLEM SETTING

Before we go on, let's take a minute and look at an example problem. Let's say that the Dean of the College of Business wants a listing of all students. There exists a sequential file of all students (see Data File A). We are told that the DEAN-FILE is blocked using the largest factor allowed on the system. We check and find that the largest block size is 6,200 bytes (for example).

Given this information, we would draw this system flowchart:

**FIGURE 4.4**
System Flowchart for
Student List Program

The corresponding detail program flowchart is shown in Figure 4.5.

The system flowchart says that the DEAN-FILE will be used as input to a program and the output will be a report. Let's go one step further and look at the program.

**FIGURE 4.5**
**Detail Program Flowchart
for Student List Program**

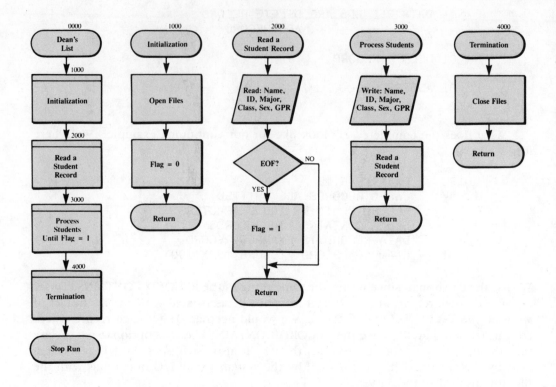

```
//GO.DEAN        DD      DSN=A159.STUDENTS. . .

//GO.REPORT      DD      SYSOUT=A,DCB=(BLKSIZE=133,RECFM=FA)
                  .
                  .
                  .

        IDENTIFICATION DIVISION.

        PROGRAM-ID.     DEANLIST.
        AUTHOR.         MICHAEL RYAN.
        DATE-WRITTEN.   MARCH 28, 1988.
        DATE-COMPILED.

       *REMARKS.
       *              THIS PROGRAM READS THE DEAN'S STUDENT
       *              FILE AND LISTS ALL STUDENTS ON A
       *              REPORT.

        ENVIRONMENT DIVISION.

        CONFIGURATION SECTION.
        SOURCE-COMPUTER.        IBM.
        OBJECT-COMPUTER.        IBM.
        SPECIAL-NAMES.          C01 IS TOP-OF-PAGE.

        INPUT-OUTPUT SECTION.
        FILE-CONTROL.
            SELECT DEAN-FILE        ASSIGN TO DA-S-DEAN.
            SELECT REPORT-FILE      ASSIGN TO UT-S-REPORT.
```

```
DATA DIVISION.

FILE SECTION.

FD   DEAN-FILE                           <----- filename from SELECT
     LABEL RECORDS ARE OMITTED
     RECORD CONTAINS 47 CHARACTERS
     BLOCK CONTAINS 131 RECORDS          <----- max 6200/47
     DATA RECORD IS STUDENT-RECORD.

01   STUDENT-RECORD          PIC X(47).

FD   REPORT-FILE
     LABEL RECORDS ARE OMITTED
     DATA RECORD IS REPORT-RECORD.

01   REPORT-RECORD           PIC X(133).
```

Take a moment to go back and see how everything fits together. I hope you see this relationship. If not please go back and review the material.

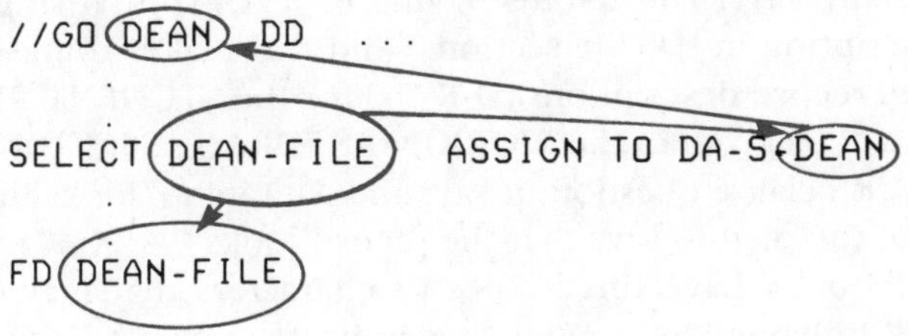

**FIGURE 4.6**
Relationship among DD, SELECT, and FD

The relationship is needed since the FDs give very valuable information about the file: record size, blocking and so forth. In fact, if we didn't provide information via the RECORD CONTAINS clause and the BLOCK CONTAINS clause, we would have to supply that information about the file in the DD statement. The system needs that information, and we must either tell it with our FD or with our JCL via a DCB (data control block). For instance, our JCL statement for DEAN-FILE might be:

```
//GO.DEAN   DD   DSN=A159.STUDENTS,
//              DCB=(LRECL=47,BLKSIZE=6157,RECFM=F)
//GO.REPORT DD   . . .
```

where the DCB is saying

LOGICAL RECORD LENGTH (LRECL) = 47 characters
BLOCK SIZE in characters (BLKSIZE) = 6157 characters
     [47 × 131 = 6157]
RECORD FORMAT (RECFM) IS FIXED (same size)

My preference is to supply the information via the FD, but either is OK. You should know and use your employer's standards.

## TIP

If you want to specify blocking within the JCL instead of within the program, simply specify a blocking factor of 0 in the FD.

## GENERAL RECORD DESCRIPTION (G-R-Ds)

The 01s associated with the FDs say a mouthful. What is PICTURE? What is X(47) or, for that matter, X(133)? Why not show the data fields that make up the STUDENT-RECORD? What is the REPORT-RECORD's format? These are very important questions, and we will answer all of them.

The form of the 01s that I use does not allow for reference to individual data fields. I choose to do it this way to avoid some problems with record descriptions given in the File Section. For instance, the value clause may not be used in the File Section. So I elect to provide all detail data descriptions in the working storage section. . .for now, anyway. This avoids having to learn special situations involved in giving detail description in the file section. And this makes things easier to learn. Therefore, the detail record descriptions (D-R-Ds) for the STUDENT-RECORD and the REPORT-RECORD will be given in the WORKING-STORAGE SECTION.

As to the PICTURE clause question, it says the data item "looks like this." So for STUDENT-RECORD, the picture says that the record looks like X(47). But what does that mean? In COBOL we have three types of characters that may be used: alphabetic, numeric and alphanumeric. Well, we indicate which to the compiler by a code:

A – alphabetic
9 – numeric
X – alphanumeric

Therefore, X(47) means that the data element, in this case, STUDENT-RECORD, is made up of 47 alphanumeric characters. Similarly, X(133) says our report records (lines) are made up of 133 alphanumeric characters.

The 01s associated with our files are GENERAL RECORD DESCRIPTIONS (G-R-Ds) which satisfy the compiler and help us avoid some problems. (Take my word for that for now.) But we still need to reference the data fields, and we cannot with G-R-Ds. We still need detail record descriptions (D-R-Ds) to be able to reference the data field and do what we need to do for the report.

## WORKING-STORAGE SECTION

The **WORKING-STORAGE SECTION** is organized into two major parts. All 01 record descriptions follow all independent record descriptions, 77 level items, if 77s are used. So a typical **WORKING-STORAGE SECTION** might look like:

```
WORKING-STORAGE SECTION.

77   Independent record
77   Independent record
01   D-R-D
01   D-R-D
01   D-R-D
```

All our D-R-Ds will be done in this section of the DATA DIVISION. (Assume for now that we are not using REPORT SECTION or SCREEN SECTION.) The section will contain our record descriptions for all input and output records. We will also have need for other records, but, the bottom line is that we need to learn how to code detail record descriptions.

## DETAIL RECORD DESCRIPTIONS (D-R-Ds)

Have you ever developed an outline for a story or for a chapter in a textbook? Does the following outline format say anything to you?

```
I                 <------- major topic
    A             <------- subtopic
    B             <------- subtopic
        1             <------- subtopic
        2             <------- subtopic
            a             <------- subtopic
            b
    C             etc
        1
        2
        3
    D
```

Does it communicate anything by itself? Without our ever knowing what we are outlining, it does tell a story, doesn't it? It says that topic I is made up of four major topics: A, B, C, D. It also says that major topic B is itself made up of two major subtopics: 1, 2. And 2 is also made up of two subtopics: a, b. And finally, C is made up of subtopics: 1, 2, 3. Well, a detail record description says the same thing! Look at this comparison.

```
I             01        <---- record level
    A             03        <---- subtopic
    B             03        <---- subtopic
        1             05        <---- subtopic
        2             05        <---- subtopic
            a                 07
            b                 07
    C             03        etc
        1             05
        2             05
        3             05
    D             03
```

What does the D-R-D say? The record, 01, is made up of four major parts, 03s. The second 03 is made up of two parts, 05s. The second 05 is itself made up of two part, 07s. The English outline not only shows the major parts, but it also shows the relationships among the parts. So does the D-R-D in COBOL!

### Group Level and Elementary Level Items

In COBOL we have two types of data elements that make up a record description: group level items and elementary level items. A group level item is one that is broken down into parts, or subdivided. An elementary level item is one that is not subdivided. Only elementary level items may contain a PICTURE clause.

So the next question is, which of the items in our example are group level items and which are elementary level items? Remember that all record descriptions are defined at the 01 level, and all data fields are defined using 02–49 levels. In fact, the 01s must begin in the A margin, and all 02–49s must begin in the B margin.

Therefore, the 01 is in the A margin and the 03s are in column 12, the beginning of the B margin. So, what margin are the 05s in? The 07s? You say the C and D margins? No, they are still in the B margin. We indent them for our eyes only, not the compiler's. In fact, the compiler would be just as happy with:

```
01
   03
   03
   05
   05
   07
   07
   03
   05
   05
   05
   03
```

But don't do it that way. Use our standards. However, this does bring up a very important point. How does the compiler recognize a group level item from an elementary level item? It does so by the relative level number values.

**Rule:** When you classify a data entry, look at the next entry. If the level number of the entry is larger than the one you are classifying, than the one you are classifying is a group level item. If not, it is an elementary level item.

Looking at this from the programmer's perspective:

**Rule:** If you are making an item a group, subdivide it. Follow the item with a larger level number.

Both rules say the same thing. So the indentation is for readability's sake only. It has no functional meaning to the D-R-D.

Anyway, which are our group and elementary levels, and which may contain a picture clause? The following record description shows all this.

```
01                              Group
     03                         Elementary – picture
     03                         Group
          05                    Elementary – picture
          05                    Group
               07              Elementary – picture
               07              Elementary – picture
     03                         Group
          05                    Elementary – picture
          05                    Elementary – picture
          05                    Elementary – picture
     03                         Elementary – picture
```

I think it's time to do one.  Let's continue with the DEAN-LIST problem.  Here are the data fields and types:

| | |
|---|---|
| Name | X |
| Social security number | X |
| Major code | 9 |
| Class code | 9 |
| Sex code | 9 |
| GPR | 9 (four decimal places) |

```
WORKING-STORAGE SECTION.

01   STUDENT-RECORD-IN.
     03   NAME
```

What's next?  Don't we need more information?  Sure we do!  We need to know the size of each field and the relative position in the record of each field.

| Column | Description | Type |
|---|---|---|
| 1–20 | Name | X |
| 25–33 | Social security number | X |
| 36 | Major Code | 9 |
| 38 | Class Code | 9 |
| 40 | Sex Code | 9 |
| 43–47 | GPR (four decimals) | 9 |

Now we can finish.

```
01   STUDENT-RECORD-IN.
     03   NAME                     PIC X(20).
     03   SOCIAL-SECURITY-NUMBER   PIC X(9).
     03   MAJOR-CODE               PIC 9(1).
     03   CLASS-CODE               PIC 9(1).
     03   SEX-CODE                 PIC 9(1).
     03   GPR                      PIC 9(1)V9(4).
```

Do you agree with that?  Well, if you did, don't feel bad.  Most people do at first.  But, something is missing.  The definition of a data field is dependent, for location in the record, on the previous item(s).  Therefore, the description above incorrectly says:

| Name | is in column 1–20 | . . . OK |
|------|-------------------|----------|
| SS-number | is in column 21–29 | . . . OOPS |
| Major-code | is in column 30 | . . . OOPS |

.

.

We forgot about the empty columns between the data fields. Here is what the correct D-R-D would be:

```
01   STUDENT-RECORD-IN.
     03   NAME                         PIC X(20).
     03   FILLER                       PIC X(4).
     03   SOCIAL-SECURITY-NUMBER       PIC X(9).
     03   FILLER                       PIC X(2).
     03   MAJOR-CODE                   PIC 9(1).
     03   FILLER                       PIC X(1).
     03   CLASS-CODE                   PIC 9(1).
     03   FILLER                       PIC X(1).
     03   SEX-CODE                     PIC 9(1).
     03   FILLER                       PIC X(1).
     03   GPR                          PIC 9(1)V9(4).
```

Let's look at it closely again. Why did we use 03 and not, say, 02 or 05? Why did we use PIC instead of PICTURE? What is the GPR's picture? And what is FILLER?

The reason for 03 is simply by choice and standard. You should always leave room between levels. So, 02 was out of the question. I could have used 05. In fact, some people prefer 05. That's OK. Use whatever you're comfortable with. . .or whatever your prof wants.

However, if you choose to use 05, then you should use all 05s. Remember about level number significance. Don't, for instance, say:

```
03   NAME
     05   SOCIAL-SECURITY-NUMBER
     07   MAJOR-CODE
```

.

.

That would mistakenly say that NAME is made up of SOCIAL-SECURITY-NUMBER, which is in turn made up of MAJOR-CODE. That's obviously not correct.

However, if we wanted to report the social security number as 999-99-9999, then, we would need to be able to reference each part separately so that the D-R-D would be:

```
01   STUDENT-RECORD-IN.
     03   NAME                         PIC X(20).
     03   FILLER                       PIC X(4).
     03   SOCIAL-SECURITY-NUMBER.
          05   SSN-PART-1              PIC X(3).
          05   SSN-PART-2              PIC X(2).
          05   SSN-PART-3              PIC X(4).
     03   FILLER                       PIC X(2).
     03   MAJOR-CODE                   PIC 9(1).
     03   FILLER                       PIC X(1).
     03   CLASS-CODE                   PIC 9(1).
     03   FILLER                       PIC X(1).
     03   GPR                          PIC 9(1)V9(4).
```

With this D-R-D the whole social security number can still be referenced (the 03 level) *and* the individual parts can be referenced. You should also notice that the 03 level for social security number no longer has a picture clause. Why? Because it is now a group level item. The compiler allows PICTURE clauses only on elementary level items. It can determine the size of the social security number by the sum of the parts.

### Implied Decimal

Well, this brings us to the picture on GPR. We are describing a field that has four decimal positions and has a total of five positions in size. So, would 9(5) do? No, even though my parents would have been happier with my undergraduate GPR with that picture! I guess you can anticipate the use of the V. It simply identifies the LOGICAL position for the decimal point. Notice I said logical. The decimal is not in the data. We want it implied in that position. COBOL doesn't like physical decimals in the data. Look at these examples:

| Data Value | Picture | Interpretation |
|------------|---------|----------------|
| 12345 | 9(3)V9(2) | 9(3)^9(2) |
| 123.45 | 9(3)V9(2) | ERROR |

## TIP

**All numeric data is right justified in their field.**

Can you also anticipate what the word FILLER is used for? You're right if you said it is used to show that a field exists but does not need to be referenced. Thank goodness for fillers. Just think of all the data names it saves us from thinking up. In fact, in COBOL '85 we can actually leave the word FILLER off. I'm not sure how I feel about that yet, but I think I'm going to like it.

I guess I should say something more about the other picture clauses. In fact, we should note that PIC is OK to use instead of PICTURE. Either way, be consistent in a program for readability's sake. (The compiler doesn't care if you mix them.) Anyway, what is X(4) or 9(3)? Remember X(47) and X(133)? Well, X(4) says the data field is made up of four alphanumeric characters; 9(3) says three numeric characters. We could say the same thing with

$$
\begin{array}{cc}
\text{XXXX} & 999 \\
\text{or} & \text{or} \\
\text{X(2)XX} & \text{9(1)9(1)9(1)}
\end{array}
$$

But why do that? Our standards say to use the multiplier form: 9(3), etc. I think it makes it easier to read and maintain a program if you don't mix techniques.

For instance, how many characters are in the following record? 35, 50, 55, or 65?

```
01   PAY-RECORD-IN.
     03   EMPLOYEE-NAME              PIC X(30).
     03   FILLER                    PIC XXXX.
     03   SOCIAL-SECURITY-NUMBER.
          05   PART-1               PIC X(3).
          05   PART-2               PIC XX.
          05   PART-3               PIC X(4).
     03   FILLER                    PIC X(4).
     03   HOURS-WORKED              PIC 999.
     03   FILLER                    PIC X(5).
     03   RATE-OF-PAY               PIC 999V9(2).
     03   FILLER                    PIC X(5).
```

What did you come up with 65? It gets confusing with the various PICTURE clauses being used, doesn't it? If all were in multiplier form, all you would have to do is add up the numbers in parentheses. You would not have to count positions.

## DETAIL RECORD DESCRIPTIONS. . .OUTPUT RECORDS

The detail record description that we designed and discussed to this point was for input. That is, it described our input records that make up the DEAN-FILE. Remember the following system flowchart (Figure 4.7):

**FIGURE 4.7**
**System Flowchart for Student List Program with Explanation**

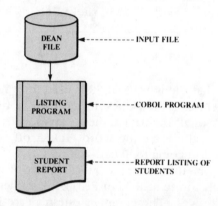

The flowchart shows that the COBOL program will use the DEAN-FILE as input and produce the Student Report as output. Since files are made up of records and COBOL processes files one record at a time, you would expect to have one detail record description for input and at least one for output. Why at least one? Well, let's take a look at the report design. From the detail flowchart we know that the following fields are to be reported for each student. However, we should lay out the report to see it and to get the dean's approval. Why go through all the trouble and find out the dean doesn't like our report format? Assume the following report layout was approved by the dean:

CBA STUDENT LISTING

| NAME | ID | MAJOR | CLASS | SEX | GPR |
|------|-----|-------|-------|-----|-----|
| . | . | . | . | . | . |
| . | . | . | . | . | . |
| . | . | . | . | . | . |

- The page heading should be on line 3 of the first page. (We will look at putting headings on all pages a little later in the text.)
- The column headings should be on line 6.
- The actual body of the report should be double-spaced.
- The columns should be equally spaced.

You notice that the report includes both page and column headings. Does our detail flowchart indicate them? No, it doesn't. So we need to modify the flowchart. The easiest way would be to add the two writes, page heading and column headings, to the initialization module (Figure 4.8). Why two writes? Remember that each write symbol is associated with a record, in this case a line on the report, or more specifically, with each differently formatted line.

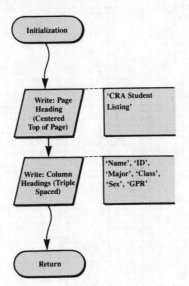

**FIGURE 4.8**
**Modified INITIALIZATION Module**

How many D-R-Ds for output do we need? Three:

- One for the page heading
- One for the column headings
- One for the body of the report

Let's start our D-R-Ds with the one used to list the students. After all, it should look a lot like the D-R-D for input. The best way to do this would be to use a printer layout form and locate the data columns. In fact, I would locate all the elements of the report. Figure 4.9 shows these results.

So, using the information on the printer layout form, we would generate the following D-R-D for output.

```
01    STUDENT-RECORD-OUT.
      03    FILLER                      PIC X(  )
      03    NAME-OUT                    PIC X(20).
      03    FILLER                      PIC X(  )
      03    SOCIAL-SECURITY-NUMBER.
            05    SSN-1                 PIC X(3).
            05    SSN-2                 PIC X(2).
            05    SSN-3                 PIC X(4).
      03    FILLER                      PIC X(  )
      03    MAJOR-CODE                  PIC 9(1).
```

**FIGURE 4.9**
Printer Layout Form for
Detail Line of Student List
Program

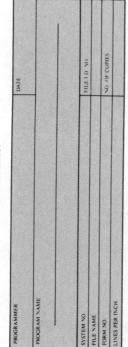

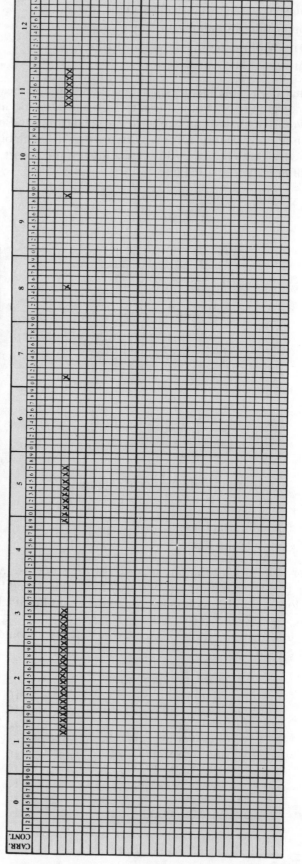

```
        03   FILLER                      PIC X(  )
        03   CLASS-CODE                  PIC 9(1).
        03   FILLER                      PIC X(  )
        03   SEX-CODE                    PIC 9(1).
        03   FILLER                      PIC X(  )
        03   G-P-R                       PIC 9(1).9(4).
        03   FILLER                      PIC X(  )
```

I know I've left some things off. But first things first. Can you see the format of the record? Each data field is included, and each is separated by a FILLER. You also probably noticed that the FILLER lines are missing periods. Well, I did that on purpose. We need to add something to all the FILLER lines! But, first the FILLER sizes. Just count the spaces between data fields on the printer layout form and fill in the blanks. Notice that I evenly spaced the fields as requested by the dean.

```
  01   STUDENT-RECORD-OUT.
        03   FILLER                      PIC X(15) VALUE SPACES.
        03   NAME-OUT                    PIC X(20).
        03   FILLER                      PIC X(13) VALUE SPACES.
        03   SOCIAL-SECURITY-NUMBER.
             05   SSN-1                  PIC X(3).
             05   SSN-2                  PIC X(2).
             05   SSN-3                  PIC X(4).
        03   FILLER                      PIC X(13) VALUE SPACES.
        03   MAJOR-CODE                  PIC 9(1).
        03   FILLER                      PIC X(13) VALUE SPACES.
        03   CLASS-CODE                  PIC 9(1).
        03   FILLER                      PIC X(13) VALUE SPACES.
        03   SEX-CODE                    PIC 9(1).
        03   FILLER                      PIC X(13) VALUE SPACES.
        03   G-P-R                       PIC 9(1).9(4).
        03   FILLER                      PIC X(15) VALUE SPACES.
```

Do you agree with all the sizes of the fillers? I could have done it a little differently. For instance, all the fillers could have been 13, and the four extra spaces could have been left to the end, or four of the fields could have been made 14, and so on. I chose to put two extra at the beginning and the end.

### The VALUE Clause

Did you notice the **VALUE SPACES** clause? I put it on each of the FILLER lines because I want spaces between my data fields. Look at the data flow indicated on the system flowchart. The data is coming into our program from the DEAN-FILE. We designed a D-R-D to handle the records for input. We have just finished our D-R-D for output for the body of the report. This is shown graphically in Figure 4.10.

We have two areas in memory set up to handle our input and output. Why two? . . . two different formats. We want the output to be pretty for the dean. So we make it more readable and edit the fields where appropriate. Therefore, we need two D-R-DS. However, how does the data get from the input D-R-D area to the output D-R-D area? Magic? No, we need to move it from one area to the other before we write. So each data field is now moved something like this:

```
    MOVE NAME TO NAME-OUT.
```

That causes the contents of NAME to be moved to NAME-OUT. Similarly, we move the rest of the data. Now, assuming we write the record at this point in time (without the VALUE SPACES clause), what would we get? We would get our data fields and whatever was in the filler areas from some previous program. In other words, since we didn't put something into these areas in our program, we get whatever was left there, or trash.

**FIGURE 4.10**
Depiction of Input and
Output Record Areas in
Memory

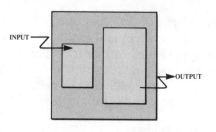

Now, use the VALUE SPACES clause, and what happens? We get spaces between all our data fields, not trash. Why? Because the VALUE clause says to put into this field the specified literal, data name, or figurative constant.

$$\underline{\text{VALUE}} \text{ IS [ ALL ]} \begin{Bmatrix} \text{data-name} \\ \text{literal} \\ \text{figurative constant} \end{Bmatrix}$$

### The Data Names

By now you probably noticed my use of data names in STUDENT-RECORD-IN and STUDENT-RECORD-OUT. Why did I use the same data-names for some fields and different data-names for others? I did it to illustrate some points about data-name referencing in COBOL. Remember that we said in Chapter 1 that all references to data-names in COBOL must be unique. If the data-name is not unique, we must do something to make the reference unique. For instance, if I said to my class, "Bob, you have an A in this class and are excused for the rest of the semester," you can bet that every Bob would assume I meant him and leave the class. My reference would not be unique if there were more than one Bob in class. If I said, "Bob Anderson," then that Bob would know that I meant him. I made my reference unique by using his last name.

Well, I must do the same thing in COBOL. If I said:

```
MOVE NAME TO NAME-OUT
```

COBOL would not have a problem knowing what to do. However, if I said:

```
MOVE MAJOR-CODE TO MAJOR-CODE
```

What would COBOL assume I wanted? During compilation the compiler replaces our data-names with memory addresses. Assume that the addresses are as shown below:

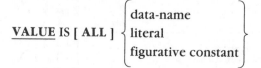

Then, would the compiler interpret our move as:

```
MOVE 1000 TO 5000
```

or

```
MOVE 5000 TO 1000
```

It doesn't know what we want. And, do you know what happens when the compiler does not know what we want? It gives us error messages. And, as you will find out, COBOL is prolific with its error messages.

How do we fix this error? We could change the data-names to MAJOR-CODE-IN and MAJOR-CODE-OUT. Or we could leave them the same (not unique) and make our reference unique by saying:

```
MOVE MAJOR-CODE OF STUDENT-RECORD-IN TO
     MAJOR-CODE OF STUDENT-RECORD-OUT.
```

With either change the compiler is now happy! Oh, by the way, do you see now why record names must be unique? They are a data field's last name.

With all this in mind, do you understand that GPR and G-P-R are unique? Anything to make them different. Let me suggest that one pretty good technique is to add -IN and -OUT to the data fields in the corresponding input and output D-R-Ds.

Speaking of GPR, what is the PICTURE clause saying? For input we used 9(1)V9(4), yet for output we used 9(1).9(4). Well, the decimal point in the PICTURE is considered an edit character (one of many we will study). Unlike the V, which says to imply a decimal, the period (.) says to print a decimal. This brings up our next topic, edit characters.

## EDITING

In COBOL we have the ability to edit input data fields and output data fields. For input or internal use, we deal with decimal points and signs. For output we really try to make data more readable and pretty; we eliminate leading zeros; we actually print decimal points. We can include dollar signs, commas, plus and minus signs, and, for the accountants in the group, we even have the ability to indicate CR and DR (DB in COBOL).

So you see that our intent for editing input is to achieve correctness, while for output it is also to make data pretty. The following chart shows the edit characters that we will look at:

*Edit Characters*

| Input | |
|---|---|
| V | implied decimal point |
| S | to indicate a signed data field |

## Output

### Zero Suppression

| | |
|---|---|
| Z and floating Z | suppresses the printing of leading zeros |
| $ | prints a single dollar sign |
| floating $ | suppresses the printing of leading zeros and prints one $ sign |
| * | prints a single asterisk |
| floating * | suppresses the printing of leading zeros and prints one * for each zero replaced |

### Insertion

| | |
|---|---|
| . | prints a decimal point |
| , | prints a comma, if a digit prints to the left |
| B | causes a blank to be inserted |
| 0 | causes a zero to be inserted |
| / | causes a slash to be inserted |

### Sign Control

| | |
|---|---|
| + | will cause either a " + " sign or "−" sign to print, depending on the value of the data moved into the field |
| − | causes a "−" sign to print if the value of data moved into the field is negative; if positive, *no* sign will print |
| CR | will print only if the data value is negative |
| DB | will print only if the data value is negative |

### *Input Editing*

The two edit characters used for input data are the V and the S. These two characters are also used for temporary storage data names. In both cases the data fields are for internal use and not for reporting. So why not use the decimal point and a plus or minus sign instead? Well, COBOL requires that all data that will be used mathematically must be numeric. And a numeric field that has been **edited** with a decimal point and/or a plus or minus sign *is not* numeric. In order for COBOL to print a decimal or plus or minus, it must include the character in the field. Therefore, the value in the field no longer just contains numbers. It contains numbers and decimals and/or signs. Therefore, for those data fields intended for mathematical operations, we use the V and/or S, and the compiler recognizes the V as an implied decimal point and an S as a signed field and represents them correctly in memory (without actual decimal or sign). In fact neither the V or S represent a storage position: S9(4)V9(2) is six(6) positions not 8. The following are examples:

| | |
|---|---|
| 9(4)V9(2) | numeric field with 2 decimal places |
| 9(4) | numeric field |
| S9(4) | signed numeric field |
| 9(2).9(2) | numeric edited field |
| +9(3) | numeric edited field |

### Output Editing

The two most common groups of edit characters used for reporting are zero suppression and insertion characters. (There is some overlap.) The third group of characters is devoted to sign control. Two of the characters are particularly intended for accounting reports.

### Zero Suppression

Most of us would agree that a field on a report would look best without leading zeros. That is to say, the following unedited results would not be very appealing:

| Data | Sending Field | Receiving Field | Output Results |
|---|---|---|---|
| 1234 | 9(4) | 9(5) | 01234 |
| 1234 | 9(2)V9(2) | 9(4).9(2) | 0012.34 |
| 12345.67 | 9(6)V9(2) | 9(6).9(2) | 012345.67 |

The output isn't very pretty, is it? Wouldn't you prefer this?

1234

12.34

$12,345.67

I think these are easier to read and more meaningful. I can tell dollar values from non-dollar values. Leading zeros are messing up things. How do we get better results? With the Z and dollar sign ($) edit characters.

**The Z and Floating Z.**     The Z may be used to the right and left of the decimal point. It will cause a leading zero *not* to print. Or, another way of thinking about it is that the zero will be replaced with a space. Therefore:

| Data | Sending Field | Receiving Field | Results |
|---|---|---|---|
| 1234 | 9(5) | Z(1)9(4) | 1234 |
| 1234 | 9(5) | Z(5) | 1234 |

Both of these obviously cause the same results to occur. Both suppressed the leading zero in the leftmost position. However, the second would suppress leading zeros in all other positions also. Therefore:

| Data | Sending Field | Receiving Field | Results |
|------|---------------|-----------------|---------|
| 5 | 9(5) | Z(1)9(4) | 0005 |
| 5 | 9(5) | Z(5) | 5 |

See the difference in using one Z and the floating Z?

Remember that **leading** zeros are suppressed. So any embedded zeros are still printed. You would probably not like it if your pay for the period was $1,000.00, and the edit field used to print it was $ZZZZ.99, causing your check to be $1    .00. It's only leading zeros that are suppressed.

---

## TIP

**Leave one 9 to the left of the decimal point. That causes a zero value to print as 0 and not a blank.**

---

**The $ (Dollar Sign) and Floating $ (Dollar Sign).**     Since we brought up the topic of pay, you realize that some numbers on reports are dollar values. It would seem appropriate to be able to label them as such with a dollar sign. Well, we have a choice between doing it with a stationary dollar sign or a floating dollar sign.

If on a report we wanted the following:

```
$     57.95
$    112.13
$49010.03
```

What PICTURE clause would do it for us? How about $9(5).99? No, since that would allow leading zeros to print, resulting in:

```
$00057.95
$00112.13
$49010.13
```

Well, what about $(6).99? Will that work? It causes:

```
$57.95
$112.13
$49010.03
```

That looks good, but it's not what we wanted! Try this logic. We want a stationary dollar sign, and we want to suppress leading zeros. So, let's use a combination of dollar signs and floating Z, $Z(5).99. Results look like this:

```
$     57.95
$    112.13
$49010.03
```

We did it! It took a combination to get what we wanted. Now, what if we wanted the dollar sign to print right up next to the number instead of being stationary? How about this picture clause, $(6).99? Yes, this would do it. In fact, look back at the example using this picture. The dollar sign is printed to the left of the number. And, since the numbers have different sizes, the dollar sign floats from one position to another.

You should note two things about the dollar sign. It must have a position to print in, and, as a floating edit character, it suppresses leading zeros. Here are some examples:

| Sending Data | Receiving Field | Field | Results |
|---|---|---|---|
| 12345 | 9(5) | $Z(5) | $12345 |
| 123.45 | 9(5)V9(2) | $Z(5).9(2) | $   123.45 |
| 123.45 | 9(5)V9(2) | $(6).9(2) | $123.45 |

A couple of special notes. Notice that the total number of print positions in the receiving field had to increase by one, since the dollar sign has to have a position to print in. Also, you may not float both a dollar sign and Z in the same picture, and neither should be to the right of a nine (9). Here are some examples of *invalid* pictures:

| | |
|---|---|
| 9(4)Z(2).9(2) | ← Z used to the right of 9 |
| ZZ99ZZ.99 | ← Z used to the right of 9 |
| $$$ZZZ.99 | ← both Z and $ may not float |
| ZZZ$$$.99 | ← both Z and $ may not float |

**The * (Asterisk).**    This character is primarily used for check writing. If you were to print $    5.00 on a check, someone could add some digits with an appropriate typewriter and end up with a check for $9995.00. And, while that person was in South America, you would be trying to explain to your boss how it was COBOL's fault! Seriously, COBOL does let us avoid this problem. We use the asterisk (*).

The asterisk will print in every leading zero position. Therefore, a picture of ***9 would cause the value 0123 to print as *123. Here are some other examples:

| Data | Sending Field | Receiving Field | Results |
|---|---|---|---|
| 1234.56 | 9(4)V9(2) | $****.9(2) | $1234.56 |
| 5.00 | 9(4)V9(2) | $****.9(2) | $***5.00 |
| 5 | 9(4) | ***9 | ***5 |

## Insertion Characters

Let's turn our attention to the set of edit characters called insertion characters. As the name implies, these edit characters will be inserted between two digit/character positions according to certain guidelines.

**The Decimal.**    As we noted earlier, the decimal will print in the position indicated in the picture clause. When data is moved from one field to another, the decimal point also serves the purpose of data alignment—the decimal points are lined-up, and then the data is moved. (More about the move a little later.)

Let's look at some examples:

| Data | Sending Field | Receiving Field | Results |
|---|---|---|---|
| 12345 | 9(5) | Z(5) | 12345 |
| 123ˏ45 | 9(3)V9(2) | 9(3).9(2) | 123.45 |
| 123ˏ45 | 9(3)V9(2) | 9(5) | 00123 |
| 12345 | 9(5) | 9(3).9(2) | 345.00 |
| 123ˏ45 | 9(3)V9(2) | .9(2) | .45 |

Notice how the decimal points are aligned and then the data is positioned around it. Notice, even when a V or decimal is not part of the picture, first, third, and fourth examples, the decimal is assumed to the right of the rightmost digit.

One way to think about how this works is to move the data, squeeze in the decimal, and then remove all data that no longer fits. For instance:

| 123ˆ45 | 9(3)V9(2) | 9(3).9(2) | 123.45 |
|---|---|---|---|
| 123ˆ45 | 9(3)V9(2) | 9(1).9(1) | 3.4 |

In the first example, the decimal pushes its way between the 3 and 4. It does the same in the second example, but the 1 and 2 and 5 have been truncated because of the picture size.

**The Comma.**    The comma is also an insertion character, but unlike the decimal point, it **does not** always print. Why? Well, the rule says that the comma will be printed where it is shown in the picture **if** a digit prints to its left. Therefore, with a picture of Z,ZZZ,ZZ9.99, a value of 1 would **not** cause the printing of either comma. In fact, it would take a value of at least 1000 to cause a comma to print and a value of 1 million to cause both commas to print. Here are some examples:

| Data | Sending Field | Receiving Field | Results |
|---|---|---|---|
| 12345 | 9(5) | 99,999 | 12,345 |
| 5 | 9(5) | 99,999 | 00,005 |
| 5 | 9(5) | ZZ,ZZ9 | 5 |
| 1234ˏ56 | 9(4)V9(2) | $,ZZZ.99 | −ERROR− |
| 1234ˏ6 | 9(4)V9(2) | $,$$$.99 | −ERROR− |
| 123456789 | 9(9) | ZZZ,ZZZ,ZZ9 | 123,456,789 |

Most of the examples, I think, explain themselves. But do notice how the comma is inserted in between two digits when there is one to its left. Look at the second example. Why did the comma print? You say the zero is not significant. You're right! But, the rule says nothing about significance. It just says a DIGIT to the left; any DIGIT, including a zero.

What's wrong with the fourth example? Well, the stationary dollar sign says it will print in that position. Therefore, how will the comma print, since a digit can never print to its left? (The same rule applies to the fifth example.)

**The B (Blank).**    There are those occasions when we would like a string of digits/characters separated by some special character for readability's sake. Wasn't that what the decimal and comma did? Sure it was. But, in some cases, neither of these is appropriate. Which social security number looks best?

491,09,1205

or

491.09.1205

or

491 09 1205

I think the third one is easiest to read. Well, guess what the edit character B does for us? It causes a blank to be inserted wherever we use it in the picture clause. Therefore:

| Data | Sending Field | Receiving Field | Results |
| --- | --- | --- | --- |
| 491091205 | 9(9) | 9999B99999 | 4910 91205 |
| 491091205 | 9(9) | 9(3)B9(2)B9(4) | 491 09 1205 |
| 12345 | 9(5) | ZZ,BZZB,Z9 | 1, 23 ,45 |
| ABCDE | X(5) | X(3)BX(2) | ABC DE |

The first two examples illustrate a likely use of the blank. The third example shows an exaggerated use to illustrate that the blank may be used with other edit characters. It just inserts itself into the data. The fourth shows that the B may be used with alphanumeric data fields.

**The 0 (Zero).**   Guess what the insertion character 0 does? You're right! It prints in the position in which it is used in the picture clause so that a picture of 99009 would cause two zeros to print in the positions shown. Some examples would be:

| Data | Sending Field | Receiving Field | Results |
| --- | --- | --- | --- |
| 12345 | 9(5) | 9900999 | 1200345 |
| 123ᴧ45 | 9(3)V99 | 90909.909 | 10203.405 |
| 123ᴧ45 | 9(3)V99 | 9(3).00 | 123.00 |

Do you get the idea? It works much like the other insertion characters. But this one was designed with our accounting friends in mind. Why do I say that? Look at the third example. See how that picture causes 00 to print to the right of the decimal point? If you have had an accounting course, you remember how they like to report data to the nearest dollar, etc. The 9(3).00 allows us to do that. Why not just use 9(3)? Well, the accountants like two decimal places **printed** and not just left off. Therefore, we want the report to be to the nearest dollar, but we want two places printed. Are we between a rock and a hard place? No, we have the insertion character zero to rescue us.

**The / (Slash).**   I could probably just say go back and read the blank section, replacing the B with the /. You know, with a word processor I could just do a find/replace and have this part already written and typed. Let me just say the slash will print where it is shown in the picture. Examples:

| Data | Sending Field | Receiving Field | Results |
|---|---|---|---|
| 12345 | 9(5) | 99/999 | 12/345 |
| 120588 | 9(6) | 99/99/99 | 12/05/88 |
| 491091205 | 9(9) | 9(3)/9(2)/9(4) | 491/09/1205 |
| ABCDE | X(5) | X(3)/X(2) | ABC/DE |

The slash is nice for reporting dates, as in the second example above. Even the social security number reads better with slashes than with nothing.

I should note that the slash is a feature of COBOL '74 and does not work on earlier compilers.

### Sign Control Characters

**The Plus and Minus Signs.**    We have occasion from time to time to print signed numbers instead of unsigned numbers. Our reports don't always just include positive numbers, which is what is implied by unsigned numbers. So to print, we use the plus and minus signs as edit characters. Both may be used on either side of the decimal. Both may also be used as floating edit characters. They may also be used in combination with other characters.

The basic rules for when the signs print are:

- If a plus sign is used, the symbol + will print for a positive value **and** the symbol – will print for a negative number.

- If, however, you just want the – symbol to print for negative values and **no** sign to print for positive numbers, you use the  minus sign instead of the plus sign.

For instance:

| Data | Sending Field | Receiving Field | Results |
|---|---|---|---|
| +123.45 | S9(3)V9(2) | +9(3).9(2) | +123.45 |
| +123.45 | S9(3)V9(2) | –9(3).9(2) | 123.45 |
| –123.45 | S9(3)V9(2) | +9(3).9(2) | –123.45 |
| –123.45 | S9(3)V9(2) | –9(3).9(2) | –123.45 |
| +123.45 | S9(3)V9(2) | 9(3).9(2)+ | 123.45+ |
| +123.45 | S9(3)V9(2) | 9(3).9(2)– | 123.45 |
| –123.45 | S9(3)V9(2) | 9(3).9(2)+ | 123.45– |
| –123.45 | S9(3)V9(2) | 9(3).9(2)– | 123.45– |

## TIP

When you design output, be consistent in your use of plus and minus signs. Always use them either to the left or to the right of the decimal, not both.

**The CR (Credit) and DB (Debit).**    These two edit characters have their basis in accounting. You should remember from accounting that certain accounts normally have a credit balance while others have a debit balance. This comes from the basic accounting equation.

$$ASSETS = LIABILITIES + EQUITY$$

Since this is an equation, if you decrease one side, you must decrease the other and the same for increases. But, the question is, what does it take to increase and/or decrease an asset account? A liability account? Do you remember an asset account normally has a debit (DB) balance while a liability account normally has a credit (CR) balance? Therefore, to decrease an asset, we credit (CR) the account, while to decrease a liability account we debit (DB) it.

| ASSETS | = | | LIABILITIES | + | | EQUITY | |
|---|---|---|---|---|---|---|---|
| Debit to Increase | Credit to Decrease | | Debit to Decrease | Credit to Increase | | Debit to Decrease | Credit to Increase |

So, to look at a snapshot of the equation, we might have:

$$\$100,000 = \$60,000 + \$40,000$$

Now, if you paid off a liability of $10,000, how would that be shown in the equation? The liabilities would be decreased by $10,000 DB and the assets would be decreased by a $10,000 CR. This is shown below:

| ASSETS | | = | LIABILITIES | | + | EQUITY | |
|---|---|---|---|---|---|---|---|
| (DB) +100,000 | (CR) | | (DB) | (CR) +60,000 | | (DB) | (CR) +40,000 |
| | −10,000 | | −10,000 | | | | |

So we subtract from our asset and our liability account. But in one case the action is a credit while the other is a debit. So, how do we cause this in COBOL?

The DB or CR will print **only** for a negative value. Neither will print for a positive value. Therefore, on a report if we want to show a value to be a credit to an account when the value is negative (asset account) and to show a value to be a debit to an account when the value is negative (liability account), then we should edit the data field with CR or DB.

```
03  ASSET-TRANS      PIC ZZ,ZZZ.99 CR
```

and

```
03  LIAB-TRANS       PIC ZZ,ZZZ.99 DB
```

Therefore, the negative $10,000 would show as 10,000 CR for the asset and 10,000 DB for the liability. In both cases, the corresponding account balances would be reduced.

Here are some other examples:

| Data | Sending Field | Receiving Field | Results |
|------|------|------|------|
| +123.45 | S9(3)V99 | $(4).99 DB | $123.45 |
| −123.45 | S9(3)V99 | $(4).99 DB | $123.45 DB |
| +123.45 | S9(3)V99 | $(4).99 CR | $123.45 |
| −123.45 | S9(3)V99 | $(4).99 CR | $123.45 CR |

## *TIP*

**Notice the sign, S, is on the sending field. Without it, the use of DB, CR, and for that matter, + and −, is meaningless.**

## DETAIL RECORD DESCRIPTIONS FOR HEADINGS

Remember that we were discussing D-R-Ds for output and had concluded that our example needs three:

- page heading
- column headings
- body of the report

Well, believe it or not, we just finished the discussion of D-R-D for the body of the report. Sounded innocent when we started, didn't it? But, it got us into a pretty lengthy discussion of editing. That's OK. We needed that knowledge to make our report look nice. Now, it is time to work at headings. This discussion will be shorter!

Unlike the D-R-D for the body of the report, record descriptions used for writing headings don't write variable values. They write constants. Consequently, the fields don't need to be referenced, and the constants can be set with the VALUE CLAUSE.

```
01   PAGE-HEADING.
     03   FILLER          PIC X(57) VALUE SPACES.
     03   FILLER          PIC X(19) VALUE
               'CBA STUDENT LISTING'.
     03   FILLER          PIC X(57) VALUE SPACES.
```

See what I mean about not having to reference the 03 levels? All I want to do is write the record with the values shown. Do you also see where I got the picture sizes? The page heading was 19 (count the characters). That left 114 characters for the other two 03s, or 57 for each, to center the heading.

That's pretty straightforward. What about the column headings? Well, they are pretty easy, also. Basically, you do the same thing, but figuring spacing is harder. First, you don't just space the column headings themselves. You must place them over the columns of data. So I would have laid out the full report on my printer layout form: page heading, column headings and data fields. In particular, the body of the report and the column headings should be designed together.

However, since we already have the STUDENT-RECORD-OUT designed, can we design the column headings record for it? I think for this simple example we can.

```
01   COLUMN-HEADINGS.
     03   FILLER            PIC X(23) VALUE SPACES.
     03   FILLER            PIC X(4)  VALUE 'NAME'.
     03   FILLER            PIC X(24) VALUE SPACES.
     03   FILLER            PIC X(2)  VALUE 'ID'.
     03   FILLER            PIC X(15) VALUE SPACES.
     03   FILLER            PIC X(5)  VALUE 'MAJOR'.
     03   FILLER            PIC X(9)  VALUE SPACES.
     03   FILLER            PIC X(5)  VALUE 'CLASS'.
     03   FILLER            PIC X(10) VALUE SPACES.
     03   FILLER            PIC X(3)  VALUE 'SEX'.
     03   FILLER            PIC X(11) VALUE SPACES.
     03   FILLER            PIC X(3)  VALUE 'GPR'.
     03   FILLER            PIC X(19) VALUE SPACES.
```

So far so good, I hope! Do you see that the record format matches the STUDENT-RECORD-OUT. The trick is to fill in the PICs on the FILLER lines with the VALUE SPACES clauses. How do we do that? If we had used the printer layout form, which I suggest you use, we simply counted the spaces. So you can place them on the form and come back. Now, the pictures on the FILLER lines with VALUE SPACES should make sense to you.

## DETAIL RECORD DESCRIPTIONS. . .OTHER

As you might suspect, the three D-R-Ds we have looked at are very common. But there are others. Look at the Circle Club program in Appendix C. You should recognize all the record descriptions except for TOTAL-LINE. Notice that TOTAL-LINE has both a heading (description) and a variable. Up to now, our D-R-D contained one or the other, but not both. Its format allows us to print a line that contains a variable and a line description of that variable.

What if the dean had asked us to count the number of students and report the count on the bottom of the last page as follows:

```
THE TOTAL NUMBER OF STUDENTS IS     XXXX
```

Then, the D-R-D would look like the one from the CIRCLE CLUB program (Appendix C):

```
01   STUDENT-COUNT-LINE.
     03   FILLER            PIC X(10) VALUE SPACES.
     03   FILLER            PIC X(33) VALUE
             'THE TOTAL NUMBER OF STUDENTS IS '.
     03   STUDENT-COUNT-OUT PIC ZZZ9.
     03   FILLER            PIC X(86) VALUE SPACES.
```

While looking at this program, you might have noticed yet another different D-R-D . . . 01 DUMMY-LINE, and you also possibly noticed 01 STAR-LINE. These are a little different from the others we have studied.

The DUMMY-LINE is used to write a line of blanks. There are times that such a need arises. A good example occurs if you are double-spacing the body of a report and you want the first line of the body triple-spaced from the heading. There is also a case where we want to leave one page and go to another, but we don't want to write on the first line of the next page. This case is probably hard for you to see, since it is related to the way a COBOL WRITE verb is handled. So, for now, just take my word on it.

What about the STAR-LINE? See how it was used in the report design? We separated the TOTAL-LINE from the body with a line of stars (asterisks). So, the record description contains 114 asterisks surrounded by spaces. One hundred fourteen (114) is not a magic number. We are limited to 128 characters for a non-numeric literal, so I could have gone as high as 128. Anyway, I used PIC X(114).

Can you imagine having now to say VALUE followed by 114 asterisks in quotes? Well, COBOL again has a nice feature that helps us avoid that problem. It is called the ALL option. Saying PIC X(114) VALUE ALL '*' will cause all 114 positions to contain an asterisk. If you wanted some other character, say "−" all you would need to change in the program would be the "*" to a "−" Nice, isn't it? You could even say something like ALL '*−', and the results would be as you suspect . . . a line (114 characters) of *−*−*− etc.

The other two record descriptions you see in Circle Club deal with the date. 01 DATE-STORE is simply a D-R-D that has three data fields. And 01 DATE-LINE is used to write the date and page number. It is similar to the TOTAL-LINE in that both literals, DATE and PAGE, and variables, DATE-OUT and PAGE-OUT, are written.

As you suspect, we could go on and on with variation after variation of D-R-D. Basically, you are writing out either spaces, literals, or data values. This is done either separately or in some combination as required by the particular report design. You should look at the design and identify differently formatted lines. Generally, you will need a separate D-R-D for each of the different formats. For example, look at Figure 4.11 How many D-R-Ds would we need?

**FIGURE 4.11**
**Example Report Spacing Layout to Demonstrate Need for D-R-Ds**

```
Line 4                          EXAMPLE REPORT

Line 8              ID  NAME  ADDRESS  STATE  AMOUNT

Line 11                       first line of body
                              (double-spaced)

           *******************************************
                        (double-spaced from body)

Line # + 2      THE TOTAL NUMBER OF PEOPLE IS XXXXX
```

How many D-R-Ds did you come up with? Five? Six? Well, in a way both are correct for now. Here are the D-R-Ds you will need:

- Report title . . . EXAMPLE REPORT
- Column headings . . . ID NAME etc.
- Body of the report . . . detail lines
- Slash line (/)
- Total line

Does everyone agree with those? Five differently formatted lines, five D-R-Ds. What about the sixth line? If you said a blank line, you're right. We will need it to skip down from the top of the page and to triple-space between the column headings and the first detail line.

When we get into the language a little further and we start doing some math and start working with tables, we will look at yet some other D-R-Ds. It would be one of those take my word for it cases if we looked at them now. So be aware that we are just finished for now.

## THE LINKAGE SECTION

This section is used for systems using subprograms. A subprogram is a separate program that is executed by another program, usually called a main program. Symbolically, Figure 4.12 shows this relationship (two programs with a communications link between them):

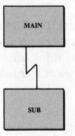

**FIGURE 4.12**
Main Program and
Subprogram Relationship

What's being communicated? Well, one thing would be the passing of data/information back and forth between them by specific data names used for this purpose. In the main program the data names are found in the WORKING-STORAGE SECTION. Guess where they are found in the subprogram? In the LINKAGE SECTION! Why? Well, the data locations are allocated when the main program is compiled, and the sub is given access just to those locations instead of separate locations being allocated in the sub itself. Look at Figure 4.13. It shows this sharing of data locations.

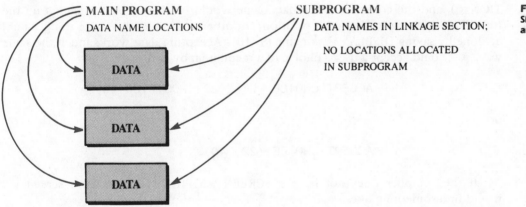

**FIGURE 4.13**
Sharing Data between Main
and Subprogram

I will discuss this section in more detail in the chapter on subprogramming, but you should know that the D-R-Ds in the linkage section look just like all the others we have studied.

## THE REPORT SECTION

The **REPORT SECTION** of the DATA DIVISION is used in programs using the REPORT WRITER feature of COBOL. Again, I will discuss this section fully in the REPORT WRITER Appendix. However, I thought I would mention a couple of things dealing with D-R-Ds.

Level numbers are still used in the report section. However, each 01 is designated as being a detail line or heading line or footing line. Then, within each 01, we'll specify the fields, as we've done before, but with a difference. Look at this D-R-D for the an example page heading.

```
01   PAGE-HEADING TYPE IS HEADING.
     05   LINE NUMBER PLUS 4.
          10    COLUMN NUMBER IS 59   PIC  X(14) VALUE
                     'EXAMPLE REPORT'.
```

I guess the differences are obvious: the TYPE clause on the 01, no data name of FILLER on the 10, just a column number specification. We even specify the line to print on with the 05 entry. Come to think about it, the D-R-D is more than a little different. So, let's stop for now and leave our full discussion for later.

## THE SCREEN SECTION

This section, like the others, is associated with a particular feature of COBOL. In this case it is associated with interactive COBOL. That is, its specific function is for communication between programs and users. Unlike the other section, though, it is not a COBOL standard. It has not been accepted by the CODASYL Committee. Since it is not a standard feature, it is impossible to discuss it as we have the other sections.

Basically, the COBOL compilers that allow for interactive communications do so with the DISPLAY and ACCEPT verbs. With them we can display and accept detail records and data names. Therefore, we could say DISPLAY data-name LINE 5 POSITION 10, and the contents of the data-name would be shown on the screen on the fifth line beginning in the tenth position. In other compilers this same thing would be done by saying DISPLAY data-name (5, 10). Accepting data works much the same way. We could accept a user's choice of a menu item by saying:

```
ACCEPT CHOICE   LINE 22   POSITION 40
```

or

```
ACCEPT CHOICE (22, 40)
```

If the compiler does not have a SCREEN SECTION, to describe a screen we would find something like:

```
DISPLAY 'MAIN MENU'              LINE 5   POSITION 35 ERASE
        '1-PROCESS TRANSACTIONS' LINE 8   POSITION 30
        '2-PRODUCE REPORTS'      LINE 10  POSITION 30
        '3-PROCESS INQUIRY'      LINE 12  POSITION 30
        '9-EXIT PROGRAM'         LINE 14  POSITION 30.
```

To accept the user's choice, we could code:

```
DISPLAY 'Please enter your choice. . .1, 2, 3, or 9'
                                 LINE 20 POSITION 30.
ACCEPT CHOICE                    LINE 20 POSITION 70.
```

With a SCREEN SECTION in the DATA DIVISION, I could code a record that would do the same for me:

```
SCREEN SECTION.
   01   MENU-SCREEN.
        05   BLANK SCREEN.
        05   LINE 5   COLUMN 35   VALUE
                'MAIN MENU'.
        05   LINE 8   COLUMN 30   VALUE
                '1-PROCESS TRANSACTIONS'.
        05   LINE 10 COLUMN 30   VALUE
                '2-PRODUCE REPORTS'.
        05   LINE 12 COLUMN 30   VALUE
                '3-PROCESS INQUIRY'.
        05   LINE 14 COLUMN 30   VALUE
                '9-EXIT PROGRAM'.
   01   ACCEPT-MESSAGE.
        05   LINE 20 COLUMN 30   VALUE
                'Please enter your choice. . .1, 2, 3, or 9'.
   01   ACCEPT-CHOICE-SCREEN.
        05   LINE 20 COLUMN 70   TO CHOICE.
```

Then, procedurally, we would code:

```
DISPLAY MENU-SCREEN.
DISPLAY ACCEPT-MESSAGE.
ACCEPT  ACCEPT-CHOICE-SCREEN.
```

I guess you can see the similarities. One technique is more procedure oriented, while the SCREEN SECTION allows us to do most of the description in the DATA DIVISION.

There are other features that I will discuss in Appendix F on interactive programming.

## SUMMARY

This chapter included several major topics and many related subtopics. We approached the material along the COBOL organization of sections. We looked at the FILE SECTION, WORKING-STORAGE SECTION, LINKAGE SECTION, REPORT SECTION, and the SCREEN SECTION. The FILE and WORKING-STORAGE sections took up most of the chapter, and rightly so. The other three sections are discussed more fully in later parts of the text. We simply introduced them here because we were discussing the DATA DIVISION.

The first section of the DATA DIVISION is the FILE SECTION. As the name implies, it describes files prepared for processing. The file description (FD), including the optional clauses of RECORD CONTAINS and BLOCK CONTAINS, were discussed fully. This discussion led us to record descriptions and the use of level numbers.

In the chapter I adopted a policy that all detail descriptions of data records (D-R-Ds) would, for now, be done in the WORKING-STORAGE SECTION. All we would do in the FILE SECTIONs (FDs) would be general record descriptions (G-R-Ds). I did this because the value clause may not be used in the File Section.

We discussed the functional similarities between an outline and a detail record description (D-R-D) and saw how the level numbers tell a story in and of themselves. We can see the data relationships by examining the relative values, 03, 05, etc., of the data fields. Once we understood the basic structure of record descriptions, we looked at several types—input record descriptions, detail line (body) record descriptions, page and column headings and total lines. We also said that there would be others as we cover new material.

The discussion of record descriptions necessitated the introduction and study of editing and the use of edit characters. We studied the characters by organizing them into two major groups—those used for input and those used for output. For input we studied S and V. Output edit characters were divided into subgroups—zero suppression (Z, $), insertion (. , B, 0), and sign control (+, −, CR, DB).

Other features used in record descriptions were also studied. The FILLER, VALUE CLAUSE, and the ALL were major topics of discussion. We saw how the FILLER is used for those fields that do not need to be referenced procedurally. The VALUE CLAUSE was very useful for assigning values to data fields and even for assigning spaces to fields including FILLER lines.

Associated with the VALUE CLAUSE is the ALL. It allows us a shortcut for assigning values to a field. Instead of explicitly having to list all characters in a literal, we can simply say ALL '*', and no matter how many positions are in the picture, we fill it all with asterisks.

In the WORKING-STORAGE SECTION we also mentioned 77 level items. I purposely didn't discuss these in the chapter because they are used primarily for math. Therefore, I will discuss them when we need them.

The next two sections, LINKAGE and REPORT, were functionally described, but no detail discussion was provided because both are discussed when we use them in the text.

Finally, we discussed, a little more fully, the SCREEN SECTION. The first thing you probably noticed was that this section is not a COBOL standard. (However, as PC COBOL becomes more popular I believe a standard will be adopted.)

The topic of interactive COBOL involves the use of the DISPLAY and ACCEPT verbs. While I showed both, the full forms are left for later. We also saw that compilers that incorporate a SCREEN SECTION and those that don't handle communications differently. The concept is the same; the technique varies. We saw a comparison which also exposed some screen options to aid in screen design. However, I again decided to put off fully discussing these features until the section on interactive COBOL. That's when we need it!

## EXERCISES

### Chapter Review Questions

1. Which of the following sections is not a standard in COBOL?
    a.   WORKING-STORAGE
    b.   FILE
    c.   REPORT
    d.   LINKAGE
    e.   SCREEN

2. Which data element is defined with a 01 level indicator?

   a. File
   b. Record
   c. Field
   d. Independent record
   e. None of the above

3. Which FD would be appropriate for the following: SELECT MASTER-FILE ASSIGN TO DA-S-MASTER?

   a. FD MASTER . . .
   b. FD MASTER FILE . . .
   c. FD DA-S-MASTER . . .
   d. FD MASTER-FILE . . .
   e. None of the above

4. If a tape has a density of 5,000 BPI and you wrote 1,000, 200 character records on the file unblocked, how many inches of tape would be required (assume 1″ gaps)?

   a. 40″
   b. 1,000″
   c. 240″
   d. 200″
   e. 1,040″

5. What would you answer be if you used a blocking factor of 100 records?

   a. 10″
   b. 40″
   c. 1050″
   d. 50″
   e. 210″

6. An alphanumeric field is designed with a picture of:

   a. 9s
   b. Zs
   c. As
   d. Xs
   e. None of the above

7. A data item that is subdivided is called a(n):

   a. D-R-D
   b. G-R-D
   c. Group
   d. Elementary
   e. Both a and c are true

8. Which picture clause is a different size?

   a. 9(5)V9(2)
   b. 99999V9(2)
   c. 9(2)9(3)V9(2)
   d. 99999V9(9)
   e. Both b and d

9. Generally you would need how many D-R-Ds for each differently formatted output line?

    a.    No general relationship exist

    b.    One, except for summary reports

    c.    One, except for detail reports

    d.    Two; one for the headings and one for the body

    e.    One

10. To give a data field an initial value of blanks you could use:

    a.    . . . VALUE 'SPACES'

    b.    . . . VALUE INITIALIZE

    c.    . . . VALUE SPACES

    d.    . . . VALUE BLANKS

    e.    . . . VALUE 'BLANKS'

11. All references to a data name must be made:

    a.    With unique data names

    b.    Unique

    c.    With elementary level items

    d.    With group level items

    e.    None of the above

12. Which of the following EDIT Characters may be used for INPUT Records?

    a.    $

    b.    Z

    c.    V

    d.    S

    e.    Both c and d

13. In order to write a line like the one shown:

```
TOTAL NET PAY IS $105,923.15
```

would require:

    a.    Two D-R-Ds

    b.    One D-R-D

    c.    Must be done on two lines

    d.    You cannot write a literal and a data value with one D-R-D

    e.    None of the above

14. The LINKAGE SECTION is used for:

    a.    Interactive programming

    b.    Linking files with DSNs

    c.    Designing Screens

    d.    Subprogramming

    e.    Both a and c

15. The DISPLAY and ACCEPT VERBS are used extensively with:
   a. Subprogramming to pass data between paragraphs
   b. REPORT WRITER feature to present reports
   c. SCREEN SECTION and Interactive Programs
   d. WORKING-STORAGE SECTION for Counting
   e. None of the above

## Discussion Questions

1. Compare a G-R-D with a D-R-D.
2. Explain the relationship among the FD, SELECT and DD statements.
3. Briefly explain the advantages and disadvantages of blocking.
4. Briefly explain why a reference to a data name must be unique.
5. Give one D-R-D, using level numbers only, that contains exactly 3 group level items and 7 elementary level items.

## Practice Problems

Use the following record layout for Questions 1–3.

| Columns | Description | Type |
|---------|-------------|------|
| 1–30 | Name | X |
| 35–40 | Account-ID | 9 |
| 35–38 | Account-Number | |
| 39–40 | Sequential-Number | |
| 45 | Account-Type-Code | 9 |
| | 1-checking | |
| | 2-savings | |
| | 3-new | |
| 50 | Account-Class-Code | 9 |
| | 1-Individual | |
| | 2-Business | |
| 55–60 | Account Balance | 9 |

1. Design a D-R-D that could be used for input of the record above.
2. Design a D-R-D that could be used for output of the records. You should use appropriate spacing and editing.
3. Design a D-R-D that could be used for column headings for the records.
4. Re-design the D-R-D in 2 to accommodate type and class descriptions instead of codes. You should also print the Account-ID as 999-99.
5. Assume the records are for a customer file whose data set name is CUST, write the DD, SELECT, FD to allow for processing the file.

6. Given the following, show the requested answers: (Assume all numeric fields are right justified and all alphanumeric fields are left justified)

| | Data | Sending Field | Receiving Field | Output Results |
|---|---|---|---|---|
| 1. | 12345 | 9(5) | Z(5) | _____ |
| 2. | 12345 | 9(3)V9(2) | 9(5).9(2) | _____ |
| 3. | 12345 | 9(3)V9(2) | 9(5).00 | _____ |
| 4. | −12345 | S9(3)V9(2) | 9(3).9(2) | _____ |
| 5. | −12345 | S9(3)V9(2) | 9(3).9(2)− | _____ |
| 6. | 12345 | 9(3)V9(2) | $9(3).9(2) | _____ |
| 7. | 12345 | 9(5) | 9(7) | _____ |
| 8. | 12345 | 9(3)V9(2) | 9(7)V9(4) | _____ |
| 9. | 12345 | 9(3)V9(2) | $$$,$$9.9(2) | _____ |
| 10. | 7654321 | 9(5)V9(2) | $$$,$$9.9(2) | _____ |
| 11. | 7654321 | 9(5)V9(2) | 9(2).9(1) | _____ |
| 12. | 7654321 | 9(5)V9(2) | Z(7).9(2) | _____ |
| 13. | −7654321 | S9(5)V9(2) | ZZZZ9.99CR | _____ |
| 14. | −7654321 | S9(5)V9(2) | ZZZZ9.99DB | _____ |
| 15. | +7654321 | S9(5)V9(2) | ZZZZ9.99CR | _____ |
| 16. | ABCDE | X(5) | X(5) | _____ |
| 17. | ABCDE | X(5) | X(3) | _____ |
| 18. | ABC | X(3) | X(2) | _____ |
| 19. | ABC | X(5) | X(5) | _____ |
| 20. | ABCDE | X(5) | XBXBXBX | _____ |

## Programming Assignments

1. Given the following PROCEDURE DIVISION, write the COBOL program to read the Inventory File, Data Set C, and list all the records on a report. The Report should have the page heading "INVENTORY LISTING" centered on the first line of the page. Column heading should be printed and be triple-spaced from the page heading. For the Column headings use the field descriptions given in the data set description. The detail lines should be single spaced. The data is Data Set C.

```
PROCEDURE DIVISION.
MAIN-PARA.
    PERFORM INIT-PARA.
    PERFORM HEADINGS-PARA.
    PERFORM READ-PARA.
    PERFORM PROCESS-PARA
        UNTIL FLAG = 1.
    PERFORM TERMINATION-PARA.

INIT-PARA.
    OPEN INPUT INVENTORY-FILE.
    OPEN OUTPUT REPORT-FILE.

HEADINGS-PARA.
    WRITE REPORT-LINE FROM PAGE-HEADING
        AFTER PAGE-TOP.
    WRITE REPORT-LINE FROM COLUMN-HEADINGS
        AFTER ADVANCING 3 LINES.
    WRITE REPORT-LINE FROM BLANK-LINE
        AFTER ADVANCING 1 LINE.
```

```
READ-PARA.
      READ INVENTORY-FILE INTO INVENTORY-RECORD-WS
            AT END
                  MOVE 1 TO FLAG.

PROCESS-PARA.
      MOVE ITEM-NUMBER-IN TO ITEM-NUMBER-OUT.
      MOVE DESCRIPTION-IN TO DESCRIPTION-OUT.
      MOVE QUANTITY-ON-HAND TO QUANTITY-ON-HAND-OUT.
      MOVE COST-PER-UNIT TO COST-PER-UNIT-OUT.
      MOVE REORDER-POINT-IN TO REORDER-POINT-OUT.
      MOVE SUPPLIER-CODE-IN TO SUPPLIER-CODE-OUT.
      MOVE BUYER-CODE-IN TO BUYER-CODE-OUT.
      WRITE REPORT-LINE FROM INVENTORY-RECORD-OUT-WS
            AFTER ADVANCING 1 LINE.
      PERFORM READ-PARA.

TERMINATION-PARA.
      CLOSE INVENTORY-FILE
            REPORT-FILE.
```

2. Using the PROCEDURE DIVISION in Problem 1 as your model, write a COBOL program to read the Personnel File, Data Set B, and write a listing of all employees. You should use appropriate file and data names for this data set. The page heading should be printed on the first line of the page and should read "EMPLOYEE LISTING". The column heading should be separated from the page heading by five blank lines. Use the field descriptions as the column headings. The first detail line should be triple spaced from the column headings. The detail lines should be double spaced from each other.

# PROCEDURE DIVISION

**OBJECTIVES**     This chapter starts our coverage of the PROCEDURE DIVISION. I say starts because you will soon realize that most of the rest of the book will discuss tools and techniques that will end up as code in the PROCEDURE DIVISION. Don't get me wrong. We will still discuss many other aspects of the DATA DIVISION, but it will be in relation to solving a particular application. Therefore, we will be looking at more PROCEDURE DIVISION features to support our problem solutions.

Even with the admission that this is only a start, Chapter 5 is a full one. It introduces the overall features of the PROCEDURE DIVISION. It also ties it to the hierarchy chart and flowchart. You will see that the PROCEDURE DIVISION is made up of sections, paragraphs, sentences, and statements. Then you will study many of the verbs from three categories: input/output, data manipulation and logic/control. You won't study all the verbs to the same extent, since we need full chapters for some. However, we will look extensively at those verbs that will allow us to write a simple program: OPEN, CLOSE, READ, WRITE, MOVE, PERFORM. Introductory coverage is provided for others like ADD, SUBTRACT, MULTIPLY, DIVIDE, COMPUTE, and IF, while others are just mentioned.

## TOPICS

- **relationship of PROCEDURE DIVISION to hierarchy chart and flowchart**
- **paragraphs and sections**
- **qualification of data items for moving**
- **group vs. corresponding moves**

- **reading data**
- **writing data**
- **decision making**
- **logic flow control**
- **DO WHILE logic construct**
- **verbs and sentence structure**

## KEY WORDS

- **PROCEDURE DIVISION**
- **READ. . .INTO**
- **WRITE. . .FROM**
- **ADD**
- **SUBTRACT**
- **MULTIPLY**
- **DIVIDE**
- **COMPUTE**

- **IF. . .ELSE**
- **MOVE**
- **STOP RUN**
- **EXIT, EXIT PROGRAM**
- **OPEN**
- **CLOSE**
- **DISPLAY**
- **ACCEPT**

## INTRODUCTION

Well, we finally get to the COBOL division that allows us to do the data manipulation required to solve a problem. This division is directly related to the flowchart (most of the time). There is almost a one-to-one match, one symbol for one line of code.

As with all the previous divisions, the PROCEDURE DIVISION is made up of sections, paragraphs, sentences and statements. However, until we get to the SORT Chapter, we will not use sections in this division, so each module in our hierarchy chart and the corresponding flowchart module will be coded as a paragraph. Those paragraphs will include all I/O, data manipulation and logic control necessary to code a solution to a problem.

## RELATIONSHIP TO HIERARCHY CHART AND FLOWCHART

The relationships among the hierarchy chart, flowchart, and procedural code are important ones. Look at Figure 5.1 to make sure you see the relationships.

Each module in the chart has an associated flowchart module; for instance, 0000-MAIN. We saw this relationship in Chapter 1. The relationship continues and expands to include the PROCEDURE DIVISION. Do you see it? The hierarchy module leads to a flowchart module that in turn we code into a paragraph by the same name and number. Figure 5.1 shows just one module as an example, but the same relationship holds true for all the modules. You would expect to find a flowchart module for each hierarchy module, and, similarly, you will find a paragraph for each flowchart module.

This close relationship is why flowcharts remain popular. It is easy to see the paragraphs that will be needed in the PROCEDURE DIVISION. Furthermore, maintenance is made easier when hierarchy charts and flowcharts or pseudocode are included in the system documentation. THE COBOL VERBS Within the PROCEDURE DIVISION we find the action or actions needed to solve the problem. We have organized these into procedural modules called paragraphs. And we have seen that paragraphs are made up of sentences. The COBOL sentences, like English sentences, include verbs. In fact, our COBOL sentences in the **PROCEDURE DIVISION** generally take the form:

FIGURE 5.1
Relationship of Hierarchy
Chart, Flowchart, and
PROCEDURE DIVISION

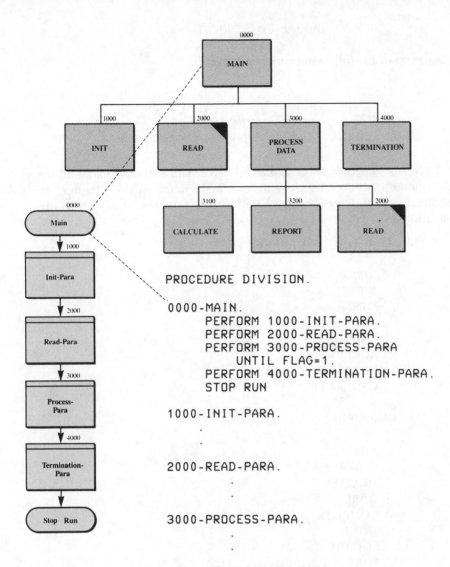

```
PROCEDURE DIVISION.

0000-MAIN.
     PERFORM 1000-INIT-PARA.
     PERFORM 2000-READ-PARA.
     PERFORM 3000-PROCESS-PARA
        UNTIL FLAG=1.
     PERFORM 4000-TERMINATION-PARA.
     STOP RUN

1000-INIT-PARA.
     .
     .

2000-READ-PARA.
     .
     .

3000-PROCESS-PARA.
     .
     .

4000-TERMINATION-PARA.
     .
```

**OPERATOR** and **OPERAND(S)**

or, in terms more like those of COBOL:

**VERB** and **OBJECT(S)**

or, more informally:

**WHAT WE WANT TO DO** and **WHAT TO DO IT TO**

For instance:

```
        READ STUDENT-FILE.
```

and

ADD 1 TO STUDENT—COUNT.

are made up of the following verbs and objects.

| Verb | Object |
|------|--------|
| READ | STUDENT-FILE |
| ADD | 1 TO STUDENT-COUNT |

There are generally three classes of verbs, and we will look at all the verbs eventually.  Some of the verbs we will look at in detail in this chapter; others we just introduce now, and yet others we will wait to study until we get to the appropriate applications.

- INPUT/OUTPUT (I/O) VERBS

  READ
  WRITE
  OPEN
  CLOSE
  DISPLAY
  ACCEPT
  REWRITE
  GENERATE

- DATA MANIPULATION VERBS

  ADD
  SUBTRACT
  MULTIPLY
  DIVIDE
  COMPUTE
  MOVE
  SEARCH
  SORT

- LOGIC and CONTROL VERBS

  IF
  EVALUATE (COBOL '85)
  PERFORM
  GO TO
  STOP RUN
  EXIT
  EXIT PROGRAM
  TERMINATORS (COBOL '85)
  INITIATE
  TERMINATE

Note:  There are other verbs that don't strictly fall into one of the classes: COPY and CALL are examples.

## I/O VERBS

As you can see, there are several input/output (I/O) verbs available in COBOL. Of particular interest now are READ, WRITE, OPEN and CLOSE. DISPLAY and ACCEPT will also be examined. However, REWRITE and GENERATE will be left until later in the appropriate chapters.

**OPEN.**    Before any file can be used in COBOL, it must first be opened—not only opened, but opened for the appropriate use. That is, we must specify if we intend to use the file for input, output, input and output at the same time, or extend (a COBOL '85 feature usually used with MICRO COBOL).

Looking at the system flowchart in Figure 5.2, we see three files:

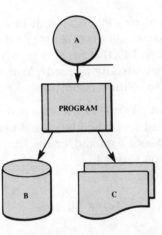

**FIGURE 5.2**
**System Flowchart Showing Three Files**

Can you tell how they are to be used? File A is input to the program, while both File B and File C are output from the program. Therefore, we would expect appropriate OPEN statement(s) before the files are used.

The general format of OPEN is:

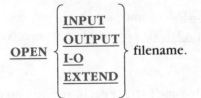

Therefore, we could code:

```
OPEN INPUT A-FILE.
OPEN OUTPUT B-FILE.
OPEN OUTPUT C-FILE.
```

That's simple enough, you say, but don't forget to do it before you try to use the files.

In fact, what if the system flowchart showed a case where the data in File A (tape) was simply being replicated on File B (disk), and the report was a listing of the contents of File B? Then, technically, the flowchart should be changed to the one in Figure 5.3.

**FIGURE 5.3**
Modified System Flowchart
Showing File B as an Input
and Output File

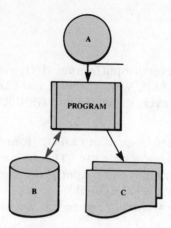

Figure 5.3 now correctly shows File B as both an output and an input file (not at the same time). Therefore, we would first **OPEN** File B as output to write to it. Then we would **OPEN** it for input to READ it back in to WRITE the report. But you cannot issue an **OPEN** if the file is already opened. You must CLOSE the file and then **OPEN** it again, which brings us to the CLOSE verb.

**CLOSE.**     You can think of **CLOSE** as the matched set to OPEN. That is to say, every file that has been opened must then be closed before a program is stopped. If not, the results may be the loss of data and/or the file. [Note: COBOL '85 will automatically **CLOSE** the files if you forget.]

The format of **CLOSE** is:

<u>CLOSE</u> filename.

Notice that the file usage specification found in OPEN is not part of **CLOSE**. All we need to do is **CLOSE**!

**READ.**     Once we have opened a file for input, we may issue **READ** commands for the file. There are two formats of the **READ** verb available for sequential files:

<u>READ</u> filename
[ <u>AT END</u> executable statement(s) ] .

and

<u>READ</u> filename [ <u>INTO</u> detail-record-description ]
[ <u>AT END</u> executable statement(s) ] .

The difference between the two formats is the location of the record of data after the **READ** is executed. In the first format, the data record is in the area described by the 01 associated with the file in the FILE SECTION. But remember, we agreed to have all detail descriptions in working storage. So we would then have to move the data to working storage in order to reference the individual data fields.

With the **READ...INTO** format, the data record ends up in the D-R-D specified with the **INTO**. Since that is where we want it, this is the format I will use until later in the text when it is more appropriate to use the first form.

However, you should realize that the D-R-D could have been coded in the FILE SECTION. This would allow the use of the first format. It would also reduce the amount of memory required for the program. (We wouldn't need the D-R-D in working storage.)

So why not do it this way? Well, for input it might be nice, but with print files, there are exceptions to the rules that we would have to study. For instance, the VALUE CLAUSE may not be used in the FILE SECTION. Therefore, all D-R-Ds used for headings would have to be coded in the WORKING-STORAGE SECTION anyway. So, for now, I think going with the second format keeps things simpler.

**WRITE.** As with READ, once a file has been opened, in this case for output, we may **WRITE** records to it. Again, we are talking only about sequential files. This includes print files. There are two formats of **WRITE** to look at first:

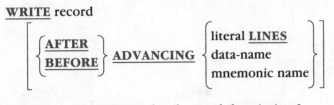

Remember from our flowchart discussions that each **WRITE** causes a record to be written to the file. In the case of a print file, it causes a line to be written. What's the difference between the two formats? Notice that the second format uses the **FROM** option. Looks like the INTO form of the READ verb, doesn't it? Well, they are functionally related. With the READ. . .INTO, we put data into a D-R-D in working storage. With the **WRITE. . .FROM** we cause the data in a D-R-D in working storage to be written to a file. But why use the second format instead of the first format?

The first format simply says **WRITE** record. This implies that the record contains the data to be written, and since the record referenced must be the record associated with the file in the FILE SECTION that we are writing to, how does the data get there? First we would have to move it there and then **WRITE**. That's not really as bad as it sounds, since we will have to do the same with the D-R-D. However, remember that there are special rules that apply to the FILE SECTION, and to standardize our input/output, I will use the INTO form of the READ and the **FROM** form of the **WRITE**. Once we become comfortable with what is happening with the data, we will apply the other formats. They do have some nice features themselves.

Example

Let's take a moment. . .well, probably longer, but it sounds good to just say a moment. . .and look at OPEN, CLOSE, READ. . .INTO and WRITE. . .FROM within the context of the DEAN-LIST program in the previous chapter. Briefly, we have the following:

```
SELECT DEAN-FILE      ASSIGN TO DA-S-DEAN.        <----- input file
SELECT REPORT-FILE    ASSIGN TO UT-S-REPORT.      <----- output file
```

```
DATA DIVISION.

FILE SECTION.

FD   DEAN-FILE
     LABEL RECORDS ARE OMITTED
     RECORD CONTAINS 47 CHARACTERS
     BLOCK CONTAINS 131 RECORDS
     DATA RECORD IS STUDENT-RECORD.

01   STUDENT-RECORD              PIC X(47).          <----- G-R-D

FD   REPORT-FILE
     LABEL RECORDS ARE OMITTED
     DATA RECORD IS REPORT-RECORD.

01   REPORT-RECORD              PIC X(133).         <----- G-R-D


WORKING-STORAGE SECTION.

01   STUDENT-RECORD-IN.                             <----- D-R-D for
     03   NAME                   PIC X(20).             input
     03   FILLER                 PIC X(4).              record
     03   SOCIAL-SECURITY-NUMBER PIC X(9).
     03   FILLER                 PIC X(2).
     03   MAJOR-CODE             PIC 9(1).
     03   FILLER                 PIC X(1).
     03   CLASS-CODE             PIC 9(1).
     03   FILLER                 PIC X(1).
     03   SEX-CODE               PIC 9(1).
     03   FILLER                 PIC X(1).
     03   GPR                    PIC 9(1)V9(4).

01   STUDENT-RECORD-OUT.                            <----- D-R-D for
     03   FILLER                 PIC X(15)  VALUE SPACES.  body of
     03   NAME-OUT               PIC X(20).              report
     03   FILLER                 PIC X(13)  VALUE SPACES.
     03   SOCIAL-SECURITY-NUMBER-OUT.
          05   SSN-1             PIC X(3).
          05   SSN-2             PIC X(2).
          05   SSN-3             PIC X(4).
     03   FILLER                 PIC X(13)  VALUE SPACES.
     03   MAJOR-CODE-OUT         PIC 9(1).
     03   FILLER                 PIC X(13)  VALUE SPACES.
     03   CLASS-CODE-OUT         PIC 9(1).
     03   FILLER                 PIC X(13)  VALUE SPACES.
     03   SEX-CODE-OUT           PIC 9(1).
     03   FILLER                 PIC X(13)  VALUE SPACES.
     03   G-P-R                  PIC 9(1).9(4).
     03   FILLER                 PIC X(15)  VALUE SPACES.

01   PAGE-HEADING.                                  <----- D-R-D for
     03   FILLER                 PIC X(57)  VALUE SPACES.  page
     03   FILLER                 PIC X(19)  VALUE           heading
               'CBA STUDENT LISTING'.
     03   FILLER                 PIC X(51)  VALUE SPACES.
```

```
    01  COLUMN-HEADINGS.                                    <----- D-R-D for
        03  FILLER              PIC X(23)    VALUE SPACES.   column
        03  FILLER              PIC X(4)     VALUE 'NAME'.   headings
        03  FILLER              PIC X(24)    VALUE SPACES.
        03  FILLER              PIC X(2)     VALUE 'ID'.
        03  FILLER              PIC X(15)    VALUE SPACES.
        03  FILLER              PIC X(5)     VALUE 'MAJOR'.
        03  FILLER              PIC X(9)     VALUE SPACES.
        03  FILLER              PIC X(5)     VALUE 'CLASS'.
        03  FILLER              PIC X(10)    VALUE SPACES.
        03  FILLER              PIC X(3)     VALUE 'SEX'.
        03  FILLER              PIC X(11)    VALUE SPACES.
        03  FILLER              PIC X(3)     VALUE 'GPR'.
        03  FILLER              PIC X(19)    VALUE SPACES.
```

Given those file descriptions and D-R-Ds, the PROCEDURE DIVISION looks like this:

```
PROCEDURE DIVISION.

0000-MAIN-PARA.

    PERFORM 1000-INIT-PARA.
    PERFORM 2000-HEADINGS-PARA.
    PERFORM 3000-READ-PARA.
    PERFORM 4000-PROCESS-PARA
        UNTIL FLAG=1.
    PERFORM 5000-TERMINATION-PARA.
    STOP RUN.

1000-INIT-PARA.

    OPEN INPUT  DEAN-FILE.
    OPEN OUTPUT REPORT-FILE.

2000-HEADINGS-PARA.

    WRITE REPORT-RECORD FROM BLANK-LINE
        AFTER ADVANCING TO-PAGE-TOP.
    WRITE REPORT-RECORD FROM PAGE-HEADING
        AFTER ADVANCING 5 LINES.
    WRITE REPORT-RECORD FROM COLUMN-HEADINGS
        AFTER ADVANCING 3 LINES.

3000-READ-PARA.

    READ DEAN-FILE INTO STUDENT-RECORD-IN        We'll look
        AT END                    <--------------  at this
            MOVE 1 TO FLAG.                        later.

4000-PROCESS-PARA.

    MOVE NAME TO NAME-OUT.
    MOVE SOCIAL-SECURITY-NUMBER TO SOCIAL-SECURITY-NUMBER-OUT.
    MOVE MAJOR-CODE TO MAJOR-CODE-OUT.
    MOVE CLASS-CODE TO CLASS-CODE-OUT.
    MOVE SEX-CODE TO SEX-CODE-OUT.
    MOVE GPR TO G-P-R.
```

```
WRITE REPORT-RECORD FROM STUDENT-RECORD-OUT                    We'll look
    AFTER ADVANCING 2 LINES.              <---------   at this
PERFORM 3000-READ-PARA.                                        later.

5000-TERMINATION-PARA.

    CLOSE DEAN-FILE.
    CLOSE REPORT-FILE.
```

You should note that 1000-INIT-PARA is executed first. That causes both files to be opened. DEAN-FILE is opened for input and REPORT-FILE is opened for output. This says that we intend to **READ** from DEAN-FILE and **WRITE** to REPORT-FILE. Look at paragraphs 3000 and 4000 to see that this is the case!

I also want to point out that the last thing done (before stopping) is 5000-TERMINATION-PARA. That causes both files to be closed just as the rules require.

With READ, you saw the use of the **AT END** clause. This clause is used to sense the end of a file (EOF) and allow the programmer to do something when it occurs. We also saw AFTER ADVANCING used with WRITE to control spacing on a page. We will discuss both of these options in the next chapter in the context of an application. We will see what we may do at EOF, and we will finally tackle the SPECIAL NAMES clause.

We will study the verbs more completely in the next chapter. For now, remember the following relationships:

first    OPEN files for input or output
then     READ/WRITE data records
last     CLOSE all opened files

**DISPLAY.**    This verb is used to send output to a printer or some other output device. It is typically used for low volume output situations. Typically, we use DISPLAY for:

- printing an error message
- debugging
- interactive programs (screens)
- file dumps (small files)

---

## TIP

**It is not good practice to use the DISPLAY as a means of writing reports or for writing the contents of large files. Use the WRITE verb to do those things.**

---

The format of the DISPLAY is:

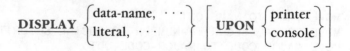

$$\underline{\text{DISPLAY}} \left\{ \begin{array}{l} \text{data-name,} \cdots \\ \text{literal,} \cdots \end{array} \right\} \left[ \underline{\text{UPON}} \left\{ \begin{array}{l} \text{printer} \\ \text{console} \end{array} \right\} \right]$$

Therefore, to see the contents of a record, we could say:

```
DISPLAY STUDENT-RECORD-IN
```

Note: The default setting is dependent on the installation. I'm assuming printer in this case.

However, the record just prints as is. . .no formatting and left justified on the line.

You could do the following and label it; this is good practice if you are displaying several data items:

```
DISPLAY "STUDENT-RECORD-IN CONTAINS ", STUDENT-RECORD-IN.
```

This will print the contents of STUDENT-RECORD-IN, but it also prints the literal "STUDENT-RECORD-IN". This helps you to read the output.

If all you wanted to see was each student's name and did not necessarily need the whole record, you could code it this way:

```
DISPLAY 'STUDENT NAME IS ', NAME.
```

I should tell you that you may not DISPLAY files. That is, you may not say:

```
DISPLAY filename
```

But, of course, you may **DISPLAY** the file's contents one record at a time by placing:

```
DISPLAY record-name
```

into the process loop.

Using **DISPLAY** in an interactive environment allows for screen displays. We said some of this earlier when we discussed the SCREEN SECTION. **DISPLAY** takes on many other options. Appendix F will show this use of **DISPLAY**.

---

## *TIP*

You may also use the DISPLAY to help debug your program. Place a DISPLAY para-name in each paragraph, for instance, to see the logic path your program is following.

---

**ACCEPT.**    If DISPLAY is for output, **ACCEPT** is for input to the program. You may input from the system and/or the keyboard.

One frequent use of **ACCEPT** is to get the current date for date-stamping reports. In fact, we may **ACCEPT** the day and time also.

ACCEPT looks like this:

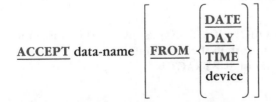

So we could **ACCEPT** the current date from the system with:

ACCEPT CURRENT-DATE FROM DATE.

where CURRENT-DATE is described in the WORKING-STORAGE SECTION.

**ACCEPT** is also used in interactive programs, where we can **ACCEPT** data from the keyboard. For instance, we could say:

ACCEPT STUDENT-RECORD-IN FROM CONSOLE.

This would allow us to enter the students' records from the console (keyboard). I don't recommend this way of entering data, since the same test data would have to be entered each time the program is executed. However, there is a better way to use **ACCEPT** in conjunction with COBOL '85 and the SCREEN SECTION. We will look at this in Appendix F.

## DATA MANIPULATION VERBS

As the name implies, this group of verbs is used to manipulate data. We will study most of these in later chapters. In fact, some have full chapters devoted to them, including SORT. However, I do want to introduce them to you briefly.

### Math Verbs

This is a subgrouping of the manipulation class by function: math. In COBOL we have several math verbs available.

- **ADD**
- **SUBTRACT**
- **MULTIPLY**
- **DIVIDE**
- **COMPUTE**

The math chapter looks at all these extensively, so all we will do here is take a brief look. One general rule that applies to all math verbs is that *only* numeric literals or data-names whose pictures are numeric (9, V, S) may be used in mathematical expressions.

**ADD and SUBTRACT.**     We are allowed to **ADD/SUBTRACT** two or more data names and/or numeric literals.

The general format of ADD is:

$$\underline{ADD} \left\{ \begin{array}{l} \text{data-name}_1 \; \cdots \\ \text{numeric literal} \end{array} \right\} \underline{TO} \; \text{data-name}_2 \; [ \; \underline{GIVING} \; \text{data-name.} \; ]$$

Note: In '74 COBOL, if GIVING is used, TO must not be used. However, COBOL '85 does allow both in the same statement.

The general format of SUBTRACT is:

$$\underline{\text{SUBTRACT}} \begin{Bmatrix} \text{data-name}_1 \cdots \\ \text{numeric literal} \end{Bmatrix} \underline{\text{FROM}} \text{ data-name}_2 \text{ [ } \underline{\text{GIVING}} \text{ data-name. ]}$$

Note: Both the **FROM** and **GIVING** may be used together.

**MULTIPLY and DIVIDE.**     Like ADD and SUBTRACT, these two verbs are very similar in their use (except for the obvious functional difference). In both cases we may **MULTIPLY OR DIVIDE** two, only two data names and/or numeric literals.

The general format of **MULTIPLY** is:

$$\underline{\text{MULTIPLY}} \begin{Bmatrix} \text{data-name}_1 \\ \text{numeric literal} \end{Bmatrix} \underline{\text{BY}} \begin{Bmatrix} \text{data-name}_2 \\ \text{numeric literal} \end{Bmatrix} \text{ [ } \underline{\text{GIVING}} \text{ data-name. ]}$$

Note: If the object of the BY is a numeric literal, then **GIVING** must be used. Both **BY** and **GIVING** may be used together.

The general format of **DIVIDE** is:

$$\underline{\text{DIVIDE}} \begin{Bmatrix} \text{data-name}_1 \\ \text{numeric literal} \end{Bmatrix} \begin{Bmatrix} \underline{\text{BY}} \\ \underline{\text{INTO}} \end{Bmatrix} \begin{Bmatrix} \text{data-name}_2 \\ \text{numeric literal} \end{Bmatrix} \text{ [ } \underline{\text{GIVING}} \text{ data-name. ]}$$

Note: With the **BY** option, data-name$_1$ is divided **BY** data-name$_2$. While with the **INTO** data-name$_2$ is divided by data-name$_1$. The **INTO** is the most used format of the verb. And, if the **BY** is used, the **GIVING** option must be used. On the other hand, with the **INTO**, the **GIVING** must be used only if the object of the **INTO** is a numeric literal.

You have probably noticed that all these verbs do one math function only: either ADD or SUBTRACT or MULTIPLY or DIVIDE. What if we needed to do more than one, say some equation like:

$$Y = \frac{A^2 + B^3 (A - C^2)^2}{(A + B)^2 (B - C)^2}$$

Could you do it with the math verbs discussed so far? Sure! But it would take a little work. You would have to do something like this:

```
MULTIPLY A BY A GIVING A-SQ
MULTIPLY B BY B GIVING B-SQ
MULTIPLY B BY B-SQ GIVING B-CUBED
MULTIPLY C BY C GIVING C-SQ
SUBTRACT C-SQ FROM A GIVING DIFF
MULTIPLY DIFF BY DIFF GIVING DIFF-SQ
MULTIPLY B-CUBED BY DIFF-SQ GIVING RESULT-1
ADD A-SQ TO RESULT-1
ADD A TO B GIVING SUM-1
MULTIPLY SUM-1 BY SUM-1 GIVING SUM-1-SQ
SUBTRACT C FROM B GIVING DIFF-2
MULTIPLY DIFF-2 BY DIFF-2 GIVING DIFF-2-SQ
MULTIPLY SUM-1-SQ BY DIFF-2-SQ GIVING RESULT-2
DIVIDE RESULT-2 INTO RESULT-1 GIVING Y
```

See what I mean about a little work? Well, guess what? We don't have to do it that way; we have **COMPUTE**!

**COMPUTE.**     With this verb we are to perform multiple math functions in one expression. And these expressions look like math expressions that we have used outside of the COBOL world.

The equation above would be:

$$COMPUTE \ Y = (A ** 2 + (B ** 3 * (A - C ** 2) ** 2)) \ / \ (((A + B) ** 2) * (B - C) ** 2).$$

That looks a little easier! Well, shorter anyway than what we had before. All those symbols, **, *, /, +, – are the operators we may use with **COMPUTE**.

The general format of **COMPUTE** is:

<u>COMPUTE</u> data-name$_1$ = arithmetic expression.

where data-name$_1$ is just a storage location for the results and, therefore, it need not be numeric but may be numeric edited (Zs, $s, ., etc.). The arithmetic expression may involve some or all of the operators:

| | |
|---|---|
| ** | exponentiation (raising to a power) |
| * | multiplication |
| / | division |
| + | addition |
| – | subtraction |

and numeric literals and/or data-names (numeric only).

Well, enough about the math verbs for now. You may want to go ahead and look at the math chapter to get the full picture if you are dying of curiosity.

### Move Verbs

The next subgroup within the data manipulation class are the **MOVE** verbs. With **MOVE** we are able to take data from one location and copy it into another. This could involve moving data from an input record area to an output record area. It could involve moving data from a temporary work area, like a 77, to an output record area.

We need to examine the types of the **MOVE** verb available to us:

- simple **MOVE**
- qualified **MOVE**
- group level **MOVE**
- corresponding **MOVE**

And, we need to examine moving data types also. That is to say, we need to examine issues involved in moving:

| | | |
|---|---|---|
| numeric | to numeric | 9 → 9 |
| numeric | to numeric edited | 9 → 9, Z, $, etc. |
| alphanumeric | to alphanumeric | X → X |

As you can see, there are plenty of combinations to deal with. Don't let that worry you. For the most part, the three I just showed you are the ones used most often.

**Simple MOVE.** I have stressed the fact that in COBOL all data references must be unique. Either the data names themselves make the reference unique by being unique, or we must do something special in the reference to handle data names that are not unique.

If the data names are unique, then a simple **MOVE** is all that is required.

The format of the simple **MOVE** is:

$$\underline{\text{MOVE}} \left\{ \begin{array}{l} \text{data-name} \\ \text{literal} \end{array} \right\} \underline{\text{TO}} \text{ data-name, } \cdots$$

Given the following record descriptions, which data fields can be moved with the simple **MOVE**?

```
01   EXAMPLE-IN                      01   EXAMPLE-OUT
     03   A                               03   AA
     03   B                               03   B
     03   C                               03   C-C
     03   D                               03   D
```

Well, we could say:

```
     MOVE  A  TO  AA.
     MOVE  B  TO  B.
     MOVE  C  TO  C-C.
     MOVE  D  TO  D.
```

However, do they all work? No! The first and third are OK, since each data-name is unique (A, AA; C, C-C). The second and fourth moves are not OK since B and D are not unique. Remember that the reference must be unique! If B in 01 EXAMPLE-IN is at location 1000, and B in 01 EXAMPLE-OUT is at location 5000, what would the compiler do? Should it generate:

```
     MOVE  location 1000 TO location 5000
```

or

```
     MOVE  location 5000 TO location 1000
```

We looked at this problem in an earlier chapter while discussing uniqueness of references. But it's important enough to show again. The compiler doesn't know which to do, so it gives us an error message. What do we do? Well, we may change the data names, making them unique, or change to a different **MOVE** verb.

**Qualified MOVE.** Actually, this **MOVE** type gets its name because of the way we must reference the data names in question. As we just saw, B and D were not unique, and the simple **MOVE** did not work.

The format of this **MOVE** is:

$$\underline{\text{MOVE}} \text{ data-name} \left\{ \begin{array}{l} \underline{\text{OF}} \text{ record-name} \\ \underline{\text{IN}} \text{ group-name} \end{array} \right\} \underline{\text{TO}} \text{ data-name} \left\{ \begin{array}{l} \underline{\text{OF}} \text{ record-name} \\ \underline{\text{IN}} \text{ group-name} \end{array} \right\} .$$

Therefore, I would **MOVE** B and D as follows:

```
MOVE B OF EXAMPLE-IN TO B OF EXAMPLE-OUT.
MOVE D OF EXAMPLE-IN TO D OF EXAMPLE-OUT.
```

Now, the compiler can handle the statements because the references are unique.

By the way, what if there were another data item called A in another record other than EXAMPLE-IN? How would we MOVE A now? Here's how!

```
MOVE A IN EXAMPLE-IN TO AA.
```

Do you see that I had to qualify only A and not AA? That brings up another issue. May you qualify even if qualifying is not needed? Yes! In fact, some people say that you should always qualify so that the reader is always sure what record the item is in, and so that the reader of the PROCEDURE DIVISION statements knows without having to search for the D-R-D.

**Group Level MOVE.**    As the name implies, the group level MOVE is a move that references at least one group level item. (Remember that a group level item is one that is subdivided.) Let's look at our example records. . .I've changed them!

```
01   EXAMPLE-IN                    01   EXAMPLE-OUT
     03   A                             03   AA
     03   B                             03   B
          05   M                             05   M
          05   N                             05   N
     03   C                             03   C-C
     03   D                             03   DD
          05   X                             05   XX
          05   Y                             05   YY
```

Now, if I said:

```
MOVE D TO DD.
```

What would happen? Since both are group level items, the contents of group D will be moved into group DD one character (byte) at a time, starting with the leftmost byte. We will see in a moment that a group MOVE works just like an alphanumeric MOVE (X → X) regardless of the data types involved.

How about the other group item?

```
MOVE B TO B.
```

Oops! B is not unique. Let's try again.

```
MOVE B OF EXAMPLE-IN TO B OF EXAMPLE-OUT.
```

What is this?. . .a qualified group MOVE! That's correct. I guess you see that qualification does not belong to anyone verb. It is dictated by the reference requirements.

I need to make another point here. To do this, let's put pictures on the items:

```
03   D.                            03   DD.
     05   X   PIC X(4).                 05   XX   PIC X(5).
     05   Y   PIC X(2).                 05   YY   PIC X(5).
```

When the "MOVE D TO DD" is executed, the six bytes of D get moved to the ten bytes of DD. Look at Figure 5.4.

FIGURE 5.4
Example of a Group Move

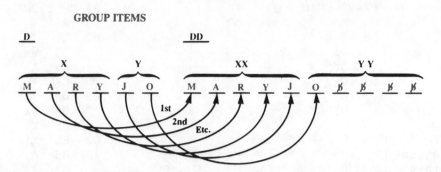

Well, all the data moved. But, did we get what we wanted? XX now has "MARYJ" and YY now has "Obbbb". You must insure with a group **MOVE** that the group corresponds or at least know that the results may be different from what you expected.

## TIP

**Do not use the group MOVE. While simple MOVEs take more code, they add to the readability of the code. A group MOVE causes data to be moved implicitly. I like explicit MOVEs!**

**MOVE CORRESPONDING.**    How do I have a different format and still **MOVE** a group without needing a separate **MOVE** for each field? The **MOVE CORRESPOND-ING**, that's how! The rule for the **MOVE CORRESPONDING** says that the data names must correspond. This does **not** say that the data types (X, 9, A, etc.) must correspond. Be careful about subordinate groups. . .groups within the group(s) being moved. The general format calls for the data names to be group level items. The for-mat is:

$$\underline{MOVE} \left\{ \begin{array}{l} \underline{CORRESPONDING} \\ \underline{CORR} \end{array} \right\} \text{group-name} \underline{TO} \text{ group-name}.$$

Going back to the records in the group **MOVE** discussion, what would be moved if I said:

```
MOVE CORRESPONDING B OF EXAMPLE-IN TO B OF EXAMPLE-OUT.
```

The contents of M in EXAMPLE-IN would be moved to M in EXAMPLE-OUT and the same for N. Graphically:

```
03  B                                03  B
    05   M    ----------------->         05   M
    05   N    ----------------->         05   N
```

How about "**MOVE CORRESPONDING** D TO DD."? If you said nothing will MOVE, you're right. There is no correspondence! How about "**MOVE CORRE-SPONDING** EXAMPLE-IN TO EXAMPLE-OUT."?

```
01    EXAMPLE-IN                                01    EXAMPLE-OUT
      03   A                                          03   AA
      03   B                                          03   B
           05   M      -------------->                     05   M
           05   N      -------------->                     05   N
      03   C                                          03   C-C
      03   D                                          03   D
           05   X                                          05   XX
           05   Y                                          05   YY
 I    ┌ 03   E                                       03   EE
added  │    05   W                                        05   W
this  └     05   Z                                        05   Z
```

That's all folks!  That's all that corresponds!  You ask, why not W and Z?  Since they do not have the same group name, they don't correspond.  They are in a subordinate group, and the group names do not correspond.

However, I loaded the example to illustrate the different issues.  The **MOVE CORRESPONDING** is great in those cases where much of the data in an input record is just being moved to the output record and printed.  The data item is not involved in any math or logic operations.  For instance, take a look at the following example:

```
01    INVENTORY-RECORD-IN              01    INVENTORY-RECORD-OUT
      03   DESCRIPTION                       03   DESCRIPTION
      03   FILLER                            03   FILLER
      03   ITEM-NUMBER                       03   ITEM-NUMBER
      03   FILLER                            03   FILLER
      03   SUPPLIER-CODE                     03   SUPPLIER-CODE
      03   FILLER                            03   FILLER
      03   WAREHOUSE-CODE                    03   WAREHOUSE-CODE
      03   FILLER                            03   FILLER
      03   Q-O-H                             03   Q-O-H
      03   FILLER                            03   FILLER
      03   COST-PER-UNIT                     03   COST-PER-UNIT
```

How could we **MOVE** all input fields to output?  With six qualified moves. . .or, with one **MOVE CORRESPONDING**!

```
MOVE CORRESPONDING INVENTORY-RECORD-IN TO
                   INVENTORY-RECORD-OUT.
```

Nice, isn't it?  I love things that reduce my work requirements.  But, it's not all gravy!  What if you needed to calculate the total inventory cost?  Say:

```
COMPUTE TOTAL-INVENTORY-COST = TOTAL-INVENTORY-COST
        + (Q-O-H * COST-PER-UNIT).
```

Then, we have problems.  Why?  Which Q-O-H and COST-PER-ITEM are we referencing?  It's the same old problem about unique names.  On the one hand, we want all the data names the same to make moving them easy.  On the other hand, we need to reference two of the data fields in the COMPUTE.  What do we do?  We could change the COMPUTE to read:

```
COMPUTE TOTAL-INVENTORY-COST = TOTAL-INVENTORY-COST
      + (Q-O-H OF INVENTORY-RECORD-IN
      * COST-PER-UNIT OF INVENTORY-RECORD-IN).
```

Or, we could make these two fields unique:

```
         .                           .
         .                           .
         .                           .
03   Q-O-H-IN                  03   Q-O-H-OUT
         .                           .
         .                           .
         .                           .
03   COST-PER-UNIT-IN          03   COST-PER-UNIT-OUT
```

Now, our references to the data fields in the COMPUTE do not need qualification. But the **MOVE CORRESPONDING** moves only corresponding data items, so we would have to add two simple moves to move Q-O-H-IN and COST-PER-UNIT-IN. We would now need three moves:

```
MOVE CORRESPONDING INVENTORY-RECORD-IN TO
     INVENTORY-RECORD-OUT.
MOVE Q-O-H-IN TO Q-O-H-OUT.
MOVE COST-PER-UNIT-IN TO COST-PER-UNIT-OUT.
```

I think either is OK. My purpose here was to point out the choices, not make a decision for you.

## *TIP*

**Like the group move, the MOVE CORRESPONDING causes an implicit move. Use it sparingly.**

### *Moving and Data Types*

Up to this point, I have avoided data types almost entirely. But, we must consider data types because COBOL has some specific Dos and Don'ts. Figure 5.5 shows which are allowed and which are not.

| FROM \ TO | NUMERIC | NUMERIC EDITED | ALPHANUMERIC | ALPHABETIC |
|---|---|---|---|---|
| NUMERIC | OK | OK | INTEGERS ONLY | NO |
| NUMERIC EDITED | COBOL '85 ONLY | NO | OK | NO |
| ALPHANUMERIC | NU | NO | OK | OK |
| ALPHABETIC | NO | NO | OK | OK |

**FIGURE 5.5**
**Table of Allowable MOVEs**

As you can see from the figure, the three moves that we use most are OK. My point is that those, $9 \rightarrow 9$, $9 \rightarrow 9$ edited, and $X \rightarrow X$, are not the only ones that are OK. There are others that are allowed.

**Numeric Moves.**   Let's now take a closer look at how data values are moved from one field to another.  There are a few rules that apply here:

- Align the decimal places in both the sending and receiving fields.
- Data is moved from right to left on the left of the decimal.
- Data is moved from left to right on the right of the decimal.
- If the sending field is larger than the receiving field, high-order digits will be truncated (cut off).
- If the sending field is smaller than the receiving field, the receiving field is filled with zeros.

Examples:

| Data | Sending Field | Receiving Field | Results | |
|------|---------------|-----------------|---------|---|
| 1234 | 9(4) | 9(4) | 1234 | ← data fits |
| 1234 | 9(4) | 9(6) | 001234 | ← fill with 0s |
| 1234 | 9(4) | 9(2) | 34 | ← truncation |
| 1234.56 | 9(4)V9(2) | 9(4).9(2) | 1234.56 | ← data fits |
| 1234 | 9(4) | 9(4).9(2) | 1234.00 | ← fill with 0s |
| 1234.56 | 9(4)V9(2) | 9(6).9(4) | 001234.5600 | ← fill with 0s |
| 1234.56 | 9(4)V9(2) | 9(2).9(1) | 34.5 | ← truncation |

Do you see how the decimal points are aligned and the data moved in both directions from the decimal point?  See how we pad with zeros and truncate, depending on relative size of the fields?

**Numeric Edited Moves.**   You have actually already seen these when we looked at edit characters.  But, let's take a quick look again.

Examples:

| Data | Sending Field | Receiving Field | Results |
|------|---------------|-----------------|---------|
| 1234.56 | 9(4)V9(2) | $(4)9.99 | $1234.56 |
| 1234 | 9(4) | Z(5)9 | bb1234 |

Remember this?  The rules for moving numeric data still apply, but we also apply the editing rules.  You might want to look back at the edit characters.

**Alphanumeric Moves.**   Moving data from one alphanumeric data item to another also has some basic rules:

- Data is moved one byte at a time from left to right.
- If the receiving field is larger than the sending field, then it is right filled with blanks.
- If the receiving field is smaller than the sending field, then truncation of the rightmost digit(s) occurs.

Examples:

| Data | Sending Field | Receiving Field | Results |
|------|---------------|-----------------|---------|
| READY | X(5) | X(5) | READY |
| READY | X(5) | X(4) | READ |
| READY | X(5) | X(6) | READY⌀ |

A special note about group level moves. . .remember that I said they work like alphanumeric moves. They act like X → X no matter what the picture clauses of the elementary level items might be!

For example:

```
03  GROUP-A.                    03  GROUP-B.
    05  A   PIC 9(4).               05  A   PIC X(8).
    05  B   PIC X(2).               05  B   PIC 9(4).
```

Moving GROUP-A TO GROUP-B would cause:

Group sizes:     X(6)      ⟶      X(12)
                           TO
Data value:     1234AB    ⟶      1234AB⌀⌀⌀⌀⌀⌀

It moves the data all right, but if we now tried to do math with B of GROUP-B, we would get an error, since it contains blanks. Be careful where you use group moves!

**Alphabetic Moves.**    These data fields are moved according to the rules of alphanumeric moves.

## LOGIC AND CONTROL VERBS

Many verbs fall into this category. Two of the major ones are the IF and the PERFORM verbs. They require much explanation. Others do not require much in formal discussion. Yet others are associated with particular features of COBOL. They will be discussed fully with those features.

**IF.**    In COBOL and other languages, **IF** is our way to make decisions. (IF is not a verb in English, but within our COBOL sentence definition, IF is considered a COBOL verb.) We use several forms of **IF**s:

- simple **IF**
- IF. . .then. . .ELSE
- nested **IF**

The format of the simple form of **IF** is:

IF condition
    executable statements.

An example of the first form would be:

```
IF GPR > 3.5
   ADD 1 TO TOP-STUDENT-COUNT.
```

The second format looks like:

**IF** condition

executable statement(s)

**ELSE**

executable statement(s).

An example of this format follows:

```
IF SEX-CODE = 1
   ADD 1 TO MALE-COUNT
ELSE
   ADD 1 TO FEMALE-COUNT.
```

And, the third format is just a combination of these:

**IF** condition$_1$

executablestatement(s)

**IF** condition$_2$

executable statement(s)

**IF** condition$_3$

executable statement(s)

**ELSE**

executable statement(s)

**ELSE**

executable statement(s)

**ELSE**

executable statement(s).

An example would be:

```
IF MAJOR-CODE = 3
   ADD 1 TO FINANCE-COUNT
   IF GPR > 3.00
      ADD 1 TO GOOD-FINANCE-STUDENT
      IF SEX-CODE = 2
         ADD 1 TO GOOD-FINANCE-FEMALE-COUNT
      ELSE
         ADD 1 TO GOOD-FINANCE-MALE-COUNT
   ELSE
      ADD 1 TO FAIR-FINANCE-STUDENT
ELSE
   ADD 1 TO OTHER-MAJOR.
```

There are several shapes we could show for the nested IF format, but I think you get the idea.

The IF statement is called a condition statement. What it does is cause a condition (or conditions) to be evaluated. If the condition is true, do something and if the condition is false, the computer must do something else. This can best be shown with the flowchart segment in Figure 5.6.

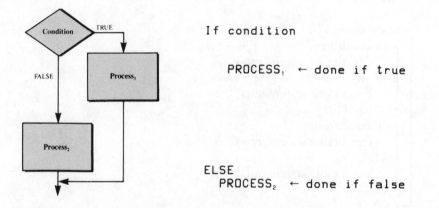

```
If condition

      PROCESS₁  ← done if true




   ELSE
      PROCESS₂  ← done if false
```

**FIGURE 5.6**
**Example IF Structure Shown
with Flowchart and Code**

As you can see, we need a whole chapter to cover the IF. . .different forms, relational operators, END-IF, NEXT SENTENCE, and the COBOL '85 CASE structure, EVALUATE. So, in Chapter 8 we will take an in-depth look at the IF and its features.

**GO TO.**    This is the way we have in COBOL of branching from one point to another. The format of **GO TO** is:

$$\underline{GO\ TO} \left\{ \begin{array}{l} \text{paragraph-name} \\ \text{section-name} \end{array} \right\}.$$

Do you recall that one of the goals of structured programming is to minimize the use of **GO TO**? Well, I suggest you don't use the **GO TO** except in a couple of places. These are with the SORT and with subprograms.

**EXIT and EXIT PROGRAM.**    These two are used for entirely different reasons. **EXIT** is used in COBOL when a paragraph is needed at an end of a section for branching to (GO TO). The paragraph has no other function but to allow us to get to the end of a section. This paragraph is not allowed to be empty. COBOL does not like lonely paragraphs. So, guess what we put into the paragraph?. . .the verb **EXIT**.

For example:

```
        LAST-PARA.
            EXIT.
```

**EXIT** does nothing except keep us from having an empty paragraph.

**EXIT PROGRAM**, on the other hand, does have a very important function. It causes the return to a calling program from the called program. This verb is used with subprograms. It will be discussed fully in that chapter.

**INITIATE and TERMINATE.**    These verbs are associated with REPORT WRITER They will be discussed in an appendix.

### Scope Terminators

All these verbs are used with other verbs to show where the verb's scope ends.  They are COBOL '85 features, but I think a look at some at this point is important.

**END-IF.**    END-IF helps identify the end of an IF without having to end the sentence.  For instance:

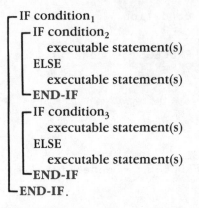

```
┌─ IF condition₁
│  ┌─ IF condition₂
│  │     executable statement(s)
│  │  ELSE
│  │     executable statement(s)
│  └─ END-IF
│  ┌─ IF condition₃
│  │     executable statement(s)
│  │  ELSE
│  │     executable statement(s)
│  └─ END-IF
└─ END-IF .
```

Without **END-IF**, this structure is not possible.  You see, I need to have two complete IF. . .then. . .ELSE structures within condition₁.  Take the first **END-IF** out of the sentence.  The IF condition₃ is now part of the ELSE (false) of the condition₂ statement.  That's not what we wanted.

Look at it the way Figure 5.7 shows it.

See the difference?  Before the **END-IF**, we had to structure the logic as in Figure 5.8.

We will look at this more in the IF Chapter.

**END-READ.**    This one is another of my favorites because it solves a problem of logic structure we have had up until COBOL '85.

What if you had a READ verb within an IF?

```
IF condition₁
     .
     .
     .
  READ filename INTO D-R-D
     AT END executable statement(s)
  ADD . . . . .
  MULTIPLY . . . . .
     .
     .
     .
ELSE
     .
     .
     .
```

What is going to happen?  When condition₁ is true, the READ will be done and if the READ is successful, then the ADD and MULTIPLY will be done.  Right?  Wrong!  The ADD and MULTIPLY are actually conditioned on the AT END (EOF).  Now, let's use the **END-READ**.

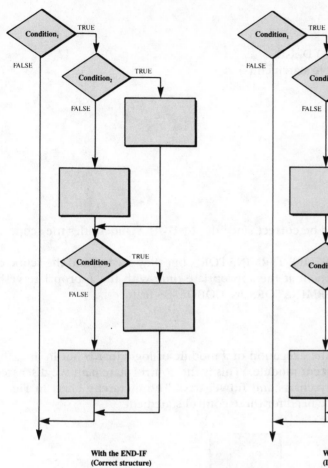
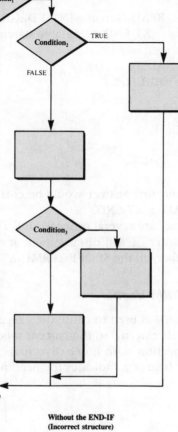

With the END-IF
(Correct structure)

Without the END-IF
(Incorrect structure)

**FIGURE 5.7**
Logic Structure with and
without the END-IF

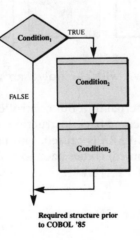

Required structure prior
to COBOL '85

**FIGURE 5.8**
Required Logic Flow to
Accomplish END-IF Structure
with COBOL '74

```
IF condition₁
      .
      .
      .
   READ filename INTO D-R-D
      AT END executable statement(s)
   END-READ
   ADD . . . . .
   MULTIPLY . . . . .
      .
      .
ELSE
      .
      .
```

Now your first answer would be correct since the **END-READ** identifies the scope of the READ. . .AT END.

There are several other SCOPE TERMINATORS, but they are beyond the scope of this chapter.  I will discuss them at the appropriate time with the appropriate verb. Remember, all the SCOPE TERMINATORS are COBOL '85 features.

### PERFORM Verbs

**PERFORM** is used to cause the execution of a module of logic that is not in line, the module is external to the current module.  This is the control statement we discussed in connection with hierarchy charts and flowcharts.  The hierarchy chart in Figure 5.9, for instance, indicates the need for three control statements.

**FIGURE 5.9**
**Hierarchy Chart Showing the Need for Three PERFORMs**

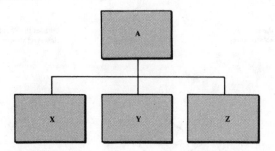

This logic would be shown with the flowchart and COBOL coded as shown in Figure 5.10.

The three modules are external to A but controlled by A.  I guess you could think of **PERFORM** as a go-to-and-come-back instruction.  That is, that during the execution of A-PARA, a branch to X-PARA is caused, but, unlike the situation with GO TO, once X-PARA is completed, control comes back to A-PARA.

There are several forms of **PERFORM**:

- simple **PERFORM**
- **PERFORM** some number of times
- **PERFORM THROUGH**
- **PERFORM UNTIL**
- **PERFORM VARYING** (covered with the tables chapter)
- in line **PERFORM**  (COBOL '85)

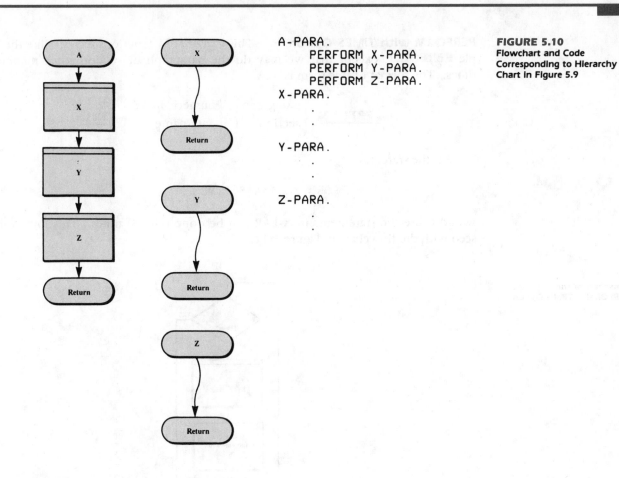

```
A-PARA.
   PERFORM X-PARA.
   PERFORM Y-PARA.
   PERFORM Z-PARA.
X-PARA.
   .
   .
   .
Y-PARA.
   .
   .
   .
Z-PARA.
   .
   .
   .
```

**FIGURE 5.10**
Flowchart and Code
Corresponding to Hierarchy
Chart in Figure 5.9

**Simple PERFORM.**    The simple **PERFORM** says, "Go to the paragraph or section specified, execute it and come back to the statement following the **PERFORM**." The general format of **PERFORM** is:

$$\underline{\textbf{PERFORM}} \quad \left\{ \begin{array}{l} \text{paragraph} \\ \text{section} \end{array} \right\}$$

So, **PERFORM** X-PARA will cause everything in X-PARA to be executed. But how is the end of X-PARA known? In other words, what is the range of the **PERFORM**? The end of one paragraph occurs when the next paragraph is reached. The end of one section—a group of paragraphs—occurs when the next section is reached. Graphically, it looks like this:

       **PERFORM X-PARA.**

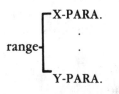

**PERFORM with TIMES Option.**    This **PERFORM** functions exactly like the simple **PERFORM**, except that we may do the paragraph or section some number of times. The format of this form is:

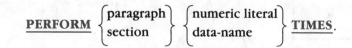

$$\underline{\text{PERFORM}} \begin{Bmatrix} \text{paragraph} \\ \text{section} \end{Bmatrix} \begin{Bmatrix} \text{numeric literal} \\ \text{data-name} \end{Bmatrix} \underline{\text{TIMES}}.$$

So, the statement:

```
PERFORM X-PARA 5 TIMES.
```

would cause the statements in X-PARA to be done five (5) times. This logic can be seen with the flowchart in Figure 5.11.

**FIGURE 5.11**
**Flowchart of the**
**PERFORM. . .TIMES Option**

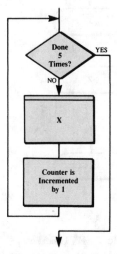

Note:  The counter is set up by
COBOL, not by us in our
program!

We could also write:

```
PERFORM X-PARA n TIMES.
```

This allows us to vary the number of times X-PARA is done when the **PERFORM** is executed. We must supply a value for n before the **PERFORM** is executed. So, if n = 3, this **PERFORM** and the previous one are functionally the same. However, this form gives us more flexibility. We can change the value of n during the program's execution and thereby change the number of times X-PARA is executed. We can even do it **0 TIMES**.

**PERFORM THROUGH.**    This is an interesting option of the **PERFORM**, and in fact, may be used with all other forms. The effect of the **THROUGH** is to define the range of the to **PERFORM** routine to include multiple paragraphs or sections. Its basic format is:

$$\underline{\text{PERFORM}} \begin{Bmatrix} \text{paragraph} \\ \text{section} \end{Bmatrix} \begin{Bmatrix} \underline{\text{THROUGH}} \\ \underline{\text{THRU}} \end{Bmatrix} \begin{Bmatrix} \text{paragraph} \\ \text{section} \end{Bmatrix}.$$

If we said:

        PERFORM A–PARA THROUGH Z–PARA.

What would we cause to be executed? We must look at the order of the paragraphs to be specific. But, in general terms, we would cause A-PARA, Z-PARA and every paragraph physically between to be executed. Look at this and see it graphically.

        PERFORM A-PARA THROUGH Z-PARA.

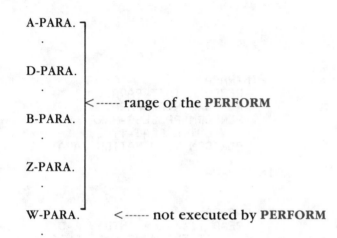

**TIP**

**Perform Through is not recommended in structured programming standards, because it leads to implicit execution of paragraphs.**

**PERFORM UNTIL.**     This **PERFORM** is the **PERFORM** that matches the DO WHILE structure. Its format is:

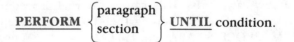

$$\text{PERFORM} \begin{Bmatrix} \text{paragraph} \\ \text{section} \end{Bmatrix} \text{UNTIL condition.}$$

The added feature here is the UNTIL   The **PERFORM** says: **PERFORM** the paragraph or section until some condition is met. It is important to understand that the **PERFORM...UNTIL** is the DO WHILE logic construct (besides giving me a good exam question). Why? Because it tests before performing. Remember that the DO WHILE is symbolized as in Figure 5.12.

The condition may be a single or compound condition. It is tested first, and if the condition is not met, the procedure is executed. The condition is tested again, and the process continues until the condition is met. At that time control passes to the statement following the **PERFORM**

A good example of this **PERFORM** is the code for the module in our flowchart that says "UNTIL EOF" or "UNTIL FLAG = 1". For instance, see Figure 5.13.

**FIGURE 5.12**
The DOWHILE and the
PERFORM...UNTIL

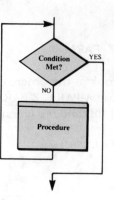

```
PERFORM procedure
    UNTIL condition
```

**FIGURE 5.13**
Example Flowchart and Code
for the PERFORM...UNTIL
Incorporating the EOF FLag

```
MAIN-PARA.
    PERFORM INIT-PARA.
    PERFORM READ-PARA.
    PERFORM PROCESS-PARA.
        UNTIL FLAG=1.
    PERFORM TERMINATION-PARA.

INIT-PARA.
    .

READ-PARA.
    READ filename INTO D-R-D
        AT END MOVE 1 to FLAG.
PROCESS-PARA.
    .
    PERFORM READ-PARA.

TERMINATION-PARA.
    .
```

I hope you see how each **PERFORM** causes external procedures to be executed and how the **PERFORM...UNTIL** is doing the same thing except that it will continue to **PERFORM** PROCESS-PARA until FLAG = 1. When does FLAG = 1?...when the data runs out! See the AT END on the READ verb? That's what sets it to 1!

Figure 5.12 shows that the **PERFORM...UNTIL** is executed by testing first, doing the procedure, and re-testing. In COBOL '85 we have been given the option of changing when the test is done. We may say test before or test after. The test before is the default, and so test before is still the DO WHILE construct. However, the test after makes the **PERFORM** a DO UNTIL construct since the procedure is done at least once, and then the condition is tested.

**In-Line PERFORM.**     This is another feature of COBOL '85. Instead of having to **PERFORM** an external module to do something, we can include the something within the **PERFORM**. For example:

```
PERFORM UNTIL ANSWER = 'YES'
    ADD AMOUNT TO TOTAL
    ACCEPT ANSWER
END-PERFORM
```

Without this new feature, we would have had to code:

```
PERFORM ADD-PARA.
    UNTIL ANSWER = 'YES'.
        .
        .

    ADD-PARA.
        ADD AMOUNT TO TOTAL.
        ACCEPT ANSWER.
```

To summarize the topic of **PERFORM** verbs, we can say that they control the execution of an external module of logic. There are several different forms, but they all have the characteristic of a go-to-and-come-back command.

Each **PERFORM** has a range of control. A **PERFORM** of a paragraph stops at the next paragraph, while a **PERFORM** of a section stops at the next section. We also have the **PERFORM THROUGH**, which starts at one paragraph and goes through the last one stated in the **PERFORM**.

We also looked at the **PERFORM UNTIL**. This is our DO WHILE structure because it tests first and then may execute and re-test as does the DO WHILE logic construct. We saw that COBOL '85 allows us to test after as well.

Another COBOL '85 feature is the in line **PERFORM**. It allows us to include the statements to be executed within the **PERFORM** statement itself.

**STOP RUN.**    This statement ends the execution of the program. You may have more than one STOP RUN, but I don't suggest it. It leads to sloppy code. The format of this verb is:

STOP RUN.

## AN EXAMPLE

Let's code the solution to the dean's request for a student listing, except that the dean just wants all students with GPR > 3.00. He also wants a count of all students. We will use the same FDs and D-R-D that we have been using, so I'll just note them and concentrate on the PROCEDURE DIVISION.

The hierarchy chart and flowchart are shown in Figures 5.14 and 5.15, respectively.

**FIGURE 5.14**
**Hierarchy Chart For Student**
**Listing Problem**

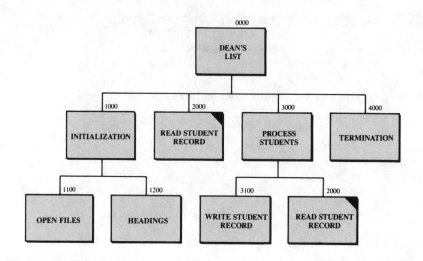

**FIGURE 5.15**
**Flowchart for Student Listing**
**Problem**

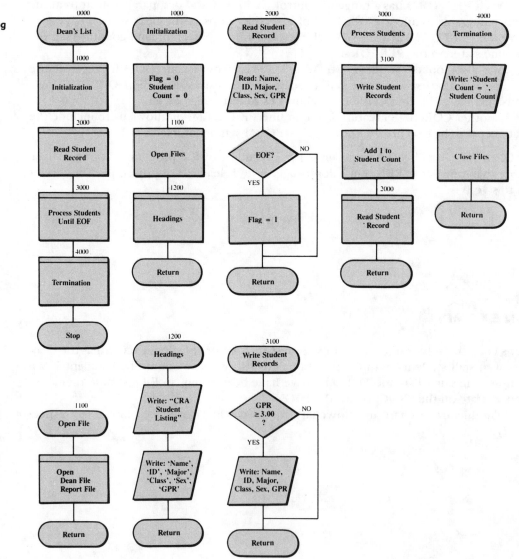

```
IDENTIFICATION DIVISION.

PROGRAM-ID. LISTING.

AUTHOR.    KEVIN.

ENVIRONMENT DIVISION.

CONFIGURATION SECTION.
        .
        .

INPUT-OUTPUT SECTION.

    SELECT DEAN-FILE    ASSIGN TO DA-S-DEAN.
    SELECT REPORT-FILE  ASSIGN TO UT-S-REPORT.

DATA DIVISION.

FILE SECTION.

FD  DEAN-FILE
        .
        .

01  STUDENT-RECORD              PIC X(47).

FD  REPORT-FILE
        .
        .

01  REPORT-RECORD              PIC X(133).

WORKING-STORAGE SECTION.

77  STUDENT-COUNT              PIC 9(4)    VALUE 0.
77  FLAG                       PIC 9(1)    VALUE 0.

01  STUDENT-RECORD-IN.
    03
    03                same as before
    03

01  STUDENT-RECORD-OUT.
    03
    03                same as before
    03

01  PAGE-HEADING.
        .
        .                same as before

01  COLUMN-HEADINGS.
        .
        .                same as before
```

```
01   STUDENT-COUNT-LINE.
     03   FILLER                        PIC X(56)   VALUE SPACES.
     03   FILLER                        PIC X(17)   VALUE
              'STUDENT COUNT IS  '.
     03   STUDENT-COUNT-OUT             PIC ZZZ9.
     03   FILLER                        PIC X(56)   VALUE SPACES.

PROCEDURE DIVISION.

0000-MAIN-PARA.
     PERFORM 1000-INIT-PARA.
     PERFORM 2000-READ-PARA.
     PERFORM 3000-PROCESS-STUDENT-PARA
         UNTIL FLAG=1.
     PERFORM 4000-TERMINATION-PARA.
     STOP RUN.

1000-INIT-PARA.
     PERFORM 1100-OPEN-FILES-PARA.
     PERFORM 1200-HEADINGS-PARA.

1100-OPEN-FILES-PARA.
     OPEN INPUT  DEAN-FILE.
     OPEN OUTPUT REPORT-FILE.

1200-HEADINGS-PARA.
     WRITE REPORT-RECORD FROM BLANK-LINE
         AFTER PAGE-TOP.
     WRITE REPORT-RECORD FROM PAGE-HEADING
         AFTER 5.
     WRITE REPORT-RECORD FROM COLUMN-HEADINGS
         AFTER 3.

2000-READ-PARA.
     READ DEAN-FILE INTO STUDENT-RECORD-IN
         AT END
             MOVE 1 TO FLAG.

3000-PROCESS-STUDENTS-PARA.
     PERFORM 3100-WRITE-STUDENT-RECORD-PARA.
     ADD 1 TO STUDENT-COUNT.
     PERFORM 2000-READ-PARA.

3100-WRITE-STUDENT-RECORD-PARA.
     IF GPR > 3.00
         MOVE NAME                     TO NAME-OUT
         MOVE SOCIAL-SECURITY-NUMBER TO
             SOCIAL-SECURITY-NUMBER-OUT
         MOVE MAJOR-CODE               TO MAJOR-CODE-OUT
         MOVE CLASS-CODE               TO CLASS-CODE-OUT
         MOVE SEX-CODE                 TO SEX-CODE-OUT
         MOVE GPR                      TO G-P-R
         WRITE REPORT-RECORD FROM STUDENT-RECORD-OUT
             AFTER 2.
```

```
4000-TERMINATION-PARA.
    MOVE STUDENT-COUNT TO STUDENT-COUNT-OUT.
    WRITE REPORT-RECORD FROM STUDENT-COUNT-LINE
        AFTER 5.
    CLOSE DEAN-FILE.
    CLOSE REPORT-FILE.
```

This example, hierarchy chart, flowchart and code should illustrate the relationships among these elements that are so important. It should also illustrate how most of the verbs we talked about in the chapter work together.

## SUMMARY

The PROCEDURE DIVISION of the COBOL program is where we code the logic to our problem solutions. It is made up, as are the other divisions, of sections, paragraphs, sentences and statements.

Each of these sentences is made up of a verb and some object the verb acts on. I organized and grouped the verbs into three types for discussion. We talked about the input/output verbs, in particular READ, WRITE, OPEN and CLOSE. We found out that before a file may be used, we must OPEN it, and then before we STOP RUN we must CLOSE it.

Speaking of using the files, we talked at length about READ and WRITE. While I pointed out that there are two forms of each, I decided to standardize and use the READ...INTO and WRITE...FROM forms. These seem to work the same way, and they kept us from having to learn exceptions to rules (for now anyway).

Once we understood how to get data into and out of our program, we looked at the data-manipulation types of verbs. These included MOVEs and the math verbs. We looked more closely at MOVE verbs because of the nature of COBOL data records that requires us to move data around. We saw the different forms of MOVE and where and how those forms might be used: the simple MOVE for unique items, qualified MOVE for non-unique items and the MOVE CORRESPONDING for lazy (not really lazy, but very smart and careful) movers. We also looked at moves and data types: $9 \rightarrow 9$, $X \rightarrow X$, and so on. This topic sort of tied up our earlier discussion on edit characters.

We looked briefly at the math verbs, but left full discussion till the Math Chapter. However, we did see that we have a variety of verbs, including the COMPUTE verb, which looks much like the LET in BASIC or the assignment statement in FORTRAN.

The third class was the control and logic class—that group of verbs that help logic flow and control logic flow. The two major verbs we studied were IF and PERFORM. Again, we spent more time with PERFORM. Because of our modular approach to coding, we needed the verb that allows us to use that structure. We saw again that many forms are available. While that's true, we also saw that there are similarities: their range and go-to-and-come-back features. The two most-used forms seem to be the simple PERFORM and the PERFORM UNTIL. The UNTIL form is the DO WHILE structured programming construct. We put it to use with our programs to implement the lead read technique that we discussed in Chapter 2. We also saw a couple of '85 features for the PERFORM: test before and test after options and the inline PERFORM.

We just took a brief introductory look at the IF verb. The full discussion with all the options and rules will be covered in a chapter on the IF statement.

## SAMPLE PROGRAM

The following is a complete running COBOL program using many of the features and techniques discussed in this Chapter.

```
PP 5740-CB1 RELEASE 2.4                    IBM OS/VS COBOL  JULY  1, 1982      16.52.35  DATE OCT 19,1988


        1                    16.52.35        OCT 19,1988


00001              IDENTIFICATION DIVISION.
00002
00003              PROGRAM-ID.
00004                        BILLING.
00005              AUTHOR.
00006                        GEORGE FOWLER.
00007              INSTALLATION.
00008                        TEXAS A & M UNIVERSITY.
00009              DATE-WRITTEN.
00010                        SEPTEMBER 8, 1985.
00011              DATE-COMPILED. OCT 19,1988.
```

```
        2         BILLING        16.52.35        OCT 19,1988


00013              ******************************************************************
00014              *                                                                *
00015              *  LAB ASSIGNMENT                                                 *
00016              *  DATE ASSIGNED                                                  *
00017              *  DATE DUE                                                       *
00018              *  PURPOSE:          THIS IS A BILLING PROGRAM FOR THE   CIRCLE  *
00019              *     CLUB RESTAURANT AND BAR. IT CALCULATES THE TOTAL AMOUNT DUE *
00020              *     FROM EACH CUSTOMER AND A GRAND TOTAL DUE FROM ALL ACCOUNTS. *
00021              *     THERE ARE DISCOUNTS ALLOWED UNDER CERTAIN CONDITIONS.  THEY *
00022              *     ARE:                                                        *
00023              *        2 PERCENT FOR A RESTRAURANT BILL OVER $200.00           *
00024              *        5 PERCENT FOR A BAR BILL OVER $400.00                   *
00025              *        3 PERCENT FOR A TOTAL BILL OVER $1,000.00 AFTER         *
00026              *          OTHER DISCOUNTS HAVE BEEN SUBTRACTED.                 *
00027              *                                                                *
00028              *     INPUT FILE SPECIFICATIONS:                                 *
00029              *        CARD COLUMNS                    DESCRIPTION             *
00030              *           1- 3                      MEMBERSHIP NUMBER         *
00031              *           5-29                      MEMBER NAME               *
00032              *          31-48                      MEMBER ADDRESS            *
00033              *          49-53                      RESTAURANT BILL           *
00034              *          55-59                      BAR BILL                  *
00035              *          61-65                      ANY OTHER CHARGES         *
00036              *          67-72                      PAST DUE AMOUNT           *
00037              *                                                                *
00038              *  THE OUTPUT CONTAINS MEMBERSHIP NUMBER,  NAME,  ADDRESS,  AND  *
00039              *  AMOUNT DUE.    THE SUMMARY CONTAINS THE TOTAL AMOUNT DUE FROM *
00040              *  ALL CUSTOMERS.                                                *
00041              *                                                                *
00042              ******************************************************************
```

*(continued)*

```
     3         BILLING        16.52.35       OCT 19,1988

00044          *********************************************************
00045          *                                                       *
00046          *                   ENVIRONMENT DIVISION                *
00047          *                                                       *
00048          *********************************************************
00049           ENVIRONMENT DIVISION.
00050
00051           CONFIGURATION SECTION.
00052
00053           SOURCE-COMPUTER.
00054                     IBM-370.
00055           OBJECT-COMPUTER.
00056                     IBM-370.
00057           SPECIAL-NAMES.
00058                     C01 IS TOP-OF-NEXT-PAGE.
00059
00060           INPUT-OUTPUT SECTION.
00061
00062           FILE-CONTROL.
00063
00064               SELECT INPUT-FILE
00065                   ASSIGN TO DA-S-INFILE.
00066
00067               SELECT OUTPUT-FILE
00068                   ASSIGN TO UT-S-OUTFILE.
00069
```

```
     4         BILLING        16.52.35       OCT 19,1988

00071          *********************************************************
00072          *                                                       *
00073          *                   DATA DIVISION                       *
00074          *                                                       *
00075          *********************************************************
00076           DATA DIVISION.
00077
```

```
     5         BILLING        16.52.35       OCT 19,1988

00079           FILE SECTION.
00080
00081           FD  INPUT-FILE
00082               RECORD CONTAINS 80 CHARACTERS
00083               BLOCK CONTAINS 77 RECORDS
00084               LABEL RECORDS ARE OMITTED
00085               DATA RECORD IS RECORD-IN.
00086
00087           01  RECORD-IN          PIC X(80).
00088
00089           FD  OUTPUT-FILE
00090               LABEL RECORDS ARE OMITTED
00091               DATA RECORD IS OUTPUT-RECORD.
00092
00093           01  OUTPUT-RECORD       PIC X(133).
00094
```

*(continued)*

```
        6        BILLING       16.52.35      OCT 19,1988

00096        ****************************************************************
00097        *                                                              *
00098        *                    WORKING STORAGE SECTION                   *
00099        *                                                              *
00100        ****************************************************************
00101        WORKING-STORAGE SECTION.
00102
00103           01   ACCUMULATORS.
00104                03   TOTAL-BILL            PIC 9(6)V99   VALUE ZERO.
00105                03   TOTAL-AMT-DUE         PIC 9(6)V99   VALUE ZERO.
00106                03   PAGE-NUM              PIC 9(8)      VALUE ZERO.
00107
00108           01   INDICATORS-GROUP.
00109                03   ARE-THERE-MORE-RECORDS  PIC X(3)    VALUE 'YES'.
00110                     88   MORE-RECORDS                   VALUE 'YES'.
00111                     88   NO-MORE-RECORDS                VALUE 'NO '.
00112
00113           01   INPUT-RECORD.
00114                03   MEMBER-NUMBER-IN      PIC 9(3).
00115                03   FILLER                PIC X(1).
00116                03   NAME-IN               PIC X(25).
00117                03   FILLER                PIC X(1).
00118                03   MEMBER-ADDRESS-IN     PIC X(18).
00119                03   REST-BILL             PIC 9(3)V99.
00120                03   FILLER                PIC X(1).
00121                03   BAR-BILL              PIC 9(3)V99.
00122                03   FILLER                PIC X(1).
00123                03   OTHER-CHARGES         PIC 9(3)V99.
00124                03   FILLER                PIC X(1).
00125                03   AMT-OUTSTANDING       PIC 9(4)V99.
00126                03   FILLER                PIC X(8).
```

```
        7        BILLING       16.52.35      OCT 19,1988

00128           01   DETAIL-LINE.
00129                03   FILLER                PIC X(22)  VALUE SPACES.
00130                03   MEMBER-NUMBER-OUT     PIC 9(3).
00131                03   FILLER                PIC X(19)  VALUE SPACES.
00132                03   NAME-OUT              PIC X(26).
00133                03   FILLER                PIC X(10)  VALUE SPACES.
00134                03   MEMBER-ADDRESS-OUT    PIC X(19).
00135                03   FILLER                PIC X(13)  VALUE SPACES.
00136                03   AMT-DUE               PIC $$$.$$$.99.
00137                03   FILLER                PIC X(11)  VALUE SPACES.
00138
00139           01   TITLE.
00140                03   FILLER                PIC X(61)  VALUE SPACES.
00141                03   FILLER                PIC X(11)  VALUE
00142                     'CIRCLE CLUB'.
00143                03   FILLER                PIC X(61)  VALUE SPACES.
00144
00145           01   HEADER.
00146                03   FILLER                PIC X(15)  VALUE SPACES.
00147                03   FILLER                PIC X(17)  VALUE
00148                     'MEMBERSHIP NUMBER'.
00149                03   FILLER                PIC X(18)  VALUE SPACES.
00150                03   FILLER                PIC X(4)   VALUE 'NAME'.
00151                03   FILLER                PIC X(30)  VALUE SPACES.
00152                03   FILLER                PIC X(7)   VALUE 'ADDRESS'.
00153                03   FILLER                PIC X(22)  VALUE SPACES.
00154                03   FILLER                PIC X(10)  VALUE 'AMOUNT DUE'.
00155                03   FILLER                PIC X(10)  VALUE SPACES.
00156
00157           01   TOTAL-LINE.
00158                03   FILLER                PIC X(36)  VALUE SPACES.
00159                03   FILLER                PIC X(43)  VALUE
00160                     'THE TOTAL AMOUNT DUE FROM ALL CUSTOMERS IS'.
00161                03   AMOUNT                PIC $$$$.$$9.99.
00162                03   FILLER                PIC X(43)  VALUE SPACES.
00163
00164           01   BLANK-LINE                 PIC X(133) VALUE SPACES.
```

*(continued)*

```
       8         BILLING        16.52.35      OCT 19,1988

00166        01  STAR-LINE.
00167            03  FILLER                   PIC X(9)    VALUE SPACES.
00168            03  FILLER                   PIC X(114) VALUE ALL '*'.
00169            03  FILLER                   PIC X(10)  VALUE SPACES.
00170
00171        01  DATE-STORE.
00172            03  YR                       PIC 9(2).
00173            03  MON                      PIC 9(2).
00174            03  DIA                      PIC 9(2).
00175
00176        01  DATE-LINE.
00177            03  FILLER                   PIC X(3)    VALUE SPACES.
00178            03  FILLER                   PIC X(6)    VALUE 'DATE: '.
00179            03  DATE-OUT.
00180                05  MON                  PIC 9(2).
00181                05  DIA                  PIC /9(2)/.
00182                05  YR                   PIC 9(2).
00183            03  FILLER                   PIC X(106) VALUE SPACES.
00184            03  FILLER                   PIC X(6)    VALUE 'PAGE: '.
00185            03  PAGE-OUT                 PIC 9(2).
00186            03  FILLER                   PIC X(2)    VALUE SPACES.
00187
```

```
       9         BILLING        16.52.35      OCT 19,1988

00189        ***************************************************************
00190        *                                                             *
00191        *                    PROCEDURE DIVISION                       *
00192        *                                                             *
00193        ***************************************************************
00194
00195        PROCEDURE DIVISION.
00196
00197
00198        0000-MAIN-DRIVER.
00199            PERFORM 1000-INITIALIZATION.
00200            PERFORM 2000-CLUB-CUSTOMER-PROCESS
00201                UNTIL NO-MORE-RECORDS.
00202            PERFORM 9900-TERMINATION.
00203            STOP RUN.
```

```
      10         BILLING        16.52.35      OCT 19,1988

00205        ***************************************************************
00206        *                                                             *
00207        *   1000 INITIALIZATION                                       *
00208        *                                                             *
00209        *     - OPENS THE INPUT AND OUTPUT FILES                      *
00210        *     - WRITES THE FIRST PAGE HEADER                          *
00211        *     - READS FIRST RECORD                                    *
00212        *                                                             *
00213        ***************************************************************
00214
00215        1000-INITIALIZATION.
00216            OPEN  INPUT INPUT-FILE
00217                  OUTPUT OUTPUT-FILE.
00218            WRITE OUTPUT-RECORD FROM BLANK-LINE
00219                AFTER TOP-OF-NEXT-PAGE.
00220            PERFORM 8600-DATE-PAGE-HEADINGS.
00221            WRITE OUTPUT-RECORD FROM TITLE
00222                AFTER ADVANCING 3 LINES.
00223            WRITE OUTPUT-RECORD FROM HEADER
00224                AFTER ADVANCING 3 LINES.
00225            PERFORM 8000-READ-RECORD.
00226
```

*(continued)*

```
    11          BILLING        16.52.35      OCT 19,1988

00228        ************************************************************
00229        *                                                          *
00230        *    2000 CLUB CUSTOMER PROCESS                            *
00231        *                                                          *
00232        *    THIS PARAGRAPH IS PERFORMED UNTIL THERE ARE NO MORE MASTER *
00233        *    RECORDS.  IT:                                         *
00234        *                                                          *
00235        *    - PERFORMS THE CALCULATION PARAGRAPH                  *
00236        *    - PERFORMS THE DETAIL WRITING PARAGRAPH               *
00237        *    - PERFORMS THE READ PARAGRAPH                         *
00238        *                                                          *
00239        ************************************************************
00240
00241        2000-CLUB-CUSTOMER-PROCESS.
00242            PERFORM 3000-CALCULATION-PARA.
00243            PERFORM 4000-ROUTINE-WRITING-ANSWER.
00244            PERFORM 8000-READ-RECORD.
00245
```

```
    12          BILLING        16.52.35      OCT 19,1988

00247        ************************************************************
00248        *                                                          *
00249        *    3000 CALCULATION PARA                                 *
00250        *                                                          *
00251        *    - CALCULATES THE BAR BILL DISCOUNTS                   *
00252        *    - CALCULATES THE CUSTOMER'S TOTAL BILL AMOUNT         *
00253        *    - ACCUMULATES THE GRAND TOTAL BILL AMOUNT             *
00254        *                                                          *
00255        ************************************************************
00256
00257        3000-CALCULATION-PARA.
00258            IF REST-BILL IS GREATER THAN 200
00259                MULTIPLY 0.98 BY REST-BILL.
00260            IF BAR-BILL > 400
00261                MULTIPLY .95 BY BAR-BILL.
00262            ADD REST-BILL, BAR-BILL, OTHER-CHARGES GIVING TOTAL-BILL.
00263            IF TOTAL-BILL GREATER THAN 1000
00264                MULTIPLY TOTAL-BILL BY 0.97 GIVING TOTAL-BILL.
00265            ADD AMT-OUTSTANDING TO TOTAL-BILL.
00266            ADD TOTAL-BILL TO TOTAL-AMT-DUE.
```

```
    13          BILLING        16.52.35      OCT 19,1988

00268        ************************************************************
00269        *                                                          *
00270        *    4000 ROUTINE WRITING ANSWER                          *
00271        *                                                          *
00272        *    - MOVES INPUT FIELDS TO OUTPUT LINE                   *
00273        *    - MOVES CUSTOMER'S TOTAL BILL AMOUNT TO OUTPUT LINE   *
00274        *    - WRITES DETAIL LINE                                  *
00275        *                                                          *
00276        ************************************************************
00277
00278        4000-ROUTINE-WRITING-ANSWER.
00279            MOVE TOTAL-BILL TO AMT-DUE.
00280
00281        ************************************************************
00282        *                                                          *
00283        * NOTE:    WHEN TOTAL-BILL IS MOVED TO AMT-DUE, A  PROBLEM COULD *
00284        * OCCUR  BECAUSE  THE  PICTURE  FOR  TOTAL-BILL  IS ONE CHARACTER *
00285        * LARGER THAN THE PICTURE  FOR  AMT-DUE  AND  YOU COULD LOSE THE *
00286        * HIGH ORDER DIGIT OF THE LARGER PICTURE.                  *
00287        *                                                          *
00288        ************************************************************
00289
00290            MOVE MEMBER-NUMBER-IN TO MEMBER-NUMBER-OUT.
00291            MOVE NAME-IN TO NAME-OUT.
00292            MOVE MEMBER-ADDRESS-IN TO MEMBER-ADDRESS-OUT.
00293            WRITE OUTPUT-RECORD FROM DETAIL-LINE
00294                AFTER ADVANCING 2 LINES.
```

*(continued)*

```
   14        BILLING        16.52.35        OCT 19,1988

00296            8000-READ-RECORD.
00297                READ INPUT-FILE INTO INPUT-RECORD
00298                    AT END
00299                        MOVE 'NO ' TO ARE-THERE-MORE-RECORDS.
00300
00301            8600-DATE-PAGE-HEADINGS.
00302                ACCEPT DATE-STORE FROM DATE.
00303                MOVE CORRESPONDING DATE-STORE TO DATE-OUT.
00304                ADD 1 TO PAGE-NUM.
00305                MOVE PAGE-NUM TO PAGE-OUT.
00306                WRITE OUTPUT-RECORD FROM DATE-LINE
00307                    AFTER ADVANCING 1 LINES.
```

```
   15        BILLING        16.52.35        OCT 19,1988

00309        ********************************************************************
00310        *                                                                  *
00311        *   9900 TERMINATION                                               *
00312        *                                                                  *
00313        *    - MOVES GRAND TOTAL BILLING AMOUNT TO SUMMARY LINE            *
00314        *    - WRITES GRAND TOTAL LINES                                    *
00315        *    - CLOSES FILES                                               *
00316        *                                                                  *
00317        ********************************************************************
00318
00319            9900-TERMINATION.
00320                WRITE OUTPUT-RECORD FROM STAR-LINE
00321                    AFTER ADVANCING 3 LINES.
00322                MOVE TOTAL-AMT-DUE TO AMOUNT IN TOTAL-LINE.
00323
00324        ********************************************************************
00325        *                                                                  *
00326        * NOTE: THE ABOVE MOVE STATEMENT IS A SIMPLE MOVE, WE ARE MOVING   *
00327        * DATA FROM ONE  LOCATION  TO  ANOTHER  WITH  BOTH  DATA  NAMES    *
00328        * (TOTAL-AMT-DUE AMOUNT) BEING UNIQUE; THAT IS, THEY APPEAR ONLY   *
00329        * ONCE IN THE DATA DIVISION.                                       *
00330        *                                                                  *
00331        ********************************************************************
00332
00333                WRITE OUTPUT-RECORD FROM TOTAL-LINE
00334                    AFTER ADVANCING 3 LINES.
00335                CLOSE INPUT-FILE, OUTPUT-FILE.
```

*(continued)*

```
DATE: 10/19/88                                                                    PAGE: 01

                                        CIRCLE CLUB

   MEMBERSHIP NUMBER              NAME                    ADDRESS              AMOUNT DUE

           586               LANZA, MARIO           101 CARUSO WAY             $963.22

           355               BEASLEY, REGGIE R.     2035 HARVEY                $341.07

           004               RASKOLNIKOV, FYODOR    4321 GULAG MANOR           $136.19

           996               IVANOVNA, ALYONA       401 HAY MARKET             $963.47

           829               SMITHE, BYRON L.       90 DEVONSHIRE            $1,857.94

           193               RANCHER, TEX A.        740 GUERNSEY               $263.44

           811               CORTEZ, SIGNIO H.      1818 CHEVERALLA             $61.65

           045               MUDD, HARCORT FENTON   2111 NAGGA WAY           $9,196.32

           355               RICH, RICHY            1 PROFLIGATE PL.            $60.98

           492               MOON, WARREN           50 ZENITH RD.             $515.58

           933               MCHALE, KEVIN          5 SECOND LANE           $5,622.81

           810               KELLY, GENE            53 RAINDANCE DR.           $19.88

           500               KIRKPATRICK, GENE      1300 PENN AVE.          $1,983.76

           287               DROVELL, ROBERT H.     77 SUNSET STRIP           $254.19

           001               MONT BENI, DONATELLO   100 GRAND TOWER         $1,274.99

           900               KIPLING, KIMBALL       25 INDIA AVE.               $9.00

           503               KAFKA, FRANZ           75 PARADISE COURT          $45.00

           984               BLAIR, ERIC            15 BUTTER DR.             $189.23

           345               TWAIN, MARK            39 RIVER ROAD             $282.50

           489               ORWELL, GEORGE         51 FLY STREET           $1,838.00

           543               CLEMENS, SAMUEL        93 BOAT AVE.              $581.40


*******************************************************************************************

        THE TOTAL AMOUNT DUE FROM ALL CUSTOMERS IS  $26,460.62
```

## Chapter Review Questions

1.  Which of the following is not an I/O Verb?

    a.  SORT
    b.  READ. . .INTO
    c.  WRITE. . .FROM
    d.  CLOSE
    e.  OPEN

2.  Which of the following is not a DATA MANIPULATION Verb?

    a.  COMPUTE
    b.  MOVE
    c.  ADD
    d.  IF
    e.  DIVIDE

3.  Which of the following verbs handles the case construct?

    a.  IF
    b.  PERFORM
    c.  GO TO
    d.  EVALUATE
    e.  Both a and d

4.  With an ADD you may:

    a.  Add only two numeric literals
    b.  Add only two numeric data names
    c.  Add only two numeric data names and/or literals
    d.  Add two or more numeric data names and/or literals
    e.  None of the above

5.  A group MOVE:

    a.  Moves all corresponding data names from one group to another
    b.  Works like an X MOVE
    c.  Works like a 9 MOVE
    d.  Works like a MOVE CORRESPONDING
    e.  None of the above

6.  Which of the following is true about a numeric move?

    a.  Data is moved in both directions from the decimal
    b.  The decimals are aligned before data is moved
    c.  Truncation may occur with both the high order and low order positions
    d.  A larger receiving field is left filled with zeros and right filled with zeros
    e.  All of the above are true

7.  The END-IF scope terminator:

    a.  Allows for multiple IF THEN ELSE structures within a true or false path
    b.  Eliminates multiple IF THEN ELSE structures within a true or false path
    c.  Has been eliminated from COBOL '85
    d.  May only be used with nested PERFORM
    e.  None of the above

8. The range of a PERFORM whose object is a paragraph is:
   a.  Determined with the END-PERFORM scope terminator
   b.  Determined by a period
   c.  The next paragraph
   d.  The next perform
   e.  None of the above

9. The PERFORM. . .UNTIL matches which structured programming construct?
   a.  DO UNTIL
   b.  DO WHILE
   c.  CASE
   d.  SEQUENCE
   e.  IF-THEN-ELSE

10. The PERFORM. . .THROUGH causes:
    a.  A set of paragraphs to be done
    b.  A set of sections to be done
    c.  Structured programming purist to cringe
    d.  A implicit set of paragraphs/sections to be done
    e.  All of the above

11. A command to open a file that is already open:
    a.  Restarts the file at the first record
    b.  Will cause an error
    c.  Will be ignored
    d.  Will operate as a close followed by an open
    e.  None of the above

12. The CLOSE verb must also specify how the file was used . . . CLOSE INPUT filename etc.
    a.  True
    b.  False

13. The READ. . .INTO format causes the data to be placed (end up in) into:
    a.  The G-R-D
    b.  The D-R-D
    c.  WORKING STORAGE
    d.  The input buffer
    e.  Both b and c

14. The WRITE. . .FROM writes the contents of:
    a.  The G-R-D
    b.  The D-R-D
    c.  The file
    d.  The output buffer
    e.  None of the above

15. The verb used for low volume output is the:
    a.  ACCEPT verb
    b.  WRITE verb
    c.  PERFORM verb
    d.  DISPLAY verb
    e.  Both a and d

16. The need to use the qualified move is caused by:
    a.  Unique data name
    b.  The COBOL '85 Compiler
    c.  Non-Unique data name
    d.  Numeric data name
    e.  None of the above

17. A group level move requires that both data names referenced be group level items.
    a.  True
    b.  False

18. If two group items have the same format and data names, the group move and move corresponding would cause the same result.
    a.  True
    b.  False

19. Which of the following is true of an alphanumeric move where the sending field is larger than the receiving field?
    a.  The receiving field will be right filled with spaces
    b.  Low-order truncation will occur.
    c.  The receiving field will be left filled with spaces
    d.  High-order truncation will occur
    e.  None of the above

20. A group level move works like a(n):
    a.  Numeric move
    b.  Alphanumeric move
    c.  Numeric edited move
    d.  Literal move
    e.  None of the above

## Discussion Questions

1. Briefly contrast a group move with a move corresponding.
2. Briefly explain the relationship of the hierarchy chart, flowchart and procedure division.
3. Explain the purpose of the OPEN and CLOSE verbs.
4. Show why the COMPUTE verb is necessary in COBOL.
5. Briefly explain a numeric move.
6. Give an example of a DO WHILE Construct.
7. Give an example of a DO UNTIL Construct.
8. Explain how COBOL '85 has enhanced the PERFORM.

## Practice Problems

1. Given the following code convert it to eliminate the GO TO's.

```
PARA-A.
    IF  A = B
        GO TO PARA-B
    ELSE
        GO TO PARA-C.
```

```
PARA-B.
    :
    GO TO PARA-D.

PARA-C.
    :
    :

PARA-D.
```

2. For the example shown in Figures 5.14 and 5.15, convert the hierarchy chart, flowchart and code to write only female, senior, information system majors with a GPR > 3.5.

3. For the same example, convert the hierarchy chart, flowchart and code to also write all students that do not have a GPR > 3 to a separate report.

4. Given the following "code", show the corresponding hierarchy chart.

```
0000-MAIN-PARA
    PERFORM 1000-INIT-PARA.
    PERFORM 2000-READ-PARA.
    PERFORM 3000-PROCESS-PARA.
        UNTIL FLAG = 1.
    PERFORM 4000-TERMINATION-PARA.

1000-INIT-PARA.
    :

2000-READ-PARA.
    :

3000-PROCESS-PARA.
    PERFORM 3100-CALC-PARA.
    PERFORM 3200-WRITE-PARA.
    PERFORM 2000-READ-PARA.

3100-CALC-PARA.
    PERFORM 3110-COMPUTE-PARA.
    PERFORM 3120-SUM-PARA.
    :

3110-COMPUTE-PARA.
    :

3120-SUM-PARA.
    :

3200-WRITE-PARA.
    :
```

5. Using the customer file from Chapter 4's problems, design a HIPO, detail flowchart and COBOL program to do the following:

    a.    Write a detail listing of all checking customers.

    b.    Write a summary report to include:
   - total customers by type
   - total customers by class
   - total account balance by type
   - grand total account balance

## Programming Assignments

1. Write the complete COBOL program to read the Dean File, Data Set A form 2, and write a listing of all students who have at least 100 hours taken. Hint: use IF HOURS-TAKEN > 99 . . . in the process paragraph. You should use "STUDENT LISTING" as the page heading and appropriate column headings.

2. Write the complete COBOL program to read the Inventory File, Data Set C, and write a report of all items. The report should only include the item number, item description quantity on hand, cost per unit and the total item cost. The total item cost is calculated as MULTIPLY QUANTITY-ON-HAND-IN BY COST-PER-UNIT-IN GIVING TOTAL-ITEM-COST. You should use "COST REPORT" as the page heading and appropriate column headings. The detail lines should be double spaced.

# PROCESSING A SEQUENTIAL FILE—DETAIL AND TOTAL TIMES

**_OBJECTIVES_**    The objectives for this chapter focus on the processing of a sequentially organized data file.  We will look at a problem and let it guide us in our discussion of the COBOL elements and tools needed to code the solution.

You will start by developing the solution using your tools: hierarchy chart, IPO and flowcharts.  Then you will look at the COBOL code for the problem.  In doing so you will study the AT END clause of the READ verb.  You will also study the carriage control features available with the WRITE verb's AFTER clause.  In fact, you will finally see what the SPECIAL-NAMES clause is for.

One major objective of the chapter is the presentation of a sequential file model. You will see how the processing of a sequential file follows a model or standard approach.  I will show you this model with the hierarchy chart, the flowchart and the PROCEDURE DIVISION.  This model should help you conceptualize your approach to sequential file processing.  It will be used extensively throughout the rest of the text.

Finally, you will look at the real world of COBOL.  You will study the need for, and the benefits of, standards.  You will also look again at program development, but from a different perspective.  Then you will be shown the basics of JCL and some of the most-used options, particularly those that we will use in this text.

## TOPICS

- **End of file**
- **Detail time**
- **Total time**
- **Carriage control**
- **SPECIAL-NAMES option**

- **Data paths**
- **Sequential file model**
- **Program development**
- **Running a COBOL program**
- **JCL**

---

*KEY WORDS*

- **AT END**
- **AFTER ADVANCING**
- **SPECIAL-NAMES**

- **READ. . .INTO**
- **WRITE. . .FROM**
- **DD**
- **DSN**

---

## INTRODUCTION

Processing data that is on a sequential file, or data that has a sequential organization, even if the data is on a direct access device, is one of the major application areas in data processing. Many batch systems rely on data organized sequentially; systems like payroll and inventory tend to use sequential files.

A sequential file allows for records to be processed one record at a time, starting with the first and proceeding to the end of the file. Payroll and inventory systems usually involve a master file that contains all the master records. That is, in the payroll file you would expect a record for each employee, and in the inventory file you would likewise expect one record for each item in inventory.

## DETAIL AND TOTAL TIME

Generally speaking, when we write programs to process sequential files, two major times are discussed: **detail time** and **total time**. **Detail time** involves all those actions required to be done to each record's detail data—all those actions required to provide the necessary output.

For instance, for an inventory file, we might produce a report containing:

| Inventory File Record | | Output Report Record |
|---|---|---|
| ITEM NUMBER | → | ITEM NUMBER |
| ITEM DESCRIPTION | → | ITEM DESCRIPTION |
| QUANTITY ON HAND | → | QUANTITY ON HAND |
| COST PER ITEM | → | COST PER ITEM |
| | | ITEM'S TOTAL COST |
| SUPPLIER CODE | → | SUPPLIER CODE |

We would READ an inventory record, MOVE all input to output, calculate the item's total cost, and WRITE the record. We would do this for each record in the file. All of that occurs during **detail time**. What happens during **total time**?

Assume that we wanted a grand total of our inventory costs. How would we accomplish the task? Could we wait until after end of file to sum the individual items for a total cost? Do we write the grand total after processing each record? Well, these are all very good questions, so let's look at each.

In order to accomplish the task of providing the grand total cost, we would need to do two things. First, we would accumulate the sum of each item's total cost. Then, when we had done that for each item, we would write the total. So, the question now is when to do these things. We *cannot* wait until after end of file to accumulate the grand total cost. We must provide a means for summing during **detail time**; otherwise, we would lose the data needed from previous records. Since we "READ. . .INTO" the same detail record description, we replace the previous data with the newly-read data. So, even though we *do not print* the total until *after the end of file*, **total time**, we must prepare for the printing during **detail time**.

### The Problem

Let's pose a situation and see how we would approach it to provide a solution. Since we looked at the inventory problem earlier, let's examine it more closely now.

Assume that the manager has requested that we write a program to provide her with a listing of all the inventory items, to include all input data and the items' total cost. She would also like to have the grand total cost of the inventory presented.

**The Hierarchy Chart.** Our first step should be to make sure we understand the problem and all the separate tasks required. We can accomplish this by laying out a hierarchy chart as in Figure 6.1.

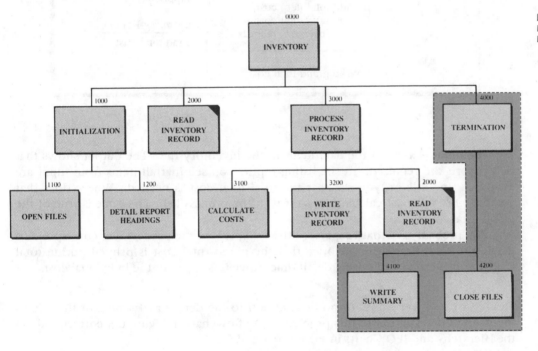

**FIGURE 6.1**
Hierarchy Chart for Inventory Problem

The hierarchy chart is similar to what we have been using. It shows the lead read, module 2000, and includes the necessary process modules, 3000, 3100 and 3200, to solve the problem. Primarily, I want you to notice that I have indicated the modules used in detail time and total time.

This hierarchy chart shows that we have broken the problem into four major tasks: INITIALIZATION, READING, PROCESSING THE RECORDS, and TERMINATION. Looks familiar, doesn't it? (Most sequential file-processing problems generally look like this.) We then broke down modules 1000, 3000, and 4000 into parts needed for the solution.

Notice that I set off the chart graphically into two parts. One part includes modules 0000 through 3200. These correspond to detail time, while the second part, consisting of modules 4000, 4100 and 4200, correspond to total time.

**The IPO Chart.**    Our next step is to develop our IPO Chart. Using the form used in Chapter 2, our IPO Chart for this problem should look something like what is shown in Figure 6.2.

**FIGURE 6.2**
IPO Chart for Inventory
Problem

| PROGRAM: | Inventory List Including Cost | |
|---|---|---|
| **INPUT** | **PROCESS** | **OUTPUT** |
| **Inventory File**<br>item number<br>item description<br>quantity on hand<br>cost per unit<br>supplier code | Write detail report headings<br>Read inventory records<br>Calculate total item cost:<br>  Total item cost =<br>    quantity on hand ×<br>      cost per unit<br>Calculate grand total cost:<br>  Add total item cost<br>    to grand total cost<br>Write inventory records<br><br>Write grand total cost | **Inventory Listing Report**<br>item number<br>item description<br>quantity on hand<br>cost per unit<br>total item cost<br>supplier code<br><br>**Summary Report**<br>Grand total cost |

The input is a list of the data items in the inventory file. The output shows that two reports are required. In the listing report you see that all items from input are included. In addition you see that the total item cost is needed. Where does that come from? We must calculate it, so it is in the process list. The same is true of the grand total cost.

You probably see that I separated the two parts of the process that correspond to detail and total time again. Notice that the grand total cost is printed during total time, but it is calculated during detail time, since it is a sum of the individual costs.

**Flowchart.**    Let's now turn our attention to the details and timing of the details involved in the solution to this problem. The flowchart in Figure 6.3 corresponds to the Hierarchy and IPO Charts in Figures 6.1 and 6.2.

The flowchart in Figure 6.3 shows all the events and the sequence the events should follow for our solution. The next step might be to code the solution. However, we saw earlier in the text that we need some specifications first. We need the format of INVENTORY-FILE, and we need to know what report format the manager wants. The INVENTORY-RECORD is shown in Data File C, and the report formats are shown in Figure 6.4.

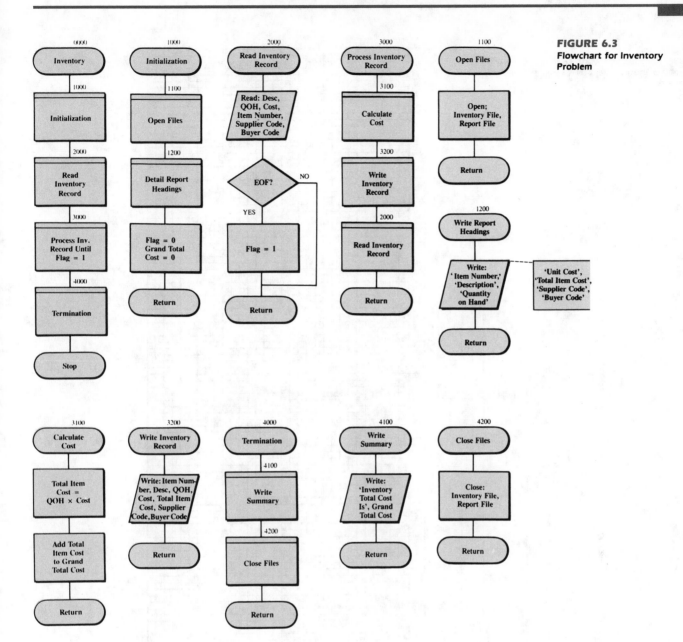

**FIGURE 6.3**
**Flowchart for Inventory Problem**

**FIGURE 6.4**
**Printer Layout for Inventory**
**Problem Showing Report**
**Designs**

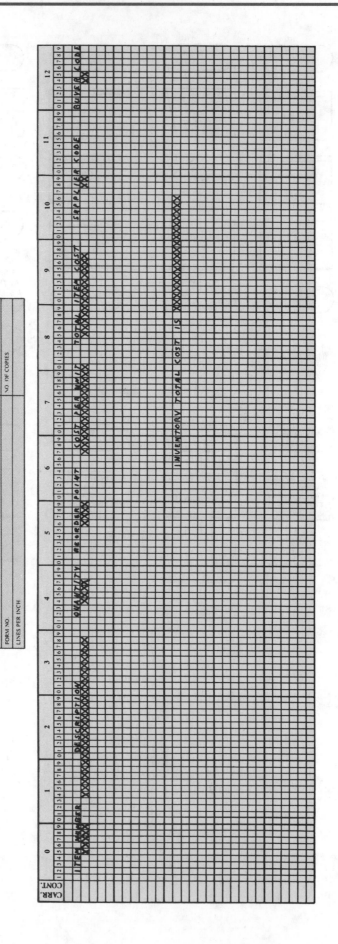

### What COBOL Tools are Needed?

Before we start to code, we need to examine what procedural tools we will need. From the flowchart we can see that we will need the following tools:

| Tool | For |
| --- | --- |
| PERFORM | Module control |
| PERFORM...UNTIL | Looping |
| OPEN | To initialize files |
| CLOSE | To close files |
| READ | To read data records |
| WRITE | To write records |
| COMPUTE | To calculate item cost |
| ADD | To get grand total |
| MOVE | To move data from input to output |
| STOP RUN | To stop the program |

Most of these tools we looked at in the previous chapter. However, we said we would look more thoroughly at some features of the READ and WRITE verbs in this chapter. Also, while we introduced the ADD and COMPUTE in Chapter 5, these verbs will be studied in detail in the next chapter. So, I will use them here but discuss their intricacies later.

Let's now develop the code for the solution to the problem. Let's look at the first two divisions. About the only thing to note is that I have two SELECTs. Make sense? Sure, we have only two files, one input and one output.

```
        IDENTIFICATION DIVISION.
            .
            .
        PROGRAM-AD.      INVLIST.
            .
            .

        ENVIRONMENT DIVISION.

        CONFIGURATION SECTION.
            .
        SPECIAL-NAMES.
            C01 IS PAGE-TOP.
            .
            .

        INPUT-OUTPUT SECTION.
            SELECT INVENTORY-FILE    ASSIGN TO DA-S-INV.
            SELECT REPORT-FILE       ASSIGN TO UT-S-REPORT.
```

Now let's look at the DATA DIVISION together. Do you agree with the two FDs? We have said several times that we require one FD for each SELECT.

```
DATA DIVISION.

FILE SECTION.
FD  INVENTORY-FILE
    LABEL RECORDS ARE OMITTED
    RECORD CONTAINS 50 CHARACTERS
    BLOCK CONTAINS 100 RECORDS
    DATA RECORD IS INVENTORY-RECORD.

01  INVENTORY-RECORD            PIC X(35).

FD  REPORT-FILE
    LABEL RECORDS ARE OMITTED
    DATA RECORD IS REPORT-RECORD.

01  REPORT-RECORD               PIC X(133).

WORKING-STORAGE SECTION.

*************************************************************
77  FLAG                        PIC 9(1)      VALUE 0.
77  TOTAL-ITEM-COST             PIC 9(8)V9(2) VALUE 0.
77  GRAND-TOTAL-COST            PIC 9(10)V9(2) VALUE 0.

*                 OR            <------------ NOTE: you may    *
                                             use either
                                             technique
01  INDICATORS.
    03  FLAG                    PIC 9(1)      VALUE 0.

01  COSTS.
    03  TOTAL-ITEM-COST         PIC 9(5)V9(2) VALUE 0.
    03  GRAND-TOTAL-COST        PIC 9(8)V9(2) VALUE 0.


*************************************************************

01  INVENTORY-RECORD-IN.
    03  ITEM-NUMBER             PIC 9(5).
    03  DESCRIPTION             PIC X(25).
    03  QOH                     PIC 9(4).
    03  UNIT-COST               PIC 9(6)V9(2).
    03  ROP                     PIC 9(4).
    03  SUPPLIER-CODE           PIC 9(2).
    03  BUYER-CODE              PIC 9(2).

01  INVENTORY-RECORD-OUT.
    03  FILLER                  PIC X(4)      VALUE SPACES.
    03  ITEM-NUMBER-OUT         PIC 9(5).
    03  FILLER                  PIC X(5)      VALUE SPACES.
    03  DESCRIPTION-OUT         PIC X(25).
    03  FILLER                  PIC X(5)      VALUE SPACES.
    03  QOH-OUT                 PIC Z(3)9(1).
    03  FILLER                  PIC X(8)      VALUE SPACES.
    03  ROP-OUT                 PIC ZZZ9.
    03  FILLER                  PIC X(8)      VALUE SPACES.
    03  UNIT-COST-OUT           PIC $(2),$(3),$(2)9.99.
    03  FILLER                  PIC X(4)      VALUE SPACES.
```

```
        03   TOTAL-ITEM-COST-OUT        PIC $(2),$(3),$(2)9.99.
        03   FILLER                     PIC X(10)        VALUE SPACES.
        03   SUPPLIER-CODE-OUT          PIC 9(1).
        03   FILLER                     PIC X(14)        VALUE SPACES.
        03   BUYER-CODE-OUT             PIC X(2).
        03   FILLER                     PIC X(8)         VALUE SPACES.

    01  COLUMN-HEADINGS.
        03   FILLER                     PIC X(2)         VALUE SPACES.
        03   FILLER                     PIC X(11)        VALUE 'ITEM NUMBER'.
        03   FILLER                     PIC X(8)         VALUE SPACES.
        03   FILLER                     PIC X(11)        VALUE 'DESCRIPTION'.
        03   FILLER                     PIC X(10)        VALUE SPACES.
        03   FILLER                     PIC X(8)         VALUE 'QUANTITY'.
        03   FILLER                     PIC X(2)         VALUE SPACES.
        03   FILLER                     PIC X(13)        VALUE
                 'REORDER POINT'.
        03   FILLER                     PIC X(3)         VALUE SPACES.
        03   FILLER                     PIC X(13)        VALUE
                 'COST PER UNIT'.
        03   FILLER                     PIC X(3)         VALUE SPACES.
        03   FILLER                     PIC X(15)        VALUE
                 'TOTAL ITEM COST'.
        03   FILLER                     PIC X(4)         VALUE SPACES.
        03   FILLER                     PIC X(13)        VALUE
                 'SUPPLIER CODE'.
        03   FILLER                     PIC X(4)         VALUE SPACES.
        03   FILLER                     PIC X(10)        VALUE
                 'BUYER CODE'.
        03   FILLER                     PIC X(4)         VALUE SPACES.

    01  GRAND-TOTAL-COST-LINE.
        03   FILLER                     PIC X(66)        VALUE SPACES.
        03   FILLER                     PIC X(24)        VALUE
                 'INVENTORY TOTAL COST IS '.
        03   GRAND-TOTAL-COST-OUT       PIC $(3),$(3),$(3),$(2)9.99.
        03   FILLER                     PIC X(25)        VALUE SPACES.

    01  BLANK-LINE.
        03   FILLER                     PIC X(133)       VALUE SPACES.
```

I'm sure you saw the OR in WORKING-STORAGE SECTION. That's not a COBOL technique. I'm simply showing you that you could set up those data values either way.

The question is, however, why do we need FLAG, TOTAL-ITEM-COST and GRAND-TOTAL-COST? Well, FLAG is used as our end of file indicator. We set it up and initialize it to zero so that we can set it to one when end of file occurs.

What about the other two fields? Look back at the IPO and flowchart. Didn't we need two cost items? Well, we need two data fields to use to accumulate them. Since we are accumulating numbers, we must also initialize them to zero. By the way, didn't we initialize those three items in the flowchart in the INITIALIZATION module? We sure did. So, all we are doing now is what we planned with our problem-solving tools.

However, since I've initialized them with the VALUE clause, I don't have to show the process procedurally. I know, I have said the flowchart matches one for one with the PROCEDURE DIVISION. Well, this is an exception. We may initialize during compilation with the VALUE clause.

### The Procedure Division

I'm going to concentrate on the PROCEDURE DIVISION, but please make sure you understand all the entries in the previous divisions. Remember, of course, that I'm going to discuss the SPECIAL-NAMES entry of the ENVIRONMENT DIVISION in conjunction with the WRITE verb in a moment.

So, let's take a paragraph by paragraph look at the PROCEDURE DIVISION.

```
PROCEDURE DIVISION.

0000-MAIN-PARA.
    PERFORM 1000-INITIALIZATION-PARA.
    PERFORM 2000-READ-INV-RECORD-PARA.
    PERFORM 3000-PROCESS-INV-RECORDS-PARA
            UNTIL FLAG=1.
    PERFORM 4000-TERMINATION-PARA.
    STOP RUN.

1000-INITIALIZATION-PARA.
    PERFORM 1100-OPEN-FILES-PARA.
    PERFORM 1200-HEADINGS-PARA.

1100-OPEN-FILES-PARA.
    OPEN INPUT  INVENTORY-FILE.
    OPEN OUTPUT REPORT-FILE.

1200-HEADINGS-PARA.
    WRITE REPORT-RECORD FROM BLANK-LINE
        AFTER PAGE-TOP.
    WRITE REPORT-RECORD FROM COLUMN-HEADINGS
        AFTER 5.
    WRITE REPORT-RECORD FROM BLANK-LINE
        AFTER 1.

2000-READ-INV-RECORD-PARA.
    READ INVENTORY-FILE INTO INVENTORY-RECORD-IN
        AT END
            MOVE 1 TO FLAG.

3000-PROCESS-INV-RECORDS-PARA.
    PERFORM 3100-CALCULATE-COST-PARA.
    PERFORM 3200-WRITE-INV-RECORD-PARA.
    PERFORM 2000-READ-INV-RECORD-PARA.

3100-CALCULATE-COST-PARA.
    COMPUTE TOTAL-ITEM-COST = QOH * UNIT-COST.
    ADD TOTAL-ITEM-COST TO GRAND-TOTAL-COST.

3200-WRITE-INV-RECORD-DATA.
    MOVE ITEM-NUMBER     TO  ITEM-NUMBER-OUT.
    MOVE DESCRIPTION     TO  DESCRIPTION-OUT.
    MOVE QOH             TO  QOH-OUT.
    MOVE UNIT-COST       TO  UNIT-COST-OUT.
    MOVE ROP             TO  ROP-OUT.
```

```
        MOVE TOTAL-ITEM-COST   TO  TOTAL-ITEM-COST-OUT.
        MOVE SUPPLIER-CODE     TO  SUPPLIER-CODE-OUT.
        WRITE REPORT-RECORD FROM  INVENTORY-RECORD-OUT
            AFTER 2.

    4000-TERMINATION-PARA.
        PERFORM 2100-WRITE-SUMMARY-PARA.
        PERFORM 4200-CLOSE-FILES-PARA.

    4100-WRITE-SUMMARY-PARA.
        MOVE GRAND-TOTAL-COST TO GRAND-TOTAL-COST-OUT.
        WRITE REPORT-RECORD FROM GRAND-TOTAL-COST-LINE.

    4200-CLOSE-FILES-PARA.
        CLOSE INVENTORY-FILE
              REPORT-FILE.
```

**Paragraph 0000.**      In this paragraph we used four PERFORMs to control the four main tasks in our problem. The PERFORM for 3000-PROCESS-INV-RECORDS-PARA is a PERFORM. . .UNTIL, since we want to continue to process inventory records until there are no more. And, of course, when we are finished with all our tasks, we stop the program.

A special note of caution here: One error that we all make from time to time is that we get so excited about finishing our code, we forget the STOP RUN. That means that once the 4000-TERMINATION-PARA is completed, execution falls through to 1000-INITIALIZATION-PARA. Oops! You can see that would cause some funny results.

**Paragraphs 1100 and 1200.**      In paragraph 1100 we find two OPEN verbs, one for each file. We also specified the appropriate usage for each. This is required of us in order to READ the INVENTORY-FILE and to WRITE the reports.

Once the file is opened, we prepare for our detail report by writing the column headings. In paragraph 1200 you notice three WRITE verbs. The first causes a blank line to be written. The second writes the actual headings, and the third writes another blank line.

**The AFTER Clause.**      The last two WRITEs used familiar **AFTER** statements. **AFTER 5** says to advance to the fifth line following the current line and WRITE. **AFTER 1** says to advance one line and WRITE. But what in the world does **AFTER PAGE-TOP** mean? Just what it says. . .before writing, skip to the top of the next page.

Remember the format of the **AFTER** clause is:

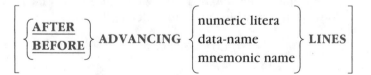

The full WRITE command, including the **AFTER** option, says:

"WRITE a record of data FROM the detail record specified AFTER ADVANCING some specified number of LINES." So, we might WRITE something like AFTER ADVANCING X LINES. Therefore, we will WRITE the column headings AFTER ADVANCING 5 LINES. So, if we were on the line specified by the arrow, ←, we would leave 4 blank lines:

Advance

| | | current line ← |
|---|---|---|
| 1 | → | blank line |
| 2 | → | blank line |
| 3 | → | blank line |
| 4 | → | blank line |
| 5 | → | column headings |

The general rule to follow may be stated two ways:

- **AFTER** n LINES will leave n−1 blank lines.

or

- **AFTER** n + 1 LINES will leave n blank lines.

**Lines Options.** We have three ways to specify the number of lines: numeric literal, data-name or a mnemonic name. The first two are straightforward. AFTER numeric literal **LINES** we have used many times. But what if we want to write something on the nth line, depending on the situation? We will code AFTER n **LINES**, as long as n has a valid numeric value, before we execute the WRITE.

**SPECIAL-NAMES** The third option is the one we have been waiting for. It's the one that says AFTER PAGE-TOP. PAGE-TOP is a name associated with a specific carriage control channel. We made the association in the ENVIRONMENT DIVISION with the **SPECIAL-NAMES** clause. We coded:

```
SPECIAL-NAMES.
    C01 IS PAGE-TOP.
```

What we said with that code is that when we say AFTER PAGE-TOP we want the printer to skip to channel 1.

Imagine for a moment that a carriage control tape is aligned with the top of the printed page. On the tape we may punch holes in twelve channels (columns). Now, say that we punched a hole in column 1 and aligned it with the top of the paper. As we write to the printer, both advance. Then, when we want to get to the next page, how may we do it? Well, we could count the lines we have used, calculate the difference by subtracting the count from 65 (lines per page), and then WRITE. . .AFTER difference **LINES**. Or, we could associate some data name called a mnemonic name with channel one and code WRITE. . .AFTER PAGE-TOP, where PAGE-TOP is that mnemonic name. This would cause the printer to advance until channel one is sensed which would align the page at the top. Now, I should point out that there is no magic to the mnemonic name, PAGE-TOP. We could say AFTER DOG or AFTER CAT, and it would work just as well if we had coded:

```
C01 IS DOG.
```

or

```
C01 IS CAT.
```

But don't use these names. I'm just trying to show you that it is the association with C01 that is important, not the name. I like PAGE-TOP or other things like TO-PAGE-TOP, GOING-TO-THE-TOP, etc., because of how they would read when used with the AFTER: AFTER ADVANCING TO-PAGE-TOP, for instance, reads nicely.

**Carriage Control.**      All this knowledge is well and good. But how do our commands get to the printer? They get there with our record. In fact, the first character of our record contains the information about skipping to the next page or 5 lines or n lines, etc. This information is called **carriage control** information. It is interpreted by the printer's control unit and our commands become physical realities.

So, when we studied D-R-D for output and I said that each record should begin with at least a FILLER of X(1), you now see why. When the WRITE is executed, the **carriage control** character is placed into the first byte of the record. If we had data in that position, we would lose it. In fact, the first position does not print. Even though our print line is X(133), we print only in the last 132 positions. The first position is not printed. It contains the **carriage control** character, and it would mess up our reports if it printed. For example,

```
01   EXAMPLE-RECORD.
     03 NAME-OUT. . . . . . . .
```

and if we put TEDDY in NAME-OUT we would get EDDY, which probably would not make TEDDY happy!

**Paragraph 2000.**      As the name implies, this paragraph contains our READ verb. It says to READ a record from INVENTORY-FILE and place it into INVENTORY-RECORD-IN. Which record? The next record! This is a sequential file, and we get one record at a time in sequence starting with the first.

**AT END Clause.**      What happens when there is no next record? In other words, what happens when we reach the end of file (EOF)? In our example we control what happens with the **AT END** clause. The general format of the **AT END** is:

$$\left[ \underline{\text{AT END}} \text{ executable statement(s).} \right]$$

Notice that the **AT END** is optional, but if you don't use it, it will cause your program to bomb, or to get ABENDED, by the system. So, I suggest that you always control what happens at EOF by using the **AT END** clause. We use it to set FLAG to 1 to control our loop process. Once it is set to 1, the PERFORM. . .UNTIL is satisfied and control passes to the next statement.

**Paragraph 3000.**      This paragraph is done over and over for each INVENTORY-RECORD. We coded three PERFORMs in the paragraph, one for each module controlled by this module: calculation of cost, writing each record and reading the next record. In fact, this paragraph is like a small main module.

**Paragraph 3100.**      The math for our solution is placed in this paragraph. We used the COMPUTE to calculate each item's total cost, and then, we used the ADD to keep our running sum of the item's total cost. That will be our GRAND-TOTAL-COST. See how English-like and easy to read COBOL is? We haven't really studied the math verbs fully, but these make sense to us.

**Paragraph 3200.**      We have looked extensively at the MOVE verb and the WRITE verb, so that at least their formats are recognizable. But are we sure what they are doing?

The easiest way to show you is to remind you that we READ. . .INTO INVENTORY-RECORD-IN (paragraph 2000), and we WRITE. . .FROM STUDENT-RECORD-OUT. Therefore, we need to MOVE the data from the input record to the output record. That explanation is OK for every MOVE except one. Why do we need to MOVE TOTAL-ITEM-COST? Why not just use the output description,

TOTAL-ITEM-COST-OUT in our COMPUTE statement? The key is in their respective PICTURE clauses. One is numeric, while the other is numeric edited. And, since only numeric items may be used mathematically, we need both descriptions. Furthermore, look at the ADD! We need to do math with TOTAL-ITEM-COST, but we want to print it with dollar signs and a decimal point. That requires both descriptions, one for calculations, TOTAL-ITEM-COST, and one for reporting, TOTAL-ITEM-COST-OUT.

**Paragraph 4000.**    When we finish processing each INVENTORY-RECORD in INVENTORY-FILE, we are finished with detail time, and we are ready for total time. Therefore, we have two things left to do: WRITE the total and CLOSE the files, both of which are done in this paragraph.

**Paragraph 4100.**    In this paragraph we MOVE the grand total value to the output record we designed. Then we WRITE it. Notice that I don't calculate the grand total here. It must have already been calculated, since it's too late to calculate it now. We are finished processing the individual records.

**Paragraph 4200.**    Once we have finished processing and reporting the next to the last thing we need to do is to execute a CLOSE statement for each of our files: INVENTORY-FILE and REPORT-FILE. The last thing to do is execute the STOP RUN.

### The Program in Summary

Well, what do you think?. . .not bad, really, just a little long. But try something. Let a non-COBOL friend read the PROCEDURE DIVISION. See if your friend can tell what the program is doing. I bet you will be pleasantly surprised. It's exactly this readability that makes COBOL popular. It is also what makes it easy to maintain!

Anyway, by now you should be starting to see how the tools, the HIPO, the flowchart and the COBOL program go together—the modules and the paragraphs in particular. While this was your first look, can you see how the PROCEDURE DIVISION is put together? It is made up of the MAIN-DRIVER followed by the paragraphs it controls. In turn, these paragraphs are followed by the ones they control, and so forth. Do you see how the numbering system helps with the order of things? The only exception was the one common module, 2000-READ-INV-REC-PARA.

### Data Path

One major item I want to cover with you at this time is the concept of **data path** You have seen that we READ. . .INTO one area, MOVE to another, and then WRITE from that other area. In Chapter 5 we saw why. But let's understand data flow a little better. If you understand this one concept at this point in your COBOL life, it will save you hours of debugging time later.

**Input Data Path.**    Let me present the READ verb again:

READ filename INTO DETAIL-RECORD-DESCRIPTION (D-R-D).

The data path for input can then be shown as follows:

$$\text{FILE} \xrightarrow{\text{READ}} \text{G-R-D} \xrightarrow{\text{INTO}} \text{D-R-D}$$

In other words, the READ causes data from a file to be placed into the GENERAL-RECORD-DESCRIPTION (G-R-D), input buffer; then, when the INTO is executed, the data is moved (group MOVE) from the G-R-D to the D-R-D.

**Output Data Path.**     What do you suppose the output data path looks like? First, let me present the WRITE again:

WRITE G-R-D FROM D-R-D.

The data path would be:

$$FILE \xleftarrow{\text{WRITE}} G\text{-}R\text{-}D \xleftarrow{\text{FROM}} D\text{-}R\text{-}D$$

It's just the opposite of the READ. Data from the D-R-D is moved (group MOVE) to the G-R-D, output buffer, and then written to the file.

Let's look at these two paths together:

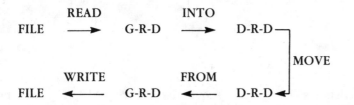

So we READ data INTO a D-R-D and WRITE data FROM a different D-R-D. How do we get data from one to the other? Most of the time we use the MOVE verb. So, do you see that to process the sequential INVENTORY-FILE we basically READ, MOVE and WRITE?

At this point, let me ask you an interesting question. What would it take to list a set of employees or students, or for that matter, any sequential file? READ, MOVE, AND WRITE? Well, that might be a little oversimplified, but my point is that processing a sequential file is fairly generic.

## SEQUENTIAL FILE MODEL

Let's try to develop a model to use for processing sequential files. In order to do this, we must identify the common characteristics:

- Sequentially organized file
- READ one record at a time
- Process the record
- WRITE a detail report of all or some of the records
- Repeat the last three steps until out of data
- WRITE summary report(s) if required

For instance, if we were to list all employees who work for a company, we would READ each record, process it, and then WRITE it. Or, what if we were asked to list all the students in the DEAN-FILE, or maybe only list the honor (GPR > 3.00) students? We would still READ each record, process it and WRITE it (if moved). In fact, we could generalize further, since writing a detail report is not always required.

What does all this mean? Well, I'm showing you a way to approach sequential file problems that might save you time and effort. Let's look at our model's common characteristics in a hierarchy chart (Figure 6.5).

**FIGURE 6.5**
**Hierarchy Chart for**
**Sequential File Model**

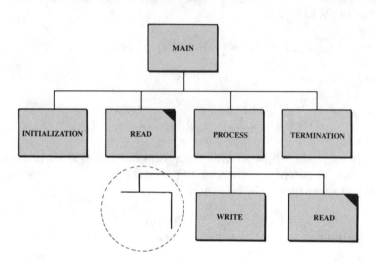

This chart shows that for any sequential file we will have some initialization, a common READ module, a process module, and a termination module controlled by a main module. Within the process module, we will usually have WRITE and always READ. Writing in this manner is called the lead read technique. We simply fill in the blank with the module or modules required for the particular problem.

Figure 6.6 shows the flowchart for the model. It also shows that we just have to fill in the process module with the logic needed to solve the particular problem. But generally the main module would look similar to what Figure 6.7 shows. The READ module would have the READ logic, and we would just fill in the I/O block to fit our problem.

Finally, Figure 6.7 shows the model in the PROCEDURE DIVISION. Notice that the process paragraph just has to be filled in. Whatever we need to solve our particular problem we code into the blank. It's almost like a fill-in-the-blank question.

I don't mean to oversimplify. The general hierarchy chart, flowchart and PRO-CEDURE DIVISION apply all right, but the logic needed to fill in the blank may be very complex. I'm not saying all sequential file problems are easy; I'm just saying that we have a model to follow to which we add the required code.

### Using the Sequential File Model

Without getting into much detail, let me illustrate the use of the model by listing all employees from an Employee File. The PROCEDURE DIVISION code to list the employees is shown below.

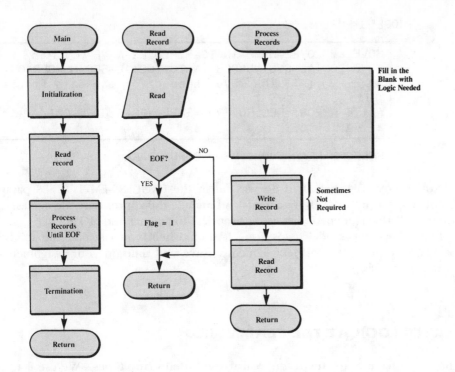

**FIGURE 6.6**
**Flowchart for Sequential File Model**

**FIGURE 6.7**
**PROCEDURE DIVISION for Sequential File Model**

```
PROCEDURE DIVISION.

MAIN-PARA.
        .
        .
        PERFORM READ-PARA.
        PERFORM PROCESS-PARA
           UNTIL FLAG=1.
           .
           .
        STOP RUN.

        READ-PARA.
           READ filename INTO G-R-D
              AT END
                 MOVE 1 TO FLAG.
```

```
PROCESS-PARA.




        PERFORM READ-PARA.
```

Fill in this blank with the detail needed

```
PROCEDURE DIVISION.
     MAIN-PARA.

           .
           .
        PERFORM READ-EMPLOYEE-RECORDS-PARA.
        PERFORM PROCESS-EMPLOYEES
           UNTIL FLAG=1.
           .
           .
        STOP RUN.

READ-EMPLOYEE-RECORDS-PARA.
     READ EMPLOYEE-FILE INTO EMPLOYEE-RECORD-IN
         AT END
             MOVE 1 TO FLAG.
```

PROCESS-EMPLOYEES.

```
MOVE EMPLOYEE-NAME-IN TO EMPLOYEE-NAME-OUT.
MOVE SOCIAL-SEC-NUMBER-IN TO SOCIAL-SEC-NUMBER-OUT.
MOVE  .  (all the moves needed for the data fields)
      .
WRITE REPORT-RECORD FROM EMPLOYEE-RECORD-OUT
     AFTER 2.
```

PERFORM READ-EMPLOYEE-RECORDS-PARA.

Notice how all we had to do was fill in the PROCESS-EMPLOYEES paragraph with the appropriate MOVE statements and include the appropriate file names? What if we were listing students? Just use appropriate file names and MOVEs.

I sure hope the model helps you. It should help you visualize the solution to sequential-file problems and, consequently, save you time on your assignments and maybe even your exams!


## A QUICK LOOK AT THE REAL WORLD

I know you have heard the term "real world" used many times. We use it to mean the world different from Academics; we don't mean that the Academic world is unreal. Now I want to look at the real world a little to let us see how it compares to our academic programming world.

Our academic world is one in which you face four or five classes a semester, work part-time in a lot of cases, and have other involvements such as dating, marriage, family, sports and professional organizations like Data Processing Management Association (DPMA) and Association for Computing Machinery (ACM). One of your classes is usually a computer class. Let's say for example that computer class is (what else?) a COBOL class. You find that you go to class, listen to lecture, have a program assigned, code the program (hierarchy chart, IPO, flowchart first!), run the program, debug the program and then turn it in. Your instructor gives you your gold star and that assignment is over.

In the real world you also get assignments that you code and test. However, once you are sure of the results, you don't turn an assignment in and forget about it. You turn it over to the user, and the program goes into production. Then it has to be maintained, and if it bombs, guess who gets called? This is the process that is different from the academic world. You don't just get your gold star and go on to your next assignment; you live with the consequences of what you write.


### *Programming Standards*

One other area that *may be* different between Academics and industry is the use of programming standards. Industry uses these standards to try to insure that the many systems are being developed and maintained in a consistent fashion.

The standards in Appendix D are a sample of what we might find in industry. They establish the packet to be put together for each program. They also establish what design tools will be used for program development: tools like hierarchy charts, IPO charts, flowcharts, pseudocode and others.

Coding standards are also included typically in a corporation's standards. As can be seen in Appendix D, our standards cover such things as:

- data name formation
- length and abbreviations
- use of appropriate suffix: -file, -record
- one statement per line
- no continuation symbols
- in-line comments
- paragraph numbering system
- indentation
- others

I will use the standards in my examples so that you may get used to them. Try to familiarize yourself with the standards as soon as possible. However, you will notice that the standards cover items of COBOL that you have not seen yet. So, just scan those until you need them.

## Program Development

How do we, or should we, go about the task of developing a program? I think of the task in three parts:

- solution design
- coding and testing
- putting it into production

Let's discuss them.

**Solution Design.**    This is that part we have talked at length about—using the design tools. Before we start to code and test, someone should have taken all the specifications established during system analysis and, using hierarchy charts, IPOs, flowcharts and layout forms or some other appropriate tools, established the logic design.

**Coding and Testing.**    Using the design developed. The programmer sets down the code that corresponds to the solution. Sometimes, because of language limitations or quirks, the way code is implemented may vary from the design. These differences must be noted. Remember, once the program gets into production, the flowcharts and other items will become part of the documentation package. If the code and tools don't match, that will make maintenance harder.

Once the program is coded, we run it using test data: data whose outcome is known, that tests all possible logic paths through the program. If we don't test all logic paths, we usually get calls late at night when the program bombs.

During testing we have several types of errors to handle:

- compiler syntax errors
- execution time errors
- logic errors

Most of us have experienced these at some time in our programming lives. Compiler errors are those that arise because we coded something the compiler could not interpret. For instance, if we coded the following:

```
CALCULATE TOTAL = QOH * COST.
```

The word calculate is not a COBOL verb. We intended to code COMPUTE and didn't. Another example is:

```
WRITE REPORT-FILE FROM STUDENT-RECORD-OUT
      AFTER ADVANCING 2 LINES.
```

What's wrong with this statement? Well, we referenced the file name instead of the name of the G-R-D associated with the file. This is a good example of COBOL syntax errors.

On the other hand, execution time errors mean that we got by the compiler and went into execution. During execution, however, we did something the operating system did not like. For instance:

- READ from a file that's not opened
- WRITE to a file opened for input
- Do math with data names that contain other than numbers. (This is one of my favorites. It is known as a SOC7, pronounced "sock seven". This is a system completion code of 007 which is the code for "invalid data in arithmetic operation" on an IBM operating system.)
- MOVE a numeric edited item to a numeric item (although COBOL '85 allows this)

These errors tend to be a little more difficult to find and correct, since they involve the operating system. However, the system gives you some information about what statement was being executed when the error occurred. So, if we get a SOC7 from the system and are told that it was executing line 714, we would look at the statement on line 714. That line might be "ADD 1 TO KOUNT" The only possibility of bad data is with the data name KOUNT. We look back to find our DATA DIVISION entry and find "77 KOUNT  PIC 9(3)". What's wrong? We forgot to initialize KOUNT. So, we fix our program by adding "VALUE 0" to the 77 level data item. Then we re-run our program.

## TIP

**Look at other counters to see if you find similar problems.**

During this part we will also find design errors; errors that include spacing or incorrect headings, and others. These are also fixed and tested again.

**Putting it into Production.**      Once we are satisfied with the program and/or system of programs, we turn it over to the user. Then the user starts using the program periodically, say daily. What does this involve? For one thing, it *does not* involve compiling the program every time the user runs it. That would be wasting resources—people and machine. All the user needs to do is execute the program with today's data.

Let's look at what that means. During the coding and testing of the program, we would symbolically do as shown in Figure 6.8.

Notice that we keep returning to the coding step and re-compiling. We have to. We are making changes to our COBOL program. So we have to re-compile. In fact, it is entirely possible that we introduce new syntax errors while fixing system or logic errors.

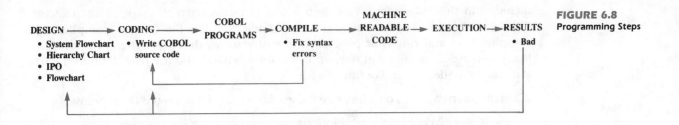

**FIGURE 6.8**
Programming Steps

However, once we are happy with the results, there is no need to check our syntax. No new code is being added. We, the users, are just going to execute the program again and again and again. So what happens now? The machine readable code is put into a library for the user. This is the production library we talked about in Chapter 3. The source code (COBOL program) is *not* placed in the production library. Therefore, all the user may do is execute the program. Re-compilation is not allowed in the production environment.

## RUNNING A COBOL PROGRAM

Once we code the COBOL program, how do we run it (compile and execute)? Well, this will vary from computer to computer. What's required on an IBM mainframe is different from what's required on an IBM-PC. Since I'm focusing on the IBM mainframe using MVS Operating System, that will continue to be my focus in this section. However, I will indicate differences where appropriate.

Running the COBOL program involves three elements:

- JCL – Job Control Language
- COBOL source program
- data

Let's discuss them.

### Job Control Language (JCL)

As the name says, JCL is a language—one with a specific purpose. Using it allows us to communicate information about our program, called a job, to the operating system. We must tell it some things, while others it assumes, and yet others are optional. The particular JCL discussed is for an IBM environment.

**Definition.**    While you now know what the letters JCL stand for and that you must provide information to the operating system, what is JCL? JCL consists of several control statements that:

- introduce the computer job to the operating system
- provide accounting information
- direct the operating system on what to do
- request hardware devices
- specify all input/output requirements

Part of the design of the Job Control Language is to have identifiable control statements that provide a means for doing each of the above. There is a statement that identifies the job called a JOB statement. The accounting information is usually included in this statement. You then tell the system what to do with the execute (EXEC) statement. For instance, you would tell it to use the COBOL compiler and compile, load and run your program. In order to do this, the program more than likely will use input files and output files. Guess what? You use data definition (DD) statements to identify and define the files.

**JCL Statements.** To summarize these statements, I have listed them below:

- JOB – marks beginning of job; provides accounting information
- EXEC – identifies the program/procedure to run (COBOL, Fortran, or some object program)
- DD – describes each data set used in the program

An example set of JCL to run a program is shown below. The program is the Circle Club program that uses the membership file as input and a printed report as output.

```
//DEMO    JOB  (P007,101A,S05,002,JB),'CIRCLE CLUB'
//CIRCLE EXEC COBCLG
//COB.SYSIN DD DSN=USR.P007.JB.CIRCLPR
//GO.MEMBER DD DSN=USR.P007.JB.CIRDATA,
//    DISP=SHR
//GO.REPORT DD SYSOUT=A DCB=(BLKSIZE=133,RECFM=FA)
```

Don't get all involved with the syntax and options for a minute. First, I want you to see the three types of statements: the JOB statement, EXEC statement, and the three DD statements.

**The JOB Statement.** On the JOB statement you probably noticed several entries. You expected to provide accounting information, but other information is also provided. This may vary from system to system, depending on the accounting package being used. So, let's look at this JOB statement, remembering that you should check your system's requirements.

```
//DEMO      JOB (P007,101A,S05,002,JB),'CIRCLE CLUB'
```

where

| | |
|---|---|
| DEMO | is the job name |
| JOB | is the type of statement |
| P007 | is the account number for the user |
| 101A | is a "mail box" location for the output |
| S05 | is an estimated job time requirement (five seconds in this example) |
| 002 | is the estimated number of lines (in thousands) required for the job |
| JB | is the user's initials |
| 'CIRCLE CLUB' | is a job label which must be in quotes |

**The EXEC Statement.** The EXEC statement is used to specify what we want done. That is, do we want to compile a program or just run an executable module (load module)? In our case we want three things done: *C*ompile, *L*ink edit, and *G*o. Let's look at the statement:

```
//CIRCLE   EXEC COBCLG
```

where

| | |
|---|---|
| **CIRCLE** | is the name of the step in the DEMO JOB.  Jobs may have more than one step. |
| **EXEC** | is the type of statement |
| **COB** | says to use the COBOL compiler called **COB**.  You should be aware that several COBOL compilers may be available on your system.  You'll need to find the appropriate one. |
| **C** | says to *C*ompile the program |
| **L** | *L*oad or link edit says to create a load module that includes the object program and other external routines needed for execution |
| **G** | says to run the program (*G*o) |

**The DD Statements.**       There are three **DD** statements, and they all describe data sets.  One describes a data set to be used during compilation (COB.), while the other two are data sets to be used when the program runs (GO.).

The **COB.SYSIN DD** statement tells the system that the COBOL compiler's input is the following data set specified with the DSN.  Let's look at it together.

```
//COB.SYSIN   DD   DSN=USR.P007.JB.CIRCLPR
```

| | |
|---|---|
| **COB.SYSIN** | says that the **DD** specifies the *SYS*tem *IN*put for the compiler |
| **DD** | identifies the type of statement |
| **DSN** | stands for *D*ata *S*et *N*ame and tells the compiler where to find the source program |
| **USR.** | identifies the data set as a user's |
| **P007.** | the user's account number for the source program location |
| **JB.** | the user's initials |
| **CIRCLPR.** | the file name that the source program is saved under on the user's account |

So, when the compiler needs the source program to start compiling, it knows exactly where to locate it.

Now, let's turn our attention to the two **GO. DD** statements.  The first one shown is:

```
//GO.MEMBER   DD DSN=USR.P007.JB.CIRDATA
//    DISP=SHR
```

where

| | |
|---|---|
| **GO.MEMBER** | says that this data set is to be used during execution.  The name MEMBER is the external name referenced in the SELECT clause of the COBOL program. |
| **DD** | identifies the type of statement |
| **DSN** | stands for *D*ata *S*et *N*ame |

USR.P007.JB.CIRDATA

> identifies the unique data set as a user data set for user P007.JB with a file name of CIRDATA

So, you would expect that we would have the following SELECT clause in the COBOL program:

        SELECT MASTER-FILE  ASSIGN TO DA-S-MEMBER.

Then, when a READ is executed, READ MASTER-FILE, a record of data is READ from CIRDATA since MASTER-FILE and CIRDATA are linked together with the external file name or DD name, MEMBER.

The second DD looks a little different in that it contains a DCB, **D**ata **C**ontrol **B**lock specification. Since it is to be our printer file, it takes this form and doesn't reference a DSN because a permanent data set is not created. The statement is:

        //GO.REPORT   DD SYSOUT=A DCB=(BLKSIZE=133,RECFM=FA)

where

| | |
|---|---|
| **GO.REPORT** | is the DD name of our print file |
| **DD** | is the type of statement |
| **SYSOUT=A** | says that we want to use the *SYS*tem *OUT*put device A. On most systems, A is the printer, but you should make sure it is the same on your system. |
| **DCB** | specifies that the *D*ata *C*ontrol *B*lock characteristics are as follows: |

- BLKSIZE=133

  states that the block contains 133 characters, or 1 record, and

- RECFM=FA

  states that the records are fixed length records (all the same length)

Again, you would expect that an appropriate SELECT clause would be included in the COBOL program that would allow for printed reports; something like this:

        SELECT REPORT-FILE  ASSIGN TO UT-S-REPORT.

When we write a record to the report file, it is sent to the system output device, the printer in our case. The printer and REPORT-FILE are linked together with the external name REPORT, which explains how you get the reports printed.

**Format and Syntax.**     It's time to take a look at the format and syntax of JCL statements. The general format of a JCL statement is:

        //NAME      OPERATION  OPERAND  COMMENTS

All the statements start with a slash in columns 1 and 2, followed by a name for the statement. This is followed by an operation field; an example would be DD. The third field is an operand(s) field. The last field is an optional comments field. I've listed some rules below:

- // starts in column 1.
- The name field must start in column 3 and be 1 to 8 characters in length.
- The operation field specifies the type of statement: JOB, EXEC, DD and must be preceded by at least one blank and start before column 16.
- The operand field(s) contain parameters separated by commas (no spaces). Examples of these are DSN, DCB, etc. The operand fields(s) must be preceded by at least one blank. The comments field is optional. It may be used with any of the statements. It too must be preceded by a space.
- The statements must be in columns 1 through 71.
- Continuation is accomplished by ending the previous line with a comma and starting another line with double slashes in columns 1 and 2, skipping at least 1 space, but starting before column 16 and continuing with the next parameter or entry. For example,

```
//GO.EXAMPLE   DD   DSN=USR.P007.JB.EXPDATA,
//     DCB=(LRECL=80,BLKSIZE=4000,RECFM=FB,DSORG=PS),
//     DISP=(NEW,CATLG,DELETE),
//     SPACE=(TRK,(1)),
//     UNIT=DISK
```

would be appropriate for the JCL to create a new file. It requires several more entries than we have looked at. (I have placed each on a separate line. I think it's easier to read that way, but it is not required.) Do you see how each of the first four lines ends with a comma and that all lines start with //? The last four lines have a blank after the slash which says it is a continuation of this DD statement.

As you might imagine, there are many, many, many options available to describe data sets. I will not cover all of them since that is beyond the scope of this text. However, I want to point out the most commonly used options for the DD statement.

**The Data Set Name (DSN).**      You have seen this earlier. It is the name of the data set. It includes the user's unique account identification and the file name.

**The Data Control Block (DCB).**      The *Data Control Block* is used to describe to the system information about the file's data contents; that is, record length, blocking factors and format. While I'll show you these, I also want to point out that the DCB may be eliminated by specifying those items in the FD for the file. Remember the RECORD CONTAINS clause and the BLOCK CONTAINS clause?

There are two schools of thought on whether to use the **DCB** or not. I prefer to use the FD to specify the file characteristics since it helps the readability of the program. The specs are more English-like and handy for maintenance. On the other hand, by having the specs done external to the program, some changes can be made to the data set without having to change and recompile the program.

## TIP

Specify a BLOCK CONTAINS of zero in a FD, and you are saying that the DCB information is in the JCL.

Following is a list of the DCB options:

| | |
|---|---|
| LRECL | specifies the *L*ogical *REC*ord *L*ength in bytes |
| BLKSIZE | specifies the *BL*oc*K SIZE* in bytes |
| RECFM | specifies the *REC*ord *For*Mat as: |

F *F*ixed length

FB *F*ixed length and *B*locked

V *V*ariable length

VB *V*ariable length and *B*locked

DSORG        specifies the organization of the data as:

DA *D*irect *A*ccess (disk, etc.) (most random data sets)

IS *I*ndexed *S*equential (most indexed data sets)

PS *P*hysical *S*equential (most sequential data sets)

BUFNO      specifies the number of I/O buffers (usually the default is two)

**The Disposition (DISP).** The disposition, **DISP**, of a data set must be specified. You must specify the current status, the status if a job runs, and the status if it abends. Some options are shown below:

Current status options:

| | |
|---|---|
| NEW | a new file is to be created |
| OLD | the file already exists |
| SHR | the file exists and may be shared between jobs |

Status upon successful completion of job:

| | |
|---|---|
| DELETE | used for temporary files |
| PASS | pass the data set to the next job step; used with multiple step jobs |
| CATLG | add the data set to the user's catalog |

Status upon abnormal termination of job:

| | |
|---|---|
| DELETE | delete the file, don't keep it |
| KEEP | keep the file (even though it may be incomplete) |

Therefore, **DISP = (NEW,CATLG,DELETE)** says that EXPDATA is a new (**NEW**) file and should be cataloged (**CATLG**) if the program runs successfully or should be deleted (**DELETE**) if the job fails.

**The Space.** The **SPACE** parameter specifies the amount of spaces required to store the file on a disk. The options are:

| | |
|---|---|
| TRK | the number of tracks needed; minimum is one track |
| CYL | the number of cylinders needed |

**The Unit.** The last parameter is the **UNIT** parameter. For our purposes this will be DISK, but it could be tape or some other valid media.

**JCL Summary.** JCL is our way of communicating information about our program and specifying the resources our program will need. Generally, we will need the following statements to run our programs during development:

| JOB | statement |
|---|---|
| EXEC | COBCLG statement |
| COB.SYSIN | DD statement to identify our program |
| GO. | DD statements for each input and output data set, including print files. If our program uses two input files, one output file, and two printer files (simultaneously), then, you would expect five GO. statements. |

Once a program, load module, is put into the production library, the JCL requirements change. You no longer need to compile and link edit the source program. In fact, you don't have the source program in the production library. The example set of JCL to run a job in the production environment might be:

```
//PAY     JOB (accounting info),'PAYROLL'
//STEP   EXEC PGM=PAYROLL
//GO.MEMBER   DD DSN=USR.P007.JB.MASTDATA,DISP=SHR
//GO.REPORT   DD SYSOUT=A DCB=(BLKSIZE=133,RECFM=FA)
```

Notice that the EXEC statement changes. The EXEC *does not* reference the COBOL compiler but a program called PAYROLL. It must be an executable module (already compiled and link edited). The COB.SYSIN DD statement is eliminated since the source program is not needed. However, both GO. statements are still there. Why? You need them for the GO step.

## SUMMARY

In this chapter you saw the approach I intend to use for most other chapters. That is, I put forth a problem and then examined the COBOL statements needed for its solution. In this way I hope to give you a reason for studying a COBOL verb or feature.

After I posed the problem, you spent much time studying the concepts of detail and total times. In doing so you looked at the AT END option of the READ and the AFTER OPTION of the WRITE. This led you into a complete discussion of carriage control including the SPECIAL-NAMES option.

Once we discussed the READ and WRITE verbs fully, you were shown the idea of data paths. That is, how does data get from a file into memory and then back out again? You saw that the input data path and output data paths were opposites and how the MOVE verb plays an important role.

Probably the most important concept we discussed was the sequential file model. We established the model to help in approaching sequential file processing. By using the model we saw that all sequential file processing has much in common and in fact, the particular needs for a problem become a fill-in-the-blank with the model.

Finally, you got to a topic that is a favorite of most people, JCL. While I didn't present all of JCL and its options, I did give you a look at what it takes to run a program. You studied the general form of JCL statements and looked at the three types: JOB, EXEC, and DD. You also saw several of the options that are commonly used with the DD statement. The options DSN, DCB, DISP, SPACE, and UNIT were presented.

I hope this chapter has given you insight into the basics of a sequential file handling program. It should also have given you an understanding of what it takes to run a program.

## EXERCISES

### Chapter Review Questions

1. Detail Time is defined as:
    a. All the code used to produce output
    b. All the processing needed to produce summary reports
    c. All the processing required to be done on each record
    d. All the processing required to be done to produce headings
    e. None of the above

2. Total Time is defined as:
    a. All processing done after EOF
    b. All processing done before EOF
    c. Only that processing not involving detail records
    d. Only that processing that produces totals
    e. None of the above

3. Carriage Control is provided with:
    a. The AT END CLAUSE
    b. THE AFTER CLAUSE
    c. THE CARRIAGE CLAUSE
    d. THE CONTROL CLAUSE
    e. None of the above

4. Which of the following is not a valid AFTER CLAUSE?
    a. AFTER SPECIAL-NAMES.
    b. AFTER NUMBER-OF-NAMES.
    c. AFTER MOUSE.
    d. AFTER 10 LINES.
    e. AFTER N LINES.

5. The AT END CLAUSE is used to:
    a. Check for End of Page
    b. Check for End of File
    c. Check for End of Paragraph
    d. Check for End of Sections
    e. All of the above

6. The path data follows on input may be depicted as:
    a.       READ
        FILE  ⟶  G-R-D

    b.       INTO
        FILE  ⟶  D-R-D

    c.       FROM          READ
        FILE  ⟶  G-R-D  ⟶  D-R-D

    d.       READ          INTO
        FILE  ⟶  G-R-D  ⟶  D-R-D

    e. None of the above

7. In general the execution of a READ from a sequential file causes:

    a.   The next record to be READ
    b.   The first record to be READ
    c.   The next record in key order to be READ
    d.   The last record to be READ
    e.   None of the above

8. Which of the following is true about the sequential file model?

    a.   Works with sequentially organized files
    b.   Incorporates the lead read technique
    c.   Works like a fill-in-the-blank question
    d.   Allows for detail and total time processing
    e.   All of the above are true

9. Which of the following is a programming standard?

    a.   One statement per line
    b.   In-line comments should be short and descriptive
    c.   File names should incorporate the suffix, -FILE
    d.   Record names should incorporate the suffix, -RECORD
    e.   All of the above

10. One of the most common errors during development is the use of invalid data in an arithmetic operation known as a:

    a.   SOC7
    b.   System Completion Code of 007
    c.   SOC1
    d.   System Completion Code of 001
    e.   Both a and b

11. Which of the following would be errors that could occur during development?

    a.   Logic
    b.   Execution Time
    c.   Syntax
    d.   Compile Time
    e.   All of the above

12. Which of the following statements is true about a program in production?

    a.   Logic errors may occur
    b.   Syntax errors may occur
    c.   The program may be re-compiled
    d.   Execution time errors may occur
    e.   Both a and d are true

13. Which of the following is not a function of JCL?

    a.   Provide accounting information
    b.   Request hardware devices
    c.   Specify all input/output requirements
    d.   Introduce the computer job to the system
    e.   Provide payment of job cost

14. The //COB.SYSIN DD Statement is used to identify:
    a.   The object program
    b.   The input data file
    c.   The source program
    d.   The compiler to be used
    e.   None of the above

15. Which of the following information is not specified with the DCB?
    a.   Blocking
    b.   Record format
    c.   Record length
    d.   File name
    e.   Organization

16. Which of the following is an appropriate disposition for a file that will be created by a program?
    a.   DISP = SHR
    b.   DISP = NEW
    c.   DISP = (NEW,CATLG,DELETE)
    d.   DISP = (OLD,CATLG,DELETE)
    e.   None of the above

17. The //GO.   DD statements are used to specify:
    a.   All input files
    b.   All output files
    c.   Only files used during execution
    d.   All report files
    e.   All of the above

18. The JCL statement that could be used to run a program that's in a production library would be:
    a.   //PROG EXEC COBCLG...
    b.   //PROG EXEC PGM = CIRCLE...
    c.   //PROG EXEC PGM = COBCLG...
    d.   //COB.PROG EXEC PGM = CIRCLE...
    e.   None of the above

## Discussion Questions

1. Briefly contrast detail and total time.
2. Briefly explain why module 3000 contains a perform 2000?
3. Briefly explain the relationship of the SPECIAL-NAMES paragraph and the WRITE verb. How is carriage control a related topic?
4. Briefly define the sequential file model.
5. Briefly discuss program development.
6. Briefly discuss how a COBOL program is run.
7. Briefly discuss the JCL statements we studied: JOB, EXEC, and DD.

## Practice Problems

1. Write the JCL to run a program given the following specifications:
   - source program is in USR.S100.AB.PROG
   - two input files: USR.P500.SS.DATA1 and USR.P600.ZZ.DATA2
   - three report files needed
   - one new disk file needed to be saved as: USR.S100.AB.NEW

2. What would be the DCB equivalent for the following FD?

```
FD  INVENTORY-FILE
    LABEL RECORDS ARE OMITTED
    RECORD CONTAINS 73 CHARACTERS
    BLOCK CONTAINS 60 RECORDS
    DATA RECORD IS INVENTORY-RECORD.

01  INVENTORY-RECORD PIC X(73).
```

3. Write a COBOL program to read the Personnel file shown in Data File B and write a report of all employees. A summary report should also be written to provide a count of the number of employees

## Programming Projects

The following assignments rely on the data dictionary, library elements and data sets found in the Project Sets Section of your text.

1. Do the JCL Assignment for either the Project Management System, Project A or for the Employee System, Project B.
2. Do the Input/Output Assignment for the Project Management System, Project A.
3. Do the Input/Output Assignment for the Employee System, Project B.

# MATH VERBS

**OBJECTIVES**     In this chapter you will study the math verbs available in COBOL: ADD, SUBTRACT, MULTIPLY, DIVIDE and COMPUTE. You will also study many of the options available with these verbs.

Several situations illustrating the various issues involved in using the math verbs will also be presented. You will see that all data items involved in math operations must have numeric picture clauses. They may not be numeric edited or anything else that is not numeric.

You will study 77 levels, accumulators and counters. In the chapter you will see how and why accumulators and counters are needed. You will see that their description may be accomplished in several ways including D-R-Ds and 77 levels.

At the end of the chapter you will briefly look at data representation in COBOL. You will find that we have been defaulting to a particular representation: Display or Zoned Decimal. And you will see that other usage clause options such as paced decimal and binary are not only available but also useful in particular situations.

## TOPICS

- **Mathematical operations**
- **Accumulators**
- **Counters**
- **Reporting**
- **Data representation**
- **Hierarchy of operators**

## KEY WORDS

- **ADD**
- **SUBTRACT**
- **MULTIPLY**
- **DIVIDE**
- **COMPUTE**
- **\*\*, \*, /, +, −**
- **Parentheses**
- **ROUNDED**
- **ON SIZE ERROR**
- **77 Level**
- **USAGE**
- **COMP**
- **COMP-3**
- **DISPLAY**

## INTRODUCTION

In most data processing problems, manipulating data mathematically is required. In Chapter 5 we introduced the verbs ADD, SUBTRACT, MULTIPLY, DIVIDE and COMPUTE, and you saw that they were classified as data manipulation verbs. In this chapter we will take a closer look at all the math verbs and the options available when using them.

## THE PROBLEM

Let's revisit the inventory problem we looked at in Chapter 6. The problem was to read an inventory file and provide a listing of all items. The list was to include all input fields plus each item's total cost. The manager also requested that the total cost of the inventory be reported as well.

### The HIPO

The Hierarchy Chart and IPO (HIPO) for the inventory problem are shown in Figures 6.1 and 6.2, respectively, in Chapter 6.

### The Flowchart

Figure 6.3 of Chapter 6 shows the detailed program flowchart for the inventory problem.

### The Code

Also, you should look back at Chapter 6 and see the code for the problem's solution. In it I did all the D-R-Ds and included the PROCEDURE DIVISION statements required for the solution. However, I didn't explain the 3100 module, repeated below from Chapter 6, that contained the math statements required by this solution: ADD and COMPUTE.

```
3100-CALCULATE-COST-PARA.
    COMPUTE TOTAL-ITEM-COST = QOH * UNIT-COST.
    ADD TOTAL-ITEM-COST TO GRAND-TOTAL-COST.
```

Since this is the math chapter, I will now more fully develop the concepts needed to do math in COBOL.

## THE MATH VERBS

The COBOL math verbs are:

ADD
SUBTRACT
MULTIPLY
DIVIDE
COMPUTE

Using these verbs you do all math in COBOL: you add with the ADD, subtract with the SUBTRACT, multiply with the MULTIPLY, divide with the DIVIDE and perform multiple operations with the COMPUTE. However, no matter which verb you use, certain rules apply to all the math verbs. These rules are listed below.

- Only numeric items, literals or data-names may be used in math operations.
- All operators in COMPUTE must be preceded and followed by at least one blank space.
- Division by zero is not permitted. If it is done, on purpose or because of bad data, it will result in an error. Such errors can be trapped by using the ON SIZE ERROR option.
- Numeric edited data-names may not be used mathematically.
- The size of the data field required to contain the result must be determined by the programmer.
- Intermediate results will carry only as much significance as the most significant data field/literal involved in that operation or final result field.
- Final results on all math verbs may be rounded.
- With the ADD, SUBTRACT, MULTIPLY and DIVIDE, the results will be stored in the final data-name referenced.

### The ADD Verb

With the **ADD** verb you are able to perform only addition. However, the number of items you add together is unlimited. You may add one or more data-names and/or numeric literals. The different formats of the ADD are as follows:

$$\underline{\text{ADD}} \left\{ \begin{array}{l} \text{data-name} \\ \text{numeric literal} \end{array} \right\} \left[ , \left\{ \begin{array}{l} \text{data-name} \\ \text{numeric literal} \end{array} \right\} \cdots \right]$$

**TO** data-name [ **ROUNDED** ] ,

$$\left[ \text{data-name} [\underline{\text{ROUNDED}}] \cdots [ \text{ON } \underline{\text{SIZE}} \ \underline{\text{ERROR}} \text{ executable statement(s) } ] \right]$$

$$\underline{\text{ADD}} \left\{ \begin{array}{l} \text{data-name} \\ \text{numeric literal} \end{array} \right\} \left[ , \left\{ \begin{array}{l} \text{data-name} \\ \text{numeric literal} \end{array} \right\} \cdots \right]$$

**GIVING** data-name [ **ROUNDED** ] ,

$$\left[ \text{data-name} [\underline{\text{ROUNDED}}] \cdots [ \text{ON } \underline{\text{SIZE}} \ \underline{\text{ERROR}} \text{ executable statement(s) } ] \right]$$

Notice that the only difference between the two formats is the use of the **TO** or the **GIVING**. They may not be used together in COBOL '68 or '74, but they may be used together in COBOL '85.

Generally, the first format says to **ADD** two or more data items to another data-name or data-names and round the results if asked to do so. The second format says to **ADD** two or more data items and place the results in the data-name(s) specified with the **GIVING**. Of course, the result may be rounded if you wish.

Let's look at some examples in order to make some sense out of these rules. If you wanted to **ADD** a set of values in COBOL, you could code:

**ADD** A B C 5.3 TO D.

This would cause the value of A to be added to the value of D, and then the value of B to be added to D, and then the value of C to be added to D, and the number 5.3 to be added to D. The final result would be stored in location D. Assuming that A has a value of 10, B has a value of 5, C has a value of 2, and D has a value of 100, the final result stored in D would be:

$$10 + 5 + 2 + 5.3 + 100 = 122.3$$

The value of D is used in the calculation, but it is replaced by the final result.

Well, what if you needed the *original* value of D later in the program? Then you would use format 2 of the **ADD**.

**ADD** A B C 5.3 D GIVING ANSWER.

This would provide the same answer, 122.3, but you would retain the original value of D, 100, by causing the result to be stored in ANSWER. Notice that ANSWER did not participate in the math; it was just a storage location. By the way, could the PICTURE on ANSWER be numeric edited? Yes it could, since it's just a storage location.

You might think of the steps this way: Remember from your introduction to programming class that math takes place in a register called an accumulator. You may think of the **ADD. . .TO** as shown below:

| | | |
|---|---|---|
| LOAD | D | places the value of D in the accumulator |
| ADD | A | adds the contents of location A to the accumulator's contents |
| ADD | B | adds the contents of location B to the accumulator's contents |
| ADD | C | adds the contents of location C to the accumulator's contents |
| ADD | 5.3 | adds the value 5.3 to the accumulator's contents |
| STORE | D | stores the results in D |

In the second case, the **ADD. . .GIVING**, the steps would be:

| | |
|---|---|
| LOAD | A |
| ADD | B |
| ADD | C |
| ADD | D |
| ADD | 5.3 |
| STORE | ANSWER |

Notice that the same values are added together, but the last instruction, STORE, places the result in ANSWER instead of D; that's what saves the original value of D for you.

What if you wanted the final answer rounded? You could have asked for it with the **ROUNDED** option. In other words you could code: **ADD A B C 5.3 GIVING ANSWER ROUNDED**. Instead of 122.3, you would have gotten 122. **ROUNDED** works as you would expect. If the value to the right of the position you are rounding to *is* larger than four, then the system rounds up by one. If the value *is not* larger than four, it *does not* round up.

Below are some examples to show this rule:

| Picture of Result Fields | Results (Before Storing) | Actual Value Stored in Result Field |
|---|---|---|
| 9(2)V9(2) | 73.5849 | 73.58 |
| 9(2)V9(2) | 73.5862 | 73.59 |

Notice that the result field retained only two decimal positions. Therefore, without rounding, both results would have been 73.58. However, with rounding, you don't just lose the two low order digits. The most significant of the low order digits to be dropped is examined for possible rounding to the least significant digit kept. In the first example, the four is not greater than four, so the eight is not increased by one. In the second example the six is greater than four, and the eight is increased to nine.

The ON **SIZE ERROR** option on the **ADD**, and for that matter on all the math verbs, checks for result fields that are too small.

In the case of the **ADD**, if the PICTURE clause on ANSWER in our example was PIC 9(2)V9(2), then the value of 122.3 would cause an error. It would be too large to be stored in the result field. If you wanted to report the occurrence of an error instead of ignoring it, you might specify an action to be done when an error occurs.

An example of an **ADD** statement with all options would be:

```
ADD A B 1.7 GIVING C ROUNDED
    ON SIZE ERROR
        DISPLAY 'ERROR OCCURRED'
        DISPLAY 'THE SIZE OF THE RESULT IS TOO LARGE
                FOR C'.
```

### The SUBTRACT Verb

The first cousin to ADD is **SUBTRACT**. With the **SUBTRACT** you may subtract two or more numeric items, data-names and/or literals. The formats of the **SUBTRACT** are given below:

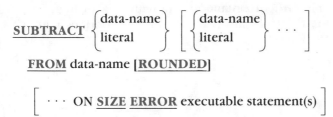

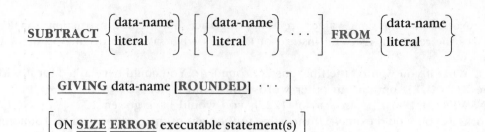

Notice that the difference between the two forms is the use of the **GIVING** in the second format. Also notice that the **FROM** and **GIVING** may be used together.

Generally, **SUBTRACT** causes all the values to the left of **FROM** to be subtracted from the data-name to the right of **FROM**. The result is then stored in the last data-name, and it may be **ROUNDED** if you wish.

Some examples may be helpful. What if you wanted to code D minus A minus B minus 5.3 with the **SUBTRACT** VERB? You could code:

```
SUBTRACT A B 5.3 FROM D.
```

If A is 10, B is 5, and D's original value is 100, what will the result be? It will be 79.7 (100 − 10 − 5 − 5.3). Do you see the similarity between the ADD and SUBTRACT? It doesn't stop here. What if the original value of D was to be retained? How would you change the **SUBTRACT**? Remember this problem with the ADD? You used the **GIVING** option. You do the same with the **SUBTRACT**.

```
SUBTRACT A B 5.3 FROM D GIVING ANSWER.
```

Now the value 79.7 is stored in ANSWER, and the original value of D is preserved. And, again, since ANSWER is just a storage location, its PICTURE may be edited.

The **ROUNDED** option and the ON **SIZE ERROR** option work the same way with **SUBTRACT** as with ADD.

An example of **SUBTRACT** with all options is shown below:

```
SUBTRACT A B 5.3 FROM D GIVING ANSWER ROUNDED
        ON SIZE ERROR DISPLAY 'AN ERROR OCCURRED'
                      DISPLAY 'THE FINAL RESULT IS TOO
                               LARGE TO STORE IN ANSWER'.
```

The result is rounded. Then, if it will not fit into the result field, the displays will be executed.

### The MULTIPLY Verb

If ADD and SUBTRACT are first cousins, so are **MULTIPLY** and DIVIDE. With **MULTIPLY** you multiply *only two* numeric data items: data-names and/or literals. You may also use the **ROUNDED** and ON **SIZE ERROR** options with **MULTIPLY**. The format of MULTIPLY is:

$$\text{MULTIPLY} \begin{Bmatrix} \text{data-name} \\ \text{literal} \end{Bmatrix} \underline{\text{BY}} \begin{Bmatrix} \text{data-name} \\ \text{literal} \end{Bmatrix}$$

$$\Big[\, \underline{\text{GIVING}}\ \text{data-name}\ [\ \underline{\text{ROUNDED}}\ ] \,\Big] \cdots$$

$$\Big[\, \text{ON}\ \underline{\text{SIZE ERROR}}\ \text{executable statement} \,\Big]$$

The way the MULTIPLY works is that the two data items are multiplied and the results are stored in the data-name following BY *or* the data-names(s) specified by GIVING. As before, you may ask for the result to be ROUNDED. Following are some examples of valid MULTIPLYs:

```
                                        ANSWER STORED IN
MULTIPLY A  BY B                             B
MULTIPLY A  BY B   GIVING C ROUNDED          C
MULTIPLY 10 BY B                             B
MULTIPLY 10 BY 20 GIVING C                   C
```

## TIP

**Instead of multiplying two numeric literals, just move the answer to the final result field.**

Some examples of *invalid* uses of the MULTIPLY are:

```
MULTIPLY A BY 10           [no place to store results]
MULTIPLY A BY B  GIVING 100 [no place to store results]
```

ON SIZE ERROR plays an important role with MULTIPLY. In fact, with MULTIPLY and DIVIDE, size errors are most common. You can imagine why. Since we must anticipate the result size and use the appropriate picture size, we are more likely to misjudge. So be careful.

### The DIVIDE Verb

The first cousin of MULTIPLY also works with *only two* numeric data items. You may divide one by or into another. The result is stored in the data-name to the right of INTO or in the data-name(s) specified by GIVING. Of course, you may ask for the result, the quotient, to be ROUNDED. The formats of DIVIDE are shown below:

$$\underline{\text{DIVIDE}} \begin{Bmatrix} \text{data-name} \\ \text{literal} \end{Bmatrix} \underline{\text{INTO}} \begin{Bmatrix} \text{data-name} \\ \text{literal} \end{Bmatrix}$$

$$\Big[\, \underline{\text{GIVING}}\ \text{data-name}\ [\ \underline{\text{ROUNDED}}\ ] \,\Big] \cdots$$

$$\Big[\, \text{ON}\ \underline{\text{SIZE ERROR}}\ \text{executable statement(s)} \,\Big]$$

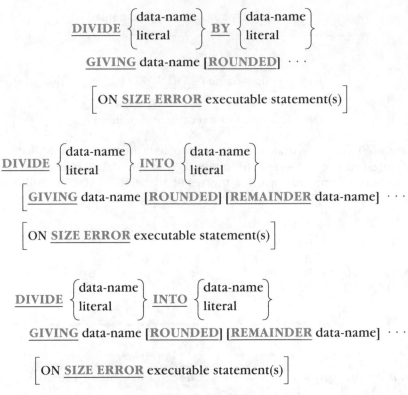

The first thing you noticed, I'm sure, is all the formats. Well, don't let it bother you. There's not that much difference among them. Notice the use of either **INTO** or **BY**. The most commonly used format is **INTO**. How does **DIVIDE** get evaluated? Let's assume that A has a value of two, and B has a value of six. Then the statement **DIVIDE** A INTO B would result in an answer of three, and it would be stored in B. As has been the case with the other verbs, if we wanted to keep the original value of B, we could code the statement as:

```
DIVIDE A INTO B GIVING C.
```

Now the answer would be stored in C, allowing B to retain its original value.

How does the **BY** option make a difference? Well, **DIVIDE** A BY B would result in an answer of 1/3 (2/6); the divisor and dividend are interchanged. However, the **DIVIDE** as shown would cause an error, because if you use the **BY** option you *must* use **GIVING**. So the correct **DIVIDE** using **BY** would be:

```
DIVIDE A BY B GIVING C.
```

In all cases you may specify the **ROUNDED** option and the ON **SIZE ERROR** option. Please be careful in determining the size of the result field, especially when dividing by a decimal value less than one.

A special option unique to **DIVIDE** is the **REMAINDER** option. What happens when you cause ten to be divided by three? The answer would be 3.333. . . . What you may have wanted is the whole number result *with* the remainder value. That is, you wanted the following:

```
DIVIDE 3 INTO 10 GIVING ANSWER
      REMAINDER LEFT-OVER.
```

where we have

```
03   ANSWER      PIC 9(2).
03   LEFT-OVER   PIC 9(2).
```

ANSWER will have a value of three, and LEFT-OVER will have a value of one. See how that worked? Instead of the .3333. . ., we retained the remainder in LEFT-OVER as a whole number.

Now, what would happen if we did the following:

```
DIVIDE 5 INTO 44 GIVING ANSWER ROUNDED
    REMAINDER LEFT-OVER.
```

Well, the use of **ROUNDED** and **REMAINDER** together requires us to be careful. Is the rounding first or is the remainder figured first? Look at the short division version:

$$
\begin{array}{r}
8.8 \\
5\,\overline{\smash{)}\,44.0} \\
\underline{40\phantom{.0}} \\
4 \;\leftarrow\; \text{(remainder)}
\end{array}
$$

If the rounding to nine is first, then what would be the remainder? It works the other way: 1) The remainder is determined, causing a four to be placed in LEFT-OVER. 2) Then the value 8.8 is **ROUNDED** to nine.

Some examples of valid **DIVIDE**s are:

```
                                    ANSWER STORED IN
DIVIDE A INTO B.                         B
DIVIDE A INTO B  GIVING C.               C
DIVIDE 5 INTO B.                         B
DIVIDE 5 INTO 10 GIVING C.               C
DIVIDE A BY   B  GIVING C.               C
DIVIDE A BY   2  GIVING C.               C
DIVIDE A INTO B  GIVING C  ROUNDED       C
DIVIDE A BY   B  GIVING C  ROUNDED       C
DIVIDE A INTO B  GIVING C  ROUNDED       C
         REMAINDER LEFT-OVER.
DIVIDE A BY   B  GIVING C  ROUNDED       C
         REMAINDER LEFT-OVER.
```

## TIP

**Use one form or the other. Mixing INTO and BY will cause problems and cost valuable programming time—yours.**

Some examples of *invalid* **DIVIDE**s follow:

```
DIVIDE A   INTO  10.    [no place for result]
DIVIDE A   BY    2.     [BY requires GIVING]
DIVIDE 10  INTO  200.   [no place for result]
```

---

### TIP

As with MULTIPLY, don't divide two literals.  Just move the literal result to a storage location.

---

A full example of a **DIVIDE** would be:

```
DIVIDE KOUNT INTO TOTAL GIVING AVERAGE ROUNDED
       REMAINDER LEFT-OVER
       ON SIZE ERROR DISPLAY 'AN ERROR OCCURRED'
                    DISPLAY 'THE RESULT COULD NOT BE
                             CONTAINED IN THE RESULT
                             FIELD AVERAGE'.
```

This full example causes rounding, keeps the remainder (if any) and checks for size error.  If the result is too large, the error message will be displayed.

---

### TIP

In the case of division, either with DIVIDE or with COMPUTE, division by zero will cause you headaches.  Avoid it.

---

### The COMPUTE Verb

How would you code the following equation using the ADD, SUBTRACT, MULTIPLY and/or DIVIDE verbs?

$$Y = \frac{A^3 + B^2 - C^4}{B^2 (A - C^2)^3}$$

It can be done, but it takes a little effort and time!  For instance, the code would look something like:

```
MULTIPLY A    BY A    GIVING A-SQ.
MULTIPLY A    BY A-SQ GIVING A-CUBED.
MULTIPLY B    BY B    GIVING B-SQ.
MULTIPLY C    BY C    GIVING C-SQ.
MULTIPLY C-SQ BY C-SQ GIVING C-FOURTH.
                .
                .
                .
```

Get the idea?  It would take a few more statements than we would anticipate with a higher level language like COBOL.  If you're not already put off by the number of statements required above, what if I added the calculation of the square root of the equation as shown?

$$Y = \sqrt{\frac{A^3 + B^2 - C^4}{B^2 (A - C^2)^3}}$$

Do you give up? While some of us remember how to do long-hand fractional powers with the approximation technique, most of us are more familiar with the square root key on a calculator. We want something in COBOL that allows us an easier way of handling this type of expression. There is a key word, **COMPUTE**.

With the **COMPUTE** verb you are allowed to perform several mathematical functions in one statement. So, unlike the other math verbs that allow only one function, **COMPUTE** allows you to do all those and also exponentiation (power functions) together in one statement.

The general format of the **COMPUTE** is:

**COMPUTE data-name [ ROUNDED ] = mathematical expression**

**COMPUTE** works like the FORTRAN assignment statement and the BASIC Let statement. The mathematical expression is evaluated, and the result is stored in the data-name on the left of the equals sign.

How do you code mathematical expressions in the **COMPUTE** statement? You do it with symbols that represent particular math operations. These symbols (operators) are shown in Figure 7.1.

| | |
|---|---|
| ** | EXPONENTIATION |
| * | MULTIPLICATION |
| / | DIVISION |
| + | ADDITION |
| - | SUBTRACTION |

**FIGURE 7.1**
Math Operators

These operators are used to form expressions similar to:

```
COMPUTE ANSWER = A + B - C / D * E ** 2.
```

Now, which operation is done first? Since changing the order in which we evaluate the operators changes the answer, order is important. COBOL, like other computer languages, has a hierarchy of operators. Figure 7.2 shows this hierarchy.

| | |
|---|---|
| ** | Highest level operator |
| *, / | |
| +, - | Lowest level operator |

**FIGURE 7.2**
Hierarchy of Operators

Figure 7.2 says that exponentiation is the highest level operation. It will normally be done first in an expression. The multiplication and division operators are the next level. They will be done after all exponentiation. However, don't misread Figure 7.2. There is no preference between operators on the same level in the hierarchy. There is only preference among levels. Therefore, there is no preference between the * and the /, or between the + and −. Let's look at the example

COMPUTE again and indicate the order in which the operators will be executed (Figure 7.3).

**FIGURE 7.3**
**Example of Operator
Execution Order**

COMPUTE ANSWER = A  +  B  –  C  /  D  *  E  **  2.

Assume the following values:

COMPUTE ANSWER = 20  +  14  –  10  /  5  *  3  **  2.

```
                          result 2   result 1
                             2          9
                          └─────┬─────┘
        result 4              result 3
          34                    18
        └──────────┬───────────┘
                result 5
                  16
```

Notice:

- The E ** 2 (3 ** 2 = 9) is done first because it is the highest level operator.
- C/D (10 / 5 = 2) is done next because, if multiple operators at the same hierarchical level exist, then they are executed left to right within the statement.
- Result 2 * Result 1 is done third (2 * 9 = 18).
- A and B are then added producing Result 4 (20 + 14 = 34).
- Result 3 is subtracted from Result 4 producing the final result (34 – 18 = 16).

Do you see how the hierarchy of operators works? It's important, since you will be building these expressions. A feature that might help is the use of parentheses. They may be used to improve readability and/or change the order in which operators are executed. For instance, what if your intention in Figure 7.3 had been to raise everything to the left of the ** to the second Power? The normal order caused you to raise only E to the power of 2. You would fix this problem with the use of the parentheses as shown in Figure 7.4. Notice how the final result is now 784 instead of 16.

**FIGURE 7.4**
**Example of Operator
Execution Order Using
Parentheses**

COMPUTE ANSWER = (A  +  B  –  C  /  D  *  E)  **  2

Assume the following values:

COMPUTE ANSWER = (20  +  14  –  10  /  5  *  3)  **  2

```
                          result 1
                             2
                          └─────┐
        result 3              result 2
          34                    6
        └──────────┬───────────┘
                result 4
                  28
                └────────┬────────┘
                      result 5
                        784
```

Now the parentheses cause the exponentiation to be done fifth instead of first, but that's what you wanted. Some general rules for the use of parentheses are appropriate here:

- Parentheses must be used in pairs—one left, one right.
- The leftmost left parenthesis must be preceded by at least one blank space and the rightmost right parenthesis must be followed by at least one blank space.
- Execution starts from the innermost set of parentheses and works outward.
- Sets of parentheses at the same level are evaluated left to right.
- The hierarchy of operators still holds within each set of parentheses.

Let's visualize the idea of nested parentheses. Figure 7.5 shows a COMPUTE statement with parentheses only.

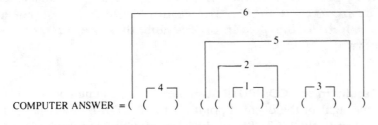

Note: Numbers indicate order parentheses are evaluated.

**FIGURE 7.5**
**Nested Parentheses**

I've labeled the parentheses for ease of reference. Don't do that when coding, or the compiler will choke! The innermost set of parentheses is the one labeled 1. The expression within it will be done first. If that expression were A + B * C, the * would be done first. The parentheses labeled 2 and 3 are at the same level as are parentheses 4 and 5. Our rules say that 2 will be done first, then 3. At the next level, 4 will be done, followed by 5. These work this way because they were evaluated in left to right order. The last one to be evaluated is 6.

So much for all these rules and generic examples. Let's do the problem I posed, the one that we started with just the ADD, SUBTRACT, MULTIPLY and DIVIDE verbs. Here is *an* answer:

```
COMPUTE Y = (A** 3 + B ** 2 - C ** 4) /
            (B ** 2 * (A - C ** 2) ** 3).
```

While that is a correct answer, we could have used parentheses to try to make it more readable:

```
COMPUTE Y = ((A** 3) + (B ** 2) - (C ** 4)) /
            ((B ** 2) * (A - (C ** 4))) ** 3.
```

This form groups the operations visually for the reader.

## TIP

**Use parentheses to help readability. If it's easier to read, then it's probably easier to understand. That reduces errors.**

What about the equation that included the square root? Well, remember COBOL does not have a square root key. We accomplish the square root by raising the expression to the 1/2 power. Therefore, the equation would be:

```
COMPUTE Y = ((A ** 3 + B ** 2 - C ** 4) /
              (B ** 2 * (A - C ** 2) ** 3)) **.5 .
```

Notice the extra parentheses. The **.5 could have been coded as **(1/2).

---

### TIP

**Code fractional powers, or roots, with parentheses or use the decimal equivalents. Thus $\sqrt{a}$ is coded a\*\*(1/2) or a\*\*.5. Also $\sqrt{a^3}$ is coded a\*\*(3/2) or a\*\*1.5. For example, if you coded 100\*\*1/2, this would not give the desired result of 10. The result would be 50 since the 100 would be raised to the power of one and then the result would be divided by two.**

---

**Intermediate Results in the COMPUTE Statement.** The number of positions to the left and to the right of the decimal point for the PICTURE of a data item should be equal to the larger of the PICTUREs of the items involved in a particular operation or the final storage location. Consider an application that said a retirement deduction would be equal to 3.5% of gross pay. Given the following:

|  |  |  | Assumed Value |
|---|---|---|---|
| 03 | GROSS-PAY | PIC 9(5)V99. | 1000.00 |
| 03 | RETIREMENT-PERCENT | PIC 99V99. | 3.50 |

.

.

and

.

| 03 | RETIREMENT-AMOUNT | PIC 9(5)V99. | 0.00 |
|---|---|---|---|

```
COMPUTE RETIREMENT-AMOUNT = GROSS-PAY *
                            (RETIREMENT-PERCENT/100).
```

The **COMPUTE** statement would produce:

```
RETIREMENT-AMOUNT = 1000 * (3.5/100)
                  = 1000 * .035
                  = 30
```

Since the intermediate result needed three decimal places and the maximum involved was two, the intermediate result became $30. The **COMPUTE** should have been coded as:

```
COMPUTE RETIREMENT-AMOUNT = (GROSS-PAY*RETIREMENT-PERCENT)
                            /100.
```

This would produce:

```
RETIREMENT-AMOUNT = (1000 * 3.5)/100
                  = 3500/100
                  = 35.00
```

This is the result you would expect. This is one of the reasons some people use the **COMPUTE** only for power functions.

## ACCUMULATING, COUNTING AND CONSTANTS

Math is used in a program to provide answers to some relationship. However, besides computing something like GROSS-PAY or RETIREMENT-AMOUNT, you also need to accumulate values, count the occurrences of things and set up constants.

### *Accumulating*

Let's get back to the inventory problem I described earlier in the chapter. In particular, I want to get back to the math required. Recall that you needed to calculate the item cost for each item in the inventory, and you needed to accumulate the total inventory cost. In paragraph 3100 I coded the following:

```
3100-CALCULATE-COST-PARA.
    COMPUTE TOTAL-ITEM-COST = QOH * UNIT-COST.
    ADD TOTAL-ITEM-COST TO GRAND-TOTAL-COST.
```

Both of these statements are clear. COMPUTE generates an item's total cost by multiplying the number of units on hand, QOH, by the cost of each unit, UNIT-COST. This TOTAL-ITEM-COST is accumulated in GRAND-TOTAL-COST, which will contain the total cost of the inventory once all items are processed at EOF.

My question to you is this. Where are each of these data- names defined?

| Data-Name | | Described in | Picture |
|---|---|---|---|
| QOH | → | INVENTORY-RECORD-IN | 9s |
| UNIT-COST | → | INVENTORY-RECORD-IN | 9s, V |
| TOTAL-ITEM-COST | → | independent record description | 9s, V |
| GRAND-TOTAL-COST | → | independent record description | 9s, V |

(Look back at the code in Chapter 6.)

I think everyone understands the first two, QOH and UNIT-COST. But why didn't I define TOTAL-ITEM-COST in INVENTORY-RECORD-OUT? Why didn't I define GRAND-TOTAL-COST in GRAND-TOTAL-COST-LINE? Look at the PICTURE clauses of the corresponding fields in those two records. They are edited in both cases. Can you use numeric edited data items in math operations? No. Both TOTAL-ITEM-COST and GRAND-TOTAL-COST need to be numeric; therefore, they may not be edited. But you want to report them edited with dollar signs, decimal points, and so on. You seem to be between a rock and a hard place. Not quite! You set up temporary work locations that allow you to do math with the data items and then move their contents to the appropriate output records at EOF.

**77 Levels.** You need temporary storage areas. What do you do? Look at the program code. I showed two ways of doing this. Either way is fine. Let's look at the second way first. I grouped data items by function and put them into detail record descriptions like this:

```
01   COSTS.
     03   TOTAL-ITEM-COST      PIC 9(5)V9(2) VALUE 0.
     03   GRAND-TOTAL-COST     PIC 9(8)V9(2) VALUE 0.
```

This method is OK since they are both cost fields. Using the D-R-D to set up these accumulators is different from what we have done so far. In other 01s the fields were positioned in relation to one another based on relative location in the record. In this case, what's the record? That's my point. They are independent and could be physically reversed.

However, another way to define them independently is the **77 level** item. 77s are called independent record descriptions. Since the two cost items are not presented together, why not describe them independently? You can. I showed the corresponding 77 level entries first in the code because if 77s are used in a program, they must appear first in WORKING-STORAGE. They were coded as shown below:

```
77   TOTAL-ITEM-COST      PIC 9(5)V9(2) VALUE 0.
77   GRAND-TOTAL-COST     PIC 9(8)V9(2) VALUE 0.
```

Notice that except for the level indicators, the actual description is the same. Which is better? Let me just say that both are OK. If you use the 01 form, insure that the detail-record-description contains related accumulators and counters, etc. If you use 77 levels, try to alphabetize them so that you can find them easily when you are trying to reference them. Both ways are used. My point is that no matter which you or your prof decides upon, you need to understand why they are needed.

## TIP

**If you use 01 record descriptions to define your accumulators, place them first in WORKING-STORAGE. This will save you time in debugging.**

### Counting

Everything that I discussed about accumulators applies to counting. After all, counting is a type of accumulation. However, with the discussion of counting we can look at a special situation. For this let's go back to the DEAN-FILE. Let's assume you wanted the average GPR for the college's students. What would be required? You would need to accumulate the GPR's for all students, count the students and then calculate the average GPR (sum/count) after EOF. Therefore, you would have the following descriptions and code:

```
WORKING-STORAGE SECTION.

77   STUDENT-COUNT       PIC 9(4)      VALUE 0.
77   TOTAL-GPR           PIC 9(5)V9(4) VALUE 0.
         .
         .
         .
01   STUDENT-RECORD-IN.
         .
         .
     03   GPR             PIC 9(1)V9(4).
```

```
01   AVERAGE-LINE.
        .
        .
     03   AVERAGE-GPR           PIC 9(1).9(4).
        .
        .


PROCEDURE DIVISION.

MAIN-PARA.

        .
        .
     PERFORM READ-STUDENT-RECORDS.
     PERFORM PROCESS-STUDENTS
        UNTIL FLAG=1.
     PERFORM SUMMARY.
        .
        .
        .

PROCESS-STUDENTS.

        .
        .
     ADD 1 TO STUDENT-COUNT.
     ADD GPR TO TOTAL-GPR.
        .
        .
     PERFORM READ-STUDENT-RECORDS.

SUMMARY.
     COMPUTE AVERAGE-GPR = TOTAL-GPR/STUDENT-COUNT.
     WRITE . . . FROM AVERAGE-LINE
           . . . .
```

Does all that look OK to you? I just filled in the essential parts for our discussion. I also used the sequential file model for your benefit. The thing I want you to notice is that neither the STUDENT-COUNT nor the TOTAL-GPR was reported; yet you needed to describe them, didn't you? Is my description of AVERAGE-GPR OK where it is? It's edited! But it's OK, since it is only used for storing the answer.

## THE ISSUE OF DATA REPRESENTATION

Up to this point in our discussion and use of data items, I have not concerned myself with how the values have been stored internally. Obviously, I assumed that the numbers used in our mathematical operations were numeric. But what do the numbers look like in memory, and do looks affect our math?

### The USAGE Clause

There are several ways that numbers may be represented in memory. How you cause an item to be stored affects how it is handled mathematically. The general format of the **USAGE** clause, which may be used with any group or elementary item you have used in the DATA DIVISION, follows.

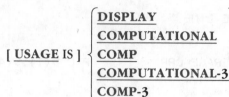

··· [ USAGE IS ] DISPLAY / COMPUTATIONAL / COMP / COMPUTATIONAL-3 / COMP-3

**DISPLAY.**    The **DISPLAY** option is the default.  Since I never specified a **USAGE** clause with any of the data elements, I in essence used **DISPLAY** in all cases.  This format is also known as ZONED DECIMAL format because each digit in the number is represented in a byte of memory where the first four bits represent a zone and the last four bits represent a decimal number.

Let's look at some numbers represented this way.  You must recall a few things.  First, I will be using the EBCDIC code. (The discussion also holds for ASCII code.)  Second, remember that these codes use eight-bit bytes.  Remember that the EBCDIC code for an unsigned number, say 5, is F5.  This could be written as: 11110101.  Also, recall that the byte is divided into two equal parts of four bits each, called nibbles.  Using the positional value of the binary numbering system, 1111 is 15 and 0101 is 5.  But how is 15 an F?  Remember the hexadecimal numbering system?  10 is an A, 11 is a B, and so forth until 15 is F.

So, when you say F5 you just mean a byte of memory represented in hexadecimal.  Therefore, the number 12345 would be represented in ZONED DECIMAL as F1F2F3F4F5.  It requires five bytes to store this number.  Before COBOL can do math with this number, it must first remove the zones (except for one).  This is called packing, because it now takes less memory to store the same number.  The packed result of the number

| BYTE | BYTE | BYTE | BYTE | BYTE | |
|------|------|------|------|------|---|
| F1 | F2 | F3 | F4 | F5 | = 5 BYTES |

would be

| BYTE | BYTE | BYTE | |
|------|------|------|---|
| 12 | 34 | F5 | = 3 BYTES |

**COMPUTATIONAL-3.**    This format, as you have probably guessed, represents the data in PACKED DECIMAL format. This helps in two ways. It saves storage and speeds up our math operations.

Remember I said that before math is done with a ZONED DECIMAL data field, it had to be packed. Well, if you described the data fields involved as **COMP-3**, the packing would not be required. Look at the example, assuming the following data elements:

```
    03   GROSS-PAY           PIC 9(5)V9(2).


    03   TOTAL-GROSS-PAY     PIC 9(8)V9(2)  VALUE 0.
```

Then saying ADD GROSS-PAY TO TOTAL-GROSS-PAY would cause the following actions:

- TOTAL-GROSS-PAY would be packed.
- GROSS-PAY would be packed.
- TOTAL-GROSS-PAY and GROSS-PAY would be added.
- TOTAL-GROSS-PAY would be unpacked.
- GROSS-PAY would be unpacked.

Had you described the two data elements as :

```
03   GROSS-PAY              PIC 9(5)V9(2) USAGE COMP-3.


03   TOTAL-GROSS-PAY     PIC 9(8)V9(2) USAGE COMP-3
                  VALUE 0.
```

The actions caused upon execution would change to:

- GROSS-PAY and TOTAL-GROSS-PAY are added.

(That's it, folks! No other action required!) See the benefits? It uses less storage and makes for faster math.

**COMPUTATIONAL.** This specification allows us to store the numeric data in binary form. For now you will have to trust me when I say that there are times when representing data in binary is best for what you are doing. They are very nice for subscripts. But we won't get to that chapter for a while yet. So suffice it to say that USAGE COMPUTATIONAL allows us to represent data in binary.

## SUMMARY

In this chapter we looked at the COBOL math verbs ADD, SUBTRACT, MULTIPLY, DIVIDE and COMPUTE. We also looked at related topics such as accumulating and counting, 77 level items, data representation and reporting.

You saw that no matter which verb you used, all data items actually involved in the mathematical operations must be numeric. With all the verbs except the COMPUTE, the GIVING option is used to preserve data values by storing the final results in a separate location.

The COMPUTE verb is the most robust in allowing math operations. In it you may ADD (+), SUBTRACT (−), MULTIPLY (*), DIVIDE (/) and raise to a power (**). You saw that these operators follow a hierarchy and that the hierarchy may be altered with the use of parentheses.

Then, you looked at the topic of accumulating and counting. You saw that in COBOL you sometimes need two areas for a data item: one for math and one for reporting. You also saw that accumulators and counters used to generate an answer and not actually reported themselves still require definition in WORKING-STORAGE. We did this both with a D-R-D, with an 01 and with a new item, the 77 level.

Finally, you took a brief look at data representation. You saw that we have been working with data in one format, ZONED DECIMAL, and that other formats are available: BINARY and PACKED DECIMAL. You saw that, for doing math, data represented as PACKED DECIMAL actually reduces storage requirements and reduces the time of execution for the math verbs by not requiring packing and unpacking.

While we examined COMP-3 fully, I asked you to wait for the discussion. COMP-3 is handy for use with subscripts, and that topic comes later.

## SAMPLE PROGRAM

The following is a complete running COBOL program using many of the features and techniques discussed in this chapter.

```
PP 5740-CB1 RELEASE 2.4                    IBM OS/VS COBOL  JULY  1, 1982        14.25.42  DATE OCT 25,1988

       1                        14.25.42      OCT 25,1988

00001           IDENTIFICATION DIVISION.
00002
00003           PROGRAM-ID. MATH.
00004           AUTHOR. FOWLER.
00005           DATE-WRITTEN.  JULY 1988.
00006           DATE-COMPILED. OCT 25,1988.
00007           REMARKS.
00008
00009           ****************************************************************
00010           *                                                              *
00011           *   ASSIGNMENT NUMBER                                          *
00012           *   DATE ASSIGNED                                              *
00013           *   DATE DUE                                                   *
00014           *   PURPOSE:   THIS IS A GRADE POINT RATIO CALCULATION PROGRAM.*
00015           *             THE GRADE POINT RATIO IS DETERMINED BY DIVIDING  *
00016           *             THE NUMBER OF GRADE POINTS EARNED BY THE NUMBER   *
00017           *             OF CREDIT HOURS TAKEN.                           *
00018           *                                                              *
00019           *                                                              *
00020           *                                                              *
00021           *     INPUT FILE SPECIFICATIONS:                               *
00022           *         CARD COLUMNS                    DESCRIPTION           *
00023           *     ------------------                  -----------          *
00024           *            1-30                     STUDENT'S NAME           *
00025           *            31-39                    STUDENT'S ID NUMBER      *
00026           *            40-40                    STUDENT'S MAJOR CODE     *
00027           *            41-41                    STUDENT'S CLASS CODE     *
00028           *            42-42                    STUDENT'S SEX CODE       *
00029           *            43-45                    CREDIT HOURS TAKEN       *
00030           *            46-48                    GRADE POINTS EARNED      *
00031           *                                                              *
00032           *   THE OUTPUT CONTAINS STUDENT'S ID NUMBER, STUDENT'S NAME,   *
00033           *   MAJOR CODE, CLASS CODE, SEX CODE, AND THE GRADE POINT RATIO.*
00034           *                                                              *
00035           *                                                              *
00036           *   A SUMMARY LINE, WHICH CONTAINS THE AVERAGE STUDENT GRADE    *
00037           *   POINT RATIO, WILL BE PRINTED AT THE BOTTOM OF THE REPORT.   *
00038           ****************************************************************
00039
```

```
       2        MATH            14.25.42       OCT 25,1988

00041           ENVIRONMENT DIVISION.
00042
00043           CONFIGURATION SECTION.
00044
00045           SOURCE-COMPUTER. IBM.
00046           OBJECT-COMPUTER. IBM.
00047           SPECIAL-NAMES.    C01 IS PAGE-TOP.
00048
00049           INPUT-OUTPUT SECTION.
00050
00051           FILE-CONTROL.
00052
00053               SELECT DEAN-FILE
00054                   ASSIGN TO DA-S-DEAN.
00055
00056               SELECT REPORT-FILE
00057                   ASSIGN TO UT-S-REPORT.
00058
```

*(continued)*

```
    3         MATH          14.25.42      OCT 25,1988

00060           DATA DIVISION.
00061
00062           FILE SECTION.
00063
00064           FD   DEAN-FILE
00065                LABEL RECORDS ARE OMITTED
00066                RECORD CONTAINS 48 CHARACTERS
00067                BLOCK CONTAINS 100 RECORDS
00068                DATA RECORD IS STUDENT-RECORD.
00069
00070           01   STUDENT-RECORD PIC X(48).
00071
00072
00073           FD   REPORT-FILE
00074                LABEL RECORDS ARE OMITTED
00075                DATA RECORD IS REPORT-LINE.
00076
00077           01   REPORT-LINE PIC X(133).
00078
```

```
    4         MATH          14.25.42      OCT 25,1988

00080           WORKING-STORAGE SECTION.
00081
00082           77   END-OF-FILE-FLAG          PIC 9              VALUE O.
00083           77   GPR                       PIC 9(1)V9(4).
00084           77   TOTAL-CREDIT-HOURS        PIC 9(5)           VALUE O.
00085           77   TOTAL-GRADE-POINTS        PIC 9(5)           VALUE O.
00086
00087           01   PAGE-HEADING.
00088                05 FILLER                 PIC X(47)          VALUE SPACES.
00089                05 FILLER                 PIC X(39)          VALUE
00090                      'DEANFILE STUDENT LISTING AND GPR REPORT'.
00091                05 FILLER                 PIC X(47)          VALUE SPACES.
00092
00093           01   HEADINGS.
00094                03 FILLER                 PIC X(13)          VALUE SPACES.
00095                03 FILLER                 PIC X(4)           VALUE 'NAME'.
00096                03 FILLER                 PIC X(41)          VALUE SPACES.
00097                03 FILLER                 PIC X(2)           VALUE 'ID'.
00098                03 FILLER                 PIC X(14)          VALUE SPACES.
00099                03 FILLER                 PIC X(5)           VALUE 'MAJOR'.
00100                03 FILLER                 PIC X(8)           VALUE SPACES.
00101                03 FILLER                 PIC X(7)           VALUE 'CLASS'.
00102                03 FILLER                 PIC X(7)           VALUE SPACES.
00103                03 FILLER                 PIC X(4)           VALUE 'SEX'.
00104                03 FILLER                 PIC X(11)          VALUE SPACES.
00105                03 FILLER                 PIC X(3)           VALUE 'GPR'.
00106
00107           01   STUDENT-RECORD-IN.
00108                03 NAME-IN                PIC X(30).
00109                03 ID-IN                  PIC X(9).
00110                03 MAJOR-IN               PIC 9(1).
00111                03 CLASS-IN               PIC 9(1).
00112                03 SEX-IN                 PIC 9(1).
00113                03 CREDIT-HOURS-IN        PIC 9(3).
00114                03 GRADE-POINTS-IN        PIC 9(3).
00115
00116           01   STUDENT-RECORD-OUT.
00117                03 FILLER                 PIC X(13)          VALUE SPACES.
00118                03 NAME-OUT               PIC X(30).
00119                03 FILLER                 PIC X(12)          VALUE SPACES.
00120                03 ID-OUT                 PIC X(9).
00121                03 FILLER                 PIC X(12)          VALUE SPACES.
00122                03 MAJOR-OUT              PIC 9(1).
00123                03 FILLER                 PIC X(12)          VALUE SPACES.
00124                03 CLASS-OUT              PIC 9(1).
00125                03 FILLER                 PIC X(12)          VALUE SPACES.
00126                03 SEX-OUT                PIC 9(1).
00127                03 FILLER                 PIC X(12)          VALUE SPACES.
00128                03 GPR-OUT                PIC 9(1).9(4).
00129                03 FILLER                 PIC X(12)          VALUE SPACES.
00130
```

*(continued)*

```
        5          MATH          14.25.42      OCT 25,1988


     00132          O1   AVERAGE-GRADE-POINT-LINE.
     00133               O3 FILLER              PIC X(94)       VALUE SPACES.
     00134               O3 FILLER              PIC X(21)       VALUE
     00135                    'AVERAGE STUDENT GPR: '.
     00136               O3 AVERAGE-GPR-OUT     PIC 9(1).9(4).
     00137               O3 FILLER              PIC X(4)        VALUE ' ***'.
     00138               O3 FILLER              PIC X(8)        VALUE SPACES.
     00139
     00140          O1   BLANK-LINE.
     00141               O3 FILLER              PIC X(133)      VALUE SPACES.
     00142
```

```
        6          MATH          14.25.42      OCT 25,1988


     00144          PROCEDURE DIVISION.
     00145
     00146          0000-MAIN-PARA.
     00147               PERFORM 1000-INIT-PARA.
     00148               PERFORM 8000-READ-PARA.
     00149               PERFORM 2000-PROCESS-PARA
     00150                    UNTIL END-OF-FILE-FLAG = 1.
     00151               PERFORM 3000-TERMINATION-PARA.
     00152               STOP RUN.
     00153
```

```
        7          MATH          14.25.42      OCT 25,1988


     00155          ****************************************************************
     00156          *    1000-INIT-PARA.                                           *
     00157          *                                                              *
     00158          *    THIS PARAGRAPH OPENS THE DEAN FILE AND REPORT FILE, AND   *
     00159          *    WRITES THE REPORT HEADINGS.                               *
     00160          *                                                              *
     00161          ****************************************************************
     00162
     00163          1000-INIT-PARA.
     00164               OPEN INPUT DEAN-FILE.
     00165               OPEN OUTPUT REPORT-FILE.
     00166               WRITE REPORT-LINE FROM BLANK-LINE
     00167                    AFTER PAGE-TOP.
     00168               WRITE REPORT-LINE FROM PAGE-HEADING
     00169                    AFTER 3.
     00170               WRITE REPORT-LINE FROM HEADINGS
     00171                    AFTER 3.
     00172               WRITE REPORT-LINE FROM BLANK-LINE
     00173                    AFTER 1.
     00174
```

```
        8          MATH          14.25.42      OCT 25,1988


     00176          ****************************************************************
     00177          *    2000-PROCESS-PARA.                                        *
     00178          *                                                              *
     00179          *    THIS PARAGRAPH IS A CONTROL PARAGRAPH FOR                 *
     00180          *                                                              *
     00181          *        2100-CALCULATIONS-PARA                                *
     00182          *        2200-WRITE-REPORT-PARA                                *
     00183          *        8000-READ-PARA                                        *
     00184          *                                                              *
     00185          ****************************************************************
     00186
     00187          2000-PROCESS-PARA.
     00188               PERFORM 2100-CALCULATIONS-PARA.
     00189               PERFORM 2200-WRITE-REPORT-PARA.
     00190               PERFORM 8000-READ-PARA.
     00191
```

*(continued)*

```
   9        MATH         14.25.42      OCT 25,1988

00193        ****************************************************************
00194        *   2100-CALCULATIONS-PARA.                                    *
00195        *                                                              *
00196        *   THIS PARAGRAPH CALCULATES THE STUDENT'S GPR (TO 4 DECIMAL  *
00197        *   PLACES AND ROUNDED) AND ACCUMULATES THE CREDIT HOURS AND   *
00198        *   GRADE POINTS WHICH WILL BE USED TO CALCULATE THE AVERAGE   *
00199        *   STUDENT GPR IN THE 3000-TERMINATION-PARA.                  *
00200        *                                                              *
00201        ****************************************************************
00202
00203          2100-CALCULATIONS-PARA.
00204              COMPUTE GPR ROUNDED = GRADE-POINTS-IN / CREDIT-HOURS-IN.
00205              ADD CREDIT-HOURS-IN TO TOTAL-CREDIT-HOURS.
00206              ADD GRADE-POINTS-IN TO TOTAL-GRADE-POINTS.
00207
```

```
  10        MATH         14.25.42      OCT 25,1988

00209        ****************************************************************
00210        *   2200-WRITE-REPORT-PARA.                                    *
00211        *                                                              *
00212        *   THIS PARAGRAPH MOVES THE APPROPRIATE DATA (STUDENT'S NAME, *
00213        *   ID, MAJOR CODE, CLASS CODE, SEX CODE, AND GPR) TO THE      *
00214        *   APPROPRIATE OUTPUT FIELDS IN THE DETAIL LINE AND THEN      *
00215        *   PRINTS THE DETAIL LINE.                                    *
00216        *                                                              *
00217        ****************************************************************
00218
00219          2200-WRITE-REPORT-PARA.
00220              MOVE NAME-IN TO NAME-OUT.
00221              MOVE ID-IN TO ID-OUT.
00222              MOVE MAJOR-IN TO MAJOR-OUT.
00223              MOVE CLASS-IN TO CLASS-OUT.
00224              MOVE SEX-IN TO SEX-OUT.
00225              MOVE GPR TO GPR-OUT.
00226              WRITE REPORT-LINE FROM STUDENT-RECORD-OUT
00227                  AFTER 1.
00228
```

```
  11        MATH         14.25.42      OCT 25,1988

00230        ******************************************************************
00231        *   8000-READ-PARA.                                              *
00232        *                                                                *
00233        *   THIS PARAGRAPH READS A RECORD FROM THE DEAN FILE.  WHEN THE  *
00234        *   END OF THE FILE HAS BEEN REACHED, THE END-OF-FILE-FLAG WILL  *
00235        *   BE CHANGED FROM O (WHICH INDICATES THAT THERE ARE STILL      *
00236        *   MORE RECORDS TO BE READ FROM THE FILE) TO 1 (WHICH INDI-     *
00237        *   CATES THAT THERE ARE NO MORE RECORDS TO BE READ FROM THE     *
00238        *   FILE.                                                        *
00239        *                                                                *
00240        ******************************************************************
00241
00242          8000-READ-PARA.
00243              READ DEAN-FILE INTO STUDENT-RECORD-IN
00244                  AT END
00245                      MOVE 1 TO END-OF-FILE-FLAG.
00246
```

*(continued)*

```
   12        MATH          14.25.42     OCT 25,1988

00248        ******************************************************
00249        *  3000-TERMINATION-PARA.                            *
00250        *                                                    *
00251        *  THIS PARAGRAPH USES THE ACCUMULATED CREDIT HOURS AND GRADE *
00252        *  POINTS TO CALCULATE THE AVERAGE STUDENT GPR.  THE AVERAGE  *
00253        *  STUDENT GPR IS PRINTED WITH THREE ASTERISKS TO THE RIGHT   *
00254        *  TO DISTINGUISH IT FROM AN ORDINARY DETAIL LINE.  LAST, THE *
00255        *  FILES ARE CLOSED.                                 *
00256        *                                                    *
00257        *  NOTE:   THE RESULTS OF THE DIVISION (TO DETERMINE THE AVER- *
00258        *          AGE STUDENT GPR) ARE STORED DIRECTLY IN THE EDITED  *
00259        *          OUTPUT FIELD INSTEAD OF BEING STORED IN AN INTER-   *
00260        *          MEDIATE FIELD AND THEN BEING MOVED TO AN EDITED     *
00261        *          OUTPUT FIELD.                             *
00262        *                                                    *
00263        ******************************************************
00264
00265        3000-TERMINATION-PARA.
00266            DIVIDE TOTAL-GRADE-POINTS BY TOTAL-CREDIT-HOURS
00267                GIVING AVERAGE-GPR-OUT ROUNDED.
00268            WRITE REPORT-LINE FROM AVERAGE-GRADE-POINT-LINE
00269                AFTER 3.
00270            CLOSE DEAN-FILE.
00271            CLOSE REPORT-FILE.
```

```
                DEANFILE STUDENT LISTING AND GPR REPORT

    NAME                        ID         MAJOR    CLASS    SEX      GPR
    THOMAS WILKINSON         123456789       4        4       1      3.7619
    DON VILLANOSKI          987654321       1        1       1      2.7500
    MICHAEL FOWLER          555555555       2        2       1      3.8966
    TIA FOWLER              888888888       3        3       2      3.4943
    CLINT SMITH             333333333       2        3       1      1.9839
    HOWARD PORTER           454545454       1        1       1      2.3158
    APRIL JONES             777777777       2        3       2      2.8025
    APRIL JACKS             787878778       4        4       2      2.5649
    BRYAN MANN              232323232       3        1       1      2.6667
    ZEKE MORGAN             434356569       2        2       1      2.8947
    BILL ADAM               102302220       4        4       1      2.8092
    JILL MATSON             010101206       2        1       2      2.8947
    TINA MARIO              000000222       4        3       2      2.3380
    CLYDE FELD JR.          129834765       4        2       1      2.9057
    GEORGE MARINAKIES       100010055       5        1       1      2.7083
    JAMES PAPPAS            342537891       5        3       1      2.3253
    STEVE PARKS             908765101       1        1       2      3.8000
    LYNDA MATHER            203040506       3        3       2      2.7538
    KEVIN MCKENN            444455555       2        3       1      3.4933
    IRENE SMITH             001122334       4        1       2      2.0000
    EMILY LYLE              999888777       1        1       2      2.2667
    PEG PORTERHOUSE         123321123       3        4       2      2.9703
    DAN ROBESON             656765679       4        3       1      2.2400
    DANA MILLS              908070600       4        4       2      2.7500
    GEORGE RYAN             564731009       1        2       1      2.4000
    BILLY BOB BARRETT       111000222       1        4       1      2.2500
    MARY JO MARTINEZ        102938475       2        4       2      2.3077
    POLLY ANN FLOWERS       501112234       4        4       2      2.5773
    MATHEW ALTMEN           980980980       5        3       1      3.2258
    DIANE LAWERNCE          263718818       5        2       2      2.5714
    SARA WALKER             828347561       5        3       2      3.5375
    MARIA SANTIAGO          777345777       5        2       2      2.4444
    ANTONIO MARTINEZ        773330666       5        3       1      3.0000
    ROBERTO SMITH           311230099       4        4       1      2.9000
    ANDY BUENZA             000001111       1        2       1      2.7429
    MARIA SANCHEZ           501155003       4        3       2      3.2000
    STACY PHARR             444344344       2        4       2      3.5263
    MICHAEL RYAN            717273747       2        1       1      3.2727
    MARY LITTLE             394958690       2        4       2      3.1579
    ANNIE MARINOS           010203040       2        1       2      2.2727
    C. H. FLOWER            404040404       2        4       1      2.6887
    ROY JOICE               102450555       1        4       1      3.5045
    DAVID LETTER            978675643       3        1       1      2.0000
    JANE CATES              132435467       3        1       2      2.7600
    KEN MARTINEZ            002903992       3        4       1      2.7704
    GEORGE COMONOS          516972420       4        1       1      3.2400
    SESSIE PARSONS          808188808       4        2       2      2.5106
    PEGGY MARTTA            222288885       5        4       2      2.0635
    THOMAS THOMPSON         844839931       5        1       1      2.2857
    WAYNE HEDDER            246808642       5        4       1      3.9694


                                    AVERAGE STUDENT GPR: 2.8570 ***
```

## EXERCISES

### Chapter Review Questions

1. The data name used to store the result in a COMPUTE:
    a.  May be edited
    b.  Must be numeric
    c.  May be a numeric literal
    d.  May be alphanumeric
    e.  None of the above

2. The data name specified by the GIVING option:
    a.  Must be numeric
    b.  May be edited
    c.  Is involved in the calculation of the answer
    d.  May be a numeric literal
    e.  None of the above

3. In order to preserve all initial values in the SUBTRACT statement which option must be used?
    a.  FROM
    b.  GIVING
    c.  ROUNDED
    d.  ON SIZE ERROR
    e.  None of the above

4. With the multiply you are allowed to:
    a.  Get the product of two or more numeric data names
    b.  Get the product of two or more numeric literals
    c.  Get the product of two or more numeric data names and/or literals
    d.  Use numeric and nonnumeric data names
    e.  None of the above

5. If an ADD used the ROUNDED option and a result of 473.5 was to be stored what would the final ANSWER (PIC 9(3)) contain?
    a.  473.5
    b.  473
    c.  474
    d.  Cannot be rounded with .5
    e.  None of the above

6. Similar to the ADD, the SUBTRACT may not incorporate both the FROM and GIVING in the same statement.
    a.  True
    b.  False

7. The ON SIZE ERROR option:
    a.  Checks for final result fields that are too big
    b.  Checks for final result fields that are too small
    c.  Checks for intermediate result fields that are the wrong size
    d.  Both a and b are checked for
    e.  None of the above

8. DIVIDE 5 INTO 10 and DIVIDE 5 BY 10 both provide the same answer of:

    a.   5
    b.   .5
    c.   Both a and b
    d.   2.0
    e.   None of the above

9. The math verb that allows for multiple math operations in one statement is the:

    a.   ADD
    b.   SUBTRACT
    c.   MULTIPLY
    d.   DIVIDE
    e.   COMPUTE

10. Which of the following depicts the hierarchy of operators (from highest to lowest)?

| a. ** | b. – | c. ** | d. +,– | e. *,/ |
|-------|------|-------|--------|--------|
| * | + | *,/ | /,* | ** |
| + | / | +,– | ** | +,– |
| / | * | | | |
| – | ** | | | |

11. Using parentheses in a compute:

    a.   Enhances readability
    b.   Modifies the order of execution
    c.   Is superfluous
    d.   Is required
    e.   a, b and c all could be true

12. When you need to report a count in COBOL, how many data-names would you need for the count?

    a.   One
    b.   Two
    c.   Depends on the type of count
    d.   Depends on whether the count is on a summary report or detail report
    e.   None of the above

13. If you use 77 level items in a program they:

    a.   May be used in the FILE SECTION
    b.   May be used anywhere in the WORKING-STORAGE SECTION
    c.   Must appear last in the WORKING-STORAGE SECTION
    d.   Must appear first in the WORKING-STORAGE SECTION
    e.   None of the above

14. The default data representation for a numeric field is:

    a.   COMP
    b.   COMP-1
    c.   Binary
    d.   Zoned Decimal
    e.   Packed Decimal

15. A more efficient data representation for a numeric field that is to be used mathematically is:
    a. Display
    b. COMP
    c. COMP-3
    d. COMP-4
    e. None of the above

## Discussion Questions

1. Briefly explain the evaluation of a compute that has nested parentheses.
2. Briefly explain how 77 level item's may be avoided.
3. Briefly contrast the DISPLAY and COMP-3 options.
4. Explain the hierarchy of operators.
5. Explain the use of the GIVING option.

## Practice Problems

1. Given the following equations, convert them into appropriate COBOL math statements:
    a. $Y = A + B$
    b. $TOTAL = A + B + 5.9 + C$
    c. $ANSWER = A + \dfrac{B \times C}{D} - E^2$
    d. $Y = A$
    e. $Y = A - \dfrac{B}{C^2} + D$
    f. $Y^2 = \dfrac{C}{D} - A$
    g. $ANS = (A + B) / (D - E)^2 (A - D)^3 (B + E)^2 / (A - E)$
    h. $Y = (A + B)^3 (C - D) (E + A) (A - C)^2$
       (Do with and without COMPUTE)

2. Evaluate the following using the values given for each problem:

   A = 10   C = 3
   B = 2    D = 4

   | | | Answer | Stored In |
   |---|---|---|---|
   | a. | COMPUTE Y = A + B – (D – B) ** B | _____ | _____ |
   | b. | COMPUTE ANS = (A – D) ** 2 / C | _____ | _____ |
   | c. | MULTIPLY D BY C GIVING F | _____ | _____ |
   | d. | ADD A B C TO D | _____ | _____ |
   | e. | SUBTRACT B D FROM A GIVING F | _____ | _____ |
   | f. | COMPUTE ANS ROUNDED = (D + C = B) ** 2 / (A – B * C) | _____ | _____ |
   | g. | DIVIDE B INTO A | _____ | _____ |
   | h. | COMPUTE ANS = (A – D + B) ** 2 / (((D * C) ** 2 – (A * D + D)) ** .5 – B) | _____ | _____ |

3. Write the following program or program segments:
    a. Write the Procedure Division statements necessary to read the Inventory data file, Data File C and write a report that list all data. For each item add the extension of total cost (QOH × Cost Per Unit).

b.    Write the Procedure Division statements necessary to read the Inventory data file, Data File C, and list all items below their ROP.  A summary report should be included that shows:

      1.    Count of items to be ordered

      2.    Percent of total items below ROP

c.    Using the Dean File Data Set (Form 2), write the procedure division statements necessary to calculate and print each student's GPR.  Show the average GPR as a Column Total.

## Programming Projects

The following assignments rely on the data dictionary, library elements and data sets found in the Project Sets Section of your text.

1. Do the Project Management Math Assignment in Project A.

2. Do the Employee System Math Assignment in Project B.

## 8

# MAKING DECISIONS IN COBOL—THE IF VERB

**OBJECTIVES**   So far all our logic paths have been straightforward. The sequence construct has been our logic structure to this point. The only deviation has been the PERFORM. . .UNTIL, which controls an iterative or looping construct.

The main purpose of this chapter is to examine the IF verb which allows for alternative logic paths. You will see various IF structures, and you will see how these structures are coded. In fact, you will see a particular structure that causes us trouble in COBOL, and also see how a COBOL '85 feature will help us avoid this trouble.

Throughout the chapter you will see segments of COBOL programs illustrating solutions to a variety of problems. You will also have a complete running program at the end of the chapter.

## TOPICS

- IF structures
- IF THEN ELSE
- nested IFs
- relational operators
- logical operators
- numeric comparisons
- nonnumeric comparisons

- counting and accumulating
- class test
- sign test
- condition names
- END-IF
- CASE structure

## KEY WORDS

- IF
- ELSE
- EQUAL TO (=)
- LESS THAN (<)
- GREATER THAN (>)
- NOT
- AND

- OR
- NUMERIC
- ALPHABETIC
- POSITIVE
- NEGATIVE
- EVALUATE

## INTRODUCTION

The IF statement in COBOL is a very useful and powerful tool. Through the IF you are able to build logic structures that allow for multiple logic paths. You recall, I'm sure, that one of the basic logic constructs of structured programming is the selection construct. This construct is handled with the IF verb.

Through the IF statement, you may select among paths of logic. You will also see that this selection involves the testing of conditions. These conditions may be simple conditions involving EQUAL TO (=), LESS THAN (<), and/or GREATER THAN (>) relationships. The conditions may also be complex; they may allow the use of the logical operators AND and OR. In fact, our conditions may also test for the state of a data item. Is it NUMERIC or ALPHABETIC? Is it POSITIVE or NEGATIVE?

The logic power afforded by IF is tremendous. The logic structures you may build can become very sophisticated and very complex. By combining the relational and logical operators for the selection of separate paths which themselves have complex conditions for the selection of paths, you can get very complex in a hurry. Such complex structures are called nested IFs. They are very popular, and they are used often.

With the IF our conditions may be easy to read, depending on the data-names involved. That is, IF GROSS-PAY > 50 is relatively easy to understand. However, IF GP > 50 might not be as readily understood. Major culprits in our use of the IF statement are abbreviations or codes. Statements like IF MAJOR-CODE = 1, or worse, IF MC = 1 cannot be understood unless you know the code. Wouldn't IF ACCOUNTING-MAJOR make more sense? Sure it would. Well, COBOL helps make more sense with condition names. We will study them too.

Finally, you will be shown a very important new feature of COBOL, the EVALUATE verb. This verb lets us handle one of the other structured programming logic constructs, the CASE structure.

## THE PROBLEM

Through the Math Chapter all our problems could be solved without our having to make decisions (except in the case of the PERFORM. . .UNTIL). Let's look at another situation. Say the dean asked you to list all the students in the dean's file. The dean also asked for a count of all students and the average GPR for all students.

That's the type of problem we have been working. For each student in the file, you would:

```
ADD 1 TO STUDENT-COUNT.
ADD GPR TO TOTAL-GPR.
```

Once you reached the end of file, you could calculate the average GPR and write both the STUDENT-COUNT and average GPR.

Now, what if the dean changed his mind and decided he wanted a count of students by major? That is, he wanted to know how many students were Accounting majors and how many were Information System majors, and so on (see Data File A). This is a little more complex. You need to build your logic to choose among all the major codes so that you can count each student according to his or her MAJOR-

CODE. Well, guess what? You need to build separate logic paths for each value of MAJOR-CODE. How do you do that? With the IF verb!

## THE IF STRUCTURE

When you studied the programming logic structures, I discussed the selection construct and said that its common name is the **IF THEN ELSE**. The basic format is given below.

<u>IF</u> condition  
    executable statement   ◄——true path  
    ⎡ executable statement ⎤  
    ⎣    . . .           ⎦

<u>ELSE</u> condition  
    executable statement   ◄——false path  
    ⎡ executable statement ⎤  
    ⎣    . . .           ⎦

The **IF** is interpreted this way: If the condition is true, then the executable statement(s) immediately following the condition and preceding the **ELSE** are executed. If the condition is false, then the executable statement(s) following the **ELSE** are executed.

Let's look at an example: Assume that a student's GPR is 3.5. The following illustrates how the **IF** is evaluated.

```
IF GPR > 3.00
    ADD 1 TO HONOR-STUDENT-COUNT
ELSE
    ADD 1 TO REGULAR-STUDENT-COUNT.
```

Since GPR is a 3.5 (we looked in memory and saw the value with our special eyes!!), the condition is true and the ADD is executed so that student is counted as an honor student.

Suppose now that we look into memory again and see a GPR for the next student of 1.95. Now the condition is false, and the ADD will be executed so that student is counted as a regular student.

### Typical IF Structures

See how that works? Well, let's make sure by looking at some popular IF structures. However, please keep in mind that no matter which structure you use or how complex the condition, the **IF** still says, "if true follow one execution path, and if false follow another execution path."

**Do Something Extra Structure.** This structure can best be seen by representing it with a flowchart.

You can see from Figure 8.1 that when the condition is true, the yes branch, PROCESS$_1$ and PROCESS$_2$ are extra compared with the no branch.

**FIGURE 8.1**
Do Something Extra IF
Structure

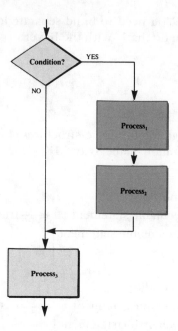

An example of this form would be the case for calculating overtime pay when the number of hours worked is greater than 40. Figure 8.2 shows both the flowchart and **IF** statement that corresponds to this example.

**FIGURE 8.2**
Overtime Pay Example of IF

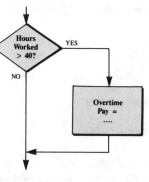

```
IF HOURS-WORKED > 40
   COMPUTE OVERTIME-PAY = ...
```

Noticed the **IF**, didn't you? You're right! I didn't use an **ELSE**. Well, there is nothing ELSE to do. But besides that problem, do you understand the example? I hope so.

Now, back to the ELSEless **IF**. Technically, every **IF** should be matched with an **ELSE**. Purists in structured programming insist on it. So Figure 8.2 could have been shown as I indicate in Figure 8.3.

Notice that the logic shown in the flowchart *did not* change. The **IF** did. I added a feature: **NEXT SENTENCE**. It causes execution to go to the next sentence. Since the **IF** is a COBOL sentence, it ends with a period. Therefore, using **NEXT SENTENCE** simply does what it says. It may be used for either path, true or false, but if used, it must be the only statement in that path.

Which is better? I don't use the **NEXT SENTENCE** illustrated in Figure 8.3. I like the **IF** in Figure 8.2. In both cases the sentence following the **IF** will be done next, so why add extra code that, in my opinion, does nothing for readability? However, my bias doesn't make it the best. Use whatever you are comfortable with or whatever your instructor requires.

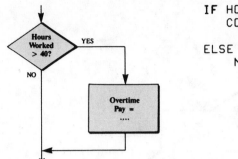

```
IF HOURS-WORKED > 40
        COMPUTE OVERTIME-PAY =...

ELSE
        NEXT SENTENCE.
```

**FIGURE 8.3**
**Overtime Pay Example of IF ELSE**

**Do One or the Other Structure.**  The next structure is an extension of the first. However, unlike the first structure, each logic path has something to be done.  Figure 8.4 shows this structure.

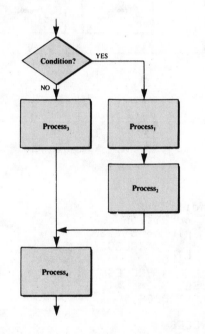

```
IF condition
        PROCESS₁
        PROCESS₂

ELSE
        PROCESS₃.

PROCESS₄.
```

**FIGURE 8.4**
**Do One or the Other IF Structure**

See where it gets its name?  If the condition is true, PROCESS₁ and PROCESS₂ are done.  If false, PROCESS₃ is done.  But never are all three processes done on the same pass.  Either PROCESS₁ and PROCESS₂ or PROCESS₃ is done.  In both cases PROCESS₄ will be done.

**The Nested IF.**  Up to this point I have talked just about processes being done. What may those processes be?  Any executable statement: READ, WRITE, ADD, MOVE and even another **IF**, hence the name Nested **IF**, one **IF** condition on another (Figure 8.5).

Interpreting this structure just follows what we have done earlier.  If Condition₁ is true, then Condition₂ is checked.  If Condition₂ is true, then Condition₃ is checked.  If Condition₃ is true, then PROCESS₄ is done.  In other words, for PROCESS₄ to be done, all conditions have to be true.  When is PROCESS₁ done?  When Condition₁ is false.  PROCESS₂ is done when Condition₁ is true and Condition₂ is false.  And, PROCESS₃ is done when Condition₁ and Condition₂ are true while Condition₃ is false.  All logic paths come together to do PROCESS₅.

What does the **IF** sentence look like?  It's sort of neat looking (Figure 8.6).

**FIGURE 8.5**
Flowchart Showing Nested IF
Structure

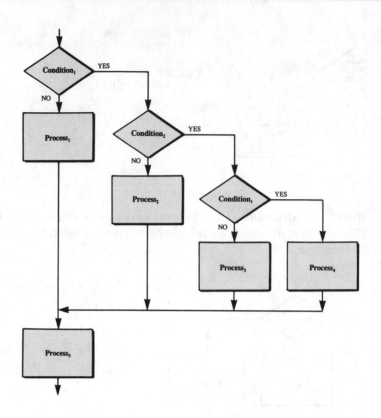

**FIGURE 8.6**
"Code" for Nested IF

```
IF condition₁
   IF condition₂
      IF condition₃
            PROCESS₄
      ELSE
            PROCESS₃
   ELSE
         PROCESS₂
ELSE
      PROCESS₁.
```

A couple of notes are needed here. First, all the **ELSE**s match up with an **IF**. In fact, that's a requirement of COBOL. However, the indentation and alignment, each **IF** with its **ELSE**, are standards used in this text. Notice also that the **ELSE**, here and in previous examples, is on a line by itself. It might help to look at the standards again (Appendix D).

Figure 8.7 shows another form of nesting.

The difference in the two nesting examples is that Figure 8.6 shows nesting on the yes path, while Figure 8.7 shows nesting on the no path. You should note that by combining Figure 8.6 and Figure 8.7 you would have nesting on both logic paths. This type of logic structure is not only possible but common.

### The Operators

Now that you have seen several of the IF structures and studied some of the rules associated with using the IF, it is time to turn your attention to the conditions. All our examples showed conditions being tested and branches being taken based on whether the conditions were true or false. The conditions in COBOL may be built using relational operators and logical operators.

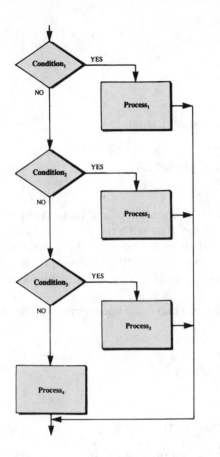

**FIGURE 8.7**
Nesting on the No Path

```
IF condition₁
    PROCESS₁
ELSE
    IF condition₂
        PROCESS₂
    ELSE
        IF condition₃
            PROCESS₃
        ELSE
            PROCESS₄
```

**Relational Operators.**    There are have several relationships that may be tested for in IF conditions. You build these relational tests using the following operators:

| | |
|---|---|
| $=$ | **EQUAL TO** |
| $>$ | **GREATER THAN** |
| $<$ | **LESS THAN** |
| NOT $=$ | **NOT EQUAL TO** (less than or greater than) |
| NOT $>$ | **NOT GREATER THAN** (equal to or less than) |
| NOT $<$ | **NOT LESS THAN** (equal to or greater than) |
| $> =$ | ('85 COBOL for greater than or equal to) |
| $< =$ | ('85 COBOL for less than or equal to) |

For instance, you can build the following conditions.

```
IF MAJOR-CODE = 2 . . .
```

or

```
IF MAJOR-CODE NOT = REQUESTED-MAJOR . . .
```

Generally, you can build relationships by comparing:

- two data-names
- a data-name with a literal where both are numeric
- a data-name with a literal where both are nonnumeric

- a data-name with an expression
- a literal with an expression
- two expressions

Examples of these would be:

```
IF LINE-COUNT    > MAXIMUM-LINES . . .
IF LINE-COUNT    = 25 . . .
IF SEX-CODE      = 'F' . . .
IF SALARY-LIMIT  < YTDE + SALARY . . .
IF HRS-WK - 40   > 10 . . .
```

A good use and example of the relational operator would be to control the number of detail lines written per page. Let's say that with the required headings, page and column, you design the detail report to allow for no more than 20 detail lines.

What have we been doing so far? This is something I have just ignored until now. I just printed headings on the first page of the report and just kept printing going from page to page continuously.

Let's look at our sequential file model and make the appropriate changes.

```
PERFORM 1000-HEADING-PARA.
PERFORM 2000-READ-PARA.
PERFORM 3000-PROCESS-PARA
    UNTIL FLAG = 1.

1000-HEADINGS-PARA.
    WRITE REPORT-LINE FROM TITLE-LINE
        AFTER PAGE-TOP.
    WRITE REPORT-LINE FROM COLUMN-HEADINGS
        AFTER 4.

2000-READ-PARA.
    READ . . .

3000-PROCESS-PARA.
    MOVE(s)
            .
            .
            .
    IF LINE-COUNT = 20
        PERFORM 1000-HEADINGS-PARA
        MOVE 0 TO LINE-COUNT.

    WRITE . . .

    ADD 1 TO LINE-COUNT.

    PERFORM 2000-READ-PARA.
```

Notice that I have used a generic example. The control of lines on a page is independent of the type of data. Look at 3000-PROCESS-PARA. Without the IF and ADD, it's the old MOVE, WRITE, READ, PROCESS module. However, by adding one to LINE-COUNT every time a line is written, I can check the number of lines that have been written before I write the next line. So, when LINE-COUNT equals 20, the headings will be written and LINE-COUNT will be set back to zero.

> ## TIP
>
> Don't forget to reset line count back to zero. If you don't, then once you write the headings on the second page of the detail report, you won't write them again because line count will not equal 20 again.

**Logical Operators.**        Now that you have seen the relational operators, it's time to show you how to build compound conditions. That is, you may need to check two or more conditions in an IF statement.

The logical operators available to us are the AND and OR. So we may build statements that say:

$$\text{IF condition}_1 \text{ AND condition}_2$$

$$\text{IF condition}_1 \text{ OR condition}_2$$

We can even combine them by saying:

$$\text{IF condition}_1 \text{ AND condition}_2 \text{ OR condition}_3 \cdots$$

Of course, the conditions still use the relational operators we discussed in the previous section. As you can tell, we can handle complex logic with the IF.

How are AND and OR evaluated? For AND, both conditions must be true for the IF to be true. With OR, either of the conditions *or both* must be true for the IF to be true. Figure 8.8 shows this rule.

### EVALUATION OF <u>AND</u> LOGICAL OPERATOR

#### LOGICAL RELATION

IF condition$_1$ AND condition$_2$

| | | |
|---|---|---|
| true | true | → evaluated as: true |
| true | false | → false |
| false | true | → false |
| false | false | → false |

### EVALUATION OF <u>OR</u> LOGICAL OPERATOR

#### LOGICAL RELATION

IF condition$_1$ OR condition$_2$

| | | |
|---|---|---|
| true | true | → evaluated as: true |
| true | false | → true |
| false | true | → true |
| false | false | → false |

**FIGURE 8.8**
Logical Operators AND and OR

Figure 8.8 shows that an AND relationship is true in one case and false in three cases, while with OR the IF is evaluated as true in three cases and false in only one case.

Assuming that a student's record from DEAN-FILE had a MAJOR-CODE of 2, a CLASS-CODE of 4 and a SEX-CODE of 1, how would the following IFs be evaluated?

| Statement | Evaluated as |
|---|---|
| IF MAJOR-CODE = 2 AND CLASS-CODE = 4 | TRUE<br>since both are true |
| IF CLASS-CODE = 4 AND SEX-CODE = 2 | FALSE<br>since SEX-CODE = 1 |
| IF MAJOR-CODE = 3 OR SEX-CODE = 1 | TRUE<br>since SEX-CODE = 1 |
| IF MAJOR-CODE = 3 OR CLASS-CODE = 4<br>AND SEX-CODE = 2 | FALSE |

The first three are understandable from our discussion. However, in the last example, I threw you a curve. To evaluate that IF statement, you must have some information. In particular, you must know that there is a hierarchy of logical operators. All **AND**s are evaluated first, and then the **OR**s are evaluated. Multiple operators of the same hierarchial level are evaluated from left to right. It doesn't stop there. We can change the hierarchy by using parentheses.

Let's look at some examples in Figures 8.9 and 8.10.

**FIGURE 8.9**
**Example of Order of Evaluation of ANDs and ORs**

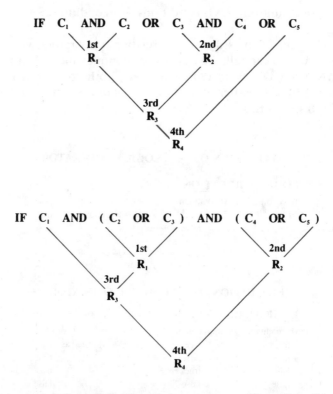

**FIGURE 8.10**
**Effect of Parentheses on Logical Operator Hierarchy**

Figure 8.9 is straightforward. The first operator evaluated is $C_1$ AND $C_2$. Second to be evaluated is $C_3$ AND $C_4$. Then, the leftmost OR, $R_1$ OR $R_2$, is evaluated and finally, the last to be evaluated is $R_3$ OR $C_5$.

## TIP

To evaluate a complex IF, evaluate the ANDs first and rewrite the IF statement as you go. Doing so, the following IF would be handled as:

*(continued)*

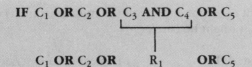

Do this until you have nothing but ORs. Then it is easy to evaluate since any one true makes the IF true.

By the way, do you now see why the IF statement, IF MAJOR-CODE = 3 OR CLASS-CODE = 4 AND SEX-CODE = 2, was false? Well, let's examine it.

IF  MAJOR-CODE = 3  **OR**  CLASS-CODE = 4 **AND** SEX-CODE = 2

false          OR                    false

Since at least one true is required for the IF to be true, you have a false case.

## TIP

**When you build IF relations, try to keep them simple.**

How would you code the following logic? Count all students (DEAN-FILE) that are not Accounting or Information Systems majors. Would you code:

```
IF MAJOR-CODE NOT = 1 OR MAJOR-CODE NOT = 2
    ADD 1 TO KOUNT.
```

If that's what you would code, your answer would be wrong. Try this. What if MAJOR-CODE was 5? Then you would correctly ADD 1 TO KOUNT. However, what if MAJOR- CODE was 2? You would incorrectly ADD 1 TO KOUNT. You don't agree, do you? This is a very common mistake. The IF reads correctly, but the combination of NOT logic and the logical operators always seems to cause a problem. A code of 2 means that it is not = 1. Therefore, the IF is true, since all that is required for an OR relation is one condition to be true. So be careful!

## TIP

**Using logical operators with NOT logic tends to tie your minds into knots. If you must use NOT—OR logic, make sure to use parentheses.**

Now that you have seen both relational and logical operators you might have a question about the nested IF and an IF with the AND logical operator. Are they the same? Not quite! Look at the example in Figure 8.11.

Notice the difference? The nested IF allows you to do some process on each of the condition's no paths. On the other hand, the AND allows the choice of only one path or the other. It does not allow you the numerous paths offered by the nested IF. Look at it in code. It might be clearer.

| Nested IF | Logical AND Operator |
|---|---|
| IF condition$_1$ | IF condition$_1$ and condition$_2$ |
|    IF condition$_2$ |    and condition$_3$ |
|       IF condition$_3$ |       PROCESS$_1$ |
|          PROCESS$_4$ | ELSE |
|       ELSE |       PROCESS$_2$. |
|          PROCESS$_3$ | |
|    ELSE | |
|       PROCESS$_2$ | |
| ELSE | |
|    PROCESS$_1$. | |

One method is not better than the other. They both have their application. However, they are not the same. So be careful.

**FIGURE 8.11**
**Comparison of Nested If with IF. . .AND**

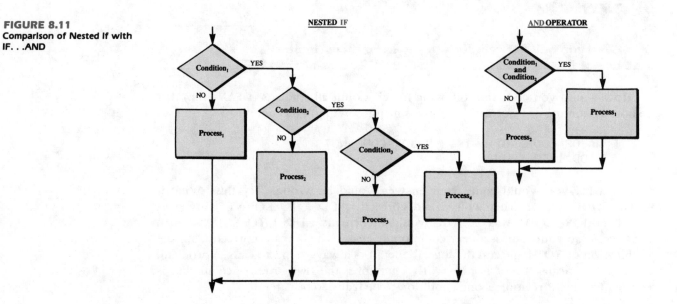

### Types of Comparisons

So far you have seen how to use the relational and logical operators with the IF statement. We need now to look at the operands involved in the relational operations. We need to discuss numeric comparisons, and nonnumeric comparisons and mixing of operand types.

**Numeric.** The operands used in a relational test may both be numeric. They may be either numeric data-names or numeric literals. The evaluation is done as you would expect. Let's study a few.

In the statement IF A = B

| when A = | and B = | is evaluated as: |
|----------|---------|------------------|
| 5        | 5       | true             |
| 5.1      | 5       | false            |
| 5.0      | 5       | true             |
| 5.00     | 5.01    | false            |

That's pretty much as expected. However, you may have trouble if you mix types of operands; that is, compare a numeric data-name with a nonnumeric literal. For instance:

In the statement IF A = '5'

| when A = | and PIC | is evaluated as: |
|----------|---------|------------------|
| 5        | 9(1)    | true             |
| 5        | 9(4)    | false            |

The second example is false because the two values compared are actually 0005 = '5'. And, since one of the operands is nonnumeric, the comparison is done from the leftmost byte, one byte at a time. Therefore, 0 is not equal to 5 and the IF is false.

## TIP

**Always make both operands numeric for a numeric test. Don't mix operands!**

**Nonnumeric.** As with the numeric operands, both should be nonnumeric. They may be either nonnumeric data-names or nonnumeric literals. The evaluation of a nonnumeric test is done starting from the leftmost byte until a non-equal is found. Let's look at some examples (assume a PIC X(4)).

In the statement IF X = Y

| when X = | and Y = | is evaluated as |
|----------|---------|-----------------|
| CATƀ     | DOGƀ    | false           |
| CATƀ     | CATƀ    | true            |
| CATS     | CATƀ    | false           |

The first two examples are clear. CAT is not equal to DOG and CAT is equal to CAT. The third example illustrates that the values have to be exactly equal to compare equal. What if X had a PIC X(6) and Y a PIC X(4)?

$$\text{IF X} \quad = \quad \text{Y}$$
assumed value        catƀƀƀƀ   catƀ

Would this statement be true or false? True; unequal size does not affect the evaluation of the contents.

Equal comparisons are not the only thing we use. How does the computer evaluate inequalities? That is:

$$IF \quad A < B$$
$$\text{assumed value} \quad CAT < DOG$$

Is DOG < CAT or not? The comparison starts with the leftmost byte, so the question really becomes is D < C? No, it's not. But it's not just because I say so. It's because of the collating sequence used by the system.

Remember the brief look at EBCDIC representation of numbers? All characters have a certain code also, and in EBCDIC an A comes before a B and so forth. The code for an A is 11000001 and for a B is 11000010. So, B is greater than A. And C is greater than B and so forth through Z.

What about fields of different lengths? Say we compare two fields that contain the following values:

JOE SMITH        JOE SMITHVILLE

How do they compare? Well, SMITH would evaluate as less-than, because the equality would hold for each character through the H. Then, a blank would be compared with a V and a blank comes before a V in the collating sequence.

Have you forgotten that we started this whole discussion because the dean wanted to know the number of students within each major? Well, I haven't forgotten. We are now ready to look at the logic using pseudocode.

```
SET counts to 0.
READ 1st record.
DO WHILE not EOF
    IF MAJOR-CODE = 1
        ADD 1 to ACCOUNTING-COUNT
    ELSE
        IF MAJOR-CODE = 2
            ADD 1 to INFO-SYSTEMS-COUNT
        ELSE
            IF MAJOR-CODE = 3
                ADD 1 to FINANCE-COUNT
            ELSE
                IF MAJOR-CODE = 4
                    ADD 1 to MANAGEMENT-COUNT
                ELSE
                    ADD 1 to MARKETING-COUNT.
    READ a record.
END DO.
WRITE counts.
```

Now, what would the procedural code look like? Here is one possibility using the sequential file model.

```
PERFORM 1000-READ-PARA.
PERFORM 2000-PROCESS-PARA
    UNTIL FLAG = 1.
    .
    .
```

```
1000-READ-PARA.
    READ-DEAN-FILE . . .

2000-PROCESS-PARA.,
    IF MAJOR-CODE = 1
        ADD 1 TO ACCOUNTING-COUNT
    ELSE
        IF MAJOR-CODE = 2
            ADD 1 TO INFO-SYSTEMS-COUNT
        ELSE
            IF MAJOR-CODE = 3
                ADD 1 TO FINANCE-COUNT
            ELSE
                IF MAJOR-CODE = 4
                    ADD 1 TO MANAGEMENT-COUNT
                ELSE
                    ADD 1 TO MARKETING-COUNT.

    PERFORM 1000-READ-PARA.
```

Do you agree that the preceding code solves our problem? It does! It causes one to be added to the appropriate count, depending upon the student's major code value. Therefore, for every student who has a major code of 2, a one will be added to INFO-SYSTEMS-COUNT. It works the same for all the major codes. So, once all students have been processed, we wind up with the five counts the dean wanted.

## TIP

**The logical association between a code and corresponding data-name is the programmers responsibility.**

### Data Validation

One of the application areas that is very common in data processing is the validation of data. Generally, these validation tests fall into the following categories:

- sequence test
- presence test
- range test
- reasonableness test
- type test

**Sequence Testing.**     Many applications require that the data be in either ascending sequence or descending sequence. That is, some key field, say employee number, is used to order the file. Then the programs using that ordered file check to insure that the data is in sequence.

The process paragraph will have an IF check similar to the following:

```
IF EMPLOYEE-NUMBER NOT > PREVIOUS-EMPLOYEE-NUMBER
    PERFORM ERROR-PARA
ELSE
    PERFORM GO-AHEAD-AND-PROCESS-PARA.
```

**Presence Testing.**　This test does exactly what it says. It checks to see if a field that is supposed to contain data does in fact contain data. An IF statement like the following one could be used:

```
IF STUDENT-NAME = SPACES
    PERFORM BAD-NAME-PARA.
```

**Range Testing.**　In range testing you are trying to ensure that data fields are within a certain expected range of values. For instance, I do a range test on my student's exam grades with an IF statement like:

```
IF EXAM1 < 0 OR EXAM1 > 100
    PERFORM BAD-EXAM-PARA.
```

**Reasonableness Testing.**　This test is used to ensure, or try to ensure anyway, that data fields contain a reasonable value. For instance, in a payroll program we might check to make sure that the net pay is not greater than some set value.

```
IF FACULTY-NET-PAY > 1000 OR
    GRADUATE-ASSISTANT-NET-PAY > 2000
        PERFORM UNREASONABLE-PAY-PARA.
```

So, if a faculty member's salary is over 1,000 dollars, we report it as unreasonably high and don't print the check. We do the same for a graduate student if the pay is over 2,000 dollars. Just kidding about the limits, but do you see what we mean by reasonable?

**Type Test.**　Within the type test you find two tests: the sign test and the class test. The sign test is testing to see if a value is positive or negative. The general format is:

$$\underline{\text{IF}}\text{ data-name IS } [\ \underline{\text{NOT}}\ ]\ \left\{ \begin{array}{l} \underline{\text{POSITIVE}} \\ \underline{\text{NEGATIVE}} \end{array} \right\}$$

executable statement(s)

$$\left[ \begin{array}{l} \underline{\text{ELSE}} \\ \text{executable statement(s)} \end{array} \right].$$

You may test a field that is signed or unsigned. But if the field is unsigned, the value is always evaluated as positive, except for a zero which is considered neither positive nor negative.

The class test allows you to test a data field to see if it's numeric or alphabetic. The general format for this test is:

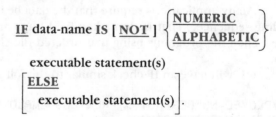

$$\underline{\text{IF}}\text{ data-name IS } [\ \underline{\text{NOT}}\ ]\ \left\{ \begin{array}{l} \underline{\text{NUMERIC}} \\ \underline{\text{ALPHABETIC}} \end{array} \right\}$$

executable statement(s)

$$\left[ \begin{array}{l} \underline{\text{ELSE}} \\ \text{executable statement(s)} \end{array} \right].$$

A field is considered to be NUMERIC if it contains the digits 0–9 and a sign. The field tested may have either a PIC of 9 or a PIC of X.

A field is considered to be ALPHABETIC if it contains the characters A–Z and the blank. The field tested may have either a PIC of X or a PIC of A.

---

## TIP

If you write a data validation program, use PIC X for all fields. That way a check for range or reasonableness does not have to be preceded by a numeric test.

---

Let's look at some examples of these tests:

| Data Item Value | Test | Results |
|---|---|---|
| 1234 | NUMERIC | True |
| 1234 | NOT NUMERIC | False |
| ABCD | ALPHABETIC | True |
| ABCD | NOT ALPHABETIC | False |
| +1234 | NUMERIC | True |
| AB12 | NUMERIC | False |
| AB12 | ALPHABETIC | False |
| AB12 | NOT NUMERIC | True |
| AB12 | NOT ALPHABETIC | True |

---

## TIP

Testing a field as NOT ALPHABETIC is not the equivalent of testing a field as NUMERIC. The field could be ALPHANUMERIC. Always check for a numeric field directly; that is, IF data-name NUMERIC.

---

### Condition Names

As you have probably noticed, many fields in input files contain codes instead of full descriptions. That is, codes of 1 and 2 for male and female or codes of 1, 2, 3, 4 and 5 for major are not unusual.

Using the codes in the program leads to IF statements that may be unclear or requires the reader to know all the codes in order to check logic structure. Remember our solution to the count of students within each major? It involved several of these IFs:

```
IF MAJOR-CODE = 1
    ADD 1 TO ACCOUNTING-COUNT
ELSE
    IF MAJOR-CODE = 2
        ADD 1 TO INFO-SYSTEMS-COUNT
    ELSE
        .
        .
```

The reader might not remember if 1 is for Accounting or not. Wouldn't it be nice to be able to make it more understandable? I mean, wouldn't

```
IF ACCOUNTING-STUDENT
      ADD 1 TO ACCOUNTING-COUNT
ELSE
      IF INFO-SYSTEMS-STUDENT
            ADD 1 TO INFO-SYSTEMS-COUNT
      ELSE
                  .
                  .
```

be easier to understand? I think so, and I'm sure you do also. Therefore, the next question I expect is how do you do that? My answer is very easily!

First of all, what I used is called a condition name. It's called that because it may be used only with condition statements:

IF condition name

or

PERFORM · · · UNTIL condition name

A condition name *is not* a data location. It is a name associated with a particular value a data-name may have. So, it's the name of a value, not the name of a location. It is set up in the DATA DIVISION using 88 level indicators. The format of 88 level items is:

88 condition name __VALUE__ literal.

The best way to see this is with an example. Let's code the condition names for our student's major code.

```
01    STUDENT-RECORD-IN.
      03    NAME-IN            PIC X(30).
      03    ID-IN             PIC X(9).
      03    MAJOR-CODE        PIC 9(1).
            88   ACCOUNTING-STUDENT      VALUE 1.
            88   INFO-SYSTEMS-STUDENT    VALUE 2.
            88   FINANCE-STUDENT         VALUE 3.
            88   MANAGEMENT-STUDENT      VALUE 4.
            88   MARKETING-STUDENT       VALUE 5.
      03    CLASS-CODE        PIC 9(1).
      03    SEX-CODE          PIC 9(1).
      03    GPR               PIC 9(1)V9(4).
```

This record now contains condition names associated with the value of MAJOR-CODE. When you say:

IF FINANCE-STUDENT

it is the same as saying:

```
        IF MAJOR-CODE = 3
```

But the condition name makes the IF more easily understood.

Could you have done the same with CLASS-CODE and SEX-CODE? Sure, you could have. For instance:

```
03    CLASS-CODE              PIC 9(1).
      88 FRESHMAN             VALUE 1.
      88 SOPHOMORE            VALUE 2.
                   .
                   .
```

Could you have done it with the MAJOR-CODE if it had a picture of X? Yes, you could have.

```
03    MAJOR-CODE             PIC X(1).
      88  ACCOUNTING-STUDENT         VALUE '1'.
      88  INFO-SYSTEMS-STUDENT       VALUE '2'.
                   .
                   .
```

The difference is that the value is a nonnumeric literal instead of a numeric literal.

What if the codes for male and female were M and F? Then the code would be:

```
03    SEX-CODE              PIC X(1).
      88  MALE              VALUE 'M'.
      88  FEMALE            VALUE 'F'.
```

## TIP

**Make sure that the literal matches the PIC clause in type: PIC 9 for numeric literal and PIC X for nonnumeric literal.**

A nice application for 88 levels is with end of file checking. Instead of having to say UNTIL FLAG = 1, you can now use something more easily understood. Assume you have the following record description:

```
01    ARE-THERE-MORE-RECORDS      VALUE 'YES'.
      88   MORE-RECORDS           VALUE 'YES'.
      88   NO-MORE-RECORDS        VALUE 'NO'.
```

Then we could code the PERFORM. . .UNTIL and the READ as follows:

```
        PERFORM 1000-READ-PARA.
        PERFORM 2000-PROCESS-PARA
            UNTIL NO-MORE-RECORDS.

    1000-READ-PARA.
        READ DEAN-FILE INTO STUDENT-RECORD-IN
            AT END
                MOVE 'NO' TO ARE-THERE-MORE-RECORDS.
```

Notice that I used the condition name associated with the value 'NO' with the UNTIL. I initialized the data-name ARE-THERE-MORE-RECORDS to 'YES' and then moved 'NO' to ARE-THERE-MORE-RECORDS at end of the file.

## TIP

**Use data-names for indicators and switches that ask a question. It helps readability!**

The use of condition names is not limited to making condition testing more understandable and readable. They are also nice for data validation. The value we associate with a condition name may actually be more than a literal. In reality, we may specify values three ways:

- as literals
- as a range of values
- as a set of values

For instance, with the MAJOR-CODE I could have added another 88 level shown in the manner below:

```
03   MAJOR-CODE                        PIC 9(1).
     88
        .
        .
     88  VALID-MAJOR-CODE              VALUE 1, 2, 3, 4, 5.
```

Now, to check to see if I have a valid code, I don't have to ask:

```
IF MAJOR-CODE NOT = 1 AND MAJOR-CODE NOT = 2
        AND MAJOR-CODE NOT = 3 AND MAJOR-CODE NOT = 4
        AND MAJOR-CODE NOT = 5
    PERFORM BAD-CODE-PARA
ELSE
        .
        .
```

or

```
IF NOT ACCOUNTING-STUDENT AND NOT INFO-SYSTEMS-STUDENT
        .
        .
```

With the additional 88, I can simply code:

```
IF NOT VALID-MAJOR-CODE
    PERFORM BAD-CODE-PARA
ELSE
        .
        .
```

Isn't it easier to code the IF to validate the codes using the 88 with the set of values? I could also have coded the 88 with a range by saying:

```
88   VALID-MAJOR-CODE     VALUE 1 THROUGH 5.
```

This allows for the same easy code.

Be careful using ranges. If the class codes were F, S, J and N for the four classes, and you coded:

```
88 VALID-CLASS-CODE        VALUE 'F' THROUGH 'S'
```

a value of 'G' would be considered valid since it's in the range. A set would be needed in this case.

## COBOL '85—THE END-IF

Earlier in the text I mentioned that a new feature afforded by COBOL '85 was the use of scope terminators. They are identifiers that mark the range of a statement. One such scope terminator is the **END-IF**. In order to use it, you must match it with an IF statement. The following shows its format:

> **IF** condition
>
> executable statement(s)
>
> **ELSE**
>
> executable statement(s)
>
> **END**-IF.

What good is it? Let's look at a logic situation that I have avoided up until now. The flowchart in Figure 8.12 graphically shows the situation.

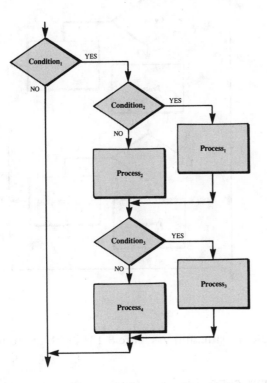

**FIGURE 8.12**
**Logic Structure Illustrating Need for END-IF**

Now try to code the logic using COBOL '74.

```
IF C₁
     IF C₂
          P₁
     ELSE
          P₂
     IF C₃
          P₃
     ELSE
          P₄
ELSE
     NEXT SENTENCE.
```

Does the code do what the flowchart calls for? No, it doesn't! Assume $C_1$ is true. Then, assume $C_2$ is true. That would cause $P_1$ to be done, which would then end the IF. However, in the flowchart we wanted to check $C_3$ also. In the code $C_3$ will be tested only if $C_1$ is true and $C_2$ is false. You see the IF $C_3$ is actually nested in the ELSE for IF $C_2$. In other words, the code looks like the logic in Figure 8.13 instead of Figure 8.12 as needed. I've highlighted the logic path that is wrong.

**FIGURE 8.13**
**Logic Structure Showing**
**Limitation of COBOL '74**
**IF Structure**

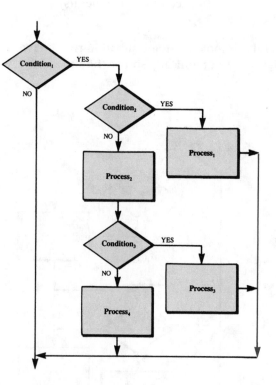

How do we handle the situation in Figure 8.13? With the following code:

```
IF C₁
     PERFORM CHECK-SECOND-CONDITION
     PERFORM CHECK-THIRD-CONDITION
ELSE
     NEXT SENTENCE.
```

So we place the second and third conditions in their own paragraphs. Seems like the long way around, doesn't it? Well, COBOL '85 comes to the rescue with the END-IF. Here's the logic using COBOL '85.

```
IF C₁
    IF C₂
        P₁
    ELSE
        P₂
    END-IF
    IF C₃
        P₃
    ELSE
        P₄
    END-IF
ELSE
    NEXT SENTENCE
END-IF.
```

Now, the **END-IF** has defined the scope of IF $C_2$. It allows IF $C_3$ to also be tested when IF $C_1$ tests true.

## THE EVALUATE VERB IN COBOL '85

I would be remiss if I did not mention, at least briefly, the **EVALUATE** verb while I'm in the IF chapter. In Chapter 2 we looked at structured programming and identified one of the logic structures as the CASE structure. I called it the nested IF THEN ELSE construct. COBOL '85 gives us a direct way of handling the CASE. No longer do we have to use nested IFs or, what's worse, the GO TO DEPENDING.

A format of the **EVALUATE** verb is given below:

<u>**EVALUATE**</u> data-name
    <u>**WHEN**</u> literal
        executable statement(s)
    $\left[\begin{array}{l}\underline{\textbf{WHEN}}\text{ literal} \\ \text{executable statement(s)} \\ \quad \cdots \end{array}\right]$

So we may now code the CASE as:

```
EVALUATE MAJOR-CODE
    WHEN 1
        ADD 1 TO ACCOUNTING-COUNT
    WHEN 2
        ADD 1 TO INFO-SYSTEMS-COUNT
    WHEN 3
        ADD 1 TO FINANCE-COUNT
    WHEN 4
        ADD 1 TO MANAGEMENT-COUNT
    WHEN 5
        ADD 1 TO MARKETING-COUNT.
```

We could have also coded:

```
EVALUATE MAJOR-CODE
    WHEN ACCOUNTING-STUDENT
        ADD 1 TO ACCOUNTING-COUNT
                .
                .
```

Finally, COBOL has a CASE verb. You will find it helps the code's readability over nested IFs.

## SUMMARY

This chapter introduced the IF verb. But we didn't just discuss syntax and rules; we looked at several logic structures.

We examined the "Do Something Extra" structure and the "Do One Instruction Set or Another" structure. Both of these structures are common to programming. They are easily handled in COBOL.

Once we looked at structure, we studied the operators: relational and logical. The relational operators we studied were the EQUAL TO (=), LESS THAN (<) and GREATER THAN (>). We examined the results of comparisons with these operators and even discussed NOT logic: NOT =, NOT < AND NOT >. We also saw two new operators available in COBOL '85; < = and > =.

After fully examining the relational operators, we studied the logical operators: AND and OR. Using these required you to understand that a hierarchy exists. All ANDs are done before the ORs. All logical operators of the same level are evaluated left to right. You then saw how the logical and relational operators, when used together, can be used to build very sophisticated relationships.

Once we understood the operators, our next topic was data validation. We looked at several tests available to us: sequence tests to test if records are in ascending or descending key order; presence tests to see if a field is blank; range tests to check if a data item is within some range of values; reasonableness tests to check and see if a value is within reason; and type tests that allow us to check to see if a data item is numeric or alphabetic and the sign test to see if a data item is positive or negative.

These discussions led us to the topic of condition names, 88 levels. These were a whole new idea in names. That is, they are not data-names, but names for values that data-names may have. We saw that 88 levels made IF statements more easily understood. But you also saw that they were handy for data validation as well. We could easily build condition names for valid values, sets of values and ranges of values that made the IF test so much easier than explicitly checking for each value.

The last topics in the chapter were COBOL '85 enhancements: END-IF and EVALUATE. We saw how the END-IF is used and how it helps solve one of the common logic situations that is found in most programs; the need to nest two complete IF THEN ELSEs within another IF.

The EVALUATE is COBOL '85's answer to the CASE construct. We saw how it is used in a COBOL program as an alternative to nested IFs and the GO TO DEPENDING.

# SAMPLE PROGRAM

The following is a complete running COBOL program using many of the features ·:chniques discussed in this Chapter.

```
  PP 5740-CB1 RELEASE 2.4                      IBM OS/VS COBOL   JULY 1, 1982      21.51.04  DATE NOV 10,1988

       1                      21.51.04      NOV 10,1988

  00001            IDENTIFICATION DIVISION.
  00002
  00003            PROGRAM-ID. IF-LOGIC.
  00004            AUTHOR. FOWLER.
  00005            DATE-WRITTEN.  JULY 1988.
  00006            DATE-COMPILED. NOV 10,1988.
  00007            REMARKS.
  00008
  00009            ********************************************************
  00010            *                                                      *
  00011            *   ASSIGNMENT NUMBER                                  *
  00012            *   DATE ASSIGNED                                      *
  00013            *   DATE DUE                                           *
  00014            *   PURPOSE:   THIS IS A GRADE POINT RATIO CALCULATION PROGRAM. *
  00015            *             THE GRADE POINT RATIO IS DETERMINED BY DIVIDING  *
  00016            *             THE NUMBER OF GRADE POINTS EARNED BY THE NUMBER  *
  00017            *             OF CREDIT HOURS TAKEN. IN ADDITION, THE MAJOR    *
  00018            *             CODE, CLASS CODE, AND SEX CODE WILL BE CONVERTED *
  00019            *             TO THE ACTUAL NAMES ASSOCIATED WITH THE CODES.   *
  00020            *                                                      *
  00021            *   INPUT FILE SPECIFICATIONS:                         *
  00022            *       CARD COLUMNS               DESCRIPTION          *
  00023            *   --------------------------     -----------          *
  00024            *          1-30                    STUDENT'S NAME       *
  00025            *         31-39                    STUDENT'S ID NUMBER  *
  00026            *         40-40                    STUDENT'S MAJOR CODE *
  00027            *         41-41                    STUDENT'S CLASS CODE *
  00028            *         42-42                    STUDENT'S SEX CODE   *
  00029            *         43-45                    CREDIT HOURS TAKEN   *
  00030            *         46-48                    GRADE POINTS EARNED  *
  00031            *                                                      *
  00032            *   THE OUTPUT CONTAINS STUDENT'S ID NUMBER, STUDENT'S NAME, *
  00033            *   MAJOR NAME, CLASS NAME, SEX, AND THE GRADE POINT RATIO.  *
  00034            *                                                      *
  00035            *                                                      *
  00036            *   A SUMMARY LINE, WHICH CONTAINS THE AVERAGE STUDENT GRADE *
  00037            *   POINT RATIO, WILL BE PRINTED AT THE BOTTOM OF THE REPORT. *
  00038            ********************************************************
  00039
```

```
       2       IF-LOGIC      21.51.04        NOV 10,1988

  00041            ENVIRONMENT DIVISION.
  00042
  00043            CONFIGURATION SECTION.
  00044
  00045            SOURCE-COMPUTER. IBM.
  00046            OBJECT-COMPUTER. IBM.
  00047            SPECIAL-NAMES.    C01 IS PAGE-TOP.
  00048
  00049            INPUT-OUTPUT SECTION.
  00050
  00051            FILE-CONTROL.
  00052
  00053                SELECT DEAN-FILE
  00054                    ASSIGN TO DA-S-DEAN.
  00055
  00056                SELECT REPORT-FILE
  00057                    ASSIGN TO UT-S-REPORT.
  00058
```

*(continued)*

```
     3          IF-LOGIC        21.51.04      NOV 10,1988

00060          DATA DIVISION.
00061
00062          FILE SECTION.
00063
00064          FD  DEAN-FILE
00065              LABEL RECORDS ARE OMITTED
00066              RECORD CONTAINS 48 CHARACTERS
00067              BLOCK CONTAINS 100 RECORDS
00068              DATA RECORD IS STUDENT-RECORD.
00069
00070          01  STUDENT-RECORD PIC X(48).
00071
00072
00073          FD  REPORT-FILE
00074              LABEL RECORDS ARE OMITTED
00075              DATA RECORD IS REPORT-LINE.
00076
00077          01  REPORT-LINE PIC X(133).
00078
```

```
     4          IF-LOGIC        21.51.04      NOV 10,1988

00080          WORKING-STORAGE SECTION.
00081
00082          77  END-OF-FILE-FLAG          PIC 9            VALUE O.
00083          77  GPR                       PIC 9(1)V9(4).
00084          77  TOTAL-CREDIT-HOURS        PIC 9(5)         VALUE O.
00085          77  TOTAL-GRADE-POINTS        PIC 9(5)         VALUE O.
00086          77  ACCOUNTING-KOUNT          PIC 9(2)         VALUE O.
00087          77  INFORMATION-SYSTEMS-KOUNT PIC 9(2)         VALUE O.
00088          77  FINANCE-KOUNT             PIC 9(2)         VALUE O.
00089          77  MANAGEMENT-KOUNT          PIC 9(2)         VALUE O.
00090          77  MARKETING-KOUNT           PIC 9(2)         VALUE O.
00091
00092          01  ARE-THERE-MORE-RECORDS    PIC X(3)         VALUE 'YES'.
00093              88  MORE-RECORDS                           VALUE 'YES'.
00094              88  NO-MORE-RECORDS                        VALUE 'NO'.
00095
00096          01  DETAIL-PAGE-HEADING.
00097              05 FILLER                 PIC X(47)        VALUE SPACES.
00098              05 FILLER                 PIC X(39)        VALUE
00099                      'DEANFILE STUDENT LISTING AND GPR REPORT'.
00100              05 FILLER                 PIC X(47)        VALUE SPACES.
00101
00102          01  HEADINGS.
00103              03 FILLER                 PIC X(10)        VALUE SPACES.
00104              03 FILLER                 PIC X(4)         VALUE 'NAME'.
00105              03 FILLER                 PIC X(36)        VALUE SPACES.
00106              03 FILLER                 PIC X(2)         VALUE 'ID'.
00107              03 FILLER                 PIC X(18)        VALUE SPACES.
00108              03 FILLER                 PIC X(5)         VALUE 'MAJOR'.
00109              03 FILLER                 PIC X(16)        VALUE SPACES.
00110              03 FILLER                 PIC X(5)         VALUE 'CLASS'.
00111              03 FILLER                 PIC X(10)        VALUE SPACES.
00112              03 FILLER                 PIC X(3)         VALUE 'SEX'.
00113              03 FILLER                 PIC X(10)        VALUE SPACES.
00114              03 FILLER                 PIC X(3)         VALUE 'GPR'.
00115              03 FILLER                 PIC X(9)         VALUE SPACES.
00116
00117          01  SUMMARY-KOUNT-HEADING.
00118              03 FILLER                 PIC X(55)        VALUE SPACES.
00119              03 FILLER                 PIC X(23)        VALUE
00120                      'STUDENT COUNTS BY MAJOR'.
00121              03 FILLER                 PIC X(55)        VALUE SPACES.
00122
00123          01  STUDENT-RECORD-IN.
00124              03 NAME-IN                PIC X(30).
00125              03 ID-IN                  PIC X(9).
00126              03 MAJOR-IN               PIC 9(1).
00127              03 CLASS-IN               PIC 9(1).
00128                  88  FRESHMAN                           VALUE 1.
00129                  88  SOPHOMORE                          VALUE 2.
00130                  88  JUNIOR                             VALUE 3.
00131                  88  SENIOR                             VALUE 4.
00132              03 SEX-IN                 PIC 9(1).
00133              03 CREDIT-HOURS-IN        PIC 9(3).
```

*(continued)*

```
     5       IF-LOGIC       21.51.04      NOV 10,1988

00134              03 GRADE-POINTS-IN        PIC 9(3).
00135
00136      01  STUDENT-RECORD-OUT.
00137              03 FILLER                 PIC X(10)      VALUE SPACES.
00138              03 NAME-OUT               PIC X(30).
00139              03 FILLER                 PIC X(7)       VALUE SPACES.
00140              03 ID-OUT                 PIC X(9).
00141              03 FILLER                 PIC X(7)       VALUE SPACES.
00142              03 MAJOR-NAME-OUT         PIC X(19).
00143              03 FILLER                 PIC X(7)       VALUE SPACES.
00144              03 CLASS-NAME-OUT         PIC X(9).
00145              03 FILLER                 PIC X(7)       VALUE SPACES.
00146              03 SEX-OUT                PIC X(6).
00147              03 FILLER                 PIC X(7)       VALUE SPACES.
00148              03 GPR-OUT                PIC 9(1).9(4).
00149              03 FILLER                 PIC X(9)       VALUE SPACES.
00150
00151      01  ACCOUNTING-LINE.
00152              03 FILLER                 PIC X(40)      VALUE SPACES.
00153              03 FILLER                 PIC X(49)      VALUE
00154                   'TOTAL NUMBER OF STUDENTS IN ACCOUNTING'.
00155              03 FILLER                 PIC X(2)       VALUE ': '.
00156              03 ACCOUNTING-KOUNT-OUT   PIC Z9.
00157              03 FILLER                 PIC X(40)      VALUE SPACES.
00158
00159      01  INFORMATION-SYSTEMS-LINE.
00160              03 FILLER                 PIC X(40)      VALUE SPACES.
00161              03 FILLER                 PIC X(49)      VALUE
00162                   'TOTAL NUMBER OF STUDENTS IN INFORMATION SYSTEMS'.
00163              03 FILLER                 PIC X(2)       VALUE ': '.
00164              03 INFO-SYSTEMS-KOUNT-OUT PIC Z9.
00165              03 FILLER                 PIC X(40)      VALUE SPACES.
00166
00167      01  FINANCE-LINE.
00168              03 FILLER                 PIC X(40)      VALUE SPACES.
00169              03 FILLER                 PIC X(49)      VALUE
00170                   'TOTAL NUMBER OF STUDENTS IN FINANCE'.
00171              03 FILLER                 PIC X(2)       VALUE ': '.
00172              03 FINANCE-KOUNT-OUT      PIC Z9.
00173              03 FILLER                 PIC X(40)      VALUE SPACES.
00174
```

```
     6       IF-LOGIC       21.51.04      NOV 10,1988

00176      01  MANAGEMENT-LINE.
00177              03 FILLER                 PIC X(40)      VALUE SPACES.
00178              03 FILLER                 PIC X(49)      VALUE
00179                   'TOTAL NUMBER OF STUDENTS IN MANAGEMENT'.
00180              03 FILLER                 PIC X(2)       VALUE ': '.
00181              03 MANAGEMENT-KOUNT-OUT   PIC Z9.
00182              03 FILLER                 PIC X(40)      VALUE SPACES.
00183
00184      01  MARKETING-LINE.
00185              03 FILLER                 PIC X(40)      VALUE SPACES.
00186              03 FILLER                 PIC X(49)      VALUE
00187                   'TOTAL NUMBER OF STUDENTS IN MARKETING'.
00188              03 FILLER                 PIC X(2)       VALUE ': '.
00189              03 MARKETING-KOUNT-OUT    PIC Z9.
00190              03 FILLER                 PIC X(40)      VALUE SPACES.
00191
00192      01  AVERAGE-GRADE-POINT-LINE.
00193              03 FILLER                 PIC X(97)      VALUE SPACES.
00194              03 FILLER                 PIC X(21)      VALUE
00195                   'AVERAGE STUDENT GPR: '.
00196              03 AVERAGE-GPR-OUT        PIC 9(1).9(4).
00197              03 FILLER                 PIC X(4)       VALUE ' ***'.
00198              03 FILLER                 PIC X(5)       VALUE SPACES.
00199
00200      01  BLANK-LINE.
00201              03 FILLER                 PIC X(133)     VALUE SPACES.
00202
```

*(continued)*

```
        7         IF-LOGIC        21.51.04        NOV 10,1988

    00204          PROCEDURE DIVISION.
    00205
    00206          0000-MAIN-PARA.
    00207              PERFORM 1000-INIT-PARA.
    00208              PERFORM 8000-READ-PARA.
    00209              PERFORM 2000-PROCESS-PARA
    00210                  UNTIL NO-MORE-RECORDS.
    00211              PERFORM 3000-TERMINATION-PARA.
    00212              STOP RUN.
    00213
```

```
        8         IF-LOGIC        21.51.04        NOV 10,1988

    00215          ******************************************************************
    00216          *  1000-INIT-PARA.                                               *
    00217          *                                                                *
    00218          *  THIS PARAGRAPH OPENS THE DEAN FILE AND REPORT FILE AND        *
    00219          *  WRITES THE REPORT HEADINGS.                                   *
    00220          *                                                                *
    00221          ******************************************************************
    00222
    00223          1000-INIT-PARA.
    00224              OPEN INPUT DEAN-FILE.
    00225              OPEN OUTPUT REPORT-FILE.
    00226              WRITE REPORT-LINE FROM BLANK-LINE
    00227                  AFTER PAGE-TOP.
    00228              WRITE REPORT-LINE FROM DETAIL-PAGE-HEADING
    00229                  AFTER 3.
    00230              WRITE REPORT-LINE FROM HEADINGS
    00231                  AFTER 3.
    00232              WRITE REPORT-LINE FROM BLANK-LINE
    00233                  AFTER 1.
    00234
```

```
        9         IF-LOGIC        21.51.04        NOV 10,1988

    00236          ******************************************************************
    00237          *  2000-PROCESS-PARA.                                            *
    00238          *                                                                *
    00239          *  THIS PARAGRAPH IS A CONTROL PARAGRAPH FOR                     *
    00240          *                                                                *
    00241          *      2100-CALCULATIONS-PARA                                    *
    00242          *      2200-CONVERT-MAJOR-CODE-PARA                              *
    00243          *      2300-CONVERT-CLASS-CODE-PARA                              *
    00244          *      2400-CONVERT-SEX-CODE-PARA                                *
    00245          *      2500-WRITE-REPORT-PARA                                    *
    00246          *      8000-READ-PARA                                           *
    00247          *                                                                *
    00248          ******************************************************************
    00249
    00250          2000-PROCESS-PARA.
    00251              PERFORM 2100-CALCULATIONS-PARA.
    00252              PERFORM 2200-CONVERT-MAJOR-CODE-PARA.
    00253              PERFORM 2300-CONVERT-CLASS-CODE-PARA.
    00254              PERFORM 2400-CONVERT-SEX-CODE-PARA.
    00255              PERFORM 2500-WRITE-REPORT-PARA.
    00256              PERFORM 8000-READ-PARA.
    00257
```

*(continued)*

```
   10        IF-LOGIC        21.51.04        NOV 10,1988

00259        ***************************************************************
00260        *    2100-CALCULATIONS-PARA.                                  *
00261        *                                                             *
00262        *    THIS PARAGRAPH CALCULATES THE STUDENT'S GPR (TO 4 DECIMAL *
00263        *    PLACES AND ROUNDED) AND ACCUMULATES THE CREDIT HOURS AND  *
00264        *    GRADE POINTS WHICH WILL BE USED TO CALCULATE THE AVERAGE  *
00265        *    STUDENT GPR IN THE 3000-TERMINATION-PARA.                 *
00266        *                                                             *
00267        ***************************************************************
00268
00269           2100-CALCULATIONS-PARA.
00270              COMPUTE GPR ROUNDED = GRADE-POINTS-IN / CREDIT-HOURS-IN.
00271              ADD CREDIT-HOURS-IN TO TOTAL-CREDIT-HOURS.
00272              ADD GRADE-POINTS-IN TO TOTAL-GRADE-POINTS.
00273
```

```
   11        IF-LOGIC        21.51.04        NOV 10,1988

00275        ***************************************************************
00276        *    2200-CONVERT-MAJOR-CODE-PARA                             *
00277        *                                                             *
00278        *    THIS PARAGRAPH CONVERTS THE MAJOR CODES INTO THE ACTUAL   *
00279        *    NAMES ASSOCIATED WITH THE CODE AND MOVES THEM TO AN OUTPUT*
00280        *    FIELD IN THE DETAIL LINE. IT ALSO ACCUMULATES A COUNT OF  *
00281        *    STUDENTS WITHIN EACH OF THE MAJORS.                       *
00282        *                                                             *
00283        *       MAJOR CODE                MAJOR NAME                   *
00284        *       ==========                ==========                  *
00285        *           1                     ACCOUNTING                  *
00286        *           2                     INFORMATION SYSTEMS         *
00287        *           3                     FINANCE                     *
00288        *           4                     MANAGEMENT                  *
00289        *           5                     MARKETING                   *
00290        *                                                             *
00291        *    NESTED IF STATEMENTS ARE USED TO IMPROVE THE EFFICIENCY OF*
00292        *    THE PROGRAM CODE.                                        *
00293        *                                                             *
00294        *    NOTE:  THE LOGIC IN THIS PARAGRAPH ASSUMES THAT THERE IS  *
00295        *           PERFECT DATA FOR THE MAJOR CODE (I.E. IT ASSUMES   *
00296        *           THAT THERE WILL ONLY BE VALID CODES - 1 2 3 4 5 -  *
00297        *           FOR THE MAJOR CODES).  BECAUSE OF THIS ASSUMPTION  *
00298        *           ONLY 4 COMPARISONS ARE NEEDED.                     *
00299        *                                                             *
00300        *                                                             *
00301        ***************************************************************
00302
00303           2200-CONVERT-MAJOR-CODE-PARA.
00304              IF MAJOR-IN = 1
00305                 MOVE '      ACCOUNTING' TO MAJOR-NAME-OUT
00306                 ADD 1 TO ACCOUNTING-KOUNT
00307              ELSE
00308                 IF MAJOR-IN = 2
00309                    MOVE 'INFORMATION SYSTEMS' TO MAJOR-NAME-OUT
00310                    ADD 1 TO INFORMATION-SYSTEMS-KOUNT
00311                 ELSE
00312                    IF MAJOR-IN = 3
00313                       MOVE '        FINANCE' TO MAJOR-NAME-OUT
00314                       ADD 1 TO FINANCE-KOUNT
00315                    ELSE
00316                       IF MAJOR-IN = 4
00317                          MOVE '     MANAGEMENT' TO MAJOR-NAME-OUT
00318                          ADD 1 TO MANAGEMENT-KOUNT
00319                       ELSE
00320                          MOVE '      MARKETING' TO MAJOR-NAME-OUT
00321                          ADD 1 TO MARKETING-KOUNT.
00322
```

*(continued)*

```
     12        IF-LOGIC       21.51.04      NOV 10,1988

00324         *****************************************************************
00325         *  2300-CONVERT-CLASS-CODE-PARA                                  *
00326         *                                                                *
00327         *  THIS PARAGRAPH CONVERTS THE CLASS CODES INTO THE ACTUAL       *
00328         *  NAMES ASSOCIATED WITH THE CODE AND MOVES THEM TO AN OUTPUT    *
00329         *  FIELD IN THE DETAIL LINE.                                     *
00330         *                                                                *
00331         *            CLASS CODE              CLASS NAME                  *
00332         *            ==========              ==========                  *
00333         *                1                   FRESHMAN                    *
00334         *                2                   SOPHOMORE                   *
00335         *                3                   JUNIOR                      *
00336         *                4                   SENIOR                      *
00337         *                                                                *
00338         *  THE IF STATEMENTS IN THIS PARAGRAPH UTILIZE CONDITION-NAME    *
00339         *  CONDITIONS TO FACILITATE IN THE READABILITY OF THE CODE.      *
00340         *  EACH CONDITION-NAME HAS A CORRESPONDING 88-LEVEL ENTRY IN     *
00341         *  THE DATA DIVISION (SEE STUDENT-RECORD-IN).  ONCE AGAIN        *
00342         *  NESTED IF'S HAVE BEEN USED TO IMPROVE THE EFFICIENCY OF       *
00343         *  THE PROGRAM CODE.                                             *
00344         *                                                                *
00345         *  NOTE:   THE LOGIC IN THIS PARAGRAPH ASSUMES THAT THERE IS     *
00346         *          PERFECT DATA FOR THE CLASS CODE (I.E. IT ASSUMES      *
00347         *          THAT THERE WILL ONLY BE VALID CODES - 1 2 3 4 -       *
00348         *          FOR THE CLASS CODES).  BECAUSE OF THIS ASSUMPTION     *
00349         *          ONLY 3 COMPARISONS ARE NEEDED.                        *
00350         *                                                                *
00351         *                                                                *
00352         *****************************************************************
00353
00354          2300-CONVERT-CLASS-CODE-PARA.
00355              IF FRESHMAN
00356                 MOVE 'FRESHMAN' TO CLASS-NAME-OUT
00357              ELSE
00358                 IF SOPHOMORE
00359                    MOVE 'SOPHOMORE' TO CLASS-NAME-OUT
00360                 ELSE
00361                    IF JUNIOR
00362                       MOVE ' JUNIOR' TO CLASS-NAME-OUT
00363                    ELSE
00364                       MOVE ' SENIOR' TO CLASS-NAME-OUT.
00365
```

```
     13        IF-LOGIC       21.51.04      NOV 10,1988

00367         *****************************************************************
00368         *  2400-CONVERT-SEX-CODE-PARA                                    *
00369         *                                                                *
00370         *  THIS PARAGRAPH CONVERTS THE SEX CODES INTO THE ACTUAL NAMES   *
00371         *  ASSOCIATED WITH THE CODE AND MOVES THEM TO AN OUTPUT  FIELD   *
00372         *  IN THE DETAIL LINE.                                           *
00373         *                                                                *
00374         *            SEX CODE                SEX                         *
00375         *            ==========              =======                     *
00376         *                1                   MALE                        *
00377         *                2                   FEMALE                      *
00378         *                                                                *
00379         *  AGAIN, NESTED IF'S HAVE BEEN USED TO IMPROVE THE EFFICIENCY   *
00380         *  THE PROGRAM CODE.                                             *
00381         *                                                                *
00382         *  NOTE:   THE LOGIC IN THIS PARAGRAPH ASSUMES THAT THERE IS     *
00383         *          PERFECT DATA FOR THE SEX CODE (I.E. IT ASSUMES        *
00384         *          THAT THERE WILL ONLY BE VALID CODES - 1 2 -           *
00385         *          FOR THE SEX CODES).  BECAUSE OF THIS ASSUMPTION       *
00386         *          ONLY 1 COMPARISON IS NEEDED.                          *
00387         *                                                                *
00388         *                                                                *
00389         *****************************************************************
00390
00391          2400-CONVERT-SEX-CODE-PARA.
00392              IF SEX-IN = 1
00393                 MOVE ' MALE' TO SEX-OUT
00394              ELSE
00395                 MOVE 'FEMALE' TO SEX-OUT.
00396
```

*(continued)*

```
        14          IF-LOGIC        21.51.04        NOV 10,1988

00398           ***************************************************************
00399           *  2500-WRITE-REPORT-PARA.                                    *
00400           *                                                             *
00401           *  THIS PARAGRAPH MOVES THE APPROPRIATE DATA (STUDENT'S NAME, *
00402           *  ID, AND GPR) TO THE APPROPRIATE OUTPUT FIELDS IN THE DETAIL*
00403           *  AND THEN PRINTS THE DETAIL LINE.                           *
00404           *                                                             *
00405           ***************************************************************
00406
00407           2500-WRITE-REPORT-PARA.
00408               MOVE NAME-IN TO NAME-OUT.
00409               MOVE ID-IN TO ID-OUT.
00410               MOVE GPR TO GPR-OUT.
00411               WRITE REPORT-LINE FROM STUDENT-RECORD-OUT
00412                   AFTER 1.
00413
```

```
        15          IF-LOGIC        21.51.04        NOV 10,1988

00415           ***************************************************************
00416           *  8000-READ-PARA.                                            *
00417           *                                                             *
00418           *  THIS PARAGRAPH READS A RECORD FROM THE DEAN FILE.  WHEN THE*
00419           *  END OF THE FILE HAS BEEN REACHED, THE END OF FILE FLAG     *
00420           *  (ARE-THERE-MORE-RECORDS) WILL HAVE THE VALUE 'NO' MOVED TO *
00421           *  IT TO INDICATE THAT THERE ARE NO-MORE-RECORDS TO BE READ   *
00422           *  FROM THE FILE.                                             *
00423           *                                                             *
00424           *  NOTE: IN THIS PROGRAM CONDITION-NAME CONDITIONS ARE USED TO*
00425           *        SIGNIFY THE END-OF-FILE (SEE 0000-MAIN-PARA) AND     *
00426           *        SUBSEQUENTLY THE END OF THE FILE PROCESSING. THE     *
00427           *        CONDITION-NAME CONDITIONS HAVE CORRESPONDING 88-LEVEL*
00428           *        ITEMS CODED IN THE DATA DIVISION.                    *
00429           *                                                             *
00430           ***************************************************************
00431
00432           8000-READ-PARA.
00433               READ DEAN-FILE INTO STUDENT-RECORD-IN
00434                   AT END
00435                       MOVE 'NO' TO ARE-THERE-MORE-RECORDS.
00436
00437
```

```
        16          IF-LOGIC        21.51.04        NOV 10,1988

00439           ***************************************************************
00440           *  3000-TERMINATION-PARA                                      *
00441           *                                                             *
00442           *  THIS PARAGRAPH IS A CONTROL PARAGRAPH FOR                  *
00443           *                                                             *
00444           *        3100-WRITE-AVERAGE-GPR-PARA                          *
00445           *        3200-WRITE-KOUNT-SUMMARY-PARA                        *
00446           *                                                             *
00447           *  THE DEAN FILE AND REPORT FILE ARE THEN CLOSED AFTER THE    *
00448           *  ABOVE PARAGRAPHS ARE PERFORMED                             *
00449           ***************************************************************
00450
00451           3000-TERMINATION-PARA.
00452               PERFORM 3100-WRITE-AVERAGE-GPR-PARA.
00453               PERFORM 3200-WRITE-KOUNT-SUMMARY-PARA.
00454               CLOSE DEAN-FILE.
00455               CLOSE REPORT-FILE.
00456
```

*(continued)*

```
   17        IF-LOGIC        21.51.04      NOV 10,1988

00458        ****************************************************************
00459        *  3100-WRITE-AVERAGE-GPR-PARA                                 *
00460        *                                                              *
00461        *  THIS PARAGRAPH USES THE ACCUMULATED CREDIT HOURS AND GRADE  *
00462        *  POINTS TO CALCULATE THE AVERAGE STUDENT GPR.  THE AVERAGE   *
00463        *  STUDENT GPR IS PRINTED WITH THREE ASTERISKS TO THE RIGHT    *
00464        *  TO DISTINGUISH IT FROM AN ORDINARY DETAIL LINE.             *
00465        *                                                              *
00466        *  NOTE:   THE RESULTS OF THE DIVISION (TO DETERMINE THE AVER- *
00467        *          AGE STUDENT GPR) ARE STORED DIRECTLY IN THE EDITED  *
00468        *          OUTPUT FIELD INSTEAD OF BEING STORED IN AN INTER-   *
00469        *          MEDIATE FIELD AND THEN BEING MOVED TO AN EDITED     *
00470        *          OUTPUT FIELD.                                       *
00471        *                                                              *
00472        ****************************************************************
00473        3100-WRITE-AVERAGE-GPR-PARA.
00474            DIVIDE TOTAL-GRADE-POINTS BY TOTAL-CREDIT-HOURS
00475                GIVING AVERAGE-GPR-OUT ROUNDED.
00476            WRITE REPORT-LINE FROM AVERAGE-GRADE-POINT-LINE
00477                AFTER 3.
00478
```

```
   18        IF-LOGIC        21.51.04      NOV 10,1988

00480        ****************************************************************
00481        *  3200-WRITE-KOUNT-SUMMARY-PARA                               *
00482        *                                                              *
00483        *  THIS PARAGRAPH WRITES A SUMMARY REPORT WHICH LISTS THE      *
00484        *  NUMBER OF STUDENTS IN EACH MAJOR.                           *
00485        *                                                              *
00486        ****************************************************************
00487        3200-WRITE-KOUNT-SUMMARY-PARA.
00488            WRITE REPORT-LINE FROM SUMMARY-KOUNT-HEADING
00489                AFTER PAGE-TOP.
00490            WRITE REPORT-LINE FROM BLANK-LINE
00491                AFTER 1.
00492            MOVE ACCOUNTING-KOUNT TO ACCOUNTING-KOUNT-OUT.
00493            WRITE REPORT-LINE FROM ACCOUNTING-LINE
00494                AFTER 2.
00495            MOVE INFORMATION-SYSTEMS-KOUNT TO INFO-SYSTEMS-KOUNT-OUT.
00496            WRITE REPORT-LINE FROM INFORMATION-SYSTEMS-LINE
00497                AFTER 2.
00498            MOVE FINANCE-KOUNT TO FINANCE-KOUNT-OUT.
00499            WRITE REPORT-LINE FROM FINANCE-LINE
00500                AFTER 2.
00501            MOVE MANAGEMENT-KOUNT TO MANAGEMENT-KOUNT-OUT.
00502            WRITE REPORT-LINE FROM MANAGEMENT-LINE
00503                AFTER 2.
00504            MOVE MARKETING-KOUNT TO MARKETING-KOUNT-OUT.
00505            WRITE REPORT-LINE FROM MARKETING-LINE
00506                AFTER 2.
```

*(continued)*

```
                    DEANFILE STUDENT LISTING AND GPR REPORT


        NAME                    ID          MAJOR             CLASS       SEX      GPR

        THOMAS WILKINSON      123456789     MANAGEMENT          SENIOR      MALE     3.7619
        DON VILLANOSKI        987654321     ACCOUNTING          FRESHMAN    MALE     2.7500
        MICHAEL FOWLER        555555555  INFORMATION SYSTEMS    SOPHOMORE   MALE     3.8966
        TIA FOWLER            888888888     FINANCE             JUNIOR      FEMALE   3.4943
        CLINT SMITH           333333333  INFORMATION SYSTEMS    JUNIOR      MALE     1.9839
        HOWARD PORTER         454545454     ACCOUNTING          FRESHMAN    MALE     2.3158
        APRIL JONES           777777777  INFORMATION SYSTEMS    JUNIOR      FEMALE   2.8025
        APRIL JACKS           787878778     MANAGEMENT          SENIOR      FEMALE   2.5649
        BRYAN MANN            232323232     FINANCE             FRESHMAN    MALE     2.6667
        ZEKE MORGAN           434356569  INFORMATION SYSTEMS    SOPHOMORE   MALE     2.8947
        BILL ADAM             102302220     MANAGEMENT          SENIOR      MALE     2.8092
        JILL MATSON           010101206  INFORMATION SYSTEMS    FRESHMAN    FEMALE   2.9947
        TINA MARIO            000000222     MANAGEMENT          JUNIOR      FEMALE   2.3380
        CLYDE FELD JR.        129834765     MANAGEMENT          SOPHOMORE   MALE     2.9057
        GEORGE MARINAKIES     100010055     MARKETING           FRESHMAN    MALE     2.7083
        JAMES PAPPAS          342537891     MARKETING           JUNIOR      MALE     2.3253
        STEVE PARKS           908765101     ACCOUNTING          FRESHMAN    FEMALE   3.8000
        LYNDA MATHER          203040506     FINANCE             JUNIOR      FEMALE   2.7538
        KEVIN MCKENN          444455555  INFORMATION SYSTEMS    JUNIOR      MALE     3.4933
        IRENE SMITH           001122334     MANAGEMENT          FRESHMAN    FEMALE   2.0000
        EMILY LYLE            999888777     ACCOUNTING          FRESHMAN    FEMALE   2.2667
        PEG PORTERHOUSE       123321123     FINANCE             SENIOR      FEMALE   2.9703
        DAN ROBESON           656765679     MANAGEMENT          JUNIOR      MALE     2.2400
        DANA MILLS            908070600     MANAGEMENT          SENIOR      FEMALE   2.7500
        GEORGE RYAN           564731009     ACCOUNTING          SOPHOMORE   MALE     2.4000
        BILLY BOB BARRETT     111000222     ACCOUNTING          SENIOR      MALE     2.2500
        MARY JO MARTINEZ      102938475  INFORMATION SYSTEMS    SENIOR      FEMALE   2.3077
        POLLY ANN FLOWERS     501112234     MANAGEMENT          SENIOR      FEMALE   2.5773
        MATHEW ALTMEN         980980980     MARKETING           JUNIOR      MALE     3.2258
        DIANE LAWERNCE        263718818     MARKETING           SOPHOMORE   FEMALE   2.5714
        SARA WALKER           828347561     MARKETING           JUNIOR      FEMALE   3.5375
        MARIA SANTIAGO        777345777     MARKETING           SOPHOMORE   FEMALE   2.4444
        ANTONIO MARTINEZ      773330666     MARKETING           JUNIOR      MALE     3.0000
        ROBERTO SMITH         311230099     MANAGEMENT          SENIOR      MALE     2.9000
        ANDY BUENZA           000001111     ACCOUNTING          SOPHOMORE   MALE     2.7429
        MARIA SANCHEZ         501155003     MANAGEMENT          JUNIOR      FEMALE   3.2000
        STACY PHARR           444344344  INFORMATION SYSTEMS    SENIOR      FEMALE   3.5263
        MICHAEL RYAN          717273747  INFORMATION SYSTEMS    FRESHMAN    MALE     3.2727
        MARY LITTLE           394958690  INFORMATION SYSTEMS    SENIOR      FEMALE   3.1579
        ANNIE MARINOS         010203040  INFORMATION SYSTEMS    FRESHMAN    FEMALE   2.2727
        C. H. FLOWER          404040404  INFORMATION SYSTEMS    SENIOR      MALE     2.6887
        ROY JOICE             102450555     ACCOUNTING          SENIOR      MALE     3.5045
        DAVID LETTER          978675643     FINANCE             FRESHMAN    MALE     2.0000
        JANE CATES            132435467     FINANCE             FRESHMAN    FEMALE   2.7600
        KEN MARTINEZ          002903992     FINANCE             SENIOR      MALE     2.7704
        GEORGE COMONOS        516972420     MANAGEMENT          FRESHMAN    MALE     3.2400
        SESSIE PARSONS        808188808     MANAGEMENT          SOPHOMORE   FEMALE   2.5106
        PEGGY MARTTA          222288885     MARKETING           SENIOR      FEMALE   2.0635
        THOMAS THOMPSON       844839931     MARKETING           FRESHMAN    MALE     2.2857
        WAYNE HEDDER          246808642     MARKETING           SENIOR      MALE     3.9694


                                                  AVERAGE STUDENT GPR: 2.8570 ***
```

```
                    STUDENT COUNTS BY MAJOR


        TOTAL NUMBER OF STUDENTS IN ACCOUNTING          :  8

        TOTAL NUMBER OF STUDENTS IN INFORMATION SYSTEMS : 12

        TOTAL NUMBER OF STUDENTS IN FINANCE             :  7

        TOTAL NUMBER OF STUDENTS IN MANAGEMENT          : 13

        TOTAL NUMBER OF STUDENTS IN MARKETING           : 10
```

## EXERCISES

### Chapter Review Questions

1. Which of the following is not a relational operator?

   a. Equal to
   b. And
   c. Less than
   d. Greater than
   e. =

2. Which of the following are logical operators?

   a. And
   b. Or
   c. =
   d. <
   e. Both a and b

3. Which of the following is true?

   a. Every IF must have an ELSE
   b. Only nested IFs must have ELSEs
   c. The ELSE is only part of COBOL '85
   d. The ELSE is being replaced by the END-IF
   e. All of the above are false

4. The do something extra structure is best described as:

   a. Separate executable statements to be done for each logic path
   b. Only the true path causes executable statements to be done
   c. Only the false path causes executable statements to be done
   d. Both b and c
   e. None of the above

5. The nested IF structure can be replaced by using the AND logical operator.

   a. True
   b. False

6. In an IF that uses both AND and OR, which is evaluated first?

   a. ORs
   b. ANDs
   c. In order from left to right
   d. In the order determined by the relational operators
   e. None of the above

7. Comparison of two alphanumeric fields is done:

   a. From right to left, one byte at a time
   b. From left to right, one byte at a time
   c. Only if both fields are the same size
   d. Only numeric fields may be compared
   e. None of the above

8. Using IF logic, How many IFs and ADDs and 77 level items would be needed to count something that had ten possible values. (Assume data is valid)?

    a.    10 IFs, 10 ADDs, 10 77s
    b.    9 IFs, 10 ADDs, 10 77s
    c.    9 IFs, 9 ADDs, 9 77s
    d.    9 IFs, 9 ADDs, 10 77s
    e.    None of the above

9. Checking a data field to see if it's blank or not is called:

    a.    Sequence Testing
    b.    Reasonableness Testing
    c.    Type Testing
    d.    Range Testing
    e.    None of the above

10. In a check printing routine, checking the size of the dollar value would be an example of:

    a.    Size Testing
    b.    Type Testing
    c.    Reasonableness Testing
    d.    Range Testing
    e.    None of the above

11. A class test would check to see if a field is:

    a.    Numeric
    b.    Positive
    c.    Alphabetic
    d.    Negative
    e.    Both a and c are class test

12. An 88 Level Item:

    a.    Is a subdivision of a 77 level
    b.    Is a condition name
    c.    May only be used in IF's and PERFORMS
    d.    May contain a picture clause
    e.    None of the above

13. The VALUE clause for an 88 to be used to check for a valid MAJOR CODE of A, I, F, M and K would be

    a.    VALUE 'A' THROUGH 'K'
    b.    VALUE A, I, F, M, K
    c.    VALUE A, OR I, OR F, OR M, OR K
    d.    VALUE 'A', 'I', 'F', 'M', 'K'
    e.    None of the above

14. An 88's values may be specified as:

    a.    A numeric literal
    b.    A nonnumeric literal
    c.    A range of values
    d.    A set of values
    e.    All of the above

15. The END-IF
    a.    Is just used for readability
    b.    Helps build logic structure
    c.    Is not yet available in COBOL '85
    d.    Is being replaced by the ELSE
    e.    None of the above

16. The EVALUATE verb allows for coding which structured programming construct more directly?
    a.    IF Then Else
    b.    DoWhile
    c.    DoUntil
    d.    Case
    e.    All of the above

## Discussion Questions

1. Briefly compare the NESTED IF with the EVALUATE for handling the CASE CONSTRUCT.
2. Briefly explain why the compound condition "AND" is not the same as the NESTED IF.
3. Briefly explain how the END-IF adds more power to the IF structures we may use.
4. Briefly make a case for:
    a.    Always using NEXT SENTENCE
    b.    Never using NEXT SENTENCE
5. Briefly explain the use of AND and OR in the same IF STATEMENT.

## Practice Problems

1. Write the procedure division statements necessary to read the Dean File, Data File A Form 1, and count the number of students by:
    a.    Major,
    b.    Class,
    c.    Sex,
    d.    Class within Major and
    e.    Sex within Class within Major

2. Write the procedure division statements necessary to read the Inventory File, Data File C, and accumulate the total value of inventory that each buyer is responsible for. Also provide a count of the items by supplier and by buyer.

3. Write the procedure division statements necessary to read the Personnel File, Data File B, and list all employees. However all department and store codes should be converted to appropriate descriptions.

## Programming Projects

The following assignments rely on the data dictionary, library elements and data sets found in the Project Sets Section of your text.

1. Do the Logic Assignment for the Project Management System in Project A.
2. Do the Logic Assignment for the Employee System in Project B.

# CONTROL BREAK

**_OBJECTIVES_**   Up to now, we have simply been writing reports without much more than putting page and column headings on them. In industry, reports need to be easy to read and understand. Anything we can do in data processing to make it possible for users to understand reports is well worth the effort.

Therefore, we will look at grouping information on reports and presenting these groups on the report to enhance the usefulness of the reports. We will study control-break logic and concepts. We will see that ordered data is required, but once it is appropriately ordered, we can key on values in data fields to do special things for the different groupings of data: headings, totals, paging and so on.

## TOPICS

- **hierarchical relationship in control fields**
- **single-level control break**
- **multiple-level control breaks**
- **using nested PERFORMs for control**

- **headings**
- **totaling, counts**
- **group indication**
- **key fields**
- **ordered data**

## KEY WORDS

- **group indicator**
- **control break**
- **control totals**

## THE PROBLEM

In the business world, it is not enough just to write the requested reports with all the correct results. The reports need to be pretty. That is, they should be easy to read, and results should be easy to find.

One technique used extensively to make reports is called control-break logic. This logic allows for reports to be grouped by using a data field as a key. For instance, assume the dean file has been sorted (we will study how in a later chapter) by major. It would be nice to use the major field to enhance the appearance of our report; a listing of all students in major order. Using the major field in this fashion is what is referred to as control-break logic.

## SINGLE-LEVEL CONTROL BREAK

Let's look at a specific problem. Assume the Dean wants a report of all students ordered by major. The listing should include all the input data for each student, and the students should be listed alphabetically. Each major should start a new page with all headings included on each page. Since this problem includes a break on only one variable, major, it is called a single-level control break problem.

### Understanding the Concept

Before we look at the solution to the problem, let's look at a few terms and concepts. In a control-break problem, a field in the record is usually specified as the control field. It must be a field that the file was ordered (sorted) on. Can you imagine the problem of reporting the students by major if the students were not sorted by major? It would be impossible! (I shouldn't say that. Nothing is impossible. It would just be very, very difficult.)

### Group Indication

What are we going to include on the report for each student? Name, ID, Major, Classification, Sex, and GPR? That seems correct, since the dean wanted all data. However, should we report the major with each student or just once for each group of students? It seems redundant to list ACCOUNTING with each of several hundred accounting majors. Why not just include ACCOUNTING as a heading and not print it for each student? As you might suspect, this technique has a special phrase to describe it. It is called group indication. Figure 9.1 shows how the report should look.

Let's look at the ordered file. Assume that DEAN-FILE has already been sorted by major. Since you are now experts on sorting, the following illustrations should not bother you.

FIGURE 9.1
Report Format

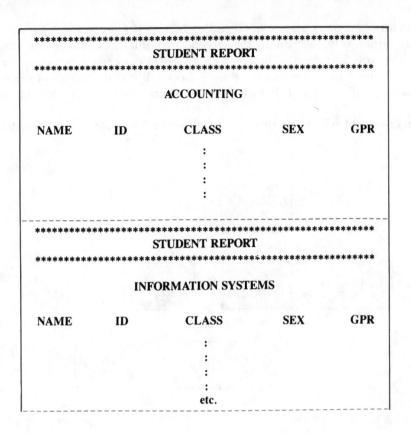

```
****************************************************************
                        STUDENT REPORT
****************************************************************

                          ACCOUNTING

  NAME         ID        CLASS         SEX        GPR
                           :
                           :
                           :
```

```
****************************************************************
                        STUDENT REPORT
****************************************************************

                     INFORMATION SYSTEMS

  NAME         ID        CLASS         SEX        GPR
                           :
                           :
                           :
                           :
                          etc.
```

SORTED MAJOR CODE ORDER
1
1
1
1
1
1
2
2
2
2
2
2
3
3
3
3
3
3
4
4
4
4
5
5
5
5
5

Notice that the major codes are in ascending order. However, the logic we will look at works either way, ascending or descending. But first, where are the control breaks? Can you find them? There is a control break at each major change: 1 to 2, 2 to 3, 3 to 4. and 4 to 5. Do you see those? Good! But that's not all of them. Would you believe me if I told you that the EOF is a break also? That's a change from 5 to EOF.

Where should we start? How about with the hierarchy chart shown in Figure 9.2?

**FIGURE 9.2**
**Single-Level Control-Break Hierarchy Chart**

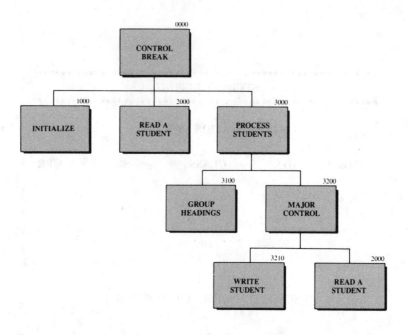

Notice the similarities between the control-break chart and the simple input/output chart in Chapter 2. We just had to add a level to the chart. If we were just going to list the students without concern for control breaks, then the headings would go up one level and the move, write and read modules would also move up a level. Why? Because we don't need the major control module any more. Go with me to the next step before you panic. Let's look at the pseudocode for the logic:

```
INITIALIZATION
READ 1st STUDENT RECORD
DO WHILE MORE RECORDS
    SET MAJOR-TEST TO MAJOR-CODE
    HEADINGS - PAGE AND COLUMN
    DO UNTIL MAJOR-CODE NOT = MAJOR-TEST
        OR NO MORE RECORDS
            MOVE INPUT DATA TO OUTPUT RECORD
            WRITE STUDENT RECORD
            READ STUDENT RECORD(2nd THROUGH Nth)
    END DO
END DO
```

How is this different from a simple listing? Let's reminisce for a minute. Remember this from Chapter 2?

```
INITIALIZE
HEADINGS
READ 1st STUDENT RECORD
DO WHILE MORE RECORDS
     MOVE INPUT DATA TO OUTPUT RECORD
     WRITE STUDENT RECORD
     READ STUDENT RECORD(2nd THROUGH Nth)
END DO
```

All that really changes is the second DO. That should make sense, since it was controlling the major break.

When you compare the two sets of pseudocode you should realize that, when we added the control on major, we just needed to add that control on our move and write logic. No longer could we just write each record; we had to write each record depending on that record's major code.

It's time to look at the COBOL code to express this logic. You will notice in the code that follows that I use the lead read model again. After all, the DEAN-FILE is a sequential file. Since you are familiar with the model, I will concentrate on the control-break elements in the procedure division.

```
0000-MAIN-PARA.
     PERFORM 1000-INIT-PARA.
     PERFORM 2000-READ-PARA.
     PERFORM 3000-PROCESS-STUDENTS
         UNTIL NO-MORE-RECORDS.

1000-INIT-PARA.
     .
     .
     .

2000-READ-PARA.
     READ DEAN-FILE INTO STUDENT-RECORD
         AT END
                 MOVE 'NO' TO ARE-THERE-MORE-RECORDS.

3000-PROCESS-STUDENTS.
     MOVE MAJOR-CODE TO MAJOR-TEST.
     PERFORM 3100-HEADINGS-PARA.
     PERFORM 3200-MAJOR-BREAK
         UNTIL MAJOR-CODE NOT = MAJOR-TEST
         OR NO-MORE-RECORDS.

3100-HEADINGS-PARA.
     IF MAJOR-CODE = 1
        MOVE 'ACCOUNTING' TO MAJOR-TITLE
     ELSE
        IF MAJOR-CODE = 2
           MOVE 'INFORMATION SYSTEMS' TO MAJOR-TITLE
        ELSE
           IF MAJOR-CODE = 3
              MOVE 'FINANCE' TO MAJOR-TITLE
           ELSE
              IF MAJOR-CODE = 4
                 MOVE 'MANAGEMENT' TO MAJOR-TITLE
              ELSE
                 MOVE 'MARKETING' TO MAJOR-TITLE.
```

```
        WRITE REPORT-LINE FROM PAGE-HEADING
            AFTER PAGE-TOP.
        WRITE REPORT-LINE FROM COLUMN-HEADINGS
            AFTER 5.

    3200-MAJOR-BREAK.
        PERFORM 3210-MOVE-AND-WRITE.
        PERFORM 2000-READ-PARA.

    3210-MOVE-AND-WRITE.
        MOVE NAME-IN TO NAME-OUT.
        MOVE ID-IN TO ID-OUT.
        MOVE CLASS-IN TO CLASS-OUT.
        MOVE SEX-IN TO SEX-OUT.
        MOVE GPR-IN TO GPR-OUT.
        WRITE REPORT-LINE FROM STUDENT-RECORD-OUT
            AFTER 2.
```

The best way to explain the concept is to step through the logic with you. I'll assume you recognize the overall coding. MAIN-PARA is OK as is. The same can be said about INIT-PARA and READ-PARA. In fact, you should feel comfortable with the MAJOR-BREAK paragraph. Except for its name, it's just our old move and write paragraph.

The 3000-PROCESS-STUDENTS paragraph is the kicker. The first line sets a test value. Every time we enter this paragraph we set the test value to the new major code. We then use it to write the corresponding heading. Then we control the PER-FORM with it. That is, we stay in the control of the PERFORM-3200-MAJOR-BREAK until the major code changes. That's a control break! Therefore, every time the major code changes, the PERFORM is satisfied and control passes back to the PER-FORM that got us there, the PERFORM PROCESS-PARA. This PERFORM continues sending us back until there are no more records to process.

Every time we go back to PROCESS-PARA, we do the headings for a new major (IF MAJOR-CODE = 1 MOVE 'ACCOUNTING' TO MAJOR-TITLE etc.) and reset the test value (MOVE MAJOR-CODE TO MAJOR-TEST). Now the only thing that satisfies the PERFORM is a change in MAJOR-CODE or running out of data. Let's play computer and execute the code ourselves.

| | |
|---|---|
| 1st | Initialization is performed (open files etc.). |
| 2nd | The first record is read. |
| 3rd | The PERFORM PROCESS-PARA is executed. |
| 4th | The test value is set. |
| 5th | The headings paragraph is executed. |
| 6th | The appropriate major's description is moved to the title. |
| 7th | The page and column headings are written. |
| 8th | The 3200-MAJOR-BREAK paragraph is done. |
| 9th | The data is moved and written. |
| 10th | The next record is read. |
| 11th | Control passes back to the perform and the conditions are tested. |

NOTE: Steps 9 through 11 are repeated until one of the conditions is met.

| | |
|---|---|
| 12th | When major changes, then steps 3 through 8 are repeated. |

or

12th    When EOF is reached the PERFORM PROCESS-PARA is satisfied and control passes to the statement following the PERFORM.  The logic is finished.

A complete COBOL program for the one-level control break problem is included at the end of the chapter.

## MULTI-LEVEL CONTROL BREAKS

We are now ready to tackle the problem of multiple control breaks.  In our previous discussion we looked at a situation that was predicated on the major code changing: a one-level control break.  Now we want to look at more than one level, say class within major, or sex within class within major.

I guess it goes without saying that while I'm referring to the DEAN-FILE again, it really does not matter.  Pick a file, any sequential file.  If the records have appropriate fields (related for reporting purposes), then the techniques apply.  We could just as easily report salesman within department within store within region within district.  It's not the fields that are important, it's the concept.  It works no matter what the fields are.

### Applying the Single-Level Concept

As with single-level control-break logic, there are some terms and concepts we need to examine.  We will continue to talk about group indication, but because of having multiple control breaks, we will have group indication at multiple levels.  This will necessitate making distinctions between major and minor keys, for clarity.  Therefore, we might say the report is to be major group indicated by major-code, and class-code is to be minor group indicated.

### Hierarchical Relationship Between Levels

The hierarchical relationship between codes is a significant concept with multiple control breaks.  We assume that, for a major break, all lower levels are assumed to have broken as well.  For the sex within class within major example, if major changes, then both class and sex are also assumed to have  changed.  If class breaks, then a sex change is assumed.  Be patient with this concept.  I will show it to you in an example a little later.

### The Problem

Let's continue using the DEAN-FILE.  Assume that the dean asks us for a report of students.  However, he wants the report ordered by classification within major.  Furthermore, he wants the report major group indicated by major code, and the minor group indicated by classification code.  Figure 9.3 shows the report design he sketches out for us.

Notice that he has indicated in his design not only that he wants groups indicated by major and class codes, but that he also wants it done in a particular fashion.  That is, the major is to be a title, and each major starts a new page, while classification is a column heading.  However, the classification is written only for the first student in the minor group: freshman, sophomore, junior, senior.  Meeting this request combines the two techniques we discussed for single-level control breaks.  We will look at yet another style in a little bit.

GROUP INDICATOR ⟶

GROUP INDICATOR ⟶

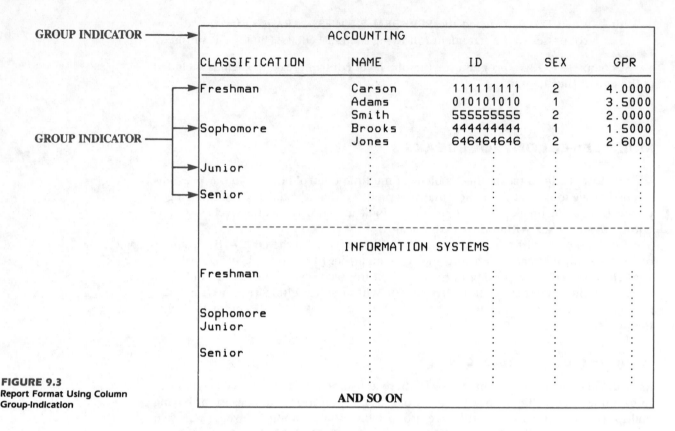

**FIGURE 9.3**
Report Format Using Column
Group-Indication

Assume that the data file has been sorted by some appropriate technique that places the sorted records on a file called NEW-FILE. (If the data were to be sorted in the control-break program, you would use sort techniques discussed in the Sort Chapter.)

If we took NEW-FILE home with us and sat in our favorite chair, we would notice as we read the file that the major codes and class codes are as shown in Figure 9.4.

Since I didn't want to bore you with 6,000 records, I just depicted a sample of what NEW-FILE records would look like. Where are the control breaks? See the little <s I used in the figure? Those are the control breaks. Notice that for the minor key, class, we have more breaks than with the major key, major. That makes sense, doesn't it? The data is sorted by class within major. Therefore the major is held constant and the minor is sorted within it. Doesn't this result in more breaks for the minor key? Sure it does!

### The Hierarchy Chart

Leading to our code, let's look again at the appropriate hierarchy first (Figure 9.5). See how the depth has increased? I have more levels in this hierarchy chart than for the single-level control-break chart. But look at the change. All I did was add the extra module (3210) to control the move and write (3211) and the read (2000) modules. Didn't we add another group to control by? Well then, it should follow that we would need to add to our hierarchy chart.

| Record | Sorted Major Codes | Sorted Class Codes |
|--------|-------------------|-------------------|
| 1 | 1 | 1 |
| 2 | 1 | 1 < |
| 3 | 1 | 2 < |
| 4 | 1 | 3 < |
| 5 | 1 | 4 |
| 6 | 1 | 4 |
| 7 | 1 < | 4 < |
| 8 | 2 | 1 |
| 9 | 2 | 1 |
| 10 | 2 | 1 < |
| 11 | 2 | 3 |
| 12 | 2 | 3 |
| 13 | 2 | 3 < |
| 14 | 2 < | 4 < |
| 15 | 3 | 1 < |
| 16 | 3 | 2 |
| 17 | 3 | 2 |
| 18 | 3 | 2 < |
| 19 | 3 | 3 |
| 20 | 3 < | 3 < |
| 21 | 4 | 3 |
| 22 | 4 | 3 |
| 23 | 4 | 3 < |
| 24 | 4 | 4 |
| 25 | 4 < | 4 < |
| 26 | 5 | 1 < |
| 27 | 5 | 2 < |
| 28 | 5 | 3 < |
| 29 | 5 | 4 |
| 30 | 5 < | 4 < |

**FIGURE 9.4**
*Records Sorted by Class within Major Showing Control Breaks (<)*

This is what happens to the pseudocode.

```
Initialization
Read 1st student record
Do while more records
    Set major-test to major-code
    Write major group headings—page and column
    Do until major-code not = major-test
       or no more records
        Set class-test to class-code
        Move class description to output
        Do until class-code not = class-test
            or major-code not = major-test
            or no more records
            Move input data to output record
                (except for class and major)
            Write student record
            Move spaces to output class description
            Read next student record (2nd – Nth)
        End Do
    End Do
End Do
```

**FIGURE 9.5**
**Multiple Control-Break**
**Hierarchy Chart**

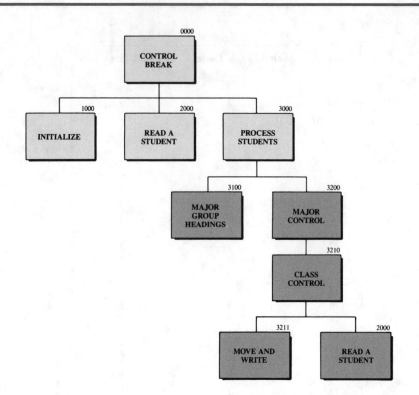

Again you should see that the move and write logic just keeps moving down. Another do while to control class breaks was added. Let's take a moment and digest all this graphically. Figure 9.6 shows the different breaks.

**FIGURE 9.6**
**Nested Loops Used to Depict**
**Control Breaks**

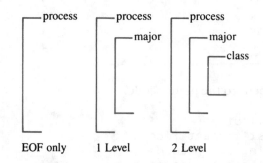

The EOF-only graphic hopes to show that the looping control is just controlled by reading the end of the file. There is no special control break. (I might argue that EOF is a control break even here.) The 1 Level graphic on the other hand shows a nested level within the EOF level. We have imposed an additional requirement on our processing. Furthermore, the 2 Level shows yet another control level on our processing. In fact, this depiction could be used for as many levels as you would like.

### Coding the Multi-Level Control Break

Let's approach this a little differently than we did the single level. It should give you another perspective. Figure 9.7 shows our sequential file model without any control break (except for EOF).

Recognize the model? Remember, all we have to do is fill in the blank with whatever processing we need to do for a particular problem. In this case, we would simply include the moving and writing of student records.

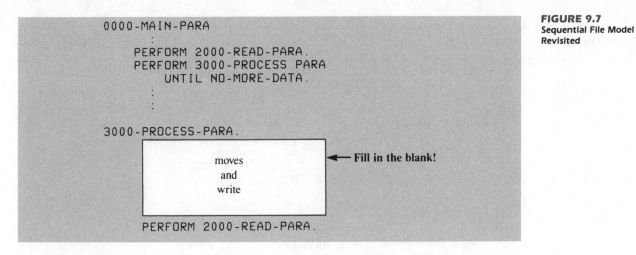

0000-MAIN-PARA

    PERFORM 2000-READ-PARA.
    PERFORM 3000-PROCESS PARA
        UNTIL NO-MORE-DATA.


3000-PROCESS-PARA.

moves
and
write

← **Fill in the blank!**

PERFORM 2000-READ-PARA.

**FIGURE 9.7**
Sequential File Model
Revisited

What would happen with one-level control-break requirements?  Let's do it!
(Figure 9.8)

0000-MAIN-PARA.
    :
    PERFORM 2000-READ-PARA.
    PERFORM 3000-PROCESS-PARA
        UNTIL NO-MORE-DATA.
    :

3000-PROCESS-PARA.

    PERFORM 3100-MAJOR-BREAK
            UNTIL MAJOR-CODE NOT = MAJOR-TEST     ← **Fill in the blank!**
            OR NO-MORE-DATA.


3100-MAJOR-BREAK.

        moves and write


PERFORM 2000-READ-PARA.

**FIGURE 9.8**
Sequential File Model
Showing One-Level Control-
Break Code

See what happens?  The fill-in-the-blank becomes more extensive because we
added the additional PERFORM for the control break.  Can you imagine what happens for the two-level control break?  Let's take a look with Figure 9.9.  But if you
understood the previous example, multiple levels are duck soup!

The fill-in-the-blank just gets bigger and bigger, but it's still the sequential file
model.  We just keep adding control levels.  This matches our control break requirements; PERFORM 3100. . . and PERFORM 3110. . . are the controls for major break
and class break, respectively.  What about sex within class within major?  Try it yourself.  Then ask your professor if you're not sure, but I'm confident you can do it.

**FIGURE 9.9**
Sequential File Model
Showing Multi-Level Control-
Break Code

```
0000-MAIN-PARA.
      :
      PERFORM 2000-READ-PARA.
      PERFORM 3000-PROCESS PARA
          UNTIL NO-MORE-DATA.
      :
      :
3000-PROCESS-PARA.

      PERFORM 3100-MAJOR-BREAK
              UNTIL MAJOR-CODE NOT = MAJOR TEST
              OR NO-MORE-DATA.
```

◄——Fill in the blank!

```
3100-MAJOR-BREAK.

      PERFORM 3110-CLASS-BREAK
          UNTIL CLASS-CODE NOT = CLASS-TEST
      OR MAJOR-CODE NOT = MAJOR TEST
      OR NO-MORE-DATA.
              .
3110-CLASS-BREAK.


              moves and write



PERFORM 2000-READ-PARA.
```

Well, let's get back to the COBOL code for the two-level control break.

```
          0000-MAIN-PARA.
1             PERFORM 1000-INITIALIZATION.
2             PERFORM 2000-READ-PARA.
3             PERFORM 3000-PROCESS PARA
                  UNTIL NO-MORE-DATA.
              :
              :
          1000-INITIALIZATION.
              :
              :

          2000-READ-PARA.
4             READ DEAN-FILE INTO STUDENT-RECORD-IN
                  AT END MOVE 'NO ' TO ARE-THERE-MORE-RECORDS.

          3000-PROCESS-PARA.
5             MOVE MAJOR-CODE TO MAJOR-TEST.
6             PERFORM 3100-MAJOR-HEADINGS.
7             PERFORM 3200-MAJOR-BREAK
                  UNTIL MAJOR-CODE NOT = MAJOR-TEST
                  OR NO-MORE-DATA.
```

```
        3100-MAJOR-HEADINGS.
8           IF MAJOR-CODE = 1
                MOVE 'ACCOUNTING' TO MAJOR-TITLE
            ELSE
                IF MAJOR-CODE = 2
                    MOVE 'INFORMATION SYSTEMS' TO MAJOR-TITLE
                ELSE
                    IF MAJOR-CODE = 3
                        MOVE 'FINANCE' TO MAJOR-TITLE
                    ELSE
                        IF MAJOR-CODE = 4
                            MOVE 'MANAGEMENT' TO MAJOR-TITLE
                        ELSE
                            MOVE 'MARKETING' TO MAJOR-TITLE.
9           WRITE REPORT-LINE FROM PAGE-HEADING
                AFTER PAGE-TOP.
10          WRITE REPORT-LINE FROM COLUMN-HEADINGS
                AFTER 5.


        3200-MAJOR-BREAK.
11          MOVE CLASS-CODE TO CLASS-TEST.
12          IF CLASS-CODE = 1
                MOVE 'FRESHMAN' TO CLASSIFICATION-OUT
            ELSE
                IF CLASS-CODE = 2
                    MOVE 'SOPHOMORE' TO CLASSIFICATION-OUT
                ELSE
                    IF CLASS-CODE = 3
                        MOVE 'JUNIOR' TO CLASSIFICATION-OUT
                    ELSE
                        MOVE 'SENIOR' TO CLASSIFICATION-OUT.
13          PERFORM 3210-CLASS-BREAK
                UNTIL CLASS-CODE NOT = CLASS-TEST
                OR MAJOR-CODE NOT = MAJOR-TEST
                OR NO-MORE-DATA.


        3210-CLASS-BREAK.
14          PERFORM 3211-MOVE-AND-WRITE.
15          PERFORM 2000-READ-PARA.


        3211-MOVE-AND-WRITE.
16          MOVE NAME-IN TO NAME-OUT.
17          MOVE ID-IN   TO ID-OUT.
18          MOVE SEX-IN  TO SEX-OUT.
19          MOVE GPR-IN  TO GPR-OUT.
20          WRITE REPORT-LINE FROM STUDENT-RECORD-OUT
                AFTER 2.
21          MOVE SPACES TO CLASSIFICATION-OUT.
```

Notice that neither MAJOR nor CLASS is moved in module 3211. CLASS was moved in 3200 module (outside the loop) so that the first time through the loop, the classification is written. However, after that, spaces are moved to CLASSIFICATION-OUT, in module 3211, which causes spaces to be written for each subsequent record in the same class. This is a powerful technique for group indication.

Let's step through the code together using the ordered NEW-FILE shown earlier in this discussion (Figure 9.4). I have also taken the liberty of numbering the lines of code we just looked at to be able to make references to particular lines of code.

Lines 1 through 4 are our standard beginning for our sequential file model. Line 4 causes the first record to be read. In line 5 the major-test value is initialized to the major code in the current record, 1. Line 6 writes the headings. Notice that it causes lines 8 through 10 to be executed. Line 8 is interesting. The set of IFs move the appropriate major description to the title.

Now we get to the heart of the code, line 7. Notice that this PERFORM is conditioned on one of two happenings. MAJOR-CODE changes, or there is no more data. Therefore, the first time through, first student record, the PERFORM is not satisfied, since MAJOR-CODE and MAJOR-TEST are both 1. (We just made them equal in line 5.)

Lines 11 though 13 are executed next. Line 11 is familiar. It sets the CLASS-TEST value to the current CLASS-CODE, 1 at this point. The set of IFs stating in line 12, though familiar, seems out of place. It is placed here, out of the write loop, so that we don't write the classification for every student. . .just for the first student in the group. Therefore, it initializes CLASSIFICATION-OUT, which will write the first time through the loop. Then, in line 21, it is set to spaces.

The PERFORM in line 13 is our next level control break. It is satisfied when CLASS changes or MAJOR changes or we run out of data.

I can hear you now. Why do we check major also? Well, let's look at an exaggerated example. What if all accounting majors were seniors and what if all information systems majors were also seniors? The data would look something like Figure 9.10.

**FIGURE 9.10**
**Control Breaks with No Class Breaks**

| Name | Major Code | Class Code |
|------|-----------|-----------|
| Joe  | 1 | 4 |
| :    | 1 | 4 |
| :    | 1 | 4 |
| :    | : | 4 |
| :    | : | 4 |
| Bob  | 1 < | 4 |
| Mary | 2 | 4 |
| :    | 2 | 4 |
| :    | 2 | 4 |
| :    | : | 4 |
| Bill | 2 < | 4 |
| :    | 3 < | 4 |
| :    | : | 4 |

Notice there are no breaks in CLASS. Therefore, the PERFORM on line 13 would never catch a break if MAJOR wasn't also checked. We would miss the MAJOR control break between ACCOUNTING and INFORMATION SYSTEMS. Do you see that? Give it another look, because it is important. This is the hierarchical relationship I spoke of earlier. A change in MAJOR forces a change in CLASS. Look at Figure 9.11.

The INFORMATION SYSTEM major is missing! We just reported Mary's and Bill's major as ACCOUNTING. Just another way to see why we need to check MAJOR at the CLASS break level?

Let's continue with our data. For the first record we will reach line 13 with class and major equal to 1 and their test values also equal to 1. Of course we are not at EOF yet. Therefore, we execute lines 14 and 16 through 21 and then read the next record, line 15. At this point control goes back to the PERFORM at line 13. Has major or class changed? Have we reached EOF? Well, look at the second record: Major code is still 1, class code is still 1, and obviously it's not EOF.

FIGURE 9.11
Example of Hierarchical
Relationship Requirement

```
                    ACCOUNTING

Class     Name        ID      SEX      GPR
Senior    Joe         ...     ...      ...
            :
          Bob
          Mary
            :
          Bill
            :
            :
```

Since a break didn't occur we stay in the loop—lines 14 and 16 through 21 and 15 in that order. See how the classification is written only the first time, since line 12 is not in the loop.

The second time we execute line 15, we will read record 3. Does a break occur? Yes, it does. The class code changes to 2. Therefore, the PERFORM on line 13 is satisfied, and control passes back to the PERFORM on line 7. Since MAJOR-CODE did not change, this PERFORM is not satisfied. It is executed again, and this causes lines 11 through 13 to be executed.

Are you with me? This is very important! Line 11 will reinitialize CLASS-TEST to the current CLASS-CODE, now a 2. The class description is moved to the output record in line 12, and the PERFORM is started again. Is it satisfied? No, none of the conditions are met. Therefore, we are in the loop again, lines 14 and 16 through 21 and 15. We stay in this loop until a break occurs. This happens with record 4, another class break.

Finally, we read record 8. This causes both a class break and a major break. Therefore, the PERFORM on line 13 is satisfied. But we also satisfy the PERFORM on line 7, since the major changed also. This causes control to return to line 3. Is this PERFORM satisfied? No, we still have data. Therefore, lines 5, 6, and 7 are done again. This reinitializes MAJOR-TEST to the current value of MAJOR-CODE, writes the headings for the new major, and re-enters the PERFORM on line 7. Since it is not satisfied, it causes lines 11, 12, 13 to be executed. This in turn resets the CLASS-TEST and CLASSIFICATION-OUT, and the PERFORM on line 13 starts our loop of lines 14 and 16 through 21 and 15 again.

We stay in this loop until record 11 is read. It is a class break. Another class break occurs at record 14. Record 15 causes both a major and class break, since both codes change. Follow the logic through to record 21. Notice that the class does not change, but the major does. What happens? Remember the hierarchy of control breaks. A break at one level assumes that all levels below also break. Therefore the PERFORM on line 13 should be satisfied, because we check for major changes also. Therefore, we go back to line 7 and check this PERFORM's conditions. Is it satisfied? Yes. Major changed; therefore, control goes back to line 3. Since we are not out of data, this PERFORM is not satisfied and the whole logic is restarted.

One last thing should be noted. Does the logic handle EOF correctly? When an attempt is made to read the 31st record, the EOF will be sensed. Therefore, the PERFORMs at line 13 and at line 7 and at line 3 are all satisfied (all check for EOF), and the control-break logic is finished.

## GROUP INDICATION OF ANOTHER FASHION

Recall that I said we would look at reporting of data for multiple control breaks that was different. The difference is not to use the major break as a title. In fact all control breaks are still shown in the detail report but are group indicated and not used as report titles. How? Well, each control-break key is listed only for the first record in the group.

Figure 9.12 shows the two-level group we just worked through using the new report format. Notice that both control-break keys are column headings. But only the first report line for a group contains information. That is, we don't keep writing "ACCOUNTING" for all accounting students. Neither do we keep writing "FRESH-MAN" or "SOPHOMORE" or "JUNIOR" or "SENIOR." Just once is best!

**FIGURE 9.12**
**Group-Indication Report**

```
                     DEAN'S STUDENT REPORT
        MAJOR       CLASS    NAME        ID      SEX       GPR
        ACCOUNTING  FRESHMAN JOE      557534081  MALE     1.0000
                             BETH     333333333  FEMALE   4.0000
                      :        :          :         :        :
                    SOPHOMORE JILL    123456789  FEMALE   3.5000
                             JAN      444444555  FEMALE   2.6000
                                                           :
                    JUNIOR   BOB      666666666  MALE     4.0000
                             MARY     101010101  FEMALE   3.0000
                      :        :          :         :        :
                    SENIOR   SAM      554433220  MALE     1.5000
                             CHARLES  430043430  MALE     2.3000
                      :        :          :         :        :

        INFO.SYSTEMS FRESHMAN MICHAEL  .........
                               :          :         :        :
```

As a special note: Could this have been done with one level? Sure it could. This is what I was talking about earlier in our single-level control-break discussion. Could this form be used for three, four, or more level breaks? Sure it can. In fact, most people like this form over the other. It's a matter of choice or possible corporate standards. Which is my preference? As you probably expected, I like the first approach. Using the major break group indication as a title just appeals to me.

## CONTROL TOTALS

I don't want to leave you with the impression that control-break logic is simply a technique for managing report formats for titles and detail lines. It's not. What about reporting counts and/or totals for control groups? Does our logic work to allow for control totals? It works very well.

### A Problem

Let's pose a problem. What if the dean wanted the students group indicated by class within major? In addition, he wants the total number of students in each major group. He wants this count written at the bottom of the group. In other words, the report would look as shown in Figure 9.13.

```
                    ACCOUNTING

CLASS           NAME        ID      SEX     GPR
FRESHMAN        .....
                              :
                              :

SOPHOMORE                     :
                              :
JUNIOR                        :
                              :
SENIOR                        :
                              :

        TOTAL NUMBER OF ACCOUNTING MAJORS IS xxxx

------------------------------------------------------------

                  INFORMATION SYSTEMS

CLASS           NAME        ID      SEX     GPR
                           :
                           :
                           :
                           :
                           :

TOTAL NUMBER OF INFORMATION SYSTEMS MAJORS IS xxxxx

------------------------------------------------------------
```

**FIGURE 9.13**
Report Showing Control
Totals

## Hierarchy Chart for Control Totals

Probably the easiest way to show this additional requirement is to look at both the hierarchy chart in Figure 9.14 and pseudocode that follows.

```
    Initialization
    Read 1st student record
    Do while more records
        Set major-test to major-code
        Write major group headings—page and column
        Do until major-code not = major-test
            or no more records
            Set class-test to class-code
            Move class description to output
            Do until class-code not = class-test
                or major-code not = major-test
                or no more records
                Add 1 to student-count
                Move input data to output record
                    (except for class and major)
                Write student record
                Move spaces to output class description
                Read next student record (2nd – Nth)
            End Do (class loop)
        End Do (major loop)
        Write student-count
        Set student-count to 0
    End Do (EOF loop)
```

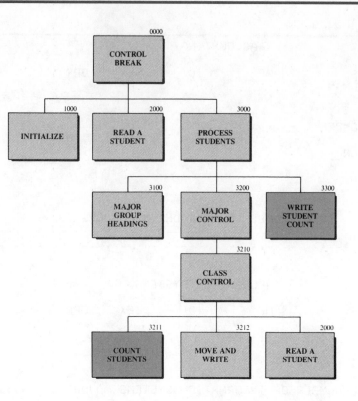

You should recognize both the chart and the pseudocode. In the hierarchy chart I added two modules—3300 and 3211. One does the counting and one writes the count. Since I'm counting individual students, module 3211 appears at the detail level of the hierarchy chart. How about writing the count? Why did I put it at 3300? Think of it this way: Module 3200 controls a loop that breaks for each change in major. When that occurs, I have the corresponding count of students to report (not before). Therefore I don't want the WRITE STUDENT COUNT module within the loop.

If that still bothers you a little, look at the pseudocode. See the ADD? It's at the innermost level, the detail level. Since we pass through the logic for each student, the count will reflect the number of students processed. However, we want the count for each major, not a grand total. Don't panic! Look at the Write student-count and the Set student-count to 0. Notice that they are both done only when the major changes (breaks). Therefore, for each change in major, we write the corresponding count and reset the count to 0. When we do this, what value is in student-count for each major break? The number of students in that major.

### Pseudocode for Multiple Control Totals

What would it take to write the counts for each class and each major? What about including the grand total of all students? If you understood the previous example, then you should not have too much trouble generalizing the technique. We need an ADD for the particular count. Then, when the break for the corresponding count occurs, we write it and reset the count to zero. For instance, the following pseudocode depicts this generalization with three levels—sex within class within major.

```
            :
    Read . . .
    Do while more records
            :
        Do until major changes
            or no more records
                :
            Do until class changes
                or major changes
                or no more records
                    :
                Do until sex changes
                    or class changes
                    or major changes
                    or no more records
                        :
                    Add 1 to sex-count
                    Add 1 to class-count
                    Add 1 to major-count
                    Add 1 to grand-total-count
                    Read . . .
                End Do (sex loop)
                Write sex-count
                Set sex-count to 0
            End Do (class loop)
            Write class-count
            Set class-count to 0.
        End Do (major loop)
        Write major-count
        Set major-count to 0
    End Do (EOF loop)
    Write grand-total-count
```

Don't get heartburn trying to digest all this in one gulp. Look at it for a while. Step through it with some data. You need to give it time to settle.

Now that it's settled, let's step through it together. Use the data set shown in Figure 9.15.

OK, are you ready? We enter the outer PERFORM, and, since we have data to process, we enter the next level and, in fact, since we can see the data we will go all the way into the innermost loop and process the first student. Doing this will cause all four counts to be equal to 1. Now we stay in this inner loop until a break occurs. Looking at our data, when does the first break occur? It occurs after the third student is processed, since the fourth record causes the sex to change (1 to 2).

OK then, since sex changed, we end the sex loop and write the sex count (3) and reset it to 0. Since class or major didn't change, we just re-enter the sex loop and continue processing students.

At this point take a close look at the count values shown with the data. See how major count and class count are still increasing, (they did not break) while sex count starts over at 1. That's correct, isn't it? We are counting a new group of students within the same class and major. Let's go on.

Reading the fifth record causes a break in both class (1 to 2) and sex (2 to 1). Does our logic work? The changes cause the exit from the sex loop. That in turn results in the writing of sex count (1) and the setting of sex count back to 0. But it doesn't stop there. The class loop is also exited. Why? Class changed! Therefore, we would write class count (4) and reset it to 0 also. Now we restart the class loop *and* the sex loop. Processing the fifth record causes major count to be 5, class count to be 1 and sex count to be 1. Why? Since both class and sex broke, the counts start over. However, major didn't break, so it continues to increase. After all, the five students are all in the same major, so major count should be 5.

**FIGURE 9.15**
Data for Control-Break Example

| Record | Major | Class | Sex | Grand total | Major count | Class count | Sex count |
|--------|-------|-------|-----|-------------|-------------|-------------|-----------|
| 1 | 1 | 1 | 1 | 1 | 1 | 1 | 1 |
| 2 | 1 | 1 | 1 | 2 | 2 | 2 | 2 |
| 3 | 1 | 1 | 1 | 3 | 3 | 3 | 3 |
| 4 | 1 | 1 | 2 | 4 | 4 | 4 | 1 |
| 5 | 1 | 2 | 1 | 5 | 5 | 1 | 1 |
| 6 | 1 | 3 | 2 | 6 | 6 | 1 | 1 |
| 7 | 1 | 4 | 2 | 7 | 7 | 1 | 1 |
| 8 | 2 | 1 | 1 | 8 | 1 | 1 | 1 |
| 9 | 2 | 1 | 1 | 9 | 2 | 2 | 2 |
| 10 | 2 | 2 | 1 | 10 | 3 | 1 | 1 |
| 11 | 2 | 3 | 1 | 11 | 4 | 1 | 1 |
| 12 | 2 | 4 | 2 | 12 | 5 | 1 | 1 |
| 13 | 2 | 4 | 2 | 13 | 6 | 2 | 2 |
| 14 | 3 | 1 | 1 | 14 | 1 | 1 | 1 |
| 15 | 3 | 1 | 1 | 15 | 2 | 2 | 2 |
| 16 | 3 | 4 | 1 | 16 | 3 | 1 | 3 |
| 17 | 3 | 4 | 2 | 17 | 4 | 2 | 1 |
| 18 | 3 | 4 | 2 | 18 | 5 | 3 | 2 |
| 19 | 4 | 1 | 1 | 19 | 1 | 1 | 1 |
| 20 | 4 | 1 | 2 | 20 | 2 | 2 | 1 |
| 21 | 4 | 2 | 1 | 21 | 3 | 1 | 1 |
| 22 | 4 | 2 | 2 | 22 | 4 | 2 | 1 |
| 23 | 4 | 3 | 1 | 23 | 5 | 1 | 1 |
| 24 | 4 | 4 | 2 | 24 | 6 | 1 | 1 |
| 25 | 4 | 4 | 2 | 25 | 7 | 2 | 2 |
| 26 | 5 | 1 | 2 | 26 | 1 | 1 | 1 |
| 27 | 5 | 2 | 1 | 27 | 2 | 1 | 1 |
| 28 | 5 | 3 | 1 | 28 | 3 | 1 | 1 |
| 29 | 5 | 4 | 1 | 29 | 4 | 1 | 1 |
| 30 | 5 | 4 | 2 | 30 | 5 | 2 | 1 |

Note: < indicates control breaks

What happens when the sixth record is read? Both class and sex change again. So we would write and reset the counts as with the fifth record. But look at what happens when the seventh record is read. Only class changed (3 to 4). So does our logic work? You bet it does. Why? Well, remember our control break hierarchy. . .every control break assumes all levels below also break. Therefore, the change in class causes us to exit the sex loop (look at the or class change on the DO). This again causes us to write the sex count (1) and reset it to 0. It then causes us to exit the class loop and write the class count (1) and reset it to 0 also. What about the major count? It keeps increasing. Major has not changed.

Guess what's next? You're right. . .a major change. However, by now, you know what is going to happen. All counts will be written and reset to 0 (major count = 7, class count = 1, and sex count = 1). After writing the count and processing the eighth record, all counts would be equal to what? If you said 1, you're right. We are starting a whole new major, class and sex group.

You should follow through with the rest of the data and verify the count values. I want to jump to the EOF. So far we continued to process records because we had data to process. But when we try to read the 31st record we reach the EOF. Therefore, the EOF causes all levels to break. This in turn causes all current values of counts to be written (major count = 5, class count = 2, sex count = 1). But you would expect that. However, the EOF loop is now exited and guess what happens? The grand total (30) is written and the logic finished.

## COUNT EFFICIENCY

Some of you are probably wondering about my example, in particular the way I accumulated my counts. I didn't say my example was the best way to do it. I just felt like using the four individual ADDs would be the easiest to start with. But let's modify it a little.

Let me ask you a question. How many ADDs were executed for the thirty (30) records? Each ADD was executed once for each pass through the sex loop. That's thirty times for each ADD or a total of 120 (4 × 30) ADDs executed. If we had processed 25,000 student records, we would execute 100,000 ADDs. I could go on to bigger numbers, but I think you see my point about the number of ADDs. Can we do it more efficiently? Let's see!

By having all our counts at the lowest detail level we add 1 to each count for every student. If the major, class, and sex remain the same, we are being redundant in our counting. Why add 1 to all three counts? Why not just add 1 to one count until a change occurs? Look at the pseudocode below that illustrates more efficient counting.

```
        :
    Read . . .
    Do while more records
        :
        Do until major changes
            or no more records
            :
            Do until class changes
                or major changes
                or no more records
                :
                Do until sex changes
                    or class changes
                    or major changes
                    or no more records
                    :
                    Add 1 to sex-count
                    Read . . .
                End Do (sex loop)
                Write sex-count
                Add sex-count to class-count
                Set sex-count to 0
            End Do (class loop)
            Write class-count
            Add class-count to major-count
            Set class-count to 0
        End Do (major loop)
```

```
              Write major-count
              Add major-count to grand-total-count
              Set major-count to 0
       End Do (EOF loop)
       Write grand-total-count
```

You probably notice that I removed all ADDs except ADD 1 TO SEX-COUNT from the innermost loop, sex loop. Think about it. What am I counting? All students of the same major, class, sex group. Then when sex changes, I add sex count to class count. Why? All these students are still in the same major and class group. . .I've just had a change—say from male to female—within freshman accounting students. Now when class changes, I added class count to major count. Again this is correct, because all students so far are in the same major group. That is, all students are still, say, finance majors. And finally (you guessed it) when major changes, major count is added to the grand total.

Algebraically, we have done the following:

GRAND TOTAL = SUM OF MAJOR COUNTS
MAJOR COUNT = SUM OF CLASS COUNTS WITHIN MAJORS
CLASS COUNT = SUM OF SEX COUNTS WITHIN CLASSES
SEX COUNT = SUM OF STUDENTS WITHIN SEX

Given this technique, how many ADDs are executed for the 30 students? The ADD 1 TO SEX COUNT is still done for each student, so that's 30 ADDs. However, ADD SEX COUNT TO CLASS COUNT is done only for each change in sex . . . 23 in our example. Following through with this reasoning, the ADD CLASS COUNT TO MAJOR COUNT is done for each class break . . . 18 and the major count is added to grand total for each major break . . . 5. How many total ADDs are executed? 76 (30 + 23 + 18 + 5). That's better than 120, isn't it? What if we had the 25,000 students data set? If we assume the same number of control breaks, then the number of ADDs would be:

```
25,000  individual students
    23  sex breaks
    18  class breaks
     5  major breaks
25,046  ADDs executed
```

Now I know you would agree with this increase in efficiency, (25,046 compared to 4 × 25,000 = 100,000).

## TIP

**At each level the following four steps are done:**

1. **Print the total.**
2. **Add the total to next higher level.**
3. **Zero the total.**
4. **Initialize the test field.**

## Code for Controls and Totals

I guess it's time to look at the PROCEDURE DIVISION code to handle this logic. The code necessary for handling three-level control breaks, with totals for all levels plus a grand total, is shown below.

```
00000-MAIN-PARA.
    PERFORM 10000-INITIALIZATION.
    PERFORM 20000-READ-PARA.
    PERFORM 30000-PROCESS PARA
        UNTIL NO-MORE-DATA.
    PERFORM 40000-WRITE-GRAND-TOTAL.   <---- causes GRAND-TOTAL to
    :                                         be written after EOF


10000-INITIALIZATION.
    :
    :

20000-READ-PARA.
    READ DEAN-FILE INTO STUDENT-RECORD-IN
        AT END
            MOVE 'NO ' TO ARE-THERE-MORE-RECORDS.


30000-PROCESS-PARA.
    MOVE MAJOR-CODE TO MAJOR-TEST.
    PERFORM 31000-MAJOR-HEADINGS.
    PERFORM 32000-MAJOR-BREAK
        UNTIL MAJOR-CODE NOT = MAJOR-TEST
        OR NO-MORE-DATA.
    PERFORM 33000-WRITE-MAJOR-COUNT.   <----- causes MAJOR-TOTAL
                                              to be written for
31000-MAJOR-HEADINGS.                         each major break
    IF MAJOR-CODE = 1
        MOVE 'ACCOUNTING' TO MAJOR-TITLE
    ELSE
        IF MAJOR-CODE = 2
            MOVE 'INFORMATION SYSTEMS' TO MAJOR-TITLE
        ELSE
            IF MAJOR-CODE = 3
                MOVE 'FINANCE' TO MAJOR-TITLE
            ELSE
                IF MAJOR-CODE = 4
                    MOVE 'MANAGEMENT' TO MAJOR-TITLE
                ELSE
                    MOVE 'MARKETING' TO MAJOR-TITLE.
    WRITE REPORT-LINE FROM PAGE-HEADING
        AFTER PAGE-TOP.
    WRITE REPORT-LINE FROM COLUMN-HEADINGS
        AFTER 5.
```

```
32000-MAJOR-BREAK.
    MOVE CLASS-CODE TO CLASS-TEST.
    IF CLASS-CODE = 1
        MOVE 'FRESHMAN' TO CLASSIFICATION-OUT
    ELSE
        IF CLASS-CODE = 2
            MOVE 'SOPHOMORE' TO CLASSIFICATION-OUT
        ELSE
            IF CLASS-CODE = 3
                MOVE 'JUNIOR' TO CLASSIFICATION-OUT
            ELSE
                MOVE 'SENIOR' TO CLASSIFICATION-OUT.
    PERFORM 32100-CLASS-BREAK
        UNTIL CLASS-CODE NOT = CLASS-TEST
        OR MAJOR-CODE NOT = MAJOR-TEST
        OR NO-MORE-DATA.
    PERFORM 32200-WRITE-CLASS-COUNT.    <----- causes CLASS-COUNT to
                                              be written for each
                                              class break or major
                                              break
32100-CLASS-BREAK.
    MOVE SEX-CODE TO SEX-TEST.
    IF SEX-CODE = 1
        MOVE 'MALE' TO SEX-OUT
    ELSE
        MOVE 'FEMALE' TO SEX-OUT.
    PERFORM 32110-SEX-BREAK
        UNTIL SEX-CODE NOT = SEX-TEST
        OR CLASS-CODE NOT = CLASS-TEST
        OR MAJOR-CODE NOT = MAJOR-TEST
        OR NO-MORE-DATA.
    PERFORM 32120-WRITE-SEX-COUNT.      <----- causes SEX-COUNT to
                                              be written for each
                                              sex break or class
31110-SEX-BREAK.                              break or major break
    PERFORM 32111-MOVE-AND-WRITE.
    PERFORM 20000-READ-PARA.

32111-MOVE-AND-WRITE.
    ADD 1 TO SEX-COUNT.
    MOVE NAME-IN TO NAME-OUT.
    MOVE ID-IN    TO ID-OUT.
    MOVE SEX-IN   TO SEX-OUT.
    MOVE GPR-IN   TO GPR-OUT.
    WRITE REPORT-LINE FROM DETAIL-LINE-OUT
        AFTER 2.
    MOVE SPACES TO CLASSIFICATION-OUT.

32120-WRITE-SEX-COUNT.
    MOVE SEX-COUNT TO SEX-COUNT-OUT.
    WRITE REPORT-LINE FROM SEX-LINE
        AFTER 2.
    ADD SEX-COUNT TO CLASS-COUNT.
    MOVE 0 TO SEX-COUNT.
```

```
32200-WRITE-CLASS-COUNT.
    MOVE CLASS-COUNT TO CLASS-COUNT-OUT.
    WRITE REPORT-LINE FROM CLASS-LINE
        AFTER 2.
    ADD CLASS-COUNT TO MAJOR-COUNT.
    MOVE 0 TO CLASS-COUNT.

33000-WRITE-MAJOR-COUNT.
    MOVE MAJOR-COUNT TO MAJOR-COUNT-OUT.
    WRITE REPORT-LINE FROM MAJOR-LINE
        AFTER 2.
    ADD MAJOR-COUNT TO GRAND-TOTAL.
    MOVE 0 TO MAJOR-COUNT.

40000-WRITE-GRAND-TOTAL.
    MOVE GRAND-TOTAL TO GRAND-TOTAL-OUT.
    WRITE REPORT-LINE FROM GRAND-LINE
        AFTER 2.
```

If you understood the discussion up to this point, then the code should not cause you a problem. It simply follows the expressed logic from our pseudocode. One thing you probably saw that was different was the paragraph numbering system. I had to go to a five-digit number because of the levels required in my solution.

## SUMMARY

In this chapter we examined the topic of control breaks. We examined how to do it ourselves. You should know that there is a special feature of COBOL called REPORT WRITER that is very handy for control-break problems. If you are interested, you should study the Appendix on Report Writer.

Coding the logic for control break ourselves involved nested PERFORMs. This hierarchical relationship was discussed fully with several examples. The concept of control breaks can be summarized as follows:

In our sequential file model the process paragraph would contain the MOVEs and WRITE for our detail line followed by our READ control. This would simply list our records without paying special attention to breaks/changes in data values—like changes in major code, etc.

If we now want to pay attention to change, we need more control over our report. Therefore, we added another level of control—PERFORM. . .UNTIL a change in data value. The MOVEs and WRITEs now were further down in our control structure. If we added a second control-break field, say class within major, we simply added another level of control—PERFORM. . .UNTIL. This concept and approach applied for 1, 2, or as many control-break levels as needed.

As you can probably tell, I think the topic of control breaks is a fun topic. It gives us the power to make our reports look really nice, and in so doing, make them more understandable and meaningful.

## SAMPLE PROGRAM

The following is a complete running COBOL program using many of the features and
techniques discussed in this chapter.

```
PP 5740-CB1 RELEASE 2.4                    IBM OS/VS COBOL  JULY  1, 1982      14.50.21  DATE OCT 25,1988

    1                      14.50.21      OCT 25,1988

00001          IDENTIFICATION DIVISION.
00002          PROGRAM-ID. CNTRLBRK.
00003          AUTHOR. FOWLER.
00004          DATE-WRITTEN. AUGUST 1988.
00005          DATE-COMPILED. OCT 25,1988.
00006          REMARKS.
00007
00008          ****************************************************************
00009          *                                                              *
00010          *   ASSIGNMENT NUMBER                                          *
00011          *   DATE ASSIGNED                                              *
00012          *   DATE DUE                                                   *
00013          *   PURPOSE:   THIS IS A COMPANY PERSONNEL EARNINGS PROGRAM.   *
00014          *             IT WILL REPORT THE NAME, SOCIAL SECURITY NUMBER, *
00015          *             AND YEAR-TO-DATE EARNINGS OF EACH EMPLOYEE AS WELL*
00016          *             AS THE DEPARTMENT SUBTOTALS, STORE SUBTOTALS, AND *
00017          *             A COMPANY TOTAL.  THE INFORMATION WILL BE REPORTED*
00018          *             BY DEPARTMENT WITHIN STORE USING A CONTROL BREAK  *
00019          *             FORMAT.                                          *
00020          *                                                              *
00021          *                                                              *
00022          *   INPUT FILE SPECIFICATIONS:                                 *
00023          *        CARD COLUMNS                     DESCRIPTION           *
00024          *   -------------------------             -----------          *
00025          *            1-30                    EMPLOYEE'S NAME            *
00026          *           31-39                    EMPLOYEE'S SOC SEC NUM     *
00027          *           40-40                    STORE CODE                *
00028          *           41-41                    DEPARTMENT CODE           *
00029          *           42-50                    YTD EARNINGS              *
00030          *                                        (TO 2 DECIMAL PLACES) *
00031          *                                                              *
00032          *   THE FIRST DETAIL LINE OF EACH PAGE, STORE, AND DEPARTMENT  *
00033          *   WILL BE GROUP INDICATED.                                   *
00034          *                                                              *
00035          ****************************************************************
00036
```

```
    2         CNTRLBRK         14.50.21        OCT 25,1988

00038          ENVIRONMENT DIVISION.
00039
00040          CONFIGURATION SECTION.
00041
00042          SOURCE-COMPUTER. IBM.
00043          OBJECT-COMPUTER. IBM.
00044          SPECIAL-NAMES.   C01 IS PAGE-TOP.
00045
00046          INPUT-OUTPUT SECTION.
00047
00048          FILE-CONTROL.
00049
00050              SELECT PERSONNEL-FILE
00051                  ASSIGN TO DA-S-PERSON.
00052
00053              SELECT REPORT-FILE
00054                  ASSIGN TO UT-S-REPORT.
00055
00056
```

*(continued)*

```
     3        CNTRLBRK        14.50.21        OCT 25,1988

00058          DATA DIVISION.
00059
00060          FILE SECTION.
00061
00062     FD   PERSONNEL-FILE
00063               LABEL RECORDS ARE OMITTED
00064               RECORD CONTAINS 50 CHARACTERS
00065               BLOCK CONTAINS 100 RECORDS
00066               DATA RECORD IS PERSONNEL-RECORD.
00067     01   PERSONNEL-RECORD                 PIC X(50).
00068
00069
00070     FD   REPORT-FILE
00071               LABEL RECORDS ARE OMITTED
00072               DATA RECORD IS PERSONNEL-REPORT-RECORD.
00073     01   PERSONNEL-REPORT-RECORD          PIC X(133).
00074
00075
```

```
     4        CNTRLBRK        14.50.21        OCT 25,1988

00077          WORKING-STORAGE SECTION.
00078
00079          77   DEPARTMENT-SUBTOTAL             PIC 9(9)V9(2).
00080          77   STORE-SUBTOTAL                  PIC 9(9)V9(2).
00081          77   COMPANY-TOTAL                   PIC 9(9)V9(2).
00082          77   PREVIOUS-DEPARTMENT-CODE        PIC 9.
00083          77   PREVIOUS-STORE-CODE             PIC 9.
00084          77   LINE-COUNT                      PIC 99.
00085
00086          01   PERSONNEL-RECORD-IN.
00087               05   NAME-IN                    PIC X(30).
00088               05   SOCIAL-SECURITY-NUMBER-IN  PIC X(9).
00089               05   STORE-IN                   PIC S(1).
00090               05   DEPT-IN                    PIC 9(1).
00091               05   YTDE-IN                    PIC 9(7)V9(2).
00092
00093
00094          01   ARE-THERE-MORE-RECORDS          PIC X(3) VALUE 'YES'.
00095               88 MORE-RECORDS                          VALUE 'YES'.
00096               88 NO-MORE-RECORDS                       VALUE 'NO'.
00097
00098          01   DETAIL-LINE.
00099               05   FILLER                     PIC X(7)  VALUE SPACES.
00100               05   STORE-NUMBER-OUT           PIC 9     BLANK WHEN ZERO.
00101               05   FILLER                     PIC X(6)  VALUE SPACES.
00102               05   DEPARTMENT-NUMBER-OUT      PIC 9     BLANK WHEN ZERO.
00103               05   FILLER                     PIC X(6)  VALUE SPACES.
00104               05   NAME-OUT                   PIC X(30).
00105               05   FILLER  .                  PIC X(6)  VALUE SPACES.
00106               05   SOCIAL-SECURITY-NUMBER-OUT PIC 9(9).
00107               05   FILLER                     PIC X(6)  VALUE SPACES.
00108               05   YTD-EARNINGS-OUT           PIC $$,$$$,$$9.99.
00109               05   FILLER                     PIC X(48) VALUE SPACES.
00110
00111          01   BLANK-LINE.
00112               05   FILLER                     PIC X(133)  VALUE SPACES.
00113
00114          01   PAGE-HEADING.
00115               05   FILLER                     PIC X(35) VALUE SPACES.
00116               05   FILLER                     PIC X(30) VALUE
00117                         'COMPANY EMPLOYEE YTD EARNINGS '.
00118               05   FILLER                     PIC X(34) VALUE
00119                         'LISTING BY DEPARTMENT WITHIN STORE'.
00120               05   FILLER                     PIC X(34) VALUE SPACES.
00121
```

*(continued)*

```
     5          CNTRLBRK        14.50.21      OCT 25,1988

00123          01  COLUMN-HEADING.
00124              05  FILLER                      PIC X(5)  VALUE SPACES.
00125              05  FILLER                      PIC X(5)  VALUE 'STORE'.
00126              05  FILLER                      PIC X(2)  VALUE SPACES.
00127              05  FILLER                      PIC X(5)  VALUE 'DEPT.'.
00128              05  FILLER                      PIC X(4)  VALUE SPACES.
00129              05  FILLER                      PIC X(4)  VALUE 'NAME'.
00130              05  FILLER                      PIC X(28) VALUE SPACES.
00131              05  FILLER                      PIC X(17) VALUE
00132                      'SOCIAL SECURITY #'.
00133              05  FILLER                      PIC X(3)  VALUE SPACES.
00134              05  FILLER                      PIC X(12) VALUE
00135                      'YTD EARNINGS'.
00136              05  FILLER                      PIC X(48) VALUE SPACES.
00137
00138          01  DEPARTMENT-SUBTOTAL-LINE.
00139              05  FILLER                      PIC X(21) VALUE SPACES.
00140              05  FILLER                      PIC X(19) VALUE
00141                      'DEPARTMENT SUBTOTAL'.
00142              05  FILLER                      PIC X(2)  VALUE SPACES.
00143              05  FILLER                      PIC X(47) VALUE ALL '*'.
00144              05  FILLER                      PIC X(2)  VALUE SPACES.
00145              05  DEPARTMENT-SUBTOTAL-OUT     PIC $$$$,$$$,$$9.99.
00146              05  FILLER                      PIC X(27) VALUE SPACES.
00147
00148          01  STORE-SUBTOTAL-LINE.
00149              05  FILLER                      PIC X(21) VALUE SPACES.
00150              05  FILLER                      PIC X(14) VALUE
00151                      'STORE SUBTOTAL'.
00152              05  FILLER                      PIC X(7)  VALUE SPACES.
00153              05  FILLER                      PIC X(47) VALUE ALL '*'.
00154              05  FILLER                      PIC X(23) VALUE SPACES.
00155              05  STORE-SUBTOTAL-OUT          PIC $$$$,$$$,$$9.99.
00156              05  FILLER                      PIC X(6)  VALUE SPACES.
00157
00158          01  COMPANY-TOTAL-LINE.
00159              05  FILLER                      PIC X(21) VALUE SPACES.
00160              05  FILLER                      PIC X(13) VALUE
00161                      'COMPANY TOTAL'.
00162              05  FILLER                      PIC X(8)  VALUE SPACES.
00163              05  FILLER                      PIC X(47) VALUE ALL '*'.
00164              05  FILLER                      PIC X(23) VALUE SPACES.
00165              05  COMPANY-TOTAL-OUT           PIC $$$$,$$$,$$9.99.
00166              05  FILLER                      PIC X(6)  VALUE ' ***'.
00167
00168          01  COMPANY-UNDERLINE.
00169              05  FILLER                      PIC X(112) VALUE SPACES.
00170              05  FILLER                      PIC X(15)  VALUE ALL '-'.
00171              05  FILLER                      PIC X(6)   VALUE SPACES.
00172
```

```
     6          CNTRLBRK        14.50.21      OCT 25,1988

00174          PROCEDURE DIVISION.
00175
00176          0000-MAIN-PARA.
00177              PERFORM 1000-INIT-PARA.
00178              PERFORM 8000-READ-PARA.
00179              PERFORM 2000-PROCESS-PARA
00180                  UNTIL NO-MORE-RECORDS.
00181              PERFORM 3000-TERMINATE-PARA.
00182              STOP RUN.
00183
```

*(continued)*

```
    7          CNTRLBRK        14.50.21        OCT 25,1988

00185          ********************************************************
00186          *  1000-INIT-PARA                                      *
00187          *                                                      *
00188          *  THIS PARAGRAPH OPENS THE INPUT AND OUTPUT FILES, ZEROS OUT  *
00189          *  THE COMPANY TOTAL, AND WRITES THE REPORT HEADINGS.  *
00190          *                                                      *
00191          ********************************************************
00192
00193          1000-INIT-PARA.
00194              OPEN INPUT PERSONNEL-FILE
00195                  OUTPUT REPORT-FILE.
00196              MOVE ZERO TO COMPANY-TOTAL.
00197              WRITE PERSONNEL-REPORT-RECORD FROM BLANK-LINE
00198                  AFTER PAGE-TOP.
00199              WRITE PERSONNEL-REPORT-RECORD FROM PAGE-HEADING
00200                  AFTER 3.
00201              WRITE PERSONNEL-REPORT-RECORD FROM COLUMN-HEADING
00202                  AFTER 3.
00203              WRITE PERSONNEL-REPORT-RECORD FROM BLANK-LINE
00204                  AFTER 1.
00205              MOVE 8 TO LINE-COUNT.
00206
```

```
    8          CNTRLBRK        14.50.21        OCT 25,1988

00208          ********************************************************
00209          *  8000-READ-PARA                                      *
00210          *                                                      *
00211          *  THIS PARAGRAPH READS A RECORD FROM THE PERSONNEL INPUT FILE.*
00212          *                                                      *
00213          ********************************************************
00214
00215          8000-READ-PARA.
00216              READ PERSONNEL-FILE INTO PERSONNEL-RECORD-IN
00217                  AT END
00218                      MOVE 'NO' TO ARE-THERE-MORE-RECORDS.
00219
```

*(continued)*

```
     9      CNTRLBRK      14.50.21      OCT 25,1988

00221        ****************************************************************
00222        *  2000-PROCESS-PARA                                           *
00223        *                                                              *
00224        *  THIS PARAGRAPH IS THE MAJOR FIELD BREAK PARAGRAPH.  IN THIS *
00225        *  PARAGRAPH THE MAJOR FIELD HOLDER (PREVIOUS-STORE-CODE) IS   *
00226        *  SET TO ALLOW THE COMPARISON OF THE VALUE OF THE CURRENT     *
00227        *  RECORD'S STORE TO THE PREVIOUS RECORD'S STORE.  THE STORE   *
00228        *  SUBTOTAL IS ZEROED OUT (AS WE ARE STARTING WITH A NEW STORE *
00229        *  AT THIS POINT).                                             *
00230        *                                                              *
00231        *  THE PARAGRAPH THEN TRANSFERS CONTROL TO THE                 *
00232        *  2100-DEPARTMENT-BREAK-PARA WHICH WILL CONTINUE TO BE PER-   *
00233        *  FORMED UNTIL A MAJOR CONTROL BREAK IS ENCOUNTERED (THE PRE- *
00234        *  VIOUS RECORD'S STORE IS NOT EQUAL TO THE CURRENT RECORD'S   *
00235        *  STORE) OR THE END OF THE FILE IS REACHED.                   *
00236        *                                                              *
00237        *  AT THE TIME THAT A MAJOR CONTROL BREAK IS ENCOUNTERED THE   *
00238        *  STORE SUBTOTAL WILL BE ADDED TO THE COMPANY TOTAL AND       *
00239        *  WRITTEN AS A SUBTOTAL LINE ON THE REPORT. THE LINE COUNT    *
00240        *  WILL BE INCREMENTED BY 3 TO REFLECT THE WRITTEN SUBTOTAL    *
00241        *  LINE.                                                       *
00242        *                                                              *
00243        *  NOTE THAT IN THIS PARAGRAPH THE STORE-IN IS MOVED TO THE    *
00244        *  STORE-NUMBER-OUT THIS IS DONE SO THE FIRST DETAIL LINE OF   *
00245        *  EACH STORE WILL CONTAIN THE STORE NUMBER (SEE COMMENTS FOR  *
00246        *  2110-ADD-MOVE-AND-WRITE-PARA FOR FURTHER COMMENTS REGARDING *
00247        *  GROUP INDICATION).                                          *
00248        *                                                              *
00249        ****************************************************************
00250
00251        2000-PROCESS-PARA.
00252            MOVE STORE-IN TO PREVIOUS-STORE-CODE.
00253            MOVE STORE-IN TO STORE-NUMBER-OUT.
00254            MOVE ZERO TO STORE-SUBTOTAL.
00255            PERFORM 2100-DEPARTMENT-BREAK-PARA
00256                UNTIL STORE-IN NOT = PREVIOUS-STORE-CODE
00257                   OR NO-MORE-RECORDS.
00258            ADD STORE-SUBTOTAL TO COMPANY-TOTAL.
00259            MOVE STORE-SUBTOTAL TO STORE-SUBTOTAL-OUT.
00260            WRITE PERSONNEL-REPORT-RECORD FROM STORE-SUBTOTAL-LINE
00261                AFTER 1.
00262            WRITE PERSONNEL-REPORT-RECORD FROM BLANK-LINE
00263                AFTER 1.
00264            ADD 3 TO LINE-COUNT.
00265
```

*(continued)*

```
        10      CNTRLBRK       14.50.21      OCT 25,1988

00267        ****************************************************************
00268        *  2100-DEPARTMENT-BREAK-PARA                                  *
00269        *                                                              *
00270        *  THIS PARAGRAPH IS THE MINOR FIELD BREAK PARAGRAPH.  IN THIS *
00271        *  PARAGRAPH THE MINOR FIELD HOLDER (PREVIOUS-DEPARTMENT-CODE) *
00272        *  IS SET TO ALLOW THE COMPARISON OF THE VALUE OF THE CURRENT  *
00273        *  RECORD'S DEPARTMENT TO THE PREVIOUS RECORD'S DEPARTMENT.    *
00274        *  THE DEPARTMENT SUBTOTAL IS ZEROED OUT (AS WE ARE STARTING   *
00275        *  WITH A NEW DEPARTMENT WITHIN THE STORE AT THIS POINT).      *
00276        *                                                              *
00277        *  THE PARAGRAPH THEN TRANSFERS CONTROL TO THE                 *
00278        *  2110-ADD-MOVE-AND-WRITE-PARA WHICH WILL CONTINUE TO BE PER- *
00279        *  FORMED UNTIL A MAJOR CONTROL BREAK IS ENCOUNTERED (THE PRE- *
00280        *  VIOUS RECORD'S STORE IS NOT EQUAL TO THE CURRENT RECORD'S   *
00281        *  STORE), OR A MINOR CONTROL BREAK IS ENCOUNTERED (THE PRE-   *
00282        *  VIOUS RECORD'S DEPARTMENT IS NOT EQUAL TO THE CURRENT       *
00283        *  RECORD'S DEPARTMENT), OR THE END OF THE FILE IS REACHED.    *
00284        *                                                              *
00285        *  AT THE TIME THAT A MAJOR CONTROL BREAK IS ENCOUNTERED OR    *
00286        *  AT THE TIME THAT A MINOR CONTROL BREAK IS ENCOUNTERED THE   *
00287        *  DEPARTMENT SUBTOTAL WILL BE ADDED TO THE STORE SUBTOTAL AND *
00288        *  THE DEPARTMENT SUBTOTAL WILL BE WRITTEN AS A SUBTOTAL LINE  *
00289        *  ON THE REPORT.  THE LINE COUNT WILL BE INCREMENTED BY 3 TO  *
00290        *  REFLECT THE WRITTEN SUBTOTAL LINE.                          *
00291        *                                                              *
00292        *  NOTE THAT IN THIS PARAGRAPH THE DEPT-IN IS MOVED TO THE     *
00293        *  DEPARTMENT-NUMBER-OUT. THIS IS DONE SO THE FIRST DETAIL LINE*
00294        *  EACH STORE OR DEPARTMENT WILL CONTAIN THE DEPARTMENT NUMBER.*
00295        *  (SEE COMMENTS FOR  2110-ADD-MOVE-AND-WRITE-PARA FOR FURTHER *
00296        *  COMMENTS REGARDING GROUP INDICATION).                       *
00297        *                                                              *
00298        ****************************************************************
00299
00300        2100-DEPARTMENT-BREAK-PARA.
00301            MOVE DEPT-IN TO PREVIOUS-DEPARTMENT-CODE.
00302            MOVE DEPT-IN TO DEPARTMENT-NUMBER-OUT.
00303            MOVE ZERO TO DEPARTMENT-SUBTOTAL.
00304            PERFORM 2110-ADD-MOVE-AND-WRITE-PARA
00305                UNTIL DEPT-IN NOT = PREVIOUS-DEPARTMENT-CODE
00306                    OR STORE-IN NOT = PREVIOUS-STORE-CODE
00307                    OR NO-MORE-RECORDS.
00308            ADD DEPARTMENT-SUBTOTAL TO STORE-SUBTOTAL.
00309            MOVE DEPARTMENT-SUBTOTAL TO DEPARTMENT-SUBTOTAL-OUT.
00310            WRITE PERSONNEL-REPORT-RECORD FROM DEPARTMENT-SUBTOTAL-LINE
00311                AFTER 2.
00312            WRITE PERSONNEL-REPORT-RECORD FROM BLANK-LINE
00313                AFTER 1.
00314            ADD 3 TO LINE-COUNT.
00315
```

*(continued)*

```
      11        CNTRLBRK         14.50.21        OCT 25,1988

00317         ************************************************************
00318         *   2110-ADD-MOVE-AND-WRITE-PARA                           *
00319         *                                                          *
00320         *   IN THIS PARAGRAPH THE YEAR-TO-DATE EARNINGS ARE ADDED TO
00321         *   DEPARTMENTAL SUBTOTAL AND THE NAME, SOCIAL SECURITY NUMBER, *
00322         *   AND YEAR-TO-DATE-EARNINGS ARE MOVED TO THEIR RESPECTIVE *
00323         *   OUTPUT FIELDS.  IF THE LINE COUNT IS GREATER THAN 55, THE *
00324         *   9000-NEW-PAGE-PARA WILL BE PERFORMED.  THE DETAIL LINE IS *
00325         *   THEN WRITTEN, THE LINE COUNT IS INCREMENTED BY 1, AND THE *
00326         *   NEXT RECORD IS READ.                                    *
00327         *                                                          *
00328         *   NOTE THAT IN THIS PARAGRAPH ZEROES ARE MOVED TO THE STORE *
00329         *   NUMBER OUT AND THE DEPARTMENT NUMBER OUT.  BOTH OF THESE *
00330         *   FIELDS CONTAIN A "BLANK WHEN ZERO" CLAUSE.  AS LONG AS A *
00331         *   CONTROL BREAK HAS NOT BEEN ENCOUNTERED (OR THE BEGINNING OF *
00332         *   A NEW PAGE) THESE FIELDS WILL ALWAYS PRINT AS BLANK SPACES. *
00333         *   THIS IS HOW THE GROUP INDICATION IS ACHIEVED.           *
00334         *                                                          *
00335         ************************************************************
00336
00337          2110-ADD-MOVE-AND-WRITE-PARA.
00338              ADD YTDE-IN TO DEPARTMENT-SUBTOTAL.
00339              MOVE NAME-IN TO NAME-OUT.
00340              MOVE SOCIAL-SECURITY-NUMBER-IN TO SOCIAL-SECURITY-NUMBER-OUT.
00341              MOVE YTDE-IN TO YTD-EARNINGS-OUT.
00342              IF LINE-COUNT IS GREATER THAN 55
00343                  PERFORM 9000-NEW-PAGE-PARA.
00344              WRITE PERSONNEL-REPORT-RECORD FROM DETAIL-LINE
00345                  AFTER 1.
00346              ADD 1 TO LINE-COUNT.
00347              MOVE ZEROES TO STORE-NUMBER-OUT, DEPARTMENT-NUMBER-OUT.
00348              PERFORM 8000-READ-PARA.
00349
```

```
      12        CNTRLBRK         14.50.21        OCT 25,1988

00351         ************************************************************
00352         *   9000-NEW-PAGE-PARA                                     *
00353         *                                                          *
00354         *   THIS PARAGRAPH IS PERFORMED WHEN THE NUMBER OF LINES ON A *
00355         *   PAGE EXCEEDS 55.  WHEN THIS OCCURS, THE REPORT SKIPS TO A *
00356         *   NEW PAGE AND THE HEADINGS ARE WRITTEN.  NOTE THAT THE   *
00357         *   STORE-IN AND THE DEPT-IN ARE MOVED TO THE STORE-NUMBER-OUT *
00353         *   AND THE DEPARTMENT-NUMBER-OUT (RESPECTIVELY).  THIS IS DONE *
00359         *   SO THE FIRST DETAIL LINE OF THE NEW PAGE WILL BE GROUP  *
00360         *   INDICATED.  AFTER THIS THE LINE COUNT IS RESET TO 2.    *
00361         *                                                          *
00362         ************************************************************
00363
00364          9000-NEW-PAGE-PARA.
00365              WRITE PERSONNEL-REPORT-RECORD FROM COLUMN-HEADING
00366                  AFTER PAGE-TOP.
00367              WRITE PERSONNEL-REPORT-RECORD FROM BLANK-LINE
00368                  AFTER 1.
00369              MOVE STORE-IN TO STORE-NUMBER-OUT.
00370              MOVE DEPT-IN TO DEPARTMENT-NUMBER-OUT.
00371              MOVE 2 TO LINE-COUNT.
00372
```

*(continued)*

```
13        CNTRLBRK        14.50.21      OCT 25,1988

00374          *****************************************************************
00375          *  3000-TERMINATE-PARA                                          *
00376          *                                                               *
00377          *  IN THIS PARAGRAPH THE COMPANY TOTAL (YTD EARNINGS) IS        *
00378          *  WRITTEN UNDER A DOTTED LINE (TO DELINEATE IT FROM THE OTHER  *
00379          *  SUBTOTALS). THE INPUT AND OUTPUT FILES ARE THEN CLOSED.      *
00380          *                                                               *
00381          *****************************************************************
00382
00383           3000-TERMINATE-PARA.
00384               MOVE COMPANY-TOTAL TO COMPANY-TOTAL-OUT.
00385               WRITE PERSONNEL-REPORT-RECORD FROM COMPANY-UNDERLINE
00386                   AFTER 0.
00387               WRITE PERSONNEL-REPORT-RECORD FROM COMPANY-TOTAL-LINE
00388                   AFTER 3.
00389               CLOSE PERSONNEL-FILE
00390                   REPORT-FILE.
```

```
                  COMPANY EMPLOYEE YTD EARNINGS LISTING BY DEPARTMENT WITHIN STORE

STORE   DEPT.   NAME                   SOCIAL SECURITY #   YTD EARNINGS
  1       1     ROY DEJOIE                 564732337          $987.50
                RICHARD LONG               222222222       $15,000.00

                DEPARTMENT SUBTOTAL  *************************************************   $15,987.50

          2     MARY JONES                 918273645            $9.00
                IRENE HIGGS                000110011         $3,500.00
                HOWARD PORTER              329020045         $2,500.00

                DEPARTMENT SUBTOTAL  *************************************************    $6,009.00

          3     JILL BOTTOMS               678098098           $75.50
                DONNA FRASER               525354555         $3,000.00

                DEPARTMENT SUBTOTAL  *************************************************    $3,075.50

          4     JOHN PEARSON               342134333       $800,000.00
                DEAN DECENSA               102938476        $69,500.50

                DEPARTMENT SUBTOTAL  *************************************************  $869,500.50

                STORE SUBTOTAL       *************************************************                $894,572.50

  2       1     JOANN ALTMEN               304050607     $1,500,000.00

                DEPARTMENT SUBTOTAL  *************************************************  $1,500,000.00

          2     KEVIN MCKENSIE             345123322          $987.50

                DEPARTMENT SUBTOTAL  *************************************************      $987.50

          3     LICA HOEKSTRA              389120987          $987.50

                DEPARTMENT SUBTOTAL  *************************************************      $987.50

          4     TOM DEATS                  811122900        $7,000.00
                MICHAEL FOWLER             584934566     $9,000,000.00
                TIA FOWLER                 654321234       $300,000.00

                DEPARTMENT SUBTOTAL  *************************************************  $9,307,000.00

                STORE SUBTOTAL       *************************************************              $10,808,975.00

  3       1     JOE SMITH                  111111111        $1,000.00
                ROD ALTMEN                 546820988     $3,000,650.00
                POLLY ANN FOWLER           981209334            $5.00
```

(continued)

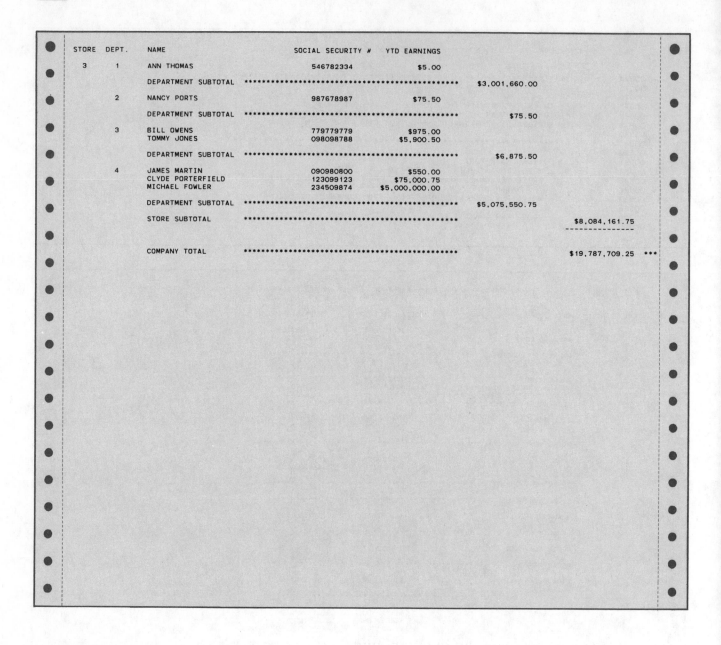

```
STORE  DEPT.   NAME                         SOCIAL SECURITY #   YTD EARNINGS

  3      1     ANN THOMAS                       546782334            $5.00

                DEPARTMENT SUBTOTAL  ***************************************************   $3,001,660.00

         2     NANCY PORTS                      987678987           $75.50

                DEPARTMENT SUBTOTAL  ***************************************************      $75.50

         3     BILL OWENS                       779779779          $975.00
               TOMMY JONES                      098098788        $5,900.50

                DEPARTMENT SUBTOTAL  ***************************************************   $6,875.50

         4     JAMES MARTIN                     090980800          $550.00
               CLYDE PORTERFIELD                123099123       $75,000.75
               MICHAEL FOWLER                   234509874    $5,000,000.00

                DEPARTMENT SUBTOTAL  ***************************************************   $5,075,550.75

                STORE SUBTOTAL       ***************************************************        $8,084,161.75
                                                                                               ---------------

                COMPANY TOTAL        ***************************************************        $19,787,709.25  ***
```

### Chapter Review Questions

1. Control-break logic requires:
    a. The sorting of data within the same program
    b. Ordered data
    c. Nested IFs
    d. The use of the CONTROL verb
    e. None of the above

2. Group indication refers to:
    a. The use of a control-break field to label a group
    b. Reporting the control-break field just once for each group
    c. The group of records in the file
    d. The group of records on a report
    e. Both a and b are true

3. The hierarchy relationship assumes that:
    a. For a major break all lower levels also break
    b. For a minor break all higher levels also break
    c. All levels above and below also break
    d. All fields at the same level also break
    e. None of the above

4. The technique to code multiple-level control-break logic uses:
    a. Nested IFs
    b. Nested PERFORMs
    c. Nested SORTs
    d. Serial IFs
    e. Serial PERFORMs

5. For a 5-level control break requiring counts for each control-break level and a grand total could be done with how many ADDs?
    a. 6
    b. 5
    c. 1
    d. 0
    e. None of the above

6. The technique for summing at the control level to accomplish the process of control totals is :
    a. More efficient than including all ADDs at the lowest control level
    b. Less efficient than including all ADDs at the lowest level
    c. Requires less ADD statements
    d. Requires more ADD statements
    e. None of the above

7. Accumulation of a grand total is done at:
    a. End of file
    b. The detail level
    c. The highest control level
    d. The lowest control level
    e. Both b and c may be used

8. Multi-level control-break logic is an extension of single-level control-break logic.
    a. True
    b. False

9. EOF is a control break.
    a. True
    b. False

10. To keep from printing the group indicator for each record in a group:
    a. The value is initialized outside the control loop
    b. Spaces are moved to the field after each write
    c. Nothing special is needed
    d. The printing can not be avoided
    e. Both a and b are needed

11. The PERFORMs used to control the control-break logic could all be replaced with IFs.
    a. True
    b. False

12. The PERFORM—UNTIL EOF is actually a control break.
    a. True
    b. False

13. Within a control-break algorithm the number of lines printed per page would be controlled with:
    a. An IF statement on the WRITE
    b. BY the WRITE itself
    c. By the lowest level PERFORM in the control-break structure
    d. By the highest level PERFORM in the control-break structure
    e. None of the above

14. In order to apply control-break logic, the data file would have to be in the required order.
    a. True
    b. False

15. Which of the following is not done for CONTROL TOTALS?
    a. Print the TOTAL
    b. ADD the TOTAL to the next higher level
    c. Zero the TOTAL
    d. ADD 1 to each TOTAL FIELD
    e. Initialize the Field

## Discussion Questions

1. Briefly explain the hierarchical relationship used for multiple-level control breaks.
2. Contrast the control-total methods discussed in the chapter.
3. Briefly explain how control totals may be calculated.

## Practice Problems

1. Write the procedure division code to produce a report of all employees in the Personnel File, Data File B. Group-indicate the report on store and department within store.

2. Write a COBOL program to read the Inventory File, Data File C, and produce a report listing all inventory items alphabetically. The report should be group-indicated by buyer and supplier within buyer. A summary report should show total inventory cost by supplier.

## Programming Projects

The following assignments rely on the data dictionary, library elements and data sets found in the Project Sets Section of your text.

1. Do the Control-Break Assignment for the Project Management System in Project A.

2. Do the Control-Break Assignment for the Employee System in Project B.

# THE REAL WORLD OF COBOL

# THE REAL WORLD OF COBOL

# COPY LIBRARIES AND THE REAL WORLD OF COBOL

**10**

***OBJECTIVES***   Throughout the text you have seen entire COBOL programs developed. You have also written complete programs yourself (I hope). You have studied the development and production library environment and its relation to COBOL programming in the real world.

In this chapter we will study systems of programs, instead of just a series of single programs. We will look at several programs that are all part of a system, such as an inventory system, a payroll system or a personnel information system. These systems have a common characteristic. Each system of programs typically requires the use of a common set of files: a master file (for instance, containing a record for each inventory item) and a transaction file (containing actions to be taken on the master: sales, etc.). These common files lend themselves to the use of a new library, the copy library.

We will study how to set up and use the copy library. We will see the companion documentation, the data dictionary, that is essential when using a copy library.

You will see how using the copy library helps system development and maintenance and leads to program standardization.

## TOPICS

- development library revisited
- production library revisited
- copy library
- data dictionary
- system of programs

- JCL
- development enhancement
- maintenance enhancement
- standardization

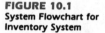

**KEY WORDS**

- library
- COPY
- data dictionary

- //SYSLIB statement
- library member
- PDS (partitioned data set)

## THE REAL WORLD OF COBOL

After graduating, you will go to work and get your first assignment, and you will probably find that you are part of a project team working on a system. This system will involve multiple programs. The one you will be assigned will be just one of many.

Let's assume that the system you will work on will be an inventory system as depicted in the system flowchart in Figure 10.1.

**FIGURE 10.1**
**System Flowchart for Inventory System**

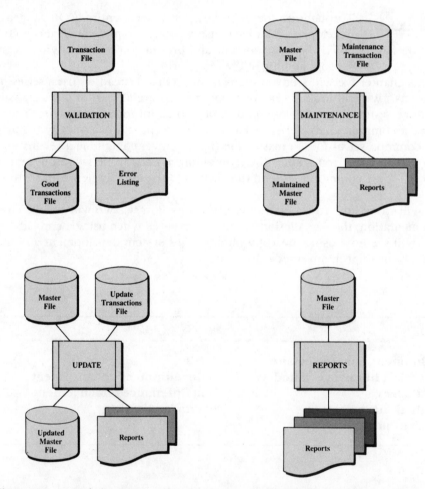

There are several things you should notice. First, there are four programs in the system. Second, three of the programs use the same master file. Third, all the programs write reports. Using the techniques you have studied so far and applying them to this system, you should not be surprised if the project leader gives you and three others your assignments. These would include the file designs, report designs and other specifications, such as hierarchy, IPO and flow charts.

Given all this, you and your team members would go to your desks and program. Each of you would test your programs using the development library (test-data sets, etc.). Once everyone was happy with the system, it would go into production and you would go to your next project.

Is that the real world? To some extent it is; however, what happens one, two or three years down the road when the system is to be revised? Will that task be easy? Did the system development allow for ease of maintenance? Did you and your team members use common data-names? The answer to these questions is very likely no. Is there a better way? Yes, there is!

While in school you probably didn't have to worry beyond getting your programming assignment turned in, getting your gold star and picking up your next assignment. In the real world you must go beyond the school view to a broader view, a real world view.

## THE PROBLEM

So your view needs to change. Therefore, how do you develop systems that go beyond getting your gold star? How do you design for standardization and ease of maintenance?

Wouldn't it be nice if all the file names were the same in each program? Wouldn't it also be nice if all common data fields were defined with the same data names? Sure it would! But how does the project leader insure your team will follow guidelines such as these? Does the project leader get a baseball bat and hold it over your head? After all, the programs will work whether or not the standards are followed.

No, a bat won't be necessary. All the project leader needs to do is place all the common code into a library and give everyone a list of what is there. Then you and your team can simply copy the code into your programs instead of writing unique code yourselves.

Guess what that technique uses? You're right: a copy library, data dictionary and the COBOL COPY verb.

## THE DEVELOPMENT AND PRODUCTION LIBRARIES

You should recall our previous discussions of these two libraries. It is important enough for us to revisit them.

You use the development library during the development of your programs. In that environment you code your program, compile it and run it against test-data files. All compilation and logic errors, you hope, are fixed during development.

Once your program is running correctly and has been fully tested, it is placed into production. Remember that only the object program, which is the result of compilation, is placed into production. The source program is kept in either the development library or a separate historical library for later reference.

The major point that I want you to recall is that the source program is used during development and the object program is used in production.

## THE COPY LIBRARY

As with the other libraries, the copy library is a collection of files. In order for you to use the COBOL COPY verb, you must have a copy library. The content of the copy library is a collection of files that contain COBOL source code. The COPY verb tells the system to go to the library specified with the JCL and copy the library member, file, into the source program. The copied member replaces the COPY itself.

How is the copy library developed? The project leader or systems analyst works out the file and record designs for a system. These FDs and D-R-Ds are keyed and saved as files in the copy library. For instance, let's assume that the following FD for the inventory master file and the following D-R-D for the master inventory record are saved as members of a library called INVLIB.

```
FD   INVENTORY-FILE                          <---- INVMAST
     LABEL RECORDS ARE OMITTED
     RECORD CONTAINS 40 CHARACTERS
     BLOCK CONTAINS 100 RECORDS
     DATA RECORD IS INVENTORY-RECORD.
01   INVENTORY-RECORD             PIC X(40).



01   INVENTORY-RECORD-IN.                    <---- INVRECIN
     03   ITEM-NUMBER             PIC X(5).
     03   ITEM-DESCRIPTION        PIC X(25).
     03   QOH                     PIC 9(4).
     03   UNIT-COST               PIC 9(4)V9(2).
```

Assume the FD was saved as INVMAST and that INVENTORY-RECORD-IN was saved as INVRECIN. Therefore, a listing of the contents, known as the directory, of INVLIB (inventory library) would show that it has two members.

Directory for INVLIB:

INVMAST

INVRECIN

## TIP

**Eight characters are typically used to form the member names and the library name because most systems limit such names to eight characters. Check your system to see what you may use.**

Given this directory, you as a programmer could include both of these members in your source program by simply saying COPY INVMAST and COPY INVRECIN at the appropriate place in your program. Instead of having to code the FD and D-R-D, you simply say COPY member-name. In fact, each member of the project team who uses the master file could do the same thing and get the same code.

Once each of you on the team copies the FD and D-R-D, what names would you use in your programs for the file and data fields? You're right! Each of you would use the same names. Then going back to do system maintenance, or in fact just going back reviewing the system, will be so much easier, since all programs in the system use the same data names for the same files and fields.

### The COPY Verb

COPY may be used to copy source code from a library into all divisions except the IDENTIFICATION DIVISION. The COBOL COPY verb may be used to copy SELECTs, FDs, 77 level items, D-R-Ds, and PROCEDURE DIVISION code. About the only other limitation is that the copied source code may not contain a COPY. In other words, nested copies are not allowed.

The general format of the COPY verb is shown below:

$$\underline{\text{COPY}} \text{ member-name } \left[ \genfrac{}{}{0pt}{}{\underline{\text{OF}}}{\underline{\text{IN}}} \text{ library-name} \right]$$

The member-name is the name of the source code that the programmer wants copied into the program. If there is only one library, the optional specification of library-name is not needed. However, if more than one library is available, one may be specified with the OF or IN option.

---

## TIP

**Make sure that the member-name you use in a COPY is part of the library. A common error is to COPY the FD file name instead of the member-name the FD was saved under.**

---

In our example we have only INVLIB, so we could use either form. The JCL to support copying from INVLIB would be as shown below:

```
//COPYEX        JOB (P007,101,S05,002,JB),'COPYEXAMPLE'
//COPYPROG      EXEC COBCLG
//COB.SYSLIB    DD DSN=USR.S100.PL.INVLIB,. . .
//COB.SYSIN     DD DSN=USR.P007.JB.INVENT,. . .
//GO.MASTER     DD DSN=USR.S100.PL.INVMAST,. . .
//GO.TRANS      DD DSN=USR.S100.PL.TRANSACT,. . .
//GO.RPT        DD DCB=. . .
```

Notice the JCL. You know what all of it is for except for the //COB.SYSLIB statement. But even that statement contains a familiar entry; the DSN. This new JCL statement just says that the library is known by the data set name of USR.S100.PL.INVLIB.

Did you notice that the library, master file and transaction file are in the same account while the program is in a different account? This is normal. The project leader sets up the library and the data sets in an account that may be accessed by all team members.

What does the code that uses the library look like? It looks like what you would expect with a small change. So let's look at the code together.

```
            IDENTIFICATION DIVISION.

            PROGRAM-ID.     COPYEX.
            AUTHOR.         MRF.
                  .
                  .
                  .

            ENVIRONMENT DIVISION.

            CONFIGURATION SECTION.
                  .
                  .
            INPUT-OUTPUT SECTION.

                SELECT INVENTORY-FILE    ASSIGN TO DA-S-MASTER.
                SELECT TRANSACTION-FILE  ASSIGN TO DA-S-TRANS.
                SELECT REPORT-FILE       ASSIGN TO UT-S-RPT.
                  .
                  .
                  .

            DATA DIVISION.

            FILE SECTION.

                COPY INVMAST.           (or COPY INVMAST OF INVLIB.)

            FD  TRANSACTION-FILE
                  .
                  .
                  .

            FD  REPORT-FILE
                  .
                  .
                  .

            WORKING-STORAGE SECTION.
                  .
                  .
                COPY INVRECIN.          (or COPY INVRECIN OF INVLIB.)
                  .
                  .
                  .

            PROCEDURE DIVISION.
                  .
                  .
                  .

            2000-READ-PARA.
                READ INVENTORY-FILE INTO INVENTORY-RECORD-IN
                    AT END
                      .  .  .
```

Notice that two COPYs were used, one for each library member (the FD and D-R-D). As a programmer, I love it. All that I have to do is say COPY instead of coding the FD and D-R-D. I don't even have to make up data names for the items. Even that has been done for me by the system analyst or the project leader with the library!

What happens now? Well, you just compile your program as always. The COPY will bring in the source code from the library. The full program is compiled, and as usual a listing is provided. What does the listing look like? Take a look.

```
        IDENTIFICATION DIVISION.
            .
            .
            .

        ENVIRONMENT DIVISION.
            .
            .
            .

        DATA DIVISION.
        FILE SECTION.

C       FD  INVENTORY-FILE
C           LABEL RECORDS ARE OMITTED
C           RECORD CONTAINS 40 CHARACTERS
C           BLOCK CONTAINS 100 RECORDS
C           DATA RECORD IS INVENTORY-RECORD
C       01  INVENTORY-RECORD              PIC X(40).
            .
            .
            .

        WORKING-STORAGE SECTION.
            .
            .
            .

C       01  INVENTORY-RECORD-IN.
C           03  ITEM-NUMBER               PIC X(5).
C           03  ITEM-DESCRIPTION          PIC X(25).
C           03  QOH                       PIC 9(4).
C           03  UNIT-COST                 PIC 9(4)V9(2).
            .
            .
            .

        PROCEDURE DIVISION.
            .
            .
            .
```

Notice that everything is like your coding except that the COPY verbs have been replaced by the library members. See how the copied code is identified in the listing with the C in column 1? That is usually what happens but it is not a standard. I have included a version of the CIRCLE CLUB program at the end of the chapter that includes copies for you to see the real thing.

In the example, I included the library members, the pre-compiled source listing showing the COPY verb in several places and the compiled listing showing the program that now includes the members. The complete before and after listings should help your understanding of this powerful tool. By the way, you should notice that the output provided by this version of the CIRCLE CLUB program is exactly the same as the CIRCLE CLUB program in Appendix C.

### Data Dictionary

A little earlier I made the statement that I loved the COPY because it saved me some coding and saved me from having to make up some data names. Well, that's fine, but if we don't make up the names, how do we write code that needs to reference those data items? For instance, how could we have coded the READ statement if we didn't know the file name and the D-R-D name? We couldn't. As a programmer you not only need to know the library name and the member names to use the COPY verb, you must also know all the data names. This information is supplied to the programmer via a document called the data dictionary.

The data dictionary contains an entry for each library member. While different formats are used, each contains approximately the same information. This includes:

- member-name
- record name or file name
- elements function: input, output, so on
- brief description, including record and block size for files
- a list of data elements:

  data names
  description of each data-name
  PICTURE clause for each elementary item
  VALUE clause when appropriate
  record redefinition where appropriate

For example, the data dictionary for the INVLIB would look like that shown in Figures 10.2 and 10.3.

**FIGURE 10.2**
**Data Dictionary Entry for INVMAST Member of INVLIB**

```
FILE DESCRIPTION:  INVENTORY-FILE

MEMBER NAME:       INVMAST

FUNCTION:          INPUT


PURPOSE:   DESCRIBES THE INVENTORY MASTER FILE AND
           SPECIFIES DATA CONTROL BLOCK INFORMATION -
           LABEL RECORDS ARE OMITTED
           RECORD CONTAINS 40 CHARACTERS
           BLOCK CONTAINS 100 RECORDS
           DATA RECORD IS INVENTORY-RECORD


RECORD DESCRIPTION:

DATA-NAME              DESCRIPTION              PICTURE


INVENTORY-RECORD    INVENTORY-FILE RECORD       X(40)
```

You can see how as a programmer you can now code since the data dictionary provides all the information needed for the library members. You can now refer to the quantity on hand as QOH and be correct. Before you had the data dictionary, you might have guessed and used Q-O-H. Close, but by now you know that close doesn't count with the compiler.

**FIGURE 10.3**
Data Dictionary Entry for
INVRECIN Member of INVLIB

```
RECORD NAME:   INVENTORY-RECORD-IN

MEMBER NAME:   INVRECIN

FUNCTION:      DETAIL RECORD DESCRIPTION


PURPOSE:   WORKING STORAGE DETAIL RECORD DESCRIPTION
           FOR INVENTORY-FILE


RECORD DESCRIPTION:

DATA-NAME            DESCRIPTION                PICTURE


ITEM-NUMBER          UNIQUELY IDENTIFIES AN
                     ITEM OF INVENTORY          X(5)

ITEM-DESCRIPTION     DESCRIBES THE ITEM         X(25)

QOH                  QUANTITY ON HAND IN
                     UNITS                      9(4)

UNIT-COST            AVERAGE COST OF A
                     UNIT OF THIS ITEM          9(4)V9(2)
```

So, to summarize, you may copy source code from a library. However, you must have a data dictionary to know what names to use in your code. And, it almost goes without saying, the data dictionary must be kept up to date at all times.

## System Considerations

What should be placed into a copy library? I imagine you could get as many different answers as number of people asked. But let me try to generalize for you and give you some examples of some candidates beyond what we have already seen.

I believe that all files that are to be used in a system should be included in the library. The exception to this would be report and temporary files. Temporary files are typically used by a single program for only one run. There would be little need to make a standard description available to all programmers for such a file. Using a similar argument, most reports are unique to a program and are not good candidates for a copy library. However, many corporations have report format standards: common report banners that include date and page number and common footings that may include company name. These record descriptions, however, would be good candidates for inclusion in a copy library.

## SUMMARY

The COBOL COPY verb is a very powerful programming tool. It should be considered when systems are designed. Use of COPY helps reduce coding time during system development. It helps standardize code, which is a great aid to system maintenance.

The COPY verb is used to copy the source code from the system library. Source code is saved as a file, each of which is known as a library member. These members may be copied into the ENVIRONMENT, DATA or PROCEDURE DIVISIONs. They are compiled with the rest of the program and are identified on the source listing with a C in column 1.

Using the COPY verb requires that the project leader supply the programmers with a data dictionary that includes an entry for each library member. The data dictionary includes such information as the file or record name, function of the member, member-name (needed for the COPY), and all data names, descriptions, and PICTURE clauses.

Use of the COPY verb enhances system development and maintenance.

## SAMPLE PROGRAMS

The following programs and library elements are complete running programs illustrating the use of the COPY verb and a copy library. The first program is a listing before compilation showing the actual COPY verbs. This is followed by the library elements to be copied as they appear in the library. The last program is a listing showing the results of compilation. The copies are replaced by the source code from the library and indicated as such by the C in column one of the listing.

## Source Program with COPY Verbs

```
                                              REVISED 01/10/88   *
     IDENTIFICATION DIVISION.

     PROGRAM-ID.
                    DEMOCODE.
     AUTHOR.
                    GEORGE FOWLER.
     INSTALLATION.
                    TEXAS A & M UNIVERSITY.
     DATE-WRITTEN.
                    SEPTEMBER 8, 1985.
     DATE-COMPILED.
          EJECT
     ****************************************************************
     *                                                             *
     *   ASSIGNMENT NUMBER                                         *
     *   DATE ASSIGNED                                            *
     *   DATE DUE                                                 *
     *   PURPOSE:           THIS IS A BILLING PROGRAM FOR THE   CIRCLE *
     *   CLUB RESTAURANT AND BAR. IT CALCULATES THE TOTAL AMOUNT DUE *
     *   FROM EACH CUSTOMER AND A GRAND TOTAL DUE FROM ALL ACCOUNTS. *
     *   THERE ARE DISCOUNTS ALLOWED UNDER CERTAIN CONDITIONS.  THEY *
     *   ARE:                                                     *
     *       2 PERCENT FOR A RESTAURANT BILL OVER $200.00         *
     *       5 PERCENT FOR A BAR BILL OVER $400.00                *
     *       3 PERCENT FOR A TOTAL BILL OVER $1,000.00 AFTER       *
     *         OTHER DISCOUNTS HAVE BEEN SUBTRACTED.               *
     *                                                             *
     *   INPUT FILE SPECIFICATIONS:                               *
     *       CARD COLUMNS                       DESCRIPTION        *
     *          1- 3                            MEMBERSHIP NUMBER  *
     *          5-29                            MEMBER NAME        *
     *         31-48                            MEMBER ADDRESS     *
     *         49-53                            RESTAURANT BILL    *
     *         55-59                            BAR BILL           *
     *         61-65                            ANY OTHER CHARGES  *
     *         67-72                            PAST DUE AMOUNT    *
     *                                                             *
     *   THE OUTPUT CONTAINS MEMBERSHIP NUMBER,  NAME,  ADDRESS,  AND *
     *   AMOUNT DUE.   THE SUMMARY CONTAINS THE TOTAL AMOUNT DUE FROM *
     *   ALL CUSTOMERS.                                           *
     *                                                             *
     ****************************************************************
          EJECT
     ****************************************************************
     *                                                             *
     *              ENVIRONMENT DIVISION                          *
     *                                                             *
     ****************************************************************
     ENVIRONMENT DIVISION.


     CONFIGURATION SECTION.

     SOURCE-COMPUTER.
                    IBM-370.
     OBJECT-COMPUTER.
                    IBM-370.
     SPECIAL-NAMES.
                    CO1 IS TO-TOP-OF-PAGE.
```

*(continued)*

```
 61.
 62.            INPUT-OUTPUT SECTION.
 63.
 64.            FILE-CONTROL.
 65.
 66.                SELECT CUSTOMER-FILE
 67.                    ASSIGN TO DA-S-INFILE.
 68.
 69.                SELECT REPORT-FILE
 70.                    ASSIGN TO UT-S-OUTFILE.
 71.
 72.                EJECT
 73.        ****************************************************************
 74.        *                                                              *
 75.        *                      DATA DIVISION                           *
 76.        *                                                              *
 77.        ****************************************************************
 78.
 79.        DATA DIVISION.
 80.
 81.        FILE SECTION.
 82.
 83.        COPY CUSTFD.
 84.
 85.        FD  REPORT-FILE
 86.            LABEL RECORDS ARE OMITTED
 87.            DATA RECORD IS REPORT-RECORD.
 88.
 89.        01  REPORT-RECORD        PIC X(133).
 90.
 91.                EJECT
 92.        ****************************************************************
 93.        *                                                              *
 94.        *                 WORKING STORAGE SECTION                      *
 95.        *                                                              *
 96.        ****************************************************************
 97.        WORKING-STORAGE SECTION.
 98.
 99.        77  TOTAL-BILL              PIC 9(6)V99   VALUE ZERO.
100.        77  TOTAL-AMT-DUE           PIC 9(6)V99   VALUE ZERO.
101.        77  PAGE-NUM                PIC 9(8)      VALUE ZERO.
102.        77  REPORT-NAME             PIC X(50)     VALUE
103.                        ' CIRCLE CLUB REPORT'.
104.
105.        01  INDICATORS-GROUP.
106.            03  ARE-THERE-MORE-RECORDS    PIC X(3)    VALUE 'YES'.
107.                88 MORE-RECORDS                       VALUE 'YES'.
108.                88 NO-MORE-RECORDS                    VALUE 'NO '.
109.
110.                EJECT
111.        ****************************************************************
112.        *                                                              *
113.        *                 CUSTOMER INPUT RECORD DESIGN                 *
114.        *                                                              *
115.        ****************************************************************
116.
117.        COPY CUSTWS.
118.
119.                EJECT
120.        ****************************************************************
121.        *                                /                             *
```

*(continued)*

```
122.      *                        OUTPUT RECORD DESIGN                        *
123.      *                                                                    *
124.      **********************************************************************
125.
126.          01  DETAIL-LINE.
127.              03  FILLER                   PIC X(22)  VALUE SPACES.
128.              03  MEMBER-NUMBER-OUT        PIC 9(3).
129.              03  FILLER                   PIC X(19)  VALUE SPACES.
130.              03  NAME-OUT                 PIC X(26).
131.              03  FILLER                   PIC X(10)  VALUE SPACES.
132.              03  MEMBER-ADDRESS-OUT       PIC X(19).
133.              03  FILLER                   PIC X(12)  VALUE SPACES.
134.              03  AMT-DUE                  PIC $$$$,$$$.99.
135.              03  FILLER                   PIC X(11)  VALUE SPACES.
136.
137.          01  TITLE.
138.              03  FILLER                   PIC X(61)  VALUE SPACES.
139.              03  FILLER                   PIC X(11)  VALUE
140.                      'CIRCLE CLUB'.
141.              03  FILLER                   PIC X(61)  VALUE SPACES.
142.
143.          01  COLUMN-HEADINGS.
144.              03  FILLER                   PIC X(15)  VALUE SPACES.
145.              03  FILLER                   PIC X(17)  VALUE
146.                      'MEMBERSHIP NUMBER'.
147.              03  FILLER                   PIC X(18)  VALUE SPACES.
148.              03  FILLER                   PIC X(4)   VALUE 'NAME'.
149.              03  FILLER                   PIC X(30)  VALUE SPACES.
150.              03  FILLER                   PIC X(7)   VALUE 'ADDRESS'.
151.              03  FILLER                   PIC X(22)  VALUE SPACES.
152.              03  FILLER                   PIC X(10)  VALUE 'AMOUNT DUE'.
153.              03  FILLER                   PIC X(10)  VALUE SPACES.
154.              EJECT
155.          01  STAR-LINE.
156.              03  FILLER                   PIC X(15)  VALUE SPACES.
157.              03  FILLER                   PIC X(101) VALUE ALL '*'.
158.              03  FILLER                   PIC X(17)  VALUE SPACES.
159.
160.
161.          01  TOTAL-LINE.
162.              03  FILLER                   PIC X(36)  VALUE SPACES.
163.              03  FILLER                   PIC X(43)  VALUE
164.                      'THE TOTAL AMOUNT DUE FROM ALL CUSTOMERS IS'.
165.              03  AMOUNT                   PIC $$$$,$$9.99.
166.              03  FILLER                   PIC X(43)  VALUE SPACES.
167.
168.          EJECT
169.      **********************************************************************
170.      *                                                                    *
171.      *                        PAGE BANNERS                                *
172.      *                                                                    *
173.      **********************************************************************
174.
175.          01  DATE-STORE.
176.              03  YEAR-STORE               PIC 9(2).
177.              03  MONTH-STORE              PIC 9(2).
178.              03  DAY-STORE                PIC 9(2).
179.
180.      COPY PAGEBAN1.
181.
182.      COPY PAGEBAN2.
```

*(continued)*

```
183.
184.          COPY PAGEBAN3.
185.
186.
187.              EJECT
188.      ***********************************************************
189.      *                                                         *
190.      *                  PROCEDURE DIVISION                     *
191.      *                                                         *
192.      ***********************************************************
193.
194.      PROCEDURE DIVISION.
195.
196.
197.      0000-MAIN-DRIVER.
198.          PERFORM 1000-INITIALIZATION.
199.          PERFORM 2000-CLUB-CUSTOMER-PROCESS
200.              UNTIL NO-MORE-RECORDS.
201.          PERFORM 3000-TERMINATION.
202.          STOP RUN.
203.          EJECT
204.      ***********************************************************
205.      *                                                         *
206.      *    1000 INITIALIZATION                                  *
207.      *                                                         *
208.      *    - OPENS THE INPUT AND OUTPUT FILES                   *
209.      *    - WRITES THE FIRST PAGE COLUMN-HEADINGS              *
210.      *    - READS FIRST RECORD                                 *
211.      *                                                         *
212.      ***********************************************************
213.
214.      1000-INITIALIZATION.
215.          OPEN  INPUT CUSTOMER-FILE
216.                OUTPUT REPORT-FILE.
217.          ACCEPT DATE-STORE FROM DATE.
218.          MOVE YEAR-STORE   TO YEAR-OUT.
219.          MOVE MONTH-STORE TO MONTH-OUT.
220.          MOVE DAY-STORE    TO DAY-OUT.
221.           MOVE REPORT-NAME TO REPORT-NAME-OUT.
222.          PERFORM 1100-PAGE-HEADING.
223.          PERFORM 8000-READ-RECORD.
224.
225.      1100-PAGE-HEADING.
226.          ADD 1 TO PAGE-NUM.
227.          MOVE PAGE-NUM TO PAGE-OUT.
228.          WRITE REPORT-RECORD FROM PAGE-BANNER-1
229.              AFTER ADVANCING TO-TOP-OF-PAGE.
230.          WRITE REPORT-RECORD FROM PAGE-BANNER-2
231.              AFTER ADVANCING 1 LINE.
232.          WRITE REPORT-RECORD FROM PAGE-BANNER-3
233.              AFTER ADVANCING 1 LINE.
234.          WRITE REPORT-RECORD FROM PAGE-BANNER-1
235.              AFTER ADVANCING 1 LINE.
236.          WRITE REPORT-RECORD FROM COLUMN-HEADINGS
237.              AFTER ADVANCING 3 LINES.
238.          EJECT
239.      ***********************************************************
240.      *                                                         *
241.      *  2000 CLUB CUSTOMER PROCESS                             *
242.      *                                                         *
243.      *    THIS PARAGRAPH IS PERFORMED UNTIL THERE ARE NO MORE MASTER  *
```

*(continued)*

```
244.     *     RECORDS.  IT:                                          *
245.     *                                                            *
246.     *     - PERFORMS THE CALCULATION PARAGRAPH                   *
247.     *     - PERFORMS THE DETAIL WRITING PARAGRAPH                *
248.     *     - PERFORMS THE READ PARAGRAPH                          *
249.     *                                                            *
250.     **************************************************************
251.
252.          2000-CLUB-CUSTOMER-PROCESS.
253.              PERFORM 2100-CALCULATION-PARA.
254.              PERFORM 2200-ROUTINE-WRITING-ANSWER.
255.              PERFORM 8000-READ-RECORD.
256.
257.          EJECT
258.     **************************************************************
259.     *                                                            *
260.     *   2100 CALCULATION PARA                                    *
261.     *                                                            *
262.     *     - CALCULATES THE BAR BILL DISCOUNTS                    *
263.     *     - CALCULATES THE CUSTOMER'S TOTAL BILL AMOUNT          *
264.     *     - ACCUMULATES THE GRAND TOTAL BILL AMOUNT              *
265.     *                                                            *
266.     **************************************************************
267.
268.          2100-CALCULATION-PARA.
269.              IF REST-BILL IS GREATER THAN 200
270.                  MULTIPLY 0.98 BY REST-BILL.
271.              IF BAR-BILL > 400
272.                  MULTIPLY .95 BY BAR-BILL.
273.              ADD REST-BILL, BAR-BILL, OTHER-CHARGES GIVING TOTAL-BILL.
274.              IF TOTAL-BILL GREATER THAN 1000
275.                  MULTIPLY TOTAL-BILL BY 0.97 GIVING TOTAL-BILL.
276.              ADD AMT-OUTSTANDING TO TOTAL-BILL.
277.              ADD TOTAL-BILL TO TOTAL-AMT-DUE.
278.          EJECT
279.     **************************************************************
280.     *                                                            *
281.     *   2200 ROUTINE WRITING ANSWER                              *
282.     *                                                            *
283.     *     - MOVES INPUT FIELDS TO OUTPUT LINE                    *
284.     *     - MOVES CUSTOMER'S TOTAL BILL AMOUNT TO OUTPUT LINE    *
285.     *     - WRITES DETAIL LINE                                   *
286.     *                                                            *
287.     **************************************************************
288.
289.          2200-ROUTINE-WRITING-ANSWER.
290.              MOVE TOTAL-BILL TO AMT-DUE.
291.
292.     **************************************************************
293.     *                                                            *
294.     * NOTE:    WHEN TOTAL-BILL IS MOVED TO AMT-DUE, A  PROBLEM COULD *
295.     * OCCUR  BECAUSE  THE  PICTURE  FOR  TOTAL-BILL  IS ONE CHARACTER *
296.     * LARGER  THAN THE PICTURE  FOR  AMT-DUE  AND  YOU COULD LOSE THE *
297.     * HIGH ORDER DIGIT OF THE LARGER PICTURE.                    *
298.     *                                                            *
299.     **************************************************************
300.
301.              MOVE MEMBER-NUMBER-IN TO MEMBER-NUMBER-OUT.
302.              MOVE NAME-IN TO NAME-OUT.
303.              MOVE MEMBER-ADDRESS-IN TO MEMBER-ADDRESS-OUT.
304.              WRITE REPORT-RECORD FROM DETAIL-LINE
305.                  AFTER ADVANCING 2 LINES.
306.          EJECT
307.     **************************************************************
308.     *                                                            *
309.     *   3000 TERMINATION                                         *
310.     *                                                            *
311.     *     - MOVES GRAND TOTAL BILLING AMOUNT TO SUMMARY LINE     *
312.     *     - WRITES GRAND TOTAL LINES                             *
313.     *     - CLOSES FILES                                         *
314.     *                                                            *
315.     **************************************************************
316.
317.          3000-TERMINATION.
318.              WRITE REPORT-RECORD FROM STAR-LINE
319.                  AFTER ADVANCING 3 LINES.
320.              MOVE TOTAL-AMT-DUE TO AMOUNT IN TOTAL-LINE.
321.              WRITE REPORT-RECORD FROM TOTAL-LINE
322.                  AFTER ADVANCING 3 LINES.
323.              CLOSE CUSTOMER-FILE, REPORT-FILE.
324.
325.          8000-READ-RECORD.
326.              READ CUSTOMER-FILE INTO CUSTOMER-RECORD-IN
327.                  AT END
328.                      MOVE 'NO ' TO ARE-THERE-MORE-RECORDS.
329.
```

## Copy Library Elements

```
1.        01  PAGE-BANNER-1                    PIC X(133) VALUE ALL '-'.
```

```
1.        01  PAGE-BANNER-2.
2.            05  FILLER                       PIC X(49) VALUE SPACES.
3.            05  FILLER                       PIC X(35) VALUE
4.                    'ANTHONY AND ASSOCIATES OF AGGIELAND'.
5.            05  FILLER                       PIC X(40) VALUE SPACES.
6.            05  FILLER                       PIC X(6)  VALUE
7.                    'PAGE: '.
8.            05  PAGE-OUT                     PIC ZZ9.
```

```
1.        01  PAGE-BANNER-3.
2.            05  REPORT-NAME-OUT              PIC X(50).
3.            05  FILLER                       PIC X(75) VALUE SPACES.
4.            05  DATE-OUT.
5.                10  MONTH-OUT                PIC X(2).
6.                10  FILLER                   PIC X(1)  VALUE '/'.
7.                10  DAY-OUT                  PIC X(2).
8.                10  FILLER                   PIC X(1)  VALUE '/'.
9.                10  YEAR-OUT                 PIC X(2).
```

```
1.
2.        FD  CUSTOMER-FILE
3.            RECORD CONTAINS 72 CHARACTERS
4.            BLOCK CONTAINS 88 RECORDS
5.            LABEL RECORDS ARE OMITTED
6.            DATA RECORD IS CUSTOMER-RECORD.
7.
8.        01  CUSTOMER-RECORD              PIC X(72).
```

```
1.
2.        01  CUSTOMER-RECORD-IN.
3.            03  MEMBER-NUMBER-IN         PIC 9(3).
4.            03  FILLER                   PIC X(1).
5.            03  NAME-IN                  PIC X(25).
6.            03  FILLER                   PIC X(1).
7.            03  MEMBER-ADDRESS-IN        PIC X(18).
8.            03  REST-BILL                PIC 9(3)V99.
9.            03  FILLER                   PIC X(1).
10.           03  BAR-BILL                 PIC 9(3)V99.
11.           03  FILLER                   PIC X(1).
12.           03  OTHER-CHARGES            PIC 9(3)V99.
13.           03  FILLER                   PIC X(1).
14.           03  AMT-OUTSTANDING          PIC 9(4)V99.
```

## Compiled Program

```
PP 5740-CB1 RELEASE 2.4                    IBM OS/VS COBOL   JULY 1, 1982      22.05.12  DATE NOV 10,1988


        1                      22.05.12        NOV 10,1988

00001      *                                          REVISED 01/10/88  *
00002        IDENTIFICATION DIVISION.
00003
00004        PROGRAM-ID.
00005                    DEMOCODE.
00006        AUTHOR.
00007                    GEORGE FOWLER.
00008        INSTALLATION.
00009                    TEXAS A & M UNIVERSITY.
00010        DATE-WRITTEN.
00011                    SEPTEMBER 8, 1985.
00012        DATE-COMPILED. NOV 10,1988.
```

```
        2        DEMOCODE     22.05.12        NOV 10,1988


00014        *********************************************************
00015        *                                                       *
00016        *  ASSIGNMENT NUMBER                                    *
00017        *  DATE ASSIGNED                                        *
00018        *  DATE DUE                                             *
00019        *  PURPOSE:         THIS IS A BILLING PROGRAM FOR THE  CIRCLE *
00020        *  CLUB RESTAURANT AND BAR. IT CALCULATES THE TOTAL AMOUNT DUE *
00021        *  FROM EACH CUSTOMER AND A GRAND TOTAL DUE FROM ALL ACCOUNTS. *
00022        *  THERE ARE DISCOUNTS ALLOWED UNDER CERTAIN CONDITIONS.  THEY *
00023        *  ARE:                                                 *
00024        *      2 PERCENT FOR A RESTRAURANT BILL OVER $200.00    *
00025        *      5 PERCENT FOR A BAR BILL OVER $400.00            *
00026        *      3 PERCENT FOR A TOTAL BILL OVER $1,000.00 AFTER  *
00027        *        OTHER DISCOUNTS HAVE BEEN SUBTRACTED.          *
00028        *                                                       *
00029        *  INPUT FILE SPECIFICATIONS:                           *
00030        *      CARD COLUMNS                    DESCRIPTION       *
00031        *         1- 3                         MEMBERSHIP NUMBER *
00032        *         5-29                         MEMBER NAME       *
00033        *        31-48                         MEMBER ADDRESS    *
00034        *        49-53                         RESTAURANT BILL   *
00035        *        55-59                         BAR BILL          *
00036        *        61-65                         ANY OTHER CHARGES *
00037        *        67-72                         PAST DUE AMOUNT   *
00038        *                                                       *
00039        *  THE OUTPUT CONTAINS MEMBERSHIP NUMBER,  NAME,  ADDRESS,  AND *
00040        *  AMOUNT DUE.    THE SUMMARY CONTAINS THE TOTAL AMOUNT DUE FROM *
00041        *  ALL CUSTOMERS.                                       *
00042        *                                                       *
00043        *********************************************************
```

```
        3        DEMOCODE     22.05.12        NOV 10,1988


00045        *********************************************************
00046        *                                                       *
00047        *                 ENVIRONMENT DIVISION                  *
00048        *                                                       *
00049        *********************************************************
00050        ENVIRONMENT DIVISION.
00051
00052
00053        CONFIGURATION SECTION.
00054
00055        SOURCE-COMPUTER.
00056                    IBM-370.
00057        OBJECT-COMPUTER.
00058                    IBM-370.
00059        SPECIAL-NAMES.
00060                    C01 IS TO-TOP-OF-PAGE.
00061
00062        INPUT-OUTPUT SECTION.
00063
00064        FILE-CONTROL.
00065
00066            SELECT CUSTOMER-FILE
00067                ASSIGN TO DA-S-INFILE.
00068
00069            SELECT REPORT-FILE
00070                ASSIGN TO UT-S-OUTFILE.
00071
```

*(continued)*

```
      4        DEMOCODE        22.05.12      NOV 10,1988

00073        ********************************************************
00074        *                                                      *
00075        *                    DATA DIVISION                     *
00076        *                                                      *
00077        ********************************************************
00078
00079        DATA DIVISION.
00080
00081        FILE SECTION.
00082
00083        COPY CUSTFD.
00084 C
00085 C      FD   CUSTOMER-FILE
00086 C           RECORD CONTAINS 72 CHARACTERS
00087 C           BLOCK CONTAINS 88 RECORDS
00088 C           LABEL RECORDS ARE OMITTED
00089 C           DATA RECORD IS CUSTOMER-RECORD.
00090 C
00091 C      01   CUSTOMER-RECORD           PIC X(72).
00092
00093        FD   REPORT-FILE
00094             LABEL RECORDS ARE OMITTED
00095             DATA RECORD IS REPORT-RECORD.
00096
00097        01   REPORT-RECORD      PIC X(133).
00098
```

```
      5        DEMOCODE        22.05.12      NOV 10,1988

00100        ********************************************************
00101        *                                                      *
00102        *              WORKING STORAGE SECTION                 *
00103        *                                                      *
00104        ********************************************************
00105        WORKING-STORAGE SECTION.
00106
00107        77   TOTAL-BILL           PIC 9(6)V99  VALUE ZERO.
00108        77   TOTAL-AMT-DUE         PIC 9(6)V99  VALUE ZERO.
00109        77   PAGE-NUM              PIC 9(8)     VALUE ZERO.
00110        77   REPORT-NAME           PIC X(50)    VALUE
00111                       ' CIRCLE CLUB REPORT'.
00112
00113        01   INDICATORS-GROUP.
00114             03   ARE-THERE-MORE-RECORDS   PIC X(3)   VALUE 'YES'.
00115                  88  MORE-RECORDS                     VALUE 'YES'.
00116                  88  NO-MORE-RECORDS                  VALUE 'NO '.
00117
```

*(continued)*

```
       6        DEMOCODE       22.05.12      NOV 10,1988


00119           ********************************************************
00120           *                                                      *
00121           *            CUSTOMER INPUT RECORD DESIGN              *
00122           *                                                      *
00123           ********************************************************
00124
00125           COPY CUSTWS.
00126 C
00127 C    01  CUSTOMER-RECORD-IN.
00128 C        03   MEMBER-NUMBER-IN        PIC 9(3).
00129 C        03   FILLER                  PIC X(1).
00130 C        03   NAME-IN                 PIC X(25).
00131 C        03   FILLER                  PIC X(1).
00132 C        03   MEMBER-ADDRESS-IN       PIC X(18).
00133 C        03   REST-BILL               PIC 9(3)V99.
00134 C        03   FILLER                  PIC X(1).
00135 C        03   BAR-BILL                PIC 9(3)V99.
00136 C        03   FILLER                  PIC X(1).
00137 C        03   OTHER-CHARGES           PIC 9(3)V99.
00138 C        03   FILLER                  PIC X(1).
00139 C        03   AMT-OUTSTANDING         PIC 9(4)V99.
00140
```

```
       7        DEMOCODE       22.05.12      NOV 10,1988


00142           ********************************************************
00143           *                                                      *
00144           *               OUTPUT RECORD DESIGN                   *
00145           *                                                      *
00146           ********************************************************
00147
00148      01  DETAIL-LINE.
00149          03   FILLER                  PIC X(22)  VALUE SPACES.
00150          03   MEMBER-NUMBER-OUT       PIC 9(3).
00151          03   FILLER                  PIC X(19)  VALUE SPACES.
00152          03   NAME-OUT                PIC X(26).
00153          03   FILLER                  PIC X(10)  VALUE SPACES.
00154          03   MEMBER-ADDRESS-OUT      PIC X(19).
00155          03   FILLER                  PIC X(12)  VALUE SPACES.
00156          03   AMT-DUE                 PIC $$$$,$$$.99.
00157          03   FILLER                  PIC X(11)  VALUE SPACES.
00158
00159      01  TITLE.
00160          03   FILLER                  PIC X(61)  VALUE SPACES.
00161          03   FILLER                  PIC X(11)  VALUE
00162                    'CIRCLE CLUB'.
00163          03   FILLER                  PIC X(61)  VALUE SPACES.
00164
00165      01  COLUMN-HEADINGS.
00166          03   FILLER                  PIC X(15)  VALUE SPACES.
00167          03   FILLER                  PIC X(17)  VALUE
00168                    'MEMBERSHIP NUMBER'.
00169          03   FILLER                  PIC X(18)  VALUE SPACES.
00170          03   FILLER                  PIC X(4)   VALUE 'NAME'.
00171          03   FILLER                  PIC X(30)  VALUE SPACES.
00172          03   FILLER                  PIC X(7)   VALUE 'ADDRESS'.
00173          03   FILLER                  PIC X(22)  VALUE SPACES.
00174          03   FILLER                  PIC X(10)  VALUE 'AMOUNT DUE'.
00175          03   FILLER                  PIC X(10)  VALUE SPACES.
```

*(continued)*

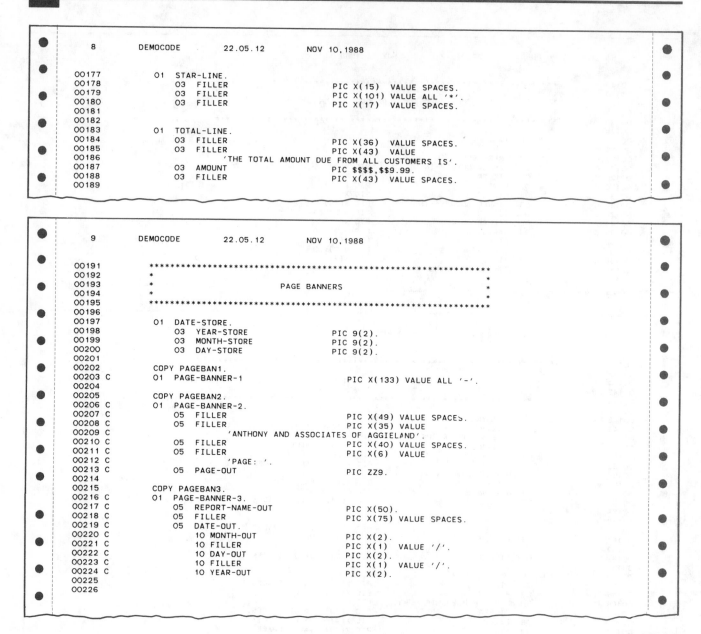

```
     8       DEMOCODE        22.05.12        NOV 10,1988

00177              01  STAR-LINE.
00178                  03  FILLER                    PIC X(15)  VALUE SPACES.
00179                  03  FILLER                    PIC X(101) VALUE ALL '*'.
00180                  03  FILLER                    PIC X(17)  VALUE SPACES.
00181
00182
00183              01  TOTAL-LINE.
00184                  03  FILLER                    PIC X(36)  VALUE SPACES.
00185                  03  FILLER                    PIC X(43)  VALUE
00186                       'THE TOTAL AMOUNT DUE FROM ALL CUSTOMERS IS'.
00187                  03  AMOUNT                    PIC $$$$,$$9.99.
00188                  03  FILLER                    PIC X(43)  VALUE SPACES.
00189
```

```
     9       DEMOCODE        22.05.12        NOV 10,1988

00191              ****************************************************************
00192              *                                                              *
00193              *                      PAGE BANNERS                            *
00194              *                                                              *
00195              ****************************************************************
00196
00197              01  DATE-STORE.
00198                  03  YEAR-STORE            PIC 9(2).
00199                  03  MONTH-STORE           PIC 9(2).
00200                  03  DAY-STORE             PIC 9(2).
00201
00202              COPY PAGEBAN1.
00203 C            01  PAGE-BANNER-1             PIC X(133) VALUE ALL '-'.
00204
00205              COPY PAGEBAN2.
00206 C            01  PAGE-BANNER-2.
00207 C                05  FILLER               PIC X(49) VALUE SPACES.
00208 C                05  FILLER               PIC X(35) VALUE
00209 C                     'ANTHONY AND ASSOCIATES OF AGGIELAND'.
00210 C                05  FILLER               PIC X(40) VALUE SPACES.
00211 C                05  FILLER               PIC X(6)  VALUE
00212 C                     'PAGE: '.
00213 C                05  PAGE-OUT             PIC ZZ9.
00214
00215              COPY PAGEBAN3.
00216 C            01  PAGE-BANNER-3.
00217 C                05  REPORT-NAME-OUT      PIC X(50).
00218 C                05  FILLER               PIC X(75) VALUE SPACES.
00219 C                05  DATE-OUT.
00220 C                    10  MONTH-OUT        PIC X(2).
00221 C                    10  FILLER           PIC X(1)  VALUE '/'.
00222 C                    10  DAY-OUT          PIC X(2).
00223 C                    10  FILLER           PIC X(1)  VALUE '/'.
00224 C                    10  YEAR-OUT         PIC X(2).
00225
00226
```

*(continued)*

```
   10          DEMOCODE       22.05.12       NOV 10,1988


00228        *****************************************************************
00229        *                                                               *
00230        *                      PROCEDURE DIVISION                       *
00231        *                                                               *
00232        *****************************************************************
00233
00234         PROCEDURE DIVISION.
00235
00236
00237         0000-MAIN-DRIVER.
00238             PERFORM 1000-INITIALIZATION.
00239             PERFORM 2000-CLUB-CUSTOMER-PROCESS
00240                 UNTIL NO-MORE-RECORDS.
00241             PERFORM 3000-TERMINATION.
00242             STOP RUN.
```

```
   11          DEMOCODE       22.05.12       NOV 10,1988


00244        *****************************************************************
00245        *                                                               *
00246        *   1000 INITIALIZATION                                         *
00247        *                                                               *
00248        *     - OPENS THE INPUT AND OUTPUT FILES                        *
00249        *     - WRITES THE FIRST PAGE COLUMN-HEADINGS                   *
00250        *     - READS FIRST RECORD                                      *
00251        *                                                               *
00252        *****************************************************************
00253
00254         1000-INITIALIZATION.
00255             OPEN  INPUT CUSTOMER-FILE
00256                   OUTPUT REPORT-FILE.
00257             ACCEPT DATE-STORE FROM DATE.
00258             MOVE YEAR-STORE  TO YEAR-OUT.
00259             MOVE MONTH-STORE TO MONTH-OUT.
00260             MOVE DAY-STORE   TO DAY-OUT.
00261              MOVE REPORT-NAME TO REPORT-NAME-OUT.
00262             PERFORM 1100-PAGE-HEADING.
00263             PERFORM 8000-READ-RECORD.
00264
00265         1100-PAGE-HEADING.
00266             ADD 1 TO PAGE-NUM.
00267             MOVE PAGE-NUM TO PAGE-OUT.
00268             WRITE REPORT-RECORD FROM PAGE-BANNER-1
00269                 AFTER ADVANCING TO-TOP-OF-PAGE.
00270             WRITE REPORT-RECORD FROM PAGE-BANNER-2
00271                 AFTER ADVANCING 1 LINE.
00272             WRITE REPORT-RECORD FROM PAGE-BANNER-3
00273                 AFTER ADVANCING 1 LINE.
00274             WRITE REPORT-RECORD FROM PAGE-BANNER-1
00275                 AFTER ADVANCING 1 LINE.
00276             WRITE REPORT-RECORD FROM COLUMN-HEADINGS
00277                 AFTER ADVANCING 3 LINES.
```

*(continued)*

```
     12        DEMOCODE        22.05.12        NOV 10,1988

00279        ****************************************************************
00280        *                                                              *
00281        *    2000 CLUB CUSTOMER PROCESS                                 *
00282        *                                                              *
00283        *    THIS PARAGRAPH IS PERFORMED UNTIL THERE ARE NO MORE MASTER *
00284        *    RECORDS.  IT:                                             *
00285        *                                                              *
00286        *    - PERFORMS THE CALCULATION PARAGRAPH                       *
00287        *    - PERFORMS THE DETAIL WRITING PARAGRAPH                    *
00288        *    - PERFORMS THE READ PARAGRAPH                              *
00289        *                                                              *
00290        ****************************************************************
00291
00292        2000-CLUB-CUSTOMER-PROCESS.
00293            PERFORM 2100-CALCULATION-PARA.
00294            PERFORM 2200-ROUTINE-WRITING-ANSWER.
00295            PERFORM 8000-READ-RECORD.
00296
```

```
     13        DEMOCODE        22.05.12        NOV 10,1988

00298        ****************************************************************
00299        *                                                              *
00300        *    2100 CALCULATION PARA                                      *
00301        *                                                              *
00302        *    - CALCULATES THE BAR BILL DISCOUNTS                        *
00303        *    - CALCULATES THE CUSTOMER'S TOTAL BILL AMOUNT              *
00304        *    - ACCUMULATES THE GRAND TOTAL BILL AMOUNT                  *
00305        *                                                              *
00306        ****************************************************************
00307
00308        2100-CALCULATION-PARA.
00309            IF REST-BILL IS GREATER THAN 200
00310                MULTIPLY 0.98 BY REST-BILL.
00311            IF BAR-BILL > 400
00312                MULTIPLY .95 BY BAR-BILL.
00313            ADD REST-BILL, BAR-BILL, OTHER-CHARGES GIVING TOTAL-BILL.
00314            IF TOTAL-BILL GREATER THAN 1000
00315                MULTIPLY TOTAL-BILL BY 0.97 GIVING TOTAL-BILL.
00316            ADD AMT-OUTSTANDING TO TOTAL-BILL.
00317            ADD TOTAL-BILL TO TOTAL-AMT-DUE.
```

*(continued)*

```
   14        DEMOCODE        22.05.12        NOV 10,1988

00319         *****************************************************************
00320         *                                                               *
00321         *   2200 ROUTINE WRITING ANSWER                                 *
00322         *                                                               *
00323         *     - MOVES INPUT FIELDS TO OUTPUT LINE                       *
00324         *     - MOVES CUSTOMER'S TOTAL BILL AMOUNT TO OUTPUT LINE       *
00325         *     - WRITES DETAIL LINE                                      *
00326         *                                                               *
00327         *****************************************************************
00328
00329         2200-ROUTINE-WRITING-ANSWER.
00330             MOVE TOTAL-BILL TO AMT-DUE.
00331
00332         *****************************************************************
00333         *                                                               *
00334         * NOTE:    WHEN TOTAL-BILL IS MOVED TO AMT-DUE, A  PROBLEM COULD *
00335         * OCCUR  BECAUSE THE  PICTURE  FOR TOTAL-BILL  IS ONE CHARACTER  *
00336         * LARGER THAN THE PICTURE  FOR  AMT-DUE  AND  YOU COULD LOSE THE *
00337         * HIGH ORDER DIGIT OF THE LARGER PICTURE.                       *
00338         *                                                               *
00339         *****************************************************************
00340
00341             MOVE MEMBER-NUMBER-IN TO MEMBER-NUMBER-OUT.
00342             MOVE NAME-IN TO NAME-OUT.
00343             MOVE MEMBER-ADDRESS-IN TO MEMBER-ADDRESS-OUT.
00344             WRITE REPORT-RECORD FROM DETAIL-LINE
00345                 AFTER ADVANCING 2 LINES.
```

```
   15        DEMOCODE        22.05.12        NOV 10,1988

00347         *****************************************************************
00348         *                                                               *
00349         *   3000 TERMINATION                                            *
00350         *                                                               *
00351         *     - MOVES GRAND TOTAL BILLING AMOUNT TO SUMMARY LINE        *
00352         *     - WRITES GRAND TOTAL LINES                                *
00353         *     - CLOSES FILES                                            *
00354         *                                                               *
00355         *****************************************************************
00356
00357         3000-TERMINATION.
00358             WRITE REPORT-RECORD FROM STAR-LINE
00359                 AFTER ADVANCING 3 LINES.
00360             MOVE TOTAL-AMT-DUE TO AMOUNT IN TOTAL-LINE.
00361             WRITE REPORT-RECORD FROM TOTAL-LINE
00362                 AFTER ADVANCING 3 LINES.
00363             CLOSE CUSTOMER-FILE, REPORT-FILE.
00364
00365         8000-READ-RECORD.
00366             READ CUSTOMER-FILE INTO CUSTOMER-RECORD-IN
00367                 AT END
00368                     MOVE 'NO ' TO ARE-THERE-MORE-RECORDS.
00369
```

*(continued)*

```
--------------------------------------------------------------------------------
                              ANTHONY AND ASSOCIATES OF AGGIELAND
CIRCLE CLUB REPORT                                                   PAGE:    1
                                                                   11/10/88
--------------------------------------------------------------------------------

   MEMBERSHIP NUMBER              NAME                 ADDRESS          AMOUNT DUE

         586             LANZA, MARIO            101 CARUSO WAY         $963.22

         355             BEASLEY, REGGIE R.      2035 HARVEY            $341.07

         004             RASKOLNIKOV, FYODOR     4321 GULAG MANOR       $136.19

         996             IVANOVNA, ALYONA        401 HAY MARKET         $963.47

         829             SMITHE, BYRON L.        90 DEVONSHIRE        $1,857.94

         193             RANCHER, TEX A.         740 GUERNSEY           $263.44

         811             CORTEZ, SIGNIO H.       1818 CHEVERALLA         $61.65

         045             MUDD, HARCORT FENTON    2111 NAGGA WAY       $9,196.32

         355             RICH, RICHY             1 PROFLIGATE PL.        $60.98

         492             MOON, WARREN            50 ZENITH RD.          $515.58

         933             MCHALE, KEVIN           5 SECOND LANE        $5,622.81

         810             KELLY, GENE             53 RAINDANCE DR.        $19.88

         500             KIRKPATRICK, GENE       1300 PENN AVE.       $1,983.76

         287             DROVELL, ROBERT H.      77 SUNSET STRIP        $254.19

         001             MONT BENI, DONATELLO    100 GRAND TOWER      $1,274.99

         900             KIPLING, KIMBALL        25 INDIA AVE.           $9.00

         503             KAFKA, FRANZ            75 PARADISE COURT       $45.00

         984             BLAIR, ERIC             15 BUTTER DR.          $189.23

         345             TWAIN, MARK             39 RIVER ROAD          $282.50

         489             ORWELL, GEORGE          51 FLY STREET        $1,838.00

         543             CLEMENS, SAMUEL         93 BOAT AVE.           $581.40

************************************************************************************

        THE TOTAL AMOUNT DUE FROM ALL CUSTOMERS IS  $26,460.62
```

**EXERCISES**

### Chapter Review Questions

1. Copy Libraries contain:
   - a. Object Code
   - b. Source Code
   - c. Both Object and Source Code
   - d. Files called members
   - e. Both b and d

2. A major benefit or benefits of using copy libraries is:
   - a. Ease of maintenance
   - b. Standardization of code
   - c. Reduced development time
   - d. Ease of making revisions during development
   - e. All of the above

3. To copy the FD for PAYROLL-FILE, called FDPAY, into your program, you could use which of the following:
   - a. COPY FD
   - b. COPY PAYROLL-FILE
   - c. COPY FD PAYROLL-FILE
   - d. COPY FDPAY
   - e. None of the above

4. A library is the same as a:
   - a. File
   - b. Record
   - c. Partitioned Data Set
   - d. Program
   - e. Data set

5. If two copy libraries contained required members, which of the following could be used?
   - a. COPY MASTREC FROM COPYLBRY.
   - b. COPY MASTREC OF COPYLBRY.
   - c. COPY MASTREC IN COPYLBRY.
   - d. COPY MASTFD, MASTREC OF COPYLBRY.
   - e. Both b and c

6. Which JCL statement could be used to allow access to COPYLBRY?
   - a. //SYSLIB. DD DSN = USR.P500.CD.COPYLBRY...
   - b. //COB.SYSIN DD DSN = USR.P500.CD.COPYLBRY...
   - c. //COB.SYSLIB DD DSN = USR.P500.CD.COPYLBRY...
   - d. //GO.SYSLIB DD DSN = USR.P500.CD.COPYLBRY...
   - e. None of the above

7. The listing of a program that included the use of the COPY would indicate all copied code by:

    a.   Placing the word copied in columns 73–78

    b.   Placing the word copy in columns 1–4

    c.   Copied code is not specially indicated

    d.   Placing a C in column 1

    e.   None of the above

8. Which of the following is not part of the data dictionary?

    a.   Level numbers

    b.   Field type and length

    c.   Data names

    d.   Purpose of member

    e.   Member-name

9. Which of the following would not normally be considered for inclusion in a copy library?

    a.   FDs

    b.   D-R-Ds

    c.   Temporary File descriptions

    d.   Common File descriptions

    e.   77 Level Items

10. Each member of a Copy Library must contain only one COBOL Element; an FD, a D-R-D but not both in one file.

    a.   True

    b.   False

11. A copy library would be used concurrently with the:

    a.   Partitioned data set

    b.   Development library

    c.   Production library

    d.   Object program

    e.   Both a and b

12. In the sample program at the end of the chapter, how many copy library elements were used?

    a.   1

    b.   2

    c.   3

    d.   4

    e.   5

13. A copy library element may contain a copy.

    a.   True

    b.   False

14. The data dictionary is only useful for documentation.

    a.   True

    b.   False

15. Which of the following file descriptions would not be a good candidate for a copy library?

    a.   Master File

    b.   Report File

    c.   Temporary File

    d.   Both a and b

    e.   Both a and c

## Discussion Questions

1. Briefly discuss how programmer teams would benefit by using copy libraries.
2. How would a system using copy libraries be:
    a.    Easier to develop?
    b.    Easier to maintain?
3. Briefly show the relationship of the COPY, data dictionary and the library members.
4. How does the copy library relate to the production and development libraries?
5. Briefly explain the role of the systems analyst and/or project leader when copy libraries are to be used in program development.

## Practice Problems

1. Change the Circle Club Program in this chapter to use the copy for:

```
01  DETAIL-LINE.
01  COLUMN-HEADINGS.
```

    Include the new library members.
2. Change the Circle Club Program to incorporate a new corporate policy that standardizes the handling of the date for all programs. The routine and record description are called DATEPROC and DATEREC respectively.
3. Develop a copy library for the Personnel File in Data File B. Show all the members, FD, D-R-D, and Page Banners for the report. Also develop the data dictionary for the members.
4. Develop the data dictionary for the example program at the end of the chapter.

## Programming Assignment

1. Write a COBOL program to read the Personnel File and list all employees on a report. Every report page should include a banner. Show the use of the copy library you designed in Practice Problem 1 above. You should also show the JCL required to access the library.

# TABLES

**_OBJECTIVES_**   In this chapter you will learn about data sets called tables in COBOL.  Tables are groups of related data items that lend themselves to certain types of problems.  These include counting, accumulating and code conversions.  You will learn how to define tables and use tables for data-dependent and logic-dependent situations.  You will also learn to report table contents.  After all, if you accumulated your answers in a table, you don't want to keep them a secret.

## TOPICS

- table definition: 1, 2, 3 levels and more
- types of tables: compile-time and execution-time
- subscripting and indexing
- data-dependent algorithms
- logic-dependent algorithms
- techniques for manipulating tables
- nested PERFORMs and PERFORM AFTER
- reporting tables
- reading into tables
- searching tables
- not-nice data requirements
- redefining data areas

## KEY WORDS

- OCCURS
- REDEFINE
- SUBSCRIPT
- INDEX and INDEXED BY
- PERFORM. . .AFTER
- SEARCH and SEARCH ALL

## THE PROBLEM

Up to this point in the text, we have worked with data names that have a particular characteristic: They could contain only one data value at a time. In many cases this is fine, but as we will see there are situations that would be easier to handle with data names that have more than one value: tables.

Let's look at the DEAN-FILE again. This file contains a record for each student in the college. Each student's record contains (among other items) name, id, major code (1-5), class code (1-4), sex code (1-2) and GPR (see Data File A Form 1 for full description).

The dean comes to you. By now he has heard you are the expert, and he asks you to provide him with a listing of all students in the college and a summary report containing a count of students in each of the five majors (Accounting, Information Systems, Finance, Marketing and Management).

Expert student that you are, you have developed the hierarchy chart and the IPO chart shown in Figures 11.1 and 11.2 and the flowchart shown in Figure 11.3. As the system analyst, you have discussed those with the dean. (The system user has agreed with the design.)

**FIGURE 11.1**
**The Hierarchy Chart for the Dean's Problem**

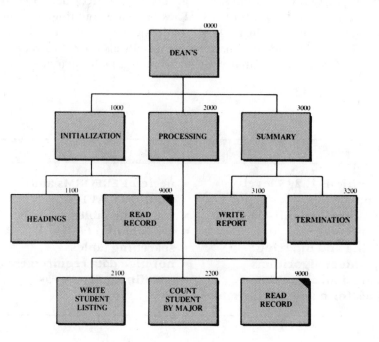

Assuming you can see in your mind's eye all the COBOL requirements through the DATA DIVISION for the problem, let's look at the PROCEDURE DIVISION statements necessary (using our sequential file model):

```
0000-DEAN-PARA.
     PERFORM  1000-INIT-PARA.
     PERFORM  2000-PROCESS-PARA
         UNTIL  NO-MORE-DATA.
     PERFORM  3000-SUMMARY-PARA.
```

**FIGURE 11.2**
The IPO Chart for the Dean's
Problem

| INPUT | PROCESS | OUTPUT |
|---|---|---|
| name<br>id<br>major code (1–5)<br>class code (1–4)<br>sex code (1–2)<br>gpr | write heading for<br>  student listing<br>initialize counts<br>read student records<br>write student records<br>count students by major<br>  if major-code = 1<br>    add 1 to acct<br>  if major-code = 2<br>    add 1 to is<br>      ⋮<br>      ⋮<br>write summary headings<br>write counts | **Student Listing**<br><br>name<br>id<br>major code<br>class code<br>sex code<br>gpr<br><br>**Summary Report**<br><br>number of accounting<br>number of info. systems<br>number of finance<br>number of management<br>number of marketing |

```
        1000-INIT-PARA.
            ⋮
            ⋮


        2000-PROCESS-PARA.
            PERFORM 2100-WRITE-STUDENT-LISTING.
            PERFORM 2200-COUNT-STUDENTS-BY-NUMBER.
            PERFORM 9000-READ-STUDENT-RECORD.

        2100-WRITE-STUDENT-LISTING.
            MOVE   NAME        TO   NAME-OUT.
            MOVE   I-D         TO   I-D-OUT.
            MOVE   MAJOR-CODE  TO   MAJOR-CODE-OUT.
            MOVE   CLASS-CODE  TO   CLASS-CODE-OUT.
            MOVE   SEX-CODE    TO   SEX-CODE-OUT.
            MOVE   GPR         TO   GPR-OUT.
            WRITE REPORT-LINE FROM STUDENT-LINE
                AFTER 2.


*
*   This module assumes IF logic and does not incorporate the use
*   of tables—yet!  This logic also assumes data is valid.
*

        2200-COUNT-STUDENTS-BY-MAJOR.
            IF  MAJOR-CODE = 1
                ADD 1  TO  ACCOUNTING-COUNT
            ELSE
                IF  MAJOR-CODE = 2
                    ADD 1  TO  FINANCE-COUNT
                ELSE
                    IF  MAJOR-CODE = 3
                        ADD 1  TO  INFO-SYS-COUNT
                    ELSE
                        IF  MAJOR-CODE = 4
                            ADD 1  TO  MANAGEMENT-COUNT
                        ELSE
                            ADD 1  TO  MARKETING-COUNT.
```

**FIGURE 11.3**
The Flowchart for the Dean's
Problem

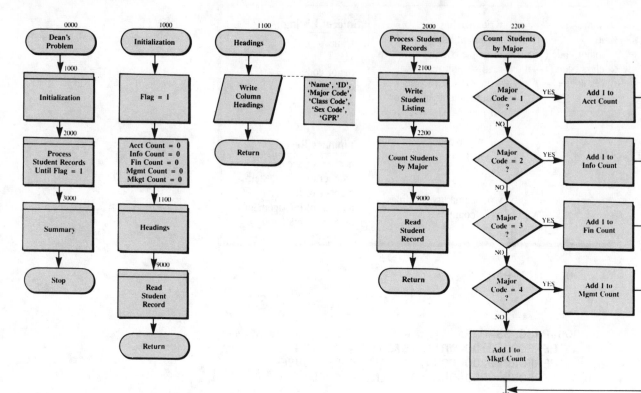

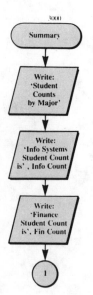

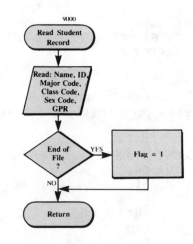

```
3000-SUMMARY-PARA.
     PERFORM 3100-WRITE-REPORT.
     PERFORM 3200-TERMINATION.

3100-WRITE-REPORT.
     PERFORM 3110-HEADINGS.
     MOVE 'THE NUMBER OF ACCOUNTING MAJORS IS '
          TO  DESCRIPTION-OUT.
     MOVE  ACCOUNTING-COUNT  TO  KOUNT-OUT.
     WRITE REPORT-LINE FROM  SUMMARY-LINE
          AFTER 2.
               :
               :
```

(repeat for each count)

I would like to concentrate on the 2200-COUNT-STUDENTS-BY-MAJOR module. What is required by this module? Four IF statements, five ADDs and five counters (77 level items). You're saying to yourself, that's not too bad. But what if instead of five codes, we had 50... still not too bad? What about 5,000? Using COBOL tables solves the problem. We will look at tables in a little bit. First, let's pose another related problem.

In module 2100-WRITE-STUDENT-LISTING, we simply wrote the codes (major code, class code, and sex code). What if the dean wanted the descriptions and not the codes? Just for the class code (1–4) alone, we would need three IF statements and four MOVEs as shown below.

```
IF  CLASS-CODE = 1
     MOVE 'FRESHMAN' TO  CLASS-OUT
ELSE
     IF  CLASS-CODE = 2
          MOVE 'SOPHOMORE' TO  CLASS-OUT
     ELSE
          IF  CLASS-CODE = 3
               MOVE 'JUNIOR   ' TO  CLASS-OUT
          ELSE
               MOVE 'SENIOR   ' TO  CLASS-OUT.
```

## TIP

**COBOL '85 allows this lengthy IF logic to be accomplished with the EVALUATE. Tables would still be preferable.**

Again, what if we had a situation that required conversion of 50 codes? 5,000 codes?... or some sufficiently large number to make you look for another way (or profession)? Both of these problems make us want to examine other COBOL features that help make this and related problems easier to handle.

## TABLES—WHAT ARE THEY?

Tables in COBOL are ways of defining a set of locations. Each location can still hold just one value at a time, but with the advantages that all the locations have the same name and each location need not be explicitly coded. Remember the mathematical notation:

$$\sum_{i=1}^{500} X_i$$

This implies that 500 Xs exist, and they all have the same name. So how do mathematicians distinguish among the Xs? They qualify each reference by adding a subscript. Therefore X4 is unique from X20. Furthermore, Xi implies that a particular value for the subscript i will be provided where and when needed.

Using COBOL notation, we could set up 500 Xs in this way:

```
01   X-TABLE.
     03   X            PICTURE 9(5)   OCCURS 500 TIMES.
```

Notice that X is just a data-name with a picture of 9(5). If the 03 ended there, you would have one location called X. This is no different from what we have been doing so far. However, we need 500 Xs, so we add something new—the OCCURS clause. It tells the compiler to set up not one, but 500 Xs. Wasn't that easy? Compared to writing 500 77s, it's duck soup!

Here are some rules for the OCCURS clause:

### OCCURS number [ TIMES ]

- The OCCURS may not be at the 01, 77, or 88 level.
- The number must be an integer value.
- If the OCCURS is a group level item, then each elementary item in the group occurs that number of times also.
- All items in the table must be referenced with subscripts
- The first table position is data-name (1), the second is data-name (2) and so on.

As with most learning experiences, we keep finding new things to study as we learn. So let's look at some rules for using subscripts in COBOL. First of all, remember that you are already expert at using subscripts in math. All you need to learn now is the COBOL compiler's rules. A subscript is simply a data-name qualifier. In COBOL all *references* to data must be unique. Therefore, since all elements of a table have the same name, the subscript is our way of distinguishing among the elements.

The thing for you to do is find the subscript key on your keyboard. Find it? Well, don't worry about it, it does not exist. So how do you handle coding subscripts in COBOL? You show subscripts by following the data-name with the subscript in parentheses. For instance, X(4) or X(10) or, in general, data-name(sub).

Here are some rules for using subscripts:

- Subscript must be a positive numeric value.
- Subscript may be a data-name with a numeric picture or a numeric literal.
- Multiple subscripts are separated by commas.
- Subscript may not be subscripted.
- Subscript may not be used with a data-name containing a REDEFINES clause or a VALUE clause (new feature allowed in '85).

## TYPES OF TABLES

In COBOL we have the ability to define two types of tables: execution-time tables and compile-time tables. An execution-time table receives its initial value during the execution of the program. On the other hand, a compile-time table, as you probably suspect, receives its initial values during the compilation of the program. Notice the key is the initial value. Procedurally a table is a table is a table. Execution-time tables are typically used as counters or accumulators where compile-time tables are typically used to keep static, unchanging values like descriptions for codes or pay rates for codes.

### Execution-Time Tables

Where do we stand now? We have two problems that tables may help with. You have looked at how to reference table elements. What do you say we quit talking (so to speak) and apply tables to the dean's problem?

First look at counting the students by major. In 2100 module, you find the IFs and ADDs. You also needed five counters for the logic to work. You still need the counters, but you will use a table instead of 77 levels. Given the table

```
01   KOUNT-TABLE.
     03   KOUNT        PIC 9(4)   OCCURS 5 TIMES.
```

this sets up a table that we can depict as shown in Figure 11.4.

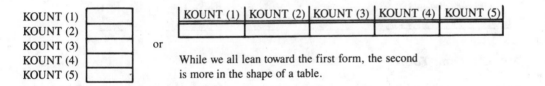

While we all lean toward the first form, the second is more in the shape of a table.

**FIGURE 11.4**
The One-Level Kount Table
Shown Two Ways

Module 2100 can be revised as shown below:

```
2100-COUNT-STUDENTS-BY-MAJOR.
     ADD 1  TO  KOUNT (MAJOR-CLASS).
```

That's it, believe it or not! Well, not quite. Our 77 level counters were initialized with the VALUE clause. In COBOL '74, we cannot use the VALUE clause with the table. (COBOL '85 allows the use of the VALUE clause in this manner.) Therefore, you must add the following logic:

```
1000-INIT-PARA.
     MOVE ZERO TO KOUNT-TABLE.
```

Even with the added MOVE verb it is still very simple. I'm sure you are now asking, "How does it work, and what would you do with 5,000 codes?"

When the 2100 module is executed, the ADD will be done. Read it as "ADD 1 TO KOUNT SUB ___" where the value of MAJOR-CODE fills in the blank. If MAJOR-CODE is a 2, then it reads "ADD 1 TO KOUNT SUB 2" which adds 1 to the contents of KOUNT (2). If MAJOR-CODE was a 4 on the next pass, then a 1 would be added to the contents of KOUNT (4). See how that works? Every time MAJOR-CODE is a 2, 1 is added to the same location. Therefore, after we are finished, KOUNT (2) will contain the number of students whose major code was a 2.

Look back at the IF logic. Every time MAJOR-CODE was a 2, you added 1 to INFO-SYS-COUNT. Notice you get the same answer. That is, INFO-SYS-COUNT is equal to KOUNT (2). How is that? Both sets of logic work with the values of MAJOR-CODE. They are both **dependent** on the **data**, in particular the value of MAJOR-CODE for each student.

What if you had 5,000 codes? Well, the "IF logic" would require:

- 5,000  77 level items,
- 4,999  IFs, and
- 5,000  ADDs

The tables approach would require:

- changing the OCCURS 5 TIMES to OCCURS 5000 TIMES.

That's it!

The OCCURS 5000 TIMES substitutes for the 77 levels. The ADD with MAJOR-CODE as a subscript is functionally 5,000 ADDs, and since the one ADD works for all 5,000, no IFs are needed. I love it. Don't you? I mean, I'm always trying to work smart instead of hard (some call it being lazy). Not only that, look at the power of this logic. It works for five (5) or five million (5,000,000). Just change the OCCURS. While I used 5,000,000 to make a point, there is an upper limit to the size of a table and this would exceed it. But you get my point on the power of the technique.

---

## TIP

**Using tables is a more robust technique than using multiple IFs.**

---

### Compile-Time Tables

What type of table did you use for the dean's problem? If you said execution-time, you are right. You gave its initial values during execution (MOVE ZERO TO KOUNT-TABLE), and it was used for counting. What type of table do you need to convert the class code to a description (the second part of the dean's problem)? You need a compile-time table!

Remember that in COBOL '74, the OCCURS clause and VALUE clause may not be used together. Yet you need both clauses to set up a compile-time table—the OCCURS to actually set up the table locations and the VALUE clause to assign the initial values. It looks like you are between a rock and a hard place. You are, but you can get around the problem by using a powerful feature of COBOL, the redefinition of a previously defined area. Let's set up the table required to convert the class codes:

```
01   CLASS-VALUES.
     03   FILLER                        PIC X(9)   VALUE 'FRESHMAN '.
     03   FILLER                        PIC X(9)   VALUE 'SOPHOMORE'.
     03   FILLER                        PIC X(9)   VALUE 'JUNIOR   '.
     03   FILLER                        PIC X(9)   VALUE 'SENIOR   '.

01   CLASS-TABLE   REDEFINES   CLASS-VALUES.
     03   CLASS-DESCRIPTION             PIC X(9)   OCCURS 4 TIMES.
```

**The Redefines.**        Notice that we first set up a record area that contains the four descriptions we need.  However, we don't have a table yet, and in fact, we just used fillers because we do not need to reference these areas in CLASS-VALUES.  The second 01 contains a new feature, **REDEFINES**.  It simply tells the compiler, "Don't set up a new area; just give a previous area another name."  So the record description of CLASS-TABLE is superimposed over CLASS-VALUES.  Functionally these are the same area.

Look at what we did in CLASS-TABLE.  It contains an OCCURS clause.  By redefining CLASS-VALUES, we get our initial values in a table.  Take a look at the results of the OCCURS, ignoring for the moment the **REDEFINES**.  A one-level table with four elements is set up as shown in Figure 11.5:

CLASS-DESCRIPTION (1)
CLASS-DESCRIPTION (2)
CLASS-DESCRIPTION (3)
CLASS-DESCRIPTION (4)

**FIGURE 11.5**
The One-Level Class
Description Table

Four locations called CLASS-DESCRIPTION now exist.  Each location can contain nine characters, PIC X(9), for a total of 36 characters.  Now look at CLASS-VALUES.  It also defines an area of 36 characters.  However, these 36 characters are given initial values as well.  Since the table is superimposed (by the REDEFINES) over this area, we end up with the table in Figure 11.6.

CLASS-DESCRIPTION (1)   FRESHMAN

CLASS-DESCRIPTION (2)   SOPHOMORE

CLASS-DESCRIPTION (3)   JUNIOR

CLASS-DESCRIPTION (4)   SENIOR

**FIGURE 11.6**
The One-Level Class
Description Table with Initial
Values

Therefore, when we reference CLASS-DESCRIPTION (3), we will get "JUNIOR   ".  This was not as easy as execution-time tables to set up, but look what it does for us procedurally!

Going back to 2100-WRITE-STUDENT-LISTING module, we find we need three **IFs** and four **MOVEs** to convert the class codes.  Assuming the compile-time table in Figure 11.6, we can rewrite the 2100 module as follows:

```
2100-WRITE-STUDENT-LISTING.
    :
    :
    MOVE CLASS-DESCRIPTION (CLASS-CODE) TO CLASS-OUT.
    :
    :
```

I told you it was powerful.  You see that if a student's class code is 2, CLASS-OUT will contain SOPHOMORE for the report.  If the next student's class code is a 4, then SENIOR will be reported.  Isn't that what you did with the IFs?  In both cases, the value of CLASS-CODE determines which literal you reported.

What would happen with 50 codes?  Procedurally, nothing would change.  The MOVE would stay the same!  However, the set up would be time-consuming to code and compilation would take longer.  While that's true, production programs do not get recompiled for each run, so that from an execution standpoint the table is still effective.

You ask, what about 5,000? You have me. I would have to make a decision between a compile-time table (a lot of code) or an execution-time table (more execution time). Using an execution-time table, I would read the 5,000 descriptions into the table in the initialization module. That saves coding, but every time the program is executed, the values must be read into the table. You see the decision: less to code vs. expanded execution time.

Let's summarize what you have studied. You started out with the Dean's request for a listing of all students in the dean file. This list included the requirement for code conversion. The Dean wanted a second report: the number of students in each of the five majors. First you examined the logic just using IFs. Just to count the students by major you needed four **IF** statements, five **ADD**s and five counter locations. Furthermore, to convert the class codes you needed three **IF**s and four **MOVE**s.

These requirements led you to examine other techniques. You used an execution-time table for the count logic and a compile-time table for the code conversion logic. The following is your revised program:

```
WORKING-STORAGE SECTION.

01   KOUNT-TABLE.
     03   KOUNT                    PIC 9(4)   OCCURS 5 TIMES.

01   CLASS-VALUES.
     03   FILLER                   PIC X(9)   VALUE 'FRESHMAN '.
     03   FILLER                   PIC X(9)   VALUE 'SOPHOMORE'.
     03   FILLER                   PIC X(9)   VALUE 'JUNIOR   '.
     03   FILLER                   PIC X(9)   VALUE 'SENIOR   '.

01   CLASS-TABLE   REDEFINES   CLASS-VALUES.
     03   CLASS-DESCRIPTION        PIC X(9)   OCCURS 4 TIMES.

*    NOTE ALL PIC CLAUSES ARE UNIFORM!

PROCEDURE DIVISION.

0000-DEAN-PARA.

     PERFORM   1000-INIT-PARA.
     PERFORM   2000-PROCESS-PARA
        UNTIL  NO-MORE-DATA.
     PERFORM   3000-SUMMARY-PARA.

1000-INIT-PARA.
     :
     :
     MOVE ZERO TO KOUNT-TABLE.

2000-PROCESS-PARA.
     PERFORM 2100-WRITE-STUDENT-LISTING.
     PERFORM 2200-COUNT-STUDENTS-BY-MAJOR.
     PERFORM 9000-READ-STUDENT-RECORD.
```

```
2100-WRITE-STUDENT-LISTING.
    MOVE   NAME                             TO  NAME-OUT.
    MOVE   I-D                              TO  I-D-OUT.
    MOVE   MAJOR-CODE                       TO  MAJOR-CODE-OUT.
    MOVE   CLASS-DESCRIPTION (CLASS-CODE)   TO  CLASS-CODE-OUT.
    MOVE   SEX-CODE                         TO  SEX-CODE-OUT.
    MOVE   GPR                              TO  GPR-OUT.

    WRITE REPORT-LINE      FROM   STUDENT-LINE
        AFTER  2.

2200-COUNT-STUDENTS-BY-MAJOR.
    ADD 1  TO  KOUNT (MAJOR-CODE).

3000-SUMMARY-PARA.
    PERFORM 3100-WRITE-REPORT.
    PERFORM 3200-TERMINATION.


3100-WRITE-REPORT.
```

[We will look at reporting tables later in this chapter.]

I should point out that this technique for code conversion is very appropriate for the control-break problems we discussed in Chapter 9. Instead of using IFs to convert the codes for reporting, as we did for each control group, we can now use compile-time tables and subscripting.

## MULTI-LEVEL TABLES

So far we have looked at one-level execution and one-level compile-time tables. In COBOL '74 we can define one, two and three levels of both types. In COBOL '85 we can have up to seven levels. The original design of COBOL '85 allowed for 48 levels. Can you imagine depicting a 48-level table? Well, believe it or not, once we study two and three levels, you will be able to handle several levels with ease. The techniques we will study will apply to seven levels or more as easily as three levels. . .you can even handle 48 levels.

What makes a table one-level, two-levels, or seven-levels? Remember level numbers? A one-level table has an OCCURS at only one level in the table. It is designed to handle one variable such as major *or* class *or* sex. A two-level table on the other hand has an OCCURS at two levels in the table. It is designed to handle two variables such as major *and* class—not separately, but in relation to each other. For instance, what if I asked you to:

- count the number of students by major

That's what you did in Figure 11.3.

Now, what if I asked you to:

- also count the number of students by class, and
- also count the number of students by sex

Could you do it? Sure you could! You would need an execution-time table for each variable. Each table would look like the one you set up for major. The ADD statements would also be similar to the ADD used to count by major:

```
                    ADD 1  TO  MAJOR-KOUNT (MAJOR-CODE).
                    ADD 1  TO  CLASS-KOUNT (CLASS-CODE).
                    ADD 1  TO  SEX-KOUNT (SEX-CODE).
```

In all cases you had to handle one variable at a time: major code, class code or sex code.

The table-handling techniques apply just as well to other codes; department within store within city for instance. It is not the codes that are important, it is the technique!

### Two-Level Tables

What if I asked you to write the code necessary to count the number of students by class within each major? In other words, "How many freshman accounting majors are there?" Notice, that's different from "How many freshman are there?" or "How many accounting majors are there?"

You now have *two* variables to handle. Let's look at a two-level table:

```
01   KOUNT-TABLE.
     03   MAJOR                                OCCURS 5 TIMES.
          05   CLASS          PIC 9(4)  OCCURS 4 TIMES.
```

KOUNT-TABLE now has an OCCURS at two levels. The way to think of this table is to remember the meaning of the level numbers. The group level 03 is made up of the elementary level 05. So each occurrence of MAJOR is made up of the four occurrences of CLASS. How do you depict a two-level execution-time table? How do you reference it? How do you initialize it? All valid questions. Let's start by drawing it in Figure 11.7.

**FIGURE 11.7**
Drawing of Two-Level Kount Table Showing Class and Major as Levels

See the two levels? Five majors at the highest level and four classes at the second level within each major. Notice that the first level of the table is the OCCURS with the level number 03. The next level is the OCCURS with the next highest level, number 05.

As to how to reference the table elements, just remember that the name of each element is that of the elementary level item. In this case, CLASS. But there are twenty elementary items and just saying CLASS *is not* enough. You must make the reference unique. In other words, qualify the reference. The question is, how? For the element marked with an X, is CLASS (3) enough? No, there are four CLASS (3)s. We must also specify which major. So we need CLASS (2,3) for second major, third class. That uniquely identifies the element.

Why CLASS (2,3) and not CLASS (3,2)? Look at the table. Which variable OCCURS first? Which variable OCCURS second? That's right, MAJOR is first and CLASS is second. Doesn't it make sense that the first subscript goes with the first-level OCCURS and the second subscript goes with the second-level OCCURS and so on until the seventh with the seventh-level (remember, COBOL '85 allows for seven levels)?

Given this relationship, I like to draw or depict multi-level tables with the lowest level drawn on its side. Take a look at the two-level KOUNT-TABLE drawn this way (Figure 11.8).

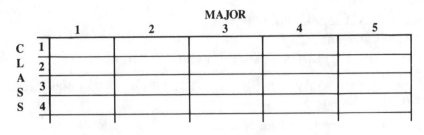

FIGURE 11.8
Two-Level Kount Table: Class within Major with Class Shown on the Side

Note: I have avoided talking rows and columns. Obviously the table could be shown with rows and columns, but row and column depiction can get complicated with multi-levels tables.

Notice that the highest level, MAJOR, is still drawn horizontally. However, the lowest level, class, is turned on its side, or vertically. Since the record description *did not* change, the references are exactly the same. That is, the first subscript goes with the first level OCCURS, MAJOR, and the second subscript goes with the second level OCCURS, CLASS. All you have done is worked smart instead of hard. By drawing class on its side, you don't have to write each class for each major, yet using this form we get the same effect.

I should point out that if you haven't already noticed, you may draw the table any way your heart and/or mind desires. It matters not how you draw it. It only matters how you describe it in the record description. After all, the drawing is to help you work with the table. It cannot be seen by the compiler.

## TIP

**For FORTRAN and BASIC Students Only!**

**If you were raised on FORTRAN or BASIC, draw the table so that the first subscript is the row and the second the column. You can easily do this by drawing it so that Class is the column and Major the row. However, your subscripts (references) are still going to be the same.**

So, how do we count the number of students by CLASS within MAJOR? Look at the code of module 2200 now:

```
2200-COUNT-STUDENTS-BY-MAJOR.
    ADD 1 TO  CLASS (MAJOR-CODE,CLASS-CODE).
```

You must have the KOUNT-TABLE previously described, and of course module 2200 is part of the full example with which you have been working.

It might be worthwhile at this point to remember what you would have had to do to solve this problem without the powerful tool of tables. You would need:

- 20    77 level items for counts
- 19    IF statements
- 20    ADD statements

What do you need using tables?

- the two-level table description
- 1 ADD statement
- MOVE ZERO TO KOUNT-TABLE. for initialization

Just for argument's sake, what if we had 1,000 majors and 500 classes within each?  Without tables you would need:

- 500,000    77 level items for counts
- 499,999    IF statements
- 500,000    ADD statements

I don't know about you, but if that were my job, I would be looking for a new one, or I would try to convince my boss to let me use tables.  Why?  Look at what I would need:

- the two-level table with the modified OCCURS
- 1 ADD statement, ADD 1 TO CLASS (MAJOR-CODE,CLASS-CODE).
- MOVE ZERO TO KOUNT-TABLE. for initialization

Those should look familiar.  They are the same code requirements we had for five majors and four classes.  I would much rather use the tables than not.  I'd rather work smart than hard; wouldn't you?

### Three-Level Tables

Let's take one more level.  What if the dean wanted to know the number of students in the college by SEX within CLASS within MAJOR?.  In other words, "How many female senior finance majors, (or whatever), are there?"  You now have a three-variable problem: SEX, CLASS and MAJOR.  Therefore you need a three-level table.  And since you will be using it to count, it is an execution-time table.

```
01   KOUNT-TABLE.
     03   MAJOR                            OCCURS 5 TIMES.
          05   CLASS                       OCCURS 4 TIMES.
               07   SEX      PIC 9(4)      OCCURS 2 TIMES.
```

Let's draw the table both ways.  Figure 11.9 shows both depictions.

I find either way easy to use because both let me see what the table looks like.  I prefer the second, because it is not as cluttered.  But again, you may draw it however it works best for you.

In case you're not sure that both drawings are the same, the element in both marked with X is referenced by:

SEX (3,1,2)

. . 3rd MAJOR, 1st CLASS, 2nd SEX

| MAJOR | 1 | | | | | | | | 2 | | | | | | | | 3 | | | | | | | | 4 | | | | | | | | 5 | | | | | | | |
|---|---|---|---|---|---|---|---|---|---|---|---|---|---|---|---|---|---|---|---|---|---|---|---|---|---|---|---|---|---|---|---|---|---|---|---|---|---|---|---|---|
| CLASS | 1 | | 2 | | 3 | | 4 | | 1 | | 2 | | 3 | | 4 | | 1 | | 2 | | 3 | | 4 | | 1 | | 2 | | 3 | | 4 | | 1 | | 2 | | 3 | | 4 | |
| SEX | 1 | 2 | 1 | 2 | 1 | 2 | 1 | 2 | 1 | 2 | 1 | 2 | 1 | 2 | 1 | 2 | 1 | 2 | 1 | 2 | 1 | 2 | 1 | 2 | 1 | 2 | 1 | 2 | 1 | 2 | 1 | 2 | 1 | 2 | 1 | 2 | 1 | 2 | 1 | 2 |

| MAJOR | | 1 | | | | 2 | | | | 3 | | | | 4 | | | | 5 | | | |
|---|---|---|---|---|---|---|---|---|---|---|---|---|---|---|---|---|---|---|---|---|---|
| CLASS | | 1 | 2 | 3 | 4 | 1 | 2 | 3 | 4 | 1 | 2 | 3 | 4 | 1 | 2 | 3 | 4 | 1 | 2 | 3 | 4 |
| S E X | 1 | | | | | | | | | | | | | | | | | | | | |
| | 2 | | | | | | | X | | | | | | | | | | | | | |

You should find SEX (5,4,1) in both. It is the same location in either drawing.

Let's apply our rule for using subscripts. That is, our position/OCCURS relationship rule: with a three-level table, the first subscript in a reference goes with the first-level OCCURS, the second subscript in a reference goes with the second-level OCCURS and the third subscript with the third-level OCCURS.

Please note that you can apply this rule to the seven levels allowed in COBOL '85. The position of the subscript goes with the level of the OCCURS. It does not matter how many levels or how we draw the table. For instance, given:

```
01   KOUNT-TABLE.
  03   COUNTRY                          OCCURS 20   TIMES.
    05   STATE                          OCCURS 50   TIMES.
      07   UNIVERSITY                   OCCURS 100  TIMES.
        09   COLLEGE                    OCCURS 20   TIMES.
          11   MAJOR                    OCCURS 5    TIMES.
            13   CLASS                  OCCURS 4    TIMES.
              15 SEX                    OCCURS 2    TIMES
                                        PIC 9(4).
```

A reference to a particular element will require seven subscripts. The first identifies the country, the second identifies the state and so forth so that we get:

```
SEX (COUNTRY-CODE, STATE-CODE, UNIV-CODE, COLLEGE-CODE,
   MAJOR-CODE, CLASS-CODE, SEX-CODE).
```

Can you imagine counting, for this example, the number of students by sex with class within major within college within university within state within country using IFs? Well, think about it! You would need:

- 80 million    77 level items $(20 \times 50 \times 100 \times 20 \times 5 \times 4 \times 2)$
- 79,999,999    IFs
- 80 million    ADDs

I don't know about you, but I *love* tables. With tables, all I need for the problem is:

- one seven-level table like the one above
- one ADD statement

```
ADD 1 TO SEX (COUNTRY-CODE, STATE-CODE, UNIV-CODE, COLLEGE-CODE,
   MAJOR-CODE, CLASS-CODE, SEX-CODE).
```

I don't even need MOVE ZERO for initialization, since COBOL '85 allows VALUE ZERO with the table.

Before we leave execution-time tables, let's look at one very important feature of all tables. Every time you execute a statement with the same value for the subscript or combination of values for the subscripts, you reference the same element. This must be true for tables to work. After all, the computer does not know or care that a MAJOR-CODE of 2 is Information Systems. All it cares about is that a code of 2 is a particular location in memory. And what you care about is that every time MAJOR-CODE is 2, you reference that same location. You have built a logical relationship. That is to say that after all data is processed from the dean's file, KOUNT (2) will contain the number of Information Systems majors.

## MULTI-LEVEL COMPILE-TIME TABLES

Compile-time tables are used for converting codes to descriptions, as we said earlier in this chapter. However, they may be used for other things. For instance, they may contain pay rates for employees so that each employee record does not contain an actual rate but a rate code. This does a couple of things:

1. It adds a level of privacy. A person looking at employee records would also have to have the table of codes to know what the employee's pay rate was.
2. It provides an easier maintenance of pay rates. If the rate for all code 5 employees changed, then only the table entry would have to be changed. All the employee records with a pay rate code of 5 would not have to be changed.

Nice, isn't it? Furthermore, if the table values were read in, the rates could be changed via a system editor and the program would not have to be recompiled with the new rate for code 5.

Let's look at a problem. What if you wanted to read a payroll file and write a report of all employees that includes all data plus the pay rate (instead of rate code)?

```
01   RATE-VALUES.
     03   FILLER              PIC 9(3)V99    VALUE  30.00.
     03   FILLER              PIC 9(3)V99    VALUE  85.50.
     03   FILLER              PIC 9(3)V99    VALUE 122.75.
     03   FILLER              PIC 9(3)V99    VALUE 172.25.

01   RATE-TABLE    REDEFINES    RATE-VALUES.
     03   RATE                PIC 9(3)V99    OCCURS 4 TIMES.

0000-MAIN-PARA.
     PERFORM 1000-INIT-PARA.
     PERFORM 2000-HEADINGS-PARA.
     PERFORM 9000-READ-EMP-RECORD-PARA.
     PERFORM 3000-WRITE-EMP-RECORD
        UNTIL NO-MORE-DATA
         :
         :
```

```
3000-WRITE-EMP-RECORD.
      MOVE   EMP-NAME          TO   EMP-NAME-OUT.
      MOVE   EMP-ADDRESS       TO   EMP-ADDRESS-OUT.
      MOVE   EMP-ID            TO   EMP-ID-OUT.
      MOVE   STORE-CODE        TO   STORE-CODE-OUT.
      MOVE   DEPARTMENT-CODE   TO   DEPARTMENT-CODE-OUT.
      MOVE   DATE-STARTED      TO   DATE-STARTED-OUT.
      MOVE   RATE (RATE-CODE)  TO   PAY-RATE-OUT.
      WRITE RPT-LINE           FROM EMP-RECORD-OUT
           AFTER 2.
      PERFORM 9000-READ-EMP-RECORD-PARA.
```

So far, you realize, this is just a one-level compile-time table. But it is not used for code conversions. . .or is it? Sure it is. The only difference is that earlier we converted a MAJOR-CODE of 1 to ACCOUNTING while here we converted a RATE-CODE of 1 to $30.00. Feel better now? You know this stuff. So, let's go ahead and expand the problem.

Our pay scale is different for each department at each store. Therefore, an employee's pay rate is determined, not by a rate code, but by which department and store he or she works in. Let's look at the table now:

```
01   RATE-VALUES.
     03   STORE-1.
          05   DEPT-1          PIC 9(3)V99     VALUE 20.00.
          05   DEPT-2          PIC 9(3)V99     VALUE 22.50.
          05   DEPT-3          PIC 9(3)V99     VALUE 27.95.
     03   STORE-2.
          05   DEPT-1          PIC 9(3)V99     VALUE 30.00.
          05   DEPT-2          PIC 9(3)V99     VALUE 32.50.
          05   DEPT-3          PIC 9(3)V99     VALUE 37.00.
     03   STORE-3.
          05   DEPT-1          PIC 9(3)V99     VALUE 35.00.
          05   DEPT-2          PIC 9(3)V99     VALUE 39.75.
          05   DEPT-3          PIC 9(3)V99     VALUE 40.25.
     03   STORE-4.
          05   DEPT-1          PIC 9(3)V99     VALUE 40.25.
          05   DEPT-2          PIC 9(3)V99     VALUE 41.00.
          05   DEPT-1          PIC 9(3)V99     VALUE 42.50.

01   RATE-TABLE     REDEFINES     RATE-VALUES.
     03   STORE                    OCCURS 4 TIMES.
          05   DEPT                OCCURS 3 TIMES.
               07   RATE           PIC 9(3)V99.
```

NOTE: I chose to use 07 RATE so that my data names would be more descriptive and easier to read.

The MOVE statement in 3000 module for the pay rate would change as indicated below:

```
3000-WRITE-EMP-RECORD.
           :
           :
      MOVE RATE (STORE-CODE,DEPARTMENT-CODE)  TO  PAY-RATE-OUT.
```

An employee working at store 2 in department 3 would have a pay rate of 37.00. You see how well that works. The employee record contains just the codes, and we convert them to a rate on the report. The only real cost comes from coding the table. But remember that is done once, and as long as the program stays in production with no change, the table does not get recompiled for each run. If the table were much longer (seven levels) or the data were very volatile (changed often), I would suggest that we read the values into the table each time the program runs.

## THE PROBLEM OF NOT-NICE DATA

The tables we have been working with so far were referenced very conveniently with input data values: **data-dependent algorithms**. The values of those data names were nice. That is, they were numeric, and they were in sequence starting with 1. Look back at our codes: 1, 2, 3, 4, and 5 for MAJOR-CODE; 1, 2, 3, and 4 for CLASS-CODE; and so on. These were nice and could be used directly as subscripts to tables that themselves had locations 1, 2, 3, 4, and so on. Now, what would happen if the MAJOR-CODEs were as follows?

> A  –  accounting
> I  –  information systems
> F  –  finance
> M  –  management
> K  –  marketing

We could not use these codes as subscripts. Where is KOUNT (MAJOR-CODE) when MAJOR-CODE is equal to "F"? The computer cannot determine a location! So you ask why anyone would establish not-nice codes like these? Research indicates that codes that are similar to what they stand for reduce recording/input errors. Furthermore, not all situations allow for nice codes—inventory item numbers, for instance. Sometimes computers convert their supplier codes that are not-nice to nice codes, but this is not easy. Large companies that use internal buyers might include as part of the item's record the initials for the buyer. You can see there may be several cases where we need to work with not-nice data.

Let's pose a problem. Given that the MAJOR-CODEs are A, I, F, M and K for the students in the dean's file (DEAN-FILE form 3), how would we count the number of students in each major? How do we convert the codes to descriptions? Well, the answer is that we must look at another COBOL tool, the SEARCH verb, and at its associated techniques.

Let's first look at the problem conceptually. If I was converting unfamiliar codes to their corresponding descriptions, I would have to look them up on a list that had both the codes and associated descriptions. I would match the code on the record with the code on the list and then copy the description. For instance, let's say a student's record contains a major code of I and we have the following list of codes and descriptions:

> A  –  Accounting
> I  –  Information Systems
> F  –  Finance
> M  –  Management
> K  –  Marketing

I would look up the I which would match the second (2) code on my list, and I would simply copy the description Information Systems to my report.

Continuing with these concepts, now that we matched the second (2) code, could we not use this knowledge to count the students by major? Sure! Just add 1 to the second (2) element of a MAJOR-KOUNT-TABLE:

```
ADD 1 TO KOUNT(MAJOR-SUB).
```

Notice the ADD looks exactly like our ADD with nice data except for the subscript:

```
ADD 1 TO KOUNT (MAJOR-CODE).
```

Instead of MAJOR-CODE, value I, we use MAJOR-SUB, value 2. Had the MAJOR-CODE been M, we would ADD 1 TO KOUNT (4) since that's the value of MAJOR-SUB. How does MAJOR-SUB get its values? We set its values when we look up the code in our list. Therefore, with MAJOR-CODE of M, we match the fourth code and we save the position value, 4, in MAJOR-SUB. With a MAJOR-CODE of A, MAJOR-SUB would be set to 1. See how that works? You should also notice that the process is consistent. Every time MAJOR-CODE is an I, MAJOR-SUB will be a 2 and so forth for all codes.

## THE SEARCH VERB

So much for talk. Let's look at the **SEARCH** verb and the COBOL equivalent to our list of codes and descriptions. The code below handles the provision of counting first. Then we'll add the code needed to handle the conversion to descriptions.

```
WORKING-STORAGE SECTION.

01   MAJOR-VALUES.
     03   FILLER              PIC X(1)   VALUE 'A'.
     03   FILLER              PIC X(1)   VALUE 'I'.
     03   FILLER              PIC X(1)   VALUE 'F'.
     03   FILLER              PIC X(1)   VALUE 'M'.
     03   FILLER              PIC X(1)   VALUE 'K'.

01   MAJOR-TABLE     REDEFINES     MAJOR-VALUES.
     03   MAJOR-KODE           PIC X(1)   OCCURS 5 TIMES
                                          INDEXED BY MAJOR-INDEX.

01   MAJOR-KOUNT-TABLE.
     03   MAJOR-KOUNT          PIC 9(4)   OCCURS 5 TIMES.
     PROCEDURE DIVISION.

     0000-MAIN-PARA.
         PERFORM 1000-INIT-PARA.
         PERFORM 2000-HEADING-PARA.
         PERFORM 9000-READ-PARA.
         PERFORM 3000-PROCESS-PARA
             UNTIL NO-MORE-DATA.
             :
             :
         STOP RUN.
```

```
1000-INIT-PARA.
     :
     :

2000-HEADING-PARA.
     :
     :

3000-PROCESS-PARA.
     SET MAJOR-INDEX TO 1.
     SEARCH MAJOR-KODE
          AT END   PERFORM 4000-NO-MATCH-FOUND-PARA
          WHEN MAJOR-CODE = MAJOR-KODE (MAJOR-INDEX)
               SET MAJOR-SUB  TO  MAJOR-INDEX
               ADD 1 TO  MAJOR-KOUNT (MAJOR-SUB).

     PERFORM 9000-READ-PARA.

4000-NO-MATCH-FOUND-PARA.
     :
     :
```

[Write record to error report]

I can hear you now. "What is all that stuff:

- SET?
- **SEARCH**?
- AT END?
- WHEN?
- INDEXED BY?"

At least I got your attention. I'm not going to leave you hanging. We will look at all the rules, but first look at the code conceptually. We said that we would look up MAJOR-CODE, find its match on our list and use that position's value as our MAJOR-SUB value for counting. That's exactly what the code does.

### Indexing

You recognize the compile-time table of codes. I added the INDEXED BY clause because the rules say that if a table is to be the object of the COBOL **SEARCH** verb, then the table must be indexed. An index works functionally like a subscript. It is usually a computer register that contains the table address in binary. This makes it a quicker reference than a subscript, since much of the time a subscript is a data-name that must first be converted to binary by the system. Indexes *may not* be used with the ADD, SUBTRACT, MULTIPLY, DIVIDE, COMPUTE, or MOVE verbs. They may be used only with the SET or PERFORM verbs. Once a data-name is defined as an index to a table, then the index and table are married. The index may be used only with the table it is indexing. However, the table may still be referenced by using one or more subscripts. We need to examine this concept further.

Let's say that MAJOR-TABLE is at the address 5001 in memory. I know that you're bothered by my use of absolute addressing instead of relative, but indexing is easier to demonstrate with an actual address, so bear with me. The index gets set to 5001 (the address of the first element). Then the addresses of the elements are calculated as 5001 plus a displacement of 0, 1, 2, 3, or 4 bytes, so that the address of the "F" is 5003 (5001 + 2).

Notice that the first element is at displacement 0 and the second is at displacement 1. Don't let this bother you. Just think of the position, like a subscript, and not the displacement when you reference an indexed table. Let the computer worry about the displacements!  Given all that, can you see that if I tried to use MAJOR-INDEX to work with some table at location 7000 I would not get the results I want? I would be looking at the wrong memory location. So keep the index with the table to which it belongs.

## TIP

**You can make a data-name contain a binary number by making its usage computational.**

Back to the code explanation.  You also recognize the count table, so let's look at the PROCEDURE code.  Since we are again working with the dean file, which is sequential, you will recognize the model.  3000-PROCESS-PARA is our focus here. You will notice two new verbs, **SET** and **SEARCH.**

### The SET Verb

The **SET** verb is our way of manipulating indexes.  Since we want to start our lookup at the first position, we SET our INDEX to 1.  This is followed by the **SEARCH** itself. Read it carefully.  It says, "Look at the MAJOR-KODE (**SEARCH**), and when you get a match between the input value for MAJOR-CODE and one of the table entries, MAJOR-KODE (MAJOR-INDEX), put the position value (MAJOR-INDEX) in a subscript (MAJOR-SUB) so that it may be used with the count table."  The AT END clause is our means of catching the situation where no match is found.

The generic form of the **SET** verb is:

$$\underline{\text{SET}} \ \text{identifier}_1 \ \left\{ \begin{array}{l} \textbf{TO} \\ \textbf{UP BY} \\ \textbf{DOWN BY} \end{array} \right\} \ \text{identifier}_2$$

where identifier$_1$ or identifier$_2$ may be an index name or a data-name, but at least one must be an index name.

$$\underline{\text{SET}} \ \text{index-name}_1 \ \text{TO} \ \text{index-name}_2.$$

or

$$\underline{\text{SET}} \ \text{index-name}_1 \ \text{TO} \ \text{data-name}_2.$$

or

$$\underline{\text{SET}} \ \text{data-name}_1 \ \text{TO} \ \text{index-name}_2.$$

The **SET** verb may also be used with numeric literals:

<u>SET</u> index-name$_1$ TO numeric literal.

### The INDEXED BY Clause

The INDEXED BY clause defines an index and associates it with a particular table level. Furthermore, each level of a table may have more than one index defined.

```
01    KOUNT-TABLE.
      03  MAJOR-KOUNT            OCCURS  5  TIMES
                                 INDEXED BY  MAJOR-INDEX.
```

Where MAJOR-INDEX is an index associated with MAJOR-KOUNT. Or,

```
01    KOUNT-TABLE.
      03  MAJOR-KOUNT            OCCURS  5  TIMES
                                 INDEXED BY  MAJOR-INDEX-1
                                             MAJOR-INDEX-2.
```

where both MAJOR-INDEX-1 and MAJOR-INDEX-2 are associated with MAJOR-KOUNT.

For a multi-level table, we associate indexes in the same way. For example:

```
01    KOUNT-TABLE.
      03  MAJOR-KOUNT            OCCURS  5  TIMES
                                 INDEXED BY  MAJOR-INDEX
          05  CLASS-KOUNT        OCCURS  4  TIMES
                                 INDEXED BY  CLASS-INDEX
              07  SEX-KOUNT      OCCURS  2  TIMES
                                 INDEXED BY  SEX-INDEX
                                 PIC 9(4).
```

This three-level table is familiar to you. So just notice the use of the INDEXED BY clause at each level, MAJOR-INDEX, CLASS-INDEX and SEX-INDEX.

To summarize, an index is defined with the INDEXED BY clause, not with a PIC clause. It is associated with a particular table level. Each table level may have more that one index. An index may be used only to reference the table it goes with, but a indexed table may still be referenced by subscripts. The value of INDEXES may be manipulated only with the SET and PERFORM verbs.

### How the Search Works

In COBOL we have two forms of the **SEARCH** verb: **SEARCH** and **SEARCH ALL**. **SEARCH** causes a serial search where **SEARCH ALL** causes a binary search.

The generic form of **SEARCH** is:

> **SEARCH** [ <u>ALL</u> ] table-entry [ <u>VARYING</u> index-name ]
>     [ <u>AT END</u> executable statement]
>     <u>WHEN</u> condition statement
>     executable statement(s).

where:

- The object of **SEARCH** is the table entry containing the OCCURS clause.

- The optional VARYING is used to vary the value of an index not associated with the table being SEARCHed or to VARY a second index associated with the SEARCH table. If the VARYING is used to vary the first or only index associated with the table it is redundant.
- The AT END is like the EOF in that it will be executed if no match is found during the SEARCH
- The WHEN statement is like the IF statement. The condition itself is an equal which must involve an indexed table entry in the table being SEARCHed. More than one WHEN may be used. They are evaluated in the order presented, and when any condition is satisfied the SEARCH conditional statements are executed and the SEARCHing stops.

### Using the Search for Counting

Now, let's look back at the 3000-PROCESS-PARA and examine the statements.

```
SET MAJOR-INDEX TO 1.
```

causes the serial search to start with the first position for each student's record. Otherwise, once we match with a MAJOR-INDEX of say 3 we would start the next serial SEARCH for the next record at 3 and would not find any accounting or information systems codes.

```
SEARCH MAJOR-KODE
```

This actually starts the lookup process of MAJOR-TABLE which will start at the value in MAJOR-INDEX. Since a VARYING is not coded, MAJOR-INDEX will be varied by the SEARCH itself.

```
AT END PERFORM 4000-NO-MATCH-FOUND-PARA
```

The AT END is executed only if the serial SEARCH does not find a match. If this happens, don't keep it a secret; report it. The 4000-NO-MATCH-FOUND-PARA should contain the logic to write the record with an appropriate error message.

The conditional part of the SEARCH is the WHEN statement:

```
WHEN MAJOR-CODE = MAJOR-KODE (MAJOR-INDEX)
```

MAJOR-CODE, you remember, caused all this. The code values are not-nice. The MAJOR-CODE is our input value. MAJOR-KODE (MAJOR-INDEX) is the table value we are hoping to match. MAJOR-INDEX starts at 1 then is varied by 1 until we either get a match or MAJOR-INDEX exceeds the number of elements specified by the OCCURS.

When we find a match, the CONDITIONed executable statements, SET and ADD, are executed. Looking closer at these two statements, we find that we are just getting around the problem that MAJOR-INDEX may be used only with MAJOR-KODES. Logically, we would like to say

```
ADD 1 TO MAJOR-KOUNT (MAJOR-INDEX).
```

since MAJOR-INDEX contains the position value for our match, and that's the value we want to use to reference our count table. But we can't use MAJOR-INDEX with the MAJOR-KOUNT-TABLE, so we first say

```
                    SET MAJOR-SUB TO MAJOR-INDEX.
```

and then use MAJOR-SUB as the subscript to MAJOR-KOUNT-TABLE. Therefore, if we match the second MAJOR-KODE, MAJOR-SUB gets set to 2 and we ADD 1 to MAJOR-KOUNT (2). Slick, isn't it? Well, if you think that's slick, look at this:
Change the count table so that it is indexed.

```
01   MAJOR-KOUNT-TABLE.
     03   MAJOR-KOUNT        PIC 9(4)   OCCURS 5    TIMES
                                        INDEXED BY KOUNT-INDEX.
```

Then 3000-PROCESS-PARA could be coded like:

```
        3000-PROCESS-PARA.
            SET KOUNT-INDEX TO 1.
            SET MAJOR-INDEX TO 1.
            SEARCH MAJOR-KODE VARYING KOUNT-INDEX
                AT END   PERFORM 4000-NO-MATCH-FOUND-PARA
                WHEN  MAJOR-CODE = MAJOR-KODE (MAJOR-INDEX)
                    ADD 1 TO  MAJOR-KOUNT (KOUNT-INDEX).
```

This code varies the index to the count table, so we just set it to 1 and it varies with MAJOR-INDEX. When the codes are equal, we just say ADD, since KOUNT-INDEX already references the appropriate position in the count table. Now, that's really slick.

### Using the Search for Descriptions

Converting not-nice codes to descriptions uses the same concept as we used for counting. However, we must do something extra in the table:

```
01   MAJOR-VALUES.
     03   FILLER            PIC X(20)   VALUE 'AACCOUNTING          '.
     03   FILLER            PIC X(20)   VALUE 'IINFORMATION SYSTEMS'.
     03   FILLER            PIC X(20)   VALUE 'FFINANCE              '.
     03   FILLER            PIC X(20)   VALUE 'MMANAGEMENT           '.
     03   FILLER            P'C X(20)   VALUE 'KMARKETING            '.

01   MAJOR-TABLE            REDEFINES   MAJOR-VALUES.
     03   MAJOR-GROUP            OCCURS 5 TIMES
                                 INDEXED BY MAJOR-INDEX.
         05   MAJOR-KODE        PIC X(1).
         05   MAJOR-NAME        PIC X(19).
```

Notice that the MAJOR-VALUES contain the major code and corresponding description. Then in the table we break these down into two parts, MAJOR-KODE and MAJOR-DESCRIPTION. This sets up a table shown in Figure 11.10.

## TIP

**Relative order in a code and its description is the programmer's responsibility.**

| | MAJOR-KODE | MAJOR-NAME |
|---|---|---|
| MAJOR-GROUP (1) | A | ACCOUNTING |
| MAJOR-GROUP (2) | I | INFORMATION SYSTEMS |
| MAJOR-GROUP (3) | F | FINANCE |
| MAJOR-GROUP (4) | M | MANAGEMENT |
| MAJOR-GROUP (5) | K | MARKETING |

**FIGURE 11.10**
One-Level Compile-Time Table Including Codes and Corresponding Names

Now that the table is set up, the major names could be reported by the following logic:

```
2000-PROC-PARA.
    PERFORM 2100-WRITE-STUDENT-LISTING.

2100-WRITE-STUDENT-LISTING.
    SET MAJOR-INDEX TO 1.
    SEARCH MAJOR-GROUP
        AT END . . .
        WHEN MAJOR-CODE = MAJOR-KODE (MAJOR-INDEX)
            MOVE MAJOR-NAME (MAJOR-INDEX) TO MAJOR-OUT.
```

Notice the similarity between this logic and the count logic. Instead of an ADD we MOVE the name to output.

## SEARCH ALL VERB

Searching a table of values for a match has so far been the exercise of starting with a particular position, normally the first, and going through the table in sequence until we have found a match or run out of table. That's not a bad technique with small tables and computers that work at a rate measured in MIPS (millions of instructions per second).

However, let's illustrate the use of the **SEARCH ALL** by looking at a special problem. What if I have an inventory file that contains a record for each of 200 items (bats, balls, gloves). Each record contains, among other things, a buyer's code (initials). The buyers are the people responsible for that item of inventory. Each buyer is responsible for many items. We may assume any number of buyers, but let's start with a small number, say 10. If we assume an equal number of items for each buyer, and we also assume that we access each item equally, then with a serial SEARCH the average comparison would be equal to 1/2 of the number of buyers (mean of a uniform distribution). That is to say if we looked up each buyer's name in the table on the average we would have to make five comparisons (10/2 = 5 comparisons).

That's why I called this a special problem. A uniform distribution is not likely. But let's look at a **SEARCH ALL** binary search and see where the five comes from. The binary search works by requiring the table values to be in order, ascending or descending. Then the search starts at the halfway point. If that's not a match, we at least know in which half of the table we might find the match. The search continues in the appropriate half, at the halfway point again. This continues until either a match is found or the match cannot be made (AT END).

Given:

```
01   BUYER-VALUES.
     03   FILLER              PIC X(22)   VALUE 'AAAMY ALLOW          '.
     03   FILLER              PIC X(22)   VALUE 'BBBOB BOYD            '.
                  ⋮
                  ⋮
     03   FILLER              PIC X(22)   VALUE 'ZZZELDA ZOE           '.

01   BUYER-TABLE      REDEFINES BUYER-VALUES.
     03   BUYER-GROUP        OCCURS 10 TIMES
                            ASCENDING KEY IS BUYER-INITIALS
                            INDEXED BY BUYER-INDEX.
          05   BUYER-INITIALS   PIC X(2).
          05   BUYER-NAME       PIC X(20).
```

Remember this from our search discussion? It's the same type of table we had before except for the ASCENDING KEY clause required by the **SEARCH ALL** logic. All it says is that the table is in ascending order according to the contents of buyer-initials, which must be a field in the table. Figure 11.11 shows this table.

**FIGURE 11.11**
Buyer Table Showing Buyer Codes and Names

|                   | BUYER-INITIALS | BUYER-NAME       |
|-------------------|----------------|------------------|
| BUYER-GROUP (1)   | AA             | AMY ALLEN        |
| BUYER-GROUP (2)   | BB             | BOB BOYD         |
| BUYER-GROUP (3)   | CC             | CHRIS CHANDLER   |
| BUYER-GROUP (4)   | DD             | DAVE DOUGAN      |
| BUYER-GROUP (5)   | LL             | LISA LANE        |
| BUYER-GROUP (6)   | MP             | MARGARET PORTER  |
| BUYER-GROUP (7)   | MR             | MICHAEL RYAN     |
| BUYER-GROUP (8)   | PP             | PETER PAUL       |
| BUYER-GROUP (9)   | SS             | SUZY SMART       |
| BUYER-GROUP (10)  | ZZ             | ZELDA ZOE        |

**SEARCH ALL BUYER-GROUP**
    AT END. . .
      WHEN BUYER-CODE = BUYER-INITIALS (BUYER-INDEX)
        MOVE BUYER-NAME (BUYER-INDEX) TO BUYER-NAME-OUT.

Assume that we have a buyer's code of LL on a record. How many comparisons would the **SEARCH ALL** make? One. That's right. Remember, this is a binary search. Therefore, the first comparison is made with BUYER-INITIALS (5) [10/2 = 5]. This would match LL and Lisa Lane would be moved to BUYER-NAME-OUT. That was easy. What if the BUYER-CODE on a record was AA? The first comparison would still be with BUYER-GROUP (5). However, it does not match and is less than LL so the code should be found in the top half of the table. The next comparison is with BUYER-GROUP (2) [5/2 = 2.5 = 2 truncated]. Then AA is compared with BUYER-GROUP (1), which is a match. How many comparisons for "PP"?

| comparison | results  |
|------------|----------|
| 1st – LL   | no match |
| 2nd – PP   | match    |

So in just two comparisons we found a match. This compares to eight with a serial search.

I can hear you now. "It took three comparisons to match AA with the **SEARCH ALL** and the **SEARCH** would have matched in one." Well, I didn't say the **SEARCH ALL** was perfect. It's just another approach that can be helpful with the appropriate data. After all, a table of 1,000 elements would take 10 comparisons maximum compared to an average of 500 comparisons with the serial SEARCH.

## SEARCHING MULTI-LEVEL TABLES

Let's assume we have different department names for each of ten colleges. Let's also assume that the college codes are nice: 1 through 10, and that the department codes are not-nice.

```
01  COLLEGE-DEPT-VALUES.
    03  COLLEGE-1.
        05  FILLER      PIC X(20)   VALUE 'AACCOUNTING        '.
        05  FILLER      PIC X(20)   VALUE 'IINFORMATION SYSTEMS'.
        05  FILLER      PIC X(20)   VALUE 'FFINANCE           '.
        05  FILLER      PIC X(20)   VALUE 'MMANAGEMENT        '.
        05  FILLER      PIC X(20)   VALUE 'KMARKETING         '.
    03  COLLEGE-2.
        05  FILLER      PIC X(20)   VALUE 'EENGLISH           '.
        05  FILLER      PIC X(20)   VALUE 'SSPEECH            '.
        05  FILLER      PIC X(20)   VALUE 'DDRAMA             '.
        05  FILLER      PIC X(20)   VALUE 'MMUSIC             '.
                  .
                  .
                  .
    03  COLLEGE-10.
        05  FILLER      PIC X(20)   VALUE 'CCHEMISTRY         '.
        05  FILLER      PIC X(20)   VALUE 'PPHYSICS           '.
        05  FILLER      PIC X(20)   VALUE 'BBIOLOGY           '.
        05  FILLER      PIC X(20)   VALUE 'GGEOLOGY           '.
        05  FILLER      PIC X(20)   VALUE 'AASTRONOMY         '.

01  COLLEGE-DEPT-TABLE         REDEFINES  COLLEGE-DEPT-VALUES.
    03  COLLEGE                OCCURS 10 TIMES
                               INDEXED BY COLLEGE-INDEX.
        05  DEPT               OCCURS 5 TIMES
                               INDEXED BY DEPT-INDEX.
            07  DEPT-KODE      PIC X(1).
            07  DEPT-NAME      PIC X(19).
```

Given this table, assume a record contains a COLLEGE-CODE and a DEPT-CODE and we want to convert the DEPT-CODE to a description. The SEARCH algorithm would be:

```
SET COLLEGE-INDEX TO COLLEGE-CODE.
SET DEPT-INDEX TO 1.
SEARCH DEPT
    WHEN DEPT-CODE = DEPT-KODE (COLLEGE-INDEX,DEPT-INDEX)
        MOVE DEPT-NAME (COLLEGE-INDEX,DEPT-INDEX)
            TO DEPT-NAME-OUT.
```

See how that works?  In order to find a department match, we set the COLLEGE-INDEX and SEARCH only within that college.  In general, to SEARCH a multi-level table you can search only one level at a time.  Therefore, all other levels must be SET prior to SEARCHing.

## MANIPULATING TABLES

Are you ready for some fun stuff?  Well, this is it.  We will massage tables to get totals in all directions: up, down, across.  We will also look at the related techniques for reporting tables.  After all, we accumulated all those counts and sums, and we need to write them out unless of course you want to keep them a secret.

If we assume we have a one-level table of student counts by major that now contains all the actual numbers, how do we calculate the total number of students?  Note that we are not doing this during detail time but at total time, after EOF.

Given the table and values in Figure 11.12, what we need to do is add up the contents of all five majors.

**FIGURE 11.12**
**One-Level Kount Table of Student Counts by Major**

```
01  MAJOR-KOUNT-TABLE.
    03  MAJOR  PIC 9(4)  OCCURS 5 TIMES.
```

| | |
|---|---|
| MAJOR (1) | 1790 |
| MAJOR (2) | 525 |
| MAJOR (3) | 610 |
| MAJOR (4) | 400 |
| MAJOR (5) | 382 |

Can you do it?  Sure you can!  Look at this:

```
ADD  MAJOR (1) MAJOR (2) MAJOR (3) MAJOR (4) MAJOR (5)
     TO TOTAL.
```

I know!  I know!  You were thinking of some fancy way, not just a plain old ADD statement.  Well, you're right.  This method was OK, but what if we wanted to do the same thing but the elements OCCURed 5,000 times?  A year from now you might be finished writing the ADD.  Let's look at a more robust and powerful approach.

First let's recognize that what we need to do is ADD the $i^{th}$ element to TOTAL for values of i from 1 to 5.  Remember,

$$\sum_{i=1}^{5} MAJOR_i$$

That's what we want to do in COBOL.  We need a new form of the PERFORM verb to help us.

### PERFORM VARYING

The format for the PERFORM VARYING is:

<u>PERFORM</u> paragraph-name

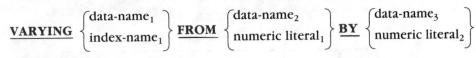

<u>UNTIL</u> condition.

You recognize the PERFORM. . .UNTIL. We just added the **VARYING** option. It works very nicely with algorithms that require subscripts and indexes. Look closer at the **VARYING** clause. Data-name$_1$ or index-name$_1$ is initialized to the **FROM** value and is incremented with the **BY** value where the FROM or BY values may be specified by a data-name or numeric literal. So if we had the following **VARYING**:

```
PERFORM  .  .  .
    VARYING I FROM 1 BY 1
       :
       :
```

We would be causing I to be initialized at 1 and then varied by 1. Looks good for our needs, doesn't it. We want to ADD MAJOR (1) and then MAJOR (2), for all majors, to TOTAL. We know where to start and what to increment by, so all we need to do is know when to stop. Guess what the condition is!

```
5000-SUMMARY-PARA.
    PERFORM 5100-GET-TOTAL
        VARYING MAJOR-SUB FROM 1 BY 1
        UNTIL MAJOR-SUB > 5.

5100-GET-TOTAL.
    ADD MAJOR (MAJOR-SUB) TO TOTAL.
```

Nice, isn't it? Let's execute it. Starting the PERFORM causes MAJOR-SUB to be initialized at 1. The condition is checked: Is MAJOR-SUB > 5? No; then the ADD is executed, causing the contents of MAJOR (1) to be ADDed to TOTAL. Then MAJOR-SUB is incremented by 1. The condition is checked. Still not > 5, so MAJOR (2)'s contents are ADDed to TOTAL. This continues until MAJOR-SUB becomes a 6, which is > 5 and satisfies the PERFORM.

Let's summarize:

| MAJOR-SUB | CONDITION | MAJOR (MAJOR-SUB) | TOTAL |
|---|---|---|---|
| 1 | > 5? no | 1,790 | 1,790 |
| 2 | > 5? no | 525 | 2,315 |
| 3 | > 5? no | 610 | 2,925 |
| 4 | > 5? no | 400 | 3,325 |
| 5 | > 5? no | 382 | 3,707 |
| 6 | > 5? yes, stop | — | 3,707 |

Now that you understand this technique, what about the case of 5,000 majors? The only thing that changes procedurally is UNTIL. It changes to MAJOR-SUB > 5000. I call that a powerful algorithm, don't you?

What if we had a two-level table like the one we have used for counting student by class within major (Figure 11.13)?

**FIGURE 11.13**
Two-Level Kount Table: Class
within Major

```
01 MAJOR-CLASS-TABLE.
   03  MAJOR              OCCURS 5 TIMES
      05  CLASS           OCCURS 4 TIMES     PIC 9(4).
```

MAJOR

| C | | 1 | 2 | 3 | 4 | 5 |
|---|---|---|---|---|---|---|
| L | 1 | | | | | |
| A | 2 | | | | | |
| S | 3 | | | | | |
| S | 4 | | | | | |

What would we have to do to get the number of students by class from this table?  We would have to ADD CLASS (1,1) to TOTAL and then CLASS (2,1) to TOTAL and then CLASS (3,1), CLASS (4,1), CLASS (5,1) all to TOTAL.  So we would be going across the table (the way I've drawn it).  A more robust view is that we want to keep the CLASS subscript constant and let the MAJOR subscript go through its entire range.  We would do this for each value of the CLASS subscript.  Let me suggest that you use this approach for all your table massaging needs.  That is, understand the relationship of the subscript values.  Once you do this, then you can code the technique.  Look at the flowchart in Figure 11.14.  It shows the logic flow, too.

## TIP

**By first understanding the relationship of the subscripts to one another, you can always build logic to control them in that way.  Usually you will find that the PERFORM VARYING is your friend in these cases.**

Now, let's code the logic shown in the flowchart.

```
5000-SUMMARY-PARA.
    PERFORM 5100-START-PROCESS
        VARYING CLASS-SUB FROM 1 BY 1
        UNTIL CLASS-SUB > 4.

5100-START-PROCESS.
    PERFORM 5110-ADD-PARA
        VARYING MAJOR-SUB FROM 1 BY 1
        UNTIL MAJOR-SUB > 5.

5110-ADD-PARA.
    ADD CLASS (MAJOR-SUB,CLASS-SUB) TO TOTAL (CLASS-SUB).
```

You should note a few things.  First, this logic uses nested PERFORMs.  Since a PERFORM. . .UNTIL keeps executing until it is satisfied, MAJOR-SUB will go from 1 to 5 for CLASS-SUB of 1.  Then CLASS-SUB will be incremented to 2, which does not satisfy the condition in the 5000 module.  This causes the 5100 module to be executed again, which restarts the MAJOR-SUB PERFORM and starts MAJOR-SUB at 1 again.  This process is repeated for each value of CLASS-SUB.

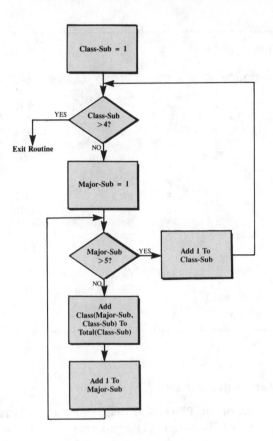

The second thing you should notice is that TOTAL is also a table. We need a total for each CLASS and we have four classes, therefore, we set up a TOTAL table with four elements.

```
01   TOTAL-TABLE.
     03   TOTAL              PIC 9(4)   OCCURS 4 TIMES.
```

The third thing to understand is the subscripting, both for CLASS and TOTAL. Why is the reference CLASS (MAJOR-SUB,CLASS-SUB) and not CLASS (CLASS-SUB,MAJOR-SUB)? The outer PERFORM in the nest varies CLASS-SUB, so shouldn't it be first in the reference? No! Remember our rule. The order of the subscripts is dependent only on the table definition. That was done with MAJOR as the first OCCURS and CLASS OCCURS within it.

As to the subscript for TOTAL, think about it. What are the four totals we are generating? They are the total students by CLASS; therefore, TOTAL should be subscripted by the CLASS subscript, CLASS-SUB. Makes sense, doesn't it? I hope so. Because if you understand these techniques for a two-level table, they can be applied to all multi-level tables.

I assume that you understand the nested PERFORMs, but let's take a closer look at the subscript values. I have shown all pertinent values in Figure 11.15.

You should also understand that, since TOTAL is subscripted with CLASS-SUB, TOTAL (CLASS-SUB) will vary as CLASS-SUB is shown to vary above.

```
                        Outer PERFORM                    Inner PERFORM
            CLASS-SUB       CONDITION    MAJOR-SUB   CONDITION    CLASS (MAJOR-SUB,CLASS-SUB)
       1st      1            > 4, no         -           -                    --
then   2nd      1             --             1        > 5, no       CLASS (1, 1)
then   3rd      1             --             2        > 5, no       CLASS (2, 1)
then   4th      1             --             3        > 5, no       CLASS (3, 1)
then   5th      1             --             4        > 5, no       CLASS (4, 1)
then   6th      1             --             5        > 5, no       CLASS (5, 1)
then   Are you wide awake?
       7th      1             --             6        > 5, YES             --
then   8th      2            > 4, no         1        > 5, no       CLASS (1, 2)
then   9th      2             --             2        > 5, no       CLASS (2, 2)
then  10th      2             --             3        > 5, no       CLASS (3, 2)
then  11th      2             --             4        > 5, no       CLASS (4, 2)
then  12th      2             --             5        > 5, no       CLASS (5, 2)
then  Are you still with me?
      13th      2             --             6        > 5, YES  ·          --
then  14th      3            > 4, no         1        > 5, no       CLASS (1, 3)
       :                      :              :           :                   :
etc.
```

**FIGURE 11.15**
**Executing Nested**
**PERFORMs**

### The Perform. . .Varying. . .After

COBOL offers us a form of the PERFORM that is nice for this type of problem. It's the PERFORM with the **AFTER** option. The general format is:

> **PERFORM** paragraph-name
>     **VARYING** data-name$_1$ **FROM** data-name$_2$ **BY** data-name$_3$
>     **UNTIL** condition$_1$
>     $\Big[$**AFTER** data-name$_4$ **FROM** data-name$_5$ **BY** data-name$_6$
>       **UNTIL** condition$_2\Big]$
>     $\Big[$**AFTER** data-name$_7$ **FROM** data-name$_8$ **BY** data-name$_9$
>       **UNTIL** condition$_3$.$\Big]$

Think of this form as a special form of nested PERFORMs. The first condition is checked first. IF it isn't satisfied, then the second condition is checked. If it isn't satisfied, then the third is tested. Specifically, Data-Name$_7$ will VARY through its entire range for each combination of values of Data-Name$_1$ and Data-Name$_4$. Data-Name$_4$ varies through its range for each value of Data-Name$_1$. Do you see the nesting?

Let's apply this form to our previous problem.

```
5000-SUMMARY-PARA.
    PERFORM 5110-ADD-PARA
        VARYING CLASS-SUB FROM 1 BY 1
            UNTIL CLASS-SUB > 4
        AFTER MAJOR-SUB FROM 1 BY 1
            UNTIL MAJOR-SUB > 5.

5110-ADD-PARA.
    ADD CLASS (MAJOR-SUB,CLASS-SUB) TO TOTAL (CLASS-SUB).
```

See how that saves us. We don't need a 5100 para anymore. (Working smart again!)

Let's make sure we understand this technique for massaging tables. So using the same table of KOUNTS, calculate the total number of students for each major (Figure 11.16).

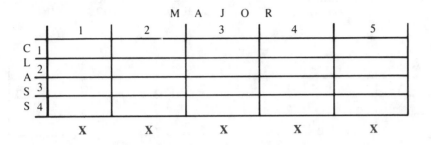

**FIGURE 11.16**
Two-Level Table Showing
Required Major Totals

Using our method, since we want the five totals indicated by the maroon Xs, we need the total table to OCCUR 5 times. Now what about the subscripts and their relationship? While MAJOR-SUB is a 1, CLASS-SUB must go through its range, 1–4. That is, MAJOR-SUB varies the slowest and CLASS-SUB varies the fastest. Therefore, given the following code, you should note several things again.

```
5000-SUMMARY-PARA.
    PERFORM 5110-ADD-PARA
        VARYING MAJOR-SUB FROM 1 BY 1
            UNTIL MAJOR-SUB > 5
        AFTER CLASS-SUB FROM 1 BY 1
            UNTIL CLASS-SUB > 4.


5110-ADD-PARA.
    ADD CLASS (MAJOR-SUB,CLASS-SUB) TO TOTAL (MAJOR-SUB).
```

Look at the order of the CLASS subscripts. They are the same as they were in the previous problem even though we are getting different totals. Look at TOTAL's subscripts. It's MAJOR-SUB. Didn't we say that we wanted the total number of MAJORs? Well then, subscripting TOTAL with MAJOR-SUB should make sense.

Does all this work for three-level tables? Sure it does! Let's look at our three-level count table and calculate the number of students by sex as indicated in Figure 11.17.

Since we want the total female and male students, we need a TOTAL that OCCURS two times. The subscript relationships need to be determined. If we go across the table (as it's drawn), then SEX-SUB would vary the slowest, MAJOR-SUB the next fastest, and CLASS-SUB the fastest. Look at the code:

```
5000-SUMMARY-PARA.
    PERFORM 5110-ADD-PARA
        VARYING SEX-SUB FROM 1 BY 1
            UNTIL SEX-SUB > 2
        AFTER MAJOR-SUB FROM 1 BY 1
            UNTIL MAJOR-SUB > 5
        AFTER CLASS-SUB FROM 1 BY 1
            UNTIL CLASS-SUB > 4.


5110-ADD-PARA.
    ADD SEX (MAJOR-SUB,CLASS-SUB,SEX-SUB) TO TOTAL (SEX-SUB).
```

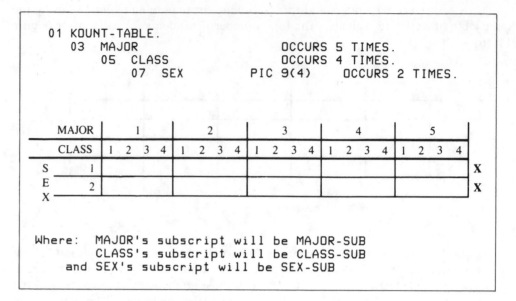

Look at a few of the subscript values to make sure the code works:

| MAJOR-SUB | CLASS-SUB | SEX-SUB |
|:---:|:---:|:---:|
| 1 | 1 | 1 |
| 1 | 2 | 1 |
| 1 | 3 | 1 |
| 1 | 4 | 1 |
| 2 | 1 | 1 |
| 2 | 2 | 1 |
| : | : | : |
| etc. | | |

Notice that the first element added to TOTAL is SEX (1,1,1). . . Well, the first one is always duck soup. Let's see if we go in the right direction. . .we do! SEX (1,2,1), SEX (1,3,1), etc. Go through the rest of it for yourself.

## TIP

**Once you have established the subscript that is to vary the slowest, you may vary the other two in either order!**

What about the subscript for TOTAL? Again we are getting the total number of female and male students, so doesn't SEX-SUB make logical sense as the subscript?

### The Impact of COBOL '85

You probably noticed that the 5100-ADD-PARA was a paragraph of just one sentence. . .the ADD. It would be nice if we didn't need an entire paragraph just for an ADD statement so that we can vary the subscripts. COBOL '85 allows for an in-line PERFORM. That is, we can put the ADD within the PERFORM, and we don't need an external module to reference. For instance:

```
PERFORM ADD CLASS (MAJOR-CODE,CLASS-CODE) TO TOTAL (MAJOR-SUB)
     VARYING MAJOR-SUB FROM 1 BY 1
          UNTIL MAJOR-SUB > 5
     AFTER CLASS-SUB FROM 1 BY 1
          UNTIL CLASS-SUB > 4
END PERFORM.
```

See how we replace the paragraph reference by placing the ADD within the PER-FORM? This eliminates the need for the 5100 module.

This device does save me some code, and I'm always saying work smart, not hard. But maybe the in-line PERFORM is not all gravy. Up to now every PERFORM was a control statement that caused the execution of a module of code. It fit nicely into our hierarchy chart and flowchart. Remember that in a hierarchy chart we show control. For instance, look at Figure 11.18.

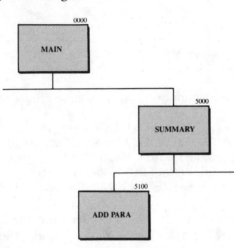

**FIGURE 11.18**
**Hierarchy Chart for External Add Module**

Each of these modules would have its own flowchart module; fitting nicely. But with the in-line PERFORM, we would not have the 5100 module. That is we would have the hierarchy chart shown in Figure 11.19 instead. Everything appears to have its pluses and minuses.

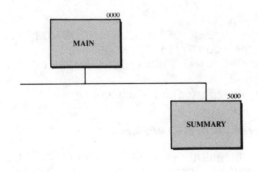

**FIGURE 11.19**
**Hierarchy Chart Showing In-Line PERFORM**

## REPORTING AND TABLES

Now that you understand how to manipulate tables to generate totals, let's look at reporting the contents of tables. After all, you went through all the trouble to accumulate the counts and/or sums in the tables. You don't want to keep them a secret. You want to write them out.

### Reporting One-Level Tables

Given that you have the MAJOR COUNT TABLE with all the counts by MAJOR already accumulated, how would you report them?

First decide how the report is to look. Assuming appropriate page headings in either example, you could write column headings with the counts under the appropriate column heading as shown in Figure 11.20.

**FIGURE 11.20**
**Column Format for Kount Report**

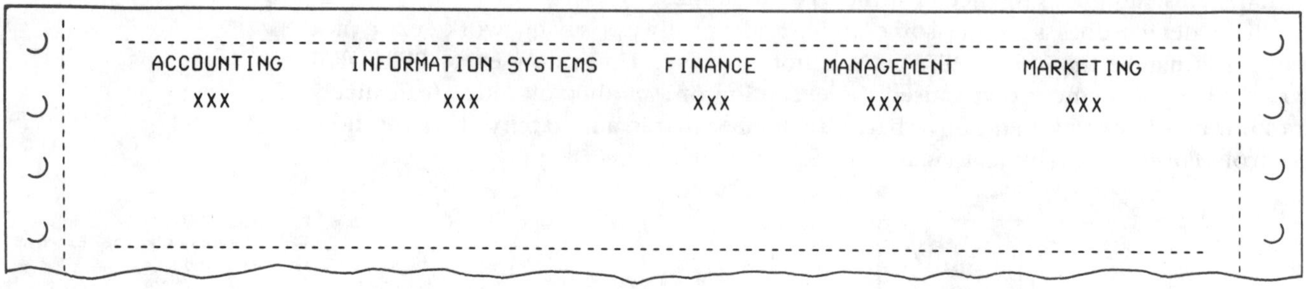

```
      ACCOUNTING      INFORMATION SYSTEMS      FINANCE      MANAGEMENT      MARKETING
         XXX                  XXX                 XXX           XXX            XXX
```

Or you could write each count on a line with an appropriate line descriptor:

```
THE NUMBER OF ACCOUNTING MAJORS IS            XXX
THE NUMBER OF INFORMATION SYSTEMS MAJORS IS   XXX
THE NUMBER OF FINANCE MAJORS IS               XXX
THE NUMBER OF MANAGEMENT MAJORS IS            XXX
THE NUMBER OF MARKETING MAJORS IS             XXX
```

I like the line descriptor format. It looks nicer and the descriptions are more informative that column headings. Furthermore, I don't think that one number makes a column. Therefore, the first form shown in Figure 11.20 is inappropriate.

The logic to write the report that we want involves using a detail record description that allows for a description and its corresponding count. Procedurally, we simply move the literal description and count to the record and write it. This logic is just like writing counts that are not in tables.

```
5000-SUMMARY-PARA.
    MOVE 'THE NUMBER OF ACCOUNTING MAJORS IS' TO DESCRIPTION.
    MOVE MAJOR-KOUNT (1) TO KOUNT-OUT.
    WRITE REPORT-LINE FROM KOUNT-LINE
        AFTER 2.
```

This procedure is repeated for each count.

### Reporting Multi-Level Tables—Two Levels

The problem of reporting multiple-level tables is a unique one. Not hard, just different. I think the best way to approach it is to look at the report format. We are to report the two-level KOUNT-TABLE of CLASS within MAJOR (Figure 11.8). Figure 11.21 shows both the drawing of the table and the report format.

Notice the similarity of the report format to the drawing of the table. There was a method to my madness in depicting tables that way!

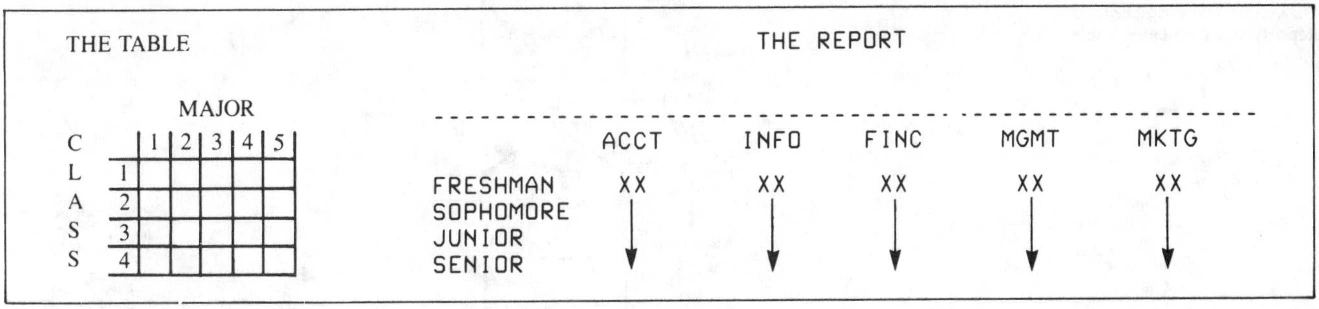

```
THE TABLE                                    THE REPORT

      MAJOR                  -----------------------------------------------
C                                    ACCT      INFO      FINC      MGMT      MKTG
L    | 1 | 2 | 3 | 4 | 5 |
A  1 |   |   |   |   |   |   FRESHMAN   XX        XX        XX        XX        XX
S  2 |   |   |   |   |   |   SOPHOMORE  |         |         |         |         |
S  3 |   |   |   |   |   |   JUNIOR     |         |         |         |         |
   4 |   |   |   |   |   |   SENIOR     ↓         ↓         ↓         ↓         ↓
```

Once we write the column headings, we have a detail line that has a descriptor, class name, and five counts. All we have to do is move all the five freshman counts, CLASS = 1, to our report line. We could approach it as we did with one-level tables. That is:

**FIGURE 11.21**
**Two-Level Table with Report Format**

```
MOVE 'FRESHMAN '   TO   DESCRIPTION.
MOVE CLASS (1,1)   TO   KOUNT-OUT-1.
MOVE CLASS (2,1)   TO   KOUNT-OUT-2.
MOVE CLASS (3,1)   TO   KOUNT-OUT-3.
MOVE CLASS (4,1)   TO   KOUNT-OUT-4.
MOVE CLASS (5,1)   TO   KOUNT-OUT-5.
WRITE RPT-LINE    FROM   KOUNT-LINE
      AFTER 2.
```

Then we would repeat this set of logic for each report line, or a total of 28 lines of code. Thank goodness for only four classes! What if we had 30 or 40 classes? We would need 210 to 280 lines of code. Not good! Let's examine the report closer. Each detail line contains a description and five counts. . . But look:

```
filler DESCRIPTION filler KOUNT filler KOUNT filler KOUNT filler KOUNT filler KOUNT filler
```

Notice the "KOUNT filler" repeating fields. In the past, when we needed a set of locations to contain different values, we used a table. A table for an output record? It works nicely. Look at the detail record description below:

```
01  KOUNT-LINE.
    03  FILLER            PIC X(10).
    03  DESCRIPTION       PIC X(19).
    03  FILLER            PIC X(05).
    03  KOUNT-GROUP       OCCURS 5 TIMES.
        05  KOUNT-OUT     PIC ZZZ9.
        05  FILLER        PIC X(6).
    03  FILLER            PIC X(49).
```

There are several items to notice. First, the KOUNT-GROUP. It OCCURS five times and allows for the five KOUNTS and fillers. Second, you notice there are no value spaces on the fillers. Well, we could use them on all fillers except the one at the 05, which is subordinate to an OCCURS. That's not acceptable in COBOL '74. COBOL '85, however, allows it. But we are using COBOL '74, so we will need to move spaces to KOUNT-LINE in the INITIALIZATION PARAGRAPH.

Let's first look at the logic. What do we need the subscripts to do to get the values out in the correct order? We need to keep CLASS-SUB at a value while MAJOR-SUB goes through its full range. Sound familiar? It should be! The logic is shown in the flowchart in Figure 11.22.

**FIGURE 11.22**
Flowchart Showing Logic for
Reporting a Two-Level Table

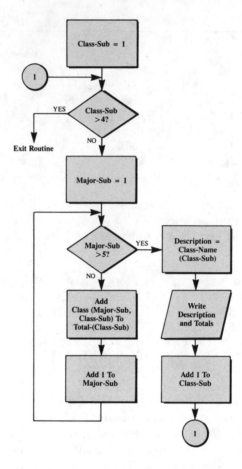

```
5000-SUMMARY-PARA.
    PERFORM 5100-START-PROCESS
        VARYING CLASS-SUB FROM 1 BY 1
        UNTIL CLASS-SUB > 4.

5100-START-PROCESS.
    PERFORM 5110-MOVE-KOUNTS-PARA
        VARYING MAJOR-SUB FROM 1 BY 1
        UNTIL MAJOR-SUB > 5.
    MOVE CLASS-NAME (CLASS-SUB) TO DESCRIPTION.
    WRITE RPT-LINE FROM KOUNT-LINE
        AFTER 2.

5110-MOVE-KOUNTS-PARA.
    MOVE CLASS (MAJOR-SUB,CLASS-SUB) TO KOUNT-OUT (MAJOR-SUB).
```

Notice the value of the subscripts which are shown in Figure 11.23.

Compare these subscript values with our previous method for writing. The same? They should be. That's the relationship we said we wanted. I told you it wasn't hard, just different.

### Reporting Three-Level Tables

Let's look now at three-level tables. Our three-level KOUNT-TABLE would make a good example. Figure 11.24 shows both the table and the report format.

| CLASS (MAJOR-SUB, | CLASS-SUB) | KOUNT-OUT (MAJOR-SUB) |
|---|---|---|
| 1 | 1 | 1 |
| 2 | 1 | 2 |
| 3 | 1 | 3 |
| 4 | 1 | 4 |
| 5 | 1 | 5 |
| WRITE | | |
| 1 | 2 | 1 |
| 2 | 2 | 2 |
| : | : | : |
| etc. | | |

**FIGURE 11.23**
**A Look at the Subscript Values for Reporting a Two-Level Table**

| | MAJOR 1 | | | | 2 | | | | 3 | | | | 4 | | | | 5 | | | |
|---|---|---|---|---|---|---|---|---|---|---|---|---|---|---|---|---|---|---|---|---|
| CLASS | 1 | 2 | 3 | 4 | 1 | 2 | 3 | 4 | 1 | 2 | 3 | 4 | 1 | 2 | 3 | 4 | 1 | 2 | 3 | 4 |
| SEX 1 | | | | | | | | | | | | | | | | | | | | |
| SEX 2 | | | | | | | | | | | | | | | | | | | | |

**FIGURE 11.24**
**Three-Level Table and Report Format**

```
                                  THE REPORT
              ---------------------------------------------------------------------------------
                    ACCOUNTING                                          INFO. SYSTEMS
              FRESHMAN  SOPHOMORE  JUNIOR  SENIOR    FRESHMAN  SOPHOMORE  JUNIOR SENIOR ..
  FEMALE         X          X         X       X          X          X         X      X     ..
  MALE           X          X         X       X          X          X         X      X     ..
```

Again, note the similarity of the table drawing and the report. Using what you learned for reporting two-level tables, you should see two detail lines, female and male, each made up of two repeating variables, CLASS within MAJOR. Can you see the record descriptions?

```
01  KOUNT-LINE.
    03  FILLER                       PIC X(2).
    03  DESCRIPTION                  PIC X(9).
    03  FILLER                       PIC X(2).
    03  MAJOR-GROUP                  OCCURS 5 TIMES.
        05  CLASS-GROUP              OCCURS 4 TIMES.
            07  KOUNT-OUT            PIC ZZZ9.
            07  FILLER               PIC X(2).


5000-SUMMARY-PARA.
    PERFORM 5100-START-PROCESS
        VARYING SEX-SUB FROM 1 BY 1                 once for each line
            UNTIL SEX-SUB > 2.

5100-START-PROCESS.
    PERFORM 5110-PROCESS-PARA
        VARYING MAJOR-SUB FROM 1 BY 1               controls the majors
            UNTIL MAJOR-SUB > 5.
```

```
            MOVE SEX-NAME (SEX-SUB) TO DESCRIPTION-OUT.
            WRITE RPT-LINE FROM KOUNT-LINE
                AFTER 2.

        5110-PROCESS-PARA.
            PERFORM 5111-MOVE-KOUNTS-PARA
                VARYING CLASS-SUB FROM 1 BY 1            controls the classes
                    UNTIL CLASS-SUB > 4.

        5111-MOVE-KOUNTS-PARA.
            MOVE SEX (MAJOR-SUB,CLASS-SUB,SEX-SUB)
                TO KOUNT-OUT (MAJOR-SUB,CLASS-SUB).
```

Each line contains room for 20 counts and a description. The nested PERFORMs simply cause the appropriate counts to be moved into those 20 locations (major x count) and then a line is written. The outer PERFORM causes this to be done twice (for male and female). This technique could be used for reporting seven-level tables. (You would need a *wide* printer.)

The subject of reporting tables is closely associated with the subject of manipulating tables. Look back and see for yourself. The number of table levels in the detail record description for the report is *one less* that the number in the table you're reporting. The line itself replaces one level, because we write that line the number of times specified in the OCCURS we eliminate. "SEX OCCURS 2 TIMES." How many lines in our report? Two. "CLASS OCCURS 4 TIMES." How many lines in that report? Four. See how that works. You should also note that the KOUNT-OUT subscript is the subscript for the level(s) in the KOUNT-LINE. Finally, which subscript varied the slowest? The one that corresponds to the detail line in the report: SEX-SUB. That's the line.

## TABLES AND THE COPY VERB

What if several programs in a system use the same compile-time table? Would this table be a candidate for inclusion in a copy library? You bet it would. Instead of every programmer having to code the table, the system analyst or project leader would design it and put it into the library. Then the time-consuming task of coding a large compile-time table would be greatly reduced. However, the need to recompile all programs using the table, when the table values change, is still with us. Remember, we are copying source code. If the source code changes, we need to recompile; but we only need to make the changes once—in a library. That's real nice!

## SUMMARY

This chapter examined the world of tables. We saw how, up to this chapter, data variables could contain only one value at a time. We also saw that some real-world problems require working with sets of values.

COBOL '74 allows for two types, and three levels, of tables. Compile-time tables receive their initial values during compilation, while execution-time tables receive their initial values during execution. Also, generally, compile-time tables are used for static values such as code description, titles, and headings. Execution-time tables tend to be used for dynamic values such as counts and totals. But beyond these distinctions, the tables are functionally used in the same way by subscripting.

Each level of a table requires a subscript. Furthermore, the order of the subscripts is dependent on the table description and not the algorithm. You saw that visually depicting the tables was an aid to using them, and I pointed out that you could choose to draw the tables many ways. I made the point several times that the drawing did not matter as long as you understood the concept. After all, the compiler cannot see your drawing.

## TIP

**If you are counting or accumulating values of data records, you are building data-dependent algorithms. On the other hand, if you are manipulating the values of a table or reporting its contents, you are building data-independent algorithms.**

In the chapter we studied data-dependent and data-independent algorithms. We also looked at the need to use the SEARCH verb to help us with the not-nice data situations.

The data-dependent algorithms were those that were used during detail time: things like counting the number of occurrences of a particular type of record (our counts by major, class, and sex) were looked at extensively. However, once these counts were completed, we needed to turn to logic to write them on reports. . .total time. These algorithms were considered not to be data dependent; that is, a data file was not being used.

Not-nice data had to be handled during detail time. Remember the problem? How do you count occurrences of an item using a data field value as a subscript if the data field contains alphabetic values or random numeric values? You convert it, that's how. But how do you convert it? Via a compile-time table and the SEARCH verb(s).

Finally, we looked at reporting, one of the data-independent situations. I introduced a technique for manipulating tables, including reporting them. In that technique we first identified the required relationship in the subscripts associated with the table level(s). Then we coded the corresponding logic. This coding required the use of either nested PERFORM...VARYING statements or the PERFORM...VARYING...AFTER. We also saw that to report multiple-level tables, an output record description that included a table was useful if not mandatory.

I hope you have given this chapter a chance. The topic is complex to start with, but once you see it, you will find it is actually rather straightforward. I find it to be one of my favorite topics to teach, probably because I find the use of tables to be one of the most powerful yet least understood topics in COBOL.

## SAMPLE PROGRAMS

The following are complete running COBOL programs using many of the features and techniques discussed in this Chapter.

## Single-Level Table With SEARCH Verb

```
PP 5740-CB1 RELEASE 2.4                    IBM OS/VS COBOL  JULY  1, 1982      21.53.59  DATE NOV 10,1988


      1                      21.53.59      NOV 10,1988


    00001          IDENTIFICATION DIVISION.
    00002
    00003          PROGRAM-ID. SEARCHING.
    00004          AUTHOR. FOWLER.
    00005          DATE-WRITTEN. AUGUST 1988.
    00006          DATE-COMPILED. NOV 10,1988.
    00007          REMARKS.
    00008
    00009          ****************************************************************
    00010          *                                                              *
    00011          *  ASSIGNMENT NUMBER                                           *
    00012          *  DATE ASSIGNED                                               *
    00013          *  DATE DUE                                                    *
    00014          *  PURPOSE:   THIS IS A GRADE POINT RATIO CALCULATION PROGRAM. *
    00015          *            THE GRADE POINT RATIO IS DETERMINED BY DIVIDING   *
    00016          *            THE NUMBER OF GRADE POINTS EARNED BY THE NUMBER   *
    00017          *            OF CREDIT HOURS TAKEN. IN ADDITION, THE MAJOR     *
    00018          *            CODE, CLASS CODE, AND SEX CODE WILL BE CONVERTED  *
    00019          *            TO THE ACTUAL NAMES ASSOCIATED WITH THE CODES     *
    00020          *            USING COMPILE-TIME TABLES.  IN ADDITION, THE      *
    00021          *            SEARCH VERB WILL BE USED TO CONVERT THE MAJOR     *
    00022          *            CODE (WHICH IS REPRESENTED IN ALPHANUMERIC FORM)  *
    00023          *            INTO THE ACTUAL MAJOR NAME.                       *
    00024          *                                                              *
    00025          *                                                              *
    00026          *   INPUT FILE SPECIFICATIONS:                                 *
    00027          *       CARD COLUMNS                    DESCRIPTION            *
    00028          *       ------------                    -----------           *
    00029          *          1-30                      STUDENT'S NAME            *
    00030          *         31-39                      STUDENT'S ID NUMBER       *
    00031          *         40-40                      STUDENT'S MAJOR CODE      *
    00032          *         41-41                      STUDENT'S CLASS CODE      *
    00033          *         42-42                      STUDENT'S SEX CODE        *
    00034          *         43-45                      CREDIT HOURS TAKEN        *
    00035          *         46-48                      GRADE POINTS EARNED       *
    00036          *                                                              *
    00037          *  THE OUTPUT CONTAINS STUDENT'S ID NUMBER, STUDENT'S NAME,    *
    00038          *  MAJOR NAME, CLASS NAME, SEX, AND THE GRADE POINT RATIO.     *
    00039          *                                                              *
    00040          *                                                              *
    00041          *  THERE IS A SUMMARY REPORT THAT IS PRINTED BY THIS PROGRAM   *
    00042          *  WHICH LISTS THE NUMBER OF STUDENTS IN EACH MAJOR AS WELL AS *
    00043          *  THE AVERAGE GRADE POINT FOR THE MAJORS.                     *
    00044          *                                                              *
    00045          ****************************************************************
    00046
```

```
      2          SEARCHIN      21.53.59      NOV 10,1988


    00048          ENVIRONMENT DIVISION.
    00049
    00050          CONFIGURATION SECTION.
    00051
    00052          SOURCE-COMPUTER. IBM.
    00053          OBJECT-COMPUTER. IBM.
    00054          SPECIAL-NAMES.   CO1 IS PAGE-TOP.
    00055
    00056          INPUT-OUTPUT SECTION.
    00057
    00058          FILE-CONTROL.
    00059
    00060              SELECT DEAN-FILE
    00061                  ASSIGN TO DA-S-DEAN.
    00062
    00063              SELECT REPORT-FILE
    00064                  ASSIGN TO UT-S-REPORT.
    00065
```

*(continued)*

```
      3        SEARCHIN       21.53.59      NOV 10,1988

00067          DATA DIVISION.
00068
00069          FILE SECTION.
00070
00071      FD  DEAN-FILE
00072          LABEL RECORDS ARE OMITTED
00073          RECORD CONTAINS 48 CHARACTERS
00074          BLOCK CONTAINS 100 RECORDS
00075          DATA RECORD IS STUDENT-RECORD.
00076
00077      01  STUDENT-RECORD PIC X(48).
00078
00079
00080      FD  REPORT-FILE
00081          LABEL RECORDS ARE OMITTED
00082          DATA RECORD IS REPORT-LINE.
00083
00084      01  REPORT-LINE PIC X(133).
00085
```

```
      4        SEARCHIN       21.53.59      NOV 10,1988

00087          WORKING-STORAGE SECTION.
00088
00089      77  GPR                     PIC 9(1)V9(4).
00090      77  MAJOR-SUB               PIC 9(2).
00091
00092      01  ARE-THERE-MORE-RECORDS  PIC X(3)        VALUE 'YES'.
00093          88  MORE-RECORDS                        VALUE 'YES'.
00094          88  NO-MORE-RECORDS                     VALUE 'NO'.
00095
00096      01  PAGE-HEADING.
00097          05  FILLER              PIC X(47)       VALUE SPACES.
00098          05  FILLER              PIC X(39)       VALUE
00099              'DEANFILE STUDENT LISTING AND GPR REPORT'.
00100          05  FILLER              PIC X(47)       VALUE SPACES.
00101
00102      01  DETAIL-REPORT-HEADINGS.
00103          03  FILLER              PIC X(10)       VALUE SPACES.
00104          03  FILLER              PIC X(4)        VALUE 'NAME'.
00105          03  FILLER              PIC X(36)       VALUE SPACES.
00106          03  FILLER              PIC X(2)        VALUE 'ID'.
00107          03  FILLER              PIC X(18)       VALUE SPACES.
00108          03  FILLER              PIC X(5)        VALUE 'MAJOR'.
00109          03  FILLER              PIC X(16)       VALUE SPACES.
00110          03  FILLER              PIC X(5)        VALUE 'CLASS'.
00111          03  FILLER              PIC X(10)       VALUE SPACES.
00112          03  FILLER              PIC X(3)        VALUE 'SEX'.
00113          03  FILLER              PIC X(10)       VALUE SPACES.
00114          03  FILLER              PIC X(3)        VALUE 'GPR'.
00115          03  FILLER              PIC X(9)        VALUE SPACES.
00116
00117      01  SUMMARY-KOUNT-HEADING-1.
00118          03  FILLER              PIC X(46)       VALUE SPACES.
00119          03  FILLER              PIC X(41)       VALUE
00120              'STUDENT COUNTS AND AVERAGE GPR''S BY MAJOR'.
00121          03  FILLER              PIC X(46)       VALUE SPACES.
00122
```

*(continued)*

```
       5        SEARCHIN        21.53.59      NOV 10,1988

00124          *
00125          *  NOTE THAT THE MAJOR CODE IS AN ALPHANUMERIC FIELD
00126          *
00127
00128          01  STUDENT-RECORD-IN.
00129              03 NAME-IN              PIC X(30).
00130              03 ID-IN                PIC X(9).
00131              03 MAJOR-IN             PIC X(1).
00132              03 CLASS-IN             PIC 9(1).
00133              03 SEX-IN               PIC 9(1).
00134              03 CREDIT-HOURS-IN      PIC 9(3).
00135              03 GRADE-POINTS-IN      PIC 9(3).
00136
00137          01  STUDENT-RECORD-OUT.
00138              03 FILLER               PIC X(10)      VALUE SPACES.
00139              03 NAME-OUT             PIC X(30).
00140              03 FILLER               PIC X(7)       VALUE SPACES.
00141              03 ID-OUT               PIC X(9).
00142              03 FILLER               PIC X(7)       VALUE SPACES.
00143              03 MAJOR-NAME-OUT       PIC X(19).
00144              03 FILLER               PIC X(7)       VALUE SPACES.
00145              03 CLASS-NAME-OUT       PIC X(9).
00146              03 FILLER               PIC X(7)       VALUE SPACES.
00147              03 SEX-OUT              PIC X(6).
00148              03 FILLER               PIC X(7)       VALUE SPACES.
00149              03 GPR-OUT              PIC 9(1).9(4).
00150              03 FILLER               PIC X(9)       VALUE SPACES.
00151
00152          01  MAJOR-NAME-VALUES.
00153              03 FILLER               PIC X(20)      VALUE 'AACCOUNTING'.
00154              03 FILLER               PIC X(20)      VALUE
00155                      'IINFORMATION SYSTEMS'.
00156              03 FILLER               PIC X(20)      VALUE 'FFINANCE'.
00157              03 FILLER               PIC X(20)      VALUE 'GMANAGEMENT'.
00158              03 FILLER               PIC X(20)      VALUE 'KMARKETING'.
00159
00160          *
00161          *  NOTE THE USE OF THE INDEXED BY TO ALLOW FOR THE USE
00162          *  OF THE SEARCH
00163          *
00164
00165          01  MAJOR-TABLE REDEFINES MAJOR-NAME-VALUES.
00166              03 MAJOR-ENTRY             OCCURS 5 TIMES
00167                                         INDEXED BY MAJOR-INDEX.
00168                  05 MAJOR-KODE           PIC X.
00169                  05 MAJOR-NAME           PIC X(19).
00170
```

*(continued)*

```
      6          SEARCHIN      21.53.59      NOV 10,1988

00172          01  CLASS-NAME-VALUES.
00173              03 FILLER                PIC X(9)      VALUE 'FRESHMAN'.
00174              03 FILLER                PIC X(9)      VALUE 'SOPHOMORE'.
00175              03 FILLER                PIC X(9)      VALUE 'JUNIOR'.
00176              03 FILLER                PIC X(9)      VALUE 'SENIOR'.
00177
00178          01  CLASS-TABLE REDEFINES CLASS-NAME-VALUES.
00179              03 CLASS-NAME            PIC X(9)
00180                                       OCCURS 4 TIMES.
00181
00182          01  SEX-VALUES.
00183              03 FILLER                    PIC X(6)      VALUE 'MALE'.
00184              03 FILLER                    PIC X(6)      VALUE 'FEMALE'.
00185
00186          01  SEX-TABLE REDEFINES SEX-VALUES.
00187              03 SEX                        PIC X(6)
00188                                            OCCURS 2 TIMES.
00189
00190          01  MAJOR-KOUNT-TABLE.
00191              03 MAJOR-KOUNT                PIC 9(2)
00192                                            OCCURS 5 TIMES.
00193
00194          01  MAJOR-CREDIT-HOUR-TABLE.
00195              03 MAJOR-HOURS                PIC 9(5)
00196                                            OCCURS 5 TIMES.
00197
00198          01  MAJOR-GRADE-POINT-TABLE.
00199              03 MAJOR-POINTS               PIC 9(5)
00200                                            OCCURS 5 TIMES.
00201
00202          01  SUMMARY-REPORT-LINE.
00203              03 FILLER                PIC X(33)     VALUE SPACES.
00204              03 FILLER                PIC X(38)     VALUE
00205                   'NUMBER OF STUDENTS AND AVERAGE GPR IN '.
00206              03 SUMMARY-NAME-OUT      PIC X(19).
00207              03 FILLER                PIC X(3)      VALUE ' : '.
00208              03 SUMMARY-KOUNT-OUT     PIC Z9.
00209              03 FILLER                PIC X(10)     VALUE SPACES.
00210              03 SUMMARY-GPR           PIC 9.9999.
00211              03 FILLER                PIC X(32)     VALUE SPACES.
00212
00213          01  BLANK-LINE.
00214              03 FILLER                PIC X(133)    VALUE SPACES.
00215
```

```
      7          SEARCHIN      21.53.59      NOV 10,1988

00217          PROCEDURE DIVISION.
00218
00219          0000-MAIN-PARA.
00220              PERFORM 1000-INIT-PARA.
00221              PERFORM 8000-READ-PARA.
00222              PERFORM 2000-PROCESS-PARA
00223                  UNTIL NO-MORE-RECORDS.
00224              PERFORM 3000-TERMINATION-PARA.
00225              STOP RUN.
00226
```

*(continued)*

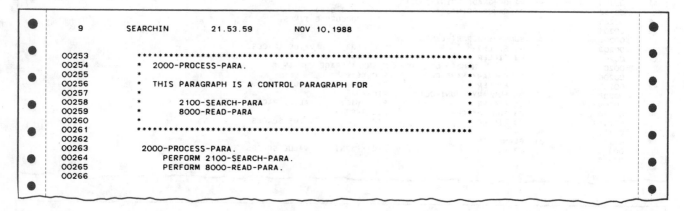

```
        8        SEARCHIN      21.53.59      NOV 10,1988

00228        ****************************************************************
00229        *   1000-INIT-PARA.                                            *
00230        *                                                             *
00231        *   THIS PARAGRAPH OPENS THE DEAN FILE AND REPORT FILE, WRITES *
00232        *   THE REPORT HEADINGS, AND ZEROS OUT THE MAJOR-KOUNT-TABLE,  *
00233        *   THE MAJOR-CREDIT-HOUR-TABLE, AND THE MAJOR-GRADE-POINT     *
00234        *   TABLE.                                                     *
00235        *                                                             *
00236        ****************************************************************
00237
00238          1000-INIT-PARA.
00239              OPEN INPUT DEAN-FILE.
00240              OPEN OUTPUT REPORT-FILE.
00241              WRITE REPORT-LINE FROM BLANK-LINE
00242                  AFTER PAGE-TOP.
00243              WRITE REPORT-LINE FROM PAGE-HEADING
00244                  AFTER 3.
00245              WRITE REPORT-LINE FROM DETAIL-REPORT-HEADINGS
00246                  AFTER 3.
00247              WRITE REPORT-LINE FROM BLANK-LINE
00248                  AFTER 1.
00249              MOVE ZEROS TO MAJOR-KOUNT-TABLE, MAJOR-CREDIT-HOUR-TABLE,
00250                  MAJOR-GRADE-POINT-TABLE.
00251
```

```
        9        SEARCHIN      21.53.59      NOV 10,1988

00253        ****************************************************************
00254        *   2000-PROCESS-PARA.                                         *
00255        *                                                             *
00256        *   THIS PARAGRAPH IS A CONTROL PARAGRAPH FOR                  *
00257        *                                                             *
00258        *        2100-SEARCH-PARA                                      *
00259        *        8000-READ-PARA                                       *
00260        *                                                             *
00261        ****************************************************************
00262
00263          2000-PROCESS-PARA.
00264              PERFORM 2100-SEARCH-PARA.
00265              PERFORM 8000-READ-PARA.
00266
```

*(continued)*

```
   10        SEARCHIN      21.53.59      NOV 10,1988

00268       **********************************************************
00269       *  2100-SEARCH-PARA.                                     *
00270       *                                                        *
00271       *  THIS PARAGRAPH SEARCHES THROUGH THE MAJOR NAME TABLE TO *
00272       *  FIND A MATCH FOR THE MAJOR-IN.  IF NO MATCH IS FOUND IN THE *
00273       *  TABLE THEN AN ERROR MESSAGE WILL BE DISPLAYED ALONG WITH *
00274       *  ERRONEOUS CODE.  IF A MATCH IS FOUND THE PROGRAM WILL  *
00275       *  CONTINUE ON TO THE 2110-MAJOR-KODE-FOUND-PARA.         *
00276       *                                                        *
00277       *  NOTE THAT THE SUBSCRIPT (MAJOR-SUB) IS SET TO THE VALUE OF *
00278       *  THE INDEX (MAJOR-INDEX) AT THE TIME THAT A MATCH IS FOUND. *
00279       *  THE COMPUTER WILL CONVERT THE DISPLACEMENT VALUE IN    *
00280       *  MAJOR-INDEX INTO AN INTEGER OCCURRENCE VALUE WHICH WILL BE *
00281       *  STORED IN MAJOR-SUB.                                   *
00282       *                                                        *
00283       *  NOTE THAT THE MAJOR-INDEX IS SET TO 1 BEFORE THE SERIAL *
00284       *  SEARCH IS INITIATED.                                   *
00285       **********************************************************
00286
00287       2100-SEARCH-PARA.
00288           SET MAJOR-INDEX TO 1.
00289           SEARCH MAJOR-ENTRY
00290               AT END
00291                   DISPLAY '* NO MATCH FOUND FOR MAJOR CODE *' MAJOR-IN
00292               WHEN MAJOR-IN = MAJOR-KODE(MAJOR-INDEX)
00293                   SET MAJOR-SUB TO MAJOR-INDEX
00294                   PERFORM 2110-MAJOR-KODE-FOUND-PARA.
00295
00296
```

```
   11        SEARCHIN      21.53.59      NOV 10,1988

00298       **********************************************************
00299       *  2110-MAJOR-KODE-PARA                                  *
00300       *                                                        *
00301       *  THIS PARAGRAPH PERFORMS A NUMBER OF STEPS ONLY IF A MATCH *
00302       *  WAS FOUND DURING THE SEARCH IN 2100-SEARCH-PARA.  IT IS A *
00303       *  CONTROL PARAGRAPH FOR                                 *
00304       *                                                        *
00305       *       2111-CALCULATIONS-PARA                           *
00306       *       2112-MOVE-AND-WRITE-PARA                         *
00307       *                                                        *
00308       **********************************************************
00309
00310       2110-MAJOR-KODE-FOUND-PARA.
00311           PERFORM 2111-CALCULATIONS-PARA.
00312           PERFORM 2112-MOVE-AND-WRITE-PARA.
00313
```

*(continued)*

```
     12        SEARCHIN       21.53.59      NOV 10,1988

00315        *****************************************************************
00316        *   2111-CALCULATIONS-PARA                                      *
00317        *                                                              *
00318        *   IN THIS PARAGRAPH THE GPR IS CALCULATED.  ALSO, THE SUB-   *
00319        *   SCRIPT (MAJOR-SUB) IS USED TO AID IN THE ACCUMULATION OF   *
00320        *   THE NUMBER OF STUDENTS BY MAJOR, THE TOTAL CREDIT HOURS BY *
00321        *   MAJOR AND THE TOTAL NUMBER OF GRADE POINTS BY MAJOR. THIS  *
00322        *   INFORMATION WILL BE USED TO PRODUCE THE SUMMARY REPORT FOR *
00323        *   THIS PROGRAM.                                              *
00324        *                                                              *
00325        *****************************************************************
00326
00327           2111-CALCULATIONS-PARA.
00328               COMPUTE GPR ROUNDED = GRADE-POINTS-IN / CREDIT-HOURS-IN.
00329               ADD 1 TO MAJOR-KOUNT(MAJOR-SUB).
00330               ADD CREDIT-HOURS-IN TO MAJOR-HOURS(MAJOR-SUB).
00331               ADD GRADE-POINTS-IN TO MAJOR-POINTS(MAJOR-SUB).
00332
00333
```

```
     13        SEARCHIN       21.53.59      NOV 10,1988

00335        *****************************************************************
00336        *   2112-MOVE-AND-WRITE-PARA                                    *
00337        *                                                              *
00338        *   IN THIS PARAGRAPH, THE CODES FOR THE MAJOR, CLASS, AND SEX *
00339        *   ARE CONVERTED TO THEIR RESPECTIVE NAMES (USING COMPILE-TIME*
00340        *   TABLES). IN ADDITION, THE REMAINING REQUIRED FIELDS ARE    *
00341        *   MOVED AND A DETAIL LINE IS WRITTEN.                        *
00342        *                                                              *
00343        *****************************************************************
00344
00345           2112-MOVE-AND-WRITE-PARA.
00346               MOVE MAJOR-NAME(MAJOR-INDEX) TO MAJOR-NAME-OUT.
00347               MOVE NAME-IN TO NAME-OUT.
00348               MOVE ID-IN TO ID-OUT.
00349               MOVE GPR TO GPR-OUT.
00350               MOVE CLASS-NAME(CLASS-IN) TO CLASS-NAME-OUT.
00351               MOVE SEX(SEX-IN) TO SEX-OUT.
00352               WRITE REPORT-LINE FROM STUDENT-RECORD-OUT
00353                   AFTER 1.
00354
00355
```

*(continued)*

```
     14        SEARCHIN        21.53.59        NOV 10,1988

00357      ****************************************************************
00358      *   8000-READ-PARA.                                           *
00359      *                                                             *
00360      *  THIS PARAGRAPH READS A RECORD FROM THE DEAN FILE.  WHEN THE *
00361      *  END OF THE FILE HAS BEEN REACHED, THE END OF FILE FLAG     *
00362      *  (ARE-THERE-MORE-RECORDS) WILL HAVE THE VALUE 'NO' MOVED TO *
00363      *  IT TO INDICATE THAT THERE ARE NO-MORE-RECORDS TO BE READ   *
00364      *  FROM THE FILE.                                             *
00365      *                                                             *
00366      ****************************************************************
00367
00368         8000-READ-PARA.
00369             READ DEAN-FILE INTO STUDENT-RECORD-IN
00370                 AT END
00371                     MOVE 'NO' TO ARE-THERE-MORE-RECORDS.
00372
```

```
     15        SEARCHIN        21.53.59        NOV 10,1988

00374      ****************************************************************
00375      *   3000-TERMINATION-PARA                                     *
00376      *                                                             *
00377      *  THIS PARAGRAPH IS A CONTROL PARAGRAPH FOR                  *
00378      *                                                             *
00379      *        3100-WRITE-SUMMARY-HEADINGS                          *
00380      *        3200-WRITE-SUMMARY-REPORT                            *
00381      *        3300-CLOSE-PARA                                      *
00382      *                                                             *
00383      ****************************************************************
00384
00385         3000-TERMINATION-PARA.
00386             PERFORM 3100-SUMMARY-HEADINGS.
00387             PERFORM 3200-WRITE-SUMMARY-REPORT
00388                 VARYING MAJOR-SUB FROM 1 BY 1
00389                 UNTIL MAJOR-SUB > 5.
00390             PERFORM 3300-CLOSE-PARA.
00391
```

```
     16        SEARCHIN        21.53.59        NOV 10,1988

00393      ****************************************************************
00394      *   3100-WRITE-SUMMARY-HEADINGS                               *
00395      *                                                             *
00396      *  THIS PARAGRAPH WRITES THE HEADINGS FOR THE SUMMARY REPORT  *
00397      *  WHICH LISTS THE TOTAL NUMBER OF STUDENTS IN EACH MAJOR AS  *
00398      *  WELL AS THE AVERAGE STUDENT GPR BY MAJOR.                  *
00399      *                                                             *
00400      ****************************************************************
00401
00402         3100-SUMMARY-HEADINGS.
00403             WRITE REPORT-LINE FROM SUMMARY-KOUNT-HEADING-1
00404                 AFTER PAGE-TOP.
00405             WRITE REPORT-LINE FROM BLANK-LINE
00406                 AFTER 1.
00407
```

*(continued)*

```
   17        SEARCHIN       21.53.59     NOV 10, 1988

00409      *******************************************************
00410      *  3200-WRITE-SUMMARY-REPORT                          '
00411      *                                                      *
00412      *  THIS PARAGRAPH WRITES THE SUMMARY LINES WHICH LIST THE
00413      *  NUMBER OF STUDENTS IN EACH MAJOR AND THE AVERAGE STUDENT *
00414      *  GPR BY MAJOR.                                       *
00415      *                                                      *
00416      *  NOTE THAT IN THIS INSTANCE A SUBSCRIPT (MAJOR-SUB) IS BEING *
00417      *  USED TO REFERENCE ENTRIES IN A TABLE THAT IS INDEXED *
00418      *  (SPECIFICALLY THE MAJOR-NAME IN THE MAJOR-TABLE).   *
00419      *                                                      *
00420      *******************************************************
00421
00422      3200-WRITE-SUMMARY-REPORT.
00423          MOVE MAJOR-NAME(MAJOR-SUB) TO SUMMARY-NAME-OUT.
00424          MOVE MAJOR-KOUNT(MAJOR-SUB) TO SUMMARY-KOUNT-OUT.
00425          DIVIDE MAJOR-POINTS(MAJOR-SUB) BY MAJOR-HOURS(MAJOR-SUB)
00426              GIVING SUMMARY-GPR ROUNDED.
00427          WRITE REPORT-LINE FROM SUMMARY-REPORT-LINE
00428              AFTER 2.
00429
00430
00431      3300-CLOSE-PARA.
00432          CLOSE DEAN-FILE.
00433          CLOSE REPORT-FILE.
```

DEANFILE STUDENT LISTING AND GPR REPORT

| NAME | ID | MAJOR | CLASS | SEX | GPR |
|---|---|---|---|---|---|
| THOMAS WILKINSON | 123456789 | MANAGEMENT | SENIOR | MALE | 3.7619 |
| DON VILLANOSKI | 987654321 | ACCOUNTING | FRESHMAN | MALE | 2.7500 |
| MICHAEL FOWLER | 555555555 | INFORMATION SYSTEMS | SOPHOMORE | MALE | 3.8966 |
| TIA FOWLER | 888888888 | FINANCE | JUNIOR | FEMALE | 3.4943 |
| CLINT SMITH | 333333333 | INFORMATION SYSTEMS | JUNIOR | MALE | 1.9839 |
| HOWARD PORTER | 454545454 | ACCOUNTING | FRESHMAN | MALE | 2.3158 |
| APRIL JONES | 777777777 | INFORMATION SYSTEMS | JUNIOR | FEMALE | 2.8025 |
| APRIL JACKS | 787878778 | MANAGEMENT | SENIOR | FEMALE | 2.5649 |
| BRYAN MANN | 232323232 | FINANCE | FRESHMAN | MALE | 2.6667 |
| ZEKE MORGAN | 434356569 | INFORMATION SYSTEMS | SOPHOMORE | MALE | 2.8947 |
| BILL ADAM | 102302220 | MANAGEMENT | SENIOR | MALE | 2.8092 |
| JILL MATSON | 010101206 | INFORMATION SYSTEMS | FRESHMAN | FEMALE | 2.8947 |
| TINA MARIO | 000000222 | MANAGEMENT | JUNIOR | FEMALE | 2.3380 |
| CLYDE FELD JR. | 129834765 | MANAGEMENT | SOPHOMORE | MALE | 2.9057 |
| GEORGE MARINAKIES | 100010055 | MARKETING | FRESHMAN | MALE | 2.7083 |
| JAMES PAPPAS | 342537891 | MARKETING | JUNIOR | MALE | 3.3253 |
| STEVE PARKS | 908765101 | ACCOUNTING | FRESHMAN | FEMALE | 3.8000 |
| LYNDA MATHER | 203040506 | FINANCE | JUNIOR | FEMALE | 2.7538 |
| KEVIN MCKENN | 444455555 | INFORMATION SYSTEMS | JUNIOR | MALE | 3.4933 |
| IRENE SMITH | 001122334 | MANAGEMENT | FRESHMAN | FEMALE | 2.0000 |
| EMILY LYLE | 999888777 | ACCOUNTING | FRESHMAN | FEMALE | 2.2667 |
| PEG PORTERHOUSE | 123321123 | FINANCE | SENIOR | FEMALE | 2.9703 |
| DAN ROBESON | 656765679 | MANAGEMENT | JUNIOR | MALE | 2.2400 |
| DANA MILLS | 908070600 | MANAGEMENT | SENIOR | FEMALE | 2.7500 |
| GEORGE RYAN | 564731009 | ACCOUNTING | SOPHOMORE | MALE | 2.4000 |
| BILLY BOB BARRETT | 111000222 | ACCOUNTING | SENIOR | MALE | 2.2500 |
| MARY JO MARTINEZ | 102938475 | INFORMATION SYSTEMS | SENIOR | FEMALE | 2.3077 |
| POLLY ANN FLOWERS | 501112234 | MANAGEMENT | SENIOR | FEMALE | 2.5773 |
| MATHEW ALTMEN | 980980980 | MARKETING | JUNIOR | MALE | 3.2258 |
| DIANE LAWERNCE | 263718818 | MARKETING | SOPHOMORE | FEMALE | 2.5714 |
| SARA WALKER | 828347561 | MARKETING | JUNIOR | FEMALE | 3.5375 |
| MARIA SANTIAGO | 777345777 | MARKETING | SOPHOMORE | FEMALE | 2.4444 |
| ANTONIO MARTINEZ | 773330666 | MARKETING | JUNIOR | MALE | 3.0000 |
| ROBERTO SMITH | 311230099 | MANAGEMENT | SENIOR | MALE | 2.9000 |
| ANDY BUENZA | 000001111 | ACCOUNTING | SOPHOMORE | MALE | 2.7429 |
| MARIA SANCHEZ | 501155003 | MANAGEMENT | JUNIOR | FEMALE | 3.2000 |
| STACY PHARR | 444344344 | INFORMATION SYSTEMS | SENIOR | FEMALE | 3.5263 |
| MICHAEL RYAN | 717273747 | INFORMATION SYSTEMS | FRESHMAN | MALE | 3.2727 |
| MARY LITTLE | 394958690 | INFORMATION SYSTEMS | SENIOR | FEMALE | 3.1579 |
| ANNIE MARINOS | 010203040 | INFORMATION SYSTEMS | FRESHMAN | FEMALE | 2.2727 |
| C. H. FLOWER | 404040404 | INFORMATION SYSTEMS | SENIOR | MALE | 2.6887 |
| ROY JOICE | 102450555 | ACCOUNTING | SENIOR | MALE | 3.5045 |
| DAVID LETTER | 978675643 | FINANCE | FRESHMAN | MALE | 2.0000 |
| JANE CATES | 132435467 | FINANCE | FRESHMAN | FEMALE | 2.7600 |
| KEN MARTINEZ | 002903992 | FINANCE | SENIOR | MALE | 2.7704 |
| GEORGE COMONOS | 516972420 | MANAGEMENT | FRESHMAN | MALE | 3.2400 |
| SESSIE PARSONS | 808188808 | MANAGEMENT | SOPHOMORE | FEMALE | 2.5106 |
| PEGGY MARTTA | 222288885 | MARKETING | SENIOR | FEMALE | 2.0635 |
| THOMAS THOMPSON | 844839931 | MARKETING | FRESHMAN | MALE | 2.2857 |
| WAYNE HEDDER | 246808642 | MARKETING | SENIOR | MALE | 3.9694 |

```
                        STUDENT COUNTS AND AVERAGE GPR'S BY MAJOR

      NUMBER OF STUDENTS AND AVERAGE GPR IN ACCOUNTING            :  8        2.7666

      NUMBER OF STUDENTS AND AVERAGE GPR IN INFORMATION SYSTEMS : 12        2.9293

      NUMBER OF STUDENTS AND AVERAGE GPR IN FINANCE              :  7        2.9220

      NUMBER OF STUDENTS AND AVERAGE GPR IN MANAGEMENT           : 13        2.7940

      NUMBER OF STUDENTS AND AVERAGE GPR IN MARKETING            : 10        2.8779
```

## Multiple Level Tables

```
PP 5740-CB1 RELEASE 2.4                    IBM OS/VS COBOL   JULY  1, 1982      14.53.29  DATE OCT 25,1988

    1                      14.53.29        OCT 25,1988

00001              IDENTIFICATION DIVISION.
00002
00003              PROGRAM-ID. TABLES.
00004              AUTHOR. FOWLER.
00005              DATE-WRITTEN. AUGUST 1988.
00006              DATE-COMPILED. OCT 25,1988.
00007              REMARKS.
00008
00009          ****************************************************
00010          *                                                  *
00011          *   ASSIGNMENT NUMBER                              *
00012          *   DATE ASSIGNED                                  *
00013          *   DATE DUE                                       *
00014          *   PURPOSE:  THIS IS A GRADE POINT RATIO CALCULATION PROGRAM. *
00015          *            THE GRADE POINT RATIO IS DETERMINED BY DIVIDING   *
00016          *            THE NUMBER OF GRADE POINTS EARNED BY THE NUMBER   *
00017          *            OF CREDIT HOURS TAKEN. IN ADDITION, THE MAJOR     *
00018          *            CODE, CLASS CODE, AND SEX CODE WILL BE CONVERTED  *
00019          *            TO THE ACTUAL NAMES ASSOCIATED WITH THE CODES     *
00020          *            USING COMPILE-TIME TABLES.                        *
00021          *                                                  *
00022          *                                                  *
00023          *   INPUT FILE SPECIFICATIONS:                     *
00024          *        CARD COLUMNS                   DESCRIPTION *
00025          *        -------------------------      ----------- *
00026          *             1-30                      STUDENT'S NAME       *
00027          *             31-39                     STUDENT'S ID NUMBER  *
00028          *             40-40                     STUDENT'S MAJOR CODE *
00029          *             41-41                     STUDENT'S CLASS CODE *
00030          *             42-42                     STUDENT'S SEX CODE   *
00031          *             43-45                     CREDIT HOURS TAKEN   *
00032          *             46-48                     GRADE POINTS EARNED  *
00033          *                                                  *
00034          *   THE OUTPUT CONTAINS STUDENT'S ID NUMBER, STUDENT'S NAME,  *
00035          *   MAJOR NAME, CLASS NAME, SEX, AND THE GRADE POINT RATIO.   *
00036          *                                                  *
00037          *                                                  *
00038          *   THERE ARE TWO SUMMARY REPORTS THAT ARE PRINTED BY THIS PRO- *
00039          *   GRAM.  THE FIRST SUMMARY REPORT LISTS THE NUMBER OF STUDENTS *
00040          *   IN EACH MAJOR.  THE SECOND SUMMARY REPORT LISTS THE NUMBER   *
00041          *   OF STUDENTS BY SEX WITHIN CLASS WITHIN MAJOR.  *
00042          ****************************************************
00043
```

```
    2        TABLES           14.53.29        OCT 25,1988

00045              ENVIRONMENT DIVISION.
00046
00047              CONFIGURATION SECTION.
00048
00049              SOURCE-COMPUTER. IBM.
00050              OBJECT-COMPUTER. IBM.
00051              SPECIAL-NAMES.   CO1 IS PAGE-TOP.
00052
00053              INPUT-OUTPUT SECTION.
00054
00055              FILE-CONTROL.
00056
00057                  SELECT DEAN-FILE
00058                      ASSIGN TO DA-S-DEAN.
00059
00060                  SELECT REPORT-FILE
00061                      ASSIGN TO UT-S-REPORT.
00062
```

*(continued)*

```
    3          TABLES        14.53.29        OCT 25,1988

00064          DATA DIVISION.
00065
00066          FILE SECTION.
00067
00068          FD  DEAN-FILE
00069              LABEL RECORDS ARE OMITTED
00070              RECORD CONTAINS 48 CHARACTERS
00071              BLOCK CONTAINS 100 RECORDS
00072              DATA RECORD IS STUDENT-RECORD.
00073
00074          01  STUDENT-RECORD PIC X(48).
00075
00076
00077          FD  REPORT-FILE
00078              LABEL RECORDS ARE OMITTED
00079              DATA RECORD IS REPORT-LINE.
00080
00081          01  REPORT-LINE PIC X(133).
00082
```

```
    4          TABLES        14.53.29        OCT 25,1988

00084          WORKING-STORAGE SECTION.
00085
00086          77  GPR                    PIC 9(1)V9(4).
00087          77  MAJOR-SUB              PIC 9(2).
00088          77  CLASS-SUB              PIC 9(2).
00089          77  SEX-SUB               PIC 9(2).
00090
00091          01  ARE-THERE-MORE-RECORDS PIC X(3)       VALUE 'YES'.
00092              88 MORE-RECORDS                       VALUE 'YES'.
00093              88 NO-MORE-RECORDS                    VALUE 'NO'.
00094
00095          01  PAGE-HEADING.
00096              05 FILLER             PIC X(47)       VALUE SPACES.
00097              05 FILLER             PIC X(39)       VALUE
00098                  'DEANFILE STUDENT LISTING AND GPR REPORT'.
00099              05 FILLER             PIC X(47)       VALUE SPACES.
00100
00101          01  DETAIL-REPORT-HEADINGS.
00102              03 FILLER             PIC X(10)       VALUE SPACES.
00103              03 FILLER             PIC X(4)        VALUE 'NAME'.
00104              03 FILLER             PIC X(36)       VALUE SPACES.
00105              03 FILLER             PIC X(2)        VALUE 'ID'.
00106              03 FILLER             PIC X(18)       VALUE SPACES.
00107              03 FILLER             PIC X(5)        VALUE 'MAJOR'.
00108              03 FILLER             PIC X(16)       VALUE SPACES.
00109              03 FILLER             PIC X(5)        VALUE 'CLASS'.
00110              03 FILLER             PIC X(10)       VALUE SPACES.
00111              03 FILLER             PIC X(3)        VALUE 'SEX'.
00112              03 FILLER             PIC X(10)       VALUE SPACES.
00113              03 FILLER             PIC X(3)        VALUE 'GPR'.
00114              03 FILLER             PIC X(9)        VALUE SPACES.
00115
00116          01  SUMMARY-KOUNT-HEADING-1.
00117              03 FILLER             PIC X(55)       VALUE SPACES.
00118              03 FILLER             PIC X(23)       VALUE
00119                  'STUDENT COUNTS BY MAJOR'.
00120              03 FILLER             PIC X(55)       VALUE SPACES.
00121
00122          01  SUMMARY-KOUNT-HEADING-2.
00123              03 FILLER             PIC X(43)       VALUE SPACES.
00124              03 FILLER             PIC X(47)       VALUE
00125                  'STUDENT COUNTS BY SEX WITHIN CLASS WITHIN MAJOR'.
00126              03 FILLER             PIC X(43)       VALUE SPACES.
00127
```

*(continued)*

```
     5         TABLES          14.53.29        OCT 25,1988


 00129           01  SUMMARY-KOUNT-HEADING-3.
 00130               03 FILLER            PIC X(22)      VALUE SPACES.
 00131               03 FILLER            PIC X(10)      VALUE 'ACCOUNTING'.
 00132               03 FILLER            PIC X(12)      VALUE SPACES.
 00133               03 FILLER            PIC X(12)      VALUE
 00134                   'INFO SYSTEMS'.
 00135               03 FILLER            PIC X(12)      VALUE SPACES.
 00136               03 FILLER            PIC X(7)       VALUE 'FINANCE'.
 00137               03 FILLER            PIC X(13)      VALUE SPACES.
 00138               03 FILLER            PIC X(10)      VALUE 'MANAGEMENT'.
 00139               03 FILLER            PIC X(13)      VALUE SPACES.
 00140               03 FILLER            PIC X(9)       VALUE 'MARKETING'.
 00141               03 FILLER            PIC X(13)      VALUE SPACES.
 00142
 00143           01  SUMMARY-KOUNT-HEADING-4.
 00144               03 FILLER            PIC X(22)      VALUE SPACES.
 00145               03 FILLER            PIC X(11)      VALUE
 00146                   'FR SO JR SR'.
 00147               03 FILLER            PIC X(11)      VALUE SPACES.
 00148               03 FILLER            PIC X(11)      VALUE
 00149                   'FR SO JR SR'.
 00150               03 FILLER            PIC X(11)      VALUE SPACES.
 00151               03 FILLER            PIC X(11)      VALUE
 00152                   'FR SO JR SR'.
 00153               03 FILLER            PIC X(11)      VALUE SPACES.
 00154               03 FILLER            PIC X(11)      VALUE
 00155                   'FR SO JR SR'.
 00156               03 FILLER            PIC X(12)      VALUE SPACES.
 00157
 00158           01  SUMMARY-REPORT-2-LINE.
 00159               03 FILLER                 PIC X(10)  VALUE SPACES.
 00160               03 SUM-REP-2-SEX-OUT      PIC X(6).
 00161               03 FILLER                 PIC X(6)  VALUE SPACES.
 00162               03 MAJOR-ENTRY-OUT        OCCURS 5 TIMES.
 00163                 05 CLASS-KOUNT-ENTRY-OUT OCCURS 4 TIMES.
 00164                   07 SUMMARY-SEX-KOUNT-OUT  PIC Z9.
 00165                   07 FILLER              PIC X(1).
 00166                 05 FILLER                PIC X(10).
 00167               03 FILLER                 PIC X(1)  VALUE SPACES.
 00168
 00169           01  STUDENT-RECORD-IN.
 00170               03 NAME-IN           PIC X(30).
 00171               03 ID-IN             PIC X(9).
 00172               03 MAJOR-IN          PIC 9(1).
 00173               03 CLASS-IN          PIC 9(1).
 00174               03 SEX-IN            PIC 9(1).
 00175               03 CREDIT-HOURS-IN   PIC 9(3).
 00176               03 GRADE-POINTS-IN   PIC 9(3).
 00177
```

*(continued)*

```
    6          TABLES        14.53.29      OCT 25,1988

00179              01  STUDENT-RECORD-OUT.
00180                  03  FILLER              PIC X(10)      VALUE SPACES.
00181                  03  NAME-OUT            PIC X(30).
00182                  03  FILLER              PIC X(7)       VALUE SPACES.
00183                  03  ID-OUT              PIC X(9).
00184                  03  FILLER              PIC X(7)       VALUE SPACES.
00185                  03  MAJOR-NAME-OUT      PIC X(19).
00186                  03  FILLER              PIC X(7)       VALUE SPACES.
00187                  03  CLASS-NAME-OUT      PIC X(9).
00188                  03  FILLER              PIC X(7)       VALUE SPACES.
00189                  03  SEX-OUT             PIC X(6).
00190                  03  FILLER              PIC X(7)       VALUE SPACES.
00191                  03  GPR-OUT             PIC 9(1).9(4).
00192                  03  FILLER              PIC X(9)       VALUE SPACES.
00193
00194              01  MAJOR-NAME-VALUES.
00195                  03  FILLER              PIC X(19)      VALUE 'ACCOUNTING'.
00196                  03  FILLER              PIC X(19)      VALUE
00197                         'INFORMATION SYSTEMS'.
00198                  03  FILLER              PIC X(19)      VALUE 'FINANCE'.
00199                  03  FILLER              PIC X(19)      VALUE 'MANAGEMENT'.
00200                  03  FILLER              PIC X(19)      VALUE 'MARKETING'.
00201
00202              01  MAJOR-TABLE REDEFINES MAJOR-NAME-VALUES.
00203                  03  MAJOR-NAME          PIC X(19)
00204                                          OCCURS 5 TIMES.
00205
00206              01  CLASS-NAME-VALUES.
00207                  03  FILLER              PIC X(9)       VALUE 'FRESHMAN'.
00208                  03  FILLER              PIC X(9)       VALUE 'SOPHOMORE'.
00209                  03  FILLER              PIC X(9)       VALUE 'JUNIOR'.
00210                  03  FILLER              PIC X(9)       VALUE 'SENIOR'.
00211
00212              01  CLASS-TABLE REDEFINES CLASS-NAME-VALUES.
00213                  03  CLASS-NAME          PIC X(9)
00214                                          OCCURS 4 TIMES.
00215
00216              01  SEX-VALUES.
00217                  03  FILLER              PIC X(6)       VALUE 'MALE'.
00218                  03  FILLER              PIC X(6)       VALUE 'FEMALE'.
00219
00220              01  SEX-TABLE REDEFINES SEX-VALUES.
00221                  03  SEX                 PIC X(6)
00222                                          OCCURS 2 TIMES.
00223
```

```
    7          TABLES        14.53.29      OCT 25,1988

00225              01  MAJOR-KOUNT-TABLE.
00226                  03  MAJOR-KOUNT         PIC 9(2)
00227                                          OCCURS 5 TIMES.
00228
00229              01  MAJOR-CLASS-SEX-KOUNT-TABLE.
00230                  03  MAJOR-CLASS-SEX-ENTRY OCCURS 5 TIMES.
00231                      05  CLASS-SEX-ENTRY   OCCURS 4 TIMES.
00232                          07  SEX-KOUNT     PIC 9(2)
00233                                            OCCURS 2 TIMES.
00234
00235              01  SUMMARY-REPORT-1-LINE.
00236                  03  FILLER              PIC X(41)      VALUE SPACES.
00237                  03  FILLER              PIC X(28)      VALUE
00238                         'TOTAL NUMBER OF STUDENTS IN '.
00239                  03  SUM-REP-1-MAJOR-OUT PIC X(19).
00240                  03  FILLER              PIC X(3)       VALUE ' : '.
00241                  03  SUM-REP-1-KOUNT-OUT PIC Z9.
00242                  03  FILLER              PIC X(40)      VALUE SPACES.
00243
00244              01  LEGEND-LINE.
00245                  03  FILLER              PIC X(40)      VALUE SPACES.
00246                  03  FILLER              PIC X(14)      VALUE
00247                         'FR = FRESHMAN'.
00248                  03  FILLER              PIC X(15)      VALUE
00249                         'SO = SOPHOMORE'.
00250                  03  FILLER              PIC X(12)      VALUE
00251                         'JR = JUNIOR'.
00252                  03  FILLER              PIC X(12)      VALUE
00253                         'SR = SENIOR'.
00254                  03  FILLER              PIC X(40)      VALUE SPACES.
00255
00256              01  BLANK-LINE.
00257                  03  FILLER              PIC X(133)     VALUE SPACES.
00258
```

*(continued)*

```
   8        TABLES         14.53.29      OCT 25,1988

00260        PROCEDURE DIVISION.
00261
00262        0000-MAIN-PARA.
00263            PERFORM 1000-INIT-PARA.
00264            PERFORM 8000-READ-PARA.
00265            PERFORM 2000-PROCESS-PARA
00266                UNTIL NO-MORE-RECORDS.
00267            PERFORM 3000-TERMINATION-PARA.
00268            STOP RUN.
00269
```

```
   9        TABLES         14.53.29      OCT 25,1988

00271        ****************************************************************
00272        *    1000-INIT-PARA.                                           *
00273        *                                                              *
00274        *    THIS PARAGRAPH OPENS THE DEAN FILE AND REPORT FILE, WRITES *
00275        *    THE REPORT HEADINGS, AND ZEROS OUT THE MAJOR-KOUNT-TABLE   *
00276        *    AND THE MAJOR-CLASS-SEX-KOUNT-TABLE.                       *
00277        *                                                              *
00278        ****************************************************************
00279
00280        1000-INIT-PARA.
00281            OPEN INPUT DEAN-FILE.
00282            OPEN OUTPUT REPORT-FILE.
00283            WRITE REPORT-LINE FROM BLANK-LINE
00284                AFTER PAGE-TOP.
00285            WRITE REPORT-LINE FROM PAGE-HEADING
00286                AFTER 3.
00287            WRITE REPORT-LINE FROM DETAIL-REPORT-HEADINGS
00288                AFTER 3.
00289            WRITE REPORT-LINE FROM BLANK-LINE
00290                AFTER 1.
00291            MOVE SPACES TO SUMMARY-REPORT-2-LINE.
00292            MOVE ZEROS TO MAJOR-KOUNT-TABLE, MAJOR-CLASS-SEX-KOUNT-TABLE.
00293
```

```
  10        TABLES         14.53.29      OCT 25,1988

00295        ****************************************************************
00296        *    2000-PROCESS-PARA.                                        *
00297        *                                                              *
00298        *    THIS PARAGRAPH IS A CONTROL PARAGRAPH FOR                 *
00299        *                                                              *
00300        *            2100-CALCULATIONS-PARA                            *
00301        *            2200-WRITE-REPORT-PARA                            *
00302        *            8000-READ-PARA                                    *
00303        *                                                              *
00304        ****************************************************************
00305
00306        2000-PROCESS-PARA.
00307            PERFORM 2100-CALCULATIONS-PARA.
00308            PERFORM 2200-WRITE-REPORT-PARA.
00309            PERFORM 8000-READ-PARA.
00310
```

*(continued)*

```
      11          TABLES          14.53.29       OCT 25,1988

00312         ***********************************************************
00313         *  2100-CALCULATIONS-PARA.                                *
00314         *                                                         *
00315         *  THIS PARAGRAPH CALCULATES THE STUDENT'S GPR (TO 4 DECIMAL *
00316         *  PLACES AND ROUNDED) AND ACCUMULATES THE COUNT OF STUDENTS *
00317         *  BY MAJOR AND BY SEX WITHIN CLASS WITHIN MAJOR. THIS INFOR- *
00318         *  MATION WILL BE USED IN THE PRINTING OF THE SUMMARY REPORTS. *
00319         *                                                         *
00320         ***********************************************************
00321
00322             2100-CALCULATIONS-PARA.
00323                 COMPUTE GPR ROUNDED = GRADE-POINTS-IN / CREDIT-HOURS-IN.
00324                 ADD 1 TO MAJOR-KOUNT(MAJOR-IN).
00325                 ADD 1 TO SEX-KOUNT(MAJOR-IN, CLASS-IN, SEX-IN).
00326
```

```
      12          TABLES          14.53.29       OCT 25,1988

00328         ***********************************************************
00329         *  2200-WRITE-REPORT-PARA.                                *
00330         *                                                         *
00331         *  THIS PARAGRAPH MOVES THE APPROPRIATE DATA (STUDENT'S NAME, *
00332         *  ID, GPR, MAJOR NAME, CLASS NAME, AND SEX) TO THE APPROPRIATE*
00333         *  OUTPUT FIELDS IN THE DETAIL LINE AND THEN PRINTS THE DETAIL *
00334         *  LINE.                                                   *
00335         *                                                         *
00336         ***********************************************************
00337
00338             2200-WRITE-REPORT-PARA.
00339                 MOVE NAME-IN TO NAME-OUT.
00340                 MOVE ID-IN TO ID-OUT.
00341                 MOVE GPR TO GPR-OUT.
00342                 MOVE MAJOR-NAME(MAJOR-IN) TO MAJOR-NAME-OUT.
00343                 MOVE CLASS-NAME(CLASS-IN) TO CLASS-NAME-OUT.
00344                 MOVE SEX(SEX-IN) TO SEX-OUT.
00345                 WRITE REPORT-LINE FROM STUDENT-RECORD-OUT
00346                     AFTER 1.
00347
```

```
      13          TABLES          14.53.29       OCT 25,1988

00349         ***********************************************************
00350         *  8000-READ-PARA.                                        *
00351         *                                                         *
00352         *  THIS PARAGRAPH READS A RECORD FROM THE DEAN FILE.  WHEN THE *
00353         *  END OF THE FILE HAS BEEN REACHED, THE END OF FILE FLAG *
00354         *  (ARE-THERE-MORE-RECORDS) WILL HAVE THE VALUE 'NO' MOVED TO *
00355         *  IT TO INDICATE THAT THERE ARE NO-MORE-RECORDS TO BE READ *
00356         *  FROM THE FILE.                                          *
00357         *                                                         *
00358         ***********************************************************
00359
00360             8000-READ-PARA.
00361                 READ DEAN-FILE INTO STUDENT-RECORD-IN
00362                     AT END
00363                         MOVE 'NO' TO ARE-THERE-MORE-RECORDS.
00364
00365
```

*(continued)*

```
   14        TABLES        14.53.29      OCT 25,1988

00367          ****************************************************************
00368          *    3000-TERMINATION-PARA                                      *
00369          *                                                               *
00370          *    THIS PARAGRAPH IS A CONTROL PARAGRAPH FOR                  *
00371          *                                                               *
00372          *          3100-WRITE-REPORT-1-HEADINGS                         *
00373          *          3200-WRITE-SUMMARY-REPORT-1                          *
00374          *          3300-WRITE-REPORT-2-HEADINGS                         *
00375          *          3400-WRITE-SUMMARY-REPORT-2                          *
00376          *          3500-CLOSE-PARA                                      *
00377          *                                                               *
00378          *    A LEGEND LINE IS PRINTED AFTER THE SECOND REPORT IS WRITTEN *
00379          *    AND THE DEAN FILE AND REPORT FILE ARE THEN CLOSED AFTER THE *
00380          *    ABOVE PARAGRAPHS ARE PERFORMED.                            *
00381          ****************************************************************
00382
00383          3000-TERMINATION-PARA.
00384              PERFORM 3100-REPORT-1-HEADINGS.
00385              PERFORM 3200-WRITE-SUMMARY-REPORT-1
00386                  VARYING MAJOR-SUB FROM 1 BY 1
00387                  UNTIL MAJOR-SUB > 5.
00388              PERFORM 3300-REPORT-2-HEADINGS.
00389              PERFORM 3400-WRITE-SUMMARY-REPORT-2
00390                  VARYING SEX-SUB FROM 1 BY 1
00391                  UNTIL SEX-SUB > 2.
00392              WRITE REPORT-LINE FROM LEGEND-LINE
00393                  AFTER 4.
00394              PERFORM 3500-CLOSE-PARA.
00395
```

```
   15        TABLES        14.53.29      OCT 25,1988

00397          ****************************************************************
00398          *    3100-WRITE-REPORT-1-HEADINGS                               *
00399          *                                                               *
00400          *    THIS PARAGRAPH WRITES THE HEADINGS FOR THE FIRST SUMMARY   *
00401          *    REPORT WHICH LISTS THE TOTAL NUMBER OF STUDENTS IN EACH    *
00402          *    MAJOR.                                                     *
00403          *                                                               *
00404          ****************************************************************
00405
00406          3100-REPORT-1-HEADINGS.
00407              WRITE REPORT-LINE FROM SUMMARY-KOUNT-HEADING-1
00408                  AFTER PAGE-TOP.
00409              WRITE REPORT-LINE FROM BLANK-LINE
00410                  AFTER 1.
00411
```

```
   16        TABLES        14.53.29      OCT 25,1988

00413          ****************************************************************
00414          *    3200-WRITE-SUMMARY-REPORT-1                                *
00415          *                                                               *
00416          *    THIS PARAGRAPH WRITES THE SUMMARY LINES WHICH LISTS THE    *
00417          *    NUMBER OF STUDENTS IN EACH MAJOR.                          *
00418          *                                                               *
00419          ****************************************************************
00420
00421          3200-WRITE-SUMMARY-REPORT-1.
00422              MOVE MAJOR-NAME(MAJOR-SUB) TO SUM-REP-1-MAJOR-OUT.
00423              MOVE MAJOR-KOUNT(MAJOR-SUB) TO SUM-REP-1-KOUNT-OUT.
00424              WRITE REPORT-LINE FROM SUMMARY-REPORT-1-LINE
00425                  AFTER 2.
00426
```

*(continued)*

```
   17        TABLES          14.53.29      OCT 25,1988

00428         ************************************************************
00429         *   3300-WRITE-REPORT-2-HEADINGS                          *
00430         *                                                         *
00431         *   THIS PARAGRAPH WRITES THE HEADINGS FOR THE SECOND SUMMARY *
00432         *   REPORT WHICH LISTS THE TOTAL NUMBER OF STUDENTS BY SEX *
00433         *   WITHIN CLASS, WITHIN MAJOR.                           *
00434         *                                                         *
00435         ************************************************************
00436
00437          3300-REPORT-2-HEADINGS.
00438              WRITE REPORT-LINE FROM SUMMARY-KOUNT-HEADING-2
00439                  AFTER PAGE-TOP.
00440              WRITE REPORT-LINE FROM SUMMARY-KOUNT-HEADING-3
00441                  AFTER 2.
00442              WRITE REPORT-LINE FROM SUMMARY-KOUNT-HEADING-4
00443                  AFTER 2.
```

```
   18        TABLES          14.53.29      OCT 25,1988

00446         ************************************************************
00447         *   3400-WRITE-SUMMARY-REPORT-2                           *
00448         *                                                         *
00449         *   THIS PARAGRAPH MOVES THE APPROPRIATE SEX TO THE SECOND *
00450         *   SUMMARY REPORT'S DETAIL LINE.  AFTER THE PROPER COUNTS HAVE *
00451         *   BEEN MOVED TO THEIR RESPECTIVE OUTPUT POSITIONS, THE SUM- *
00452         *   MARY COUNTS ARE THEN PRINTED.  BECAUSE A MULTI-LEVEL TABLE *
00453         *   IS BEING USED FOR BOTH THE ACCUMULATOR AND THE OUTPUT POSI- *
00454         *   TION IT IS NECESSARY TO USE NESTED PERFORM/VARYING'S TO *
00455         *   MANIPULATE THE SUBSCRIPTS.                            *
00456         *                                                         *
00457         ************************************************************
00458
00459          3400-WRITE-SUMMARY-REPORT-2.
00460              MOVE SEX(SEX-SUB) TO SUM-REP-2-SEX-OUT.
00461              PERFORM 3410-CLASS-SUB-VARY
00462                  VARYING MAJOR-SUB FROM 1 BY 1
00463                  UNTIL MAJOR-SUB > 5.
00464              WRITE REPORT-LINE FROM SUMMARY-REPORT-2-LINE
00465                  AFTER 2.
00466
```

*(continued)*

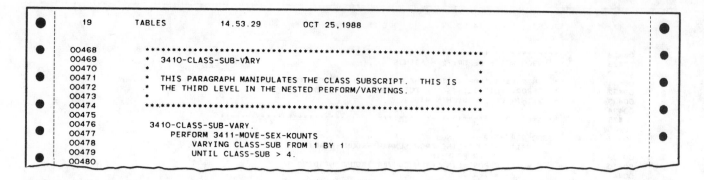

```
      19          TABLES          14.53.29      OCT 25,1988

  00468        ********************************************************
  00469        *   3410-CLASS-SUB-VARY                                 *
  00470        *                                                       *
  00471        *   THIS PARAGRAPH MANIPULATES THE CLASS SUBSCRIPT.  THIS IS  *
  00472        *   THE THIRD LEVEL IN THE NESTED PERFORM/VARYINGS.      *
  00473        *                                                       *
  00474        ********************************************************
  00475
  00476         3410-CLASS-SUB-VARY.
  00477             PERFORM 3411-MOVE-SEX-KOUNTS
  00478                 VARYING CLASS-SUB FROM 1 BY 1
  00479                 UNTIL CLASS-SUB > 4.
  00480
```

```
      20          TABLES          14.53.29      OCT 25,1988

  00482        ********************************************************
  00483        *   3411-MOVE-SEX-KOUNTS                                *
  00484        *                                                       *
  00485        *   THIS PARAGRAPH MOVES THE APPROPRIATE COUNT (NUMBER OF STU-  *
  00486        *   DENTS BY SEX WITHIN CLASS WITHIN MAJOR) TO THE APPROPRIATE  *
  00487        *   OUTPUT POSITION.                                    *
  00488        *                                                       *
  00489        ********************************************************
  00490
  00491         3411-MOVE-SEX-KOUNTS.
  00492             MOVE SEX-KOUNT(MAJOR-SUB, CLASS-SUB, SEX-SUB) TO
  00493                 SUMMARY-SEX-KOUNT-OUT (MAJOR-SUB, CLASS-SUB).
  00494
  00495
  00496
  00497
  00498         3500-CLOSE-PARA.
  00499             CLOSE DEAN-FILE.
  00500
```

*(continued)*

```
DEANFILE STUDENT LISTING AND GPR REPORT


NAME                      ID          MAJOR                  CLASS       SEX       GPR

THOMAS WILKINSON        123456789    MANAGEMENT             SENIOR      MALE      3.7619
DON VILLANOSKI          987654321    ACCOUNTING             FRESHMAN    MALE      2.7500
MICHAEL FOWLER          555555555    INFORMATION SYSTEMS    SOPHOMORE   MALE      3.8966
TIA FOWLER              888888888    FINANCE                JUNIOR      FEMALE    3.4943
CLINT SMITH             333333333    INFORMATION SYSTEMS    JUNIOR      MALE      1.9839
HOWARD PORTER           454545454    ACCOUNTING             FRESHMAN    MALE      2.3158
APRIL JONES             777777777    INFORMATION SYSTEMS    JUNIOR      FEMALE    2.8025
APRIL JACKS             787878778    MANAGEMENT             SENIOR      FEMALE    2.5649
BRYAN MANN              232323232    FINANCE                FRESHMAN    MALE      2.6667
ZEKE MORGAN             434356569    INFORMATION SYSTEMS    SOPHOMORE   MALE      2.8947
BILL ADAM               102302220    MANAGEMENT             SENIOR      MALE      2.8092
JILL MATSON             010101206    INFORMATION SYSTEMS    FRESHMAN    FEMALE    2.8947
TINA MARIO              000000222    MANAGEMENT             JUNIOR      FEMALE    2.3380
CLYDE FELD JR.          129834765    MANAGEMENT             SOPHOMORE   MALE      2.9057
GEORGE MARINAKIES       100010055    MARKETING              FRESHMAN    MALE      2.7083
JAMES PAPPAS            342537891    MARKETING              JUNIOR      MALE      2.3253
STEVE PARKS             908765101    ACCOUNTING             FRESHMAN    FEMALE    3.8000
LYNDA MATHER            203040506    FINANCE                JUNIOR      FEMALE    2.7538
KEVIN MCKENN            444455555    INFORMATION SYSTEMS    JUNIOR      MALE      3.4933
IRENE SMITH             001122334    MANAGEMENT             FRESHMAN    FEMALE    2.0000
EMILY LYLE              999888777    ACCOUNTING             FRESHMAN    FEMALE    2.2667
PEG PORTERHOUSE         123321123    FINANCE                SENIOR      FEMALE    2.9703
DAN ROBESON             656765679    MANAGEMENT             JUNIOR      MALE      2.2400
DANA MILLS              908070600    MANAGEMENT             SENIOR      FEMALE    2.7500
GEORGE RYAN             564731009    ACCOUNTING             SOPHOMORE   MALE      2.4000
BILLY BOB BARRETT       111000222    ACCOUNTING             SENIOR      MALE      2.2500
MARY JO MARTINEZ        102938475    INFORMATION SYSTEMS    SENIOR      FEMALE    2.3077
POLLY ANN FLOWERS       501112234    MANAGEMENT             SENIOR      FEMALE    2.5773
MATHEW ALTMEN           980980980    MARKETING              JUNIOR      MALE      3.2258
DIANE LAWERNCE          263718818    MARKETING              SOPHOMORE   FEMALE    2.5714
SARA WALKER             828347561    MARKETING              JUNIOR      FEMALE    3.5375
MARIA SANTIAGO          777345777    MARKETING              SOPHOMORE   FEMALE    2.4444
ANTONIO MARTINEZ        773330666    MARKETING              JUNIOR      MALE      3.0000
ROBERTO SMITH           311230099    MANAGEMENT             SENIOR      MALE      2.9000
ANDY BUENZA             000001111    ACCOUNTING             SOPHOMORE   MALE      2.7429
MARIA SANCHEZ           501155003    MANAGEMENT             JUNIOR      FEMALE    3.2000
STACY PHARR             444344344    INFORMATION SYSTEMS    SENIOR      FEMALE    3.5263
MICHAEL RYAN            717273747    INFORMATION SYSTEMS    FRESHMAN    MALE      3.2727
MARY LITTLE             394958690    INFORMATION SYSTEMS    SENIOR      FEMALE    3.1579
ANNIE MARINOS           010203040    INFORMATION SYSTEMS    FRESHMAN    FEMALE    2.2727
C. H. FLOWER            404040404    INFORMATION SYSTEMS    SENIOR      MALE      2.6887
ROY JOICE               102450555    ACCOUNTING             SENIOR      MALE      3.5045
DAVID LETTER            978675643    FINANCE                FRESHMAN    MALE      2.0000
JANE CATES              132435467    FINANCE                FRESHMAN    FEMALE    2.7600
KEN MARTINEZ            002903992    FINANCE                SENIOR      MALE      2.7704
GEORGE COMONOS          516972420    MANAGEMENT             FRESHMAN    MALE      3.2400
SESSIE PARSONS          808188808    MANAGEMENT             SOPHOMORE   FEMALE    2.5106
PEGGY MARTTA            222288885    MARKETING              SENIOR      FEMALE    2.0635
THOMAS THOMPSON         844839931    MARKETING              FRESHMAN    MALE      2.2857
WAYNE HEDDER            246808642    MARKETING              SENIOR      MALE      3.9694
```

*(continued)*

```
                    STUDENT COUNTS BY SEX WITHIN CLASS WITHIN MAJOR

           ACCOUNTING        INFO SYSTEMS        FINANCE          MANAGEMENT           MARKETING

           FR SO JR SR       FR SO JR SR         FR SO JR SR      FR SO JR SR          FR SO JR SR
  MALE      2  2  0  2        1  2  2  1          2  0  0  1       1  1  1  3           2  0  3  1
  FEMALE    2  0  0  0        2  0  1  3          1  0  2  1       1  1  2  3           0  2  1  1


           FR = FRESHMAN SO = SOPHOMORE JR = JUNIOR SR = SENIOR
```

```
                        STUDENT COUNTS BY MAJOR

     TOTAL NUMBER OF STUDENTS IN ACCOUNTING           :  8
     TOTAL NUMBER OF STUDENTS IN INFORMATION SYSTEMS  : 12
     TOTAL NUMBER OF STUDENTS IN FINANCE              :  7
     TOTAL NUMBER OF STUDENTS IN MANAGEMENT           : 13
     TOTAL NUMBER OF STUDENTS IN MARKETING            : 10
```

---

### Chapter Review Questions

1. Which of the following statements is true about tables?

   a. Three types and three levels are available in COBOL '74
   b. Forty-nine levels are available in COBOL '85
   c. The Occurs Clause must be used with the redefines clause
   d. The Occurs Clause may be used with all level numbers
   e. None of the above

2. A subscript is functionally similar to:

   a. A data-name
   b. Data-name qualification
   c. The REDEFINES
   d. The OCCURS
   e. None of the above

3. The order in which subscripts are used in a procedural reference is related to:

   a. The level of the occurs; 1st subscript with 1st level etc.
   b. The order used in a control statement like the PERFORM VARYING
   c. The algorithm
   d. The level numbers; 02 with 1st, 03 with 3rd etc.
   e. None of the above

4. Which of the following is true about subscripts?

   a. Must be a numeric value
   b. May not be subscripted
   c. Must be numeric data-name or literal
   d. Multiple subscripts are separated by commas
   e. All of the above

5. The number of IFs, ADDs and 77 level items needed to count something with 1000 different classifications without tables is (assuming good data):

   a. 999 IFs, 1,000 ADDs, 1,000 77 levels
   b. 1,000 IFs, 1,000 ADDs, 1,000 77 levels
   c. 1 IF, 1,000 ADDs, 1,000 77 levels
   d. 0 IFs, 1 ADD, 1 77 levels
   e. None of the above

6. What would it take to do Question 5 using Tables?

   a. 999, IFs, 1,000 ADDs, 1,000 77 levels
   b. 1,000 IFs, 1,000 ADDs, 1,000 77 levels
   c. 1 IF, 1,000 ADDs, 1,000 77 levels
   d. 0 IFs, 1 ADD, 1 77 levels
   e. None of the above

7. The REDEFINES:

   a. Is used to set up compile-time tables
   b. May be used at the 01 level
   c. Sets up a new area of storage
   d. Is used to set up execution-time tables
   e. Both a and b are true

8. Drawing the table must be done so that:

    a. The 1st occurs is the column

    b. The 1st occurs is the row

    c. The 1st occurs is shown on the side

    d. The 1st occurs is shown as a subset of the 2nd

    e. None of the above

9. The number of storage positions set up by a multiple-level table is determined by:

    a. Adding the occurs values

    b. Subtracting the occurs values

    c. Multiplying the occurs values

    d. Multiplying the PIC sizes by the occurs values for all levels

    e. None of the above

10. Not-nice data refers to:

    a. Data rated PG13

    b. Data that may not be used as subscripts

    c. Data in the wrong format

    d. Data that may not be redefined

    e. None of the above

11. A data-dependent algorithm is:

    a. Used during detail time

    b. Used after EOF

    c. Uses the input data

    d. Used during total time

    e. Both a and c are true

12. The INDEXED BY clause is used to set up a multiple-level table.

    a. True

    b. False

13. The SEARCH ALL causes a(n):

    a. Serial search

    b. Binary search

    c. Indexed search

    d. Chained search

    e. None of the above

14. An index name is:

    a. The same as a subscript

    b. Used in conjunction with a search

    c. Is always optional

    d. Is always required

    e. None of the above

15. A particular index name may:

    a. Only be used with the table it indexes

    b. Be used to reference any table that is searched

    c. Be used with the perform verb

    d. Be manipulated with the math verbs

    e. Both a and c

16. In order to search a multi-level table, all levels other than the level being searched:
   a. Must be set to 1
   b. Must be set to an appropriate value
   c. May be any value since they are not involved in the search
   d. Must also be the object of a search; nested search
   e. None of the above

17. The PERFORM VARYING with the after options:
   a. Is more robust than the nested performs
   b. Is less robust than the nested performs
   c. Is only a COBOL '85 feature
   d. No such option exist...but would be nice
   e. None of the above

18. The execution of the PERFORM VARYING may be described as:
   a. Initialize, Test, Perform the Procedure
   b. Perform the Procedure, Increment, Test
   c. Initialize, Test, Perform the Procedure, Increment and Test
   d. Increment, Test, Perform the Procedure
   e. None of the above

19. In order to accumulate the data at the second level of a three-level table you would:
   a. Vary the second subscript the fastest
   b. Vary the second subscript the slowest
   c. Order of varying the subscripts is unimportant
   d. Vary the first subscript the slowest
   e. Vary the third subscript the slowest

20. Which of the following is not a valid form of the SET verb?
   a. SET index-name DOWN BY 1
   b. SET index-name UP BY 1
   c. SET data-name TO index-name
   d. SET index-name TO data-name
   e. All are valid

For Questions 21 through 25 use the following table and values:

```
01   KOUNTS.
      03   LEVEL-1         OCCURS 4 TIMES.
         05   LEVEL-2      OCCURS 3 TIMES.
            07   LEVEL-3   OCCURS 2 TIMES.
               09   KOUNT  PIC 9(2).
```

| | 1 | | | 2 | | | 3 | | | 4 | | |
|---|---|---|---|---|---|---|---|---|---|---|---|---|
| | 1 | 2 | 3 | 1 | 2 | 3 | 1 | 2 | 3 | 1 | 2 | 3 |
| 1 | 5 | 1 | 4 | 3 | 4 | 5 | 5 | 3 | 3 | 4 | 1 | 3 |
| 2 | 4 | 2 | 1 | 2 | 4 | 5 | 3 | 3 | 5 | 3 | 5 | 2 |

21. What will be the value of ANSWER after the perform is executed?

```
MOVE ZERO TO ANSWER.
PERFORM GET-ANSWER
      VARYING SUB-1 FROM 1 BY 1 UNTIL SUB-1 > 4
      AFTER    SUB-2 FROM 1 BY 1 UNTIL SUB-2 > 3
      AFTER    SUB-3 FROM 1 BY 1 UNTIL SUB-3 > 2.
      .
      .
      .
GET-ANSWER.
      ADD KOUNT (SUB-1, SUB-2, SUB-3) TO ANSWER.
```

   a. 41
   b. 39
   c. 17
   d. 80
   e. None of the above

22. What will be the value of ANSWER after the perform is executed?

```
MOVE ZERO TO ANSWER.
PERFORM GET-ANSWER
      VARYING SUB-1 FROM 2 BY 2 UNTIL SUB-1 > 4
      AFTER    SUB-2 FROM 1 BY 2 UNTIL SUB-2 > 3
      AFTER    SUB-3 FROM 1 BY 1 UNTIL SUB-3 > 2.
      .
      .
      .
GET-ANSWER.
      ADD KOUNT (SUB-1, SUB-2, SUB-3) TO ANSWER.
```

   a. 41
   b. 35
   c. 23
   d. 27
   e. None of the above

23. What will be the value of the SUM-TABLE (occurs 3 times) after the perform is executed?

```
MOVE ZERO TO SUMS.
PERFORM GET-SUM
      VARYING SUB-2 FROM 1 BY 1 UNTIL SUB-2 > 3
      AFTER    SUB-3 FROM 1 BY 1 UNTIL SUB-3 > 2
      AFTER    SUB-1 FROM 1 BY 1 UNTIL SUB-1 > 4.
      .
      .
      .
GET-SUM.
      ADD KOUNT (SUB-1, SUB-2, SUB-3) TO SUM-TABLE (SUB-2).
```

| a. | | b. | | c. | | d. | | e. None of these |
|---|---|---|---|---|---|---|---|---|
| 29 | | 41 | | 17 | | 29 | | |
| 23 | | 39 | | 23 | | 28 | | |
| 28 | | 80 | | 22 | | 23 | | |

24. What will be the value of ANSWER after the perform is executed?

```
MOVE ZERO TO ANSWER.
PERFORM GET-ANSWER
    VARYING SUB-3 FROM 1 BY 1 UNTIL SUB-3 > 2
    AFTER   SUB-2 FROM 1 BY 1 UNTIL SUB-2 > 3
    AFTER   SUB-1 FROM 1 BY 1 UNTIL SUB-1 > 4.
    .
    .
    .

GET-ANSWER.
    IF KOUNT (SUB-1, SUB-2, SUB-3) > 3
        ADD KOUNT (SUB-1, SUB-2, SUB-3) TO ANSWER.
```

   a. 71

   b. 50

   c. 21

   d. 9

   e. None of the above

25. Assume you have the following table:

```
01  FREQUENCY-TABLE.
    03  FREQ OCCURS 5 TIMES PIC 9(3).
```

What will be its contents after the perform is executed?

```
MOVE ZERO TO FREQUENCY-TABLE.
PERFORM GET-FREQUENCY
    VARYING SUB-1 FROM 1 BY 1 UNTIL SUB-1 > 4
    AFTER   SUB-2 FROM 1 BY 1 UNTIL SUB-2 > 3
    AFTER   SUB-3 FROM 1 BY 1 UNTIL SUB-3 > 2.
    .
    .
    .

GET-FREQUENCY.
    MOVE KOUNT (SUB-1, SUB-2, SUB-3) TO F.
    ADD 1 TO FREQ (F).
```

| a. | b. | c. | d. | e. None of these |
|----|----|----|----|----|
| 3  | 3  | 0  | 6  | |
| 6  | 3  | 0  | 5  | |
| 21 | 7  | 0  | 7  | |
| 20 | 5  | 0  | 3  | |
| 30 | 6  | 0  | 3  | |

## Discussion Questions

1. Briefly contrast a compile-time table with an execution-time table.

2. Explain how the search may be used to search one table and vary the index of another table.

3. Contrast a data-dependent algorithm with a logic-dependent algorithm.

4. Explain the relationship of the OCCURS clause and the order of subscripts in a procedural reference.

5. Draw a two-level table two ways.

6. Define and explain the problem of "NOT-NICE DATA".

7. Contrast an index and a subscript.

8. Briefly explain the technique used to "manipulate" a multiple-level table.

9. Why is the nested perform used for reporting tables instead of the perform after?

10. How would the COPY verb help with compile-time tables?

## Practice Problems

1. Set up a table that could be used to count the number of people from each state. (Assume a state code of PIC XX.)

2. Set up a table that could be used to convert the DEAN File classification codes to their descriptions.

3. Assuming that the classification codes are:

> F – Freshman
> S – Sophomore
> J – Junior
> N – Senior

Do Problem 2 again.

4. Set up a table that could be used to accumulate the total inventory cost by supplier (assume 50 suppliers). (Data File C.)

5. Set up a payroll table for the Personnel File (Data File B). Assume that each department (10) and each store (5) has its own pay rate.

6. Write the algorithm to report the three-level table used for Chapter Review Questions 21–25 (assume you have a wide printer).

## Programming Assignments

1. Write a COBOL program to read the Inventory File (Data File C) and write a report of all inventory items. All codes should be converted to appropriate descriptions. On a summary report, print the number of items supplied by each supplier; and the value of inventory each buyer is responsible for. Also include the count of the items by supplier for each buyer.

2. Rewrite the program in 6, using buyer codes of:

> D – David
> M – Mary
> S – Steve
> G – Grace

3. Write a COBOL program to read the PERSONNEL FILE (Data File B) and write a report to include:

- number of employees from each of the 10 departments within each of the 5 stores
- total YTDE by department within store

## Programming Projects

The following assignments rely on the data dictionary, library elements and data sets found in the Project Sets Section of your text.

1. Do the Tables Assignment for the Project Management System in Project A.

2. Do the Tables Assignment for the Employee System in Project B.

# SORTING

## 12

**OBJECTIVES**    Data processing problems usually involve the need to sort data, or put it in order.  Sorting is required for processing master files for update and maintenance and for preparation of reports and files, for instance.

COBOL provides users with the SORT VERB, a very powerful tool for these instances. We will study how it is used, including all options.  I will also present four scenarios that I hope you will find to be useful as guidelines for choosing the appropriate sorting technique.

Finally, I will show you, very generally and briefly, how to sort using JCL.  I will show you two options.  One involves a system program, while another involves systems such as TSO or WYLBUR.

## TOPICS

- sorting and sort keys
- sort/merge packages
- subsets vs. entire files
- creating ordered files
- generating a new code for sorting
- COBOL sorting vs. JCL sorting
- using SECTIONs procedurally
- using the GO TO
- sorting standards and policies

## KEY WORDS

- SORT
- ASCENDING KEY
- DESCENDING KEY
- USING
- GIVING
- INPUT PROCEDURE
- OUTPUT PROCEDURE
- SD
- SORT FILE
- GO TO
- SECTION
- sort fields
- JCL

## THE PROBLEM

Up to this point in your data processing life, and in particular your COBOL life, the order in which data was presented was not important to the problem solution. However, I'm sure you can imagine that reports that are presented using some logical grouping make their readers, probably your bosses, happier! Reports that are ordered do tend to be understandable as we saw in Chapter 6.

Furthermore, data files that are in some predetermined order tend to aid processing. For instance, isn't it easier to balance your checkbook (if it's possible at all) once you order your canceled checks? I find that it is, or I guess I should say my wife says it's easier. Processing a batch of transactions against a master file becomes much easier and more efficient when the files are ordered.

So let's look at a particular problem setting. We will use the DEAN-FILE again since by now you are comfortable with its data. The dean could have wanted the data ordered by student ID, or an alphabetic listing of all students. You see that we can go on and on with possible requests from the dean. Even with our pretty simple data set, we can make many different requests that will require sorting of the DEAN-FILE. Before we look at particular solutions, however, we need to examine the COBOL SORT verb.

## SORT VERB

The heart of sorting logic in COBOL is the SORT verb. The general format is shown below:

$$
\text{\underline{SORT} filename} \\
\left\{ \begin{array}{l} \text{ON \underline{ASCENDING KEY} data-name} \cdots \\ \text{ON \underline{DESCENDING KEY} data-name} \cdots \end{array} \right\} \\
\left\{ \begin{array}{l} \text{\underline{USING} filename} \\ \text{\underline{INPUT PROCEDURE} procedure-name} \end{array} \right\} \\
\left\{ \begin{array}{l} \text{\underline{GIVING} filename} \\ \text{\underline{OUTPUT PROCEDURE} procedure-name} \end{array} \right\}
$$

Several choices must be made in coding the SORT verb. But let's understand the concept first.

The COBOL SORT actually invokes a sort/merge package. It allows a programmer to sort a set of data, using one or more key fields, into ascending or descending, or some combination, order and place the results into another file and/or write reports. So you see the sort package must know where or how it will get the data, in what order to put the data, what key fields to use for ordering, and then where to put the results.

Can you believe that you tell COBOL all this with that simple-looking verb? Look at it closely. SORT filename tells the sort package what file you want it to use as a work area. This is not your data file. It is simply a file, actually a set of files, that the sort package uses to do its work.

You wouldn't want the sort package working on your data file. You might want the original order maintained if you are simply reordering for a report or something. That's why the sort package uses a separate work file.

Next you specify the order and the key fields. That is, if you wanted the data ordered alphabetically by name you might say:

```
ASCENDING KEY   SORT-NAME
```

If you wanted the data sorted by name within major, you might say:

```
ASCENDING KEY   SORT-MAJOR SORT-NAME
```

or

```
DESCENDING KEY SORT-MAJOR
ASCENDING KEY   SORT-NAME
```

As you can see, you have a lot of flexibility regarding order and key specification.

Now you must tell the sort package how it will get the data on which it will work. You may choose between two ways. The **USING** option lets you turn over a whole file for sorting. Say:

```
USING  DEAN-FILE
```

and all the records in DEAN-FILE will be sorted.

However, if not all records are to be sorted, you can use the second option:

```
INPUT PROCEDURE   INPUT-ROUTINE
```

This allows us to specify a set of code that we write that will be executed to get the selected records to the sort package. This option provides us with more power and control, while the **USING** option is easier to code.

Once the sort package sorts the data you give it, it wants to know how to give it back to you. Again, you have two options. The first is a cousin to the **USING** option. When you say **GIVING** filename, all sorted records will be written for you to the file specified. If you just wanted a new file of all the DEAN-FILE records ordered by student ID, the **SORT** would look like:

```
SORT  SORT-FILE
     ASCENDING KEY   SORT-ID
     USING  DEAN-FILE
     GIVING NEW-FILE.
```

If you didn't want a new file, but you did want some report, then the **GIVING** option would not provide you with the control needed to write a nice report of the ordered file. You would code:

```
OUTPUT PROCEDURE   OUTPUT-ROUTINE
```

Again, this allows you to write your own logic for getting the results back from the sort package.

## COBOL SORT VERB RULES AND SYNTAX

Before we go much further, I need to give you some rules for using the SORT verb.

- The file name specified with the SORT must be described in the file section with an SD.
- The data name(s) specified with the ascending or descending key options must be defined in the record associated with the SD. They need not be unique, but if they are not, they must then be qualified.
- The file specified with the USING must be organized sequentially. (COBOL '85 allows for other organizations.)
- The file specified with the GIVING must be organized sequentially. (COBOL '85 allows for other organizations.)
- All user files specified with the USING or GIVING must have a closed status before starting the sort. The sort package will open and close the files. Therefore, if the file is already open, a system error will occur.
- The procedure name specified by the input procedure and by the output procedure must be a section in COBOL '74. However, in COBOL '85 and in some installations where '74 has been modified, the procedures need not be sections, but may be paragraphs.
- The SORT keys must not contain an OCCURS clause.
- Not more than twelve keys may be specified. (Can you imagine a need for twelve keys? I can't.)
- You must always specify one way of getting data to the sort package.
- You must always specify one way of getting results back from the sort package.

[NOTE: There are other rules. I have already mentioned some, and I will point out others as we study other sort package elements.]

## FOUR GENERAL SCENARIOS

Let's look back at our problem—that is, providing the dean with a new file of all students ordered by student ID. Look at the system flowchart in Figure 12.1.

### Using/Giving Scenario

Since all students are to be included, and a new file is to be created, what input and output techniques are best? The USING and GIVING options. The key here is that all records in DEAN-FILE are to be sorted, and all sorted records are to be included in NEW-FILE. This makes the USING/GIVING the easiest and the best technique to use in this and similar situations.

I should point out that I'm showing several general scenarios to help build a framework from which you can work. These scenarios are not all-inclusive and are not meant to be. Use them to help you in selecting the appropriate options for each particular problem situation.

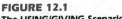

**FIGURE 12.1**
The USING/GIVING Scenario

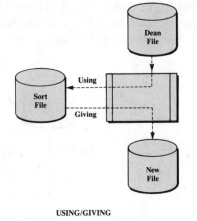

USING/GIVING

## Using/Output Procedure Scenario

What about the second situation mentioned earlier? The dean wanted an alphabetic listing of all students. Figure 12.2 shows the system flowchart for this scenario.

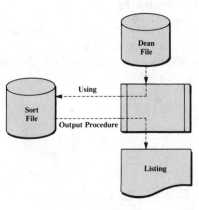

**FIGURE 12.2**
The USING/OUTPUT
PROCEDURE Scenario

USING/OUTPUT PROCEDURE

In this scenario, the entire DEAN-FILE can be used, since all records/students are to be included. However, unless you want the listing to be in an unedited disk format, you need more control of the output than the GIVING would provide. Therefore, you would use the **OUTPUT PROCEDURE** and provide the dean with a pretty report that is edited.

## Input Procedure/Giving Scenario

The dean may not be the only administrator who makes requests of you. Let's say the department head of the Information Systems (IS) department asks for a file containing IS students in alphabetic order. The system flowchart in Figure 12.3 shows this request graphically.

Notice that an **INPUT PROCEDURE** is used to get the data to the SORT file. This is done because only a subset, IS students, is needed for the sort. Could we have sorted all the records in the DEAN-FILE? Sure we could have. We could have sorted alphabetically and by major. Then we would have had to use an output procedure so that only the IS students would be written to the IS file. Since this latter technique works, why do it the first way? Assume for a minute that of the 10,000 students in the DEAN-FILE, only 500 are IS students. We would be sorting 10,000 student records on two keys in order to produce a file of 500 student records.  It makes more sense to me, and I hope to you also, to select the subset on the input side and sort only 500 records.  The results are the same but with much less sorting required.

**FIGURE 12.3**
The INPUT
PROCEDURE/GIVING
Scenario

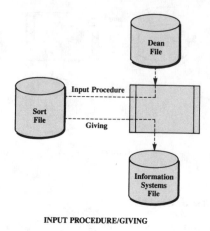

INPUT PROCEDURE/GIVING

### Input/Output Procedures Scenario

The last scenario I want to propose and discuss would involve the **INPUT** and **OUTPUT PROCEDURE**s.  If the dean asked for a report of all honors students (GPR $>=$ 3.25), you would need the ability to manipulate the data both for input to the SORT and output from the SORT.  Graphically, the system would look like that shown in Figure 12.4.

**FIGURE 12.4**
The INPUT/OUTPUT
PROCEDURE Scenario

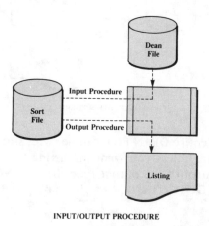

INPUT/OUTPUT PROCEDURE

Since only a subset of the DEAN-FILE (honor students) is required, the **INPUT PROCEDURE** is used.  The output request for a report requires an **OUTPUT PROCEDURE** so that a nice report can be written.

## HIERARCHY CHARTS AND FLOWCHARTS

Before we look at the logic and coding for the four scenarios, let's look at general forms for the corresponding hierarchy charts and flowcharts.  Figure 12.5 shows the hierarchy chart for the USING/GIVING scenario, while Figure 12.4 contains the hierarchy chart for the INPUT/OUTPUT techniques.

The hierarchy chart for USING/GIVING is fairly straightforward. It looks like our simple I/O hierarchy chart from Chapter 1. However, the 2000 module, which normally is PROCESS RECORDS, is replaced by SORT. That is the processing we want to do.

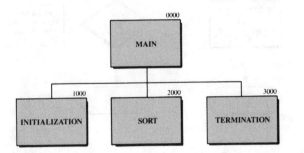

**FIGURE 12.5**
**Hierarchy Chart for USING/GIVING**

Now look at Figure 12.6. Do you see a familiar form? Notice modules 2100 and 2200. Don't they look like they could be separate hierarchy charts? If you renamed the modules to MAIN, they would each look like our standard hierarchy chart.

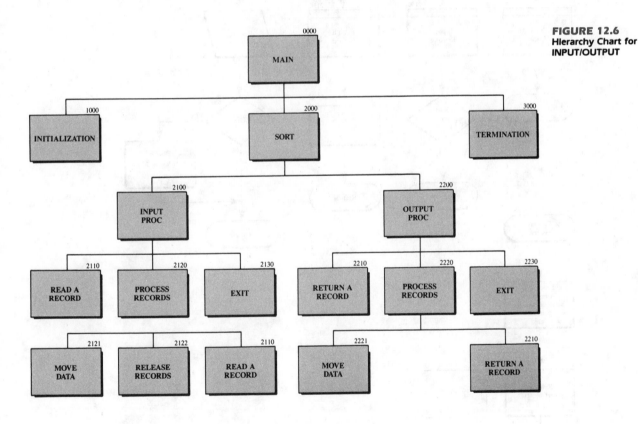

**FIGURE 12.6**
**Hierarchy Chart for INPUT/OUTPUT**

I hope this helps you understand the different sorting techniques. While I've just shown you two, the others are combinations of these. They can be derived by modifying the INPUT/OUTPUT hierarchy chart. For instance, the USING/OUTPUT hierarchy chart would not contain the 2100 modules and similarly the INPUT/GIVING would not contain the 2200 modules.

With these hierarchy charts in mind, can we develop some general logic flowcharts? Sure we can! Figure 12.7 shows the flowchart for the USING/GIVING; Figure 12.8 shows the INPUT/OUTPUT flowchart; and Figure 12.9 shows the OUTPUT PROCEDURE flowchart.

**FIGURE 12.7**
**Flowchart for USING/GIVING**

**FIGURE 12.8**
**Flowchart for INPUT PROCEDURE**

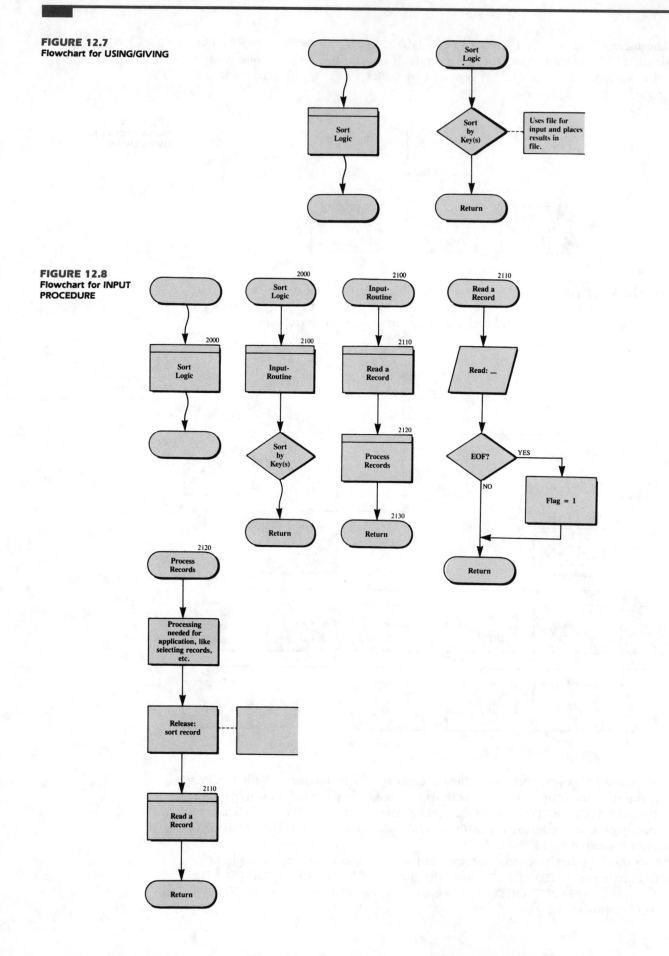

**FIGURE 12.9**
**Flowchart for OUTPUT
PROCEDURE**

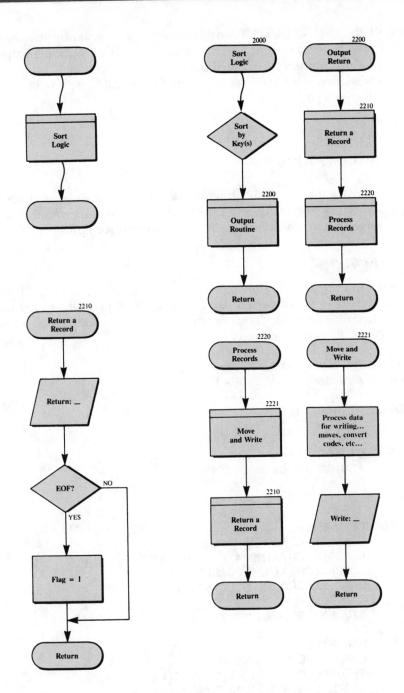

The USING/GIVING may be shown either way, (and others I'm sure). However, please note that the sort logic is performed from some module (unlabeled here). The sort logic module just shows the data files and keys. The actual logic is not shown. We will see in a later section that some believe the logic shown in the INPUT/OUTPUT flowcharts should always be shown. Then the coder may choose the appropriate COBOL technique: USING, GIVING, INPUT, OUTPUT. I lean this way also, since the complete logic is detailed separately from the COBOL source code. Either way is correct for our purposes. Check to see what technique your professor expects you to use.

Speaking of the INPUT/OUTPUT flowcharts, do you recognize it? Doesn't it look like the sequential file model or lead read technique? It is! Well, the output procedure would be more appropriately called the lead return technique. I told you that if you learned the model, you would use it over and over again. Believe me, this isn't the last place you will see it.

## CODING THE SCENARIOS

Up until now I have tried to lay some groundwork for studying the sort. I have tried to give you a framework to go from and I have tried to address for you the concepts involved. It is now time to look at the COBOL code for our scenarios.

### Code for USING/GIVING

Remember the dean's request for a file containing all students in ID order? It was the first of the four scenarios we discussed. Look back at the flowchart for that scenario (Figure 12.1). Three files are used. Therefore, how many selects and FDs do we need in this scenario? Three, also? Well, let's see.

```
            SELECT DEAN-FILE
                ASSIGN TO DA-S-DEAN.

            SELECT NEW-FILE
                ASSIGN TO DA-S-NEW.

            SELECT SORT-FILE
                ASSIGN TO DA-S-SORTWKS.
                         :
                         :

            FD  DEAN-FILE
                LABEL RECORDS ARE OMITTED
                RECORD CONTAINS 47 CHARACTERS
                BLOCK CONTAINS 100 RECORDS
                DATA RECORD IS STUDENT-RECORD.

            01  STUDENT-RECORD                    PIC X(47).

            FD  NEW-FILE
                LABEL RECORDS ARE OMITTED
                RECORD CONTAINS 47 CHARACTERS
                BLOCK CONTAINS 100 RECORDS
                DATA RECORD IS NEW-STUDENT-RECORD.

            01  NEW-STUDENT-RECORD                PIC X(47).

            SD  SORT-FILE
                DATA RECORD IS SORT-RECORD.

            01  SORT-RECORD
                03  FILLER                        PIC X(30).
                03  SORT-ID                       PIC X(9).
                03  FILLER                        PIC X(8).
                         :
                         :
```

The first two SELECTs and FDs are what you have become used to for sequential files. The corresponding FDs are also recognizable. You should note that the record and block sizes are the same. This is important, because we will be coding the sort with the USING and GIVING options.

I'm sure you noticed the third SELECT. It's for the file the sort package will use. It's not our file, but we must have a SELECT clause and an FD (file description) anyway. However, the ASSIGN clause is essentially documentation. It depends on your particular environment. Check with your professor as to your system needs. Some systems don't even require the ASSIGN! Every SELECT requires a matching FD, right? Well, almost. The SORT FILE is special. We describe the file not with an FD but with an SD for Sort File Description.

You will notice that the SORT-RECORD is not just a general record description. It contains some detail. Why? Because the sort package requires that the sort key fields referenced by the SORT verb in the PROCEDURE DIVISION *must* be described in the record associated with the SORT-FILE in the FILE SECTION. Therefore, since we are going to sort by ID, the SORT-RECORD has enough detail to locate the sort key. (It could have more.) If we had more key fields, they would also need to be specified in SORT-RECORD. Please note that we must still keep the integrity of the record size (47). Don't forget and leave off the third 03. The SORT would work, but NEW-FILE would not contain the students' codes or GPR (the last eight bytes).

Finally, we need to examine the PROCEDURE DIVISION. Since we are to provide a sorted file of all students, the USING and GIVING options are all that we need. Therefore, using the SELECTs and FD and SD, the PROCEDURE DIVISION would be as shown below.

```
PROCEDURE DIVISION.

0000-MAIN-PARA.
    PERFORM 1000-SORT-PARA.
    STOP RUN.

1000-SORT-PARA.
    SORT SORT-FILE
        ASCENDING KEY   SORT-ID
        USING   DEAN-FILE
        GIVING NEW-FILE.
```

Are you disappointed or excited? I hope excited. You just looked at the procedural code needed to sort *all* the records in DEAN-FILE into ascending ID order and put the results into a newly created file, NEW-FILE. All this with eight lines of code. Do you see why I said earlier that the USING/GIVING was the easy way of sorting?

While I have used the DEAN-FILE to illustrate the USING/GIVING scenario, it doesn't matter what the data is. If you have a sequentially-organized file and you want to create another file of all the original data, but in some different order, then the technique works.

What if 100,001 Auto Parts has an inventory file, and management wants you to create a new file, ordered by supplier? Can you see that the USING/GIVING will work? What if the original file was an accounts receivable file? A personnel file? An accounts payable file? It doesn't matter. The technique is not dependent on the type of data file. It is dependent on the file organization and the fact that all records are to be sorted and placed in another sequentially-organized file.

### Coding the USING/OUTPUT PROCEDURE Scenario

What if the dean wanted a listing or report of all students in alphabetical order? Notice that all student records are still involved in the sort, but instead of a file, a report is to be produced. Referring to our scenarios, we realize that we have a USING/OUTPUT PROCEDURE situation. This would still require a SELECT for the DEAN-FILE and SORT-FILE, but we no longer need NEW-FILE. Now we need a REPORT-FILE instead. The three SELECTs are now:

```
SELECT DEAN-FILE
     ASSIGN TO DA-S-DEAN.

SELECT SORT-FILE
     ASSIGN TO DA-S-SORTWKS.

SELECT REPORT-FILE
     ASSIGN TO DA-S-REPORT.
           .
           .
           .
```

Since we have three SELECTs, we would need the FDs and SD given below:

```
DATA DIVISION.
FILE SECTION.

FD   DEAN-FILE
     LABEL RECORDS ARE OMITTED
     RECORD CONTAINS 47 CHARACTERS
     BLOCK CONTAINS 100 RECORDS
     DATA RECORD IS STUDENT-RECORD.

01   STUDENT-RECORD                          PIC X(47).

FD   REPORT-FILE
     LABEL RECORDS ARE OMITTED
     DATA RECORD IS REPORT-RECORD.

01   REPORT-RECORD                           PIC X(133).

SD   SORT-FILE
     DATA RECORD IS SORT-RECORD.

01   SORT-RECORD
     03   SORT-NAME                          PIC X(30).
     03   FILLER                             PIC X(17).
           .
           .
           .
```

Notice that the SD for SORT-FILE is the same. However, 01 SORT-RECORD has changed. Why? Remember that the sort key field(s) must be described in the record. Since the report is required to be in alphabetic order by name, and not in order by ID, the SORT-RECORD description had to be changed.

I don't think we need to discuss the reason for applying the USING option in this problem except to say that all records are sorted. However, we do need to discuss the OUTPUT PROCEDURE. Earlier I mentioned that the OUTPUT PROCEDURE gave you more control over the data coming back from the sort package. We need this control in this problem, since we are writing a report of the sorted results. Assuming we want a nice looking, edited report, the GIVING just would not do.

Look at the OUTPUT PROCEDURE statement itself:

```
OUTPUT PROCEDURE  output-routine
```

This tells the sort package that in OUTPUT-ROUTINE you have to provide the logic/code to get the sorted records back. You do not want to use the GIVING option. You want to control the output from the sort. If you will read the OUTPUT PROCEDURE statement as if there were a PERFORM after it,

```
OUTPUT PROCEDURE  PERFORM output-routine
```

it will help you understand the control involved. That is to say it works like PERFORM output-routine, but don't code the PERFORM, or the compiler will choke, and you know what happens when the compiler chokes. . .you get error messages. Since it works like a PERFORM and the sort package requires the routines specified by the OUTPUT PROCEDURE to be a SECTION, then in order to satisfy the PERFORM, the logic needs to get to the next section.

We need to look at an example. The following PROCEDURE DIVISION statements demonstrate the OUTPUT-ROUTINE.

```
PROCEDURE DIVISION.

0000-MAIN-PARA.
    PERFORM 1000-INIT-PARA.
    PERFORM 2000-SORT-PARA.
      :
      :
    STOP RUN.

1000-INIT-PARA.
    OPEN OUTPUT REPORT-FILE.
    [Logic to write heading]

2000-SORT-PARA.
    SORT SORT-FILE
        ASCENDING KEY  SORT-NAME
        USING  DEAN-FILE
        OUTPUT PROCEDURE 2100-OUTPUT-ROUTINE.

2100-OUTPUT-ROUTINE SECTION.
2100-OUTPUT-ROUTINE-PARA.
    PERFORM 2110-RETURN-PARA.
    PERFORM 2120-WRITE-REPORT-PARA
        UNTIL NO-MORE-DATA.
    GO TO 2130-OUTPUT-ROUTINE-END-PARA.

2110-RETURN-PARA.
    RETURN SORT-FILE INTO STUDENT-RECORD-IN
        AT END
            MOVE 'NO ' TO ARE-THERE-MORE-RECORDS.
```

```
2120-WRITE-REPORT-PARA.
   [ moves ]
        :
   WRITE REPORT-RECORD FROM STUDENT-RECORD-OUT
      AFTER 2.
   PERFORM 2110-RETURN-PARA.

2130-OUTPUT-ROUTINE-END-PARA.
   EXIT.

XXXX-NEXT SECTION.
        :
        :
```

Look closely at the OUTPUT-ROUTINE logic. Recognize it? You should! It's our sequential file model. The lead read technique. . .or more appropriately, the lead return technique. That's one of the differences. To read records from the SORT-FILE a new verb is used, the **RETURN** verb. Don't let this bother you. It works just like a READ. In fact, during my lecture on this topic I first write it as a READ.

```
READ SORT-FILE INTO STUDENT-RECORD-IN
   AT END . . .
```

and then change it to a **RETURN** to make the point that they work the same way.

> **RETURN** sort-file [ **INTO** detail-record-name ]
>     AT END ···

The only other difference is (don't laugh) the **GO TO**. Why use it? Because we need it for control. If the OUTPUT-PROCEDURE acts like a PERFORM OUTPUT-ROUTINE and OUTPUT-ROUTINE is a SECTION, we need some way of getting to the next SECTION, since the range for a PERFORM section is everything up to the next section. Another way of thinking: Ignore the **GO TO**. Once the PERFORM 2120-WRITE-REPORT-PARA is satisfied, what will be done next? If you said the logic would return to the 2000-SORT-PARA, you are wrong. It will fall through to 2110-RETURN-PARA. Why? A PERFORM of a SECTION *is not* satisfied by reaching the next paragraph. Therefore, since 2110-RETURN-PARA is just a paragraph, the execution falls through. But we are finished, and we want to return to the SORT-PARA, so we need to get to the next SECTION without falling through. The only way to do this is with the **GO TO**.

The GO TO allows us to skip all paragraphs and to cause logic flow to reach the next SECTION. All we had to do was add a paragraph at the end of the SECTION to branch to. We did this with the 2130 paragraph.

Did you notice the EXIT in the 2130 paragraph? What does it do? It does nothing from an execution standpoint. It is a verb that causes nothing to happen. It is, to borrow a term from assembler, a NO OP instruction. You see, COBOL does not like lonely (empty) paragraphs. If you set up a paragraph, COBOL requires at least one entry in it. So we use **EXIT**. We could have said MOVE TOTAL TO TOTAL. That in essence does nothing and would keep COBOL happy. But why not just say EXIT? I think it's easier.

Now once we GO TO (branch to) the 2130 paragraph and do everything in it, what's next? Execution reaches the XXXX-NEXT SECTION. This will cause control to return to the SORT-PARA. That is what we wanted, and we finally caused it.

## Coding the INPUT PROCEDURE/GIVING Scenario

Yet another situation would cause you to use the third scenario. Assume the department head of Information Systems (IS) requested his or her own file. The IS file should contain all IS students in alphabetic order. Since only a subset, IS students, of the DEAN-FILE is needed, the INPUT PROCEDURE is the appropriate technique. On the output side, though, we need only to create a NEW-FILE for the department head. Assuming he wants the same record format as the DEAN-FILE, then the GIVING option is all that we need to use. The SELECT and FD for the DEAN-FILE is still required, as well as the SELECT and SD for the SORT-FILE. However, we need a SELECT and FD for the file we will create, INFO-SYSTEMS-FILE. These are shown below.

```
        SELECT DEAN-FILE
            ASSIGN TO DA-S-DEAN.

        SELECT SORT-FILE
            ASSIGN TO DA-S-SORTWKS.

        SELECT INFO-SYSTEMS-FILE
            ASSIGN TO DA-S-INFOSYS.

                :
                :

        DATA DIVISION.
        FILE SECTION.

        FD  DEAN-FILE
            LABEL RECORDS ARE OMITTED
            RECORD CONTAINS 47 CHARACTERS
            BLOCK CONTAINS 100 RECORDS
            DATA RECORD IS STUDENT-RECORD.

        01  STUDENT-RECORD                  PIC X(47).

        FD  INFO-SYSTEMS-FILE
            LABEL RECORDS ARE OMITTED
            RECORD CONTAINS 47 CHARACTERS
            BLOCK CONTAINS 100 RECORDS
            DATA RECORD IS IS-STUDENT-RECORD.

        01  IS-STUDENT-RECORD               PIC X(47).

        SD  SORT-FILE
            DATA RECORD IS SORT-RECORD.

        01  SORT-RECORD
            03  SORT-NAME                    PIC X(30).
            03  FILLER                       PIC X(17).

                :
                :
```

Notice that the FDs for DEAN-FILE and INFO-SYSTEMS-FILE are again identical in size, blocking and format. The SORT-RECORD is also the same size and format. However, the big news here is not the FDs, but the PROCEDURE DIVISION.

```
PROCEDURE DIVISION.

0000-MAIN-PARA.
    PERFORM 1000-INIT-PARA.
    PERFORM 2000-SORT-PARA.
        :
        :
    STOP RUN.

1000-INIT-PARA.
    OPEN OUTPUT REPORT-FILE.

2000-SORT-PARA.
    SORT SORT-FILE
        ASCENDING KEY SORT-NAME
        INPUT PROCEDURE 2100-SELECT-ROUTINE
        GIVING INFO-SYSTEMS-FILE.

2100-SELECT-ROUTINE SECTION.
2100-SELECT-ROUTINE-PARA.
    PERFORM 2110-READ-PARA.
    PERFORM 2120-SELECT-STUDENTS-PARA
        UNTIL NO-MORE-DATA.
    GO TO 2130-SELECT-ROUTINE-END-PARA.

2110-READ-PARA.
    READ DEAN-FILE INTO STUDENT-RECORD-IN
        AT END
            MOVE 'NO ' TO ARE-THERE-MORE-RECORDS.

2120-SELECT-STUDENTS-PARA.
    IF  INFO-SYSTEMS-STUDENT
        RELEASE SORT-RECORD FROM STUDENT-RECORD-IN.
    PERFORM 2110-READ-PARA.

2130-SELECT-ROUTINE-END-PARA.
    EXIT.

XXXX-NEXT SECTION.
        :
        :
```

I hope you recognize the overall structure. It is the sequential file model again. The major new item is the **RELEASE** verb. You should recognize everything here, syntax and logic, except for the RELEASE. Notice the format of the RELEASE. Does it look like the WRITE? It should! In fact, it works just like WRITE. This is another place that during lecture I actually write it:

```
IF  INFO-SYSTEMS-STUDENT
    WRITE SORT-RECORD  FROM  STUDENT-RECORD-IN
```

and then change it to a **RELEASE** to illustrate that they work the same. But, writing to the SORT-FILE requires us to use the **RELEASE** verb.

RELEASE sort-record [ FROM detail-record-name ]
[ AT END ··· ]

## Coding the INPUT PROCEDURE/OUTPUT PROCEDURE Scenario

The last scenario is required if the dean has asked for a list of all honors students and the students grouped by classification within major, and listed alphabetically. Sound tough? Not with COBOL. My point here is that only students with a GPR $> = 3.25$ are to be sorted, and the results are to be written to a report. Given this fact and remembering our general scenarios, we will need to use the input and output techniques.

You have already used the INPUT PROCEDURE and the OUTPUT PROCEDURE. All that's different now is that you are using them together. The SELECTs, FDs, and SD and record description should not surprise you:

```
SELECT DEAN-FILE
    ASSIGN TO DA-S-DEAN.

SELECT SORT-FILE
    ASSIGN TO DA-S-SORTWKS.

SELECT REPORT-FILE
    ASSIGN TO DA-S-REPORT.
        :
        :

DATA DIVISION.
FILE SECTION.

FD  DEAN-FILE
    LABEL RECORDS ARE OMITTED
    RECORD CONTAINS 47 CHARACTERS
    BLOCK CONTAINS 100 RECORDS
    DATA RECORD IS STUDENT-RECORD.

01  STUDENT-RECORD                      PIC X(47).

FD  REPORT-FILE
    LABEL RECORDS ARE OMITTED
    DATA RECORD IS REPORT-RECORD.

01  REPORT-RECORD                       PIC X(47).

SD  SORT-FILE
    DATA RECORD IS SORT-RECORD.

01  SORT-RECORD
    03  SORT-NAME                        PIC X(30).
    03  FILLER                           PIC X(9).
    03  SORT-MAJOR                       PIC 9(1).
    03  SORT-CLASS                       PIC 9(1).
    03  FILLER                           PIC X(6).
        :
        :
```

Most of the PROCEDURE DIVISION should also be familiar. Both the INPUT and OUTPUT PROCEDUREs have been used before, and both are applications of our sequential file model. Take a close look at the code shown below.

```
PROCEDURE DIVISION.
    0000-MAIN-PARA.
    PERFORM 1000-INIT-PARA.
    PERFORM 2000-SORT-PARA.
        :
    STOP RUN.

    1000-INIT-PARA.
        OPEN INPUT  DEAN-FILE.
        OPEN OUTPUT REPORT-FILE.
        [Logic to write heading]

    2000-SORT-PARA.
        SORT SORT-FILE
            ASCENDING KEY    SORT-MAJOR
                             SORT-CLASS
                             SORT-NAME
            INPUT  PROCEDURE  2100-HONORS-ROUTINE
            OUTPUT PROCEDURE  2200-REPORT-ROUTINE.

    2100-HONORS-ROUTINE SECTION.
    2100-HONORS-ROUTINE-PARA.
        PERFORM 2110-READ-PARA.
        PERFORM 2120-SELECT-PARA
            UNTIL NO-MORE-DATA.
        GO TO 2130-HONORS-ROUTINE-END-PARA.

    2110-READ-PARA.
        READ DEAN-FILE INTO STUDENT-RECORD-IN
            AT END
                MOVE 'NO ' TO ARE-THERE-MORE-RECORDS.

    2120-SELECT-PARA.
        IF  GPR  >  3.25
            OR  GPR  =  3.25
            RELEASE SORT-RECORD FROM STUDENT-RECORD-IN.
        PERFORM 2110-READ-PARA.

    2130-HONORS-ROUTINE-END-PARA.
        EXIT.

    2200-REPORT-ROUTINE SECTION.
    2200-REPORT-ROUTINE-PARA.
        MOVE 'YES' TO ARE-THERE-MORE-RECORDS.
        PERFORM 2210-RETURN-PARA.
        PERFORM 2220-WRITE-REPORT-PARA
            UNTIL NO-MORE-DATA.
        GO TO 2230-OUTPUT-ROUTINE-END-PARA.

    2210-RETURN-PARA.
        RETURN SORT-FILE INTO STUDENT-RECORD-IN
            AT END
                MOVE 'NO ' TO ARE-THERE-MORE-RECORDS.
```

```
2220-WRITE-REPORT-PARA.
    [ moves from student-record-in to student-record-out ]
            :
    WRITE REPORT-RECORD FROM STUDENT-RECORD-OUT
        AFTER 2.
    PERFORM 2210-RETURN-PARA.

2230-OUTPUT-ROUTINE-END-PARA.
    EXIT.

XXXX-NEXT SECTION.
    :
    :
```

Now that you have looked at the code, I'm sure you recognized it. However, I should point out one little change in case you missed it. Look at the 2130 paragraph. It is not followed by a XXXX-NEXT SECTION. We don't need it. Since the OUTPUT PROCEDURE follows and it is a SECTION, we don't need the extra NEXT SECTION.

## TIP

**Don't forget to reinitialize the EOF indicator when you use the INPUT/OUTPUT procedures together.**

## SOME OTHER THOUGHTS

I have been talking to you about four scenarios that you can use as a framework for thinking about the COBOL sort. However, don't forget that other problems might occur that seem different. Other philosophies about using the different techniques do exist. If you understand the reasons for using each technique, then other problems and philosophies will not bother you. You probably noticed that I did not worry about paging for any of the reports. All that is needed for paging is to include it with the other logic. It did not impact the discussion on the SORT, so I did not include it.

You probably also question the last report that included the honors students alphabetically listed by classification for each major. Wouldn't it have been nice to present the report incorporating this ordering? You're right. That's what we did in the control-break logic chapter.

### Sorting on Calculated Information

Often we need to sort on a data value that is not part of the record, but may be calculated. For instance, assume that DEAN-FILE contained TOTAL-HOURS-TAKEN and TOTAL-GRADE-POINTS instead of GPR. If we wanted to sort by GPR, we would have to calculate it first and add it to SORT-RECORD.

Let's assume that our DEAN-FILE FD and SORT-FILE SD are as shown below:

```
FD   DEAN-FILE
     LABEL RECORDS ARE OMITTED
     RECORD CONTAINS 49 CHARACTERS
     BLOCK CONTAINS 100 RECORDS
     DATA RECORD IS STUDENT-RECORD.
01   STUDENT-RECORD                    PIC X(49).

SD   SORT-FILE
     DATA RECORD IS SORT-RECORD.
01   SORT-RECORD.
     03   FILLER                       PIC X(42).
     03   SORT-TOTAL-HOURS-TAKEN       PIC 9(3).
     03   SORT-TOTAL-GRADE-POINTS      PIC 9(4).
     03   SORT-GPR                     PIC 9V9(4).
```

Most of the code is familiar. However, notice that the DEAN-FILE now has 49 characters (second format in Data File A) to accommodate the TOTAL-GRADE-POINTS and TOTAL-HOURS-TAKEN fields. The SORT-FILE also reflects this change, but it also has a SORT-GPR field. This is needed since the sorting is to be done on GPR. Now let's look at the procedure division code required.

```
PROCEDURE DIVISION.

0000-MAIN-PARA.
     PERFORM 1000-INIT-PARA.
     PERFORM 2000-SORT-PARA.

          .
          .

1000-INIT-PARA.
     OPEN INPUT DEAN-FILE.

          .

2000-SORT-PARA.
     SORT SORT-FILE
          ASCENDING KEY SORT-GPR
          INPUT PROCEDURE 2100-CALCULATE-ROUTINE
          .
          .

2100-CALCULATE-ROUTINE SECTION.

2100-CALCULATE-ROUTINE-PARA.
     PERFORM 2110-READ-PARA.
     PERFORM 2120-CALC-AND-WRITE-PARA
          UNTIL NO-MORE-RECORDS.

2110-READ-PARA.
     READ DEAN-FILE INTO STUDENT-RECORD-IN
          AT END
               MOVE 'NO'  TO ARE-THERE-MORE-RECORDS.
```

```
2120-CALC-AND-WRITE-PARA.
    COMPUTE GPR = TOTAL-GRADE-POINTS/TOTAL-HOURS-TAKEN.
    MOVE STUDENT-RECORD-IN TO SORT-RECORD.
    MOVE GPR TO SORT-GPR.
    RELEASE SORT-RECORD.                    <----- This form will be
    PERFORM 2110-READ-PARA.                        explained later.
```

Notice that in 2120 paragraph the GPR is calculated and then moved to the SORT-RECORD. The MOVE is done after the rest of the fields are moved with a group MOVE. Then the record is released. Don't move the GPR to SORT-GPR and then say RELEASE-SORT-RECORD FROM STUDENT-RECORD-IN. This will destroy SORT-GPR's contents, since the FROM is essentially a group MOVE. That would mean the larger SORT-RECORD would be filled with blanks.

### The Case of Different Format

Assume that the information systems (IS) department head still wants the IS student file, but he wants to eliminate the major field, since the file contains only IS majors. Or what if a listing of all students by major was requested? However, the order requested is Information Systems, Accounting, Finance, Marketing, and Management. You cannot sort the major codes (1, 2, 3, 4, 5) to get that order without first manipulating the data.

In the first case, eliminating the major code, the record size will change from 47 to 46 characters. Therefore, the GIVING technique cannot be used. So the OUTPUT PROCEDURE is needed. However, we may still use the INPUT PROCEDURE. Looking back at the INPUT/GIVING example, the coding is still correct except for a few changes.

```
FD  INFO-SYSTEMS-FILE
    LABEL RECORDS ARE OMITTED
    RECORD CONTAINS 46 CHARACTERS               <--- Notice change
    BLOCK CONTAINS 100 RECORDS                       from 47
    DATA RECORD IS IS-STUDENT-RECORD.
01  IS-STUDENT-RECORD            PIC X(46).     <--- Notice change
                                                     from 47
          .
          .


PROCEDURE DIVISION.

0000-MAIN-PARA.
    PERFORM 1000-INIT-PARA.
    PERFORM 2000-SORT-PARA.

          .
          .

    STOP RUN.

1000-INIT-PARA.
    OPEN INPUT   DEAN-FILE.
    OPEN OUTPUT  INFO-SYSTEMS-FILE.             <--- Notice change

2000-SORT-PARA.
    SORT SORT-FILE
        ASCENDING KEY  SORT-NAME
        INPUT  PROCEDURE 2100-SELECT-ROUTINE
        OUTPUT PROCEDURE 2200-WRITE-IS-FILE-ROUTINE. <--- Notice
                                                          change
```

```
2200-WRITE-IS-FILE-ROUTINE SECTION.
2200-WRITE-IS-FILE-ROUTINE-PARA.
    PERFORM 2210-RETURN-PARA.
    PERFORM 2220-WRITE-RECORD-PARA
        UNTIL NO-MORE-SORTED-RECORDS.
    GO TO 2230-WRITE-IS-FILE-ROUTINE-END.

2210-RETURN-PARA.
    RETURN SORT-FILE INTO STUDENT-RECORD-IN
        AT END
            MOVE 'NO ' TO ARE-THERE-MORE-SORTED-RECORDS.

2220-WRITE-RECORD-PARA.
    MOVE    NAME-IN          TO    NAME-OUT.
    MOVE    ID-IN            TO    ID-OUT.
    MOVE    CLASSIFICATION-IN TO   CLASSIFICATION-OUT.
    MOVE    SEX-IN           TO    SEX-OUT.
    MOVE    GPR-IN           TO    GPR-OUT.
    WRITE IS-STUDENT-RECORD FROM STUDENT-RECORD-OUT.
    PERFORM 2210-RETURN-PARA.

2230-WRITE-IS-FILE-ROUTINE-END.
    EXIT.

XXXX-NEXT SECTION.
    .
    .
```

NOTE: MAJOR was *not* moved to STUDENT-RECORD-OUT, since only one major was being selected for the sort.

## TIP

**If you select records on a field to create a new file, then that field is not included in the record in the new file.**

The changes should not make you uncomfortable. The FD for INFO-SYSTEMS-FILE has to change since the record size changes. Do you see that now? (I hope so.) Do you also see why I had to open the INFO-SYSTEMS-FILE? Since I actually handle the writing of the file in the OUTPUT PROCEDURE, I must open it. With the GIVING it was opened for me, but not with the OUTPUT PROCEDURE. And of course the major change, in lines of code anyway, is the OUTPUT PROCEDURE itself. It looks like our other OUTPUT PROCEDUREs. However, notice that major was not moved to the output record. Also notice that I write FROM STUDENT-RECORD-OUT. This implies that IS-STUDENT-RECORD and STUDENT-RECORD-OUT are the same size and format—46 characters. So not only was major not moved; there is no longer a field for it in the record.

### The Case of Non-Standard Order

So you see that one small change in record format/content required us to abandon the GIVING option. Let's look at the question of non-standard order—that is, sorting on a field when the requested order is neither ascending or descending. What do you do? Well, I guess you can try and talk the user into a more standard order. If that fails you, just bite the bullet and develop a code conversion to accomplish the sort. How? Well, let's look at the problem we posed earlier. How would we list the students in the following order?

| Requested Order | Major Code |
|---|---|
| Information System | 2 |
| Accounting | 1 |
| Finance | 3 |
| Marketing | 5 |
| Management | 4 |

Look at the requested order compared to the code. We cannot sort in ascending or descending order to get those results. Do you see the problem? It is not an unusual one. It happens more often than you might think.

Let's talk about a solution. First I need to recode the data for sorting purposes, don't I? If I generated a sort field and for all information systems students I moved a value of 1 into the field, and for all accounting majors I moved a 2, and so on, for all majors I would have a field to sort on that would give me the requested order. That is, I would have the following:

| Requested Order | Major Code | Generated Code |
|---|---|---|
| Information System | 2 | 1 |
| Accounting | 1 | 2 |
| Finance | 3 | 3 |
| Marketing | 5 | 4 |
| Management | 4 | 5 |

Let's look at our need from a COBOL perspective. Since we need to sort all students, we still need the SELECT and FD for DEAN-FILE. And, of course we still need the SORT-FILE. We also need a REPORT-FILE in order to write the report.

```
    SELECT DEAN-FILE
        ASSIGN TO DA-S-DEAN.

    SELECT SORT-FILE
        ASSIGN TO DA-S-SORTWKS.

    SELECT REPORT-FILE
        ASSIGN TO UT-S-REPORT.

FD  DEAN-FILE
    LABEL RECORDS ARE OMITTED
    RECORD CONTAINS 47 CHARACTERS
    BLOCK CONTAINS 100 RECORDS
    DATA RECORD IS STUDENT-RECORD.

01  STUDENT-RECORD                    PIC X(46).

FD  REPORT-FILE
    LABEL RECORDS ARE OMITTED
    DATA RECORD IS REPORT-LINE.
```

```
01    REPORT-LINE                          PIC X(133).

SD    SORT-FILE
      DATA RECORD IS SORT-RECORD.

01    SORT-RECORD.
      03    SORT-NAME                      PIC X(30).
      03    SORT-ID                        PIC X(9).
      03    SORT-MAJOR                     PIC 9(1).
      03    SORT-CLASS                     PIC 9(1).
      03    SORT-SEX                       PIC 9(1).
      03    SORT-GPR                       PIC 9(1)V9(4).
      03    SORT-REQ-ORDER                 PIC 9(1).
      :
      :
```

You probably noticed that SORT-RECORD changed.  I added a new field.  It's the field you will sort on to get the order requested.  You need the field to put the generated code into before releasing the record to the SORT.

So much for talking about it.  Let's look at the code.  I'm going to do something a little different with the sort record.  I'm going to build my records in it and not use the RELEASE. . .FROM technique.  I will also not use the RETURN. . .INTO.  Hold on and I'll show you why in a minute.

```
PROCEDURE DIVISION.

0000-MAIN-PARA.
    PERFORM 1000-INIT-PARA.
    PERFORM 2000-SORT-PARA.

1000-INIT-PARA.
    OPEN   INPUT   DEAN-FILE.
    OPEN   OUTPUT REPORT-FILE.
    [ WRITEs needed for headings ]

2000-SORT-PARA.
    SORT   SORT-FILE
        ASCENDING KEY   SORT-REQ-ORDER
        INPUT   PROCEDURE 2100-MAJOR-PROCESS-ROUTINE
        OUTPUT PROCEDURE 2200-REPORT-ROUTINE

2100-MAJOR-PROCESS-ROUTINE SECTION.
2100-MAJOR-PROCESS-ROUTINE-PARA.
    PERFORM 2110-READ-PARA.
    PERFORM 2120-CONVERT-CODE-PARA
        UNTIL NO-MORE-RECORDS.
    GO TO  2130-MAJOR-PROCESS-ROUTINE-END.

2110-READ-PARA.
    READ   DEAN-FILE INTO   STUDENT-RECORD-IN
        AT END MOVE 'NO ' TO ARE-THERE-MORE-RECORDS.
```

```
2120-CONVERT-CODE-PARA.
    IF  INFORMATION-SYSTEMS-STUDENT
        MOVE  1 TO  SORT-REQ-ORDER
    ELSE
        IF  ACCOUNTING-STUDENT
            MOVE  2 TO  SORT-REQ-ORDER
        ELSE
            IF  FINANCE-STUDENT
                MOVE  3 TO  SORT-REQ-ORDER
            ELSE
                IF  MARKETING-STUDENT
                    MOVE  4 TO  SORT-REQ-ORDER
                ELSE
                    MOVE  5 TO  SORT-REQ-ORDER.
    PERFORM 2121-MOVE-DATA-PARA.
    RELEASE SORT-RECORD.
    PERFORM 2110-READ-PARA.

2121-MOVE-DATA-PARA.
    MOVE  NAME-IN           TO  SORT-NAME.
    MOVE  ID-IN             TO  SORT-ID.
    MOVE  CLASSIFICATION-IN TO  SORT-CLASSIFICATION.
    MOVE  SEX-IN            TO  SORT-SEX.
    MOVE  GPR-IN  .         TO  SORT-GPR.

2130-MAJOR-PROCESS-ROUTINE-END.
    EXIT.

2200-REPORT-ROUTINE SECTION.
2200-REPORT-ROUTINE-PARA.
    PERFORM 2210-RETURN-PARA.
    PERFORM 2220-WRITE-REPORT-PARA
        UNTIL NO-MORE-SORTED-RECORDS.
    GO TO 2230-REPORT-ROUTINE-END-PARA.

2210-RETURN-PARA.
    RETURN SORT-FILE
        AT END  MOVE 'NO ' TO ARE-THERE-MORE-SORTED-RECORDS.

2220-WRITE-RECORD-PARA.
    MOVE  SORT-NAME           TO  NAME-OUT.
    MOVE  SORT-ID             TO  ID-OUT.
    MOVE  SORT-CLASSIFICATION TO  CLASSIFICATION-OUT.
    MOVE  SORT-SEX            TO  SEX-OUT.
    MOVE  SORT-GPR            TO  GPR-OUT.
    WRITE REPORT-LINE FROM STUDENT-RECORD-OUT
        AFTER 2.
    PERFORM 2210-RETURN-PARA.

2230-REPORT-ROUTINE-END-PARA.
    EXIT.

XXXX-NEXT SECTION.
    :
    :
```

You should recognize the overall logic used. However, there are several items to note. First, 2120 paragraph contains all the conversion logic to develop the **REQ**uested **ORDER** code for sorting purposes. You also notice that after all the data is moved, 2121 paragraph, SORT-RECORD, is RELEASEd to SORT-FILE. Look at the form:

```
RELEASE SORT-RECORD.
```

I don't say FROM some detail-record-description for two reasons: First, I moved all the data into the SORT-RECORD, so in essence the detail-record-description is my sort record. Since the data is already there, I don't need to say FROM. Second, if I had generated the SORT-REQ-ORDER value in SORT-RECORD and then said RELEASE SORT-RECORD *FROM* STUDENT-RECORD-IN, what would happen? FROM causes a group move, and since STUDENT-RECORD-IN is smaller (47 bytes) than SORT-RECORD (48 bytes), the receiving record is right filled with blanks. Oops! There goes the SORT-REQ-ORDER value. It is now a blank. Do you see that? It's not trivial, so take a look at the technique again. It was the technique used for the calculated GPR example also.

## SOME REAL-WORLD ISSUES

Now that we all understand the COBOL SORT and its features, what would you do about the COBOL SORT in the real world if you were the D.P. manager or if you were the CIO (Chief Information Officer). You have several choices:

- Do nothing . . . probably the most-used choice!
- Set a policy that requires all COBOL programs to use the USING/GIVING *in all* cases.
- Set a policy that requires all COBOL programs to use the INPUT/OUTPUT PROCEDURES *in all* cases.
- Set a policy that allows any appropriate technique.
- Set a policy that all sorting be done through system JCL. (We will look at this in a while.)

### Setting Policy

I was not being facetious when I said the most-used policy was probably no policy. Why worry about it? Let the programmers do it any way they want. I don't agree. Even though programmers are becoming more and more knowledgeable, they should not be "required" to make those decisions. This is the case if for no other reasons than standardization and maintenance. Can you imagine the maintenance of systems that have some programmers using JCL for sorting, while others just love the USING/GIVING and always use this technique? Some programmers have a special feeling for the INPUT/OUTPUT techniques and always use them, yet others just use whichever strikes their fancy at the moment.

Let's assume you are the CIO. What would you do? Would you always require USING/GIVING? Your programmers could make it work in all cases. It becomes cumbersome, however, to handle some cases. For instance, to write a report, they would first "give" a temporary file, then use the file to write the report. Why not just use the OUTPUT PROCEDURE and not have to use a temporary file? (But it works, doesn't it?)

What about allowing for the most appropriate COBOL sorting technique? This is a good policy if the appropriate techniques are identified. Something like the four scenarios could be used as guidelines. If guidelines are not used, standardization is lost and consequently maintenance will be more difficult.

If a policy of always using the INPUT/OUTPUT PROCEDURE is our choice, then at the worst we would write code that could be more easily done with the USING/GIVING options. In other words, our SELECT-PARA would simply contain a RELEASE and not an IF...RELEASE. While this solution requires more code, *all* cases can be handled. This policy is best, since the INPUT/OUTPUT PROCEDUREs are more robust.

Finally, how about using JCL? This is a popular policy, but using JCL for all cases can become difficult. In fact, handling code conversions and printing reports are not possible. However, the standard sort is very easy to handle using JCL. A policy to do sorting using JCL is good because it allows the programmer to reduce code, but it's not all gravy. If a COBOL program expects a sorted data file for it to work properly, then code would need to be added to insure that the data is correctly sorted. If this is not done, master files, reports, and other items may be incorrect.

## SORTING WITH JCL

I will not attempt to show all the JCL sort options, but I do think it is important for you to understand that JCL is a powerful tool for sorting data files. For instance, what would it take to sort the DEAN-FILE by major? The JCL discussed is for IBM-MVS environments. Other environments don't need this or any JCL.

```
SORT FIELDS=(40,1,CH,A)
```

This statement would work in environments that support TSO or editors like WYLBUR, but it could be set up as a separate job and would require the following:

```
1     //SORTJOB JOB (accounting information)
2     //SORTMAJ EXEC  PGM=SORT
3     //SORTIN    DD   DSN=USR.N007.JB.DEANFILE,DISP=SHR
4     //SORTOUT   DD   DSN=USR.N007.JB.NEWFILE,
5     //               DISP=(NEW,CATLG,DELETE),
6     //               SPACE=(CYL,(2,6)),UNIT=DISK,
7     //               DCB=(LRECL=47,BLKSIZE=4700,RECFM=FB)
8     //SYSIN     DD   *
9     //               SORT FIELDS=(40,1,CH,A)
10    //SYSPRINT  DD   SYSOUT=A
11    //SORTWK01  DD   UNIT=SYSDA,SPACE=(CYL,5)
12    //SORTWK02  DD   UNIT=SYSDA,SPACE=(CYL,5)
13    //SORTWK03  DD   UNIT=SYSDA,SPACE=(CYL,5)
```

Looks complicated, doesn't it? Well, it's really pretty straightforward. Let's take a look at one statement at a time:

| Statement Number | Function |
|---|---|
| 1 | Provides accounting information. |
| 2 | Executes the system sort/merge package called SORT. Note that SORT is an example and each system uses its own. |
| 3 | Specifies the name of the file to be sorted. |
| 4 | Specifies the name and parameters of the file that will contain the results. |
| 5–7 | More parameters of the new (sorted) file. |
| 8 | Tells the program (PGM) SORT that the following is its input. |
| 9 | The actual sort specifications. |
| 10 | The system output device, printer, is requested. |
| 11–13 | The SORTs work space. |

I should note that this JCL example is for an MVS environment for IBM operating system. You will have to check to see what your computer environment requires. However, the point is that no matter what JCL is needed, it's not as lengthy as a COBOL program.

Let's look closer at the SORT statement:

```
SORT FIELDS=(40,1,CH,A)
```

where:

40 identifies the beginning column of the sort field
1 specifies the length of the sort field in bytes
CH specifies the type of data
A specifies the order . . . Ascending or Descending

Not bad to sort the DEAN-FILE by major. What about by sex within class within major? Are you ready?

```
SORT FIELDS=(40,1,CH,A,41,1,CH,A,42,1,CH,A)
```

where:

40,1,CH,A is for MAJOR
41,1,CH,A is for CLASS
42,1,CH,A is for SEX

I don't know about you, but I like the JCL method. It's easy.

## SUMMARY

In this chapter, we looked at the topic of sorting. Most of the chapter was dedicated to using the COBOL SORT verb to accomplish the ordering of data; however, we did look briefly at other techniques such as a JCL sort.

The COBOL SORT is a verb that actually invokes a system sort/merge package. It makes sorting within a COBOL program relatively easy. It saves the programmer from having to write actual sort code. All the programmer needs to do is specify what fields are to be used as the sort keys, the source of the data, and where the results are to be placed. This is done through the SD and the sort sentence.

We also examined four scenarios: USING/GIVING, USING/OUTPUT PROCEDURE, INPUT PROCEDURE/GIVING, and INPUT PROCEDURE/OUTPUT PROCEDURE. We established some guidelines for their use, including subset of data vs. entire file, reporting vs. new file creation, and others summarized in Figure 12.10.

**FIGURE 12.10**
Summary of SORT Scenarios and Appropriate COBOL Techniques

| SITUATIONS/TECHNIQUES | USING | INPUT PROC. | GIVING | OUTPUT PROC. |
|---|---|---|---|---|
| Sort all records | ✓ | | | |
| Sort a subset | | ✓ | | |
| Sort in non-standard order | | ✓ | | |
| Create new file | | | ✓ | |
| Create new file – different format | | | | ✓ |
| Write report | | | | ✓ |

Once guidelines were presented, I discussed the important topic of setting sort policy. Together we looked at some choices, and I discussed the pros and cons. I concluded that a policy of no policy was to be avoided and that use of the INPUT/OUTPUT PROCEDURE for all cases was the most robust. However, I pointed out that other policies are workable.

Finally we examined sorting via JCL. We looked at the SORT FIELDS statement available with system editors. Sorting by submitting a full job was also presented for MVS. These techniques were presented for you to understand that there are alternatives to the COBOL SORT. Which is best? I'm not sure one is best in all cases, but by knowing that choices exist, you may be able now to use the most appropriate ones.

## SAMPLE PROGRAMS

The following are complete running COBOL programs using many of the features and techniques discussed in this Chapter. All programs use the Dean File in Data Set A.

## Single Key USING/GIVING Sort Program—Dean File Sorted on NAME

```
PP 5740-CB1 RELEASE 2.4                    IBM OS/VS COBOL  JULY  1, 1982      15.02.19  DATE OCT 25,1988


       1                      15.02.19       OCT 25,1988


    00001          IDENTIFICATION DIVISION.
    00002
    00003          PROGRAM-ID. UGSORT.
    00004          AUTHOR. FOWLER.
    00005          DATE-WRITTEN.  JULY 1988.
    00006          DATE-COMPILED. OCT 25,1988.
    00007          REMARKS.
    00008
    00009          *************************************************************
    00010          *                                                           *
    00011          *  ASSIGNMENT NUMBER                                        *
    00012          *  DATE ASSIGNED                                            *
    00013          *  DATE DUE                                                 *
    00014          *  PURPOSE:   THIS PROGRAM UTILIZES A USING GIVING SORT TO SORT *
    00015          *             THE STUDENTS IN THE DEANFILE (APPENDIX G)     *
    00016          *             ALPHABETICALLY (IN ASCENDING ORDER).          *
    00017          *                                                           *
    00018          *  INPUT FILE SPECIFICATIONS:                               *
    00019          *        CARD COLUMNS                      DESCRIPTION       *
    00020          *     --------------------------          -----------       *
    00021          *          1-30                           STUDENT'S NAME    *
    00022          *          31-47                          NOT USED IN THE SORT *
    00023          *                                         PROCEDURE         *
    00024          *************************************************************
    00025
```

```
       2         UGSORT        15.02.19       OCT 25,1988


    00027          ENVIRONMENT DIVISION.
    00028          CONFIGURATION SECTION.
    00029          SOURCE-COMPUTER. IBM.
    00030          OBJECT-COMPUTER. IBM.
    00031          SPECIAL-NAMES.    CO1 IS PAGE-TOP.
    00032
    00033          INPUT-OUTPUT SECTION.
    00034          FILE-CONTROL.
    00035
    00036              SELECT DEAN-FILE
    00037                  ASSIGN TO DA-S-DEAN.
    00038              SELECT NEW-FILE
    00039                  ASSIGN TO DA-S-NEWER.
    00040
    00041              SELECT SORT-FILE
    00042                  ASSIGN TO UT-S-SORTWKS.
    00043
```

*(continued)*

```
        3       UGSORT        15.02.19      OCT 25,1988

00045           DATA DIVISION.
00046           FILE SECTION.
00047
00048       FD  DEAN-FILE
00049           LABEL RECORDS ARE OMITTED
00050           RECORD CONTAINS 47 CHARACTERS
00051           BLOCK CONTAINS 100 RECORDS
00052           DATA RECORD IS STUDENT-RECORD.
00053       01  STUDENT-RECORD PIC X(47).
00054
00055       FD  NEW-FILE
00056           LABEL RECORDS ARE OMITTED
00057           RECORD CONTAINS 47 CHARACTERS
00058           BLOCK CONTAINS 100 RECORDS
00059           DATA RECORD IS NEW-RECORD.
00060       01  NEW-RECORD PIC X(47).
00061
00062       SD  SORT-FILE
00063           DATA RECORD IS SORT-RECORD.
00064       01  SORT-RECORD.
00065           03 SORT-NAME    PIC X(30).
00066           03 FILLER       PIC X(17).
00067
00068           WORKING-STORAGE SECTION.
00069
```

```
        4       UGSORT        15.02.19      OCT 25,1988

00072           PROCEDURE DIVISION.
00073           0000-MAIN-PARA.
00074               SORT SORT-FILE
00075                   ASCENDING KEY SORT-NAME
00076                   USING DEAN-FILE
00077                   GIVING NEW-FILE.
00078           STOP RUN.
```

*(continued)*

## Results—Dean File Sorted on NAME

```
 1.    ANDY BUENZA            00000111112127429
 2.    ANNIE MARINOS          01020304021222727
 3.    ANTONIO MARTINEZ       77333066653130000
 4.    APRIL JACKS            78787877844225649
 5.    APRIL JONES            77777777723228025
 6.    BILL ADAM              10230222044128092
 7.    BILLY BOB BARRETT      11100022214122500
 8.    BRYAN MANN             23232323231126667
 9.    C. H. FLOWER           40404040424126887
10.    CLINT SMITH            33333333323119839
11.    CLYDE FELD JR.         12983476542129057
12.    DAN ROBESON            65676567943122400
13.    DANA MILLS             90807060044227500
14.    DAVID LETTER           97867564331120000
15.    DIANE LAWERNCE         26371881852225714
16.    DON VILLANOSKI         98765432111127500
17.    EMILY LYLE             99988877711222667
18.    GEORGE COMONOS         51697242041132400
19.    GEORGE MARINAKIES      10001005551127083
20.    GEORGE RYAN            56473100912124000
21.    HOWARD PORTER          45454545411123158
22.    IRENE SMITH            00112233441220000
23.    JAMES PAPPAS           34253789153123253
24.    JANE CATES             13243546731227600
25.    JILL MATSON            01010120621228947
26.    KEN MARTINEZ           00290399234127704
27.    KEVIN MCKENN           44445555523134933
28.    LYNDA MATHER           20304050633227538
29.    MARIA SANCHEZ          50115500343232000
30.    MARIA SANTIAGO         77734577752224444
31.    MARY JO MARTINEZ       10293847524223077
32.    MARY LITTLE            39495869024231579
33.    MATHEW ALTMEN          98098098053132258
34.    MICHAEL FOWLER         55555555522138966
35.    MICHAEL RYAN           71727374721132727
36.    PEG PORTERHOUSE        12332112334229703
37.    PEGGY MARTTA           22228888554220635
38.    POLLY ANN FLOWERS      50111223444225773
39.    ROBERTO SMITH          31123009944129000
40.    ROY JOICE              10245055514135045
41.    SARA WALKER            82834756153235375
42.    SESSIE PARSONS         80818880842225106
43.    STACY PHARR            44434434424235263
44.    STEVE PARKS            90876510111238000
45.    THOMAS THOMPSON        84483993151122857
46.    THOMAS WILKINSON       12345678944137619
47.    TIA FOWLER             88888888833234943
48.    TINA MARIO             00000022243223380
49.    WAYNE HEDDER           24680864254139694
50.    ZEKE MORGAN            43435656922128947
```

*(continued)*

## Multiple Key USING/GIVING Sort Program—Dean File
## Sorted on SEX within CLASS within MAJOR

```
PP 5740-CB1 RELEASE 2.4                IBM OS/VS COBOL  JULY  1, 1982    15.09.19  DATE OCT 25,1988


    1                       15.09.19      OCT 25,1988


00001          IDENTIFICATION DIVISION.
00002
00003          PROGRAM-ID. UGSORT.
00004          AUTHOR. FOWLER.
00005          DATE-WRITTEN.  JULY 1988.
00006          DATE-COMPILED. OCT 25,1988.
00007          REMARKS.
00008
00009          ************************************************************
00010          *                                                          *
00011          *  ASSIGNMENT NUMBER                                       *
00012          *  DATE ASSIGNED                                           *
00013          *  DATE DUE                                                *
00014          *  PURPOSE:  THIS PROGRAM UTILIZES A USING/GIVING SORT TO SORT  *
00015          *            THE STUDENTS IN THE DEANFILE (APPENDIX G) BY SEX,  *
00016          *            WITHIN CLASS, WITHIN MAJOR (IN ASCENDING ORDER).   *
00017          *                                                          *
00018          *  INPUT FILE SPECIFICATIONS:                              *
00019          *       CARD COLUMNS                     DESCRIPTION       *
00020          *      ------------------------          -----------       *
00021          *           1-30                   STUDENT'S NAME          *
00022          *          31-39                   STUDENT'S ID NUMBER     *
00023          *          40-40                   MAJOR CODE              *
00024          *          41-41                   CLASS CODE              *
00025          *          42-42                   SEX CODE                *
00026          *          43-47                   GPR (TO 4 DEC. PLACES)* *
00027          *                                                          *
00028          ************************************************************
00029
```

```
    2         UGSORT          15.09.19      OCT 25,1988


00031          ENVIRONMENT DIVISION.
00032          CONFIGURATION SECTION.
00033          SOURCE-COMPUTER. IBM.
00034          OBJECT-COMPUTER. IBM.
00035          SPECIAL-NAMES.   CO1 IS PAGE-TOP.
00036
00037          INPUT-OUTPUT SECTION.
00038          FILE-CONTROL.
00039
00040              SELECT DEAN-FILE
00041                  ASSIGN TO DA-S-DEAN.
00042              SELECT NEW-FILE
00043                  ASSIGN TO DA-S-NEWER.
00044
00045              SELECT SORT-FILE
00046                  ASSIGN TO UT-S-SORTWKS.
00047
```

*(continued)*

```
     3        UGSORT        15.09.19      OCT 25,1988

00049           DATA DIVISION.
00050           FILE SECTION.
00051
00052      FD  DEAN-FILE
00053          LABEL RECORDS ARE OMITTED
00054          RECORD CONTAINS 47 CHARACTERS
00055          BLOCK CONTAINS 100 RECORDS
00056          DATA RECORD IS STUDENT-RECORD.
00057      01  STUDENT-RECORD PIC X(47).
00058
00059      FD  NEW-FILE
00060          LABEL RECORDS ARE OMITTED
00061          RECORD CONTAINS 47 CHARACTERS
00062          BLOCK CONTAINS 100 RECORDS
00063          DATA RECORD IS NEW-RECORD.
00064      01  NEW-RECORD PIC X(47).
00065
00066      SD  SORT-FILE
00067          DATA RECORD IS SORT-RECORD.
00068      01  SORT-RECORD.
00069          03 SORT-NAME   PIC X(30).
00070          03 SORT-ID     PIC X(9).
00071          03 SORT-MAJOR  PIC 9(1).
00072          03 SORT-CLASS  PIC 9(1).
00073          03 SORT-SEX    PIC 9(1).
00074          03 SORT-GPR    PIC 9(1)V9(4).
00075
00076           WORKING-STORAGE SECTION.
00077
00078
```

```
     4        UGSORT        15.09.19      OCT 25,1988

00080           PROCEDURE DIVISION.
00081           0000-MAIN-PARA.
00082              SORT SORT-FILE
00083                  ASCENDING KEY SORT-MAJOR
00084                                SORT-CLASS
00085                                SORT-SEX
00086                  USING DEAN-FILE
00087                  GIVING NEW-FILE.
00088              STOP RUN.
```

*(continued)*

## Results—Dean File Sorted on SEX within CLASS within MAJOR

```
 1.    DON VILLANOSKI         98765432111127500
 2.    HOWARD PORTER          45454545411123158
 3.    STEVE PARKS            90876510111238000
 4.    EMILY LYLE             99988877711222667
 5.    GEORGE RYAN            56473100912124000
 6.    ANDY BUENZA            00000111112127429
 7.    BILLY BOB BARRETT      11100022214122500
 8.    ROY JOICE              10245055514135045
 9.    MICHAEL RYAN           71727374721132727
10.    JILL MATSON            01010120621228947
11.    ANNIE MARINOS          01020304021222727
12.    MICHAEL FOWLER         55555555522138966
13.    ZEKE MORGAN            43435656922128947
14.    KEVIN MCKENN           44445555523134933
15.    CLINT SMITH            33333333323119839
16.    APRIL JONES            77777777723228025
17.    C. H. FLOWER           40404040424126887
18.    MARY JO MARTINEZ       10293847524223077
19.    STACY PHARR            44434434424235263
20.    MARY LITTLE            39495869024231579
21.    DAVID LETTER           97867564331120000
22.    BRYAN MANN             23232323231126667
23.    JANE CATES             13243546731227600
24.    LYNDA MATHER           20304050633227538
25.    TIA FOWLER             88888888833234943
26.    KEN MARTINEZ           00290399234127704
27.    PEG PORTERHOUSE        12332112334229703
28.    GEORGE COMONOS         51697242041132400
29.    IRENE SMITH            00112233441220000
30.    CLYDE FELD JR.         12983476542129057
31.    SESSIE PARSONS         80818880842225106
32.    DAN ROBESON            65676567943122400
33.    TINA MARIO             00000022243223380
34.    MARIA SANCHEZ          50115500343232000
35.    BILL ADAM              10230222044128092
36.    ROBERTO SMITH          31123009944129000
37.    THOMAS WILKINSON       12345678944137619
38.    DANA MILLS             90807060044227500
39.    POLLY ANN FLOWERS      50111223444225773
40.    APRIL JACKS            78787877844225649
41.    GEORGE MARINAKIES      10001005551127083
42.    THOMAS THOMPSON        84483993151122857
43.    DIANE LAWERNCE         26371881852225714
44.    MARIA SANTIAGO         77734577752224444
45.    JAMES PAPPAS           34253789153123253
46.    MATHEW ALTMEN          98098098053132258
47.    ANTONIO MARTINEZ       77333066653130000
48.    SARA WALKER            82834756153235375
49.    WAYNE HEDDER           24680864254139694
50.    PEGGY MARTTA           22228888554220635
```

*(continued)*

## Sort Program Using INPUT/OUTPUT Procedures

```
PP 5740-CB1 RELEASE 2.4                    IBM OS/VS COBOL  JULY  1, 1982      15.11.32  DATE OCT 25,1988


       1                    15.11.32      OCT 25,1988

   00001          IDENTIFICATION DIVISION.
   00002
   00003          PROGRAM-ID. IOSORT.
   00004          AUTHOR. FOWLER.
   00005          DATE-WRITTEN.  JULY 1988.
   00006          DATE-COMPILED. OCT 25,1988.
   00007          REMARKS.
   00008
   00009          ********************************************************
   00010          *                                                      *
   00011          *  ASSIGNMENT NUMBER                                   *
   00012          *  DATE ASSIGNED                                       *
   00013          *  DATE DUE                                            *
   00014          *  PURPOSE:   THIS PROGRAM UTILIZES A SORT WITH INPUT AND OUTPUT *
   00015          *             ROUTINES TO PRODUCE A PRINTED REPORT OF ALL  *
   00016          *             STUDENTS IN THE DEANFILE (APPENDIX G) THAT HAVE A  *
   00017          *             A 2.2500 GPR OR HIGHER. THESE STUDENTS ARE SORTED  *
   00018          *             BY SEX, WITHIN CLASS, WITHIN MAJOR (IN ASCENDING  *
   00019          *             ORDER).                                  *
   00020          *                                                      *
   00021          *  INPUT FILE SPECIFICATIONS:                          *
   00022          *      CARD COLUMNS                  DESCRIPTION        *
   00023          *      ------------                  -----------        *
   00024          *        1-30                        STUDENT'S NAME     *
   00025          *        31-39                       STUDENT'S ID NUMBER *
   00026          *        40-40                       MAJOR CODE         *
   00027          *        41-41                       CLASS CODE         *
   00028          *        42-42                       SEX CODE           *
   00029          *        43-47                       GPR (TO 4 DEC. PLACES)*
   00030          *                                                      *
   00031          ********************************************************
   00032
```

```
       2        IOSORT        15.11.32       OCT 25,1988

   00034          ENVIRONMENT DIVISION.
   00035          CONFIGURATION SECTION.
   00036          SOURCE-COMPUTER. IBM.
   00037          OBJECT-COMPUTER. IBM.
   00038          SPECIAL-NAMES.   C01 IS PAGE-TOP.
   00039
   00040          INPUT-OUTPUT SECTION.
   00041          FILE-CONTROL.
   00042
   00043              SELECT DEAN-FILE
   00044                  ASSIGN TO DA-S-DEAN.
   00045
   00046              SELECT REPORT-FILE
   00047                  ASSIGN TO UT-S-REPORT.
   00048
   00049              SELECT SORT-FILE
   00050                  ASSIGN TO UT-S-SORTWKS.
   00051
```

*(continued)*

```
    3         IOSORT        15.11.32      OCT 25,1988

00053           DATA DIVISION.
00054           FILE SECTION.
00055
00056           FD  DEAN-FILE
00057               LABEL RECORDS ARE OMITTED
00058               RECORD CONTAINS 47 CHARACTERS
00059               BLOCK CONTAINS 100 RECORDS
00060               DATA RECORD IS STUDENT-RECORD.
00061           01  STUDENT-RECORD PIC X(47).
00062
00063
00064           FD  REPORT-FILE
00065               LABEL RECORDS ARE OMITTED
00066               DATA RECORD IS REPORT-LINE.
00067           01  REPORT-LINE PIC X(133).
00068
00069           SD  SORT-FILE
00070               DATA RECORD IS SORT-RECORD.
00071           01  SORT-RECORD.
00072               03 SORT-NAME   PIC X(30).
00073               03 SORT-ID     PIC X(9).
00074               03 SORT-MAJOR  PIC 9(1).
00075               03 SORT-CLASS  PIC 9(1).
00076               03 SORT-SEX    PIC 9(1).
00077               03 SORT-GPR    PIC 9(1)V9(4).
00078
```

```
    4         IOSORT        15.11.32      OCT 25,1988

00080           WORKING-STORAGE SECTION.
00081
00082           01  HEADINGS.
00083               03 FILLER PIC X(13) VALUE SPACES.
00084               03 FILLER PIC X(4)  VALUE 'NAME'.
00085               03 FILLER PIC X(41) VALUE SPACES.
00086               03 FILLER PIC X(2)  VALUE 'ID'.
00087               03 FILLER PIC X(14) VALUE SPACES.
00088               03 FILLER PIC X(5)  VALUE 'MAJOR'.
00089               03 FILLER PIC X(8)  VALUE SPACES.
00090               03 FILLER PIC X(7)  VALUE 'CLASS'.
00091               03 FILLER PIC X(7)  VALUE SPACES.
00092               03 FILLER PIC X(4)  VALUE 'SEX'.
00093               03 FILLER PIC X(11) VALUE SPACES.
00094               03 FILLER PIC X(3)  VALUE 'GPR'.
00095
00096           01  STUDENT-RECORD-IN.
00097               03 NAME-IN    PIC X(30).
00098               03 ID-IN      PIC X(9).
00099               03 MAJOR-IN   PIC X(1).
00100               03 CLASS-IN   PIC X(1).
00101               03 SEX-IN     PIC X(1).
00102               03 GPR-IN     PIC 9(1)V9(4).
00103
00104           01  STUDENT-RECORD-OUT.
00105               03 FILLER     PIC X(13) VALUE SPACES.
00106               03 NAME-OUT   PIC X(30).
00107               03 FILLER     PIC X(12) VALUE SPACES.
00108               03 ID-OUT     PIC X(9).
00109               03 FILLER     PIC X(12) VALUE SPACES.
00110               03 MAJOR-OUT  PIC 9(1).
00111               03 FILLER     PIC X(12) VALUE SPACES.
00112               03 CLASS-OUT  PIC 9(1).
00113               03 FILLER     PIC X(12) VALUE SPACES.
00114               03 SEX-OUT    PIC 9(1).
00115               03 FILLER     PIC X(12) VALUE SPACES.
00116               03 GPR-OUT    PIC 9(1).9(4).
00117               03 FILLER     PIC X(12) VALUE SPACES.
00118
00119           01  BLANK-LINE.
00120               03 FILLER     PIC X(133) VALUE SPACES.
00121
00122           01  ARE-THERE-MORE-RECORDS        PIC X(3) VALUE 'YES'.
00123               88 MORE-RECORDS                        VALUE 'YES'.
00124               88 NO-MORE-RECORDS                      VALUE 'NO'.
00125
00126           01  ARE-THERE-MORE-SORTED-RECORDS PIC X(3) VALUE 'YES'.
00127               88 MORE-SORTED-RECORDS                  VALUE 'YES'.
00128               88 NO-MORE-SORTED-RECORDS               VALUE 'NO'.
00129
```

*(continued)*

```
        5        IOSORT        15.11.32      OCT 25,1988

  00131          PROCEDURE DIVISION.
  00132          0000-MAIN-PARA.
  00133              PERFORM 1000-INIT-PARA.
  00134              PERFORM 2000-SORT-PARA.
  00135              PERFORM 4000-TERMINATION-PARA.
  00136              STOP RUN.
  00137
  00138          1000-INIT-PARA.
  00139              OPEN INPUT DEAN-FILE.
  00140              OPEN OUTPUT REPORT-FILE.
  00141              WRITE REPORT-LINE FROM HEADINGS
  00142                  AFTER PAGE-TOP.
  00143              WRITE REPORT-LINE FROM BLANK-LINE
  00144                  AFTER 1.
  00145
  00146          2000-SORT-PARA.
  00147              SORT SORT-FILE
  00148                  ASCENDING KEY SORT-MAJOR
  00149                              SORT-CLASS
  00150                              SORT-SEX
  00151                  INPUT  PROCEDURE 2100-ALL-STUDENTS-ROUTINE
  00152                  OUTPUT PROCEDURE 2200-REPORT-ROUTINE.
  00153
  00154          2100-ALL-STUDENTS-ROUTINE SECTION.
  00155          2100-ALL-STUDENTS-PARA.
  00156              PERFORM 2110-READ-PARA.
  00157              PERFORM 2120-SELECT-PARA
  00158                  UNTIL NO-MORE-RECORDS.
  00159              GO TO 2130-ALL-STUDENTS-END-PARA.
  00160
  00161          2110-READ-PARA.
  00162              READ DEAN-FILE INTO STUDENT-RECORD-IN
  00163                  AT END MOVE 'NO' TO ARE-THERE-MORE-RECORDS.
  00164
  00165          *************************************************************
  00166          *  NOTE THAT IN THE FOLLOWING PARAGRAPH, ONLY THE STUDENT   *
  00167          *  RECORDS THAT HAVE A 2.2500 GPR OR BETTER ARE RELEASED    *
  00168          *  TO THE SORT FILE.                                        *
  00169          *                                                          *
  00170          *************************************************************
  00171
  00172          2120-SELECT-PARA.
  00173              IF GPR-IN IS GREATER THAN 2.2500
  00174                  RELEASE SORT-RECORD FROM STUDENT-RECORD-IN.
  00175              PERFORM 2110-READ-PARA.
  00176
  00177          2130-ALL-STUDENTS-END-PARA.
  00178              EXIT.
  00179
```

*(continued)*

```
     6          IOSORT          15.11.32        OCT 25,1988

00181          2200-REPORT-ROUTINE SECTION.
00182          2200-REPORT-ROUTINE-PARA.
00183              PERFORM 2210-RETURN-PARA.
00184              PERFORM 2220-WRITE-REPORT-PARA
00185                  UNTIL NO-MORE-SORTED-RECORDS.
00186              GO TO 2230-REPORT-ROUTINE-END-PARA.
00187
00188          2210-RETURN-PARA.
00189              RETURN SORT-FILE INTO STUDENT-RECORD-IN
00190                  AT END MOVE 'NO' TO ARE-THERE-MORE-SORTED-RECORDS.
00191
00192          2220-WRITE-REPORT-PARA.
00193              MOVE NAME-IN TO NAME-OUT.
00194              MOVE ID-IN TO ID-OUT.
00195              MOVE MAJOR-IN TO MAJOR-OUT.
00196              MOVE CLASS-IN TO CLASS-OUT.
00197              MOVE SEX-IN TO SEX-OUT.
00198              MOVE GPR-IN TO GPR-OUT.
00199              WRITE REPORT-LINE FROM STUDENT-RECORD-OUT
00200                  AFTER 1.
00201              PERFORM 2210-RETURN-PARA.
00202
00203          2230-REPORT-ROUTINE-END-PARA.
00204              EXIT.
00205
00206          4000-TERMINATION SECTION.
00207          4000-TERMINATION-PARA.
00208              CLOSE DEAN-FILE.
00209              CLOSE REPORT-FILE.
```

| NAME | ID | MAJOR | CLASS | SEX | GPR |
|------|-----|-------|-------|-----|------|
| DON VILLANOSKI | 987654321 | 1 | 1 | 1 | 2.7500 |
| HOWARD PORTER | 454545454 | 1 | 1 | 1 | 2.3158 |
| STEVE PARKS | 908765101 | 1 | 1 | 2 | 3.8000 |
| EMILY LYLE | 999888777 | 1 | 1 | 2 | 2.2667 |
| GEORGE RYAN | 564731009 | 1 | 2 | 1 | 2.4000 |
| ANDY BUENZA | 000001111 | 1 | 2 | 1 | 2.7429 |
| ROY JOICE | 102450555 | 1 | 4 | 1 | 3.5045 |
| MICHAEL RYAN | 717273747 | 2 | 1 | 1 | 3.2727 |
| JILL MATSON | 010101206 | 2 | 1 | 2 | 2.8947 |
| ANNIE MARINOS | 010203040 | 2 | 1 | 2 | 2.2727 |
| MICHAEL FOWLER | 555555555 | 2 | 2 | 1 | 3.8966 |
| ZEKE MORGAN | 434356569 | 2 | 2 | 1 | 2.8947 |
| KEVIN MCKENN | 444455555 | 2 | 3 | 1 | 3.4933 |
| APRIL JONES | 777777777 | 2 | 3 | 2 | 2.8025 |
| C. H. FLOWER | 404040404 | 2 | 4 | 1 | 2.6887 |
| MARY JO MARTINEZ | 102938475 | 2 | 4 | 2 | 2.3077 |
| STACY PHARR | 444344344 | 2 | 4 | 2 | 3.5263 |
| MARY LITTLE | 394958690 | 2 | 4 | 2 | 3.1579 |
| BRYAN MANN | 232323232 | 3 | 1 | 1 | 2.6667 |
| JANE CATES | 132435467 | 3 | 1 | 2 | 2.7600 |
| TIA FOWLER | 888888888 | 3 | 3 | 2 | 3.4943 |
| LYNDA MATHER | 203040506 | 3 | 3 | 2 | 2.7538 |
| KEN MARTINEZ | 002903992 | 3 | 4 | 1 | 2.7704 |
| PEG PORTERHOUSE | 123321123 | 3 | 4 | 2 | 2.9703 |
| GEORGE COMONOS | 516972420 | 4 | 1 | 1 | 3.2400 |
| CLYDE FELD JR. | 129834765 | 4 | 2 | 1 | 2.9057 |
| SESSIE PARSONS | 808188808 | 4 | 2 | 2 | 2.5106 |
| TINA MARIO | 000000222 | 4 | 3 | 2 | 2.3380 |
| MARIA SANCHEZ | 501155003 | 4 | 3 | 2 | 3.2000 |
| THOMAS WILKINSON | 123456789 | 4 | 4 | 1 | 3.7619 |
| BILL ADAM | 102302220 | 4 | 4 | 1 | 2.8092 |
| ROBERTO SMITH | 311230099 | 4 | 4 | 1 | 2.9000 |
| APRIL JACKS | 787878778 | 4 | 4 | 2 | 2.5649 |
| DANA MILLS | 908070600 | 4 | 4 | 2 | 2.7500 |
| POLLY ANN FLOWERS | 501112234 | 4 | 4 | 2 | 2.5773 |
| GEORGE MARINAKIES | 100010055 | 5 | 1 | 1 | 2.7083 |
| THOMAS THOMPSON | 844839931 | 5 | 1 | 1 | 2.2857 |
| DIANE LAWERNCE | 263718818 | 5 | 2 | 2 | 2.5714 |
| MARIA SANTIAGO | 777345777 | 5 | 2 | 2 | 2.4444 |
| JAMES PAPPAS | 342537891 | 5 | 3 | 1 | 2.3253 |
| MATHEW ALTMEN | 980980980 | 5 | 3 | 1 | 3.2258 |
| ANTONIO MARTINEZ | 773330666 | 5 | 3 | 1 | 3.0000 |
| SARA WALKER | 828347561 | 5 | 3 | 2 | 3.5375 |
| WAYNE HEDDER | 246808642 | 5 | 4 | 1 | 3.9694 |

## EXERCISES

### Chapter Review Questions

1. Which of the following statements is a reason for sorting?
   a. Easier to code program
   b. Better organized reports
   c. More understandable reports
   d. Program is easier to maintain
   e. Both b and c

2. The file name specified by the SORT:
   a. Is defined by an FD
   b. Is defined by an SD
   c. Must be opened before the sort is executed
   d. Must be blocked
   e. None of the above

3. A program to sort all the records of one file and place them in another file would best use:
   a. The input/output procedure
   b. The using/giving procedure
   c. The using/output procedure
   d. The input/giving procedure
   e. None of the above

4. The key fields specified with the ASCENDING or DESCENDING KEY clauses must be defined:
   a. In the FILE SECTION
   b. In the WORKING-STORAGE SECTION
   c. In the SORT SECTION
   d. In the order listed
   e. Both b and d

5. The statement: ASCENDING KEY-1 KEY-2 KEY-3 would result in:
   a. The data being sorted using Key-3 as the major key
   b. The data being sorted using Key-1 as the minor key
   c. The data being sorted using Key-2 as the minor key
   d. Can not tell without the D-R-D to see order of data fields
   e. None of the above

6. The file specified by the USING option in COBOL '74 must be:
   a. Sequentially organized
   b. Opened before the sort is executed
   c. Closed before the sort is executed
   d. A disk file
   e. Both a and c are true

7. The input procedure:
   a. Must specify a section name
   b. Must specify a paragraph name
   c. Executes like a perform
   d. Executes like a read
   e. Both a and c are true

8. The INPUT and OUTPUT PROCEDUREs are a form of the sequential file model.
   a. True
   b. False

9. The COBOL verb used with the sort to write records to the SORT FILE is:
   a. WRITE
   b. SORT-WRITE
   c. RELEASE
   d. RETURN
   e. None of the above

10. The COBOL verb used with the SORT to read records from the SORT FILE is:
    a. WRITE
    b. SORT-READ
    c. RELEASE
    d. RETURN
    e. None of the above

11. Since the INPUT PROCEDURE specifies a section, we must use which COBOL verb to skip to the end of the section when finished?
    a. SKIP TO
    b. PERFORM
    c. GO TO
    d. EXIT TO
    e. None of the above

12. In order to sort a file using the COBOL SORT verb, the source data file to be sorted must contain all key fields.
    a. True
    b. False

13. Sorting a file in some nonstandard order would:
    a. Require generating a coded field for sorting
    b. Have to be done with JCL
    c. Require the USING option
    d. Require a nested SORT
    e. None of the above

14. Sorting with the USING/GIVING options:
    a. Requires all three files to be the same size
    b. Requires all three files to be blocked the same
    c. Requires the record formats for the sort file and the using file to be the same
    d. Both a and c
    e. None of the above

15. The sort policy that is most robust would be to use:
    a. USING/GIVING for all sorts
    b. INPUT/OUTPUT for all sorts
    c. JCL for all sorts
    d. USING/OUTPUT for all sorts
    e. INPUT/GIVING for all sorts

16. The system statement to sort records in descending order by description, which is in columns 25–40, would be:

   a. SORT FIELDS = (16,25,D,CH)
   b. SORT FIELDS = (25,40,CH,D)
   c. SORT FIELDS = (25,16,CH,D)
   d. SORT FIELDS = (40,16,CH,A)
   e. None of the above

## Discussion Questions

1. Briefly contrast the using and input procedures.
2. Explain what characteristic would determine the use of the four sort scenarios.
3. Briefly explain the function and need for the EXIT verb.
4. Briefly explain the relationship of the sort keys specified with the sort and the D-R-D associated with the SD.
5. Explain what would need to be done to sort by a field that must be calculated.
6. Assume that in your first job after graduating, you discovered that there was no policy on sorting. For each of the policies mentioned in this chapter, defend them as appropriate for your company.

## Practice Problems

1. Write the SELECT, SD and 01, and COBOL SORT statement to sort the Personnel File, Data File B, by name within department within store.
2. Write the SELECT, SD and 01, and COBOL SORT statement to sort the Inventory File, Data File C, by total item cost.
3. Write a general SORT statement to sort two keys in ascending order, a third key in descending order and a fourth in ascending order.
4. Write the PROCEDURE DIVISION to SORT the Inventory File in Data File C, in ascending order by item number and place the results into a new file called Sorted-Inv- File.
5. Write the single statement to sort the Inventory file using the SORT FIELDS statement. The file should be sorted by description within buyer within supplier all in ascending order.

## Programming Projects

The following assignments rely on the data dictionary, library elements and data sets found in the Project Sets Section of your text.

1. Do the Sort Assignment for the Project Management System in Project A.
2. Do the Sort Assignment for the Employee System in Project B.

# MASTER FILE – TRANSACTION FILE PROCESSING

**C H A P T E R**

**13**

**OBJECTIVES** The major objective of this chapter is to examine the area of master file-transaction file processing. We will look at the concept and logic of processing a set of transactions against a sequential master file.

This kind of application is very important in business. It is easily handled with COBOL. It deals with systems classified as batch systems. We will first consider a particular class of transactions, those used to update a master file. Then we will look at a second particular class of transactions, those used to maintain a master file.

During our journey through these applications, we will also study some programming techniques and concepts. We will pay particular attention to end-of-file processing and the need for setting policies pertaining to updating and maintenance, along with its impact on system design. We will also study and use some new COBOL words.

## TOPICS

- updating a master file
- transaction processing
- maintaining a master file
- the need for record order
- the key field

- end-of-file processing; using the AND, using the OR
- batch systems
- setting policy for the system

## KEY WORDS

- batch
- update
- maintenance
- transaction
- master
- AND/OR

- key field
- ordered
- HIGH VALUES
- LOW VALUES
- delete, add, change policy

## THE PROBLEM

The setting for this chapter, batch processing systems, is often found in business. A batch processing system collects transactions in a sequential file and processes them at some time other than when they occurred, say after five o'clock in the day or over the weekend.

### Transaction File

A transaction file is a set of records containing information about the occurrence of some activity; that is, a receipt of goods or a sale of goods, or a change in description of some item (for instance, fur coat to mink coat).

### Master File

The transactions are processed against a master file. This is a collection of records that contain information about a particular element of the business. A file that contains information about employees would be the employee master file; a file that contains information about all inventory items would be the inventory master file, and so on.

Let's look at a particular problem that will allow us to study master file-transaction file processing in detail. Assume we have the inventory master file whose record format is given in Data File C. Now assume we want to design a system that includes the following programs:

> Data validation
> Update
> Maintenance
> Report generation

The system flowchart is shown in Figure 13.1.

All files are sequential, and the update and maintenance functions have been placed into separate programs. The system flowchart is shown in Figure 13.1.

### Updating the Master File

Let's first concentrate on the update program; then we will turn our attention to the maintenance program.

As you can tell, I make a distinction between update and maintenance. Update involves that class of transactions that are generated by doing business. Examples are deposits and withdrawals from bank accounts and debits and credits to a chart of accounts, and so on.

The transactions that are used to do file maintenance are not directly related to doing business. Changing the address on an employee's record, changing the supplier's name on an inventory record and deleting or adding a master record, no matter what type of application, are all examples of transactions used for file maintenance.

What type of transactions will be processed by the update program? Well, we will have only two types of update transactions for our discussions, receipts of goods and sales of goods. During processing we will be updating the appropriate master records. We will also write a transaction log and report all transactions that are wrong.

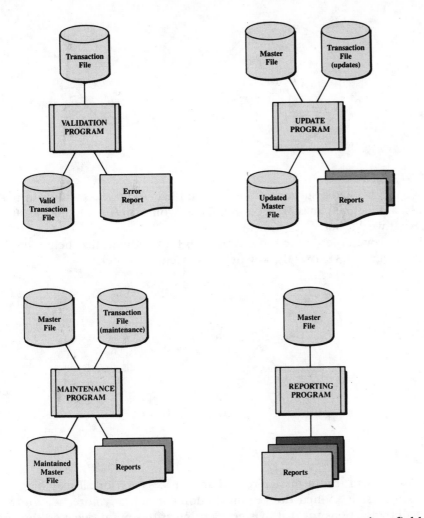

**FIGURE 13.1**
System Flowchart for
Inventory System

Now, how do we match a transaction to a master? We use a key field that uniquely identifies the master record. In our problem the item number will be the key. When we match the item number on the inventory master record with the item number on the inventory transaction record, we can then process the transaction, either a receipt or a sale. We need a code to tell us which to do, and, of course we need the quantity of the transaction. All of this requires us to have the following data in our transaction record:

| Column | Description | Type |
|--------|-------------|------|
| 1–6 | Item Number | X |
| 7 | Transaction Code | X |
| 8–10 | Quantity | 9 |

**A Case for Ordering.**     Before we go on, let me ask you something. Does the order of our master file and transaction file matter? Should they be in any specific sequence? Let's examine this issue. Assume that Figure 13.2 depicts the key field order of the respective files.

What logic process could be used to update the file? Well, we could read a master record, read each record in the transaction file to find all matches to the master record and then repeat this action for each master. In our example that means we would read the entire transaction file six times—that's 36 (6 × 6) READs. Let's examine this further.

**FIGURE 13.2**
Files in Key Field Order

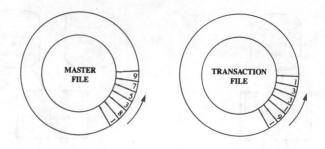

What if we had a successful business and had 1,000 transactions in this batch to process against 500 master records? That would mean 500,000 (500 × 1,000) READs. It works, but. . . .

What if we ordered the records in both files? Would that help any? You bet it would! Figure 13.3 shows the key fields in ascending order.

**FIGURE 13.3**
Ordered Master and
Transaction Files

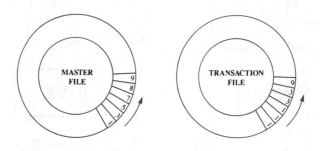

Now we can read a master record and process any or all matching transaction records against it. When the key fields don't match anymore, we know we have found all transactions for that master. Starting at this point, we read the next master record and continue with the processing. We end up having read each file just once. That's nice, isn't it?

In our first example, that means 12 READs (6 masters and 6 transactions) instead of 36. What about our 500,000 READs example? Well, we would read each record once; that means a total of 1500 READs (500 masters and 1000 transactions) instead of 500,000 READs! Therefore, I'm going to assume the master file and transaction file are sorted into ascending order based on the item number.

## TIP

**Do not confuse sequentially-organized files with sorted files. They may or may not be ordered.**

### The Three Cases

We agree on the need for ordered keys. Now what can we generalize about the processing? Well, we will be comparing the item numbers, and one of three things is possible:

master item number = transaction item number
master item number < transaction item number
master item number > transaction item number

**Master = Transaction.**     When the keys are equal, we process the current transaction and then read the next transaction. Using our example, we would read the first master, item number 1, and the first transaction, item number 1. They match, so we process the transaction. Then we would read the second transaction. It also has an item number of 1, so we would process it and then read the third transaction. Again, it is an item number of 1, so we would process it and then read the fourth transaction. The item numbers are not equal, so we would be finished with the current (first) master.

**Master < Transaction.**     With the reading of the fourth transaction record, we would have a master < transaction situation. Since this means we no longer have a transaction key that matches the current master key, we would write the current master record to the updated master file and be finished with it. Then, we would read the next master, item number 3.

The second master record key of 3 matches the transaction record key. This would cause us to process the transaction and read the next (fifth) transaction. The fifth transaction also matches the current master record key, so we would process it.

You can see that those two situations will continue to repeat themselves until the end of file is reached for one of the files or an error occurs. Let's look at the error situation first.

**Master > Transaction.**     When the master record key is greater than the transaction record key, an error has occurred. How? Let's demonstrate how by adding a transaction with an item number of 4 to our file. I've shown this in Figure 13.4.

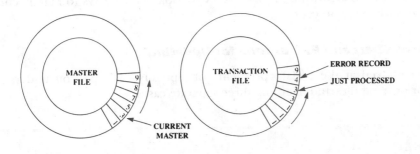

**FIGURE 13.4**
**Adding Transaction Record with Key 4**

Assume we currently have the master record with an item number of 3 and have just processed the second transaction record containing an item number of 3. Now we read the next transaction record, and the master record key is less than the transaction record key. Using our rule, we would write the updated master record, item number 3, and read the next master record, item number 5. So we now have a master record key of 5 and a transaction record key of 4. Oops! That's a master > transaction. Since both files are in ascending order, once we read a master record item number of 5, there is no way to have a matching transaction record item number of 4.

So we report the transaction as an error and read the next transaction record. This gets us back into our normal processing.

## TIP

Note that the error case would be master < transaction for files in descending order.

What caused this problem? Two possibilities come to mind: data entry mistake or the operator ran the update program in the system before running the maintenance program.

Who is at fault? In the first case, bad data should be picked up by the data validation program. Either the program has a logic problem, or data validation wasn't run.

In the second case, the operator should have had system run instructions/documentation to tell him which program to run first. Either the run instructions did not exist or they were not followed.

In any case the errors are captured and reported by the program. Now you see why we need to code for possible errors even if data has supposedly been validated.

That covers the three cases, equal, less than and greater than relationships. I've summarized them below.

| Case | Actions |
|---|---|
| 1. master key = transaction key | process transaction, read next transaction |
| 2. master key < transaction key | write current master to updated file, read next master |
| 3. master key > transaction key | report transaction as error, read next transaction |

The only thing I've left hanging is the end-of-file processing. I'll come back to it, since it is a special algorithm. In fact, we will look at two ways to handle end-of-file processing when we do get to it.

### Hierarchy Chart and Pseudocode for Updating

We have looked at the update problem conceptually. I hope you understand the need for ordered files and handling three separate cases.

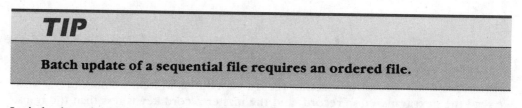

**TIP**

**Batch update of a sequential file requires an ordered file.**

Let's look at the hierarchy chart for the problem solution in Figure 13.5 and the corresponding pseudocode.

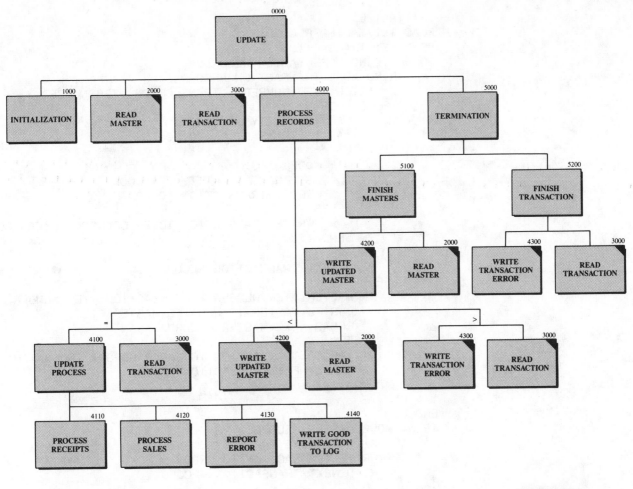

**FIGURE 13.5**
Hierarchy Chart for
Sequential File Update

```
INITIALIZE
READ 1st MASTER RECORD
READ 1ST TRANSACTION RECORD
DO UNTIL NO MORE MASTER RECORDS
     OR NO MORE TRANSACTION RECORDS
     IF MASTER ITEM NUMBER = TRANSACTION ITEM NUMBER
         IF KODE = 'R'
              ADD QUANTITY TO QOH
              WRITE TRANSACTION TO LOG
         ELSE
              IF KODE = 'S'
                   SUBTRACT QUANTITY FROM QOH
                   WRITE TRANSACTION TO LOG
              ELSE
                   WRITE TRANSACTION TO ERROR REPORT (BAD CODE)
              END-IF
         END-IF
         READ NEXT TRANSACTION RECORD
     ELSE
         IF MASTER ITEM NUMBER < TRANSACTION ITEM NUMBER
              WRITE MASTER TO UPDATED MASTER FILE
              READ NEXT MASTER RECORD
         ELSE
              WRITE TRANSACTION TO ERROR REPORT (NO MATCH)
              READ NEXT TRANSACTION RECORD
         END-IF
     END-IF
END-DO
IF NO MORE MASTER RECORDS
     DO UNTIL NO MORE TRANSACTION RECORDS
          WRITE TRANSACTION TO ERROR REPORT (NO MATCH)
          READ NEXT TRANSACTION RECORD
     END-DO
ELSE
     DO UNTIL NO MORE MASTER RECORDS
          WRITE MASTER TO UPDATED MASTER FILE
          READ NEXT MASTER RECORD
     END-DO
END-IF
CLOSE FILES
```

Notice how I've shown the three cases in the hierarchy chart. The three process cases are depicted as we discussed conceptually earlier. Now if you'll look at the pseudocode, you'll see the same design. Since pseudocode involves a sequence of instructions, I had to make a choice for my end-of-file processing. As you can see I used the OR structure. (Don't let it confuse you. I'll discuss it in a moment.)

Continuing our examination of the pseudocode, do you see our old friend the sequential file model? It's there. The only difference is that it incorporates a double lead read technique, one for each sequential file.

### COBOL Code for Update Logic

Well, it's time to convert all this wonderful design into COBOL code. Let's do that by starting with the JCL, SELECT and FDs for the update program.

## JCL, SELECT, FD

```
//GO.MASTER   DD DSN=USR.S070.MR.MASTFILE . . .
//GO.TRANS    DD DSN=USR.S070.MR.TRANFILE . . .
//GO.UPDATED  DD DSN=USR.S070.MR.UPDTFILE,
//    DISP=(NEW,CATLG,DELETE) . . .
//GO.LOGRPT   DD DCB= . . .
//GO.ERRRPT   DD DCB= . . .


        SELECT MASTER-INVENTORY-FILE    ASSIGN TO DA-S-MASTER.
        SELECT TRANSACTION-FILE         ASSIGN TO DA-S-TRANS.
        SELECT UPDATED-INVENTORY-FILE   ASSIGN TO DA-S-UPDATED.
        SELECT LOG-REPORT-FILE          ASSIGN TO UT-S-LOGRPT.
        SELECT ERROR-REPORT-FILE        ASSIGN TO UT-S-ERRRPT.


DATA DIVISION.

FILE SECTION.

FD  MASTER-INVENTORY-FILE
    LABEL RECORDS ARE OMITTED
    RECORD CONTAINS 50 CHARACTERS
    BLOCK CONTAINS 100 RECORDS
    DATA RECORD IS INVENTORY-RECORD.
01  INVENTORY-RECORD                PIC X(50).

FD  TRANSACTION-FILE
    LABEL RECORDS ARE OMITTED
    RECORD CONTAINS 10 CHARACTERS
    BLOCK CONTAINS 500 RECORDS
    DATA RECORD IS TRANSACTION-RECORD.
01 TRANSACTION-RECORD               PIC X(10).

FD  UPDATED-INVENTORY-FILE
    LABEL RECORDS ARE OMITTED
    RECORD CONTAINS 50 CHARACTERS
    BLOCK CONTAINS 100 RECORDS
    DATA RECORD IS UPDATED-RECORD.
01  UPDATED-RECORD                  PIC X(50).

FD  LOG-REPORT-FILE
        .
        .
01  LOG-RECORD                      PIC X(133).

FD  ERROR-REPORT-FILE
        .
        .
01  ERROR-RECORD                    PIC X(133).
```

Since our system flowchart, Figure 13.1, showed two input files, you should have expected the DDs, SELECTs and FDs for MASTER-INVENTORY-FILE and TRANSACTION-FILE. Also evident from the system flowchart was that we needed an updated file. That's why I've shown the DD, SELECT and FD for UPDATED-INVENTORY-FILE. Make sure you notice the disposition of the DD statement for the updated file.

Finally, we need two report files, because we develop the reports simultaneously. That is, as we process a transaction, we might need either of the report files, log or error. Since we don't know which, we must have both available at the same time.

**WORKING-STORAGE SECTION.**    Let's go on and look at the necessary working storage elements essential to our discussion.

```
WORKING-STORAGE SECTION.

01   INVENTORY-RECORD-WS.
     03   ITEM-NUMBER              PIC X(5).
     03   ITEM-DESCRIPTION         PIC X(25).
     03   QOH                      PIC 9(4).
     03   .
              .

01   TRANSACTION-RECORD-IN.
     03   TRAN-ITEM-NUMBER         PIC X(5).
     03   TRAN-KODE                PIC X(1).
     03   QUANTITY                 PIC 9(4).

01   ERROR-RECORD-OUT.
     03   FILLER                   PIC X(10)   VALUE SPACES.
     03   TRANS-RECORD-ERROR       PIC X(10).
     03   FILLER                   PIC X(30)   VALUE SPACES.
     03   ERROR-MESSAGE            PIC X(30).
     03   FILLER                   PIC X(53)   VALUE SPACES.

01   LOG-RECORD-OUT.
     03   FILLER                   PIC X(30).
     03   TRANS-RECORD-GOOD
          05   TRAN-ITEM-NUMBER-OUT  PIC X(5).
          05   FILLER                PIC X(5)     VALUE SPACES.
          05   QUANTITY-OUT          PIC ZZZ9.
     03   FILLER                   PIC X(30).
     03   ACTION-TAKEN             PIC X(17).
     03   FILLER                   PIC X(42).
```

I've included only the D-R-D for the master record, transaction record and for both reports. Also, notice that I didn't use the suffix -IN for the master. Since I will also write from this record, I used the suffix -WS (working storage). The two report records allow for reporting the results of processing the transactions.

**PROCEDURE DIVISION.**    Now let's look at the PROCEDURE DIVISION for the solution. You will notice that it parallels the pseudocode closely. Also notice that, as with the earlier segments, the procedure code itself consists of code segments. The full running program is at the end of the chapter.

```
PROCEDURE DIVISION.

0000-MAIN-PARA.
     PERFORM 1000-INIT-PARA.
     PERFORM 2000-READ-MASTER.
     PERFORM 3000-READ-TRANSACTION.
```

```
        PERFORM 4000-PROCESS-PARA
            UNTIL NO-MORE-MASTER-RECORDS
            OR NO-MORE-TRANSACTION-RECORDS.
        PERFORM 5000-EOF-PROCESSING.
            .
            .


    1000-INIT-PARA.
            .
            .


    2000-READ-MASTER.
        READ MASTER-INVENTORY-FILE INTO INVENTORY-RECORD-WS
            AT END
                MOVE 'NO' TO ARE-THERE-MORE-MASTERS.

    3000-READ-TRANSACTION.
        READ TRANSACTION-FILE INTO TRANSACTION-RECORD-IN
            AT END
                MOVE 'NO' TO ARE-THERE-MORE-TRANSACTIONS.

    4000-PROCESS-PARA.
        IF ITEM-NUMBER = TRAN-ITEM-NUMBER              <---- equal case
            PERFORM 4100-UPDATE-PARA
            PERFORM 3000-READ-TRANSACTION
        ELSE
            IF ITEM-NUMBER < TRANS-ITEM-NUMBER    <---- less than case
                PERFORM 4200-WRITE-UPDATED-MASTER
                PERFORM 2000-READ-MASTER
            ELSE
                PERFORM 4300-NO-MATCH-ERROR-PARA <---- greater than case
                PERFORM 3000-READ-TRANSACTION.

    4100-UPDATE-PARA.
        IF RECEIPT
            PERFORM 4110-RECEIPT-PARA
        ELSE
            IF SALE
                PERFORM 4120-SALE-PARA
            ELSE
                PERFORM 4130-BAD-CODE-PARA.

        IF ERROR-MESSAGE = SPACES
            MOVE TRANSACTION-RECORD-IN TO TRANS-RECORD-GOOD
            WRITE LOG-RECORD FROM LOG-RECORD-OUT
                AFTER 2.
        MOVE SPACES TO ERROR-MESSAGE.

    4110-RECEIPT-PARA.
        ADD QUANTITY TO QOH.
        MOVE 'QUANTITY ADDED' TO ACTION-TAKEN.

    4120-SALE-PARA.
        SUBTRACT QUANTITY FROM QOH.
        MOVE 'QUANTITY SUBTRACTED' TO ACTION-TAKEN.
```

```
4130-BAD-CODE-PARA.
    MOVE 'BAD CODE' TO ERROR-MESSAGE.
    MOVE TRANSACTION-RECORD-IN TO TRANS-RECORD-ERROR.
    WRITE ERROR-RECORD FROM ERROR-RECORD-OUT
        AFTER 2.


4300-NO-MATCH-ERROR-PARA.
    MOVE 'NO MATCH FOUND' TO ERROR-MESSAGE.
    MOVE TRANSACTION-RECORD-IN TO TRANS-RECORD-ERROR.
    WRITE ERROR-RECORD FROM ERROR-RECORD-OUT
        AFTER 2.
```

So far so good! I've coded the solution in a modular way to show all the parts clearly. You can see the heart of our logic in 4000-PROCESS-PARA. It contains the three cases—equal to, less than and greater than. The three corresponding modules 4100, 4200 and 4300, handle the logic for the three cases.

**EOF Using OR.**     The big thing that I have not discussed is the end-of-file (EOF) processing. So, let's do it! In 0000-MAIN-PARA I coded PERFORM 4000-PROCESS-PARA. . .using the OR logical operator. As soon as either file reaches EOF state, this PERFORM is satisfied, and we go to the next sentence.

Now let's think about this EOF processing. If we run out of transactions first, then all we need to do is read the rest of the masters and write them to the updated file. On the other hand, if we run out of masters first, then we must report the remaining transactions as errors (no match found). The code for this logic follows.

```
5000-EOF-PROCESSING.
    IF NO-MORE-TRANSACTIONS
        PERFORM 5100-FINISH-MASTERS
            UNTIL NO-MORE-MASTERS
    ELSE
        PERFORM 5200-FINISH-TRANSACTIONS
            UNTIL NO-MORE-TRANSACTIONS.

5100-FINISH-MASTERS.
    PERFORM 4200-WRITE-UPDATED-MASTER.
    PERFORM 2000-READ-MASTER.

5200-FINISH-TRANSACTIONS.
    PERFORM 4300-NO-MATCH-ERROR-PARA.
    PERFORM 3000-READ-TRANSACTION.
```

**EOF with AND.**     What would be different if we used the AND logical operator? Several things. Unlike the OR logic, we stay in our normal processing until both EOFs are reached. How do we do that? Well, think through this with me. In 4000-PROCESS-PARA what do we want to do if we no longer have transactions? We want the less-than relationship to be true. This would cause the writing and reading of the rest of the masters.

What do we want to do if we run out of masters first? Report the rest of the transactions as errors, the greater-than case.

So, how do we make the respective cases always true? Look at the new READs below.

```
2000-READ-MASTER.
     READ MASTER-INVENTORY-FILE INTO INVENTORY-RECORD-WS
          AT END
               MOVE 'NO' TO ARE-THERE-MORE-MASTERS
               MOVE HIGH-VALUES TO ITEM-NUMBER.

3000-READ-TRANSACTION.
     READ TRANSACTION-FILE INTO TRANSACTION-RECORD-WS
          AT END
               MOVE 'NO' TO ARE-THERE-MORE-TRANSACTIONS
               MOVE HIGH-VALUES TO TRAN-ITEM-NUMBER.
```

In both cases we move the figurative constant HIGH-VALUES, the highest ASCII value in the collating sequence, to the appropriate item number field. Since ITEM-NUMBER will always be greater than TRANS-ITEM-NUMBER after the master EOF is reached, we will execute both 4300 and 3000 modules. And, likewise, ITEM-NUMBER will always be less than TRANS-ITEM-NUMBER after the transaction EOF is reached. That will cause 4200 and 2000 to be executed on each pass. Then when both EOFs are reached, the AND is true and the procedure is exited.

Nice, isn't it? The 5000, 5100 and 5200 modules are no longer needed. We do need the two extra moves for HIGH VALUES. Nevertheless, I like it; it saves time!

### A Control Break Approach

The previous technique for updating a master file does not take full advantage of the fact that the files are ordered. That is, all transactions against a particular master record are together. The logic simply finds an equal (master = transaction), does the appropriate updating, reads the next transaction and starts the whole loop again (PERFORM PROCESS-PARA UNTIL . . .). Why not take full advantage of the transactions being ordered?

The logic just requires a little modification. We still drive the logic with our three cases. However, once we have an equal (master = transaction), we stay in an inner loop until we have a not-equal case (a control break). If we had 100 transactions against a master, we would not leave this inner loop and test for EOF each time. Let's look at this with the following pseudocode. Can you spot the inner loop easily?

```
READ 1st MASTER RECORD
READ 1st TRANSACTION RECORD
DO UNTIL NO MORE MASTERS
     OR UNTIL NO MORE TRANSACTIONS
     IF MASTER = TRANSACTION
          DO UNTIL MASTER NOT = TRANSACTION
               IF RECEIPT
                    ADD . . .
               ELSE
                    IF SALE
                         SUBTRACT . . .
                    ELSE
                         WRITE ERROR . . .
                    END-IF
               END-IF
               READ NEXT TRANSACTION
          END-DO
     END-IF
```

```
IF MASTER < TRANSACTION
    WRITE UPDATED MASTER
    READ NEXT MASTER
ELSE
    WRITE ERROR REPORT
    READ NEXT TRANSACTION
END-IF
END-DO
```

Do you see how the DO UNTIL will keep us within the equal case until the keys are no longer equal?

## FILE MAINTENANCE

Earlier in this chapter, I made the distinction between update and maintenance. We have spent considerable time on update. It is now time to look at maintenance. Recall that transactions now will be of three types:

1. Adding new master records to the file
2. Deleting master records from the file
3. Changing a field or fields on the master records

### Policy Considerations

We must finally consider policy issues. Why? Look at these situations. Will we allow an inventory record with a positive QOH to be deleted? Will we remove an employee's record from the master without considering end-of-the-year processing? Will we allow changes to the key field? All of these are important questions that need to be addressed. And, it continues with more global questions. Do we allow changes to be made to a newly added master? Do we allow a newly added master to be deleted? Again, these are important questions that must be addressed.

**Ordering of Transactions.**    Most of our policy questions can be addressed by ordering the transactions to insure certain action dictated by our policy. But the global questions boil down to management decisions. Don't let the programmers make them for you. Those decisions are too important not to be established by systems people in coordination with the user.

If we use our inventory problem as a vehicle for discussion, and we assume our transactions will consist of delete a record, add a record and change the description, we can demonstrate the importance of all the above questions.

In discussing the update process, all we said was that the files, master and transaction, needed to be in key order. In our example, they were placed in ascending order by their respective item numbers. Is that enough order for our file maintenance? Look at Figure 13.6, where a set of transactions is sorted only by item number.

Notice that I have also shown the transaction codes (A-add, C-change, D-delete). The two transactions against the master, item number of 1, pose no problem. However, look at the two transactions against item number 4. We change a field and then delete the record. (Why bother to change it first? However, that one doesn't cause a lot of trouble.) But look at the two transactions for master item number 7. The first transaction is a change which will be reported as an error, since that record is not on the master file. The second transaction adds the record to the master file. Sounds backwards, doesn't it?  It would have worked better had the two transactions been reversed, A-add, then C-change.

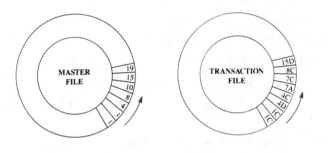

**FIGURE 13.6**
**Maintenance File Sorted Only by Item Number**

**Delete, Add, Change Policy.**     It seems to me that if we are going to allow changes to records that have been added in the same batch, we would also want to delete a record before changes are made to it.  To avoid all the unnecessary processing, the order of the transactions should be: delete, add, change.  Therefore, we need to order the transactions by transaction code within item number.  How do you sort transaction codes of A, C, D to get them in D, A, C order?  Ascending?  No!  Descending?  No!  What else is there?  Convert the codes before sorting to give the necessary order.  So, we convert Ds to 1s, As to 2s and Cs to 3s and sort in ascending order.

# TIP

**Review the Sort Chapter to see where we generated a sort field in order to be able to sort in some nonstandard order.**

Applying the new converted transaction code to our data in Figure 13.6 results in the order shown in Figure 13.7.

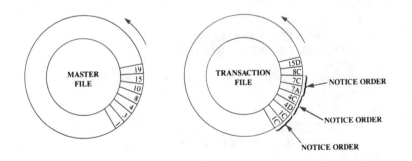

**FIGURE 13.7**
**Maintenance File Sorted by Transaction Code and Item Number**

Now we will delete item number 4 from the master file before going to all the trouble of changing it.  And we will add item number 7 to the master file and allow the subsequent change.

But what about the questions of deleting records that shouldn't be and making changes to the key field?  Both of these are programming questions.  The specifications for the program would show what is to be done.  For instance, no key field should ever be allowed to be changed with a change transaction.  It should be changed by first deleting the existing master and adding another with the new item number key.  As to the delete policy, records should not be deleted with no record of the deletion and only those that meet all criteria should be deleted.

### Logic for Doing File Maintenance

Let's look at the logic now for handling a file maintenance of the master inventory file. Our policies are:

1. Use the delete, add, change order.
2. Do not delete items with a positive QOH.
3. Do not change the item number.

What do you suppose is the heart of this logic? The same three cases we used in the update. However, let's examine the three cases in light of the maintenance situation.

**Master = Transaction.**     When an equal case arises, which transactions are allowable? Change? That's OK. Delete? That's OK if QOH is zero. Add? Oops, that's not OK. How could we add a master when it already exists? The add would be an error.

**Master < Transaction.**     This relation causes the same response it did for updating the master file. We still know we are finished with the current master.

**Master > Transaction.**     Would this still be an error as it was for updates? No, not in all cases. A change and a delete would both be errors, since they would require action on an existing master, and none exists. However, the add transaction is acceptable, since it's OK to add a new record to the file.

### Pseudocode for File Maintenance

Let's now turn our attention to the logic structure. I have shown it using the pseudocode below.

```
      .
      .
READ 1st MASTER RECORD
READ 1st TRANSACTION RECORD
DO UNTIL NO MORE MASTERS
    OR NO MORE TRANSACTIONS
    IF MASTER = TRANSACTION
       IF DELETE
           IF QOH = 0
               (DELETE THE RECORD)
               READ THE NEXT MASTER
           ELSE
               WRITE ERROR (BAD DELETE; QOH NOT = 0)
           END-IF
       ELSE
           IF CHANGE
               (CHANGE THE FIELD ON THE RECORD)
           ELSE
               WRITE ERROR (BAD TRANSACTION CODE)
           END-IF
       END-IF
       READ NEXT TRANSACTION
    ELSE
       IF MASTER < TRANSACTION
           WRITE UPDATED MASTER
           IF MASTER SAVED
               MOVE MASTER FROM SAVED LOCATION TO CURRENT MASTER
           ELSE
               READ NEXT MASTER
           END-IF
```

```
        ELSE
            IF ADD
                MOVE CURRENT MASTER TO SAVED LOCATION
                MOVE TRANSACTION TO CURRENT MASTER
            ELSE
                WRITE ERROR (BAD TRANSACTION CODE)
            END-IF
            READ NEXT TRANSACTION
        END-IF
    END-IF
END-DO
    .
    .
```

**The Add Technique.**     The majority of the pseudocode is familiar to you. The double lead read within the sequential file model is an old friend by now. The majority of the new code pertains to the policy of allowing an added record to have transactions. In order to do this, the transaction with the add code needs to become a master. However, what do we do with the current master? We save it in a temporary location. So our master read must be conditioned on whether or not we have a master saved. Symbolically, this process is shown in Figure 13.8.

**MEMORY**

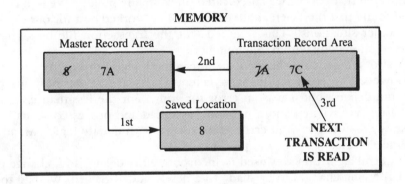
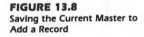

**FIGURE 13.8**
Saving the Current Master to Add a Record

In Figure 13.8 we had a master of 8 and a transaction of 7A. We have a master greater than transaction situation. That's OK, since the code is an A. First master with the item number of 8 is moved to the save location. Second, the transaction is moved to the master location and third, the next transaction is read. It's a 7C, so a change is made and the next transaction, item number of 8, is read. This causes a master < transaction. The master of 7 is now written to the updated file. That's what we wanted! The new master with item number of 7 is now part of the master. Do we just read the next master? No! Remember, we saved one. So we just move it back as shown in Figure 13.9.

**MEMORY**

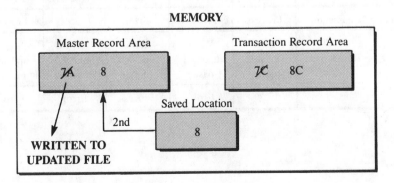

**FIGURE 13.9**
Retrieving the Saved Master after Adding a New Master

## SUMMARY

You have just studied the batch application area of master file update and maintenance. The applications require sorted sequential files. You saw that the update process included those transactions that are caused by doing business, while maintenance transactions are those that are related to keeping the static information, such as description, current.

The logic to handle updating was driven by three cases:

$$\text{master} = \text{transaction}$$
$$\text{master} < \text{transaction}$$
$$\text{master} > \text{transaction}$$

The equal case allowed for the processing of transactions like receipts and sales. When the less-than case was found, the updated master record was written to the file and the next master was read. Finally, when a greater-than case was sensed, you discovered that this is an error. You simply reported it and continued processing with the next transaction.

Maintenance of the master file also involved ordered sequential files. However, you discovered that coding was predicated on company policy. We looked at several cases and found that the delete, add, change policy worked best for our examples and in many other situations. This required that the transaction file be sorted on two keys—transaction code within item number.

You also saw that the heart of maintenance logic is driven by the same three cases. However, different actions were taken. An equal case was now acceptable for changes and deletes, but it was an error for adds. For the less-than case, the maintained master was written and a new one was read and processed. Finally, greater-than cases were not always an error as they were with update logic. An add for this case was acceptable.

A powerful algorithm was used to incorporate the delete, add, change policy. It involved allowing changes to be made to a newly added record. We had to save the current master, make the transaction the current master and change our master-read logic.

Figure 13.10 summarizes the three cases and actions taken for the transaction types for both update and maintenance.

**FIGURE 13.10**
**Summary of Actions for Update and Maintenance**

| CASES | TRANSACTION TYPES | | | | |
|---|---|---|---|---|---|
| | UPDATE | | MAINTENANCE | | |
| | RECEIPT | SALE | ADD | CHANGE | DELETE |
| Master = Transaction | Process | Process | Error | Process | Process |
| Master < Transaction | Write updated master | Write updated master | Write updated master | Write updated master | Write updated master |
| Master > Transaction | Error | Error | Process | Error | Error |

## SAMPLE PROGRAM

The following is a complete running COBOL program using many of the features and techniques discussed in this Chapter. Also included is a copy of the original Inventory File, the Transaction File and the updated Inventory File.

### The Sequential File Maintenance Program

```
PP 5740-CB1 RELEASE 2.4                    IBM OS/VS COBOL  JULY  1, 1982        21.48.38  DATE NOV 10,1988


     1                     21.48.38       NOV 10,1988

00001          IDENTIFICATION DIVISION.
00002          PROGRAM-ID. SEQMAINT.
00003          AUTHOR. FOWLER.
00004          DATE-WRITTEN. AUGUST 1988.
00005          DATE-COMPILED. NOV 10,1988.
00006          REMARKS.
00007
00008       **************************************************************
00009       *                                                            *
00010       *  ASSIGNMENT NUMBER                                         *
00011       *  DATE ASSIGNED                                             *
00012       *  DATE DUE                                                  *
00013       *  PURPOSE:   THIS IS A SEQUENTIAL FILE MAINTENANCE PROGRAM  *
00014       *             FOR THE INVENTORY MASTER FILE. QUANTITY SOLD WILL *
00015       *             BE DEDUCTED FROM THE MASTER QUANTITY ON HAND AND *
00016       *             RECEIPTS WILL BE ADDED TO THE MASTER QUANTITY ON *
00017       *             HAND.  IF AN ITEM'S QUANTITY ON HAND IS LESS THAN *
00018       *             ITS REORDER POINT AN ASTERISK WILL BE PLACED IN *
00019       *             THE STATUS FIELD TO INDICATE THIS.  WHEN THE    *
00020       *             TRANSACTION IS A RECEIPT, A NEW AVERAGE COST PER *
00021       *             UNIT WILL BE CALCULATED.                        *
00022       *                                                            *
00023       *                                                            *
00024       *                                                            *
00025       *  INPUT FILE SPECIFICATIONS:                                *
00026       *     (MASTER FILE)              DESCRIPTION                  *
00027       *     CARD COLUMNS                                           *
00028       *     --------------------       -----------                 *
00029       *         1-5                    ITEM NUMBER                  *
00030       *         6-30                   ITEM DESCRIPTION             *
00031       *        31-34                   QUANTITY ON HAND             *
00032       *        35-42                   COST PER UNIT                *
00033       *        43-46                   REORDER POINT                *
00034       *        47-48                   SUPPLIER CODE                *
00035       *        49-50                   BUYER CODE                   *
00036       *                                                            *
00037       *                                                            *
00038       *  INPUT FILE SPECIFICATIONS:                                *
00039       *     (TRANSACTION FILE)         DESCRIPTION                  *
00040       *     CARD COLUMNS                                           *
00041       *     --------------------       -----------                 *
00042       *         1-5                    TRANSACTION ITEM NUMBER*
00043       *         6-6                    TRANSACTION CODE             *
00044       *         7-10                   TRANSACTION QUANTITY         *
00045       *        11-18                   TRANSACTION COST             *
00046       *                                    PER UNIT                *
00047       *                                                            *
00048       **************************************************************
00049
```

```
     2        SEQMAINT       21.48.38       NOV 10,1988

00051          ENVIRONMENT DIVISION.
00052
00053          CONFIGURATION SECTION.
00054
00055          SOURCE-COMPUTER. IBM.
00056          OBJECT-COMPUTER. IBM.
00057          SPECIAL-NAMES.    CO1 IS PAGE-TOP.
00058
00059          INPUT-OUTPUT SECTION.
00060
00061          FILE-CONTROL.
00062
00063              SELECT INVENTORY-FILE
00064                  ASSIGN TO DA-S-INVFILE.
00065
00066              SELECT NEW-INVENTORY-FILE
00067                  ASSIGN TO DA-S-NEWFILE.
00068
00069              SELECT TRANSACTION-FILE
00070                  ASSIGN TO DA-S-TRANFILE.
00071
00072              SELECT REPORT-FILE
00073                  ASSIGN TO UT-S-REPORT.
00074
00075              SELECT ERROR-FILE
00076                  ASSIGN TO UT-S-ERROR.
00077
```

```
     3        SEQMAINT       21.48.38       NOV 10,1988

00079          DATA DIVISION.
00080
00081          FILE SECTION.
00082
00083          FD  INVENTORY-FILE
00084              LABEL RECORDS ARE OMITTED
00085              RECORD CONTAINS 50 CHARACTERS
00086              BLOCK CONTAINS 100 RECORDS
00087              DATA RECORD IS INVENTORY-RECORD.
00088          01  INVENTORY-RECORD              PIC X(50).
00089
00090          FD  NEW-INVENTORY-FILE
00091              LABEL RECORDS ARE OMITTED
00092              RECORD CONTAINS 50 CHARACTERS
00093              BLOCK CONTAINS 100 RECORDS
00094              DATA RECORD IS NEW-INVENTORY-RECORD.
00095          01  NEW-INVENTORY-RECORD          PIC X(50).
00096
00097          FD  TRANSACTION-FILE
00098              LABEL RECORDS ARE OMITTED
00099              RECORD CONTAINS 18 CHARACTERS
00100              BLOCK CONTAINS 100 RECORDS
00101              DATA RECORD IS TRANSACTION-RECORD.
00102          01  TRANSACTION-RECORD            PIC X(18).
00103
00104          FD  REPORT-FILE
00105              LABEL RECORDS ARE OMITTED
00106              DATA RECORD IS INVENTORY-REPORT-RECORD.
00107          01  INVENTORY-REPORT-RECORD       PIC X(133).
00108
00109          FD  ERROR-FILE
00110              LABEL RECORDS ARE OMITTED
00111              DATA RECORD IS ERROR-REPORT-RECORD.
00112          01  ERROR-REPORT-RECORD           PIC X(133).
00113
```

*(continued)*

```
      4       SEQMAINT       21.48.38      NOV 10,1988

00115           WORKING-STORAGE SECTION.
00116
00117       77  UPDATE-LINE-COUNT            PIC 99.
00118       77  ERROR-LINE-COUNT             PIC 99.
00119       77  TOTAL-EXTENDED-COST          PIC 9(11)V99.
00120       77  NEW-COST-PER-UNIT            PIC 9(6)V99.
00121
00122       01  INVENTORY-RECORD-IN.
00123           05  ITEM-NUMBER-IN           PIC X(5).
00124           05  ITEM-DESCRIPTION-IN      PIC X(25).
00125           05  QUANTITY-ON-HAND-IN      PIC 9(4).
00126           05  COST-PER-UNIT-IN         PIC 9(6)V9(2).
00127           05  REORDER-POINT-IN         PIC 9(4).
00128           05  SUPPLIER-CODE-IN         PIC 9(2).
00129           05  BUYER-CODE-IN            PIC 9(2).
00130
00131       01  TRANSACTION-RECORD-IN.
00132           05  TRANS-ITEM-NUMBER-IN     PIC X(5).
00133           05  TRANS-CODE-IN            PIC X.
00134               88  RECEIPT                        VALUE 'R'.
00135               88  SALE                           VALUE 'S'.
00136           05  TRANS-QUANTITY           PIC 9(4).
00137           05  TRANS-QUANTITY-ERROR REDEFINES TRANS-QUANTITY
00138                                        PIC X(4).
00139           05  TRANS-COST-PER-UNIT      PIC 9(6)V9(2).
00140           05  TRANS-COST-PER-UNIT-ERROR REDEFINES TRANS-COST-PER-UNIT
00141                                        PIC X(8).
00142
00143       01  ARE-THERE-MORE-MASTER-RECORDS  PIC X(3) VALUE 'YES'.
00144           88  MORE-MASTER-RECORDS                VALUE 'YES'.
00145           88  NO-MORE-MASTER-RECORDS             VALUE 'NO'.
00146
00147       01  ARE-THERE-MORE-TRANS-RECORDS   PIC X(3) VALUE 'YES'.
00148           88  MORE-TRANS-RECORDS                 VALUE 'YES'.
00149           88  NO-MORE-TRANS-RECORDS              VALUE 'NO'.
00150
00151       01  SUPPLIER-VALUES.
00152           05  FILLER                   PIC X(20) VALUE
00153               'ATLAS WHOLESALE CO.'.
00154           05  FILLER                   PIC X(20) VALUE
00155               'SMITH WHOLESALE INC.'.
00156           05  FILLER                   PIC X(20) VALUE
00157               'GENERAL SUPPLY CORP.'.
00158
00159       01  SUPPLIER-TABLE REDEFINES SUPPLIER-VALUES.
00160           05  SUPPLIER-NAME            PIC X(20)
00161                                        OCCURS 3 TIMES.
```

*(continued)*

```
     5      SEQMAINT      21.48.38      NOV 10,1988


00163          01  BUYER-VALUES.
00164              05  FILLER                    PIC X(20) VALUE
00165                  'THOMAS RETAIL OUTLET'.
00166              05  FILLER                    PIC X(20) VALUE
00167                  'AXEL MERCHANDISE CO.'.
00168              05  FILLER                    PIC X(20) VALUE
00169                  'GENERAL RETAIL STORE'.
00170              05  FILLER                    PIC X(20) VALUE
00171                  'TAYLOR RETAIL CORP.'.
00172
00173          01  BUYER-TABLE REDEFINES BUYER-VALUES.
00174              05  BUYER-NAME                PIC X(20)
00175                  OCCURS 4 TIMES.
00176
00177          01  DETAIL-LINE.
00178              05  FILLER                    PIC X(3)  VALUE SPACES.
00179              05  STATUS-OUT                PIC X.
00180              05  FILLER                    PIC X(4)  VALUE SPACES.
00181              05  ITEM-NUMBER-OUT           PIC 9(5).
00182              05  FILLER                    PIC X(4)  VALUE SPACES.
00183              05  ITEM-DESCRIPTION-OUT      PIC X(25).
00184              05  FILLER                    PIC X(3)  VALUE SPACES.
00185              05  QUANTITY-ON-HAND-OUT      PIC ZZZ9.
00186              05  FILLER                    PIC X(7)  VALUE SPACES.
00187              05  REORDER-POINT-OUT         PIC ZZZ9.
00188              05  FILLER                    PIC X(7)  VALUE SPACES.
00189              05  COST-PER-UNIT-OUT         PIC $$$$,$$$.99.
00190              05  FILLER                    PIC X(4)  VALUE SPACES.
00191              05  SUPPLIER-NAME-OUT         PIC X(20).
00192              05  FILLER                    PIC X(4)  VALUE SPACES.
00193              05  BUYER-NAME-OUT            PIC X(20).
00194              05  FILLER                    PIC X(7)  VALUE SPACES.
00195
00196          01  BLANK-LINE.
00197              05  FILLER                    PIC X(133)  VALUE SPACES.
00198
00199          01  ERROR-LINE.
00200              05  FILLER                    PIC X(13)  VALUE SPACES.
00201              05  ERROR-ITEM-NUMBER-OUT     PIC X(5).
00202              05  FILLER                    PIC X(11)  VALUE SPACES.
00203              05  ERROR-TRANS-CODE-OUT      PIC X.
00204              05  FILLER                    PIC X(11)  VALUE SPACES.
00205              05  ERROR-QUANTITY-OUT        PIC X(4).
00206              05  FILLER                    PIC X(11)  VALUE SPACES.
00207              05  ERROR-COST-PER-UNIT-OUT   PIC X(8).
00208              05  FILLER                    PIC X(11)  VALUE SPACES.
00209              05  ERROR-MESSAGE-OUT         PIC X(46).
00210              05  FILLER                    PIC X(12)  VALUE SPACES.
00211
```

*(continued)*

```
     6        SEQMAINT       21.48.38      NOV 10,1988

00213        01  UPDATE-REPORT-HEADING.
00214            05  FILLER                   PIC X(51) VALUE SPACES.
00215            05  FILLER                   PIC X(31) VALUE
00216                    'UPDATED INVENTORY MASTER REPORT'.
00217            05  FILLER                   PIC X(51) VALUE SPACES.
00218
00219        01  ERROR-REPORT-HEADING.
00220            05  FILLER                   PIC X(55) VALUE SPACES.
00221            05  FILLER                   PIC X(24) VALUE
00222                    'TRANSACTION ERROR REPORT'.
00223            05  FILLER                   PIC X(54) VALUE SPACES.
00224
00225
00226        01  UPDATE-COLUMN-HEADING.
00227            05  FILLER                   PIC X     VALUE SPACES.
00228            05  FILLER                   PIC X(6)  VALUE 'STATUS'.
00229            05  FILLER                   PIC X(2)  VALUE SPACES.
00230            05  FILLER                   PIC X(2)  VALUE 'ID'.
00231            05  FILLER                   PIC X(6)  VALUE SPACES.
00232            05  FILLER                   PIC X(16) VALUE
00233                    'ITEM DESCRIPTION'.
00234            05  FILLER                   PIC X(11) VALUE SPACES.
00235            05  FILLER                   PIC X(8)  VALUE 'QUANTITY'.
00236            05  FILLER                   PIC X(2)  VALUE SPACES.
00237            05  FILLER                   PIC X(10) VALUE
00238                    'REORDER PT'.
00239            05  FILLER                   PIC X(5)  VALUE SPACES.
00240            05  FILLER                   PIC X(9)  VALUE 'UNIT COST'.
00241            05  FILLER                   PIC X(4)  VALUE SPACES.
00242            05  FILLER                   PIC X(8)  VALUE 'SUPPLIER'.
00243            05  FILLER                   PIC X(16) VALUE SPACES.
00244            05  FILLER                   PIC X(5)  VALUE 'BUYER'.
00245            05  FILLER                   PIC X(22) VALUE SPACES.
00246
00247        01  ERROR-COLUMN-HEADING.
00248            05  FILLER                   PIC X(14) VALUE SPACES.
00249            05  FILLER                   PIC X(2)  VALUE 'ID'.
00250            05  FILLER                   PIC X(12) VALUE SPACES.
00251            05  FILLER                   PIC X(4)  VALUE 'CODE'.
00252            05  FILLER                   PIC X(7)  VALUE SPACES.
00253            05  FILLER                   PIC X(8)  VALUE 'QUANTITY'.
00254            05  FILLER                   PIC X(9)  VALUE SPACES.
00255            05  FILLER                   PIC X(9)  VALUE 'UNIT COST'.
00256            05  FILLER                   PIC X(10) VALUE SPACES.
00257            05  FILLER                   PIC X(13) VALUE
00258                    'ERROR MESSAGE'.
00259            05  FILLER                   PIC X(46) VALUE SPACES.
00260
```

```
     7        SEQMAINT       21.48.38      NOV 10,1988

00262            PROCEDURE DIVISION.
00263
00264            0000-MAIN-PARA.
00265                PERFORM 1000-INIT-PARA.
00266                PERFORM 2000-READ-MASTER-PARA.
00267                PERFORM 3000-READ-TRANSACTION-PARA.
00268                PERFORM 4000-COMPARISON-PROCESS-PARA
00269                    UNTIL NO-MORE-MASTER-RECORDS
00270                       OR  NO-MORE-TRANS-RECORDS.
00271                PERFORM 5000-TERMINATE-PARA.
00272                STOP RUN.
00273
```

*(continued)*

```
       8        SEQMAINT        21.48.38        NOV 10,1988

00275           *****************************************************************
00276           *   1000-INIT-PARA                                              *
00277           *                                                               *
00278           *   THIS PARAGRAPH OPENS THE TWO INPUT FILES, THE TWO OUTPUT    *
00279           *   FILES,  AND WRITES THE BOTH THE UPDATE REPORT AND ERROR     *
00280           *   REPORT HEADINGS.                                            *
00281           *                                                               *
00282           *****************************************************************
00283
00284              1000-INIT-PARA.
00285                  OPEN INPUT   INVENTORY-FILE
00286                               TRANSACTION-FILE
00287                       OUTPUT  REPORT-FILE
00288                               ERROR-FILE
00289                               NEW-INVENTORY-FILE.
00290                  PERFORM 8000-NEW-UPDATE-PAGE-PARA.
00291                  PERFORM 9000-NEW-ERROR-PAGE-PARA.
00292
```

```
       9        SEQMAINT        21.48.38        NOV 10,1988

00294           *****************************************************************
00295           *   4000-COMPARISON-PROCESS-PARA                                *
00296           *                                                               *
00297           *   IN THIS PARAGRAPH THE ITEM NUMBERS OF THE MASTER FILE AND   *
00298           *   THE TRANSACTION FILE ARE COMPARED TO DETERMINE IF THE       *
00299           *   PROCESS REQUIRED IS AN UPDATE, A WRITING OF THE MASTER      *
00300           *   RECORD TO THE NEW MASTER FILE, OR THE WRITING OF THE TRANS- *
00301           *   ACTION TO THE ERROR REPORT.                                 *
00302           *                                                               *
00303           *****************************************************************
00304
00305              4000-COMPARISON-PROCESS-PARA.
00306                  IF ITEM-NUMBER-IN > TRANS-ITEM-NUMBER-IN
00307                      PERFORM 4100-TRANS-NUMBER-ERROR-PARA
00308                  ELSE
00309                      IF ITEM-NUMBER-IN < TRANS-ITEM-NUMBER-IN
00310                          PERFORM 4200-WRITE-MASTER-TO-NEW-MAST
00311                      ELSE
00312                          PERFORM 4300-UPDATE-MASTER-PARA.
00313
```

```
      10        SEQMAINT        21.48.38        NOV 10,1988

00315           *****************************************************************
00316           *   4100-TRANS-NUMBER-ERROR-PARA                                *
00317           *                                                               *
00318           *   IN THIS PARAGRAPH, AN ERROR MESSAGE IS WRITTEN WHEN THE     *
00319           *   TRANSACTION ITEM NUMBER DOES NOT HAVE A CORRESPONDING MATCH *
00320           *   IN THE MASTER FILE.  AFTER THIS OCCURS, ANOTHER TRANSACTION *
00321           *   RECORD IS READ.                                             *
00322           *                                                               *
00323           *****************************************************************
00324
00325              4100-TRANS-NUMBER-ERROR-PARA.
00326                  MOVE TRANS-ITEM-NUMBER-IN TO ERROR-ITEM-NUMBER-OUT.
00327                  MOVE TRANS-CODE-IN TO ERROR-TRANS-CODE-OUT.
00328                  MOVE TRANS-QUANTITY-ERROR TO ERROR-QUANTITY-OUT.
00329                  MOVE TRANS-COST-PER-UNIT-ERROR TO ERROR-COST-PER-UNIT-OUT.
00330                  MOVE 'TRANSACTION DOES NOT HAVE MATCH IN MASTER FILE' TO
00331                      ERROR-MESSAGE-OUT.
00332                  IF ERROR-LINE-COUNT IS GREATER THAN 45
00333                      PERFORM 9000-NEW-ERROR-PAGE-PARA.
00334                  WRITE ERROR-REPORT-RECORD FROM ERROR-LINE
00335                      AFTER 2.
00336                  ADD 2 TO ERROR-LINE-COUNT.
00337                  PERFORM 3000-READ-TRANSACTION-PARA.
00338
```

*(continued)*

```
       11          SEQMAINT        21.48.38        NOV 10,1988

00340          ****************************************************************
00341          *   4200-WRITE-MASTER-TO-NEW-MAST                              *
00342          *                                                             *
00343          *   IN THIS PARAGRAPH, THE MASTER RECORD (WHETHER UPDATED OR   *
00344          *   NOT) IS WRITTEN TO THE NEW MASTER FILE.  IF THE REORDER    *
00345          *   POINT IS GREATER THAN THE QUANTITY ON HAND, AN ASTERISK IS *
00346          *   PRINTED IN THE STATUS COLUMN.  AFTER THIS OCCURS, ANOTHER  *
00347          *   MASTER RECORD IS READ.                                     *
00348          *                                                             *
00349          ****************************************************************
00350
00351           4200-WRITE-MASTER-TO-NEW-MAST.
00352               MOVE ITEM-NUMBER-IN TO ITEM-NUMBER-OUT.
00353               MOVE ITEM-DESCRIPTION-IN TO ITEM-DESCRIPTION-OUT.
00354               MOVE QUANTITY-ON-HAND-IN TO QUANTITY-ON-HAND-OUT.
00355               MOVE COST-PER-UNIT-IN TO COST-PER-UNIT-OUT.
00356               MOVE REORDER-POINT-IN TO REORDER-POINT-OUT.
00357               MOVE SUPPLIER-NAME (SUPPLIER-CODE-IN) TO SUPPLIER-NAME-OUT.
00358               MOVE BUYER-NAME (BUYER-CODE-IN) TO BUYER-NAME-OUT.
00359               IF REORDER-POINT-IN IS GREATER THAN QUANTITY-ON-HAND-IN
00360                   MOVE '*' TO STATUS-OUT
00361               ELSE
00362                   MOVE SPACES TO STATUS-OUT.
00363               IF UPDATE-LINE-COUNT IS GREATER THAN 45
00364                   PERFORM 8000-NEW-UPDATE-PAGE-PARA.
00365               WRITE INVENTORY-REPORT-RECORD FROM DETAIL-LINE
00366                   AFTER 2.
00367               ADD 2 TO UPDATE-LINE-COUNT.
00368               WRITE NEW-INVENTORY-RECORD FROM INVENTORY-RECORD-IN.
00369               PERFORM 2000-READ-MASTER-PARA.
00370
```

```
       12          SEQMAINT        21.48.38        NOV 10,1988

00372          ****************************************************************
00373          *   4300-UPDATE-MASTER-PARA                                    *
00374          *                                                             *
00375          *   IN THIS PARAGRAPH THE TRANSACTION CODE IS CHECKED TO SEE IF*
00376          *   THE TRANSACTION IS A RECEIPT, A SALE, OR AN INVALID TRANS- *
00377          *   ACTION.  NOTE THAT A TECHNIQUE CALLED 'ERROR TRAPPING' IS  *
00378          *   USED IN THIS CASE RATHER THAN DATA VALIDATION.  UNDER NORMAL*
00379          *   CIRCUMSTANCES THE CODE WOULD HAVE BEEN VALIDATED ALONG WITH*
00380          *   THE REST OF THE TRANSACTION RECORD FIELDS BEFORE THE RUN-  *
00381          *   NING OF THIS SEQUENTIAL FILE PROGRAM.                      *
00382          *                                                             *
00383          ****************************************************************
00384
00385           4300-UPDATE-MASTER-PARA.
00386               IF RECEIPT
00387                   PERFORM 4310-RECEIPT-PARA
00388               ELSE
00389                   IF SALE
00390                       PERFORM 4320-SALE-PARA
00391                   ELSE
00392                       PERFORM 4330-BAD-CODE-PARA.
00393               PERFORM 3000-READ-TRANSACTION-PARA.
00394
```

*(continued)*

```
        13        SEQMAINT       21.48.38        NOV 10,1988

00396        ************************************************************
00397        *   4310-RECEIPT-PARA                                      *
00398        *                                                          *
00399        *   IN THIS PARAGRAPH THE TRANSACTION QUANTITY IS ADDED TO THE *
00400        *   QUANTITY ON HAND AND A NEW AVERAGE COST PER UNIT IS    *
00401        *   DETERMINED.                                            *
00402        *                                                          *
00403        ************************************************************
00404
00405        4310-RECEIPT-PARA.
00406            COMPUTE TOTAL-EXTENDED-COST EQUAL
00407                    (COST-PER-UNIT-IN * QUANTITY-ON-HAND-IN) +
00408                    (TRANS-COST-PER-UNIT * TRANS-QUANTITY).
00409            COMPUTE NEW-COST-PER-UNIT    EQUAL
00410                    TOTAL-EXTENDED-COST /
00411                    (QUANTITY-ON-HAND-IN + TRANS-QUANTITY).
00412            MOVE NEW-COST-PER-UNIT TO COST-PER-UNIT-IN.
00413            ADD  TRANS-QUANTITY     TO QUANTITY-ON-HAND-IN.
00414
```

```
        14        SEQMAINT       21.48.38        NOV 10,1988

00416        ************************************************************
00417        *   4320-SALES-PARA                                        *
00418        *                                                          *
00419        *   THIS PARAGRAPH SUBTRACTS THE QUANTITY SOLD FROM THE QUANTITY *
00420        *   ON HAND FOR ALL SALES TRANSACTIONS.                    *
00421        *                                                          *
00422        ************************************************************
00423
00424        4320-SALE-PARA.
00425            SUBTRACT TRANS-QUANTITY FROM QUANTITY-ON-HAND-IN.
00426
```

```
        15        SEQMAINT       21.48.38        NOV 10,1988

00428        ************************************************************
00429        *   4330-BAD-CODE-PARA                                     *
00430        *                                                          *
00431        *   THIS PARAGRAPH WRITES AN ERROR MESSAGE IF THE TRANSACTION *
00432        *   CODE IS INVALID.                                       *
00433        *                                                          *
00434        ************************************************************
00435
00436        4330-BAD-CODE-PARA.
00437            MOVE TRANS-ITEM-NUMBER-IN TO ERROR-ITEM-NUMBER-OUT.
00438            MOVE TRANS-CODE-IN TO ERROR-TRANS-CODE-OUT.
00439            MOVE TRANS-QUANTITY-ERROR TO ERROR-QUANTITY-OUT.
00440            MOVE TRANS-COST-PER-UNIT-ERROR TO ERROR-COST-PER-UNIT-OUT.
00441            MOVE 'TRANSACTION CODE IS INVALID' TO
00442                ERROR-MESSAGE-OUT.
00443            IF ERROR-LINE-COUNT GREATER THAN 45
00444                PERFORM 9000-NEW-ERROR-PAGE-PARA.
00445            WRITE ERROR-REPORT-RECORD FROM ERROR-LINE
00446                AFTER 2.
00447            ADD 2 TO ERROR-LINE-COUNT.
00448
```

*(continued)*

```
    16        SEQMAINT       21.48.38      NOV 10,1988

00450        ****************************************************************
00451        *   5000-TERMINATE-PARA                                       *
00452        *                                                             *
00453        *   IN THIS PARAGRAPH THE REMAINING TRANSACTIONS (IF ALL MASTER *
00454        *   RECORDS HAVE BEEN PROCESSED) OR THE REMAINING MASTERS (IF  *
00455        *   ALL TRANSACTION RECORDS HAVE BEEN PROCESSED) ARE PROCESSED. *
00456        *   AFTER ALL RECORDS HAVE BEEN PROCESSED, THE INPUT AND OUTPUT *
00457        *   FILES ARE CLOSED.                                         *
00458        *                                                             *
00459        *                                                             *
00460        *   NOTE THE USE OF PREVIOUSLY USED MODULES (4100- AND 4200-) *
00461        *   TO COMPLETE THE SEQUENTIAL FILE MAINTENANCE PROCESS.      *
00462        *                                                             *
00463        ****************************************************************
00464
00465        5000-TERMINATE-PARA.
00466            IF NO-MORE-MASTER-RECORDS
00467                PERFORM 4100-TRANS-NUMBER-ERROR-PARA
00468                    UNTIL NO-MORE-TRANS-RECORDS
00469            ELSE
00470                IF NO-MORE-TRANS-RECORDS
00471                    PERFORM 4200-WRITE-MASTER-TO-NEW-MAST
00472                        UNTIL NO-MORE-MASTER-RECORDS.
00473
00474            CLOSE INVENTORY-FILE
00475                  TRANSACTION-FILE
00476                  REPORT-FILE
00477                  ERROR-FILE
00478                  NEW-INVENTORY-FILE.
00479
```

```
    17        SEQMAINT       21.48.38      NOV 10,1988

00481        ****************************************************************
00482        *   2000-READ-PARA                                            *
00483        *                                                             *
00484        *   THIS PARAGRAPH READS A RECORD FROM THE INVENTORY INPUT FILE.*
00485        *                                                             *
00486        ****************************************************************
00487
00488        2000-READ-MASTER-PARA.
00489            READ INVENTORY-FILE INTO INVENTORY-RECORD-IN
00490                AT END
00491                    MOVE 'NO' TO ARE-THERE-MORE-MASTER-RECORDS.
00492
00493
```

```
    18        SEQMAINT       21.48.38      NOV 10,1988

00495        ****************************************************************
00496        *   3000-READ-TRANSACTION-PARA                                *
00497        *                                                             *
00498        *   THIS PARAGRAPH READS A RECORD FROM THE TRANSACTION INPUT  *
00499        *   FILE.                                                     *
00500        *                                                             *
00501        ****************************************************************
00502
00503        3000-READ-TRANSACTION-PARA.
00504            READ TRANSACTION-FILE INTO TRANSACTION-RECORD-IN
00505                AT END
00506                    MOVE 'NO' TO ARE-THERE-MORE-TRANS-RECORDS.
00507
```

*(continued)*

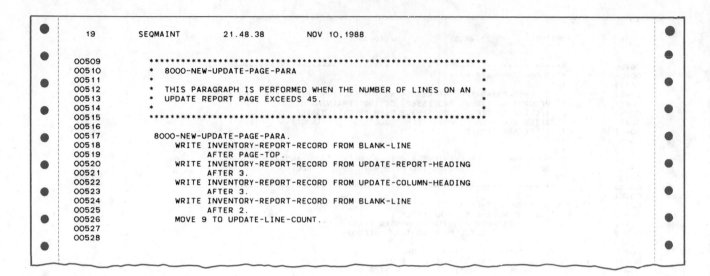

```
   19        SEQMAINT      21.48.38      NOV 10, 1988

00509        ****************************************************************
00510        *   8000-NEW-UPDATE-PAGE-PARA                                  *
00511        *                                                              *
00512        *   THIS PARAGRAPH IS PERFORMED WHEN THE NUMBER OF LINES ON AN *
00513        *   UPDATE REPORT PAGE EXCEEDS 45.                             *
00514        *                                                              *
00515        ****************************************************************
00516
00517        8000-NEW-UPDATE-PAGE-PARA.
00518            WRITE INVENTORY-REPORT-RECORD FROM BLANK-LINE
00519                AFTER PAGE-TOP.
00520            WRITE INVENTORY-REPORT-RECORD FROM UPDATE-REPORT-HEADING
00521                AFTER 3.
00522            WRITE INVENTORY-REPORT-RECORD FROM UPDATE-COLUMN-HEADING
00523                AFTER 3.
00524            WRITE INVENTORY-REPORT-RECORD FROM BLANK-LINE
00525                AFTER 2.
00526            MOVE 9 TO UPDATE-LINE-COUNT.
00527
00528
```

```
   20        SEQMAINT      21.48.38      NOV 10, 1988

00530        ****************************************************************
00531        *   9000-NEW-ERROR-PAGE-PARA                                   *
00532        *                                                              *
00533        *   THIS PARAGRAPH IS PERFORMED WHEN THE NUMBER OF LINES ON AN *
00534        *   ERROR REPORT PAGE EXCEEDS 45.                              *
00535        *                                                              *
00536        ****************************************************************
00537
00538        9000-NEW-ERROR-PAGE-PARA.
00539            WRITE ERROR-REPORT-RECORD FROM BLANK-LINE
00540                AFTER PAGE-TOP.
00541            WRITE ERROR-REPORT-RECORD FROM ERROR-REPORT-HEADING
00542                AFTER 3.
00543            WRITE ERROR-REPORT-RECORD FROM ERROR-COLUMN-HEADING
00544                AFTER 3.
00545            WRITE ERROR-REPORT-RECORD FROM BLANK-LINE
00546                AFTER 2.
00547            MOVE 9 TO ERROR-LINE-COUNT.
```

UPDATED INVENTORY MASTER REPORT

| STATUS | ID | ITEM DESCRIPTION | QUANTITY | REORDER PT | UNIT COST | SUPPLIER | BUYER |
|--------|------|------------------|----------|------------|-----------|----------|-------|
| | 02222 | ANTI-GLARE SCREEN | 15 | 5 | $383.33 | ATLAS WHOLESALE CO. | AXEL MERCHANDISE CO. |
| | 03001 | TURTLENECK SWEATER | 25 | 15 | $80.00 | ATLAS WHOLESALE CO. | THOMAS RETAIL OUTLET |
| * | 08234 | SPARK PLUGS 1 DOZ | 40 | 50 | $12.00 | ATLAS WHOLESALE CO. | GENERAL RETAIL STORE |
| | 11653 | LEATHER JACKET | 7 | 5 | $150.00 | ATLAS WHOLESALE CO. | TAYLOR RETAIL CORP. |
| | 12345 | BROWN LEATHER BELT | 20 | 15 | $15.00 | SMITH WHOLESALE INC. | THOMAS RETAIL OUTLET |
| | 12355 | BLACK LEATHER BELT | 22 | 15 | $15.00 | SMITH WHOLESALE INC. | THOMAS RETAIL OUTLET |
| * | 21100 | PRINT SILK SCARVES | 9 | 10 | $18.00 | GENERAL SUPPLY CORP. | THOMAS RETAIL OUTLET |
| | 21133 | T-SHIRT DRESSES | 8 | 5 | $21.00 | GENERAL SUPPLY CORP. | AXEL MERCHANDISE CO. |
| | 21143 | SWEATER DRESSES | 12 | 10 | $32.00 | GENERAL SUPPLY CORP. | GENERAL RETAIL STORE |
| | 22165 | DESIGNER SWEATER | 8 | 5 | $50.00 | GENERAL SUPPLY CORP. | THOMAS RETAIL OUTLET |
| | 22298 | ST COTTON SHORTS | 20 | 15 | $19.00 | GENERAL SUPPLY CORP. | TAYLOR RETAIL CORP. |
| | 22324 | BLUE JEANS PLEATS | 30 | 20 | $30.00 | SMITH WHOLESALE INC. | AXEL MERCHANDISE CO. |
| | 22346 | SOLID SWEAT SHIRTS | 23 | 15 | $22.00 | GENERAL SUPPLY CORP. | AXEL MERCHANDISE CO. |
| | 22700 | LG COTTON SHORTS | 19 | 10 | $14.00 | SMITH WHOLESALE INC. | AXEL MERCHANDISE CO. |
| | 22835 | SWEAT PANTS | 30 | 20 | $10.00 | GENERAL SUPPLY CORP. | AXEL MERCHANDISE CO. |
| | 22988 | DESIGN SWEAT SHIRT | 22 | 20 | $45.00 | ATLAS WHOLESALE CO. | GENERAL RETAIL STORE |
| | 23334 | BLUE JEANS STRAIGHT LEG | 40 | 25 | $23.00 | SMITH WHOLESALE INC. | GENERAL RETAIL STORE |
| | 23342 | DRESS BLOUSES BOWTIE | 13 | 10 | $50.00 | ATLAS WHOLESALE CO. | TAYLOR RETAIL CORP. |
| | 23444 | DESIGNER POLO SHIRTS | 32 | 25 | $50.00 | GENERAL SUPPLY CORP. | THOMAS RETAIL OUTLET |

```
                          UPDATED INVENTORY MASTER REPORT

STATUS  ID      ITEM DESCRIPTION        QUANTITY  REORDER PT    UNIT COST   SUPPLIER              BUYER

        23453   COTTON BOTTONDOWNS         38        30         $45.00      SMITH WHOLESALE INC.  AXEL MERCHANDISE CO.
        23552   DESIGNER COTTON BLOUSES    24        20         $55.00      GENERAL SUPPLY CORP.  THOMAS RETAIL OUTLET
        23664   BUDGET POLO SHIRTS         21        20         $26.00      SMITH WHOLESALE INC.  THOMAS RETAIL OUTLET
        24345   ACID WASHED JEAN JR        13        10         $18.00      SMITH WHOLESALE INC.  TAYLOR RETAIL CORP.
        24350   ACID WASHED J SKIRT        18        15         $22.00      SMITH WHOLESALE INC.  TAYLOR RETAIL CORP.
        24355   ACID WASHED MINI-SKIRT     10         8         $24.00      SMITH WHOLESALE INC.  GENERAL RETAIL STORE
```

```
                              TRANSACTION ERROR REPORT

    ID          CODE      QUANTITY      UNIT COST      ERROR MESSAGE


  02999          S          9999                       TRANSACTION DOES NOT HAVE MATCH IN MASTER FILE
  22324          B          0000         20003000      TRANSACTION CODE IS INVALID
  22700          G          0010         00005000      TRANSACTION CODE IS INVALID
  77777          Q          0010         00003000      TRANSACTION DOES NOT HAVE MATCH IN MASTER FILE
  80808          R          0020         00003000      TRANSACTION DOES NOT HAVE MATCH IN MASTER FILE
  99999          S          0025                       TRANSACTION DOES NOT HAVE MATCH IN MASTER FILE
```

## Beginning Inventory File

```
 1.     02222ANTI-GLARE SCREEN          00100004000000050102
 2.     03001TURTLENECK SWEATER         00250000800000150101
 3.     08234SPARK PLUGS 1 DOZ          00400000120000500103
 4.     11653LEATHER JACKET             00070001500000050104
 5.     12345BROWN LEATHER BELT         00200000150000150201
 6.     12355BLACK LEATHER BELT         00220000150000150201
 7.     21100PRINT SILK SCARVES         00130000180000100301
 8.     21133T-SHIRT DRESSES            00080000210000050302
 9.     21143SWEATER DRESSES            00120000320000100303
10.     22165DESIGNER SWEATER           00080000500000050301
11.     22298ST COTTON SHORTS           00200000190000150304
12.     22324BLUE JEANS PLEATS          00300000300000200202
13.     22346SOLID SWEAT SHIRTS         00230000220000150302
14.     22700LG COTTON SHORTS           00190000140000100202
15.     22835SWEAT PANTS                00300000100000200302
16.     22988DESIGN SWEAT SHIRT         00220000450000200103
17.     23334BLUE JEANS STRAIGHT LEG    00400000230000250203
18.     23342DRESS BLOUSES BOWTIE       00130000500000100104
19.     23444DESIGNER POLO SHIRTS       00320000500000250301
20.     23453COTTON BOTTONDOWNS         00380000450000300202
21.     23552DESIGNER COTTON BLOUSES    00240000550000200301
22.     23664BUDGET POLO SHIRTS         00210000260000200201
23.     24345ACID WASHED JEAN JR        00130000180000100204
24.     24350ACID WASHED J SKIRT        00180000220000150204
25.     24355ACID WASHED MINI-SKIRT     00100000240000080203
```

## Transaction File

```
 1.     02222R000500035000
 2.     02999S9999
 3.     21100S0004
 4.     22324B000020003000
 5.     22700G001000005000
 6.     77777Q001000003000
 7.     80808R002000003000
 8.     99999S0025
```

## Updated Inventory File

```
 1.     02222ANTI-GLARE SCREEN          00150003833300050102
 2.     03001TURTLENECK SWEATER         00250000800000150101
 3.     08234SPARK PLUGS 1 DOZ          00400000120000500103
 4.     11653LEATHER JACKET             00070001500000050104
 5.     12345BROWN LEATHER BELT         00200000150000150201
 6.     12355BLACK LEATHER BELT         00220000150000150201
 7.     21100PRINT SILK SCARVES         00090000180000100301
 8.     21133T-SHIRT DRESSES            00080000210000050302
 9.     21143SWEATER DRESSES            00120000320000100303
10.     22165DESIGNER SWEATER           00080000500000050301
11.     22298ST COTTON SHORTS           00200000190000150304
12.     22324BLUE JEANS PLEATS          00300000300000200202
13.     22346SOLID SWEAT SHIRTS         00230000220000150302
14.     22700LG COTTON SHORTS           00190000140000100202
15.     22835SWEAT PANTS                00300000100000200302
16.     22988DESIGN SWEAT SHIRT         00220000450000200103
17.     23334BLUE JEANS STRAIGHT LEG    00400000230000250203
18.     23342DRESS BLOUSES BOWTIE       00130000500000100104
19.     23444DESIGNER POLO SHIRTS       00320000500000250301
20.     23453COTTON BOTTONDOWNS         00380000450000300202
21.     23552DESIGNER COTTON BLOUSES    00240000550000200301
22.     23664BUDGET POLO SHIRTS         00210000260000200201
23.     24345ACID WASHED JEAN JR        00130000180000100204
24.     24350ACID WASHED J SKIRT        00180000220000150204
25.     24355ACID WASHED MINI-SKIRT     00100000240000080203
```

## EXERCISES

### Chapter Review Questions

1. A transaction file:
    a. Is synonymous with a master file
    b. Is a set of records that contain information about a element of the business
    c. Is a set of records reflecting the occurrence of some activity
    d. Must be a disk file
    e. None of the above

2. Update involves transactions that:
    a. Occur by doing business
    b. Cause static fields like descriptions to change
    c. Are the same as maintenance transactions
    d. Both a and b are true
    e. None of the above

3. The data in the master file and transaction file:
    a. Must be in ascending order
    b. Must in descending order
    c. Must be in the same order
    d. Do not need to be in any particular order
    e. Must be in the order they occurred

4. The relational case that catches errors in transaction processing when the file are in descending order would be:
    a. Master = Transaction
    b. Master < Transaction
    c. Master > Transaction
    d. Either b or c
    e. None of the above

5. The system flowchart for the update process would show how many storage files; disk or tape?
    a. 2
    b. 3
    c. 4
    d. 5
    e. 6

6. The DD statement for the updated master would have a DISP of:
    a. SHR
    b. NEW,CATLG,DELETE
    c. OLD,CATLG, KEEP
    d. SHR,OLD,KEEP
    e. None of the above

7. Creating a transaction log report and an error report:
   a. Requires two print files; two DDs
   b. May still be done with one report file
   c. Requires two programs
   d. Is never required in the same batch run
   e. None of the above

8. A batch system:
   a. Processes transactions as they occur
   b. Processes maintenance activities only
   c. Processes update activities only
   d. Processes transactions at some time after they occur
   e. None of the above

9. Using the "AND" for EOF processing:
   a. Is equivalent to using the "OR"
   b. Requires an EOF-PROCESSING paragraph
   c. Incorporates the use of HIGH-VALUES
   d. Incorporates the use of LOW-VALUES
   e. Incorporates the use of MID-VALUES

10. The overall logic structure of update processing can be referred to as a double lead read.
    a. True
    b. False

11. In doing file maintenance which of the following field types would never be changed?
    a. Description Field
    b. Quantity Field
    c. Date Field
    d. Key Field
    e. None of the above

12. In setting up run procedures, which of the following statements is true?
    a. Run update program before maintenance program
    b. Run data validation program last
    c. Run maintenance program before update program
    d. Run log program last
    e. None of the above

13. Which of the following policies for file maintenance would not allow changes to a new master in the same batch run?
    a. D, A, C
    b. A, C, D
    c. A, D, C
    d. D, C, A
    e. None of the above

14. Which of the following would be a typical maintenance policy?
    a. Use D, A, C order
    b. Do not delete records with a positive QOH
    c. Do not change the item number
    d. Sort maintenance records in the same order as master file
    e. All are typical policy statement

15. Adding a record under D, A, C policy requires:
    a. A routine for making the transaction a master
    b. No special routine
    c. A routine for saving the current master
    d. A routine for writing the transaction directly to the updated master file
    e. Both a and c are true

## Discussion Questions

1. Contrast the EOF processing using the "OR" and "AND" techniques.
2. Briefly explain how a master > transaction (files in ascending order) can occur.
3. What would happen in an environment with only one printer, if a log and error report are both required?
4. Briefly explain the advantage of the "CONTROL BREAK" method of file update.
5. What file backup is provided by normal batch processing?

## Practice Problems

1. Redo the maintenance pseudocode in the chapter incorporating the "CONTROL BREAK" method.
2. Code the three relations, M = T, M < T, M > T, for the update processing given that the files are in descending order.

## Programming Assignment

1. Write the COBOL program to do file maintenance to the PERSONNEL FILE (Data File B). You should handle the following activities:

> 'A' – Add an employee
>
> 'D' – Delete an employee ( write the record to a former employee file)
>
> 'C' – Change an employee's name

All successful activities should be written to a log report showing the maintenance record and action taken. All errors should be written to an error report showing the maintenance record and an error message. The errors you should handle are:
- No match found
- Invalid maintenance code
- Attempt to ADD an existing record
- Attempt to DELETE a non-existing record

## Programming Projects

The following assignments rely on the data dictionary, library elements and data sets found in the Project Sets Section of your text.

1. Do the File Update Assignment for the Project Management System in Project A.
2. Do the File Update Assignment for the Employee System in Project B.

# RELATIVE FILE PROCESSING

## 14

**OBJECTIVES**    The major objectives of this chapter are the study of relative files, one of the forms of random files, and the study of relative file processing. We will look at applications that use relative files sequentially and randomly. You will see the benefits and costs of relative files and briefly look at file maintenance and file update procedures using relative files.

You will also see that we may use two types of addressing methods with relative files: relative and direct. One of the direct methods will be discussed for instruction, while the relative methods will be used for the examples.

I will restrict discussion of the update and maintenance logic to the I/O routines to demonstrate the use of key access. Since the update and maintenance logic is common, for the most part, for random file processing, I will cover the details fully in the next chapter.

## TOPICS

- batch vs. real-time/on-line
- maintaining a relative file
- updating a relative file
- randomizing techniques
- direct addressing of a relative file
- relative addressing of a relative file
- access modes: sequential, random, dynamic

## KEY WORDS

- SEQUENTIAL ACCESS
- DYNAMIC ACCESS
- RANDOM ACCESS
- RELATIVE KEY
- INVALID KEY
- RELATIVE FILE
- START
- READ. . .NEXT RECORD

## THE PROBLEM SETTING

In the previous chapter, we dealt with sequential file processing. We looked at the batch application area from the perspective of maintenance and update procedures.

Batch processing is good in many applications; however, some applications are more suited to quicker response times than batch systems can provide. Can you imagine an automatic teller that worked in batch mode? Can you imagine calling up your insurance company to get some policy information and finding that the system worked in batch, requiring you to hold or call back? In both cases a quicker response is needed.

I'm sure you have read or heard about systems that provide a competitive advantage—that is, systems corporations use to allow their customers to call into their inventory system, for instance, and check the availability of an item and place an order. Can you imagine this system working in batch? Such a system also needs faster response.

We are talking about on-line systems and even on-line real-time systems.

## BATCH VS. REAL TIME

An on-line real-time system, unlike a batch system, processes transactions as they occur. That is, a sale of goods is processed at the time of the sale. A client calling into the insurance company's system gets an answer right then, not some time later.

Now, what makes it a real-time system? If in processing the transaction the system can respond in time to impact the transaction itself, it is a real-time system.

Let's look at an example. Say you go into a large national department store and pick out a garden hose to buy. You take it up to the counter and ask to charge it. When the cashier, a student (it's a university town), enters the data (item information and your account number), the data is processed. The inventory and accounts receivable files are updated. The cashier hands you your hose and you leave the store. This is an on-line system. All necessary data files are available.

However, if you had done the same thing on an on-line real-time system and you were over your credit limit, the moment the data was entered, the system would have set off alarms, locked all exterior doors, and called the manager! Seriously, the system would respond, while you were still there, saying that the transaction could not occur. Do you see what I mean about responding in time to affect the transaction itself?

Well, you have seen the need for some systems going to an on-line real-time environment. Now the question is, how do we support the environment from a file organization and hardware standpoint? Can we support an on-line real-time system with a sequential file? Let's see if we can.

Assume you went back to that store and chose a refrigerator to buy. You pick it up on your shoulder and take it to the cashier. There is someone ahead of you in line buying a garden hose. You patiently wait your turn. The cashier enters the item number of the water hose, 999998. The inventory master file is sequential, so the search begins: read, does it match, write; read, does it match, write, and so on until the match is found. If the master has 100,000 items, that would take some time. (How's your back?) Now it's your turn. The cashier enters the refrigerator's item number, 999999, and you wait and wait and wait. Finally, you can take your refrigerator home. (How's the back now?)

My point in all this is that having to read every record on a master file to make one sale seems a little ridiculous. It is! So, what do we do? We use a non-sequential file organization for the inventory master file. We use a random file organization.

A random file allows access to a record directly without the need to read each record. Each record has a unique identifier called a key, and that key is used to access any record at random. . .hence the name random file.

In other words, when the 999999 for your refrigerator is entered by the cashier, the system goes directly to that record and reads it. There is no need to read any other records.

What type of device is needed to support a random file? Could we have it on tape, or how about cards? No, those are sequential access storage devices (SASD). We need a direct access storage device (DASD) to support a random file organization.

So, to summarize, we need on-line real-time systems for some applications. To support this type of system, we need to use random file organization. And we saw to support random file organizations we need a DASD. Figure 14.1 illustrates these requirements.

| File Organization / System Types | Batch | On-Line Real Time |
|---|---|---|
| | Device Type | Device Type |
| Sequential | SASD, DASD | ----- |
| Random | DASD | DASD |

**FIGURE 14.1**
Chart Summarizing Batch and Real-Time System Requirements

Did you notice a random file being used for a batch system in Figure 14.1? There is a rule of thumb that says if 30% or fewer of the records on a master file are accessed per batch run, then a random file will be best. The number of records accessed per run is called the hit rate.

Think of it this way. If we had 100,000 master records and on the average we processed transactions against 90%, 90,000, we would waste only 10,000 READs and WRITEs, since each record has to be read and written in sequential file processing. But a sequential file isn't so bad when the hit rate is high. However, if we processed transactions against only 10%, 10,000, each run, we would be wasting 90,000 READs and WRITEs. Therefore, in an attempt to minimize I/O, we use a random file when the hit rate is low.

## FILE ORGANIZATIONS

Earlier I made the distinction between sequential files and random files. Both have their place in business data processing and both are used extensively today. In fact, in COBOL we support three organizations, one sequential and two random. In the **ORGANIZATION** clause we may say:

$$\text{ORGANIZATION IS} \begin{cases} \textbf{SEQUENTIAL} \\ \textbf{RELATIVE} \\ \textbf{INDEXED} \end{cases}$$

### Sequential File Organization

Since we have used this organization throughout the book, I want to review only a few characteristics.

- Files must be processed one record at a time in order from the beginning of the files.
- Order is not required, but essential to some applications.
- Each record usually has a unique field called the key.
- Files may be stored on sequential access storage devices or direct access storage devices.
- Organization is very good for batch systems.

### Random File Organization

This file organization is really a class of organizations. It includes relative files and indexed files. In fact, we will study two types of indexed files: indexed sequential access method, ISAM, and virtual storage access method, VSAM, files.

Some common characteristics of random files are:

- Files must be stored on direct access storage device.
- Files must have a unique field used as a key or address.
- Records may be accessed in random order.
- Random access files are essential to on-line real-time systems.

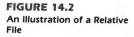

## RELATIVE FILE PROCESSING

This type of file is organized so that each record occupies a relative position in the file. The file may be thought of as a serial set of locations: 1, 2, 3, and so on. Each record in a location is accessed by the location number of the record.

To read the record that is in location 100, we simply make the record number, RELATIVE KEY, equal to 100 and issue a read. Assume that Figure 14.2 depicts a relative file.

**FIGURE 14.2**
**An Illustration of a Relative File**

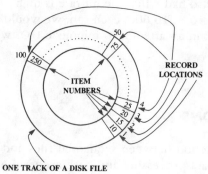

### Relative Addressing

In Figure 14.2 the first record location, 1, contains the item number 10. The second record location contains the item number 15, and so on. So when we read the contents of record location 100, we get the master record with item number 250. Now that's all well and good, but what if you wanted to update item number 20? What record position is it in? You don't know. It sure would have been nice if the item numbers matched the record numbers; that is, if our item numbers were 1, 2, 3, 4, and so on as shown in Figure 14.3.

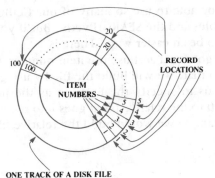

**FIGURE 14.3**
**An Illustration of Relative File Showing a Direct Relationship Between Item Number and Record Number**

ONE TRACK OF A DISK FILE

If there is a direct relationship between the item number and the record number and you want to update item number 20, you simply read the record in the 20th location. However nice that is, it is not realistic to expect item numbers to be in sequence like that. So, we need a solution. We have several. The first one involves the use of tables and a sequential address file.

If there isn't a direct correspondence between item number and record location, it is the programmer's responsibility to keep up with the relationship. Let's use Figure 14.2 to illustrate this technique.

When we build the file, we will write the records in the order indicated. So, when I write the first record, item number 10, I place the item number into the first location of a table. When I write item number 15 into the file in location 2, I place 15 into the second location in a table and so on until I have what's shown in Figure 14.4.

```
01   ADDRESS-TABLE
     05  ADDR          PIC 9(3)
              OCCURS 200 TIMES
              INDEXED BY REL-ADDR.
```

**FIGURE 14.4**
**Relative File and Address Table**

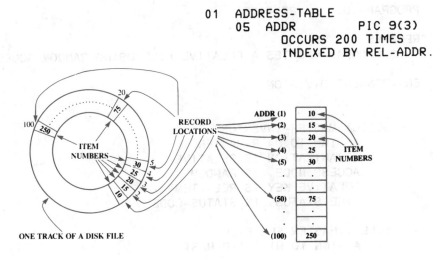

ONE TRACK OF A DISK FILE

Notice that I've kept only the item number in the table. But I kept the items in the table position that corresponds to the relative file record number for each master item. Once we are finished, the address table must be written to a file for use later.

Now the programs that use the relative master for random access will need to read the address file into an address table. When a transaction requests item number 20, the program will do a search of the address table. When a match is found, that table location value can be used to read the corresponding master record from the relative file. For instance, say a transaction item number of 20 is to be processed. Where is the master? Search the table. We match at location 3. Then, read the third record location on the relative file. What master did you get? 20? That's what you wanted.

It's sort of nice to be able to use so many of our COBOL tools at once: relative files, sequential files, tables and the SEARCH verb. But if you're like me, you're probably saying there's got to be an easier way. There is.

One such way is to go ahead and use the item number, for instance, as the record location. Sure we can do that. We will build the file by using random access instead of sequential. This allows us to specify the location as the item number's value. Now when we write record 10 to the relative file it goes into record location 10, 20 into 20, and so on. So for our example we would build the relative file shown in Figure 14.5. ure 14.5.

**FIGURE 14.5**
**Relative File Using Item**
**Number as Record Location**

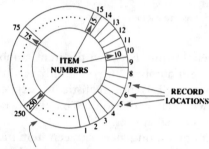

ONE TRACK OF A DISK FILE

The code for building a relative file randomly is shown below:

```
IDENTIFICATION DIVISION.

PROGRAM-ID.      RELFILE.

*REMARKS.
*THIS PROGRAM CREATES A RELATIVE FILE USING RANDOM ACCESS.

ENVIRONMENT DIVISION.
     .
     .

     SELECT MASTER-INVENTORY-FILE
         ASSIGN TO DA-R-MASTER
         ORGANIZATION IS RELATIVE
         ACCESS MODE   IS RANDOM
         RELATIVE KEY IS REL-ITEM
         FILE STATUS   IS STATUS-CODE.

     SELECT MASTER-SEQ-FILE
         ASSIGN TO UT-S-TAPEMAST.
     .
     .
```

```
DATA DIVISION.

FILE SECTION.

FD   MASTER-SEQ-FILE
     LABEL RECORDS ARE OMITTED
     RECORD CONTAINS 50 CHARACTERS
     BLOCK CONTAINS 100 RECORDS
     DATA RECORD IS SEQ-RECORD.

01   SEQ-RECORD                      PIC X(50).

FD   MASTER-INVENTORY-FILE
     LABEL RECORDS ARE OMITTED
     RECORD CONTAINS 50 CHARACTERS
     BLOCK CONTAINS 100 RECORDS
     DATA RECORD IS RELATIVE-RECORD.

01   RELATIVE-RECORD                 PIC X(50).

WORKING-STORAGE SECTION.

77   REL-ITEM                        PIC 9(4).
77   STATUS-CODE                     PIC 9(2).

01   SEQ-RECORD-IN.
     03   SEQ-ITEM-NUMBER            PIC 9(5).
     03   SEQ-ITEM-DESC              PIC X(25).
     03   SEQ-QOH                    PIC 9(4).
     03   SEQ-AVG-COST               PIC 9(6)V9(2).
     03   SEQ-ROP                    PIC 9(4).
     03   SEQ-SUPPLIER-CODE          PIC 9(2).
     03   SEQ-BUYER-CODE             PIC 9(2).

01   RELATIVE-RECORD-OUT.
     03   ITEM-NUMBER                PIC 9(5).
     03   ITEM-DESC                  PIC X(25).
     03   QOH                        PIC 9(4).
     03   AVG-COST                   PIC 9(6)V9(2).
     03   ROP                        PIC 9(4).
     03   SUPPLIER-CODE              PIC 9(2).
     03   BUYER-CODE                 PIC 9(2).


PROCEDURE DIVISION.

0000-MAIN-PARA.
     PERFORM 10000-INIT-PARA.
     PERFORM 2000-READ-PARA.
     PERFORM 3000-PROCESS-PARA
         UNTIL NO-MORE-DATA.

1000-INIT-PARA.
     OPEN INPUT  MASTER-SEQ-FILE.
     OPEN OUTPUT MASTER-INVENTORY-FILE.
```

```
2000-READ-PARA.
    READ MASTER-SEQ-FILE INTO SEQ-RECORD-IN
        AT END
            MOVE 'NO' TO IS-THERE-MORE-DATA.

3000-PROCESS-PARA.
    MOVE SEQ-ITEM-NUMBER TO REL-ITEM.     <----RECORD KEY
    MOVE SEQ-ITEM-NUMBER TO ITEM-NUMBER.
    MOVE SEQ-DESC TO DESC.
    MOVE SEQ-QOH TO QOH.
    MOVE SEQ-ROP TO ROP.
    MOVE SEQ-SUPPLIER-CODE TO SUPPLIER-CODE.
    MOVE SEQ-BUYER-CODE TO BUYER-CODE.
    MOVE SEQ-AVG-COST TO AVG-COST.
    WRITE RELATIVE-RECORD FROM RELATIVE-RECORD-OUT
        INVALID KEY
            PERFORM ERROR-PARA.
    PERFORM 2000-READ-PARA.
```

Wow! It sure works nicely, but look at all that wasted space. However, we don't need the address table and sequential file anymore, do we? Everything has its benefits and costs.

## TIP

On IBM MVS environments, you can build a relative file by using sequential access and replacing relative key with nominal key or a system utility called IDCAM (discussed in the next chapter).

## TIP

You may create an empty relative file by simply opening the file for output and then closing it. Later you may add records, using random access, to the file to build it.

### The SELECT Clause and Its Options

You probably noticed two new features of COBOL, the SELECT entries and the INVALID KEY clause. Let's look at them.

The SELECT clause for a relative file follows.

<u>SELECT</u> filename  <u>ASSIGN</u> TO DA-R-external-filename

<u>ORGANIZATION</u> IS <u>RELATIVE</u>

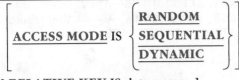

[ <u>RELATIVE KEY</u> IS data-name₁ ]

[ <u>FILE STATUS</u> IS data-name₂ ].

The **ORGANIZATION** clause specifies the file as **RELATIVE**. So does the DA-R-. With a relative file, we may access it one of three ways as indicated with the access clause: sequentially, randomly or dynamically.

With **ACCESS SEQUENTIAL** the file works much like a sequential file. A READ accesses the next record and a WRITE, under output mode, writes the next record.

**RANDOM MODE** allows the file to be accessed using the **RELATIVE KEY**. A read fetches the record at the location specified by the record key. A write places a record at that location.

**ACCESS DYNAMIC** allows us to do both sequential and random accesses in the same program. However, an attempt to read the file sequentially now requires us to use READ...NEXT RECORD. It simply says not to use **RELATIVE KEY**; just get the next logical record.

**RELATIVE KEY** is a working storage data field used for random and dynamic accesses of the file. It is not physically part of the record.

The **FILE STATUS** is a two-digit code returned to the program to tell us the status of the last I/O operation. I've included these at the end of Chapter 15 for all file organizations.

### Accessing a Relative File Sequentially

Well, I can hear you now. How do I get a sequential listing from a relative file? The answer is to use the sequential file model with ACCESS SEQUENTIAL. Even though it is a relative file, the sequential access will provide record locations 1, 2, 3 and so on in order. Nice, isn't it?

### Accessing a Relative File Randomly

What about random access? Well, to allow for accessing records at random, we must provide a value for the RECORD KEY. Following is the code to access the file randomly. A user provides the desired record's item number interactively, and the program gets it.

```
    IDENTIFICATION DIVISION
    .
    .
    .

  *REMARKS.     RANDOM ACCESS OF A RELATIVE FILE.
    .
    .
```

```
          SELECT MASTER-INVENTORY-FILE
              ASSIGN TO DA-R-MASTER
              ORGANIZATION IS RELATIVE
              ACCESS IS RANDOM     <----You could use dynamic.
              RELATIVE KEY REL-ITEM.
          .
          .
          .
      WORKING-STORAGE SECTION.

      77   REL-ITEM                          PIC 9(5).
      77   REQUESTED-ITEM                     PIC 9(5).
          .
          .
          .
      PROCEDURE DIVISION.

      0000-MAIN-PARA.
          .
          .
          .
          PERFORM 1000-ACCEPT-PARA.
          PERFORM 2000-FIND-REQUESTED-RECORD
              UNTIL REQUESTED-ITEM = 9999
          .
          .
          .
      1000-ACCEPT-PARA.
          ACCEPT REQUESTED-ITEM.              <----accepts requested
                                                   item number from
                                                   user.
      2000-FIND-REQUESTED-RECORD.
          MOVE REQUESTED-ITEM TO REL-ITEM.  <----sets the record
          READ MASTER-INVENTORY-FILE             key value.
              INTO REL-INV-RECORD-IN
                  INVALID KEY
                      DISPLAY 'RECORD DOES NOT EXIST'
                      MOVE 'NO' TO WAS-RECORD-FOUND.
          IF RECORD-FOUND
              DISPLAY REL-INV-RECORD-IN.
          PERFORM 1000-ACCEPT-PARA.
```

Do you see that an item number is accepted from the user with the ACCEPT verb? Then its value is moved to the relative key, REL-ITEM. Once that is done, a READ is issued. This either produces a record or results in an error. INVALID KEY specifies the action to be taken if an error occurs. In either case, the results are displayed. And by the way, do you recognize the logic structure? It's the sequential file model again, except that it incorporates the ACCEPT verb. So I guess we should call it the lead accept technique!

### Accessing a Relative File Dynamically

What if you wanted to process a set of transactions, batch system, against a relative master file, and, once the update and/or maintenance was done you wanted to provide a sequential list of the newly updated/maintained file? You would need to use the file both randomly and sequentially, wouldn't you? So the dynamic access mode would be needed.

```
IDENTIFICATION DIVISION.
         .
         .
         .
*REMARKS.   ACCESSING A RELATIVE FILE SEQUENTIALLY AND RANDOMLY.
         .
         .
      SELECT MASTER-INVENTORY-RECORD
            ASSIGN TO DA-R-MASTER
            ORGANIZATION IS RELATIVE
            ACCESS IS DYNAMIC            <-----Note the access mode.
            RELATIVE KEY IS REL-ITEM.
         .
         .
         .
WORKING-STORAGE SECTION.

77   REL-ITEM                    PIC 9(5).

01   TRANSACTION-RECORD-IN.
     03   TRANS-ITEM-NUMBER       PIC 9(5).
         .
         .
         .
         .
PROCEDURE DIVISION.

0000-MAIN-PARA.
         .
         .
      PERFORM 1000-INIT-PARA.
      PERFORM 2000-READ-TRANS.
      PERFORM 3000-PROCESS-PARA
          UNTIL NO-MORE-TRANS.
      PERFORM 4000-START-SEQ-LOGIC.
         .
         .
1000-INIT-PARA.
      OPEN INPUT TRANSACTION-FILE.
      OPEN I-O   MASTER-INVENTORY-FILE.

2000-READ-TRANS.
      READ TRANSACTION-FILE INTO TRANSACTION-RECORD-IN
          AT END
              MOVE 'NO' TO ARE-THERE-MORE-TRANS.

3000-PROCESS-PARA.
      MOVE 'NO' TO WAS-ERROR-FOUND.
      MOVE TRANS-ITEM-NUMBER TO REL-ITEM.
```

> You can avoid an added MOVE (as in 3000 above) by specifying RELA-TIVE KEY as TRANS-ITEM-NUMBER.

```
            READ MASTER-INVENTORY-FILE INTO REL-INVENTORY-RECORD-IN
                INVALID KEY
                    PERFORM 3100-ERROR-PARA.

            IF NO-ERROR-FOUND
                PERFORM 3200-UPDATE-PROCESS.

            PERFORM 2000-READ-TRANS.

        3100-ERROR-PARA.
            [Write error message.]
            MOVE 'YES' TO WAS-ERROR-FOUND.

        3200-UPDATE-PROCESS.
            [Logic to handle update and maintenance.]

        4000-START-SEQ-LOGIC.
            PERFORM 4100-INIT-PARA.
            PERFORM 4200-READ-MASTER-PARA.
            PERFORM 4300-LIST-MASTER
                UNTIL NO-MORE-MASTERS.
            .

            .

        4100-INIT-PARA.
            CLOSE TRANSACTION-FILE.
            CLOSE MASTER-INVENTORY-FILE.
            OPEN INPUT MASTER-INVENTORY-FILE.
```

**TIP**

> Closing and reopening the master file gets you to the first record in the file. You can do the same thing with the START verb.

```
        4200-READ-MASTER-FILE.
            READ MASTER-INVENTORY-FILE NEXT RECORD
                INTO REL-INVENTORY-RECORD-IN
                    AT END
                        MOVE 'NO' TO ARE-THERE-MORE-MASTERS.

        4300-LIST-MASTER.
            MOVE(s)
            .

            .
            WRITE REPORT-LINE FROM MASTER-RECORD-OUT
                AFTER 2.
            PERFORM 4200-READ-MASTER-PARA.
```

As you probably noticed, I've just shown you the skeleton code. From it you can see how the file is used randomly (modules 1000 through 3000). Starting with module 4000, you can see how it's used sequentially to provide a listing.

**READ. . .NEXT RECORD.**     Since the file is under ACCESS DYNAMIC, reading the file sequentially requires a different READ verb. The system needs to know how we intend to use the file. So we use the **READ. . .NEXT RECORD** format shown below.

<u>READ</u> file-name <u>NEXT</u> [ <u>RECORD</u> ] · · ·

As you can see, relative files provide much more processing flexibility than simple sequential files. But relative files sometimes are not so nice and easy to use. Remember, our example wasted a lot of space. So let's look at a different addressing scheme that goes a long way toward solving the problem of wasted space.

### Direct Addressing

This type of addressing is interesting and even sort of fun. This addressing scheme is sometimes said to be another organization type. It might be in some compilers, but ORGANIZATION IS DIRECT is not an ANSI standard. However, using direct addressing involves some standard techniques. In fact, the one depicted in Figure 14.5 is probably as direct as you can get. So I guess this one is a first cousin to an organization type.

The problem shown in Figure 14.5 was that, by using the item number itself as the record location, we wasted a lot of space. So let's do something to the item number and generate a record location instead. Let's do it so that we don't waste as much space.

**Randomizing.**     Several randomizing, or hashing, techniques are available to generate locations or addresses. I will use just one to demonstrate the concept of randomizing.

Assume you want to create a relative master file of inventory items. Figure 14.6 shows the item numbers and the resulting file. For ease of discussion, I've depicted the relative file as a vector of locations.

**ITEM NUMBERS: 4, 13, 62, 52, 98, 44**

| 0 | 44 |
| 1 | |
| 2 | 13 |
| 3 | |
| 4 | 4 |
| 5 | |
| 6 | |
| 7 | 62 |
| 8 | 52 |
| 9 | |
| 10 | 98 |

**FIGURE 14.6**
Relative File Showing Results of Hashing to Determine Record Locations

How did I come up with the file size? And, how did I pick those locations for the records?

Well, the size of the file was determined by talking to the user. She said that the inventory would never grow to more than ten items. (Hey, it's just an example!) So, in this randomizing method, the remainder method, you choose the first prime number beyond the size needed for the file, 11 in our example. Then, you divide each item number by 11 and use the resulting remainder as the address.

OK, I guess you noticed I loaded the example, since none of the divisions resulted in the same remainder, or address. I did it on purpose to demonstrate the technique without getting into all the complexities to start with.

Nevertheless, a distinct possibility is that two divisions may result in the same remainder. For instance, where would you put record 81? In location 4? No, it's not an available location. This problem involving like addresses is called synonym records. One method of solving it is to chain the records together with a system of pointers (this is beyond this text). Or you could expand the size of the file, which would reduce the number of synonyms, or you could go to another file organization like ISAM or VSAM.

## SUMMARY

Relative file processing is the first of three random file organizations that we study. In the next chapter we will look at ISAM and VSAM file organizations, referred to as indexed files.

We studied several features of relative files. The addressing methods took much of our time. We saw that using the record locations of 1, 2, 3 and so on would normally require us to maintain an address table and file in order to access the relative file.

However, if we used the item number as the record location, we no longer needed the address table and file. This led to the discussion of randomizing techniques designed to minimize wasted space. We looked at one such method, the remainder method. Several other exist, but I've left them for another course.

Finally, we looked at code segments for several applications. We created a relative file. We processed one randomly and we processed one dynamically. The bulk of the random file processing, however, is covered in Chapter 15, since the logic for all random files is very similar. In Figure 14.7, I summarize the access modes, open states and I/O operations for a relative file in order to show how they interact.

RELATIVE FILE ORGANIZATION

| ACCESS MODE | | SEQUENTIAL | | | RANDOM | | | DYNAMIC | | |
|---|---|---|---|---|---|---|---|---|---|---|
| **FILE OPENED FOR:** | | Input | Output | I/O | Input | Output | I/O | Input | Output | I/O |
| **I/O OPERATIONS ALLOWED WITH EXPECTED RESULTS** | Read | Next Record | ---- | ---- | Record Equal to Key | ---- | Record Equal to Key | Record Equal to Key | ---- | Record Equal to Key |
| | Write | ---- | Next Location | ---- | ---- | Adds a Record | Adds a Record | ---- | Adds a Record | Adds a Record |
| | Delete | ---- | ---- | Last Record Read | ---- | ---- | Deletes Key Record | ---- | ---- | Deletes Key Record |
| | Start | At Record Specified | ---- | At Record Specified | ---- | ---- | ---- | At Record Specified | ---- | At Record Specified |
| | Rewrite | ---- | ---- | Replaces Last Record | ---- | ---- | Replaces Last Record | ---- | ---- | Replaces Last Record |
| | Read... Next | Next Record | ---- | ---- | ---- | ---- | ---- | Next Record | ---- | Next Record |

**FIGURE 14.7**
**Summary of Access Mode, File Status and I/O Operations for Relative File Processing**

## SAMPLE PROGRAM

The following is a complete running COBOL program using many of the features and techniques discussed in this Chapter.

```
PP 5740-CB1 RELEASE 2.4                    IBM OS/VS COBOL  JULY 1, 1982       15.24.09  DATE OCT  9,1988


    1                        15.24.09      OCT  9,1988


00001          IDENTIFICATION DIVISION.
00002          PROGRAM-ID.  RELPROG.
00003          AUTHOR.       MICHAEL FOWLER.
00004
00005          ENVIRONMENT DIVISION.
00006
00007          CONFIGURATION SECTION.
00008
00009          SOURCE-COMPUTER.  IBM.
00010          OBJECT-COMPUTER.  IBM.
00011
00012          INPUT-OUTPUT SECTION.
00013
00014          FILE-CONTROL.
00015
00016              SELECT INVENTORY-FILE
00017                  ASSIGN TO DA-S-INVFILE.
00018
00019              SELECT RELATIVE-INVENTORY-FILE
00020                  ASSIGN TO DA-RELFILE
00021                  ORGANIZATION IS RELATIVE
00022                  ACCESS IS SEQUENTIAL
00023                  RELATIVE KEY IS REL-KEY.
00024
00025          DATA DIVISION.
00026
00027          FILE SECTION.
00028
00029          FD  INVENTORY-FILE
00030              LABEL RECORDS ARE OMITTED
00031              RECORD CONTAINS 50 CHARACTERS
00032              BLOCK CONTAINS 100 RECORDS
00033              DATA RECORD IS INVENTORY-RECORD.
00034          01  INVENTORY-RECORD.
00035              03 ITEM-NUMBER        PIC 9(5).
00036              03 DESCRIPTION        PIC X(25).
00037              03 QOH               PIC 9(4).
00038              03 COST-PER-UNIT      PIC 9(6)V9(2).
00039              03 ROP               PIC 9(4).
00040              03 SUPPLIER-CODE      PIC 9(2).
00041              03 BUYER-CODE         PIC 9(2).
00042
00043          FD  RELATIVE-INVENTORY-FILE
00044              LABEL RECORDS ARE OMITTED
00045              RECORD CONTAINS 50 CHARACTERS
00046              DATA RECORD IS RELATIVE-INV-RECORD.
00047          01  RELATIVE-INV-RECORD    PIC X(50).
00048
00049          WORKING-STORAGE SECTION.
00050
00051          77  REL-KEY          PIC 9(5).
```

*(continued)*

```
        2      RELPROG        15.24.09      OCT  9,1988

00052
00053          01  IS-THERE-MORE-DATA      PIC X(3) VALUE 'YES'.
00054              88 MORE-DATA                     VALUE 'YES'.
00055              88 NO-MORE-DATA                  VALUE 'NO'.
00056
00057          PROCEDURE DIVISION.
00058          0000-MAIN-PARA.
00059              PERFORM 1000-OPEN-PARA.
00060              PERFORM 2000-READ-PARA.
00061              PERFORM 3000-BUILD-RELATIVE-FILE
00062                     UNTIL NO-MORE-DATA.
00063              PERFORM 4000-CLOSE-PARA.
00064              STOP RUN.
00065
00066          1000-OPEN-PARA.
00067              OPEN INPUT INVENTORY-FILE.
00068              OPEN OUTPUT RELATIVE-INVENTORY-FILE.
00069
00070          2000-READ-PARA.
00071              READ INVENTORY-FILE
00072                  AT END
00073                      MOVE 'NO' TO IS-THERE-MORE-DATA.
00074
00075          3000-BUILD-RELATIVE-FILE.
00076              MOVE ITEM-NUMBER TO REL-KEY.
00077              WRITE RELATIVE-INV-RECORD FROM INVENTORY-RECORD.
00078              PERFORM 2000-READ-PARA.
00079
00080          4000-CLOSE-PARA.
00081              CLOSE INVENTORY-FILE
00082                     RELATIVE-INVENTORY-FILE.
```

## *EXERCISES*

### *Chapter Review Questions*

1. Real-time systems:

   a. Process transactions as they occur
   b. Process transactions at some later time
   c. Process updates only
   d. Process maintenances only
   e. None of the above

2. An on-line system is always real-time.

   a. True
   b. False

3. Random file organization includes:

   a. Relative
   b. Indexed
   c. VSAM
   d. ISAM
   e. All of the above

4. A random file must be stored on a:

   a. DASD
   b. SASD
   c. RASD
   d. Both a and b will do
   e. None of the above

5. A relative file may be accessed:

   a. Sequentially
   b. Randomly
   c. Dynamically
   d. Directly
   e. All of the above

6. The characteristic of a random file that makes it a relative file is:

   a. The names of your relatives are stored on it
   b. That records are stored in serially numbered locations
   c. That records are always stored using a key field value
   d. Both b and c are characteristics
   e. None of the above

7. Using the employee's social security number as the record location on a relative file:

   a. Results in very little wasted space
   b. Violates the rules for relative file formation
   c. Should be done through chaining
   d. Should be done through hashing
   e. None of the above

8. Creating a relative file may be done by:

    a. Using random access

    b. Opening and then closing the file with no other processing

    c. Opening and then closing the file with at least one write executed before closing

    d. Using sequential access

    e. All of the above

9. Direct addressing of a relative file means:

    a. Using a hashing technique for deriving the address

    b. Using a randomizing technique for deriving the address

    c. Using the key field value as the address

    d. Using the next serial location as the address

    e. Both a and b

10. Relative addressing of a relative file means:

    a. Using a hashing technique for deriving the address

    b. Using a randomizing technique for deriving the address

    c. Using the key field value as the address

    d. Using the next serial location as the address

    e. Both c and d

11. Which of the following is true about relative file accessing?

    a. Sequential access mode works like a sequential file

    b. Random access mode requires a key for access

    c. Dynamic access mode requires the READ. . .NEXT RECORD for sequential processing

    d. Dynamic access mode allows random access

    e. All of the above

12. The example program in the chapter to access a relative file randomly demonstrates a(n):

    a. Batch environment

    b. Interactive environment

    c. Lead accept technique

    d. The use of the REWRITE verb

    e. Both b and c

13. The RELATIVE KEY:

    a. Must be described in the file section

    b. May be part of the transaction record

    c. May be a 77 or 01 level item

    d. May be an 88 level

    e. Both b and c

14. READ. . .NEXT RECORD allows for sequential access of a file whose access mode is:

    a. SEQUENTIAL

    b. RANDOM

    c. DYNAMIC

    d. Both a and c

    e. None of the above

15. When more than one record has the same address, using the remainder hashing method:
    a. The records are called synonym records
    b. A bigger file must be used
    c. That cannot happen
    d. Chaining records is a solution
    e. Both a and d

## Discussion Questions

1. Define a relative file.
2. Contrast relative addressing with direct addressing.
3. Contrast sequential processing under sequential mode and dynamic mode.
4. Contrast random processing under random mode and dynamic mode.

## Practice Problems

1. Write the procedure division code to create a relative file for the DEAN-FILE (Data File A). Use an address file and place each student's record in successive locations.
2. Write the procedure division code to create a relative file using the remainder hashing technique. Use DATA FILE B. Assume that the key is an EMPLOYEE-ID of PIC 9(2) and that the manager says that there are currently 34 employees and he doesn't expect to have any more than about 45.
3. Assume you have the relative DEAN-FILE (Problem 1), write the procedure code to accept student ID's and display the information on the screen for the dean.

## Programming Assignment

1. Write a complete COBOL program to process transactions against a relative inventory file. The system also has an address file for the 50 inventory items. You should process the following transactions:

    A – ADD a record
    D – DELETE a record
    C – Change the item description
    R – Receipt of goods in units
    S – Sale of goods in units

The transactions contain the item number, code, description (if needed), and quality (if needed). Don't worry about cost for this exercise. After processing the transactions, write a report listing all records on the file.

# INDEXED FILE PROCESSING: ISAM AND VSAM

**15**

**_OBJECTIVES_**   In this chapter we will continue our study of random file processing. We will focus on a particular type of random file known as index files. The two file-management methods we will study are: Indexed Sequential Access Method (ISAM) and Virtual Storage Access Method (VSAM).

You will study both ISAM and VSAM files conceptually. However, since the codes for both are so similar, we will use VSAM organization as our vehicle to study applications.

We will look at the update and maintenance algorithms we studied earlier, except that we will have a perspective of index file organization for the master files instead of sequential file organization. You will see how I use a model that may be used for all update and maintenance logic.

During our journey, we will also look at some related topics. We will look at file status codes and their uses. We will look at the START verb and the topic of alternate keys.

_TOPICS_

- **ISAM file organization**
- **VSAM file organization**
- **maintenance of indexed files**
- **update of indexed files**
- **access modes**

- **processing model**
- **sequential processing**
- **random processing**
- **dynamic processing**

## KEY WORDS

- **INDEXED**
- **ACCESS DYNAMIC**
- **ACCESS RANDOM**
- **ACCESS SEQUENTIAL**
- **INVALID KEY**
- **ALTERNATE KEY**

- **REWRITE**
- **DELETE**
- **READ. . .NEXT RECORD**
- **FILE STATUS**
- **START**

## INTRODUCTION

I'm sure you have heard the old saying that need is the mother of invention. Well, the need to handle files randomly (and do it better than relative files allow with their need for programmers to code all the different access algorithms) led to indexed files. In particular, it led first to ISAM and then systems evolved to VSAM (again to solve a need).

The concept of indexed files was new, but the concept of indexing was not. We just needed software to support indexed file processing. It might be a good idea for us to look at the concept of indexing before we move on.

Assume that we have the table shown in Figure 15.1.

**FIGURE 15.1**
Illustration of Sorting by
Physically Moving Data
Elements

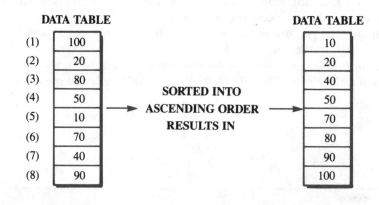

We could write the algorithm to sort the values—item numbers, for instance—into ascending or descending order. The logic could physically sort the values, or we could build another table that would contain the order necessary to provide access to the data in ascending or descending order. Figure 15.2 shows this index table.

So, to process the table with indexes requires us to step through the index table sequentially using the contents of each element as the subscript to our original table [DATA TABLE(INDEX TABLE (I))]. That will access the records in "sorted order" (shown in Figure 15.2). Neat, isn't it? Well, indexed file processing is an extension of this same concept!

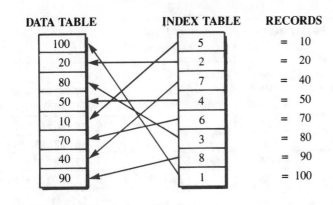

**DATA TABLE**     **INDEX TABLE**     **RECORDS**

| | | | | | |
|---|---|---|---|---|
| 100 | | 5 | | = | 10 |
| 20 | | 2 | | = | 20 |
| 80 | | 7 | | = | 40 |
| 50 | | 4 | | = | 50 |
| 10 | | 6 | | = | 70 |
| 70 | | 3 | | = | 80 |
| 40 | | 8 | | = | 90 |
| 90 | | 1 | | = | 100 |

**FIGURE 15.2**
Illustration Showing Indexes to Accomplish Sorting

## CONCEPTUAL VIEW OF ISAM

Before we get into the applications and the corresponding code, let's look at how the ISAM and VSAM operating systems handle the files. You will be happy to know that no matter how sophisticated the methods look, we as programmers do not have to do any of this. We simply specify a value for the record key and READ, WRITE, REWRITE, DELETE or WRITE!

Data records on an ISAM file are organized by cylinders. Each cylinder is composed of tracks which in turn may contain several records. For each file a cylinder index is maintained and for each cylinder an index of tracks is kept. Figure 15.3 shows an example cylinder and track index.

**CYLINDER INDEX**

| CYLINDER NUMBER | HIGHEST KEY VALUE |
|---|---|
| 1 | 75 |
| 2 | 125 |
| 3 | 252 |
| 4 | 301 |
| 5 | 450 |

**TRACK INDEX FOR CYLINDER 2**

| TRACK NUMBER | HIGHEST KEY VALUE |
|---|---|
| 1 | 82 |
| 2 | 91 |
| 3 | 105 |
| 4 | 125 |

**FIGURE 15.3**
Cylinder and Track Index Illustration

Several points need to be made. Notice that the high key values are in ascending order. That helps the system find particular records. For instance, say you want record 100. Which cylinder would it be on if it exists? Cylinder 2! Now, which track on that cylinder? Track 3! See how the order helps the search? (This is similar to the SEARCH ALL, isn't it?)

Now you must know that as records are written to create the file, no space is reserved in what is called the prime data area. However, since records will more than likely need to be added, space is set aside for those new records. This area, usually some number of tracks per cylinder, is called the overflow area.

Let's expand the track index for cylinder 2 to illustrate the prime and overflow data areas. Figure 15.4 shows the prime and overflow keys, and the actual data records, keys only, stored on that track.

Notice that in the initial status of the file, the high key values for the prime data and overflow data areas are the same; there is nothing in overflow. Also, notice that tracks 5 and 6 are the overflow tracks, and they start empty. The blank track and record pointer column for the overflow area is left blank until overflow occurs.

| Track Number | PRIME DATA AREA Highest Key Value | OVERFLOW AREA Track/ Record Pointer | Highest Key Value | Data Records (Key Only) |
|---|---|---|---|---|
| 1 | 82 | - | 82 | 76  78  80  81  82 |
| 2 | 91 | - | 91 | 84  86  87  89  91 |
| 3 | 105 | - | 105 | 93  95  99 100 105 |
| 4 | 125 | - | 125 | 110 112 118 120 125 |
| 5 | - | - | - | |
| 6 | - | - | - | |

Prime Data Tracks are 1 - 4.
Overflow Data Tracks are 5 - 6.

The data records, shown with keys only (could be item number, student id, or so on), are also shown. I've placed only five records per track for discussion. In reality, unless the records are very large, you can store many more than that (19,000 bytes/track on 3,350 disk packs).

We could depict all other cylinder and track indexes also. However, this is all we need for our conceptual discussion. So let's see how things work.

### Adding Records

What would happen if we wanted to add records 77, 117 and 97 in order to the file? Look at Figure 15.5 and follow the discussion.

| Track Number | PRIME DATA AREA Highest Key Value | OVERFLOW DATA AREA Track/ Record Pointer | Highest Key Value | Data Record Keys |
|---|---|---|---|---|
| 1 | 81 | Track 5, Record 1 | 82 | 76  **77**  78  80  81 |
| 2 | 91 | - | 91 | 84  86  87  89  91 |
| 3 | 100 | Track 5, Record 3 | 105 | 93  95  **97**  99 100 |
| 4 | 120 | Track 5, Record 2 | 125 | 110 112 **117** 118 120 |
| 5 | - | - | - | **82 125 105** |
| 6 | - | - | - | |

Several things will happen when we add these three records. Adding record 77 causes it to be squeezed between records 76 and 78. Record 97 is also squeezed into place, as is record 117. When I say squeezed between two records, I mean what actually happens is that all records that need to change locations are read and then rewritten to make room for the added record.

What happens when these records are squeezed into place? The track can hold only five records; there are now six. Well, the extra records (82, 125, 105) are all written to the overflow area. See them? But they can't just be put into overflow. The system needs to know they are there and where they are. Look at the overflow pointer. It now points to a particular location in the overflow area. So all records can still be accessed both randomly and sequentially by using the overflow pointer.

By our use of the overflow high key value, the system can still determine which track would contain a certain record. It also knows when a record from that track is in overflow (prime high key is not equal to overflow high key). This helps when we access the file sequentially. The system can still give us the records in key sequence; record 82 still follows record 81 and precedes record 84. Nice technique, isn't it?

But as you have come to expect from me, I loaded the example. I added one record per track only. What would happen if I added another set? Given the cylinder as shown in Figure 15.5, let's step through the addition of records 79, 90 and 111 as shown in Figure 15.6.

| PRIME DATA AREA | | OVERFLOW DATA AREA | | | | | | | |
|---|---|---|---|---|---|---|---|---|---|
| Track Number | Highest Key Value | Track/ Record Pointer | Highest Key Value | Data Record Keys | | | | | |
| 1 | 80 | Track 5, Record 4 | 82 | 76 | 77 | 78 | **79** | 80 | |
| 2 | 90 | Track 5, Record 5 | 91 | 84 | 86 | 87 | 89 | **90** | |
| 3 | 100 | Track 5, Record 3 | 105 | 93 | 95 | 97 | 99 | 100 | |
| 4 | 118 | Track 6, Record 1 | 125 | 110 | **111** | 112 | 117 | 118 | |
| 5 | - | - | - | 82 -- 125 -- 105 -- 81 T5, 91 -- R1 | | | | | |
| 6 | - | | | 120 T5, R2 | | | | | |

**FIGURE 15.6**
Cylinder 2's Track Indexes Showing Overflow Chaining

Adding record 79 pushed record 81 to the overflow. But notice that to keep the sequence integrity, record 81 has to point to record 82. So when record 81 moves to overflow, the pointer goes with it; then the overflow pointer is updated to point to it. Therefore, track 1's pointer changes to track 5, record 4, the location of record 81, and record 81 has a pointer to track 5, record 1, the location of record 82. See how the records are linked together? This process is called chaining.

Adding records 90 and 111 also cause records to be moved to overflow. Record 120 must take the pointer with it to keep that chain alive. In other words, each track may have a chain of records.

---

## TIP

When a record is moved to overflow, take the current pointer with it, and then update the overflow pointer.

---

### Deleting Records

Enough about adding records; let's look at deleting records. What happens when record 95 is deleted? The record is logically removed, not physically removed. In COBOL '68 it was the programmer's responsibility to make the record inactive; however, we do the same now by just saying DELETE. Some systems actually remove the record physically. This requires all the pointers to be updated as well.

A reason the record is not physically removed is to speed up processing. The removal would cause all the pointers to be updated. For instance, what would have to happen if record 120 was deleted? Its pointer (track 5, record 2) would have to be moved back to the overflow pointer, and then record 120 would be deleted. Not too bad, but it does take time.

ISAM files are wonderful, especially since we don't have to do any of the things we just studied within our programs. All we do is set a key value and access the file. Just that easy! So, why was VSAM developed if ISAM is so easy?

Let me pose a problem. Assume our inventory master file is an ISAM file, and we have added many records and deleted many others. We would have many records in overflow, and we would probably have deep chains. We would also have a lot of wasted space because of deleted records. So if our master file is very volatile, then another file organization may work better. VSAM is that other file organization.

---

## TIP

Volatile data makes VSAM a better choice than ISAM.

---

## CONCEPTUAL VIEW OF VSAM FILES

Like ISAM files, VSAM files allow for sequential and indexed processing. In order to allow for this, the VSAM operating system is organized with records grouped into intervals. Interval groups are called areas. Each area has a set of high keys called a sequence set which is similar to the track index for an ISAM file. And similarly, each VSAM file has an index set, like an ISAM file's cylinder index, that contains the high key for each area. Figure 15.7 shows these elements along with some data.

Notice how the index set contains the high key values for the four control areas. Then, in turn, for each area we have a sequence set that contains the high key for each interval in the area. Also notice that, unlike those in ISAM, the record areas contain free space. No overflow areas exist.

**INDEX SET**

| Area # | High Key |
|--------|----------|
| 1 | 325 |
| 2 | 512 |
| 3 | 700 |
| 4 | 1000 |

**SEQUENCE SET FOR AREA 1**

| High Key |
|----------|
| 120 |
| 250 |
| 325 |

**CONTROL AREA**

| | | | | | | |
|---|---|---|---|---|---|---|
| 25 | 53 | 72 | 100 | 120 | FREE | FREE |
| 125 | 150 | 173 | 201 | 215 | 240 | FREE |
| 250 | 260 | 265 | 300 | 312 | 325 | FREE |

**SEQUENCE SET FOR AREA 2**

| High Key |
|----------|
| 350 |
| 512 |
| FREE |

**CONTROL AREA**

| | | | | | | |
|---|---|---|---|---|---|---|
| 330 | 333 | 340 | 350 | FREE | FREE | FREE |
| 390 | 400 | 410 | 420 | 500 | 502 | 512 |
| FREE | FREE | FREE | FREE | FREE | FREE | FREE |

**SEQUENCE SET FOR AREA 3**

| High Key |
|----------|
| 590 |
| 650 |
| 700 |

**CONTROL AREA**

| | | | | | | |
|---|---|---|---|---|---|---|
| 515 | 520 | 527 | 532 | 540 | 580 | 590 |
| 600 | 610 | 615 | 620 | 650 | FREE | FREE |
| 660 | 663 | 670 | 700 | FREE | FREE | FREE |

**SEQUENCE SET FOR AREA 4**

| High Key |
|----------|
| 800 |
| 900 |
| 1000 |

**CONTROL AREA**

| | | | | | | |
|---|---|---|---|---|---|---|
| 710 | 720 | 735 | 775 | 800 | FREE | FREE |
| 810 | 820 | 830 | 840 | 850 | 860 | 900 |
| 910 | 970 | 1000 | FREE | FREE | FREE | FREE |

**FIGURE 15.7**
Illustration of a VSAM File

## Adding Records

Let's look at an example to see what happens when we add and delete records. Figure 15.8 shows what happened to our example, Figure 15.7, when the records 80, 345 and 130 were added to the file.

As with the ISAM file, I loaded the example. I made sure to add records that fit. But, of course, we need to address the issue of full intervals. Two things may be caused when a record is added to a full interval. Either an interval split or an area split occurs.

**Interval Split.**     When we try to add a record to a full interval and the area contains a free interval, the system splits the records between the two intervals. For instance, let's add record 510 to the second area in Figure 15.8. Since it should be squeezed between records 502 and 512 and the interval is full and a free interval exists, an interval split occurs as shown in Figure 15.9.

The set of eight records was evenly distributed between the two intervals, and the sequence set was updated to reflect the new high key values, 420 and 512.

**Area Split.**     When we try to add a record to a full interval and no free interval is available for an interval split to be done, an area split is required. An area split causes an entire new area to be created. Let's say we want to add record 815. It should go into interval 2 in area 4 (Figure 15.7). But that interval is full. You also see that a free interval does not exist. Therefore, the area is split as shown in Figure 15.10.

**FIGURE 15.8**
*Illustration of a VSAM File with Records Added*

**SEQUENCE SET FOR AREA 1**

| High Key |
|----------|
| 120 |
| 250 |
| 325 |

**CONTROL AREA**

| | | | | | | |
|------|------|------|------|------|------|------|
| 25 | 53 | 72 | **80** | 100 | 120 | FREE |
| 125 | **130** | 150 | 173 | 201 | 215 | 240 |
| 250 | 260 | 265 | 300 | 312 | 325 | FREE |

**SEQUENCE SET FOR AREA 2**

| High Key |
|----------|
| 350 |
| 512 |
| FREE |

**CONTROL AREA**

| | | | | | | |
|------|------|------|------|------|------|------|
| 330 | 333 | 340 | **345** | 350 | FREE | FREE |
| 390 | 400 | 410 | 420 | 500 | 502 | 512 |
| FREE | FREE | FREE | FREE | FREE | FREE | FREE |

**FIGURE 15.9**
*Illustration of an Interval Split*

**SEQUENCE SET FOR AREA 2**

| High Key |
|----------|
| 350 |
| **420** |
| 512 |

**CONTROL AREA**

| | | | | | | |
|------|------|------|------|------|------|------|
| 330 | 333 | 340 | 345 | 350 | FREE | FREE |
| 390 | 400 | 410 | **420** | FREE | FREE | FREE |
| **500** | **502** | **510** | **512** | FREE | FREE | FREE |

**INTERVAL SPLIT**

**INDEX SET**

| Area # | High Key |
|--------|----------|
| 1 | 325 |
| 2 | 512 |
| 3 | 700 |
| 4 | 900 |
| 5 | 1000 |

**SEQUENCE SET FOR AREA 4**

| High Key |
|----------|
| 800 |
| **830** |
| **900** |

**CONTROL AREA**

| | | | | | | |
|------|------|------|------|------|------|------|
| 710 | 720 | 735 | 775 | 800 | FREE | FREE |
| 810 | **815** | 820 | 830 | FREE | FREE | FREE |
| **840** | **850** | **860** | **900** | FREE | FREE | FREE |

**SEQUENCE SET FOR AREA 5**

| High Key |
|----------|
| 1000 |
| FREE |
| FREE |

**AREA SPLIT**

**CONTROL AREA**

| | | | | | | |
|------|------|------|------|------|------|------|
| 910 | 970 | 1000 | FREE | FREE | FREE | FREE |
| FREE | FREE | FREE | FREE | FREE | FREE | FREE |
| FREE | FREE | FREE | FREE | FREE | FREE | FREE |

**FIGURE 15.10**
*Illustration of an Area Split*

The area split was accomplished by first moving the adjacent interval to a new area and then doing an interval split. Make sure you see that! It's very important and is a lot easier read than understood.

---

## TIP

An area split on a VSAM file always involves an interval split.

### Deleting Records

What happens when a record is deleted from a VSAM file? It is removed from the file, and all records in the interval are moved up, creating free space in the interval.

## INDEXED FILE UPDATE AND MAINTENANCE

We have just finished looking at ISAM and VSAM files conceptually. It is now time to look at the COBOL elements of indexed file processing. Let's do so by looking at the following problem situation.

Assume we have a master inventory file and that we are operating within a batch system environment. I will do this to show you the maintenance and update logic. However, reading the sequential transaction file could very well be replaced by an ACCEPT of each record. Figures 15.11 and 15.12 show the batch and on-line system flowcharts, respectively.

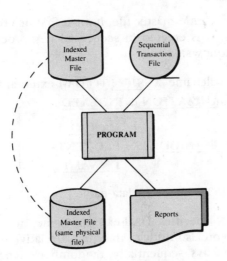

**FIGURE 15.11**
**Batch System Flowchart Using an Indexed File**

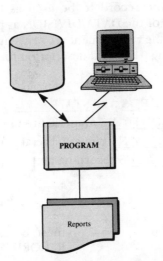

**FIGURE 15.12**
**On-Line System Flowchart Using an Indexed File**

Notice that the indexed file is shown two ways, with two files connected by a dashed line and with an arrow flowing both ways. In both cases I am depicting the fact that an indexed file is updated/maintained in place. That is, the records are written back in place, or rewritten.

> ## *TIP*
>
> In indexed file processing, updating is used to mean what update and maintenance did in sequential file processing.

## ISAM FILE PROCESSING

I will discuss ISAM file processing briefly, because there are a few features that are different from VSAM. However, the procedural features that are common for updating files will be discussed with VSAM files.

### Creating an ISAM File

Before we can process an ISAM master file, it must first be created. How do you create an ISAM file? Well, it is created in sequential key order. The general SELECT clause for an ISAM file follows.

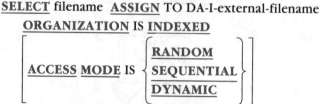

SELECT filename ASSIGN TO DA-I-external-filename
    ORGANIZATION IS INDEXED
    [ ACCESS MODE IS { RANDOM / SEQUENTIAL / DYNAMIC } ]
    [ RECORD KEY IS data-name ]

Notice that ASSIGN specifies DA-I-external-name, where the I says it is an indexed file. I assume you also noticed that, like a relative file, an ISAM file may be accessed in one of three ways, sequentially, randomly or dynamically (some '68 compilers, all '74 and '85 compilers). Finally, you see the RECORD KEY clause. It is used to specify the field within the record to be used as the key. This field must be defined in the FILE SECTION of the DATA DIVISION as part of the record description of the file. This is much like the requirement we saw with SORT keys.

The FD and corresponding 01 record description for an ISAM file would be:

FD filename
    LABEL RECORDS ARE STANDARD
    [ RECORD CONTAINS numeric literal CHARACTERS]
    [ BLOCK CONTAINS numeric literal RECORDS ]
    [ DATA RECORD IS record-name.]

```
01   record-name
     03   .
     03   .
     03   data-name      <-----must be same as specified with
     03   .                    RECORD KEY clause in SELECT
```

Since the file must be built sequentially, the procedural code will incorporate our sequential file model (again). That is, we read the records from a sequential file and write them to the ISAM file.

## TIP

A sequentially-organized file may be addressed only sequentially. However, an indexed file may be addressed sequentially and randomly.

Let's look at the logic using pseudocode.

```
INITIALIZE
READ 1st RECORD (SEQUENTIAL FILE)
DO UNTIL NO MORE RECORDS
    MOVE DATA FIELD TO RECORD KEY
    MOVE REST OF DATA
    WRITE ISAM-RECORD
        IF NOT SUCCESSFUL
            WRITE ERROR MESSAGE
        END IF
    READ NEXT RECORD (SEQUENTIAL FILE)
END DO
```

You should feel at home with this pseudocode. It looks very much like our simple READ/WRITE code from early in your COBOL life (Chapter 2). About the only difference is the IF NOT SUCCESSFUL statement.

In building an ISAM file, the record keys must be in ascending order, and they must be unique. If a particular record fails on either or both counts, the system will tell us we have used an invalid key. We simply report it. Don't keep it a secret!

Well, so much for talking in generalities. Let's build our inventory file as an ISAM file. Assume we have the sequential master sorted in ascending order (Chapter 13). Following is the code. Notice the two SELECTs in the code that follows. The first is for the sequential file that contains the inventory records. The second describes the ISAM file.

```
IDENTIFICATION DIVISION.

PROGRAM-ID.        ISAMCRT.


*REMARKS.   THIS PROGRAM BUILDS AN ISAM MASTER INVENTORY
*           FILE FROM A SEQUENTIAL MASTER INVENTORY FILE.


    SELECT SEQ-MASTER-INVENTORY-FILE  ASSIGN TO DA-S-MASTER.
    SELECT ISAM-MASTER-INVENTORY-FILE ASSIGN TO DA-I-MASTISAM
        ORGANIZATION IS INDEXED
        ACCESS IS SEQUENTIAL
        RECORD KEY IS ITEM-NUMBER.
```

The second SELECT specifies that the organization of the file is indexed. Since we build ISAM files sequentially, the access mode should not surprise you. Now the RECORD KEY is identified. Remember, the key must also be found in the FILE SECTION.

```
DATA DIVISION.

FILE SECTION.

FD   SEQ-MASTER-INVENTORY-FILE
     LABEL RECORDS ARE OMITTED
     RECORDS CONTAINS 50 CHARACTERS
     BLOCK CONTAINS 100 RECORDS
     DATA RECORD IS SEQ-RECORD.
01   SEQ-RECORD                         PIC X(50).

FD   ISAM-MASTER-INVENTORY-FILE
     LABEL RECORDS ARE STANDARD
     DATA RECORD IS ISAM-RECORD.
01   ISAM-RECORD.
     03   ITEM-NUMBER                   PIC 9(5).   <-----record key
     03   ITEM-DESC                     PIC X(25).
     03   QOH                           PIC 9(4).
     03   COST-PER-UNIT                 PIC 9(6)V9(2).
     03   ROP                           PIC 9(4).
     03   SUPPLIER-CODE                 PIC 9(2).
     03   BUYER-CODE                    PIC 9(2).

WORKING-STORAGE SECTION.
     .
     .
     .
01   SEQ-RECORD-IN.
     03   ITEM-NUMBER-IN                PIC 9(5).
     03   ITEM-DESC-IN                  PIC X(25).
     03   QOH-IN                        PIC 9(4).
     03   COST-PER-UNIT-IN              PIC 9(6)V9(2).
     03   ROP                           PIC 9(4).
     03   SUPPLIER-CODE                 PIC 9(2).
     03   BUYER-CODE                    PIC 9(2).
     .
     .
     .
```

The PROCEDURE DIVISION should look very familiar to you. Building an ISAM file requires us to read a sequential file and write the records to the ISAM file. It's the sequential file model again.

```
PROCEDURE DIVISION.

0000-MAIN-PARA.
     PERFORM 1000-INIT-PARA.
     PERFORM 2000-HEADING-PARA.
     PERFORM 3000-READ-PARA.
     PERFORM 4000-BUILD-ISAM
          UNTIL NO-MORE-DATA.
```

```
1000-INIT-PARA.
    OPEN INPUT  SEQ-MASTER-INVENTORY-FILE.
    OPEN OUTPUT ISAM-MASTER-INVENTORY-FILE.

2000-HEADING-PARA.
    [Logic to write error report heading.]

3000-READ-PARA.
    READ SEQ-MASTER-INVENTORY-FILE INTO SEQ-RECORD-IN
        AT END
            MOVE 'NO' TO ARE-THERE-MORE-RECORDS.

4000-BUILD-ISAM.
    MOVE ITEM-NUMBER-IN TO ITEM-NUMBER.     <-----sets the key
    MOVE ITEM-DESC-IN TO ITEM-DESC.               value
    MOVE QOH-IN TO QOH.
    MOVE ROP-IN TO ROP.
    MOVE SUPPLIER-CODE-IN TO SUPPLIER-CODE.
    MOVE COST-PER-UNIT-IN TO COST-PER-UNIT.
    MOVE BUYER-CODE-IN TO BUYER-CODE.
    WRITE ISAM-RECORD
        INVALID KEY                         <-----catches
            PERFORM 4100-WRITE-ERROR-PARA.        duplicate keys

    PERFORM 3000-READ-PARA.

4100-WRITE-ERROR-PARA.
    [Logic to write error message.]
```

Not bad, is it? It's just a READ/WRITE program! It does, however, illustrate the use of RECORD KEY and INVALID KEY.

### Accessing an ISAM File Sequentially

Remember my recent tip on access and organization? Well, even though the file is an indexed file, if we want to access it sequentially to write a report of it, for instance, how do we do it? Use the sequential file mode; just specify ACCESS SEQUENTIAL and open the file for input and process it as you would a sequential file.

### Accessing an ISAM File Randomly

The required logic and code to allow for random access is the same for VSAM file processing. You use random access, open the file for I/O (input and output), move an item number value from a transaction record to the record key and read the corresponding record from the ISAM file.

### Accessing an ISAM File Dynamically

This method of accessing an ISAM file allows for both sequential and random access in the same program. (While most '68 compilers now allow for dynamic access, it is not available on all of them.)

On more current compilers, we are allowed to specify dynamic access and then to use the file either randomly or sequentially. It is our responsibility to specify which we intend to use.

For random processing, with the file opened for INPUT or I/O, we use the record key value to access the file with the I/O verbs. On the other hand, for sequential processing we must tell the system not to use the record key value. We do this with the READ. . .NEXT RECORD form of the READ verb. Don't let all this worry you. I'm just mentioning this now and will discuss it fully later, since it's the same for VSAM files.

## VSAM FILE PROCESSING

A lot of the things we have discussed so far about indexed file processing hold for VSAM files as well. However, there are some differences. Creating the VSAM file requires some operating system specifications not needed for ISAM files. Another difference is found in the ASSIGN clause where the I is no longer used. And a big improvement over ISAM is the ability to specify alternate keys. Another improvement is found in the START verb with the expanded set of relational operators.

### Creating a VSAM File

When we create a VSAM file, we deal with two phases: defining the file to the system and writing the records to the file.

**IDCAMS.**   We must first define the VSAM file to the operating system by using a system utility. In the MVS environment, the utility is known as an IDCAMS. The particular utility is the DEFINE CLUSTER. I've shown an example below.

```
//CREATE    JOB (NO07,S10,001,JB),'DEFINE VSAM'
//STEP1     EXEC PGM=IDCAMS
//SYSPRINT DD   SYSOUT=A
//SYSIN     DD   *
DEFINE
    CLUSTER(
        NAME(VSM.NO07.JB.VSAMFILE)
        VOLUME(VSM001)
        RECORD SIZE(50 50)
        FREESPACE(5 5)
        INDEXED
        KEYS(5 0)
        TRACKS(1 1)
        UNIQUE)
    DATA(
        NAME(VSM.NO07.JB.VSAMFILE.DATA)UNIQUE
        INDEX(VSM.NO07.JB.VSAMFILE.INDEX)UNIQUE)
```

The DEFINE specifies a data set called a cluster with the following specifications.

| NAME | Names the data set. |
|---|---|
| VOLUME | Specifies where the data set is stored. |
| RECORD SIZE | The first number is the size of the record in bytes; second number is the number of bytes in a block. |
| FREESPACE | Specifies the amount of free space. |
| INDEXED | Says the file is indexed. |

| KEYS | The first number is the number of bytes in the key field; the second is the displacement, in bytes, from the beginning of the record. |
| TRACKS | The number of tracks needed for the file. (This is a small file.) |
| UNIQUE | Says the primary key values are unique. |
| DATA | Names the data set that will contain the data. |
| INDEX | Names the data set that will contain the indexes to the file. |

**Initializing a VSAM File.**  The first IDCAM program just defines the file. So when the program finishes executing, all we have is an empty file. Now, how do we get data into the file initially? We can write a COBOL program to do it, or we can use another utility program. The COBOL program would look almost identical to the ISAM create program. In fact, the only difference would be that the ASSIGN clause no longer requires an I. The SELECT would look like:

```
SELECT VSAM-MASTER-INVENTORY-FILE  ASSIGN TO DA-MASTVSAM
       ORGANIZATION IS INDEXED
       ACCESS MODE IS SEQUENTIAL
       RECORD KEY IS ITEM-NUMBER.
```

See how the only change (for now) is the ASSIGN? How about the FD? Well, we may use the same format except that the blocking factor is handled by the system, RECORD SIZE (50 50) in the IDCAM. Therefore, the corresponding SELECT would be the following one.

```
FD  VSAM-MASTER-INVENTORY-FILE
    LABEL RECORDS ARE STANDARD
    RECORD CONTAINS 50 CHARACTERS
    DATA RECORD IS VSAM-RECORD.
01  VSAM-RECORD.
    03  ITEM-NUMBER          PIC 9(5).
    03  ITEM-DESC            PIC X(25).
    03  QOH                  PIC 9(4).
    03  COST-PER-UNIT        PIC 9(6)V9(2).
    03  ROP                  PIC 9(4).
    03  SUPPLIER-CODE        PIC 9(2).
    03  BUYER-CODE           PIC 9(2).
```

Procedurally, you may use the code I showed you for ISAM files, except of course you must change the file names.

Now that brings up a point about the file names. How are the SELECT and DD and IDCAM DEFINE all related?

The name of the data set we set up with the IDCAM was

```
VSM.N007.JB.VSAMFILE
```

so the DD statement and SELECT would, as usual, be linked with the external file name which in turn links it to the data set name:

```
//MASTVSAM  DD   DSN=VSM.N007.JB.VSAMFILE,DISP=SHR

SELECT VSAM-MASTER-INVENTORY-FILE  ASSIGN TO DA-MASTVSAM.
```

So far so good, I hope. Now what about the other option to write the records to the empty file? It's another IDCAM utility, REPRO. I've shown it below.

```
//WRITE    JOB  (..........................)
//STEP     EXEC PGM=IDCAMS
//INPUT    DD   DSN=USR.N007.JB.MASTER
                DCB=(RECFM=FB,LRECL=50,BLKSIZE=5000)
//SYSPRINT DD   SYSOUT=A
//SYSIN    DD   *
REPRO
     INFILE(INPUT)
     OUTDATASET(VSM.N007.JB.VSAMFILE)
```

That's it! See the REPRO statement? It tells the system that the data, INFILE, is specified by the INPUT DD statement, which in turn is our sequential master file. The OUTDATASET says to put the records from the INPUT file on the VSAM file we built with the DEFINE CLUSTER IDCAM, VSM.N007.JB.VSAMFILE.

Nice, isn't it? All we need to do is run the //CREATE JOB and then the //WRITE JOB programs and we have our VSAM file. In fact, we could build a job that has two steps, one to run the IDCAMS program to define the cluster, followed by a second step to run the REPRO.

### Accessing a VSAM File Sequentially

We may access a VSAM file sequentially in two ways, using an IDCAM utility or writing a program to read the file. The IDCAM follows.

```
//PRINT    JOB  (..........................)
//STEP     EXEC PGM=IDCAMS
//SYSPRINT DD   SYSOUT=A
//SYSIN    DD   *
PRINT
     INDATASET(VSM.N007.JB.VSAMFILE)
     CHARACTER
```

Again, that's short and sweet. However, it just gives us a listing of what's on the file. It's not a pretty listing (look at the end of chapter listing).

## TIP

**Use PRINT IDCAM to get file dumps of your newly created VSAM files. It's quick and easy.**

Following is the pertinent code to provide a pretty listing of a VSAM file.

```
IDENTIFICATION DIVISION.

PROGRAM-ID.      VSAMLIST.
       .
       .

SELECT VSAM-MASTER-INVENTORY-FILE
       ASSIGN TO DA-MASTVSAM
       ORGANIZATION IS INDEXED
       ACCESS MODE IS SEQUENTIAL
       RECORD KEY IS ITEM-NUMBER.   <----optional for
                                         sequential access
       .
       .

DATA DIVISION.

FILE SECTION.

FD  VSAM-MASTER-INVENTORY-FILE
    LABEL RECORDS ARE STANDARD
    RECORD CONTAINS 50 CHARACTERS
    DATA RECORD IS VSAM-RECORD.
01  VSAM-RECORD.
    03   ITEM-NUMBER           PIC 9(5).
    03   ITEM-DESC             PIC X(25).
    03   QOH                   PIC 9(4).
    03   COST-PER-UNIT         PIC 9(6)V9(2).
    03   ROP                   PIC 9(4).
    03   SUPPLIER-CODE         PIC 9(2).
    03   BUYER-CODE            PIC 9(2).

PROCEDURE DIVISION.

0000-MAIN-PARA.
    PERFORM 1000-INIT-PARA.
    PERFORM 2000-HEADING-PARA.
    PERFORM 3000-READ-PARA.
    PERFORM 4000-PROCESS-PARA
        UNTIL NO-MORE-RECORDS.

1000-INIT-PARA.
    OPEN INPUT  VSAM-MASTER-INVENTORY-FILE.
    OPEN OUTPUT REPORT-FILE.

2000-HEADING-PARA.
    [Logic to write headings.]

3000-READ-VSAM-MASTER-INVENTORY-FILE
    AT END
        MOVE 'NO' TO ARE-THERE-MORE-RECORDS.
```

> ## TIP
>
> **Sequentially-accessed index files will provide for EOF checking.**

```
4000-PROCESS-PARA.
    MOVE ITEM-NUMBER TO ITEM-NUMBER-OUT.
    MOVE ITEM-DESC TO ITEM-DESC-OUT.
    MOVE QOH TO QOH-OUT.
    MOVE COST-PER-UNIT TO COST-PER-UNIT-OUT.
    MOVE ROP TO ROP-OUT.
    MOVE SUPPLIER-CODE TO SUPPLIER-CODE-OUT.
    MOVE BUYER-CODE TO BUYER-CODE-OUT.
    WRITE RPT-LINE FROM INVENTORY-RECORD-OUT
        AFTER 2.
    PERFORM 3000-READ-PARA.
```

Does the code look familiar? It's the sequential file model we have used over and over again. It's our old friend. But it works even with indexed files. Remember, we are using the indexed file sequentially, so it's still appropriate.

### Accessing a VSAM File Randomly

In this scenario we need to use the file in a way that lets us access records at random by specifying a key value. It is this access method that allows us to update the master file. It allows us to process transactions to allow changes, deletions, and additions of new records and to process all updates such as receipts, sales.

Earlier in this chapter, I mentioned that I would show you a model to use for updating an indexed file. Let me show you the model via pseudocode first. But before we look at the pseudocode, let's understand what needs to be done to update a VSAM file.

- Read a transaction record.
- Set the record key to the transaction value for the key field, say item number.
- Read the master record.
- If successful, process the transaction according to the transaction code; rewrite the master record.
- If not successful, report it.
- Repeat the process for all transactions.

With these general steps in mind, let's now look at the pseudocode.

```
INITIALIZE VARIABLES
READ OR ACCEPT 1st TRANSACTION          <-----ACCEPT used for
DO UNTIL NO MORE TRANSACTIONS                  interactive programs
    IF TRANSACTION CODE = 'R'
        MOVE TRANS-ITEM-NUMBER TO ITEM-NUMBER
```

```
            READ VSAM-MASTER
                IF NOT SUCCESSFUL
                    WRITE ERROR REPORT
                ELSE
                    ADD QUANTITY TO QOH
                    REWRITE VSAM-MASTER
                END IF
            END READ
        ELSE
            .
            etc.
            .

        END IF
        READ OR ACCEPT NEXT TRANSACTION
    END DO
```

**Code for Random Access.**　　　I know you're wondering why I just said "etc." for the other routines. I did it because they just repeat the ones to handle receipts. That's the model! This point will be clearer using actual code. Here goes.

```
IDENTIFICATION DIVISION.

PROGRAM-ID.        VSUPDATE.
        .

    SELECT TRANSACTION-FILE              ASSIGN TO DA-S-TRANS.
    SELECT VSAM-MASTER-INVENTORY-FILE    ASSIGN TO DA-MASTVSAM
            ORGANIZATION IS INDEXED
            ACCESS IS RANDOM
            RECORD KEY IS ITEM-NUMBER.
        .
        .


DATA DIVISION.

FILE SECTION.

FD   VSAM-MASTER-INVENTORY-FILE
        .
        .
    same as before

01   VSAM-RECORD.
     03   ITEM-NUMBER             PIC 9(5).
     03   ITEM-DESC              PIC X(25).
     03   QOH                    PIC 9(4).
     03   COST-PER-UNIT          PIC 9(6)V9(2).
     03   ROP                    PIC 9(4).
     03   SUPPLIER-CODE          PIC 9(2).
     03   BUYER-CODE             PIC 9(2).

        .
        .
```

```
PROCEDURE DIVISION.

0000-MAIN-PARA.
    PERFORM 1000-INIT-PARA.
    PERFORM 2000-HEADINGS-PARA.
    PERFORM 3000-READ-PARA.
    PERFORM 4000-PROCESS-PARA
        UNTIL NO-MORE-TRANSACTIONS.


1000-INIT-PARA.
    OPEN INPUT TRANSACTION-FILE.
    OPEN I-O   VSAM-MASTER-INVENTORY-FILE.

2000-HEADINGS-PARA.
    [Logic to write report headings.]

3000-READ-PARA.
    READ TRANSACTION-FILE INTO TRANSACTION-RECORD
        AT END
            MOVE 'NO' TO ARE-THERE-MORE-RECORDS.

4000-PROCESS-PARA.
    IF RECEIPT
        PERFORM 4100-RECEIPT-PARA
    ELSE
        IF SALE
            PERFORM 4200-SALE-PARA
        ELSE
            IF CHANGE
                PERFORM 4300-CHANGE-PARA
            ELSE
                IF DELETION
                    PERFORM 4400-DELETE-PARA
                ELSE
                    IF ADDITION
                        PERFORM 4500-ADD-PARA
                    ELSE
                        PERFORM 4600-BAD-CODE-PARA.
    PERFORM 3000-READ-PARA.

4100-RECEIPT-PARA.
    MOVE 'NO' TO WAS-AN-ERROR-FOUND.
    MOVE TRANSACTION-ITEM-NUMBER TO ITEM-NUMBER.
    READ VSAM-MASTER-INVENTORY-FILE
        INVALID KEY
            PERFORM 4110-BAD-KEY-PARA.
    IF NO-ERROR-FOUND
        ADD QUANTITY TO QOH
        REWRITE VSAM-RECORD.

4110-BAD-KEY-PARA.
    MOVE 'YES' TO WAS-AN-ERROR-FOUND.
    [Logic to write transaction to error report.]
```

```
4200-SALE-PARA.
    MOVE 'NO' TO WAS-AN-ERROR-FOUND.
    MOVE TRANSACTION-ITEM-NUMBER TO ITEM-NUMBER.
    READ VSAM-MASTER-INVENTORY-FILE
        INVALID KEY
            PERFORM 4110-BAD-KEY-PARA.
    IF NO-ERROR-FOUND
        SUBTRACT QUANTITY FROM QOH
        REWRITE VSAM-RECORD.

4300-CHANGE-PARA.
    MOVE 'NO' TO WAS-AN-ERROR-FOUND.
    MOVE TRANSACTION-ITEM-NUMBER TO ITEM-NUMBER.
    READ VSAM-MASTER-INVENTORY-FILE
        INVALID KEY
            PERFORM 4110-BAD-KEY-PARA.
    IF NO-ERROR-FOUND
        MOVE TRANS-DESC TO ITEM-DESC
        REWRITE VSAM-RECORD.
```

## TIP

The technique in 4300 could be used to change any field except for the key field.

**Using the REWRITE Verb.**      Let's take a moment here and examine those three modules. The only difference is that one says ADD, another says SUBTRACT and the third MOVEs a new description. All the other code is the same. It should be! In order to process the transaction against the appropriate master, TRANSACTION-ITEM-NUMBER is moved to the record key field, ITEM-NUMBER. Then a read is issued. If the read is successful, then the add, subtract or move is done, and the record is written back to the master. All that is common to the routines.

How do we write a record back to the file? It's done with a new verb, the REWRITE verb. Its format is given below.

REWRITE record-name [ FROM D-R-D ]

[ INVALID KEY executable statement(s) ].

The reason for REWRITE is to allow us to replace an existing record. Why not just WRITE? Because under random access, we may also add new records to the file. How? We WRITE. That's why we need the new verb, REWRITE, to replace existing records.

Before a REWRITE may be executed successfully, a successful READ must have been executed prior to executing the REWRITE. You may or may not use the INVALID KEY with REWRITE. In our routines, REWRITE will be executed only if a successful READ occurred, so I didn't use it.

**Using the DELETE Verb.**      The DELETE verb causes a record to be deleted from the file specified. Its format is as shown below:

DELETE filename [RECORD]

I suggest that you use the optional RECORD since the format without it sounds as if we are going to delete the whole file.

Let's go on with the deletion paragraph.

```
4400-DELETE-PARA.
    MOVE 'NO' TO WAS-AN-ERROR-FOUND.
    MOVE TRANSACTION-ITEM-NUMBER TO ITEM-NUMBER.
    READ VSAM-MASTER-INVENTORY-FILE
        INVALID KEY
            PERFORM R110-BAD-KEY-PARA.
    IF NO-ERROR-FOUND
        IF QOH = 0
            DELETE VSAM-MASTER-INVENTORY-FILE RECORD
            [Logic to write record to a log report.]
        ELSE
            [Logic to write message "INVALID DELETE REQUEST,
            QUANTITY ON HAND > 0".]
```

Notice the change here. I also checked to see, before deleting, that the QOH was 0. If not, I didn't delete. In either case, I reported the action taken.

Now, what about the ADD routine? Well, I could apply the same model, except the logic seems confusing. That is, the INVALID KEY would be the valid case. Since we are about to add a record, we don't want a successful read.

Let's use a more positive approach. That is, let's assume the ADD will be valid in the vast majority of cases. Only seldom do we get an error. The following code reflects this positive approach.

```
4500-ADD-PARA.
    MOVE TRANSACTION-ITEM-NUMBER TO ITEM-NUMBER.
    MOVE TRANS-DESC TO ITEM-DESC.
    MOVE QUANTITY TO QOH.
    MOVE TRANS-COST TO COST-PER-UNIT.
    MOVE TRANS-ROP TO ROP.
    MOVE TRANS-SUPPLIER-CODE TO SUPPLIER-CODE.
    MOVE TRANS-BUYER-CODE TO BUYER-CODE.
    WRITE VSAM-RECORD
        INVALID KEY
            PERFORM 4510-BAD-ADD-PARA.
```

This logic moves all the transaction data to the VSAM record. The WRITE is executed. If a duplicate exists, INVALID KEY will be executed. So, if we have an error we will still catch it, but the logic is less confusing.

### Accessing a VSAM File Dynamically

After doing the updating shown in the previous example, would you like a hard copy of the file? Wouldn't a printed report be nice to have if for no other reason than for backup?

How would you produce a pretty report? Could you just read and write the VSAM file? No! It has an access mode of random. That requires key READs. So, what do we do, memorize (save) all the record keys? No! We would be reverting to a relative file structure.

Guess what we do? First, we change the access mode to dynamic. So, the SELECT now looks like this:

```
SELECT VSAM-MASTER-INVENTORY-FILE  ASSIGN TO DA-MASTVSAM
        ORGANIZATION IS INDEXED
        ACCESS MODE IS DYNAMIC
        RECORD KEY IS ITEM-NUMBER.
```

All the logic for doing the update remains the same.  No change is needed.  Nice, isn't it? Now what happens?  We could add a PERFORM 5000-CLOSE-PARA and PER-FORM 6000-SEQ-LOGIC in the main module.

```
PROCEDURE DIVISION.

0000-MAIN-PARA.
    .
    .
    PERFORM 5000-CLOSE-PARA.
    PERFORM 6000-SEQ-LOGIC.
    .
    .

5000-CLOSE-PARA.
    CLOSE VSAM-MASTER-INVENTORY-FILE.

6000-SEQ-LOGIC.
    PERFORM 6100-INIT-PARA.
    PERFORM 6200-HEADING-PARA.
    PERFORM 6300-READ-VSAM-PARA.
    PERFORM 6400-WRITE-VSAM-LISTING
        UNTIL NO-MORE-RECORDS.

6100-INIT-PARA.
    OPEN INPUT VSAM-MASTER-INVENTORY-FILE.

6200-HEADING-PARA.
    [Logic to write headings.]

6300-READ-VSAM-PARA.
    READ VSAM-MASTER-INVENTORY-FILE NEXT RECORD
        AT END
            MOVE 'NO' TO ARE-THERE-MORE.

6400-WRITE-VSAM-LISTING.
    [Move(s) to output record.]
    WRITE RPT-LINE FROM VSAM-RECORD-OUT
        AFTER 2.
    PERFORM 6300-READ-VSAM-PARA.
```

Did you recognize the procedure?  More importantly, does it make sense?  You should pay particular attention to the fact that I first closed the VSAM file and then opened it for input.  Once that was done, I used the READ. . .NEXT RECORD form of the READ.  Why?  It tells the system that I'm not using a key read and that I just want the records in sequence.  It's that easy!

**Using the START.**    Instead of closing the file and reopening it to get to the first record position, COBOL provides another verb for our use, the START verb.  Its general format follows.

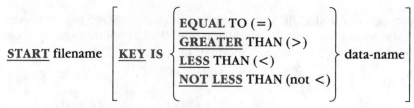

$$\underline{\text{START}} \text{ filename } \left[ \underline{\text{KEY}} \text{ IS} \left\{ \begin{array}{l} \underline{\text{EQUAL}} \text{ TO } (=) \\ \underline{\text{GREATER}} \text{ THAN } (>) \\ \underline{\text{LESS}} \text{ THAN } (<) \\ \underline{\text{NOT LESS}} \text{ THAN (not } <) \end{array} \right\} \text{data-name} \right]$$

[ <u>INVALID</u> <u>KEY</u> executable statement ] .

The START may be used only for files opened for INPUT or I/O. The file must also be accessed sequentially or dynamically. The data-name must be one of the keys associated with the file, primary or alternate.

---

## TIP

**ISAM files may use only the EQUAL TO relational operator with the START.**

---

Our procedural logic using the START would not require the OPEN or CLOSE for the MASTER file used in 5000-CLOSE-PARA and 6100-INIT-PARA. So, paragraph 5000 is no longer needed, and paragraph 6100 would now be:

```
6100-INIT-PARA.
    MOVE 0 TO ITEM-NUMBER.
    START VSAM-MASTER-INVENTORY-FILE
        KEY NOT LESS ITEM-NUMBER
        INVALID KEY
            DISPLAY 'BAD START'.
```

The rest of the logic stays the same. How does it work? Think of the value in the record key as a pointer. The START sets the pointer according to the relationship specified. In our example that would be to the first record in the file that is not less than 0. That would be our first record. If we knew that our first record was 11111, then we could have done the same thing with:

```
    MOVE 11111 TO ITEM-NUMBER.
    START VSAM-MASTER-INVENTORY-FILE
        KEY = ITEM-NUMBER
        INVALID KEY . . .
```

**Alternate Keys.**    One of the big changes that VSAM file organization offers over ISAM file organization is the ability to specify alternate keys. This is wonderful because it gives us so much more power in using an indexed file. How? Well, think of how many customers for a particular store forget their account numbers. Now, how would you access their records to answer an inquiry? Would you tell them, for instance, that you cannot accept the $10,000 payment on their account without their account number? You'd better not! You gladly accept it.

But how do you enter the payment? Your friendly systems people designed the file to allow you to enter an alternate key value—the last name—that's how! Now, you ask, won't there be duplicates? You're correct, but COBOL lets us specify that duplicates may occur.

Let's assume that for our inventory file we specified an alternate key of SUPPLIER-CODE. Now we are able to access that group of records that match a supplier. This is known as an inverted file. That's because a whole other set of indexes is generated and stored. Figure 15.13 shows an example.

FIGURE 15.13
Example Inverted File Using
SUPPLIER-CODE as Alternate
Key

| SUPPLIER CODES | INVENTORY RECORDS | | | |
|---|---|---|---|---|
| 10 | 12345 | 73014 | 54551 | ... |
| 12 | 40412 | | | |
| 25 | 91923 | 12445 | 66420 | |
| 43 | 23011 | 24443 | | |
| . | | | | |

The illustration says that there are three inventory records with supplier codes of 10 and two with supplier codes of 43 and so on. If we specify a code of 10 then issue a read, we will get the first of the three. How do we get the next two? With the READ. . .NEXT RECORD instruction.

Briefly, the code looks like that below.

```
SELECT VSAM-MASTER-INVENTORY-FILE    ASSIGN TO DA-MASTVSAM
        ORGANIZATION IS INDEXED
        ACCESS MODE IS DYNAMIC
        RECORD KEY IS ITEM-NUMBER
        ALTERNATE KEY IS SUPPLIER-CODE
                        WITH DUPLICATES.
    .
    .


PROCEDURE DIVISION.

        .
        .
        MOVE 0 TO ITEM-NUMBER.
        MOVE 10 TO SUPPLIER-CODE.
        START VSAM-MASTER-INVENTORY-FILE
            KEY = SUPPLIER-CODE.
        PERFORM 3000-READ-VSAM.
        PERFORM 4000-WRITE-RPT
            UNTIL SUPPLIER-CODE NOT = 10.
        .
        .

    3000-READ-VSAM.
        READ VSAM-MASTER-INVENTORY-FILE NEXT RECORD.

    4000-WRITE-RPT.
        [Logic to write report.]
        PERFORM 3000-READ-VSAM.
```

This logic will provide all inventory records that have a supplier code of 10. I could make it very robust by changing the MOVE 10 TO SUPPLIER-CODE to ACCEPT SUPPLIER-CODE. Then whatever valid supplier code the user enters is used in the routine.

## TRANSACTION RECORD DESCRIPTION

Look back at all the update logic for indexed files. What detail record description would be needed for the transaction record? Well, we obviously need the transaction item number. We also need the transaction code so that we know what to do. But what else do we need? Each transaction type needs something different: The sale also needs the quantity. So does the receipt. The change needs the new data value for the field being changed, and so on. Get the idea? Which transaction would dictate the format? The add would, since it requires all fields. Look at Figure 15.14. You will see a summary of transaction types and data fields needed where X indicates the field is required and * indicates that it would be required for a change to that field.

**FIGURE 15.14**
**Data Fields Needed for Transaction Types**

TRANSACTION TYPE

| DATA FIELDS | RECEIPT | SALE | CHANGE | DELETE | ADD |
|-------------|---------|------|--------|--------|-----|
| ITEM NUMBER | X | X | X | X | X |
| CODE | X | X | X | X | X |
| ITEM DESCRIPTION | | | * | | X |
| QUANTITY | X | X | | | X |
| COST PER UNIT | X | | | | X |
| ROP | | | * | | X |
| SUPPLIER CODE | | | * | | X |
| BUYER CODE | | | * | | X |

I believe that Figure 15.14 does a good job of indicating the different needs visually. So, let's get back to the detail record description. I think you would agree that the following D-R-D would work.

```
01    TRANSACTION-RECORD.
      03    TRANSACTION-ITEM-NUMBER      PIC 9(5).
      03    TRANSACTION-CODE             PIC X(1).
      03    TRANSACTION-DESC             PIC X(25).
      03    QUANTITY                     PIC 9(4).
      03    TRANS-UNIT-COST              PIC 9(6)V9(2).
      03    REORDER-POINT                PIC 9(4).
      03    TRANS-SUPPLIER-CODE          PIC 9(2).
      03    TRANS-BUYER-CODE             PIC 9(2).
```

As Figure 15.14 shows, a sale transaction would require only three fields of data and the rest would be empty. This requires that data fields be skipped when recording the transaction. This is a source of many errors. But what if each transaction had its own format? Don't get excited yet. Let's look at it together.

```
01    TRANSACTION-RECORD.
      03    TRANSACTION-ITEM-NUMBER      PIC 9(5).
      03    TRANSACTION-CODE
            88    RECEIPT       VALUE 'R'.
            88    SALE          VALUE 'S'.
            88    CHANGE        VALUE 'C'.
            88    DELETION      VALUE 'D'.
            88    ADDITION      VALUE 'A'.
```

```
03   REST-OF-RECORD                      PIC X(45).   <-----notice the
                                                              general field
03   RECEIPT-FORMAT REDEFINES REST-OF-RECORD.
     05   QUANTITY-RECEIVED              PIC 9(4).
     05   UNIT-COST                      PIC 9(6)V9(2).
     05   FILLER                         PIC X(33).

03   SALE-FORMAT REDEFINES REST-OF-RECORD.
     05   QUANTITY-SOLD                  PIC 9(4).
     05   FILLER                         PIC X(41).

03   CHANGE-FORMAT REDEFINES REST-OF-RECORD.
     05   TRANS-DESC                     PIC X(25).
     05   FILLER                         PIC X(20).

03   DELETE-FORMAT REDEFINES REST-OF-RECORD.
     05   FILLER                         PIC X(45).

03   ADD-FORMAT REDEFINES REST-OF-RECORD.
     05   DESCRIPTION-ADD                PIC X(25).
     05   QUANTITY-ADD                   PIC 9(4).
     05   COST-PER-UNIT-ADD              PIC 9(6)V9(2).
     05   ROP-ADD                        PIC 9(4).
     05   SUPPLIER-CODE-ADD              PIC 9(2).
     05   BUYER-CODE-ADD                 PIC 9(2).
```

This D-R-D has the two common fields, TRANSACTION-ITEM-NUMBER and TRANSACTION-CODE that appear first. They are followed by the rest of the record. Then, in turn, each individualized format follows by redefining the rest of the record. Therefore, in our receipt paragraph, we could say ADD QUANTITY-RECEIVED TO QOH and likewise in our sale paragraph we could code SUBTRACT QUANTITY-SOLD FROM QOH. Nice technique, isn't it? You are saying that we waste memory with the larger record, right? No! It's still the same size. Remember we are redefining, not expanding the record.

## FILE STATUS

Here is a short note about **FILE STATUS**. It is an option available on all SELECTs. It is used simply to let the system tell us what has happened on an input or output operation.

The system returns a two-digit code in the field we specified. The system uses a standard set of codes with associated values. Figure 15.15 shows the codes for the three types of file organizations we have studied.

After an attempt to read an indexed file, we receive an INVALID KEY result. All we know is that and no more. However, if we had specified the **FILE STATUS** as:

```
FILE STATUS IS COMPLETION-CODE.
```

where COMPLETION-CODE is defined in working storage, the system would have also placed the appropriate file status completion code in the data-name COMPLETION-CODE. We could then check it to see exactly what happened.

**FIGURE 15.15**
**FILE STATUS Codes and Their Interpretation**

| FILE STATUS CODES | INTERPRETATION | FILE ORGANIZATION | | |
|---|---|---|---|---|
| | | **SEQ** | **REL** | **INDEX** |
| 00 | Successful Completion | X | X | X |
| 02 | Successful Completion : Duplicate Key | | | X |
| 10 | End of File | X | X | X |
| 21 | Invalid Key: Sequence Error | | | X |
| 22 | : Duplicate Key | | X | X |
| 23 | : No Record Found | | X | X |
| 24 | : Boundary Violation | | X | X |
| 30 | I/O Error : - | X | X | X |
| 34 | : Boundary Violation | X | | |
| 9X | Varies with Installation | X | X | X |

## SUMMARY

We have looked thoroughly at the subject of indexed files. We studied both ISAM and VSAM files conceptually in order to understand what the system was doing for us. However, you saw that as much as is happening, using indexed files in COBOL is relatively easy.

You looked at building ISAM and VSAM files. In fact, you saw that indexed files can be created and initialized using system utilities called IDCAMS. I also showed you how to use indexed files sequentially, randomly and dynamically. We studied the READ, READ. . .NEXT RECORD, DELETE, SELECT, INVALID KEY, RECORD KEY and FILE STATUS for indexed files. As I did with relative files, I have summarized the access modes, type of processing, open states and I/O verbs in Figure 15.16.

**FIGURE 15.16**
**Summary of Access Mode, File Status, and I/O Operations for Indexed File Processing**

**INDEXED FILE ORGANIZATION - ISAM AND VSAM**

| ACCESS MODE | | SEQUENTIAL | | | RANDOM | | | DYNAMIC | | |
|---|---|---|---|---|---|---|---|---|---|---|
| **FILE OPENED FOR:** | | Input | Output | I/O | Input | Output | I/O | Input | Output | I/O |
| **I/O OPERATIONS ALLOWED WITH EXPECTED RESULTS** | Read | Next Record | ---- | ---- | Record Equal to Key | ---- | Record Equal to Key | Record Equal to Key | ---- | Record Equal to Key |
| | Write | ---- | Next Location | ---- | ---- | Adds a Record | Adds a Record | ---- | Adds a Record | Adds a Record |
| | Delete | ---- | ---- | Last Record Read | ---- | ---- | Deletes Key Record | ---- | ---- | Deletes Key Record |
| | Start | At Record Specified | ---- | At Record Specified | ---- | ---- | ---- | At Record Specified | ---- | At Record Specified |
| | Rewrite | ---- | ---- | Replaces Last Record | ---- | ---- | Replaces Last Record | ---- | ---- | Replaces Last Record |
| | Read... Next | Next Record | ---- | ---- | ---- | ---- | ---- | Next Record | ---- | Next Record |

I showed you that the maintenance and update functions, called update for indexed file processing, all could use a model. This model could be applied to all transaction types. However, I suggested a different algorithm for adding records.

We also looked at defining the transaction record differently. We used the REDEFINES to give us more meaningful data names and reduce data entry errors.

Finally, we looked at FILE STATUS. You saw that it is a way we have of gaining more information about input and output operations. The system gives us a two-digit code after each operation. We may check the code to get more information, beyond just invalid key, on what occurred.

## SAMPLE PROGRAM

The following is a complete running COBOL program using many of the features and techniques discussed in this Chapter. Also included is the utility program listing of the beginning Inventory File and the updated Inventory File. The Transaction File used for the update is also given.

### VSAM Program

```
PP 5740-CB1 RELEASE 2.4                        IBM OS/VS COBOL  JULY  1, 1982        16.16.03  DATE NOV 10,1988


    1                      16.16.03        NOV 10,1988


    00001          IDENTIFICATION DIVISION.
    00002          PROGRAM-ID. VSAMUPDT.
    00003          AUTHOR. FOWLER.
    00004          DATE-WRITTEN. OCTOBER 1988.
    00005          DATE-COMPILED. NOV 10,1988.
    00006          REMARKS.
    00007
    00008          ****************************************************************
    00009          *                                                              *
    00010          *   ASSIGNMENT NUMBER                                          *
    00011          *   DATE ASSIGNED                                              *
    00012          *   DATE DUE                                                   *
    00013          *   PURPOSE:   THIS IS A VSAM FILE UPDATE PROGRAM FOR THE INVEN-*
    00014          *             TORY MASTER FILE.  THE POSSIBLE TRANSACTION TYPES *
    00015          *             ARE 1) ADD A NEW RECORD TO THE MASTER FILE,      *
    00016          *             2) DELETE A RECORD FROM THE MASTER FILE, AND     *
    00017          *             3) CHANGE THE ITEM DESCRIPTION IN THE MASTER FILE.*
    00018          *                                                              *
    00019          *             THE TYPES OF ERRORS THAT ARE POSSIBLE (WHICH WILL *
    00020          *             BE WRITTEN TO AN ERROR REPORT) ARE 1) ATTEMPT TO *
    00021          *             ADD A RECORD THAT ALREADY EXISTS IN THE MASTER   *
    00022          *             FILE, 2) ATTEMPT TO DELETE A MASTER THAT DOES NOT *
    00023          *             EXIST IN THE MASTER FILE, 3) ATTEMPT TO CHANGE A *
    00024          *             RECORD THAT DOES NOT EXIST IN THE MASTER FILE, AND*
    00025          *             4) INVALID TRANSACTION CODE.                     *
    00026          *                                                              *
    00027          *                                                              *
    00028          *   INPUT FILE SPECIFICATIONS:                                 *
    00029          *     (MASTER FILE)                      DESCRIPTION           *
    00030          *       CARD COLUMNS                                           *
    00031          *     -------------------------          -----------           *
    00032          *            1-5                         ITEM NUMBER           *
    00033          *            6-30                        ITEM DESCRIPTION      *
    00034          *            31-34                       QUANTITY ON HAND      *
    00035          *            35-42                       COST PER UNIT         *
    00036          *            43-46                       REORDER POINT         *
    00037          *            47-48                       SUPPLIER CODE         *
    00038          *            49-50                       BUYER CODE            *
    00039          *                                                              *
    00040          *                                                              *
    00041          *   INPUT FILE SPECIFICATIONS:                                 *
    00042          *     (TRANSACTION FILE)                 DESCRIPTION           *
    00043          *       CARD COLUMNS                                           *
    00044          *     -------------------------          -----------           *
    00045          *            1-1                         TRANSACTION CODE      *
    00046          *            2-6                         TRANS ITEM NUMBER     *
    00047          *            7-31                        TRANS ITEM DESCRIPTION*
    00048          *            32-35                       TRANS QUANTITY ON HAND*
    00049          *            36-43                       TRANS COST PER UNIT   *
    00050          *            44-47                       TRANS REORDER POINT   *
    00051          *            48-49                       TRANS SUPPLIER CODE   *
```

*(continued)*

```
        2        VSAMUPDT        16.16.03       NOV 10, 1988


    00052          *           50-51                        TRANS BUYER CODE          *
    00053          *                                                                  *
    00054          **********************************************************************
    00055
```

```
        3        VSAMUPDT        16.16.03       NOV 10, 1988


    00057            ENVIRONMENT DIVISION.
    00058
    00059            CONFIGURATION SECTION.
    00060
    00061            SOURCE-COMPUTER. IBM.
    00062            OBJECT-COMPUTER. IBM.
    00063            SPECIAL-NAMES.   C01 IS PAGE-TOP.
    00064
    00065            INPUT-OUTPUT SECTION.
    00066
    00067            FILE-CONTROL.
    00068
    00069                SELECT INVENTORY-FILE
    00070                        ASSIGN TO INVFILE
    00071                        ORGANIZATION IS INDEXED
    00072                        ACCESS IS DYNAMIC
    00073                        RECORD KEY IS ITEM-NUMBER-KEY
    00074                        FILE STATUS IS MASTER-FILE-STATUS.
    00075
    00076                SELECT TRANSACTION-FILE
    00077                        ASSIGN TO DA-S-TRANFILE.
    00078
    00079                SELECT ERROR-FILE
    00080                        ASSIGN TO UT-S-ERROR.
    00081
```

```
        4        VSAMUPDT        16.16.03       NOV 10, 1988


    00083            DATA DIVISION.
    00084
    00085            FILE SECTION.
    00086
    00087            FD  INVENTORY-FILE
    00088                LABEL RECORDS ARE OMITTED
    00089                RECORD CONTAINS 50 CHARACTERS
    00090                DATA RECORD IS INVENTORY-RECORD.
    00091
    00092            01  INVENTORY-RECORD.
    00093                05 ITEM-NUMBER-KEY           PIC X(5).
    00094                05 FILLER                    PIC X(45).
    00095
    00096            FD  TRANSACTION-FILE
    00097                LABEL RECORDS ARE OMITTED
    00098                RECORD CONTAINS 51 CHARACTERS
    00099                BLOCK CONTAINS 100 RECORDS
    00100                DATA RECORD IS TRANSACTION-RECORD.
    00101
    00102            01  TRANSACTION-RECORD           PIC X(51).
    00103
    00104            FD  ERROR-FILE
    00105                LABEL RECORDS ARE OMITTED
    00106                DATA RECORD IS ERROR-REPORT-RECORD.
    00107
    00108            01  ERROR-REPORT-RECORD          PIC X(133).
    00109
```

*(continued)*

```
   5      VSAMUPDT       16.16.03        NOV 10,1988

00111          WORKING-STORAGE SECTION.
00112
00113          77  ERROR-LINE-COUNT              PIC 99      VALUE 99.
00114
00115          01  INVENTORY-RECORD-IN.
00116              05 ITEM-NUMBER-IN             PIC X(5).
00117              05 ITEM-DESCRIPTION-IN        PIC X(25).
00118              05 QUANTITY-ON-HAND-IN        PIC 9(4).
00119              05 COST-PER-UNIT-IN           PIC 9(6)V9(2).
00120              05 REORDER-POINT-IN           PIC 9(4).
00121              05 SUPPLIER-CODE-IN           PIC 9(2).
00122              05 BUYER-CODE-IN              PIC 9(2).
00123
00124          01  TRANSACTION-RECORD-IN.
00125              05 TRANS-CODE-IN              PIC X.
00126                  88 ADD-RECORD                         VALUE 'A'.
00127                  88 DELETE-RECORD                      VALUE 'D'.
00128                  88 CHANGE-RECORD                      VALUE 'C'.
00129                  88 VALID-TRANS-CODE                   VALUE 'A' 'D' 'C'.
00130              05 REST-OF-TRANSACTION-RECORD.
00131                  10 TRANS-ITEM-NUMBER-IN       PIC X(5).
00132                  10 TRANS-ITEM-DESCRIPTION-IN  PIC X(25).
00133                  10 TRANS-QUANTITY-ON-HAND-IN  PIC 9(4).
00134                  10 TRANS-COST-PER-UNIT-IN     PIC 9(6)V9(2).
00135                  10 TRANS-REORDER-POINT-IN     PIC 9(4).
00136                  10 TRANS-SUPPLIER-CODE-IN     PIC 9(2).
00137                  10 TRANS-BUYER-CODE-IN        PIC 9(2).
00138
00139          01  MASTER-FILE-STATUS            PIC X(2).
00140              88 SUCCESSFUL-OPERATION                   VALUE '00'.
00141
00142
00143          01  ARE-THERE-MORE-TRANS-RECORDS  PIC X(3)    VALUE 'YES'.
00144              88 MORE-TRANS-RECORDS                     VALUE 'YES'.
00145              88 NO-MORE-TRANS-RECORDS                  VALUE 'NO'.
00146
00147          01  BLANK-LINE.
00148              05 FILLER                     PIC X(133) VALUE SPACES.
00149
00150          01  ERROR-LINE.
00151              05 FILLER                     PIC X(21)   VALUE SPACES.
00152              05 ERROR-ITEM-NUMBER-OUT      PIC X(5).
00153              05 FILLER                     PIC X(20)   VALUE SPACES.
00154              05 ERROR-CODE-OUT             PIC X.
00155              05 FILLER                     PIC X(20)   VALUE SPACES.
00156              05 ERROR-MESSAGE-OUT          PIC X(46).
00157              05 FILLER                     PIC X(20)   VALUE SPACES.
00158
00159          01  ERROR-REPORT-HEADING.
00160              05 FILLER                     PIC X(55) VALUE SPACES.
00161              05 FILLER                     PIC X(24) VALUE
00162                  'TRANSACTION ERROR REPORT'.
00163              05 FILLER                     PIC X(54) VALUE SPACES.
00164
```

```
   6      VSAMUPDT       16.16.03        NOV 10,1988

00165          01  ERROR-COLUMN-HEADING.
00166              05 FILLER                     PIC X(23) VALUE SPACES.
00167              05 FILLER                     PIC X(2)  VALUE 'ID'.
00168              05 FILLER                     PIC X(20) VALUE SPACES.
00169              05 FILLER                     PIC X(4)  VALUE 'CODE'.
00170              05 FILLER                     PIC X(20) VALUE SPACES.
00171              05 FILLER                     PIC X(13) VALUE
00172                  'ERROR MESSAGE'.
00173              05 FILLER                     PIC X(46) VALUE SPACES.
00174
```

*(continued)*

```
    7        VSAMUPDT        16.16.03        NOV 10,1988

00176          PROCEDURE DIVISION.
00177
00178          0000-MAIN-PARA.
00179              PERFORM 1000-INIT-PARA.
00180              PERFORM 8000-READ-TRANSACTION-PARA.
00181              PERFORM 2000-UPDATE-PROCESS-PARA
00182                  UNTIL NO-MORE-TRANS-RECORDS.
00183              PERFORM 3000-TERMINATE-PARA.
00184              STOP RUN.
00185
```

```
    8        VSAMUPDT        16.16.03        NOV 10,1988

00187          ****************************************************************
00188          *    1000-INIT-PARA                                           *
00189          *                                                             *
00190          *    IN THIS PARAGRAPH THE INVENTORY FILE IS OPENED FOR INPUT/ *
00191          *    OUTPUT (AS IT WILL BE READ FROM AND WRITTEN TO), THE TRANS-*
00192          *    ACTION FILE IS OPENED FOR INPUT, AND THE ERROR-FILE IS    *
00193          *    OPENED FOR OUTPUT.                                        *
00194          *                                                             *
00195          ****************************************************************
00196
00197          1000-INIT-PARA.
00198              OPEN I-O    INVENTORY-FILE
00199                   INPUT  TRANSACTION-FILE
00200                   OUTPUT ERROR-FILE.
00201
```

```
    9        VSAMUPDT        16.16.03        NOV 10,1988

00203          ****************************************************************
00204          *    2000-UPDATE-PROCESS-PARA                                  *
00205          *                                                             *
00206          *    IN THIS PARAGRAPH THE TRANSACTION CODES ARE VALIDATED.    *
00207          *    IF THE CODE IS INVALID 2100-INVALID-CODE-PARA IS PERFORMED.*
00208          *    IF THE CODE IS VALID THEN IF TESTS ARE USED TO DETERMINE  *
00209          *    WHETHER THE TRANSACTION IS ADDING A RECORD, DELETING A    *
00210          *    RECORD, OR CHANGING A RECORD.  AFTER THE APPROPRIATE ACTION*
00211          *    HAS BEEN TAKEN A NEW TRANSACTION RECORD IS READ.          *
00212          *                                                             *
00213          ****************************************************************
00214
00215          2000-UPDATE-PROCESS-PARA.
00216              IF NOT VALID-TRANS-CODE
00217                  PERFORM 2100-INVALID-CODE-PARA
00218              ELSE
00219                  IF ADD-RECORD
00220                      PERFORM 2200-ADD-RECORD-PARA
00221                  ELSE
00222                      IF DELETE-RECORD
00223                          PERFORM 2300-DELETE-RECORD-PARA
00224                      ELSE
00225                          PERFORM 2400-CHANGE-RECORD-PARA.
00226              PERFORM 8000-READ-TRANSACTION-PARA.
00227
```

*(continued)*

```
   10        VSAMUPDT        16.16.03        NOV 10,1988

00229     ****************************************************************
00230     *   2100-TRANS-NUMBER-ERROR-PARA                              *
00231     *                                                            *
00232     *   IN THIS PARAGRAPH AN ERROR MESSAGE IS WRITTEN IF AN INVALID *
00233     *   TRANSACTION CODE IS DETECTED.                            *
00234     *                                                            *
00235     ****************************************************************
00236
00237      2100-INVALID-CODE-PARA.
00238          MOVE TRANS-ITEM-NUMBER-IN TO ERROR-ITEM-NUMBER-OUT.
00239          MOVE TRANS-CODE-IN TO ERROR-CODE-OUT.
00240          MOVE 'INVALID TRANSACTION CODE' TO ERROR-MESSAGE-OUT.
00241          IF ERROR-LINE-COUNT IS GREATER THAN 45
00242              PERFORM 9000-NEW-ERROR-PAGE-PARA.
00243          WRITE ERROR-REPORT-RECORD FROM ERROR-LINE
00244              AFTER 2.
00245          ADD 2 TO ERROR-LINE-COUNT.
00246
```

```
   11        VSAMUPDT        16.16.03        NOV 10,1988

00248     ****************************************************************
00249     *   2200-ADD-RECORD-PARA                                      *
00250     *                                                            *
00251     *   IN THIS PARAGRAPH THE TRANSACTION INFORMATION IS WRITTEN  *
00252     *   (AS A NEW RECORD) TO THE MASTER FILE.  IF THE ITEM NUMBER *
00253     *   IN THE TRANSACTION IS FOUND TO ALREADY EXIST, THEN 2210-  *
00254     *   ADD-ERROR-PARA IS PERFORMED.                             *
00255     *                                                            *
00256     ****************************************************************
00257
00258      2200-ADD-RECORD-PARA.
00259          MOVE TRANS-ITEM-NUMBER-IN TO ITEM-NUMBER-KEY.
00260          WRITE INVENTORY-RECORD FROM
00261              REST-OF-TRANSACTION-RECORD
00262                  INVALID KEY
00263                      PERFORM 2210-ADD-ERROR-PARA.
```

```
   12        VSAMUPDT        16.16.03        NOV 10,1988

00265     ****************************************************************
00266     *   2210-ADD-ERROR-PARA                                       *
00267     *                                                            *
00268     *   IN THIS PARAGRAPH AN ERROR MESSAGE IS WRITTEN IF THERE WAS *
00269     *   AN ATTEMPT TO ADD A RECORD THAT ALREADY EXISTS IN THE MASTER*
00270     *   FILE.                                                    *
00271     *                                                            *
00272     ****************************************************************
00273
00274      2210-ADD-ERROR-PARA.
00275          MOVE TRANS-ITEM-NUMBER-IN TO ERROR-1TEM-NUMBER-OUT.
00276          MOVE TRANS-CODE-IN TO ERROR-CODE-OUT.
00277          MOVE 'ATTEMPT TO ADD RECORD THAT ALREADY EXISTS' TO
00278              ERROR-MESSAGE-OUT.
00279          IF ERROR-LINE-COUNT IS GREATER THAN 45
00280              PERFORM 9000-NEW-ERROR-PAGE-PARA.
00281          WRITE ERROR-REPORT-RECORD FROM ERROR-LINE
00282              AFTER 2.
00283          ADD 2 TO ERROR-LINE-COUNT.
00284
```

*(continued)*

```
    13        VSAMUPDT        16.16.03        NOV 10,1988

00286        *************************************************************
00287        *    2300-DELETE-RECORD-PARA                                *
00288        *                                                           *
00289        *    IN THIS PARAGRAPH THE MASTER RECORD THAT CORRESPONDS WITH
00290        *    ITEM NUMBER IN THE TRANSACTION RECORD.  IF THE MASTER RECORD *
00291        *    SPECIFIED IN THE TRANSACTION RECORD DOES NOT EXIST IN THE    *
00292        *    MASTER FILE THEN 2310-DELETE-ERROR-PARA IS PERFORMED.   *
00293        *                                                           *
00294        *************************************************************
00295
00296        2300-DELETE-RECORD-PARA.
00297            MOVE TRANS-ITEM-NUMBER-IN TO ITEM-NUMBER-KEY.
00298            DELETE INVENTORY-FILE
00299                    INVALID KEY
00300                        PERFORM 2310-DELETE-ERROR-PARA.
00301
```

```
    14        VSAMUPDT        16.16.03        NOV 10,1988

00303        *************************************************************
00304        *    2310-DELETE-ERROR-PARA                                 *
00305        *                                                           *
00306        *    IN THIS PARAGRAPH AN ERROR MESSAGE IS WRITTEN IF THERE WAS *
00307        *    AN ATTEMPT TO DELETE A RECORD THAT DOES NOT EXIST IN THE    *
00308        *    MASTER FILE.                                            *
00309        *                                                           *
00310        *************************************************************
00311
00312        2310-DELETE-ERROR-PARA.
00313            MOVE TRANS-ITEM-NUMBER-IN TO ERROR-ITEM-NUMBER-OUT.
00314            MOVE TRANS-CODE-IN TO ERROR-CODE-OUT.
00315            MOVE 'ATTEMPT TO DELETE RECORD THAT DOES NOT EXIST' TO
00316                ERROR-MESSAGE-OUT.
00317            IF ERROR-LINE-COUNT IS GREATER THAN 45
00318                PERFORM 9000-NEW-ERROR-PAGE-PARA.
00319            WRITE ERROR-REPORT-RECORD FROM ERROR-LINE
00320                AFTER 2.
00321            ADD 2 TO ERROR-LINE-COUNT.
00322
```

```
    15        VSAMUPDT        16.16.03        NOV 10,1988

00324        *************************************************************
00325        *    2400-CHANGE-RECORD-PARA                                *
00326        *                                                           *
00327        *    IN THIS PARAGRAPH THE TRANSACTION ITEM NUMBER IS MOVED TO *
00328        *    THE MASTER KEY AND THE MASTER FILE IS READ.  IF THERE IS A  *
00329        *    A SUCCESSFUL READ (I.E. IF THERE IS A CORRESPONDING MASTER  *
00330        *    RECORD IN THE MASTER FILE) THEN THE ITEM DESCRIPTION IS     *
00331        *    CHANGED USING THE INFORMATION IN THE TRANSACTION RECORD.  IF *
00332        *    NO CORRESPONDING MASTER IS FOUND THEN 2410-CHANGE-ERROR-PARA *
00333        *    IS PERFORMED.                                           *
00334        *                                                           *
00335        *************************************************************
00336
00337        2400-CHANGE-RECORD-PARA.
00338            MOVE TRANS-ITEM-NUMBER-IN TO ITEM-NUMBER-KEY.
00339            READ INVENTORY-FILE INTO INVENTORY-RECORD-IN
00340                    INVALID KEY
00341                        PERFORM 2410-CHANGE-ERROR-PARA.
00342            IF SUCCESSFUL-OPERATION
00343                MOVE TRANS-ITEM-DESCRIPTION-IN TO ITEM-DESCRIPTION-IN
00344                REWRITE INVENTORY-RECORD FROM INVENTORY-RECORD-IN.
00345
```

*(continued)*

```
     16        VSAMUPDT       16.16.03       NOV 10,1988

00347        ***************************************************************
00348        *  2410-CHANGE-ERROR-PARA                                     *
00349        *                                                             *
00350        *  IN THIS PARAGRAPH AN ERROR MESSAGE IS WRITTEN IF THERE WAS *
00351        *  AN ATTEMPT TO CHANGE A RECORD THAT DOES NOT EXIST IN THE   *
00352        *  MASTER FILE.                                               *
00353        *                                                             *
00354        ***************************************************************
00355
00356        2410-CHANGE-ERROR-PARA.
00357            MOVE TRANS-ITEM-NUMBER-IN TO ERROR-ITEM-NUMBER-OUT.
00358            MOVE TRANS-CODE-IN TO ERROR-CODE-OUT.
00359            MOVE 'ATTEMPT TO CHANGE RECORD THAT DOES NOT EXIST' TO
00360                ERROR-MESSAGE-OUT.
00361            IF ERROR-LINE-COUNT IS GREATER THAN 45
00362                PERFORM 9000-NEW-ERROR-PAGE-PARA.
00363            WRITE ERROR-REPORT-RECORD FROM ERROR-LINE
00364                AFTER 2.
00365            ADD 2 TO ERROR-LINE-COUNT.
00366
```

```
     17        VSAMUPDT       16.16.03       NOV 10,1988

00368        ***************************************************************
00369        *  3000-TERMINATE-PARA                                        *
00370        *                                                             *
00371        *  IN THIS PARAGRAPH ALL OF THE FILES ARE CLOSED.             *
00372        *                                                             *
00373        ***************************************************************
00374
00375        3000-TERMINATE-PARA.
00376
00377            CLOSE INVENTORY-FILE
00378                  TRANSACTION-FILE
00379                  ERROR-FILE.
00380
```

```
     19        VSAMUPDT       16.16.03       NOV 10,1988

00391        ***************************************************************
00392        *  8000-READ-TRANSACTION-PARA                                 *
00393        *                                                             *
00394        *  THIS PARAGRAPH READS A RECORD FROM THE TRANSACTION INPUT   *
00395        *  FILE.                                                      *
00396        *                                                             *
00397        ***************************************************************
00398
00399        8000-READ-TRANSACTION-PARA.
00400            READ TRANSACTION-FILE INTO TRANSACTION-RECORD-IN
00401                AT END
00402                    MOVE 'NO' TO ARE-THERE-MORE-TRANS-RECORDS.
00403
```

*(continued)*

```
      20      VSAMUPDT      16.16.03      NOV 10,1988

    00405       ****************************************************************
    00406       *   9000-NEW-ERROR-PAGE-PARA                                   *
    00407       *                                                              *
    00408       *   THIS PARAGRAPH IS PERFORMED WHEN THE NUMBER OF LINES ON AN *
    00409       *   ERROR REPORT PAGE EXCEEDS 45.                              *
    00410       *                                                              *
    00411       ****************************************************************
    00412
    00413        9000-NEW-ERROR-PAGE-PARA.
    00414            WRITE ERROR-REPORT-RECORD FROM BLANK-LINE
    00415                AFTER PAGE-TOP.
    00416            WRITE ERROR-REPORT-RECORD FROM ERROR-REPORT-HEADING
    00417                AFTER 3.
    00418            WRITE ERROR-REPORT-RECORD FROM ERROR-COLUMN-HEADING
    00419                AFTER 3.
    00420            WRITE ERROR-REPORT-RECORD FROM BLANK-LINE
    00421                AFTER 2.
    00422            MOVE 9 TO ERROR-LINE-COUNT.
```

```
                         TRANSACTION ERROR REPORT

        ID               CODE                ERROR MESSAGE


      02222                A            ATTEMPT TO ADD RECORD THAT ALREADY EXISTS

      08234                Q            INVALID TRANSACTION CODE

      99999                D            ATTEMPT TO DELETE RECORD THAT DOES NOT EXIST

      99988                C            ATTEMPT TO CHANGE RECORD THAT DOES NOT EXIST
```

## Original VSAM Inventory File

```
IDCAMS  SYSTEM SERVICES                        TIME: 14:59:42    10/25/88    PAGE    2

LISTING OF DATA SET -VSM.A018.XX.VSAMFILE

KEY OF RECORD - 02222
02222ANTI-GLARE SCREEN         00100004000000050102

KEY OF RECORD - 03001
03001TURTLENECK SWEATER        00250000800000150101

KEY OF RECORD - 08234
08234SPARK PLUGS 1 DOZ         00400000120000500103

KEY OF RECORD - 11653
11653LEATHER JACKET            00070001500000050104

KEY OF RECORD - 12345
12345BROWN LEATHER BELT        00200000150000150201

KEY OF RECORD - 12355
12355BLACK LEATHER BELT        00220000150000150201

KEY OF RECORD - 21100
21100PRINT SILK SCARVES        00130000180000100301

KEY OF RECORD - 21133
21133T-SHIRT DRESSES           00080000210000050302

KEY OF RECORD - 21143
21143SWEATER DRESSES           00120000320000100303

KEY OF RECORD - 22165
22165DESIGNER SWEATER          00080000500000050301

KEY OF RECORD - 22298
22298ST COTTON SHORTS          00200000190000150304

KEY OF RECORD - 22324
22324BLUE JEANS PLEATS         00300000300000200202

KEY OF RECORD - 22346
22346SOLID SWEAT SHIRTS        00230000220000150302

KEY OF RECORD - 22700
22700LG COTTON SHORTS          00190000140000100202

KEY OF RECORD - 22835
22835SWEAT PANTS               00300000100000200302

KEY OF RECORD - 22988
22988DESIGN SWEAT SHIRT        00220000450000200103
```

*(continued)*

```
    IDCAMS  SYSTEM SERVICES                          TIME: 14:59:42    10/25/88    PAGE    3

    LISTING OF DATA SET -VSM.AO18.XX.VSAMFILE
    KEY OF RECORD - 23334
    23334BLUE JEANS STRAIGHT LEG   00400000230000250203

    KEY OF RECORD - 23342
    23342DRESS BLOUSES BOWTIE      00130000500000100104

    KEY OF RECORD - 23444
    23444DESIGNER POLO SHIRTS      00320000500000250301

    KEY OF RECORD - 23453
    23453COTTON BOTTONDOWNS        00380000450000300202

    KEY OF RECORD - 23552
    23552DESIGNER COTTON BLOUSES   00240000550000200301

    KEY OF RECORD - 23664
    23664BUDGET POLO SHIRTS        00210000260000200201

    KEY OF RECORD - 24345
    24345ACID WASHED JEAN JR       00130000180000100204

    KEY OF RECORD - 24350
    24350ACID WASHED J SKIRT       C0180000220000150204

    KEY OF RECORD - 24355
    24355ACID WASHED MINI-SKIRT    00100000240000080203

    IDC0005I NUMBER OF RECORDS PROCESSED WAS 25

    IDC0001I FUNCTION COMPLETED, HIGHEST CONDITION CODE WAS 0

    IDC0002I IDCAMS PROCESSING COMPLETE. MAXIMUM CONDITION CODE WAS 0
```

## Transaction File

```
    1.    02222R000500035000
    2.    02999S9999
    3.    21100S0004
    4.    22324B000020003000
    5.    22700G001000005000
    6.    77777Q001000003000
    7.    80808R002000003000
    8.    99999S0025
```

*(continued)*

## Updated VSAM Inventory File

```
IDCAMS  SYSTEM SERVICES                          TIME: 15:09:05     10/25/88    PAGE    2

   LISTING OF DATA SET -VSM.AO18.XX.VSAMFILE

     KEY OF RECORD - 02222
     02222ANTI-GLARE SCREEN          00100004000000050102

     KEY OF RECORD - 03001
     03001ANGORA SWEATER             00250000800000150101

     KEY OF RECORD - 08234
     08234SPARK PLUGS 1 DOZ          00400000120000500103

     KEY OF RECORD - 09999
     09999DELUXE WOOD CARVING SET    00100004000000050102

     KEY OF RECORD - 12345
     12345BROWN LEATHER BELT         00200000150000150201

     KEY OF RECORD - 12355
     12355BLACK LEATHER BELT         00220000150000150201

     KEY OF RECORD - 21100
     21100PRINT SILK SCARVES         00130000180000100301

     KEY OF RECORD - 21133
     21133T-SHIRT DRESSES            00080000210000050302

     KEY OF RECORD - 21143
     21143SWEATER DRESSES            00120000320000100303

     KEY OF RECORD - 22165
     22165DESIGNER SWEATER           00080000500000050301

     KEY OF RECORD - 22298
     22298ST COTTON SHORTS           00200000190000150304

     KEY OF RECORD - 22324
     22324BLUE JEANS PLEATS          00300000300000200202

     KEY OF RECORD - 22346
     22346SOLID SWEAT SHIRTS         00230000220000150302

     KEY OF RECORD - 22700
     22700LG COTTON SHORTS           00190000140000100202

     KEY OF RECORD - 22835
     22835SWEAT PANTS                00300000100000200302

     KEY OF RECORD - 22988
     22988DESIGN SWEAT SHIRT         00220000450000200103
```

```
IDCAMS  SYSTEM SERVICES                          TIME: 15:09:05     10/25/88    PAGE    3

   LISTING OF DATA SET -VSM.AO18.XX.VSAMFILE

   KEY OF RECORD - 23334
   23334BLUE JEANS STRAIGHT LEG  00400000230000250203

   KEY OF RECORD - 23342
   23342DRESS BLOUSES BOWTIE       00130000500000100104

   KEY OF RECORD - 23444
   23444DESIGNER POLO SHIRTS       00320000500000250301

   KEY OF RECORD - 23453
   23453COTTON BOTTONDOWNS         00380000450000300202

   KEY OF RECORD - 23552
   23552DESIGNER COTTON BLOUSES  00240000550000200301

   KEY OF RECORD - 23664
   23664BUDGET POLO SHIRTS         00210000260000200201

   KEY OF RECORD - 24345
   24345ACID WASHED JEAN JR        00130000180000100204

   KEY OF RECORD - 24350
   24350ACID WASHED J SKIRT        00180000220000150204

   KEY OF RECORD - 24355
   24355ACID WASHED MINI-SKIRT     00100000240000080203

   IDC0005I NUMBER OF RECORDS PROCESSED WAS 25

   IDC0001I FUNCTION COMPLETED, HIGHEST CONDITION CODE WAS O
```

*(continued)*

```
IDCAMS  SYSTEM SERVICES                              TIME: 15:09:05     10/25/88    PAGE    4

IDC0002I IDCAMS PROCESSING COMPLETE. MAXIMUM CONDITION CODE WAS 0
```

## Chapter Review Questions

1. ISAM stands for:

    a. Index sequential file
    b. Index sequential access method
    c. Index serial access memory
    d. Index access method
    e. None of the above

2. VSAM stands for:

    a. Virtual sequential access memory
    b. Virtual storage access method
    c. Visual serial access method
    d. Visual sequential access method
    e. None of the above

3. Using indexes for sorting:

    a. Reduces the amount of data movement
    b. Requires a second table
    c. Orders the indexes that point to the original data
    d. Is faster than a speeding bullet
    e. All of the above

4. Which of the following is true about ISAM files?

    a. Uses high key value for track and cylinder indexes
    b. Uses an overflow data area
    c. Uses a prime data area
    d. Chains records together
    e. All of the above

5. Using Figure 15.3, where would record 305 be found if it exist?

    a. Cylinder 4
    b. Cylinder 5
    c. Can not determine without track index
    d. Cylinder 1
    e. None of the above

6. Using Figure 15.6, where would record 92 be added?

    a. Track 6, Record 2
    b. Track 3, Record 1
    c. Track 5, Record 5
    d. Track 2, Record 5
    e. None of the above

7. What would be the result of a read for record 85 in Figure 15.6?

    a. EOF
    b. Invalid key
    c. File status code of 00
    d. The record is placed in the input buffer
    e. None of the above

8. A delete of a record from an ISAM file on most systems:

    a. Causes the record to be physically removed
    b. Causes the record to be logically removed
    c. Can not be done with COBOL
    d. Both a and b
    e. None of the above

9. Building an indexed file is done under sequential access.

    a. True
    b. False

10. The record key for an indexed file

    a. Is part of the record
    b. Is a 77 or 01 in working storage
    c. Is the first field in the record
    d. Is defined procedurally
    e. None of the above

11. File organization and file access must be the same; that is ORGANIZATION SEQUENTIAL and ACCESS MODE SEQUENTIAL.

    a. True
    b. False

12. Defining an VSAM file is done with:

    a. A COBOL program
    b. A system utility called PGM
    c. A system utility called IDCAM
    d. A system utility called VSAM
    e. None of the above

13. Initializing the VSAM file is done with:

    a. A COBOL program
    b. An IDCAM REPRO procedure
    c. A VSAM DEFINE procedure
    d. A system program, PGM
    e. Both a and b

14. The difference between the SELECT clause for an ISAM and a VSAM is:

    a. There is no difference
    b. The ASSIGN clause
    c. The RECORD KEY clause
    d. The ORGANIZATION clause
    e. The ACCESS MODE clause

15. A file dump of a VSAM file may be done with:

    a. A COBOL program
    b. An IDCAM, PRINT procedure
    c. An IDCAM, DUMP procedure
    d. A PGM, DUMP procedure
    e. Both a and b

16. Since a VSAM file is an indexed file, I/O procedures would never check for EOF.

    a. True
    b. False

17. In order to execute a REWRITE properly, you must first:

    a. Execute INVALID KEY

    b. Execute a READ successfully

    c. Execute a WRITE successfully

    d. Execute a RECORD KEY

    e. None of the above

18. Accessing a VSAM file both with the record key and to provide a sequential listing requires:

    a. Random access with the file opened for I-O

    b. Sequential access with the file opened for I-O

    c. Dynamic access with the file opened for output

    d. Combined access with the file opened for I-O

    e. Dynamic access with the file opened for I-O

19. The START may be used with ISAM and VSAM files.

    a. True

    b. False

20. To START a VSAM file at the beginning of the file you may:

    a. Use the START NOT < . . .

    b. CLOSE and reOPEN the file

    c. Use READ . . . NEXT RECORD

    d. Use the START > . . .

    e. Both a and b

21. The use of the ALTERNATE KEY clause allows:

    a. Two primary keys to be used alternately

    b. The VSAM file to be accessed by a secondary key

    c. The ISAM file to be accessed by a secondary key

    d. Both b and c

    e. None of the above

22. Using Figure 15.7, where would record 200 be found if it exists?

    a. Area 1

    b. Area 2

    c. Area 3

    d. Area 4

    e. None of the above

23. An area split is:

    a. Caused when an area does not have any free space

    b. Caused when an area does not have a free interval

    c. Caused when all intervals in an area are full

    d. Can not occur

    e. None of the above

24. Using Figure 15.10, what would happen if records 712, 725 and 740 were added?

    a. An interval split would occur

    b. An area split would occur

    c. Nothing, since room exists in the area

    d. A new sequential set is created

    e. None of the above

25. What would happen in Figure 15.7, if record 100 was deleted?
    a. Record 100's space would be free
    b. Record 120 would move to record 100's location
    c. Record 100 is made inactive
    d. The delete can not be used with VSAM files
    e. None of the above

## Discussion Questions

1. Briefly explain overflow chaining for an ISAM file.
2. Contrast initializing a VSAM file with a COBOL program and an IDCAM.
3. Contrast index and sequence sets with cylinder and track indexes.
4. Explain how an interval split is done.
5. Explain how a VSAM file may be accessed with a record key and sequentially in the same job.
6. Why is the index sort concept important to understanding indexed files?
7. Explain how an alternate key of major might be used for the DEAN-FILE.
8. Explain how the COPY could be used with VSAM files.
9. Explain file status codes. How could they be used? Do 88 level items help?
10. Explain the processing model for updating index files.

## Practice Problems

1. Set up the cylinder and track indexes for a file that has 10 cylinders and four tracks per cylinder. Assume that only three records fit per track and that track 0 is for the indexes and tracks 5 and 6 are for overflow. The high keys for the 10 cylinders should be: 100, 200, 300, 400, 500, 600, 700, 800, 900, 1000.
2. Now use the same data and set up the index and sequence sets for 10 areas. Each area should contain three intervals.
3. Using Figure 15.3 and 15.4 ADD the following records: 77, 90, 79, 115, 85, 122. Show the new Figure 15.4.

## Programming Assignments

1. Write the IDCAM to create a VSAM file for the DEAN-FILE in Data File A (Format 1).
2. Assume you did 1 correctly, now write the COBOL program to initialize the file.
3. Do the initialization in 2 using an IDCAM.
4. Write a COBOL program to provide a listing of students in a particular major requested by the Dean. The Dean will specify the students by indicating a major code. Assume the major code is an alternate key and accept the Dean's request interactively.

## Programming Projects

The following assignments rely on the data dictionary, library elements and data sets found in the Project Sets Section of your text.

1. Do the VSAM Assignment for the Project Management System in Project A.
2. Do the VSAM Assignment for the Employee System in Project B.

# SUBPROGRAMMING

## 16

**_OBJECTIVES_**  In this chapter we will explore the world of subprogramming. This is the world in which one program is subordinate to another. It is at the beck and call of the main program.

We will examine why this main program/subprogram world is beneficial to our data processing environment. The advantages range from development to maintenance. You will see how using subprogramming and copy libraries together is a tremendous asset to program development and maintenance.

You will study how a main program and subprogram work together, how they share data, how they communicate and how they are developed and tested.

## TOPICS

- subprogramming
- main program/subprogram relationship
- communications between programs

- using the CALL
- using the USING
- system benefits
- maintenance benefits
- using the CALL and COPY together

## KEY WORDS

- main program
- subprogram
- PROGRAM-ID
- CALL. . .USING

- PROCEDURE DIVISION. . .USING
- EXIT PROGRAM
- LINKAGE SECTION
- CANCEL

## ITS PURPOSE AND ROLE

One theme that permeates this text is structured programming. We have studied and used structured techniques throughout. Part of our discussions have dealt with independence. This independence has been aided by our control statement, the PERFORM. Those performed modules are sometimes called subroutines in other languages. Developing programs using the modular, top-down approach aids not only the development, but also the maintenance function.

Subprogramming is an extension of this philosophy. It allows system development to be done by writing the modules as programs that may be developed and tested independently of the other programs in the system. This enhances development. Eventually though, all the programs will be put through a system test, since ultimately they may all need to work together.

## SYSTEM DEVELOPMENT CONSIDERATIONS

Subprogramming has two major areas of application:

1. As programs within a system
2. As common routines within a system and/or throughout several systems

### System of Programs

In Chapter 14 our example program that accomplished update, maintenance and reporting functions was developed modularly. That is, the hierarchy chart looked something like Figure 16.1.

**FIGURE 16.1**
**Partial Hierarchy Chart**
**Illustrating Indexed Programs**
**Main Modules**

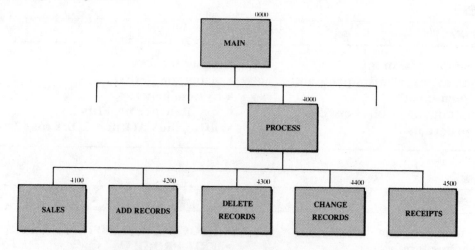

Each of the 4000 modules is executed by a PERFORM. All modules are in one program. If the project leader assigned each of the 4000 modules to individual programmers, they would all be writing code segments that would be merged into one program. None of the segments could be tested until all were written. Wouldn't it be nice if each programmer could test his or her logic independently? Sure it would. The modules being tested would be smaller and easier to test. The project leader would also have a much better idea about the progress being made. How do we do this? By making each of the modules, 4100 through 4500, a separate program. And, instead of the process module performing each, it will execute each as a subprogram.

Now each programmer will be able to develop and test programs independently. Programmers can work at their own paces. They will have more control of their jobs. This new subprogramming environment is depicted in Figure 16.2

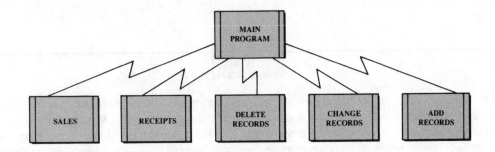

**FIGURE 16.2**
Subprogram Illustration

### Common Routine

The second major area of application is that of common routines. These routines could occur in all programs in a system or could be found in many or all systems.

One such routine that is widely found in industry is a common page header or banner. This banner is not unlike what you have seen in the data dictionaries in the Projects. The company might make a decision that all reports written must contain a banner like that shown in Figure 16.3.

```
* * * * * * * * * * * * * * * * * * * * * * * * * * * * * * * * * * * * * * * * * * * * * * * * *


Company Name                                      Date (July 7, 1988)
                                                  Page#



* * * * * * * * * * * * * * * * * * * * * * * * * * * * * * * * * * * * * * * * * * * * * * * * *
```

**FIGURE 16.3**
Example Corporate Page Banner

If every report being produced must have that banner on top of every page of every report, can you imagine all the common code that would be part of every program? Wouldn't it be best to remove all this common code and make it a subprogram? Yes it would! We have the code once instead of once for each program; probably thousands of copies. I'm assuming all the code is the same. By now, you can easily imagine the variety that could exist. So we gain in this respect also!

### COPY vs. CALL

Why not put the common code into a library and have the thousands of programs just copy it? That's very good. In fact, that is what is done in many installations. But let's look at this suggestion carefully.

Let's say a common set of source code, D-R-Ds, procedure code, etc. has been placed into a library called BANLIB. Now all the programs have **COPY** verbs in appropriate locations and all reports are meeting the corporate standards.

Now let's assume the company gets sold, and the name changes. The name that is on all reports must change. How? Just change the library element *and* have all programs copy it in. That's fine and good, but when is the copying actually done? During compilation. So every one of the programs, possibly thousands, must be recompiled. However bad recompiling sounds, the only programming change (maintenance) is done to the library element. None of the programs have to be modified. That's still great!

What if instead of a copy library approach to the common banner we used a subprogram? Now the thousands of programs just execute the banner subprogram using the **CALL** verb. This is depicted in Figure 16.4.

**FIGURE 16.4**
Relationship of Common
Subprogram to Other
Programs

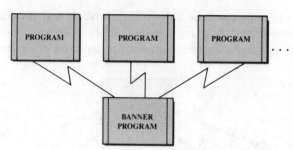

Now assume the company name is to be changed. What will that cause? The banner program will need to be modified to reflect the change. What about all the other programs? They don't have to be touched! Once the banner program is changed, it will provide the appropriate company name when it is called. How about that? That's what I call smart system design.

By using the subprogram approach, we save all the duplicate code (inherent to the technique as well), and we make maintenance so much easier. Maybe not so obvious is that development is also enhanced. Each programmer does not have to re-invent the wheel by coding the banner logic.

### COPY and CALL

I don't imply that COPY has been replaced by CALL. It hasn't. Common FDs, D-R-Ds and so on are still best handled by COPY. Logic or procedure routines such as date conversion, interest calculations and payroll table lookup are best suited to CALL. However, they also work well together.

In our previous example, what if the banner program copied the company name and procedures from a library? Now a change to company name would mean the library element would be changed and the banner program re-compiled. That's all. None of the programs have to be modified. Now that's making maintenance easy.

## TIP

**Write compile-time tables and lookup procedures into subprograms. Changes to the table values can now be made in the library.**

Well, enough talk about subprogramming in general. Let's look at the tools.

### CALL

As you probably picked up in our earlier discussions, the main program and subprogram are related via the CALL verb. In programming terms, the main program is the one doing the calling and the subprogram is the one being called.

The general format of CALL is shown below.

<u>CALL</u> program-id [ <u>USING</u> data-name$_1$, data-name$_2$ $\cdots$ ]

In the main calling program's PROCEDURE DIVISION, CALL will cause the program identified by program-id to be brought into memory and executed. That implies that the called program must be in a library in a form ready for execution, load module form. In fact, the subprogram is typically in a library called a load library. The means of getting the subprogram into a load library vary from system to system.

The following code shows the relationship of the main program, CALL, subprogram and program-id.

```
        MAIN PROGRAM           |      SUBPROGRAM
                               |
    IDENTIFICATION DIVISION.    |   IDENTIFICATION DIVISION.
        .                      |       .
        .                      |       .
    PROGRAM-ID.  MAIN.          |   PROGRAM-ID.  SUBPROG.
        .                      |       .
        .                      |       .
    DATA DIVISION.              |   DATA DIVISION.
    FILE SECTION.               |   FILE SECTION.
        .                      |       .
        .                      |       .
    WORKING-STORAGE SECTION.    |   WORKING-STORAGE SECTION.
        .                      |       .
        .                      |       .
    PROCEDURE DIVISION.         |   PROCEDURE DIVISION.
    0000-MAIN-PARA.             |   0000-MAIN-PARA.
        .                      |       .
        .                      |       .
    4000-PROCESS-PARA.          |       .
        .                      |       .
        .                      |
    CALL 'SUBPROG'.             |   9000-EXIT-PARA.
                               |       EXIT PROGRAM.
                               |
```

**USING Option.**    You probably noticed that CALL had an option available. USING is used to pass data between the main program and subprograms. In actuality, data locations are shared, with both programs having access to the same locations. If the main program puts values in certain locations, the subprograms have access to those values and vice versa.

For instance, the following illustrates CALL. . .USING.

```
    MAIN PROGRAM           |   SUBPROGRAM
        .                  |   PROGRAM-ID.   SUBPROG.
        .                  |       .
        .                  |       .
    CALL 'SUBPROG'         |   PROCEDURE DIVISION
         USING A, B.       |        USING A, B.
```

The main called the sub and made available the values in the data names A and B. Notice, though, that the subprogram also had to specify that the two data names were to be shared.

In COBOL '74 the arguments, values A and B, are shared according to the position in which they appear in the list. The names don't have to be the same. We could have said:

```
    CALL 'SUBPROG' USING A, B
```

in the main, and then

PROCEDURE DIVISION USING X, Y

in the subprogram. They would relate by position, A with X and B with Y. Whatever the main puts in A would be available to the subprogram in X.

## LINKAGE SECTION

Now that you understand that data in locations are shared, you probably realize that only one location is needed for, say, A and X in our example. But A is defined in the main program and X is defined in the subprogram. How does the compiler know not to set up another location? We tell the compiler what it needs to know by placing all shared data names in a special section in the called program, the **LINKAGE SECTION**.

Therefore, our example would now look like:

```
MAIN PROGRAM                    |   SUBPROGRAM
        .                       |        .
        .                       |   PROGRAM-ID.  SUBPROG.
        .                       |        .
WORKING-STORAGE SECTION.        |   WORKING-STORAGE SECTION.
77  A                           |        .
01  B                           |        .
        .                       |   LINKAGE SECTION.
        .                       |   01  X
        .                       |   01  Y
PROCEDURE DIVISION.             |   PROCEDURE DIVISION USING X, Y.
        .                       |
    CALL 'SUBPROG'              |
        USING A, B.             |
```

See how X and Y are defined in the **LINKAGE SECTION**. The compiler knows that a link to existing data locations is all that's needed, not new locations.

**LINKAGE SECTION** is used only in a called program. It physically follows **WORKING-STORAGE SECTION**. The data names used in the argument list must be either 77s or 01s. COBOL '85 allows for all levels to be shared. Some '74 COBOL compilers have also been modified to allow all levels to be shared.

### An Example

Let's assume that the corporate name and date are to be provided to all programs via a subprogram. The specification calls for the date to be provided in one of two formats: July 7, 1988 or 12/24/88. (Management couldn't agree on just one format.) In all cases the corporate name of Professional Systems, Inc. is to be used. Following is a main program that calls the BANPROG. The main tells the sub which date format it wants and receives back the appropriate format and corporate name.

```
IDENTIFICATION DIVISION.

PROGRAM-ID.      PAYROLL
     .
     .

ENVIRONMENT DIVISION.
     .
     .

DATA DIVISION.
     .
     .

WORKING-STORAGE SECTION.

77  FORMAT-CODE                 PIC 9(1)    VALUE 1.

01  CORPORATE-NAME              PIC X(25).
01  CONVERTED-DATE-1            PIC X(8).
01  CONVERTED-DATE-2            PIC X(18).
01  BANNER-LINE.
    03  FILLER                  PIC X(10)   VALUE SPACES.
    03  CORPORATE-NAME-OUT      PIC X(25).
    03  FILLER                  PIC X(80)   VALUE SPACES.
    03  DATE-OUT                PIC X(18).
        .
        .


PROCEDURE DIVISION.

0000-MAIN-PARA.
     .

     .
     PERFORM 7000-GET-BANNER-INFO.

7000-GET-BANNER-INFO.
    CALL 'BANPROG' USING FORMAT-CODE,
                         CORPORATE-NAME,
                         CONVERTED-DATE-1,
                         CONVERTED-DATE-2.
    MOVE CORPORATE-NAME TO CORPORATE-NAME-OUT.
    IF FORMAT-CODE = 1
        MOVE CONVERTED-DATE-1 TO DATE-OUT
    ELSE
        MOVE CONVERTED-DATE-2 TO DATE-OUT.
    WRITE RPT-LINE FROM ASTERISK-LINE
        AFTER PAGE-TOP.
    WRITE RPT-LINE FROM BANNER-LINE
        AFTER 2.
    WRITE RPT-LINE FROM ASTERISK-LINE
        AFTER 2.
```

```
        IDENTIFICATION DIVISION.

        PROGRAM-ID.      BANPROG.
              .
              .
        ENVIRONMENT DIVISION.
              .
              .
        DATA DIVISION.
              .
              .
        WORKING-STORAGE SECTION.

C       01   CORPORATE-RECORD          PIC X(25)   VALUE
C                          'INFORMATION SYSTEMS INC.'.
C       01   DATE-CONVERSION-VALUES.
C            03   FILLER               PIC X(9)    VALUE 'JANUARY'.
C            03   FILLER               PIC X(9)    VALUE 'FEBRUARY'.
C                    .
C                    .

C       01   DATES REDEFINES DATE-CONVERSION-VALUES.
C            03   MONTHS               PIC X( ) OCCURS 12 TIMES.

        01   DATE-FORM.
             03   YY-IN                PIC X(2).
             03   MM-IN                PIC X(2).
             03   DD-IN                PIC X(2).

        LINKAGE SECTION.

        77   REQUEST                   PIC 9(1).

        01   CORPORATE-NAME            PIC X(25).
        01   CONVERTED-DATE-1.
             03   MM                   PIC X(2).
             03   DD                   PIC /XX/.
             03   YY                   PIC X(2).

        01   CONVERTED-DATE-2.
             03   MONTH                PIC X(9).
             03   DAY                  PIC Z9.
             03   FILLER               PIC X(4)    VALUE ', 19'.
             03   YEAR                 PIC X(2).

        PROCEDURE DIVISION USING REQUEST,
                               CORPORATE-NAME
                               CONVERTED-DATE-1
                               CONVERTED-DATE-2.


        0000-MAIN-PARA.
            IF REQUEST = 1
                PERFORM 1000-FORM-1-PARA
            ELSE
                PERFORM 2000-FORM-2-PARA.
            MOVE CORPORATE-RECORD TO CORPORATE-NAME.
            GO TO 3000-EXIT-PARA.                    (There's the GO TO again.)
```

```
1000-FORM-1-PARA.
    ACCEPT DATE-FORM FROM DATE.      <-----Gets system date in
    MOVE YY-IN TO YY.                      YYMMDD format.
    MOVE MM-IN TO MM.
    MOVE DD-IN TO DD.

2000-FORM-2-PARA.

    [logic to convert date into second format using the month table]

3000-EXIT-PARA.
    EXIT PROGRAM.
```

Notice that in the main program, PAYROLL, when the banner information is needed, a CALL is issued to 'BANPROG.' The CALL sentence breaks down as follows:

| | |
|---|---|
| CALL 'BANPROG' | Executes the subprogram. |
| USING FORMAT-CODE | The main program specifies which date format it wants back from the subprogram. |
| CORPORATE-NAME | This is the field in which the subprogram makes the name available. |
| CONVERTED-DATE-1 | This is the field in which the subprogram returns the date in MM/DD/YY form. |
| CONVERTED-DATE-2 | This is the field in which the subprogram returns the date in July 7, 1988 form. |

Following CALL is the logic to write the banner. Notice that the returned corporate name and converted date are first moved to BANNER-LINE before it is written.

## TIP

**Think of CALL as a PERFORM since it also works like a go-to-and-come-back. When CALL is completed, control passes to the statement following the CALL.**

Now let's look at the subprogram, PROGRAM-ID. BANPROG. I want you to notice several features: the copied code, LINKAGE SECTION, PROCEDURE DIVISION USING and EXIT PROGRAM.

Since I mentioned earlier that CALL and COPY could work together to our benefit, I showed three records being copied in the example. The corporate name is copied to minimize our maintenance work when the name changes. The table of month names is also copied in to demonstrate that a standard could be used. However, in both cases I could have just as well coded the records within the subprogram.

The next new thing you saw was LINKAGE SECTION. Notice the four entries, a 77 level item and three 01s. How many data names in the USING? Four! That is why we have four entries in LINKAGE SECTION in our example. Since this is a common subprogram, its USING must accommodate all main programs that call it. And, since the data is shared by position in the argument list, the four are used.

Did you notice PROCEDURE DIVISION USING? It matches CALL USING. The data names don't match, but they match by position. By having four data names in the list, the subprogram is expecting to share four locations with the main program. In fact, all main programs that call it must have four data names in their calling list.

---

### TIP

**Just because a data-name is in the USING list does not mean it has to be used. However, a data-name may be used to pass data in both directions.**

---

I guess that you saw that I did not show the code for the 2000 paragraph. It would involve the date table. Using MM-IN's value as a subscript, we could extract the corresponding month's name. Since this is a fairly common routine, it would be a candidate to be copied.

Finally, I'm sure you saw GO TO. I used it to get to the exit paragraph so that EXIT PROGRAM could be executed. EXIT PROGRAM (GOBACK on some systems) is our way of returning to the calling program.

---

### TIP

**STOP RUN may be used, but I strongly suggest you never use one in a subprogram. You should always return to the calling program! It makes it easier to follow system logic.**

---

But I can hear you still asking why GO TO and not PERFORM? Well, this is a case where I don't want to maintain control. If I caused EXIT PROGRAM to be executed with PERFORM, the PERFORM would not be satisfied. Therefore, if the subprogram was called again during the same run and that same PERFORM was attempted again, the system would bomb. We are not allowed to re-enter a PERFORM.

So much for that, but why not just replace GO TO with EXIT PROGRAM? Well, in COBOL '74 EXIT PROGRAM must be in a paragraph by itself. However, in COBOL '85 we could do as you suggest and replace GO TO with EXIT PROGRAM.

## MULTIPLE-LEVEL CALLS

In this area of subprogramming, we have looked at the main/sub relationships. But, in fact, we can extend our discussions to several levels. That's right, a main could call a sub which, in turn, could call another sub. I've shown this relationship in Figure 16.5.

The MAIN calls SUB1 and SUB4. In turn, SUB1 calls SUB2 and SUB3, while SUB4 calls SUB3. Interesting, isn't it? Does it look like a hierarchy chart? Yes, maybe we should call it a system hierarchy chart. But I leave that for another course. My point here is that the relationship is allowable.

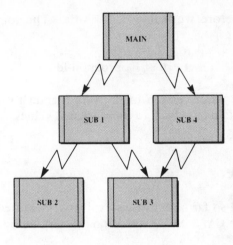

FIGURE 16.5
Multiple Levels of
Subprograms

Even though a program may be a called and a calling program at the same time, it may not call a program that called it.  That would be like talking to your friend on one phone and your friend trying to call you on another phone at the same time. The line would be busy.  Same idea with the subs: the call line is busy!  Figure 16.6 shows these illegal calls.

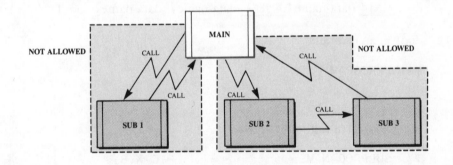

FIGURE 16.6
CALLs Not Allowed

## CANCEL

What if a calling program calls a subprogram more than once during a run?  The second time it's called, the subprogram is in the state it was in when last used.  That is, if during the first CALL certain data names were changed when they were used, they would still be in that changed state.  For instance, if you had the following:

```
77  KOUNT                  PIC 9(2)  VALUE 0.
        .
        .

    PROCEDURE DIVISION . . .
        .
        .

        ADD 1 TO KOUNT.
```

And, assume that KOUNT had reached a value of 50 when EXIT PROGRAM was executed.  Now if the program were called again, what would be the starting value of KOUNT?  0?  No, it would be 50.

So what do we do?  Well, we could always initialize all data names procedurally, or we could start with a fresh copy of the subprogram each time.  We do that with the CANCEL verb. Before we call, we CANCEL! The format of the CANCEL is shown below:

<u>CANCEL</u> program-id .

CANCEL causes a fresh version of the subprogram to be used. That, in turn, returns all values of data names back to their original values.

## A VARIABLE CALL

The calls we have used so far have always explicitly identified the subprogram being called: CALL 'SUB1' or CALL 'SUB2' or so on. Could we be more robust? We sure can.

Let's assume that a main program is to call one of several programs in an inventory system like that shown in Figure 16.2. While five subprograms exist currently, the system could grow to include others. Each time it does, the main program would have to be changed. However, we could use the CALL format shown below where data-name is given a value before CALL is executed.

<u>CALL</u> data-name [ <u>USING</u> data-name$_1$, data-name$_2$ $\cdots$ ]

Let's look at an example.

```
MAIN PROGRAM
        .
        .

WORKING-STORAGE SECTION.

77  SUBPROG-NAME                 PIC X(8).
        .
        .

PROCEDURE DIVISION.

IF REQ = 1
    MOVE 'SUB1' TO SUB-PROG-NAME
ELSE
    IF REQ = 2
        MOVE 'SUB2' TO SUB-PROG-NAME
    ELSE
            .
        etc
        .
CALL SUB-PROG-NAME.
```

This would cause SUB1 to be called when REQ is a 1. Nice, isn't it? But let's go a step further. If we accept from the user a code for the program to be executed (update, maintenance, or so on), we can use that code to get the program-id from a table of program id's, creating a very robust program. We could even oversize the table to allow for new programs that don't yet exist.

Therefore, our example might look like:

```
            MOVE PROG-NAME(REQ-PROG-CODE) TO SUB-PROG-NAME.
            CALL SUB-PROG-NAME.
```

## DEVELOPMENT AND TESTING

I've said several times that in a subprogramming development environment that one nice thing is that each program may be written and tested independently. That's much easier said than done.

For example, how would you have written and tested BANPROG? It has LINK-AGE SECTION and PROCEDURE DIVISION USING, and it does not produce any physical output. All it does is accept a request and provide a corporate name and converted date internally. How do you test it? Well, you actually make a few modifications so that it can stand alone.

Make LINKAGE SECTION a comment. Also, make PROCEDURE DIVISION USING a comment and replace it with a simple PROCEDURE DIVISION statement. In the exit paragraph make EXIT PROGRAM a comment, and replace it with STOP RUN. See where I'm going? I've made all the subprogramming elements comments and, where it was needed I replaced them with regular code.

Now, how do we check the logic? Well, I'm obviously not going to receive a request from a main program. So, let me assume first a value of one and then a value of two. For each value I'll generate the appropriate information and display it. I'll need to see if my logic worked, so I will display the results.

What would all this look like? Well, take a look. I've recoded the subprogram.

```
            IDENTIFICATION DIVISION.

            PROGRAM-ID.      BANPROG.
                  .
                  .
                  .
            DATA DIVISION.
                  .
                  .
                  .
            WORKING-STORAGE SECTION.
                  .
    C       01   CORPORATE-RECORD             PIC X(25)   VALUE
    C                          'INFORMATION SYSTEM INC.'.

    C       01   DATE-CONVERSION-VALUES.
    C            03  .
    C            03  .
    C            03  .

    C       01   DATES REDEFINES DATE-CONVERSION-VALUES.
    C            03  MONTHS                    PIC X( ) OCCURS 12 TIMES.

            01   DATE-FORM.
                 03  YY-IN                     PIC X(2).
                 03  MM-IN                     PIC X(2).
                 03  DD-IN                     PIC X(2).
```

```
*LINKAGE SECTION.

 01   REQUEST                       PIC 9(1)    VALUE 1.

 *         Use value 1 for first test, then use value 2.

 01   CORPORATE-NAME                PIC X(25).
 01   CONVERTER-DATE-1.
      03   MM                       PIC X(2).
      03   DD                       PIC /XX/
      03   YY                       PIC X(2).


 01   CONVERTED-DATE-2.
      03   MONTH                    PIC X(9).
      03   DAY                      PIC Z9.
      03   FILLER                   PIC X(4)    VALUE ', 19'.
      03   YEAR                     PIC X(2).

     PROCEDURE DIVISION.
*PROCEDURE DIVISION USING REQUEST,
*                        CORPORATE-NAME,
*                        CONVERTED-DATE-1,
*                        CONVERTED-DATE-2.

 0000-MAIN-PARA.
     IF REQUEST = 1
         PERFORM 1000-FORM-1-PARA
     ELSE
         PERFORM 2000-FORM-2-PARA.
     MOVE CORPORATE-RECORD TO CORPORATE-NAME.
     DISPLAY 'REQUEST = ', REQUEST.
     DISPLAY 'CORPORATE-NAME = ', CORPORATE-NAME.
     DISPLAY 'CONVERTED-DATE-1 = ', CONVERTED-DATE-1.
     DISPLAY 'CONVERTED-DATE-2 = ', CONVERTED-DATE-2.
     GO TO 3000-EXIT-PARA.

 1000-FORM-1-PARA.
     ACCEPT DATE-FORM FROM DATE.
     MOVE YY-IN TO YY.
     MOVE MM-IN TO MM.
     MOVE DD-IN TO DD.

 2000-FORM-2-PARA.

     [same as before]


 3000-EXIT-PARA.
 *   EXIT PROGRAM.
     STOP RUN.
```

Now that I've recoded it, does it make it a little clearer about stand-alone testing? With these modifications you can test the program by itself. Once it runs correctly, change it back; remove comments, DISPLAYs, STOP RUN, and remove VALUE clause on REQUEST.

Well, this should bring another question to your mind. What about system testing? You're right. Your program runs as a stand-alone, but it now needs to be tested as part of the system. You need to make sure the calling and called program work together. However, your program's internal logic is correct, so all you really need to do is test communication between programs.

## SUMMARY

In this chapter we examined the world of subprogramming. We looked at many topics. These included the CALL verb itself and many associated topics, including some applications.

You saw that there are two major application areas. The first was to call a program that provides a complete application function, like file update, file maintenance, and so on. The second was to use a common routine like a date conversion.

You were also shown how CALL aided system maintenance and reduced system development time. Since routines were in a subprogram, they did not have to be coded by each programmer. And, by being in one program, any changes only have to be made to that one program.

CALL and COPY work nicely together. By copying common elements into a subprogram, changes may be handled by simply revising the library element; again this provides a boost to program maintenance.

In the chapter you also studied the topics of multiple subprogram levels, where a called program could also be a calling program. However, you should remember that a called program may not call the program that called it, either directly or indirectly.

We also studied the need for CANCEL. It provides us a fresh version of a subprogram. If we don't use CANCEL, all subsequent calls to a subprogram would require procedural initialization.

Last, you got a peek at dynamic calling. That is a robust approach of determining the subprogram name during execution by using a table. This technique allows far less procedural code. One call is all that's required instead of one for each sub.

## EXERCISES

### Chapter Review Questions

1. A subprogram:
    a. May be developed independent of the main program
    b. Must be developed with the main program
    c. May only be tested with the main program
    d. Enhances system development
    e. Both a and d

2. Which of the following would be a good use of subprogramming?
    a. A common program used in several systems
    b. A common procedure routine used in several systems
    c. A common FD
    d. A common D-R-D
    e. Both a and b

3. If a subprogram uses a COPY verb:

    a. Maintenance of the program is enhanced

    b. Maintenance of the program is made more complex

    c. Maintenance is not effected

    d. An error occurs since a subprogram may not use a COPY

    e. None of the above

4. A CALL USING requires:

    a. A PROCEDURE USING

    b. A WORKING STORAGE USING

    c. A LINKAGE SECTION USING

    d. A HELLO USING

    e. None of the above

5. A CALLing program will not contain a LINKAGE SECTION.

    a. True

    b. False

6. A CALLed program may either directly or indirectly call the program that called it:

    a. Only with a Using clause

    b. Only without a using clause

    c. Only if both contain a linkage section

    d. Only if both contain an exit program

    e. None of the above

7. Data locations set up in the linkage section:

    a. Are shared by main and sub

    b. Are actually separate locations

    c. Must also be described in the called programs working storage section

    d. Must be referenced in both programs

    e. None of the above

8. A CALLed program may itself contain a CALL.

    a. True

    b. False

9. In COBOL '74, the data names listed in the CALL USING and the corresponding PROCEDURE DIVISION USING are associated by:

    a. Order

    b. Name

    c. Order in the record

    d. Order in the file

    e. None of the above

10. Re-entry to a subprogram causes:

    a. All data names to be refreshed to their initial values

    b. All data names to have the values as of their last use

    c. A subprogram may not be re-entered

    d. All LINKAGE SECTION names to be refreshed

    e. None of the above

11. The main program would not contain a CALL.

    a. True

    b. False

12. The COPY command replaces the CALL in system development.

    a. True

    b. False

13. The data names referenced in the corresponding USING clauses are:

    a. Associated by name

    b. Related by order in the USING list

    c. Associated by order in the LINKAGE SECTION

    d. Related by level number

    e. None of the above

14. A CALL statement functions like a:

    a. COPY

    b. USING

    c. PERFORM

    d. GO TO

    e. None of the above

15. The LINKAGE SECTION may contain 77 Level Items.

    a. True

    b. False

## Discussion Questions

1. Explain the function of the CANCEL Verb.
2. Explain how the use of the COPY together with a CALL might enhance a system.
3. Explain a variable CALL where the CALL verb references a data-name instead of a PROGRAM-ID.
4. Explain the testing procedures needed/used for a system that uses subprograms.
5. How would a compile-time table of pay rates be best used in the subprogramming environment? Assume many programs use the table.

## Practice Problems

1. Write a main program that calls three subprograms. The main program passes one data item to each. Each subprogram provides a particular but different function. Allow the subprograms to be called but don't worry about the particulars. Just let the subprograms return to the main program.
2. Using the DEAN-FILE in Data File A, develop a subprogram that would convert the major code to a description.
3. Do Problem 2 using the COPY for the table.

## Programming Assignments

The following assignments rely on the data dictionary, library elements and data sets found in the Project Sets Section of your text.

1. Develop a system of programs for the Personnel file in Data File B, main and subs, that would allow management to:

    a. Inquire and receive the record of a particular employee

    b. Inquire and receive a count of the number of employees

    c. Generate a listing of all employees.

Each of the requirements should be a separate subprogram with the main calling the appropriate subprogram.

2. Develop a system of programs for the Project Management System in Project A, main and sub, that would allow management to:

    a. Inquire and receive information about a particular project

    b. Receive a total of cost by each cost type

    c. Generate a listing of all projects by project type

Each of the requirements should be a separate subprogram with the main calling the appropriate subprogram.

# PROJECT
# SETS

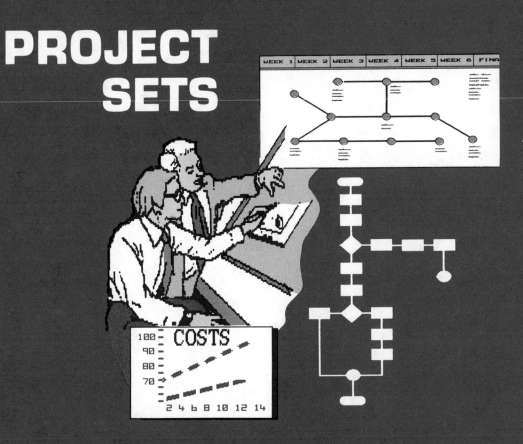

**A. THE PROJECT MANAGEMENT SYSTEM**
**B. THE EMPLOYEE SYSTEM**

# THE PROJECT MANAGEMENT SYSTEM

## Project Management Data Dictionary

| File/Record Name | Member Name |
|---|---|
| PROJECT-MASTER-FILE | PROJFD |
| PROJECT-RECORD-IN | PROJWS |
| TRANSACTION-PROJECT-FILE | TRANSFD |
| TRANS-PROJ-RECORD-IN | TRANSWS |
| MAINTENANCE-PROJECT-RECORD | MAINTFD |
| MAINT-PROJ-RECORD-IN | MAINTWS |
| PAGE-BANNER-1 | PAGEBAN1 |
| PAGE-BANNER-2 | PAGEBAN2 |
| PAGE-BANNER-3 | PAGEBAN3 |
| PAGE-FOOTER | PAGEFOOT |
| CITY-TABLE | CITYTBL |
| TYPE-TABLE | TYPETBL |
| CLASS-TABLE | CLASSTBL |
| CLIENT-TABLE | CLIENTBL |

The library elements are in your class' copy library, COPYLIB.

```
===================================================================
FILE NAME:      PROJECT-MASTER-FILE
===================================================================

MEMBER NAME:      PROJFD

===================================================================

FUNCTION:      INPUT X     OUTPUT ___     OTHER ___

===================================================================

PURPOSE:      Describes the PROJECT-MASTER-FILE and specifies
              DCB information

              RECORD CONTAINS 107 CHARACTERS
              BLOCK CONTAINS 59 RECORDS
              LABEL RECORDS ARE OMITTED
              DATA RECORD IS PROJECT-RECORD

===================================================================

                    RECORD DESCRIPTION
-------------------------------------------------------------------
DATA NAME                 DESCRIPTION                 PICTURE
-------------------------------------------------------------------

PROJECT-RECORD        Record for PROJECT-MASTER-FILE    X(107)
```

```
==================================================================
RECORD NAME:    PROJECT-RECORD-IN
==================================================================

MEMBER NAME:     PROJWS

==================================================================

FUNCTION:    INPUT ___    OUTPUT ___    OTHER X

==================================================================

PURPOSE:    Working storage record for the PROJECT MASTER
            FILE

==================================================================

                    RECORD DESCRIPTION
------------------------------------------------------------------
  DATA NAME            DESCRIPTION              PICTURE
------------------------------------------------------------------

PROJ-ID            Uniquely identifies project    X(9)

PROJ-DESC          Describes the project          X(30)

FILLER                                            X(1)

PROJ-CITY-CODE     Identifies city where project
                   is based                       X(2)
   Condition Names:
     COLLEGE-STATION           VALUE 'CS'
     HOUSTON                   VALUE 'HO'
     DALLAS                    VALUE 'DA'
     SAN-ANTONIO               VALUE 'SA'

PROJ-CLIENT-CODE   Identifies which client the
                   project is for                 X(2)

FILLER                                            X(1)

PROJ-TYPE-CODE     Identifies project type        9(1)
   Condition Names:
     SINGLE-FAMILY-UNIT        VALUE 1
     MULTI-FAMILY-UNIT         VALUE 2
     PARKS-AND-RECREATION-UNIT VALUE 3
     COMMERCIAL-UNIT           VALUE 4
     INDUSTRIAL-UNIT           VALUE 5
     VALID-PROJECT-TYPE        VALUE 1,2,3,4,5

FILLER                                            X(1)
```

```
=====================================================================
RECORD NAME:    PROJECT-RECORD-IN  cont'
=====================================================================


PROJ-CLASS-CODE            Identifies project class        9(1)
   Condition Names:
     FEDERAL-PROJECT                VALUE 1
     STATE-PROJECT                  VALUE 2
     PRIVATE-PROJECT                VALUE 3

FILLER                                                     X(1)

PROJ-MATERIALS-COST        Total materials cost to date    9(6)V99

FILLER                                                     X(1)

PROJ-PERSONNEL-COST        Total personnel cost to date    9(6)V99

FILLER                                                     X(1)

PROJ-ELECTRICAL-COST       Total electrical cost to date   9(6)V99

FILLER                                                     X(1)

PROJ-PLUMBING-COST         Total plumbing cost to date     9(6)V99

FILLER                                                     X(1)

PROJ-FRAMING-COST          Total framing cost to date      9(6)V99

FILLER                                                     X(1)

PROJ-START-DATE            Project start date
   PROJ-START-YEAR         Project start year              9(2)
   PROJ-START-MONTH        Project start month             9(2)
   PROJ-START-DAY          Project start day               9(2)

FILLER                                                     X(1)

PROJ-EST-COMP-DATE         Estimated completion date of
                           project
   PROJ-EST-COMP-YEAR      Estimated completion year       9(2)
   PROJ-EST-COMP-MONTH     Estimated completion month      9(2)
   PROJ-EST-COMP-DAY       Estimated completion day        9(2)
```

```
=====================================================================
FILE NAME:      TRANSACTION-PROJECT-FILE
=====================================================================

MEMBER NAME:        TRANSFD

=====================================================================

FUNCTION:      INPUT X     OUTPUT ---    OTHER ---

=====================================================================

PURPOSE:        Describes the TRANSACTION-PROJECT-FILE and
                specifies DCB information

                RECORD CONTAINS 18 CHARACTERS
                BLOCK CONTAINS 353 RECORDS
                LABEL RECORDS ARE OMITTED
                DATA RECORD IS TRANSACTION-PROJECT-RECORD

=====================================================================

                    RECORD DESCRIPTION
---------------------------------------------------------------------
  DATA NAME              DESCRIPTION              PICTURE
---------------------------------------------------------------------

TRANS-PROJECT-RECORD    Record for the
                        TRANSACTION-PROJECT-FILE        X(18)
```

```
=====================================================================
RECORD NAME:    TRANS-PROJ-RECORD-IN
=====================================================================

MEMBER NAME:        TRANSWS

=====================================================================

FUNCTION:      INPUT ---     OUTPUT ---    OTHER X

=====================================================================

PURPOSE:        Working storage record for the
                TRANSACTION-PROJECT-FILE

=====================================================================
```

*(continued)*

```
                        RECORD DESCRIPTION
-------------------------------------------------------------------
  DATA NAME                    DESCRIPTION                 PICTURE
-------------------------------------------------------------------

  TRANS-PROJ-ID                Associates transaction with
                               project                     X(9)

  TRANS-PROJ-CODE              Identifies type of transaction  X(1)
    Condition Names:
    CHANGE-MATERIALS-COST            VALUE 'M'
    CHANGE-PERSONNEL-COST            VALUE 'P'
    CHANGE-ELECTRICAL-COST           VALUE 'E'
    CHANGE-PLUMBING-COST             VALUE 'B'
    CHANGE-FRAMING-COST              VALUE 'F'
    VALID-TRANSACTION-CODE           VALUE 'M' 'P' 'E' 'B' 'F'

  TRANS-PROJ-AMOUNT            Indicates dollar amount of
                               transaction                 9(6)V99
```

```
==================================================================
  FILE NAME:    MAINTENANCE-PROJECT-FILE
==================================================================

  MEMBER NAME:      MAINTFD

==================================================================

  FUNCTION:     INPUT X    OUTPUT ___    OTHER ___

==================================================================

  PURPOSE:      Describes the MAINTENANCE-PROJECT-FILE and
                specifies DCB information

                RECORD CONTAINS 68 CHARACTERS
                BLOCK CONTAINS 93 RECORDS
                LABEL RECORDS ARE OMITTED
                DATA RECORD IS MAINTENANCE-PROJECT-RECORD

==================================================================

                        RECORD DESCRIPTION
-------------------------------------------------------------------
  DATA NAME                    DESCRIPTION                 PICTURE
-------------------------------------------------------------------

MAINTENANCE-PROJECT-RECORD Record for
                           MAINTENANCE-PROJECT-FILE        X(68)
```

```
==================================================================
RECORD NAME:    MAINT-PROJ-RECORD-IN
==================================================================

MEMBER NAME:    MAINTWS

==================================================================

FUNCTION:    INPUT ___    OUTPUT ___    OTHER X

==================================================================

PURPOSE:    Working storage record for the
            MAINTENANCE-PROJECT-FILE

==================================================================

                    RECORD DESCRIPTION
------------------------------------------------------------------
  DATA NAME              DESCRIPTION              PICTURE
------------------------------------------------------------------

MAINT-PROJ-ID       Associates transaction with
                    project                      X(9)

MAINT-PROJ-CODE     Identifies type of transaction  X(2)
  Condition Names:
    ADD-A-RECORD                VALUE 'AD'
    DELETE-A-RECORD             VALUE 'DE'
    CHANGE-CITY-CODE            VALUE 'CC'
    CHANGE-CLIENT-CODE          VALUE 'CL'
    CHANGE-TYPE-CODE            VALUE 'CT'
    CHANGE-EST-COMP-DATE        VALUE 'CD'
    VALID-MAINTENANCE-CODE      VALUE 'AD' 'CC' 'CL'
                                      'CT' 'CD' 'DE'


MAINT-FIELDS        Maintenance information      X(57)


------------------------------------------------------------------
  Use the following fields for ADD-A-RECORD transactions only
    (NOTE: ADD-A-RECORD-FIELDS REDEFINES MAINT-FIELDS)
------------------------------------------------------------------

ADD-ID              New project id number        X(9)
ADD-DESC            New project description      X(30)
ADD-CITY-CODE       New project city code        X(2)
ADD-CLIENT-CODE     New project client code      X(2)
ADD-TYPE-CODE       New project type code        9(1)
ADD-CLASS-CODE      New project class code       9(1)
ADD-START-DATE      New project start date       9(6)
ADD-EST-COMP-DATE   New project completion date  9(6)
```

*(continued)*

```
=============================================================
RECORD NAME:    MAINT-PROJ-RECORD-IN  cont'
=============================================================



    -----------------------------------------------------------
    Use the following field for CHANGE-CITY-CODE transactions only
        (NOTE:  CHANGE-CITY-CODE-FIELDS REDEFINES MAINT-FIELDS)
    -----------------------------------------------------------

    NEW-CITY-CODE               New city code used to replace
                                existing city code            X(2)
    -----------------------------------------------------------
    Use the following field for CHANGE-CLIENT-CODE transactions
    only
        (NOTE: CHANGE-CLIENT-CODE-FIELDS REDEFINES MAINT-FIELDS)
    -----------------------------------------------------------

    NEW-CLIENT-CODE             New client code used to replace
                                existing client code          X(2)


    -----------------------------------------------------------
    Use the following field for CHANGE-TYPE-CODE transactions only
        (NOTE:  CHANGE-TYPE-CODE-FIELDS REDEFINES MAINT-FIELDS)
    -----------------------------------------------------------

    NEW-TYPE-CODE               New type code used to replace
                                existing type code            9(1)


    -----------------------------------------------------------
    Use the following field for CHANGE-EST-COMP-DATE transactions
        (NOTE: CHANGE-EST-COMP-DATE-FIELDS REDEFINES MAINT-FIELDS)
    -----------------------------------------------------------

    NEW-EST-COMP-DATE           New estimated completion date
                                used to replace existing one

     NEW-EST-COMP-YEAR          New estimated completion year  9(2)
     NEW-EST-COMP-MONTH         New estimated completion month 9(2)
     NEW-EST-COMP-DAY           New estimated completion day   9(2)
    -----------------------------------------------------------

NOTE: NO FIELDS ARE NEEDED FOR A DELETE SINCE ALL THE DATA
      NEEDED IS THE CODE AND THE PROJECT ID BOTH OF WHICH
      ARE IN THE HEADER AREA.
```

```
================================================================
RECORD NAME:    PAGE-BANNER-1
================================================================

MEMBER NAME:    PAGEBAN1

================================================================

FUNCTION:    INPUT ___    OUTPUT ___    OTHER X

================================================================

PURPOSE:    Page banner lines 1 and 4 - line of dashes

================================================================

                    RECORD DESCRIPTION
----------------------------------------------------------------
  DATA NAME              DESCRIPTION              PICTURE
----------------------------------------------------------------

FILLER              DASHES                      X(133)
```

```
================================================================
RECORD NAME:    PAGE-BANNER-2
================================================================

MEMBER NAME:    PAGEBAN2

================================================================

FUNCTION:    INPUT ___    OUTPUT ___    OTHER X

================================================================

PURPOSE:    Page banner line 2 - contains report date and
                            page number

================================================================

                    RECORD DESCRIPTION
----------------------------------------------------------------
  DATA NAME              DESCRIPTION              PICTURE
----------------------------------------------------------------

FILLER              SPACES                      X(1)

DATE-OUT            Report date
   MONTH-OUT        Report month                9(2)
   FILLER           slash                       X(1)
   DAY-OUT          Report day                  9(2)
   FILLER           slash                       X(1)
   YEAR-OUT         Report year                 9(2)

FILLER              SPACES                      X(116)

FILLER              'PAGE: '                    X(6)

PAGE-OUT            Page number                 Z9
```

```
================================================================
RECORD NAME:     PAGE-BANNER-3
================================================================

MEMBER NAME:         PAGEBAN3

================================================================

FUNCTION:     INPUT ___    OUTPUT ___    OTHER X

================================================================

PURPOSE:      Page banner line 3 — contains report title

================================================================

                     RECORD DESCRIPTION
----------------------------------------------------------------
  DATA NAME              DESCRIPTION              PICTURE
----------------------------------------------------------------

FILLER                 SPACES                     X(42)

REPORT-TITLE           Title of report            X(50)

FILLER                 SPACES                     X(41)
```

```
================================================================
RECORD NAME:   PAGE-FOOTER
================================================================

MEMBER NAME:         PAGEFOOT

================================================================

FUNCTION:     INPUT ___     OUTPUT ___     OTHER X

================================================================

PURPOSE:      Page footer — to be printed on line 55 of every
                            report page

================================================================

                     RECORD DESCRIPTION
----------------------------------------------------------------
  DATA NAME              DESCRIPTION              PICTURE
----------------------------------------------------------------

FILLER                 SPACES                     X(111)

FILLER                 'AGATE CONSTRUCTION CO.'    X(22)
```

```
==================================================================
RECORD NAME:   CITY-TABLE
==================================================================

MEMBER NAME:      CITYTBL

------------------------------------------------------------------

FUNCTION:      INPUT ___    OUTPUT ___    OTHER X

------------------------------------------------------------------

PURPOSE:       Compile time table containing CITY-CODEs and
               corresponding city names

==================================================================

                    RECORD DESCRIPTION
------------------------------------------------------------------
  DATA NAME               DESCRIPTION              PICTURE
------------------------------------------------------------------

CITY-VALUES
                   'CSCOLLEGE STATION'            X(17)
                   'HOHOUSTON        '            X(17)
                   'DADALLAS         '            X(17)
                   'SASAN ANTONIO    '            X(17)

CITY-TABLE         REDEFINES CITY-VALUES
  CITY-ELEMENT     OCCURS 4 TIMES
                   INDEXED BY CITY-INDEX
     CITY-TBL-CODE                               X(2)
     CITY-TBL-NAME                               X(15)
```

```
==================================================================
RECORD NAME:   TYPE-TABLE
==================================================================

MEMBER NAME:      TYPETBL

------------------------------------------------------------------

FUNCTION:      INPUT ___    OUTPUT ___    OTHER X

------------------------------------------------------------------

PURPOSE:       Compile time table containing project TYPE names

==================================================================
```

*(continued)*

```
                          RECORD DESCRIPTION
    ---------------------------------------------------------------
     DATA NAME                  DESCRIPTION               PICTURE
    ---------------------------------------------------------------

    TYPE-VALUES
                          'SINGLE FAMILY      '.          X(20)
                          'MULTI-FAMILY       '.          X(20)
                          'PARKS AND RECREATION'.         X(20)
                          'COMMERCIAL         '.          X(20)
                          'INDUSTRIAL         '.          X(20)


    TYPE-TABLE            REDEFINES TYPE-VALUES
      TYPE-TBL-DESC       OCCURS 5 TIMES
                                                          X(20)
```

```
    ================================================================
     RECORD NAME:   CLASS-TABLE
    ================================================================

     MEMBER NAME:       CLASSTBL

    ================================================================

     FUNCTION:      INPUT ___    OUTPUT ___    OTHER X

    ================================================================

     PURPOSE:       Compile time table containing project CLASS
                    descriptions

    ================================================================

                          RECORD DESCRIPTION
    ---------------------------------------------------------------
     DATA NAME                  DESCRIPTION               PICTURE
    ---------------------------------------------------------------

    CLASS-VALUES
                          'FEDERAL'                       X(7)
                          'STATE  '                       X(7)
                          'PRIVATE                        X(7)

    CLASS-TABLE           REDEFINES CLASS-VALUES
      CLASS-TBL-DESC      OCCURS 3 TIMES
                                                          X(7)
```

```
================================================================
RECORD NAME:    CLIENT-TABLE
================================================================

MEMBER NAME:        CLIENTBL

================================================================

FUNCTION:     INPUT ___    OUTPUT ___    OTHER X

================================================================

PURPOSE:        Compile time table containing project CLIENT
                descriptions

================================================================

                    RECORD DESCRIPTION
----------------------------------------------------------------
  DATA NAME            DESCRIPTION              PICTURE
----------------------------------------------------------------


CLIENT-VALUES
              'TCTEXAS DEPARTMENT OF CORRECTIONS  '  X(37)
              'LULAND USE COMMISSION              '  X(37)
              'CDCOBBLESTONE DEVELOPERS           '  X(37)
              'DEPARTMENT OF EDUCATION            '  X(37)
              'TUTEXAS UTILITIES COMMISSION       '  X(37)
              'TPTEXAS PARKS AND WILDLIFE         '  X(37)
              'DCDALLAS CHAMBER OF COMMERCE       '  X(37)
              'PCPERCY CONSTRUCTION               '  X(37)
              'HCHEALTH COMMISSION                '  X(37)
              'DDDEPARTMENT OF DEFENSE            '  X(37)
              'DTDEPARTMENT OF TRANSPORTATION     '  X(37)
              'DGDEPARTMENT OF ENERGY             '  X(37)
CLIENT-TABLE             REDEFINES CLIENT-VALUES
  CLIENT-TBL-ELEMENT  OCCURS 12 TIMES
                      INDEXED BY CLIENT INDEX

      CLIENT-TBL-CODE                            X(2)
      CLIENT-TBL-DESC                            X(35)
```

# Project Management Data Sets

## Project Master File – MASTER

```
309006021REBKA POUND RESIDENTS            CSCD 1 3 02000000 00500000 00500000 03456780 00094100 868715 880201
8D0050006K M SCOTT BOOKSELLER             SACD 4 3 12533333 04753824 08475000 01500000 01075000 870110 881001
500120007CAR-APAC BODY SHOP               DACD 4 3 05000000 02500000 02540000 00500000 01200000 860431 880131
800050006MCKENZIE BAKERY                  SACD 4 3 12533333 04753824 08475000 01500000 01075000 870110 881001
500090005LIZVETA KOUNDAKJIAN RESIDENTS    SACD 1 3 30000000 08900000 02500000 02500000 00875000 861225 870513
509090005A A MICHELSON ESTATE             SACD 1 3 30000000 08900000 02500000 02500000 00875000 871225 880513
309006061JOHN MACDONALD RESIDENTS         CSCD 1 3 02000000 00500000 00500000 03456780 00094100 860715 870201
601070007J C MAXWELL RESIDENTS            SACD 5 3 35000000 10000000 09000000 10000000 00407899 860101 890531
59012007HIATUS BRAKE REPAIR SHOP          DACD 4 3 05000000 02500000 02540000 00500000 01200000 860431 880101
400004003BRUSSADR GEO-DOME AMPHITHEATER   DADC 3 2 27800090 01500000 15525043 01111111 00238574 850601 880131
243004003CHIMERA-CANARD NEWS SERVICE      DADC 3 2 27800090 01500000 15525043 01111111 00238574 870601 881231
400450031CARE-APACE RETIREMENT HOME       DADC 2 2 23700050 07500000 00500000 01500000 00950000 850101 861231
200005104GALVESTON PORT OFFICERS CLUB     HODD 5 1 04500000 12500000 00200000 00300000 00250000 870931 881001
200005004BELL-LICOSE AIR FORCE BASE       SADD 5 1 04500000 12500000 00200000 00300000 00250000 870931 881001
308005050FELICITY ICBM SILO AND GRILL     CSDD 4 1 48700315 00500000 01000000 02500000 00150000 871130 900101
308001050GALVESTON PORT SUB BASE          HODD 4 1 48700315 00500000 01000000 02500000 00150000 871130 900101
81205000BM L KING JR HIGH SCHOOL          DADE 2 1 27500000 05000000 06438123 00362713 00379432 880101 900131
700020001TEXAS POLYTECHNICAL INSTITUTE    HODE 4 2 20000000 10000000 05000000 02500000 02500000 870721 890630
800050008J. S. MILL ELEMENTARY SCHOOL     CSDE 2 1 27500000 05000000 06438123 00362713 00379432 880101 900131
600060066DEWEY DR DEWEY-NOT HIGH SCHOOL   CSDE 3 1 17500000 04500000 10000000 05000000 07000000 851010 900930
604060066PROFESSIONALISM CENTER           CSDE 3 1 17500000 04500000 10000000 05000000 07000000 851010 900930
290002001J J MCDERMOTT HUMANITIES BLDG    CSCD 4 1 04578925 12854489 01875000 00250000 00150000 870615 881231
100000300KOUNDAKJIAN PUBLIC LIBRARY       HODE 3 1 50000000 01578500 01000000 01575000 01945629 870131 900101
715020001LEIBNIZ MONADISM HIGH SCHOOL     HODE 4 2 20000000 10000000 05000000 02500000 02500000 860721 880201
200002001JOHN R BLOCKER PARK-N-WALK       CSDE 4 1 04578925 12854489 01875000 00250000 00150000 870615 881231
115000300ALBERT E SPECIAL THEORY SCHOOL   HODE 3 1 50000000 01578500 01000000 01575000 01945629 870131 900101
210003002DVORAK SOLAR CONVERSION UNIT     SADG 3 2 01578520 02500000 00450000 00120000 00300000 871220 880331
800050007BECKMAN-NADER NUCLEAR PLANT      HODG 5 2 75000000 45000000 12500000 05000000 00900000 850101 880331
412450031MOSSBAUER RESEARCH LAB           DADG 2 2 23700050 07500000 00500000 01500000 00950000 850101 871231
700124004CANARD OBSERVATORY               DADG 3 1 60000000 08500000 01000000 01000000 01000000 850101 860101
510100005JOHN HOPPER UNIVERSE CITY        SADG 4 1 30000000 05000000 05000000 07500000 00820000 851231 871231
600070007WARNIER IRON ORE MINE            SADG 5 3 35000000 10000000 09000000 10000000 00407899 860101 890531
510110006BECKMAN DISTILLATION UNIT        HODG 5 1 10000000 00050000 05000000 00050000 03885212 851231 880229
100015400EDWARD TELLER RESIDENTS          HODG 1 3 45000000 02500000 01000099 01000000 00500000 880101 880531
200003002RIVER RUN SLUECE CONTROL         SADG 3 2 01578520 02500000 00450000 00120000 00300000 851220 870131
500110006NORTH CONTRA-FLOW LANE           HODT 5 1 10000000 00050000 05000000 00050000 03885212 851231 861029
317504040MARVIN MINSKY MONORAIL           HODT 3 1 05000000 05000000 00500000 00180000 00200000 880120 900131
500100005AMIEL JORACHE BURN CLINIC        SAPC 4 1 30000000 05000000 05000000 07500000 00820000 861231 891231
812350009SINOPE COUNSELING CENTER         HOPC 4 3 12500000 01500000 00500000 00125000 00175000 860101 871231
100000100WALKER SPRINGS APARTMENTS        HOPC 2 3 22500000 15000000 00500000 00150000 02000000 870325 900101
100010200LYSITHEA WINERY                  CSPC 5 2 15000000 04375000 50000000 00500000 10000000 860903 920501
400150021STEPHEN HALES NURSERY            DAPC 4 3 00250000 00050000 01000000 01000000 00100000 850101 871101
709111202DOUG IAN RESIDENTS               HOPC 1 3 37500000 07500000 07500000 07500000 05000000 861231 890630
400650010HOEKSTRA ADOPTION AGENCY         SAPC 4 3 12500000 02000000 02500000 00150000 00950000 860921 880330
100000400EUGEN HERRIGEL RESIDENTS         HOPC 1 3 45000000 02500000 01000099 01000000 00500000 860101 870531
307004040GEORGE BUSH GARDENS              HOPC 3 1 05000000 05000000 00500000 00180000 00200000 880120 900131
700111202RICHARD STRAYER RESIDENTS        HOPC 1 3 37500000 07500000 07500000 07500000 05000000 861231 890630
800050005SPLENDOR SPRINGS REST HOME       DAPC 2 3 25000000 20000000 01500000 02000000 01500000 860201 871201
87005000SDESCATES CLEAR LENS OPTICIANS    DAPC 2 3 25000000 20000000 01500000 02000000 01500000 860201 871201
800050009J D SALAD BAR                    HOPC 4 3 12500000 01500000 00500000 00125000 00175000 850101 861231
400350021LASS ETUDE MUSIC SHOP            DAPC 4 3 00250000 00050000 01000000 01000000 00100000 850101 871101
400240010RAND ATLAS SHOP                  SAPC 4 3 12500000 02000000 02500000 00150000 00950000 860921 880130
109000100SAN ANTONIO SUARE CONDOS         SAPC 2 3 22500000 15000000 00500000 00150000 02000000 870325 900101
709113003LEVERALONE MINIMUM SECURITY      CSTC 5 2 75000000 09000000 19000000 07543434 00333333 850903 870903
200006005EUPHORIA THERAPY CENTER          DATC 4 2 01750000 02400000 02750000 03000000 00500000 840301 870630
209006005PASCAL NEURO-CARDIAC CLINIC      DATC 4 2 01750000 02400000 02750000 03000000 00500000 850301 870630
400550041TEXAS PUTATIVE PRISON FACILITY   HOTC 2 2 50000000 10000000 10000000 25000000 00100000 860228 861231
410550041DETERMINISTIC DETENTION CENTER   HOTC 2 2 50000000 10000000 10000000 25000000 00100000 860228 880131
690050055WHIPSCHNOZZEL STATE PARK         DATP 3 2 01000000 01000000 07500000 00500000 00830000 870101 880630
700111001SEYMOUR STRAYER ARBORETUM        HOTP 3 2 45000000 15000000 10000000 05000000 02500000 850410 880501
709111001TED KRISTIAN BIRD HOUSE          HOTP 3 2 45000000 15000000 10000000 05000000 02500000 850410 870501
600050055SYLVAN ROD RE-GRASS PARK         DATP 3 2 01000000 01000000 07500000 00500000 00830000 870101 880630
710124004SPINOZA SIMPLE NATURE TRAIL      DATP 3 1 60000000 08500000 01000000 01000000 01000000 870101 880101
100002200SHELLEY-GALVANI POWER PLANT      CSTU 5 2 15000000 04375000 50000000 00500000 10000000 860903 920501
590090004INFUSION FIBER OPTIC LINES       CSTU 5 2 21078000 00100000 00400000 00500032 00400000 851020 871031
700113003BRAZOS RIVER CONTROL DAM         CSTU 5 2 75000000 09000000 19000000 07543434 00333333 850903 900903
500090004DATACOM MICRO RELAY UNIT         CSTU 5 2 21078000 00100000 00400000 00500032 00400000 851020 871031
840050007ANTILLES WATER RESERVOIR         HOTU 5 2 75000000 45000000 12500000 05000000 00900000 870101 880331
```

## Sorted Project Master File – MASTSORT

```
100000100WALKER SPRINGS APARTMENTS        HOPC 2 3 22500000 15000000 00500000 00150000 02000000 870325 900101
100000200SHELLEY-GALVANI POWER PLANT      CSTU 5 2 15000000 04375000 50000000 00500000 10000000 860903 920501
100000300KOUNDAKJIAN PUBLIC LIBRARY       HODE 3 1 50000000 01578500 01000000 01575000 01945629 870131 900101
100000400EUGEN HERRIGEL RESIDENTS         HOPC 1 3 45000000 02500000 01000099 01000000 00500000 860101 870531
100010200LYSITHEA WINERY                  CSPC 5 2 15000000 04375000 50000000 00500000 10000000 860903 920501
100015400EDWARD TELLER RESIDENTS          HODG 1 3 45000000 02500000 01000099 01000000 00500000 880101 880531
109000100SAN ANTONIO SUARE CONDOS         SAPC 2 3 22500000 15000000 00500000 00150000 02000000 870325 900101
115000300ALBERT E SPECIAL THEORY SCHOOL   HODG 3 1 50000000 01578500 01000000 01575000 01945629 870131 900101
200002001JOHN R BLOCKER PARK-N-WALK       CSDE 4 1 04578925 12854489 01875000 00250000 00150000 870615 881231
200003002RIVER RUN SLUECE CONTROL         SADG 3 2 01578520 02500000 00450000 00120000 00300000 851220 870131
200004003BRUSSARD GEO-DOME AMPHITHEATER   DADC 3 2 27800090 01500000 15525043 01111111 00238574 850601 880101
200005004BELL-LICOSE AIR FORCE BASE       SADD 5 1 04500000 12500000 00200000 00300000 00250000 870931 881001
200005104GALVESTON PORT OFFICERS CLUB     HODD 5 1 04500000 12500000 00200000 00300000 00250000 870931 881001
200006005EUPHORIA THERAPY CENTER          DATC 4 2 01750000 02400000 02750000 03000000 00500000 840301 870630
209006005PASCAL NEURO-CARDIAC CLINIC      DATC 4 2 01750000 02400000 02750000 03000000 00500000 850301 870630
210003002DVORAK SOLAR CONVERSION UNIT     SADG 3 2 01578520 02500000 00450000 00120000 00300000 871220 880331
243004003CHIMERA-CANARD NEWS SERVICE      DADC 3 2 27800090 01500000 15525043 01111111 00238574 870601 881231
290002001J J MCDERMOTT HUMANITIES BLDG    CSDE 4 1 04578925 12854489 01875000 00250000 00150000 870615 881231
307004040GEORGE BUSH GARDENS              HOPC 3 1 05000000 05000000 00500000 00180000 00200000 880120 900131
308001050GALVESTON PORT SUB BASE          HODD 4 1 48700315 00500000 01000000 02500000 00150000 871130 900101
308005050FELICITY ICBM SILO AND GRILL     CSDD 4 1 48700315 00500000 01000000 02500000 00150000 871130 900101
309006021REBKA POUND RESIDENTS            CSCD 1 3 02000000 00500000 00500000 03456780 00094100 860715 880201
309006061JOHN MACDONALD RESIDENTS         CSCD 1 3 02000000 00500000 00500000 03456780 00094100 860715 870201
317504040MARVIN MINSKY MONORAIL           HODT 3 1 05000000 05000000 00500000 00180000 00200000 880120 900131
400015021STEPHEN HALES NURSERY            DAPC 4 3 00250000 00050000 01000000 01000000 00100000 850101 871101
400240010RAND ATLAS SHOP                  SAPC 4 3 12500000 02000000 02500000 00150000 00950000 860921 880130
400350021LASS ETUDE MUSIC SHOP            DAPC 4 3 00250000 00050000 01000000 01000000 00100000 850101 871101
400450031CARE-APACE RETIREMENT HOME       DADC 2 2 00000000 00000000 00000000 00000000 00000000 850101 861231
400550041TEXAS PUTATIVE PRISON FACILITY   HOTC 2 2 00000000 00000000 00000000 00000000 00000000 860228 861231
400650010HOEKSTRA ADOPTION AGENCY         SAPC 4 3 12500000 02000000 02500000 00150000 00950000 860921 880330
410550041DETERMINISTIC DETENTION CENTER   HOTC 2 2 50000000 10000000 10000000 25000000 00100000 860228 880131
412450031MOSSBAUER RESEARCH LAB           DADG 2 2 23700050 07500000 00500000 01500000 00950000 850101 871231
500090004DATACOM MICRO RELAY UNIT         CSTU 5 2 21078000 00100000 00400000 00500032 00400000 851020 871031
500090005LIZVETA KOUNDAKJIAN RESIDENTS    SACD 1 3 30000000 08900000 02500000 02500000 00875000 861225 870513
500100005AMIEL JORACHE BURN CLINIC        SAPC 4 1 30000000 05000000 05000000 07500000 00820000 861231 891231
500110006NORTH CONTRA-FLOW LANE           HODT 5 1 10000000 00050000 05000000 00050000 03885212 851231 861029
500120007CAR-APACE BODY SHOP              DACD 4 3 05000000 02500000 02540000 00500000 01200000 860431 880131
509090005A A MICHELSON ESTATE             SACD 1 3 30000000 08900000 02500000 02500000 00875000 871225 880513
510100005JOHN HOPPER UNIVERSE CITY        SADG 4 1 30000000 05000000 05000000 07500000 00820000 851231 871231
510110006BECKMAN DISTILLATION UNIT        HODG 5 1 10000000 00050000 05000000 00050000 03885212 851231 880229
590090004INFUSION FIBER OPTIC LINES       CSTU 5 2 21078000 00100000 00400000 00500032 00400000 851020 871031
590120007HIATUS BRAKE REPAIR SHOP         DACD 4 3 05000000 02500000 02540000 00500000 01200000 860431 880101
600050055SYLVAN ROD RE-GRASS PARK         DATP 3 2 01000000 01000000 07500000 00500000 00830000 870101 880630
600060066DEWEY OR DEWEY-NOT HIGH SCHOOL   CSDE 3 1 17500000 04500000 10000000 05000000 07000000 851010 900930
600070007WARNIER IRON ORE MINE            SADG 5 3 35000000 10000000 09000000 10000000 00407899 860101 890531
601070007J C MAXWELL RESIDENTS            SACD 5 3 35000000 10000000 09000000 10000000 00407899 860101 890531
604060066PROFESSIONALISM CENTER           CSDE 3 1 17500000 04500000 10000000 05000000 07000000 851010 900930
690050055WHIPSCHNOZZEL STATE PARK         DATP 3 2 01000000 01000000 07500000 00500000 00830000 870101 880630
700020001TEXAS POLYTECHNICAL INSTITUTE    HODE 4 2 20000000 10000000 05000000 02500000 02500000 870721 890630
700111001SEYMOUR STRAYER ARBORETUM        HOTP 3 2 45000000 15000000 10000000 05000000 02500000 850410 880501
700111202RICHARD STRAYER RESIDENTS        HOPC 1 3 37500000 07500000 07500000 07500000 05000000 861231 890630
700113003BRAZOS RIVER CONTROL DAM         CSTU 5 2 75000000 09000000 19000000 07543434 00333333 850903 900903
700124004CANARD OBSERVATORY               DADG 3 1 00000000 00000000 00000000 00000000 00000000 850101 860101
709111001TED KRISTIAN BIRD HOUSE          HOTP 3 2 45000000 15000000 10000000 05000000 02500000 850410 870501
709111202DOUG IAN RESIDENTS               HOPC 1 3 37500000 07500000 07500000 07500000 05000000 861231 890630
709113003LEVERALONE MINIMUM SECURITY      CSTC 5 2 75000000 09000000 19000000 07543434 00333333 850903 870903
710124004SPINOZA SIMPLE NATURE TRAIL      DATP 3 1 60000000 08500000 01000000 01000000 01000000 870101 880101
715020001LEIBNIZ MONADISM HIGH SCHOOL     HODE 4 2 20000000 10000000 05000000 02500000 02500000 860721 880201
800050005SPLENDOR SPRINGS REST HOME       DAPC 2 3 25000000 20000000 01500000 02000000 01500000 860201 871201
800050006K M SCOTT BOOKSELLER             SACD 4 3 12533333 04753824 08475000 01500000 01075000 870110 881001
800050007BECKMAN-NADER NUCLEAR PLANT      HODG 5 2 75000000 45000000 12500000 05000000 00900000 850101 880331
800050008J. S. MILL ELEMENTARY SCHOOL     CSDE 2 1 27500000 05000000 06438123 00362713 00379432 880101 900131
800050009J D SALAD BAR                    HOPC 4 3 00000000 00000000 00000000 00000000 00000000 850101 861231
800050010MCKENZIE BAKERY                  SACD 4 3 12533333 04753824 08475000 01500000 01075000 870110 881001
812050008M L KING JR HIGH SCHOOL          DADE 2 1 27500000 05000000 06438123 00362713 00379432 880101 900131
812350009SINOPE COUNSELING CENTER         HOPC 4 3 12500000 01500000 00500000 00125000 00175000 860101 871231
840050007ANTILLES WATER RESERVOIR         HOTU 5 2 75000000 45000000 12500000 05000000 00900000 870101 880331
870050005DESCATES CLEAR LENS OPTICIANS    DAPC 2 3 25000000 20000000 01500000 02000000 01500000 860201 871201
```

## Transaction File – TRANS

```
000030000B00000000
100000100P00259999
100000100B00100000
100000100D00100000
100000100M00250000
100000400P00300000
200005004F00897610
209006005E01000000
243004003P00999999
400350021H00500000
400450031F00247500
400450031P00050000
400450031F00050000
400650010E10000000
400650010F02500000
400650010JQ0999999
5RRRRRRRRKBAD DATA
500090005M00200000
500090005B00750000
500090005B00753434
500090005M00240000
500120007F00075000
500120007B00400000
600D60066YXXXXXXXX
600060066P00542000
600060066E00050000
600060066F00549000
600060066F00050000
600060066P00150000
600060066F00076000
600060066M00350000
600060066B00050000
600060066E00063200
600060066M00356000
600060066P00969000
709113003E00500000
709113003P00050000
709113003M01000000
709113003F00275000
709113003B00076823
710124004EBAD DATA
710124004EBAD DATA
710124004EBAD DATA
710124004B05000000
710124004P15000000
800050006U02500000
800050006Z00000050
800050006P02500000
890000000P00100000
```

## Maintenance File – MAINT

```
500090004CLPC
700124004DE
200006005CD880630
700124004CC3
400350021AD400350021DRIER HYDRO-DOME          HOTU23880325920101
200002001CT2
500090004CLDT
709111202CCCS
800050008DE
800050009DE
600000000CD881001
600000000AD600000000UNIV COMMENCEMENT AUDITORIUM  CSPC12880331880512
590120007CD880501
400450031DE
400550041DE
317504040CT5
300000000CT3
700000000AD700000000BERKELEY RESIDENTS          SADG33880331890331
700000000AD700000000SMART HARE TORTOISE FARM     CSTP33880331900101
700000000DE
800050009DE
600050055DE
840050007CLTP
100010200CD910501
317504040CT2
709111202XX
```

# PROJECT MANAGEMENT—PROGRAMMING PROJECTS

## PROJECT MANAGEMENT—JCL Assignment

**Problem Statement.**    The consulting firm for which you work provides an automated billing process for the Circle Club (APPENDIX C). Your firm has recently acquired a new account, the Square Club. They would like you to provide the same service for them.

Since the Square Club uses the same calculations and the member information is in the same format, you realize you can use the Circle Club program with a few minor modifications.

Basically, you will have to modify the Circle Club program itself (which is found in Appendix C), create a new data file, and modify the JCL to run the program.

Specifically, the modifications you must make for your new client are detailed below:

1. Create the new data set using the names and billing amounts listed below. The record layout is in the working storage section of the Circle Club program and in the initial comment section.

2. Change the title of the output report from "CIRCLE CLUB" to "SQUARE CLUB". (Hint: remember your output line record description should have a total of 133 characters.)

3. JCL to Run Job on MVS System.

```
//DEMO    JOB  (N007,501D,S05,002,JB),'DEMO CODE'
//STEP1   EXEC NCBCLG,REGION.GO=512K,PARM.GO='SIZE=448K'
//COB.SYSIN  DD  DSN=USR.N007.JB.CIRPRG,DISP=SHR
//GO.INFILE  DD  DSN=USR.N007.JB.CIRCLE,DISP=SHR
//GO.OUTFILE DD  SYSOUT=A,DCB=(BLKSIZE=133,RECFM=FA)
```

Where

> CIRPRG is the name of the file containing your source code.

and

> CIRCLE is the name of the data file for CIRCLE CLUB.

Save the modified program on your catalog. You may save it with your own choice of a name.

Use the data on the next page to create your new data file. Save your data file with the following specifications:

```
SAVE filename LRECL=72 (88)
```

where LRECL = 72 specifies the number of characters per record and 88 is the number of records per block.

Modify the JCL to reflect that the new program and data file are located on your account.

Square Club members and current account information: (member number, name, street address, restaurant bill, bar bill, other charges, past due amount)

```
001    Bryan, Gene,        1010 Pease St.,      $15, $10, $0,  $0
010    Manti, Vadan,       20 First Ave.,       $35, $25, $0,  $15
022    Grayson, Tim,       123 Michael Ave.,    $25, $0,  $20, $45
028    Guy, Kenneth,       89 Avenue A,         $25, $10, $5,  $0
035    Haskel, Elaine,     969 Cobol Drive,     $50, $20, $25, $0
044    Hill, George,       65 Compiler St.,     $25, $15, $0,  $0
050    Hunter, Jennifer,   156 University,      $25, $10, $0,  $0
065    Lin, Jack,          57 Unnamed Street,   $25, $10, $0,  $0
072    Lomatex, Jeannine,  91 College Dr.,      $35, $20, $0,  $25
084    McMellan, William,  101 Eastern,         $25, $10, $0,  $0
090    Mellison, Lucy,     35 Maroon Ave.,      $45, $0,  $10, $0
125    Rother, Michael,    76 Asset Parkway,    $15, $10, $0,  $30
139    North, Michael,     487 Ginger Ave.,     $25, $15, $5,  $0
154    Stewart, Mandy,     301 Data Ave.,       $25, $10, $5,  $0
165    Vasquez, Pablo,     630 Spanish Eyes,    $20, $0,  $0,  $20
```

The record layout for your new file will be the same as the input record description found in the Circle Club program. For example your first entry into your new data file should look something like this:

```
001 Bryant, Gene              1010 Pease St.    01500 01000 00000000000
```

Notice that we do not store decimals or dollars signs in our data file. We indicate where these items belong when we define the data in our program.

### PROJECT MANAGEMENT—Input/Output Assignment

**Problem Statement.**     Write a COBOL Program to print a listing of all projects. Requirements follow. All coding standards apply.

1. Project Listing Report

   This report is a listing of all the data for all projects. The format for the report is described below:

      a. A page heading of "PROJECT LISTING REPORT" should be used.
      b. Appropriate descriptive column headings should be used for the data columns.
      c. The report heading should be triple-spaced from the column headings. The body of the report should be double-spaced.

2. The data file to be used is the Project Master File, MASTER.
3. The file and record formats are given in the Data Dictionary in this Project as:

   ```
   PROJECT-MASTER-FILE
   PROJECT-RECORD-IN
   ```

4. REQUIREMENTS

   Turn in:

   - Cover sheet
   - Hierarchy chart
   - IPO chart
   - Detailed program flowchart
   - Source listing
   - Results

## PROJECT MANAGEMENT—Math Assignment

**Problem Statement.** Write a COBOL program that: (1) lists all projects on a project cost status report and (2) provides total cost figures for all associated cost fields. Output requirements are explained in the following paragraphs. All coding standards apply.

1. Project Cost Report

   The Project Cost Report is a listing of all projects in the Project Master File. The format of the report is as follows:

      a. The report should have a page heading of "PROJECT COST STATUS REPORT".
      b. Appropriate column headings should be printed for the columns required.
      c. The report should include: PROJECT-ID, PROJECT-DESCRIPTION and the FIVE COST FIELDS.
      d. At the end of the listing, a total should be printed indicating the sum of the FIVE COST FIELDS. The totals should be aligned beneath the corresponding cost field.

2. The data for this assignment is the Project Master File, MASTER.
3. The file and record formats are given in the Data Dictionary in this Project as:

   ```
   PROJECT-MASTER-FILE
   PROJECT-RECORD-IN
   ```

4. REQUIREMENTS

Turn in:

- Cover sheet
- Hierarchy chart
- IPO chart
- Detailed program flowchart
- Source listing
- Results

## PROJECT MANAGEMENT—Logic Assignment

**Problem Statement.**    Write a COBOL program that: (1) provides a project listing showing total cost, and (2) provides a summary report that gives the total number of projects in each city and the total cost by class of project. Output requirements are explained below. All coding standards apply.

1. The Total Cost Project Report

    The report is a listing of all projects in the Project Master File. The format of the report is as follows:

    a. The report should have a page heading of "TOTAL COST PROJECT REPORT".

    b. Appropriate column headings should be printed for the columns required.

    c. The report should include: PROJECT ID, CITY NAME, CLIENT NAME, PROJECT TYPE DESCRIPTION, CLASS DESCRIPTION and TOTAL COST. Notice that the city, client and type codes are to be converted to their respective names. These can be found in the Project Management Data Dictionary under:

    ```
    CITY-TABLE
    CLIENT-TABLE
    TYPE-TABLE
    CLASS-TABLE
    ```

2. The Project Summary Report

    This report includes two summaries: total number of projects in each city and total project cost by class of project. The summary should start on a separate page and include an appropriate page heading.

    a. The number of projects in each city report format is as shown:

    | Total Number of Projects | Summary |
    | --- | --- |
    | College Station | # |
    | Houston | # |
    | Dallas | # |
    | San Antonio | # |

b. The total cost by Project Class Report format is as shown:

Total Project Cost by Project    Class

| Federal | $ |
|---------|---|
| State | $ |
| Private | $ |

3. The file and record formats are given in the Data Dictionary in this Project as:

```
PROJECT-MASTER-FILE
PROJECT-RECORD-IN
```

## 4. REQUIREMENTS

Turn in:

- Cover sheet
- Hierarchy chart
- IPO chart
- Detailed program flowchart
- Source listing
- Results

### PROJECT MANAGEMENT—Control Break Assignment

**Problem Statement.**    Write a COBOL Program that: (1) writes a Project Location Report and (2) produces a Cost Summary Report. Output requirements are explained in the following paragraphs. All PEASE coding and documentation standards apply.

1. Project Location Report

Write a listing of all projects group-indicated by city. The city should be used as a title.

a. A page heading of "PROJECT CITY REPORT" should be used.
b. The name of the city should be printed two lines after the page heading.
c. The report should include: PROJECT-ID, PROJECT DESCRIPTION, TYPE and CLASS. All codes should be converted using values shown in the data dictionary.
d. Detail lines should be double-spaced.

2. Cost Summary Report

Write a report of all projects group-indicated by project type within class. Group-indicate both as columns.

a. A page heading of "COST SUMMARY REPORT" should be used.
b. The report should include: PROJECT-ID, and the FIVE COST FIELDS.
c. For each TYPE, print the TOTAL COST for each of the COST FIELDS as COLUMN TOTALS.
d. For each CLASS, print the TOTAL COST for each of the COST FIELDS also as COLUMN TOTALS.

e. Also print a Grand Total for each COST FIELD at the end of the report as COLUMN TOTALS.

3. The DATA for this assignment is the Project Master File. It must first be ordered by your professor into two files; a sorted by city file and a sorted by type within class file.

4. The file and record formats are given in the Data Dictionary in this Project as:

```
PROJECT-MASTER-FILE
PROJECT-RECORD-IN
CITY-TBL
CLASS-TBL
TYPE-TBL
```

5. REQUIREMENTS

Turn in:

- Cover sheet
- Hierarchy chart
- IPO chart
- Detailed program flowchart
- Source listing
- Results

### PROJECT MANAGEMENT—Table Processing Assignment

**Problem Statement.**    Congratulations! You have been made a senior programmer for the multi-global super-conglomerate information management firm of Pearce, Earnest and Anderson Consulting Enterprise (PEACE). Your first assignment is with a small, but potentially valuable, client—the Agate Construction Company (ACC). For the next three months or so, you'll be converting their archaic manual inventory system to a powerful, state-of-the-art computerized system.

The managing partners of PEACE have analyzed the existing system, and have set up a copy library of common COBOL code segments which you'll be using throughout the three month assignment. The copy library is in the PEACE corporate account and is saved under the name COPYLIB. You should already have the Data Dictionary that describes all the COPYLIB elements.

Your first programming assignment as a senior programmer is to write a COBOL program that generates two reports: (1) a Project Cost Status Report, and (2) a Project Cost Summary Report. Both Reports (and all subsequent reports produced for PEACE) should have the following banner and footer on every page.

1. Page Banner and Footer format

a. The page banner will consist of four lines beginning at the top of the page. The lines are: (1) a line of dashes, (2) a line containing the report date (left justified) and page number (right justified), (3) a line containing the report title (centered), and (4) a final line of dashes.

b. The footer will consist of the client company name right justified. It should be printed on line 55 of every page of all reports.

(Note: The record descriptions for the page banner and footer lines are in the COPYLIB.)

2. Project Cost Status Report

The Project Cost Status Report lists the ID number, description, client name and total cost of every project in the Project Master File. The format for the report is as follows:

    a. The page banners are described in Part 1.

    b. The column headings consist of PROJECT ID, PROJECT DESCRIPTION, PROJECT CLIENT, and TOTAL PROJECT COST. The headings should be separated from the page banner by two blank lines and should be followed by one blank line.

    c. The detail lines should be double-spaced and should contain the PROJECT ID, PROJECT DESCRIPTION, CLIENT DESCRIPTION (not the code, but the converted description) and the TOTAL PROJECT COST (sum of materials, personnel, electrical, plumbing and framing costs). There should be exactly 21 detail lines per full page.

    d. The page footer is described in Part 1.

3. Project Cost Summary Report

The Project Cost Summary Report lists the total project cost by city within project type. The format for the report is as follows:

    a. The page banners are described in Part 1.

    b. The column headings are the words 'PROJECT TYPE' followed by the city names (i.e., College Station, Houston, Dallas and San Antonio). The headings should be separated from the page banner by two blank lines and followed by three blank lines.

    c. Each detail line will contain a Project-type description, and the four total costs by city within that project-type (see attached example). Detail lines should be triple-spaced.

    d. After the last detail line, print a line showing the total project cost for each city.

    e. The page footer is described in Part 1.

4. All alphanumeric code conversions must be done with SEARCHs.
5. The data for the Project Master File is MASTER.
6. You will need the following COPYLIB elements:

```
PROJFD, PROJWS, PAGEBAN1, PAGEBAN2, PAGEBAN3, PAGEFOOT,
TYPETBL, CLIENTBL, and CITYTBL
```

7. REQUIREMENTS

    Turn in:

        • Cover sheet
        • Hierarchy chart
        • IPO chart
        • Detailed program flowchart
        • Source listing
        • Results

**Project Cost Summary Report Example**

```
----------------------------------------------------------------------------------
01/29/88                                                                   PAGE:   1
                             PROJECT COST SUMMARY REPORT
----------------------------------------------------------------------------------


  PROJECT TYPE            COLLEGE STATION        HOUSTON        DALLAS     SAN ANTONIO


  SINGLE FAMILY               48,000.34            0.00      97,000.00      576,000.00

  MULTI-FAMILY                99,000.50      150,000.00      50,000.00       32,500.00

  PARKS AND RECREATION       500,000.00       50,000.00       1,725.00            0.00

  COMMERCIAL                 790,000.00            0.00      68,700.91       61,400.00

  INDUSTRIAL                       0.00        5,000.00      15,000.00        2,946.87
                             ----------      ----------     ----------      ----------

  TOTAL                $ 1,437,000.79    $  205,000.00  $  232,425.91   $  671,846.87



                                                             AGATE CONSTRUCTION CO.
```

### PROJECT MANAGEMENT—Sorting Assignment

**Problem Statement.**     Write a COBOL program for PEASE that provides three reports: (1) a project listing of all projects in ID order (ascending), (2) a project listing of all Federal projects in project description order for each city and (3) a project listing of all projects by type of project for each class and city combination. The project should be listed in alphabetical order by description.

Requirements for the reports are given below. All coding standards apply.

1. Project Listing by ID Report

   Sort the PROJECT-MASTER-FILE in ascending order by project ordered by PROJECT-ID. All data fields should be included on the report.

   a. Use the same page banner and footer formats described in the TABLES program.
   b. Print a page heading and appropriate column headings. The page heading should be double-spaced below the banner. The column headings should be triple-spaced below the page heading and should be separated from the body of the report by two blank lines.
   c. The detailed lines should be doubled-spaced with no more than 21 detailed lines per page.
   d. Repeat all headings when starting a new page.

2. Federal Project Listing Report

   Sort all Federal Projects by description for each city. You should use the city name for sorting instead of the code. The format of the report is as follows:

   a. Use the same page banner and footer formats as in 1a. above.
   b. Print appropriate page and column headings. The spacing is as in 1b. above.

c. The detail lines should be doubled-spaced with no more than 21 per page. Include all data fields except for cost fields.

d. The report should be group-indicated using the city name as a report heading.

e. Start a new page when ever the city changes.

3. The Project Analysis Report

This report list all projects sorted by project type (descending), with project class (ascending) within city (descending). All projects should be listed in alphabetical order by description. All codes should be used for sorting but should be converted for reporting. The report should be group-indicated by type within class within city.

a. Use the same page banner and footing formats as in 1a.

b. Print appropriate page and column headings. The spacing is as in 1b.

c. The detail lines are as in 1c.

d. The report should be group-indicated using the type, class and city as columns.

e. All group-indications should be reported when starting a new page.

4. The data file is Project Master File, MASTER.

5. You will need the following COPYLIB Elements:

```
PROJFD      PROJWS      PAGEBAN1    PAGEBAN2
PAGEBAN3    PAGEFOOT    CLASSTBL    TYPETBL
CITYTBL     CLIENTBL
```

6. REQUIREMENTS

Turn in:

- Cover sheet
- Hierarchy chart
- IPO chart
- Detailed program flowchart
- Source listing
- Results

## PROJECT MANAGEMENT—Sorting and Control Break Assignment

**Problem Statement.**    Write a COBOL program that: (1) creates a sorted PROJECT-MASTER-FILE, (2) prints a PROJECT VALUATION REPORT, and (3) prints a PROJECT SCHEDULE REPORT. Output requirements are explained in the following paragraphs. All PEACE coding and documentation standards still apply.

1. Sorted PROJECT-MASTER-FILE

Sort the PROJECT-MASTER-FILE in ascending order by PROJECT-ID. Store this sorted file on your account under the file name PROJSORT. Also, print a dump of the sorted file.

2. Project Valuation Report

The Project Valuation Report is a listing of all projects sorted by total-project-cost (in descending order) within city (ascending order) within project-type (ascending order) within project-class (ascending order). The city, type and class sorts should be by code, not by description. The format for the report is as follows:

a. Use the same page banner and footer formats described in the Tables Processing Assignment.

b. Print a project class heading line double-spaced below the page banner. This line will consist of the words 'PROJECT CLASS: ' followed by the current project class description. It should be left justified.

c. Separate the column headings from the project class heading line by two blank lines. Items to be included in the column headings are: PROJECT TYPE, CITY, PROJECT DESCRIPTION, ESTINATED COMPLETION DATE and TOTAL COST.

d. The detail lines should be double-spaced, with 21 detail lines per full page. Every detail line should include the project description, estimated completion date and total cost. The city and type descriptions are group-indicators and should only be printed when the codes change. Triple-space the first record of each new project type. (See sample output for clarification.)

e. Start a new page whenever the project class code changes. Whenever you start a new page you must reprint the class heading line and the type and city descriptions.

f. After each class, print a line indicating the total project cost for that class. At the end of the report, print a grand total line indicating the cost of all projects (see sample output).

3. Project Schedule Report

The Project Schedule Report is used by ACC management to determine which projects are on schedule and which are past their originally planned completion date. It lists all projects sorted by estimated completion date (from earliest to latest) within project client. The format for the report is as follows:

a. Use the same page banner and footer formats described in Programming Assignment #1.

b. Print a client heading line double-spaced below the page banner. This line will consist of the word 'CLIENT: ' followed by the current client description, and should be left justified.

c. Separate the column headings from the client heading line by two blank lines. Items to be included in the column headings are: PROJECT STATUS, PROJECT ID, PROJECT DESCRIPTION, TOTAL COST and ESTIMATED COMPLETION DATE.

d. The detail lines should be double-spaced, with 21 detail lines per full page. Each detail line should include the project id, project description, total cost and estimated completion date.

The project status column is a group-indicator used to show which projects are late and which are still on time. You should group-indicate the late projects with the word 'LATE' and the projects that are still on schedule with the words 'ON TIME' in the project status column. Also, triple-space between the last late project and the first on-time project, of each client.

(Note: If you sort the file in ascending order by estimated completion date, all the late projects will be at the top and all the on-time projects will be at the bottom. See sample output for clarification.)

    e. Start a new page whenever the client code changes.

4. All alphanumeric code conversions must be done with SEARCHs.
5. The data for the Project Master File is MASTER.
6. You will need the following COPYLIB elements:

```
PROJFD,      PROJWS,
PAGEBAN1,    PAGEBAN2,
PAGEBAN3,    PAGEFOOT,
CLASSTBL,    TYPETBL,
CLIENTBL,    CITYTBL
```

## 6. REQUIREMENTS

Turn in:

- Cover sheet
- Hierarchy chart
- IPO chart
- Detailed program flowchart
- Source listing
- Results

## Sample Project Valuation Report

```
--------------------------------------------------------------------------------
02/15/88                                                                Page:  8
                            PROJECT VALUATION REPORT
--------------------------------------------------------------------------------

PROJECT CLASS:  LOCAL

   PROJECT            PROJECT          PROJECT         ESTIMATED
    TYPE               CITY          DESCRIPTION    COMPLETION DATE      TOTAL COST


SINGLE FAMILY      COLLEGE STATION    JOE'S HOUSE       10/12/87          500,999.99

                                      JANE'S HOUSE      05/05/88        1,200,000.00

                   HOUSTON            BOB'S HOUSE       01/12/90          750,000.00


MULTI-FAMILY       COLLEGE STATION    SPLENDOR APTS     07/15/89          500,000.00

                   SAN ANTONIO        RIVER RUN CONDOS  09/03/88        2,450,000.00



           .                    .                  .


INDUSTRIAL         SAN ANTONIO        NUCLEAR PLANT     11/21/99       10,000,000.00


                                                          AGATE CONSTRUCTION CO.
```

```
--------------------------------------------------------------------------------
02/15/88                                                                Page:  9
                            PROJECT VALUATION REPORT
--------------------------------------------------------------------------------

PROJECT CLASS:  LOCAL

   PROJECT            PROJECT          PROJECT         ESTIMATED
    TYPE               CITY          DESCRIPTION    COMPLETION DATE      TOTAL COST


INDUSTRIAL         SAN ANTONIO        SPRUCE SLUECE     04/31/90        1,450,000.00

                                      BAIRD'S SILO      05/09/93          250,000.25


                                      TOTAL COST OF LOCAL PROJECTS     $ 27,258,321.93

                                      GRAND TOTAL COST OF ALL PROJECTS $ 65,348,992.63


                                                          AGATE CONSTRUCTION CO.
```

## Sample Project Schedule Report

```
----------------------------------------------------------------------
 02/15/88                                                    Page:   1
                            PROJECT SCHEDULE REPORT
----------------------------------------------------------------------


 CLIENT: DEPARTMENT OF EDUCATION


 PROJECT                          PROJECT                          ESTIMATED
 STATUS        PROJECT ID         DESCRIPTION         TOTAL COST   COMPLETION DATE


 LATE          700040400          WOODWARD ELEMENTARY     200,000.00      10/24/86

               590000030          TODESTO ADMINISTRATIVE BLDG  575,000.45  01/31/87

               694000000          SLUMPNIK PUBLIC LIBRARY  1,200,000.00    05/20/87


 ON TIME       200000345          MT. BINGAWHACK HIGH SCHOOL  275,000.00   02/30/88

               500000000          CRAMIDIN CONTINUED ED BLDG  150,457.72   05/19/88
                        .                        .
                        .                        .
                        .                        .

 * Note: Any project with an estimated due date prior to February
 1, 1988 is considered LATE when you use the data file MASTER.
```

### PROJECT MANAGEMENT—Sequential File Update Assignment

**Problem Statement.**     Your next assignment for PEACE is to write a COBOL program that updates the ACC's Project Master File using the Transaction Project File, and produces: (1) a Project Update Activity Report, (2) a Project Update Error Report, and (3) an updated Project Master File. The record layout of the Transaction Project File is in the copy library under the element name TRANSWS. Both the master file and the transaction file are already sorted by Project ID.

All PEACE coding and documentation standards still apply. The output requirements are explained in the following paragraphs.

1. Project Update Activity Report

The Project Update Report is a listing of all valid updates processed against the Project Master File. The format for the report is as follows:

a. Use the same page banners and footer formats as in previous assignments.

b. Separate the column headings from the page banner by two blank lines. Items to be included in the column headings are: PROJECT ID, PROJECT DESCRIPTION, TYPE OF CHANGE, PREVIOUS COST ($), and UPDATED COST ($).

c. The detail lines will be double-spaced and will include the PROJECT ID, PROJECT DESCRIPTION, a description of the type of change being made, and the costs before and after the change was made.

Notice that one project may have several changes made to it. If a project has more than one change made to it, the Project ID and Project Description should only be printed on the first line for that project. All subsequent lines for the same project should contain only the description of the change and the costs before and after the change was made. Also, all subsequent lines for the same project should be single spaced.

(Note: If a project continues onto a new page, the Project ID and description should be reprinted on the new page. Also you should use a SEARCH to convert the transaction code to a description. This means you'll need to set up a compile-time table with the descriptions.)

   d. The valid transaction codes and associated transactions are:

      M – Update Materials cost
      P – Update Personnel cost
      E – Update Electrical cost
      B – Update Plumbing cost
      F – Update Framing cost

(Note: All transaction amounts should be added to the appropriate cost field.)

2. Project Update Error Report

The Project Update Error Report is a listing of all errors that occur during the update process. The format for the report is as follows:

   a. Use the standard page banner and footer formats.
   b. Separate the column headings from the page banner with two blank lines. Items to be included in the column headings are: TRANS-ACTION RECORD and ERROR DESCRIPTION.
   c. Detail lines will be double-spaced and will include the entire invalid transaction record and an error description. Although there is no need to provide column headings for the individual fields of the transaction record, you should separate the fields by inserting one blank space between each one of them. If there is more than one error in a single transaction record, only write the transaction record once, and single-space the subsequent error messages.
   d. Transaction errors that can occur are:

      1) Project not in master file – If this error occurs you do not need to check further unless of course you want to or your professor wants you to.
      2) Invalid transaction code
      3) Invalid data in transaction amount

3. Update Project Master File

An Updated Project Master File should be created in conjunction with the update process. This file should contain all of the records on the original Project Master File (not just the ones that changed). The new file should be stored in your account under the name PROJUPD.

After the update process is completed, print a report showing the contents of the Updated Project Master File. The format for this report is as follows:

   a. Page banners and footer are standard.

b. The column headings will include three rows of column numbers from 1 to 107. The column numbers should be centered on the page.

c. Double-space each detail record.

4. In each of the above reports, there should be exactly 20 detail records per full page.

5. The Project Master File is MASTSORT. The Transaction Project File is TRANS.

6. You will need the following COPYLIB elements:

All page banners and footer elements and,

```
TRANSFD TRANSWS
PROJFD
PROJWS
```

7. REQUIREMENTS

Turn in:

- Cover sheet
- Hierarchy chart
- IPO chart
- Detailed program flowchart
- Source listing
- Results

## Sample Project Update Activity Report

```
------------------------------------------------------------------------
                          STANDARD PAGE HEADER
------------------------------------------------------------------------


                                  TYPE
  PROJECT ID    PROJECT DESCRIPTION    OF CHANGE    PREVIOUS COST ($)    UPDATED COST ($)

  100000000    LOCKE'S COFFEE SHOP    ELECTRICAL      27,500.00          28,750.00

  200000000    SUZUKI ARCHERY RANGE   PLUMBING        10,000.00          15,000.00
                                      FRAMING          5,000.00           7,500.00
                                      MATERIALS       22,000.00          25,000.00
                                      PLUMBING        15,000.00          16,550.00

  300000000    SEYMOUR GLASS HOUSE    PERSONNEL       90,000.00         100,000.00
                                      MATERIALS       50,000.00          60,000.00



                .                        .               .


                .                        .               .


                .
```

### Sample Project Update Error Report

```
----------------------------------------------------------------------------
                        STANDARD PAGE HEADER
----------------------------------------------------------------------------

        TRANSACTION RECORD                    ERROR MESSAGE

        10000000A M 10000000        PROJECT NOT IN MASTER FILE

        2ZZ000000 L 030A0000        INVALID TRANSACTION CODE
                                    INVALID DATA IN TRANSACTION AMOUNT

        300000000 B BBBBBBBB        INVALID DATA IN TRANSACTION AMOUNT
```

### PROJECT MANAGEMENT—Index File Processing Assignment

**Problem Statement.**    As you know, we often use sequential file processing techniques to accomplish such high activity ratio functions as printing reports, preparing records for sorting, generating employee pay checks, etc. When we want to perform some function that has a low activity ratio, however, the use of sequential file processing may not be appropriate. For those functions, we need to consider using some technique that uses a more "direct" accessing method. Maintenance of the Agate Construction Company's Project Master File is one of those low activity ratio functions. Because of this, your PEACE supervisor has decided to make use of the indexed file organization that is available with COBOL.

Your assignment is to: (1) build a VSAM-organized Project Master File on your account using the sequentially organized master file, MASTSORT. Then, accomplish the maintenance processing, producing (2) a Project Master File Maintenance Log, and (3) a Project Master File Maintenance Error Report. And finally produce (4) a sequential listing of the Project Master File after the maintenance processing has been completed.

1. Building a VSAM-organized Project Master File

    Instructions for building a VSAM file on your account will be given in class. System utilities are included in the Chapter.

2. Project Master File Maintenance Log

    The Project Master File Maintenance Log is a report of all maintenance transactions successfully accomplished during the maintenance process. The format of the report is as follows:

    a. Use the standard page banner and footer formats.
    b. Separate the column headings from the page banner by two blank lines. Items to be included in the column headings are: PROJECT ID, MAINTENANCE DESCRIPTION, and MAINTENANCE DATA.

c. The valid transaction codes and associated transactions are:

AD – Add a Record
CC – Change City Code
CL – Change Client Code
CT – Change Type Code
CD – Change Estimated Completion Date
DE – Delete a Record

d. A detail entry will consist of either one or two lines, depending on the type of transaction.

When adding a project to the Master File, a single line consisting of the Project ID, Maintenance Description, and the new project's data will be printed.

When deleting a project from the Master File, a single line consisting of the Project ID, Maintenance Description, and the data for the project being deleted will be printed.

And when changing a City Code, Client Code, Type Code or Estimated Completion Date, for a Project, two lines will be printed. The first line will consist of the Project ID, Maintenance Description, and the word "FROM: " followed by the original data in the field being changed. The second line will consist of the word "TO: " followed by the new data. All data codes should be converted to descriptions. Single-space the second line of each change transaction. All other lines on the report should be double-spaced.

3. Project Master File Maintenance Error Report

The Project Master File Maintenance Error Report is a listing of all errors that occur during the maintenance process. The format of the report is as follows:

a. Use standard banner and footer formats.
b. Separate the column headings from the page banner by two blank lines. Items to be included in the column headings are: PROJECT ID, MAINTENANCE CODE, MAINTENANCE FIELDS, and ERROR DESCRIPTION.
c. Detail lines will be double-spaced and will consist of the Project ID, maintenance code (not description), maintenance fields, and an appropriate error message.
d. Transaction errors that can occur are:

1) Invalid add: Record already exists
2) Invalid delete: Record does not exist
3) Invalid change: Record does not exist
4) Invalid delete: Non-zero cost amount

(Note: The fourth error occurs if any one of the cost amounts in the record being deleted has a value other than zero. For example if project number 100000000 is supposed to be deleted, but it has a Framing cost of one dollar, the record cannot be deleted.)

4. Listing of the Project Master File after Maintenance Processing.

The Project Master File Listing will be printed upon completion of the maintenance process. It should be produced by sequentially accessing the VSAM-organized Project Master File. Its format is as follows:

    a. Page banners and footer are standard.

    b. The column headings will include three rows of column numbers from 1 to 107. The column numbers should be centered on the page.

    c. Double-space each detail record.

5. In each of the above reports, there should be exactly 20 detail records per full page.

6. The sequential Project Master File is MASTSORT. The Maintenance Project File is MAINT.

7. You will need the following COPYLIB elements:

All page banners and footer elements and,

```
MAINTFD      MAINTWS
TRANSWS      CLIENTBL
CITYTBL      TYPETBL
```

8. REQUIREMENTS

Turn in:

- Cover sheet
- Hierarchy chart
- IPO chart
- Detailed program flowchart
- Source listing
- Results

## Sample Project File Maintenance Log

```
--------------------------------------------------------------------------
                         STANDARD PAGE HEADER
--------------------------------------------------------------------------

   PROJECT ID          MAINTENANCE DESCRIPTION          MAINTENANCE DATA

   700900000           CHANGE CITY CODE                 FROM: HOUSTON
                                                        TO:   DALLAS

   250000000           ADD A RECORD                     250000000NEW PROJECT . . .

   310000500           DELETE A RECORD                  310000500OLD PROJECT . . .

   100000000           CHANGE CLIENT CODE               FROM:  PERCY CONSTRUCTION
                                                        TO:    DEPARTMENT OF DEFENSE

   850000000           CHANGE ESTIMATED COMPLETION DATE  FROM:  01/30/89
                                                        TO:    05/31/89
```

## Sample Project Master File Maintenance Error Report

```
---------------------------------------------------------------------------
                            STANDARD PAGE HEADER
---------------------------------------------------------------------------

                MAINTENANCE
 PROJECT ID        CODE      MAINTENANCE FIELDS        ERROR DESCRIPTION

 500000000         AD        HOUSEDATU23880101    INVALID ADD:    RECORD ALREADY EXISTS

 110000000         DE                             INVALID DELETE: RECORD DOES NOT EXIST

 400000000         CC        DE                   INVALID CHANGE: RECORD DOES NOT EXIST

 850000000         DE                             INVALID DELETE: NON-ZERO COST AMOUNT

 303030303         CD        880903               INVALID CHANGE: RECORD DOES NOT EXIST

                             .                    .

                             .                    .

                             .                    .
```

# THE EMPLOYEE SYSTEM

## Employee System
## Data Dictionary

| File/Record Name | Member Name |
|---|---|
| EMPLOYEE-SALARY-FILE | FDEMPL |
| MAINTENANCE-TRANS-FILE | FDMAINT |
| TRANSACTION-FILE | FDTRANS |
| EMPLOYEE-SALARY-VSAM-FILE | FDEMPVSM |
| EMPLOYEE-SALARY-RECORD-IN | WSEMPREC |
| TRANSACTION-RECORD-IN | TRANSREC |
| MAINTENANCE-RECORD-IN | WSMAINTR |
| PAGE-BANNER-LINE-1 | PAGEBAN1 |
| PAGE-BANNER-LINE-2 | PAGEBAN2 |
| PAGE-BANNER-LINE-3 | PAGEBAN3 |
| CITY-TABLE | CITYTBL |
| DEPARTMENT-TABLE | DEPTTBL |

The library elements are in your class' library, COPYLBRY.

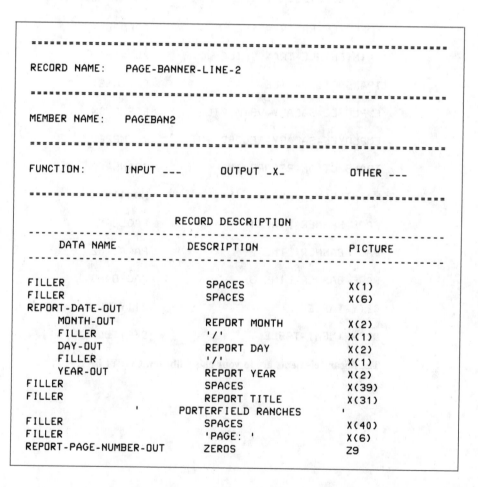

```
=========================================================

RECORD NAME:    PAGE-BANNER-LINE-1

=========================================================

MEMBER NAME:    PAGEBAN1

=========================================================

FUNCTION:    INPUT ___    OUTPUT _X_    OTHER ___

=========================================================

                    RECORD DESCRIPTION
---------------------------------------------------------
   DATA NAME           DESCRIPTION           PICTURE
---------------------------------------------------------

FILLER                  SPACES                X(2)
FILLER                  '*'                   X(128)
FILLER                  SPACES                X(3)
```

```
=========================================================

RECORD NAME:    PAGE-BANNER-LINE-2

=========================================================

MEMBER NAME:    PAGEBAN2

=========================================================

FUNCTION:    INPUT ___    OUTPUT _X_    OTHER ___

=========================================================

                    RECORD DESCRIPTION
---------------------------------------------------------
   DATA NAME           DESCRIPTION           PICTURE
---------------------------------------------------------

FILLER                  SPACES                X(1)
FILLER                  SPACES                X(6)
REPORT-DATE-OUT
    MONTH-OUT           REPORT MONTH          X(2)
    FILLER              '/'                   X(1)
    DAY-OUT             REPORT DAY            X(2)
    FILLER              '/'                   X(1)
    YEAR-OUT            REPORT YEAR           X(2)
FILLER                  SPACES                X(39)
FILLER                  REPORT TITLE          X(31)
              '         PORTERFIELD RANCHES           '
FILLER                  SPACES                X(40)
FILLER                  'PAGE: '              X(6)
REPORT-PAGE-NUMBER-OUT  ZEROS                 Z9
```

```
=====================================================================

RECORD NAME:   PAGE-BANNER-LINE-3

=====================================================================

MEMBER NAME:   PAGEBAN3

=====================================================================

FUNCTION:      INPUT ___     OUTPUT _X_        OTHER ___

=====================================================================

                          RECORD DESCRIPTION
--------------------------------------------------------------------
    DATA NAME              DESCRIPTION            PICTURE
--------------------------------------------------------------------

FILLER                       SPACES              X(2)
FILLER                        '*'                X(128)
FILLER                       SPACES              X(3)
```

```
=====================================================================

FILE NAME:     EMPLOYEE-SALARY-FILE

=====================================================================

MEMBER NAME:   FDEMPL

=====================================================================

FUNCTION:      INPUT _X_       OUTPUT ___         OTHER ___

=====================================================================

FILE DESCRIPTION:    BLOCK CONTAINS 104 RECORDS
                     RECORD CONTAINS 61 CHARACTERS
                     LABEL RECORDS ARE OMITTED
                     DATA RECORD IS EMPLOYEE-SALARY-RECORD


=====================================================================

                          RECORD DESCRIPTION
--------------------------------------------------------------------
    DATA NAME              DESCRIPTION            PICTURE
--------------------------------------------------------------------

EMPLOYEE-SALARY-RECORD        EMPLOYEE SALARY FILE   X(61)
                              RECORD
```

```
=================================================================

RECORD NAME:   EMPLOYEE-SALARY-RECORD-IN

=================================================================

MEMBER NAME:   WSEMPREC

=================================================================

FUNCTION:      INPUT ___      OUTPUT ___      OTHER _X_

=================================================================

                     RECORD DESCRIPTION
-----------------------------------------------------------------
      DATA NAME              DESCRIPTION           PICTURE
-----------------------------------------------------------------

SOCIAL-SECURITY-NUMBER-IN   SOCIAL SECURITY NUMBER
    SS-NUMBER-PART-1-IN      FIRST 3 DIGITS         X(3)
    SS-NUMBER-PART-2-IN      SECOND 2 DIGITS        X(2)
    SS-NUMBER-PART-3-IN      LAST 4 DIGITS          X(4)

EMPLOYEE-NAME-IN            EMPLOYEE'S NAME         X(20)
                           (FIRST, MIDDLE, LAST)

DATE-OF-EMPLOYMENT-IN      DATE EMPLOYEE STARTED
                           WORKING
    YEAR-OF-EMPLOYMENT-IN   YEAR  EMPLOYEE STARTED   X(2)
    MONTH-OF-EMPLOYMENT-IN  MONTH EMPLOYEE STARTED   X(2)
    DAY-OF-EMPLOYMENT-IN    DAY   EMPLOYEE STARTED   X(2)

NUMBER-OF-DEPENDENTS-IN     NUMBER OF DEPENDENTS    9(2)

RETIREMENT-PROGRAM-CODE-IN  CODE INDICATING WHICH   X(1)
                           RETIREMENT PROGRAM
                           EMPLOYEE PARTICIPATES IN

MONTHLY-PARKING-FEE-IN      MONTHLY FEE FOR PARKING 9(3)

SAVINGS-PROGRAM-PERCENTAGE-IN PERCENTAGE OF SALARY  9(3)
                           DEDUCTED FOR SAVINGS

DEPARTMENT-CODE-IN          CODE INDICATING THE     X(1)
                           DEPARTMENT IN WHICH
                           THE EMPLOYEE WORKS

CITY-CODE-IN                CODE INDICATING THE     9(1)
                           CITY IN WHICH
                           THE EMPLOYEE WORKS

MONTHLY-SALARY-IN           MONTHLY GROSS PAY       9(5)V99

YEAR-TO-DATE-EARNINGS-IN    YEARS TOTAL EARNINGS    9(6)V99
=================================================================

FILE NAME:    MAINTENANCE-TRANS-FILE

=================================================================
```

*(continued)*

```
MEMBER NAME:  FDMAINT

=================================================================

FUNCTION:     INPUT _X_        OUTPUT ___        OTHER ___

=================================================================

FILE DESCRIPTION:   BLOCK CONTAINS 100 RECORDS
                    RECORD CONTAINS 63 CHARACTERS
                    LABEL RECORDS ARE OMITTED
                    DATA RECORD IS MAINTENANCE-RECORD

=================================================================

                      RECORD DESCRIPTION
-----------------------------------------------------------------
    DATA NAME             DESCRIPTION             PICTURE
-----------------------------------------------------------------

MAINTENANCE-RECORD     MAINTENANCE TRANSACTION    X(63)
                       RECORD
```

```
=================================================================

RECORD NAME:   MAINTENANCE-RECORD-IN

=================================================================

SOURCE:        WSMAINTR

=================================================================

FUNCTION:      INPUT ___        OUTPUT ___        OTHER _X_

=================================================================

                      RECORD DESCRIPTION
-----------------------------------------------------------------
    DATA NAME             DESCRIPTION             PICTURE
-----------------------------------------------------------------

TRANS-SS-NUMBER          SOCIAL SECURITY NUMBER
   TRANS-SS-NUM-PART1       FIRST 3 DIGITS          9(3)
   TRANS-SS-NUM-PART2       SECOND 2 DIGITS         9(2)
   TRANS-SS-NUM-PART3       LAST 4 DIGITS           9(4)

MAINTENANCE-CODE         TYPE OF MAINTENANCE        X(2)
   ADD-A-RECORD             CONDITIONAL NAME        VALUE 'AD'
   DELETE-A-RECORD          CONDITIONAL NAME        VALUE 'DE'
   CHANGE-EMPLOYEE-NAME     CONDITIONAL NAME        VALUE 'CN'
   CHANGE-NO-OF-DEPENDENTS  CONDITIONAL NAME        VALUE 'CK'
   CHANGE-RETIREMENT-PRGM   CONDITIONAL NAME        VALUE 'CR'
   CHANGE-PARKING-FEE       CONDITIONAL NAME        VALUE 'CP'
   CHANGE-SAVINGS-PROGRAM   CONDITIONAL NAME        VALUE 'CS'
   CHANGE-DEPT-CODE         CONDITIONAL NAME        VALUE 'CD'
   CHANGE-CITY-CODE         CONDITIONAL NAME        VALUE 'CC'
   VALID-MAINTENANCE-CODE   CONDITIONAL NAME    VALUE 'AD"DE"CN'
                                                'CK' 'CR"CP"CS'
                                                'CD"CC'

MAINTENANCE-FIELDS       MAINTENANCE INFORMATION    X(52)
```

*(continued)*

```
-----------------------ADD transaction-----------------------

TR-NAME                      (FIRST, MIDDLE, LAST)      X(20)
TR-DATE-OF-EMPLOYMENT        DATE EMPLOYEE STARTED      X(6)
                               WORKING
TR-NUMBER-OF-DEPENDENTS      NUMBER OF DEPENDENTS       9(2)
TR-RETIREMENT-PRGM-CODE      CODE INDICATING IN WHICH   X(1)
                               RETIREMENT PROGRAM
                               EMPLOYEE PARTICIPATES
TR-MONTHLY-PARKING-FEE       MONTHLY FEE FOR PARKING    9(3)
TR-SAVINGS-PRGM-PERCENT      PERCENTAGE OF SALARY       9(3)
                               DEDUCTED FOR SAVINGS
TR-DEPARTMENT-CODE           CODE INDICATING THE        X(1)
                               DEPARTMENT IN WHICH
                               THE EMPLOYEE WORKS
TR-CITY-CODE                 CODE INDICATING THE        X(1)
                               CITY IN WHICH
                               THE EMPLOYEE WORKS
TR-MONTHLY-SALARY            MONTHLY GROSS PAY          9(5)V99
TR-YTDE                      TOTAL EARNINGS FOR YEAR    9(6)V99

-------------------DELETE transaction---------------------

FILLER                                                  X(52)

---------------CHANGE EMPLOYEE NAME    transaction---------------

TR-NEW-EMPLOYEE-NAME                                    X(20)
FILLER                                                  X(32)

--------------CHANGE NO OF DEPENDENTS transaction---------------

TR-NEW-NO-OF-DEPENDENTS                                 9(2)
FILLER                                                  X(50)

----------------CHANGE RETIREMENT PRGM transaction---------------

TR-NEW-RETIREMENT-CODE                                  X(1)
FILLER                                                  X(51)

-----------------CHANGE PARKING FEE transaction-----------------

TR-NEW-PARKING-FEE                                      9(3)
FILLER                                                  X(49)

-----------------CHANGE SAVINGS PRGM transaction-----------------

TR-NEW-SAVINGS-PROGRAM                                  X(3)
FILLER                                                  X(49)

---------------CHANGE DEPARTMENT CODE transaction---------------

TR-NEW-DEPARTMENT-CODE                                  X(1)
FILLER                                                  X(51)

------------------CHANGE CITY CODE transaction------------------

TR-NEW-CITY-CODE                                        X(1)
FILLER                                                  X(51)
```

```
===================================================================
FILE NAME:     TRANSACTION-FILE
===================================================================
MEMBER NAME:   FDTRANS
===================================================================
FUNCTION:      INPUT _X_       OUTPUT ___        OTHER ___
===================================================================
FILE DESCRIPTION:   BLOCK CONTAINS 300 RECORDS
                    RECORD CONTAINS 17 CHARACTERS
                    LABEL RECORDS ARE OMITTED
                    DATA RECORD IS TRANSACTION-RECORD
===================================================================
                     RECORD DESCRIPTION
-------------------------------------------------------------------
     DATA NAME             DESCRIPTION              PICTURE
-------------------------------------------------------------------

TRANSACTION-RECORD     TRANSACTION FILE RECORD      X(17)
```

```
===================================================================
RECORD NAME:   TRANSACTION-RECORD-IN
===================================================================
MEMBER NAME:   TRANSREC
===================================================================
FUNCTION:      INPUT ___       OUTPUT ___         OTHER _X_
===================================================================
                     RECORD DESCRIPTION
-------------------------------------------------------------------
     DATA NAME             DESCRIPTION              PICTURE
-------------------------------------------------------------------

TRANS-SS-NUMBER        SOCIAL SECURITY NUMBER       9(9)

TRANSACTION-CODE       TYPE OF UPDATE               X(1)
   INCREASE-SALARY     CONDITIONAL NAME             VALUE 'I'
   DECREASE-SALARY     CONDITIONAL NAME             VALUE 'D'
TRANSACTION-AMOUNT     AMOUNT TO INCREASE OR        9(5)V9(2)
                         DECREASE SALARY
```

```
=================================================================

FILE NAME:      EMPLOYEE-SALARY-VSAM-FILE

=================================================================

MEMBER NAME:   FDEMPVSM
=================================================================

FUNCTION:      INPUT _X_        OUTPUT X___         OTHER ___

=================================================================

FILE DESCRIPTION:   LABEL RECORDS ARE OMITTED
                    DATA RECORD IS EMPLOYEE-SALARY-VSAM-RECORD

=================================================================

                        RECORD DESCRIPTION
-----------------------------------------------------------------
    DATA NAME                   DESCRIPTION           PICTURE
-----------------------------------------------------------------

EMPLOYEE-SALARY-VSAM-RECORD    EMPLOYEE SALARY FILE
                               RECORD
   SOCIAL-SECURITY-NUMBER-VSAM                         X(9)
   FILLER                                              X(52)
```

```
=================================================================

FILE NAME:      CITY-TABLE

=================================================================

MEMBER NAME:   CITYTBL
=================================================================

FUNCTION:      INPUT ___        OUTPUT ___          OTHER X___

=================================================================

PURPOSE:       Compile time table containing city names.

=================================================================

                        RECORD DESCRIPTION
-----------------------------------------------------------------
    DATA NAME                   DESCRIPTION           PICTURE
-----------------------------------------------------------------

CITY-VALUES
                               'LONDON'               X(7)
                               'BELFAST'              X(7)
                               'SYDNEY'               X(7)
                               'DALLAS'               X(7)

CITY-TABLE                     REDEFINES CITY-VALUES
   CITY-NAME                   OCCURS 4 TIMES         X(7)
```

```
=========================================================

FILE NAME:    DEPARTMENT-TABLE

=========================================================

MEMBER NAME:  DEPTTBL

=========================================================

FUNCTION:     INPUT ---      OUTPUT ---      OTHER X---

=========================================================

PURPOSE:      Compile time table containing department codes
              and department names

=========================================================

                    RECORD DESCRIPTION
---------------------------------------------------------
     DATA NAME          DESCRIPTION           PICTURE
---------------------------------------------------------


DEPARTMENT-VALUES
                      'AACCOUNTING'           X(20)
                      'IINFORMATION SYSTEMS'  X(20)
                      'FFINANCIAL SERVICES'   X(20)
                      'SSALES'                X(20)
                      'MMARKETING'            X(20)


DEPARTMENT-TABLE            REDEFINES DEPARTMENT-VALUES
   DEPARTMENT-GROUP            OCCURS 5 TIMES
                              INDEXED BY DEPT-INDEX

      DEPT-TBL-CODE                           X(1)
      DEPT-TBL-NAME                           X(19)
```

# The Employee System
# Data Sets

## Employee File – EMPLOYEE

```
112335690CLARK, RALPH        780701042100015A3012000000620000
122389900MACALVAN, BELINDA   690115002050000F3015000000750000
145578000EVANS, DALE         790606011000005A3008000000410000
166894500LOCKE, SANDRA       711201102000015A1030000001650000
191860400HENRY, LILLIE       830912001000025M1011500000750000
226794000RODRIGUEZ, JOSE     860530011050005S3010000000540000
233459700SILVERMAN, BUBBA    671205042100025M1021000001080000
234569000WAYNE, JOE          750606031000015I3022000001180000
334892240CLARK, RALPH        850901011050005I4015000001000000
334894550CULP, BELINDA       550730031050000F3022000001100000
341181000GEYER, NELSON       550730031050000F3022000001100000
344586790MYERS, KATHY        830501001050015F4010000000500000
344894321ROBINSON, JOHN      820115002100005F4014000000745000
348904600LONG, SHELLY        780301071050015S4018500000925000
387344321ROBINSON, JOHN      820115002100005F4014000000745000
388990600ROGERS, ROBERT      771125031050015S2014000000732000
```

*(continued)*

```
389900400EASTWIND, CLINT      830912001000015M1011500000750000
390568900JONES, JANE          850201002000015I4022000001100000
432894000HARRIS, RICKY        711201102000025I1030000001650000
450182200KNAPP, KAREN         771010022100015S4019000000950000
456689000LONG, BEVERLY        790420051050000M2011000000580000
458990000WILLIAMS, DEDRA      820107061000005M4018000000950000
462912240AMOS, LOLA           850901011050005A4015000001000000
465152330DAVIS, TOMMY         690115002050000F3015000000750000
491912241WAYMACK, LES         791201031000000M4014200000340000
498239220DAVIS, ALAN          730531021050015M1010000000550000
499206600HOLDER, DEBBIE       771125031050015S2014000000732000
522136980LAMPE, GUS           790420051050000S2011000000580000
534899000WAYMACK, REBECCA     800228041050000I4017500000900000
543569000NELSON, MICKEY       760615052050015S2026500001430000
546341560BENTON, JIM BOB      760615052050015S2026500001430000
561154000IRVINE, LARRY        790606011000025I3008000000410000
567899990DERDEN, ROY          810420002050015M2013400000675000
569153340RODRIGUEZ, ALEX      860530011050015S3010000000540000
590304000ELLISON, JOHN        800228041050000I4017500000900000
634809220BIRD, BEVERLY        790807041100000F4020000001100000
676402040FULTON, EDWARD       820107061000015I4018000000950000
692185544FALCON, WANDA        830501001050015F4010000000500000
698769700LEE, SUNNY           671205042100025M1021000001080000
748665000MYERS, RALPH         750606031000005A3022000001180000
776189000GESSNER, MARK        780701042100015M3012000000620000
789345000VANSELL, RICKY       810420002050015F2013400000675000
840387290RODRIGUEZ, TOMMY     730531021050005A1010000000550000
847604600LANE, SCOTT          780301071050015S4018500000925000
899034400GERSWIN, TIA         771010022100005S4019000000950000
986190020ANDERSON, TIM        850201002000015I4022000001100000
990037890NELSON, WILL         790807041100000I4020000001100000
```

## Transaction File – TRANS

```
789345000D0015000
899034400I0001000
226794000I0005000
348904600D0010000
522136980I0100000
348904600I0050000
457001050D0050000
990037890I0500000
101010101I0001000
226794000I0005000
634809220K0100000
634809220D0005000
344894321A0010000
457995010S0010000
462912240D0000500
```

## Maintenance File – MAINT

```
     111111111ADRABBIT, PETER      880701011005011A2030000000000000
     111111111CK02
     191860400CP010
     222222222ADDOG, LOONEY        880701022000012I1005250000000000
     333333333ADMOUSE, MICHAEL     880708081015020I1400000000000000
     344894321CDA
     389900400DS
     444444444ADDUCK, DIEDRA       880708021050011A4023000000000000
     444444444CR2
     458990000AC3
     491912241DE
     499206600CS010
     555555555ADPAM, YOSEMITI      880708022010012I1090000000000000
     555555555ADPAM, YOSEMITI      880708022010012I1090000000000000
     569153340CK02
     590304000CP000
     634809220DE
     634809220DE
     666666666ADANGEL, TANSMANIAN  880701012011006I4013000001170000
     692185544CC1
     692185544CDM
     789345000CNDOG, MIGHTY
     999999999DE
```

## EMPLOYEE SYSTEMS—PROGRAMMING PROJECTS

### EMPLOYEE SYSTEM—JCL Assignment

**Problem Statement.** The consulting firm for which you work provides an automated billing process for the Circle Club (APPENDIX C). Your firm has recently acquired a new account, the Square Club. They would like you to provide the same service for them.

Since the Square Club uses the same calculations and the member information is in the same format, you realize you can use the Circle Club program with a few minor modifications.

Basically, you will have to modify the Circle Club program itself (which is found in Appendix C), create a new data file, and modify the JCL to run the program.

Specifically, the modifications you must make for your new client are detailed below:

1. Create the new data set using the names and billing amounts that follow. The record layout is in the working storage section of the Circle Club program and in the initial comment section.
2. Change the title of the output report from "CIRCLE CLUB" to "SQUARE CLUB". (Hint: remember your output line record description should have a total of 133 characters.)

3. JCL to Run Job on MVS System.

```
//DEMO    JOB  (N007,501D,S05,002,JB),'DEMO CODE'
//STEP1   EXEC NCBCLG,REGION.GO=512K,PARM.GO='SIZE=448K'
//COB.SYSIN   DD  DSN=USR.N007.JB.CIRPRG,DISP=SHR
//GO.INFILE   DD  DSN=USR.N007.JB.CIRCLE,DISP=SHR
//GO.OUTFILE  DD  SYSOUT=A,DCB=(BLKSIZE=133,RECFM=FA)
```

Where

CIRPRG is the name of the file containing your source code.

and

CIRCLE is the name of the data file for CIRCLE CLUB.

Save the modified program on your catalog. You may save it with your own choice of a name.

Use the data on the next page to create your new data file. Save your data file with the following specifications:

```
SAVE filename LRECL=72 (88)
```

where LRECL = 72 specifies the number of characters per record and 88 is the number of records per block.

Modify the JCL to reflect that the new program and data file are located on your account.

Square Club members and current account information (member number, name, street address, restaurant bill, bar bill, other charges, past due amount):

```
001    Bryan, Gene,         1010 Pease St.,      $15, $10, $0,  $0
010    Manti, Vadan,        20 First Ave.,       $35, $25, $0,  $15
022    Grayson, Tim,        123 Michael Ave.,    $25, $0,  $20, $45
028    Guy, Kenneth,        89 Avenue A,         $25, $10, $5,  $0
035    Haskel, Elaine,      969 Cobol Drive,     $50, $20, $25, $0
044    Hill, George,        65 Compiler St.,     $25, $15, $0,  $0
050    Hunter, Jennifer,    156 University,      $25, $10, $0,  $0
065    Lin, Jack,           57 Unnamed Street,   $25, $10, $0,  $0
072    Lomatex, Jeannine,   91 College Dr.,      $35, $20, $0,  $25
084    McMellan, William,   101 Eastern,         $25, $10, $0,  $0
090    Mellison, Lucy,      35 Maroon Ave.,      $45, $0,  $10, $0
125    Rother, Michael,     76 Asset Parkway,    $15, $10, $0,  $30
139    North, Michael,      487 Ginger Ave.,     $25, $15, $5,  $0
154    Stewart, Mandy,      301 Data Ave.,       $25, $10, $5,  $0
165    Vasquez, Pablo,      630 Spanish Eyes,    $20, $0,  $0,  $20
```

The record layout for your new file will be the same as the input record description found in the Circle Club program. For example your first entry into your new data file should look something like this:

```
001 Bryant, Gene       1010 Pease St.    01500 01000 00000 000000
```

Notice that we do not store decimals or dollars signs in our data file. We indicate where these items belong when we define the data in our program.

### EMPLOYEE SYSTEM—Input/Output Assignment

**Problem Statement.**    Congratulations on your progress in this course so far. Now it is time for you to write your first COBOL program. Your task is to generate the PERSONNEL SALARY REPORT for PORTERFIELD RANCHES using a data file called EMPLOYEE that has been prepared for you in the class account. The format of this file follows.

- Social Security number                    1–9
- Name (last, first, m.i.)                  10–29
- Date of employment                        30–35
- Number of dependents                      36–37
- Retirement program code                   38
- Parking fee                               39–41
- Savings program (percentage written       42–44
  in whole-number format)
- Department code                           45
- City code                                 46
- Salary (allows for two decimal places)    47–53
- Year-to-date earnings                     54–61
  (allows for two decimal places)

1. Personnel Listing Report

   The report you have to prepare should list every employee record.

   a. You should use a report heading of 'PERSONNEL SALARY REPORT FOR PORTERFIELD RANCHES'.
   b. You should use appropriate column headings for all the data fields; because of the amount of data column headings it may require more than one line.
   c. The report heading should be printed on the third line. The column headings should be triple-spaced from the heading and the first detail line.
   d. The detail line should be single-spaced.

2. REQUIREMENTS

   a. Follow programming and documentation standards.
   b. Turn in:

      - Cover sheet
      - Hierarchy chart
      - IPO chart
      - Detailed program flowchart
      - Source listing
      - Results

## EMPLOYEE SYSTEM—Math Assignment

**Problem Statement.**    The manager of PORTERFIELD RANCHES would like a PERSONNEL PAYROLL ANALYSIS. Two reports are needed: (1) a listing of all employees showing the total salary and total YTDE and (2) a summary report providing the average salary and average YTDE as well as the total number of employees.

1. Employee Listing Report

   The employee listing report is intended as a means of examining each employee's data. It also will provide a total salary figure and a total salary expense to date.

   a. The report heading should be printed on Line 5 and should read 'EMPLOYEE LISTING'.
   b. Column headings should be double-spaced from the heading and the first detail line.

    c. All data should be printed.

    d. The total salary and total YTDE should be presented as column totals and should be double-spaced from the last detail line.

2. Summary Report

This report is intended to provide further payroll information to include:

- the count of employees
- average salary
- average YTDE

    a. The report should be on a page by itself.

    b. An appropriate page heading should be used.

    c. The three required items should be presented as shown below and should be double-spaced and centered on the page.

```
THE NUMBER OF EMPLOYEES IS        X
THE AVERAGE SALARY IS             $
THE AVERAGE YTDE IS               $
```

3. The data file is EMPLOYEE.
4. REQUIREMENTS

    a. Follow programming and documentation standards.

    b. Turn in:

- Cover sheet
- Hierarchy chart
- IPO chart
- Detailed program flowchart
- Source listing
- Results

## EMPLOYEE SYSTEM—Logic Assignment

**Problem Statement.**     Even though your manager liked the Personnel Salary Report you prepared, the Personnel Department is now asking for a more detailed report. Your next task is to prepare: (1) a DETAILED PAYROLL REPORT for the Personnel Department of PORTERFIELD RANCHES, (2) a detailed summary report and (3) a department and city summary report. Once again you will be using the company employee file, EMPLOYEE. The requirements are given below:

1. Detailed Payroll Report

The information to be included in the report is the following:

    a. Each of the following items should be included on the detailed report.
- Employee name
- Employee salary
- Retirement withholding amount

This amount is equal to 12% of the salary if the retirement program code is 1, and equal to 8% of the salary if the code 2.

- Federal Income Tax amount (FIT)

Since the retirement withheld amount is tax-sheltered, it should be subtracted from the salary before calculating the FIT. Also, an adjustment for each dependent should be subtracted from the salary before applying the 15% tax rate. The necessary calculation is:

$$FIT = (Salary - (retirement\ amount$$
$$+ (\#\ of\ dependents\ *\ 1000)/12))$$
$$*\ .15$$

- Parking fee
- Amount withheld for savings premium

To calculate this amount simply apply the percentage provided in the input employee file to the salary.

- Deduction for social security (OASI)

There are three cases to consider when calculating OASI:

If YTDE > $47,500, there is no deduction.
IF YTDE < $47,500 and YTDE + Salary > $47,500,
the deduction is 5.75% of the amount that makes
YTDE = $47,500. [5.75% of (47,500 – YTDE)]

If YTDE < $47,500 and YTDE + Salary ≤ $47,500, the
deduction is 5.75% of the salary.

- Net Pay

To arrive at the net pay, subtract the total amount of the deductions from the salary.

- New YTDE

This amount is simply the previous YTDE + salary.

b. The report heading should be on line 3 and be 'PAYROLL REPORT'.
c. The column headings should be double-spaced from the heading and first detail line.

2. Payroll Summary Report

The Personnel Department would also like to have a summary report showing the total amounts for the salary, net pay, new YTDE, and each of the deduction amounts displayed as column totals. The report should list every employee's record.

a. The summary totals should be printed as column totals.
b. The column totals should be double-spaced from the last detail line.

3. Department and City Summary Report

This report is intended to provide management with payroll information pertaining to Departments and Cities. The report should provide the total salary for each city and for each department. It should also provide the total number of employees by city and by department.

a. The report should be on a page by itself with an appropriate heading.

b. The information should be presented in the following format:

|  | Number of Employees | Total Salary |
|---|---|---|
| London | X | $ |
| Belfast | X | $ |
| Sydney | X | $ |
| Dallas | X | $ |

Use the same format for Department Information.

4. The DATA FILE for this assignment is EMPLOYEE.

5. REQUIREMENTS

a. Follow programming and documentation standards.

b. Turn in:

- Cover sheet
- Hierarchy chart
- IPO chart
- Detailed program flowchart
- Source listing
- Results

### EMPLOYEE SYSTEM—Control Break Assignment

**Problem Statement.**    Write a COBOL Program to produce: (1) an Employee Location Report and (2) a Department-City Salary Summary Report. Output requirements are explained below. All coding and documentation standards apply.

1. Employee Location Report

Write a listing of all employees group-indicated by city. The city name should be used as a title.

a. A page heading of "Employee Location Report" should be used.

b. The name of the city should be triple-spaced from the page heading.

c. The report should include: Social Security Number, Employee Name, Number of Dependents and Department Name.

d. Detail lines should be double-spaced.

2. Department-City Salary Summary Report

Write a listing of all employees group-indicated by city and department within city. Group-indicate both as columns.

a. A page heading of "Salary Summary Report" should be used.

b. The report should include: Social Security Number, Name, Salary and Year-to-Date Earnings.

c. For each Department the total salary and year-to-date earnings should be reported as column totals.

d. For each City the total salary and year-to-date earnings should be reported as column totals.

e. A Grand Total of both should also be provided as column totals.

3. The DATA for this assignment is the EMPLOYEE-FILE, EMPLOYEE. It must first be ordered by your professor into a file sorted by department within city; SORTEMP.
4. The FILE and RECORD FORMATS are given in the Data Dictionary in this Project as:

```
EMPLOYEE-SALARY-FILE
EMPLOYEE-SALARY-RECORD-IN
CITY-TABLE
DEPARTMENT-TABLE
```

5. REQUIREMENTS

   a. Turn in:

   - Cover sheet
   - Hierarchy chart
   - IPO chart
   - Detailed program flowchart
   - Source listing
   - Results

## EMPLOYEE SYSTEM—Tables Assignment

**Problem Statement.** Since you have done so well in your previous assignments, your manager now wants you to prepare three analytical reports he has always wanted. The requirements are given below. You should use the coding standards. The assignment also uses a Copy Library.

1. City Report

   The City Report is a report that lists the total number of employees per city as follows:

   |         | NUMBER OF EMPLOYEES |
   |---------|---------------------|
   | LONDON  | 99999               |
   | BELFAST | 99999               |
   | SYDNEY  | 99999               |
   | DALLAS  | 99999               |

2. Department Report

   The Department Report is a report that lists the total salary per period, the average salary per period, and the average year-to-date earnings per period for each department as follows:

   | ACCOUNTING | INFO. SERVICES | FINANCE    | SALES      | MARKETING  |
   |------------|----------------|------------|------------|------------|
   | $9,999.99  | $9,999.99      | $9,999.99  | $9,999.99  | $9,999.99  |
   | $9,999.99  | $9,999.99      | $9,999.99  | $9,999.99  | $9,999.99  |
   | $9,999.99  | $9,999.99      | $9,999.99  | $9,999.99  | $9,999.99  |

3. YTDE Report

This report presents the YTDE per department within each city as follows:

```
                       LONDON    BELFAST   SYDNEY     DALLAS

ACCOUNTING            $9,999.99 $9,999.99 $9,999.99 $9,999.99
INFORMATION SYSTEMS   $9,999.99 $9,999.99 $9,999.99 $9,999.99
FINANCIAL SERVICES    $9,999.99 $9,999.99 $9,999.99 $9,999.99
SALES                 $9,999.99 $9,999.99 $9,999.99 $9,999.99
MARKETING             $9,999.99 $9,999.99 $9,999.99 $9,999.99
```

4. Notice that in every report, complete names instead of codes should be printed. The names that correspond to each code are the following:

| City Code | City Name |
| --- | --- |
| 1 | London |
| 2 | Belfast |
| 3 | Sydney |
| 4 | Dallas |

| Department Code | Information Systems |
| --- | --- |
| A | Accounting |
| I | Information Systems |
| F | Financial Services |
| M | Marketing |
| S | Sales |

5. The company has decided to standardize page banners for all reports printed. For this purpose, a library has been established so that everyone has access to copy the description of the page banners into their programs. The name of the library is COPYLBRY, and its members are PAGEBAN1, PAGEBAN2, and PAGEBAN3. A reference description of these members is attached.

6. To use members of a copy library, you must include the library in your JCL. Add the COB.SYSLIB statement to your JCL as illustrated below:

```
//DEMO      JOB  (C116,501D,S05,002,XX),'DEMO CODE'
//STEP1    EXEC  NCBCLG,REGION.GO=512K,PARM.GO='SIZE=448K'
//COB.SYSLIB  DD   DSN=USR.C112.XX.COPYLBRY,DISP=SHR
//COB.SYSIN   DD   DSN=USR.C112.XX.CIRPRG,DISP=SHR
//GO.INFILE   DD   DSN=USR.C112.XX.CIRCLE,DISP=SHR
//GO.OUTFILE  DD   SYSOUT=A,DCB=(BLKSIZE=133,RECFM=FA)
```

Using a library member is as simple as inserting one statement at the point in your program where you want the member to appear:

COPY membername

membername should be the name of the member you wish to copy at that point. In this case:

COPY PAGEBAN1

would appear in your WORKING STORAGE SECTION where you are describing your heading lines.

| Library name: | COPYLBRY |
|---|---|
| Location: | Class Account |
| Members: | PAGEBAN1 |
| | PAGEBAN2 |
| | PAGEBAN3 |

7. You may use some discretion in designing the spacing of the output reports as long as it follows the structure and layout indicated above. The fields indicated above are not necessarily large enough to accommodate the values they will contain: Adjust your picture clauses as necessary. You should include an appropriate title for each report.

8. REQUIREMENTS

    a. You must use the data file provided, EMPLOYEE.

    b. You must use the page banners from the copy library in Project B.

    c. Follow programming and documentation standards.

    d. Turn in:

- Cover sheet
- Hierarchy chart
- IPO chart
- Detailed program flowchart
- Complete source listing
- Results

9. ***BONUS

After you have completed the above requirements you may want to create a fourth report that lists the total number of employees per retirement program for each department within each city as follows:

| | LONDON | | | | | BELFAST | | | | | SYDNEY | | | | | DALLAS | | | | |
|---|---|---|---|---|---|---|---|---|---|---|---|---|---|---|---|---|---|---|---|---|
| | AC | IS | FI | SL | MK | AC | IS | FI | SL | MK | AC | IS | FI | SL | MK | AC | IS | FI | SL | MK |
| PLAN 1 | 99 | 99 | 99 | 99 | 99 | 99 | 99 | 99 | 99 | 99 | 99 | 99 | 99 | 99 | 99 | 99 | 99 | 99 | 99 | 99 |
| PLAN 2 | 99 | 99 | 99 | 99 | 99 | 99 | 99 | 99 | 99 | 99 | 99 | 99 | 99 | 99 | 99 | 99 | 99 | 99 | 99 | 99 |

******* (You have more space, so do not abbreviate as much as shown.)

## EMPLOYEE SYSTEM—Sorting Assignment

**Problem Statement.** The personnel manager with PORTERFIELD RANCHES has again asked for more information. She would like three reports: (1) a report listing all employees in Social Security number order, (2) a listing of all Dallas employees alphabetically by name for each department and (3) an alphabetical listing of all employees by department within each city.

1. Employee Listing

   This report is a listing of all employees ordered by Social Security number. It includes name, social security number, city name and department name.

   a. Use the Page Banner provided in the Copy Library described in the Data Dictionary in this Project.
   b. Use appropriate column headings. They should be double-spaced from the banner and the first detail line.
   c. The detail lines should be double-spaced with no more than 20 detail lines per page.

2. Dallas Employees Report

   This report list all Dallas Employees alphabetically for each department. All employee data should be listed.

   a. Use the Page Banner discussed in 1a. above.
   b. Is the same as 1b. above.
   c. The detail line should be double-spaced and group-indicated by department.
   d. All headings and group-indicators should be printed on a new page.

3. Department and City Report

   This report is an alphabetical listing of all employees for each department within each city. However the city names should be used for the sort.

   a. Use Page Banners as in 1a. above.
   b. Use the city name and department name as columns for group-indication.
   c. Single-space within department and double-space between cities.
   d. For each department provide a total salary figure.
   e. For each city provide a total salary.
   f. Also provide a total salary for all employees.

4. The DATA FILE is EMPLOYEE.
5. You will need the following COPYLBRY elements.

   | | | |
   |---|---|---|
   | PAGEBAN1 | FDEMPL | WSEMPREC |
   | PAGEBAN2 | CITYTBL | DEPTTBL |
   | PAGEBAN3 | | |

6. REQUIREMENTS

   a. Turn in:

   - Cover sheet
   - Hierarchy chart
   - IPO chart
   - Detailed program flowchart
   - Complete source listing
   - Results

### EMPLOYEE SYSTEM—Sorting and Control Break Assignment

**Problem Statement.**    It is time to use your latest skills in COBOL and produce a file and several new reports: the new SORTED EMPLOYEE FILE, an EMPLOYEE LISTING REPORT, a RETIREMENT PROGRAM REPORT, and an EMPLOYEE LOCATION REPORT.

1. Sorted Employee File

   Create a new file – the Sorted Employee File – in which the records are ordered by social security number, and store it in your account. Then, use this file to produce the EMPLOYEE LISTING REPORT, a listing of all the employees at PORTERFIELD RANCHES in descending social security number order. The fields to be included in this report are the SOCIAL SECURITY NUMBER, NAME, DEPARTMENT and CITY.

2. Retirement Program Report

   In the Retirement Program Report, the manager wants to group the employees by the retirement program they have chosen.

   a. A left justified subtitle will specify which group follows: 12 PERCENT GROUP for retirement program code equal to 1, or 8 PERCENT GROUP for retirement program code equal to 2. Column headings should include NAME, SOCIAL SECURITY NUMBER, NUMBER OF DEPENDENTS, SAVINGS PROGRAM, and SALARY.

   b. If you need a second page, the page banners, the subtitle and the column headings should be printed again.

3. Employee Location Report

   For the Employee Location Report, you are to print employees grouped by department within city.

   a. The cities and departments should be listed in the following order:

      | Cities | Departments |
      | --- | --- |
      | London | Information Services |
      | Belfast | Financial Services |
      | Sydney | Accounting |
      | Dallas | Marketing |
      | | Sales |

   b. Each city group should be printed on a new page with the city printed as a subtitle centered on the page. The DEPARTMENT should be the leftmost field of the detail line and should be group-indicated (should only be printed with the first employee in that department). Other fields to be included are NAME, SOCIAL SECURITY NUMBER, SALARY, and YTDE.

   c. For every city, give a total of the salaries and YTDEs.

   d. If you need a second page, the page banners, the subtitle (city), the column headings, and the group-indicator (department) should be printed again.

4. General Guidelines

   a. Notice that in every report, complete names instead of codes should be printed.

   b. Standardized page banners will again be used. The library, COPYLBRY contains the page banners as well as two new members: FDEMPL (the FD for the input file) and WSEMPREC (the detailed record description).

   c. You may use some discretion in designing the spacing of the output reports as long as it follows the structure and layout previously described. You should include an appropriate title for each report. Don't print more than 50 lines per page.

5. You will need the following COPYLBRY elements:

   | | | |
   |---|---|---|
   | PAGEBAN1 | FDEMPL | WSEMPREC |
   | PAGEBAN2 | CITYTBL | DEPTTBL |
   | PAGEBAN3 | | |

6. REQUIREMENTS

   a. You must use the data file provided, EMPLOYEE.

   b. You must use the page banners, FD, and detailed record description for the input record from the copy library through the use of the COPY statement.

   c. Follow programming and documentation standards.

   d. Turn in:

   - Cover sheet
   - Hierarchy chart
   - IPO chart
   - Detailed program flowchart
   - Complete source listing
   - Results

### EMPLOYEE SYSTEM—Sequential File Update Assignment

**Problem Statement.**     Write a COBOL program to be used for doing file updates to the Employee Master File. A Sequential File of transactions will be provided for the update. The update will be done to the employee's salary. (To illustrate update techniques we will assume that having multiple transactions per employee is valid.)

Three reports should be provided: (1) the update activity report, (2) a transaction error report and (3) an updated master file listing report. All coding standards are to be used. Reports requirements are given below:

1. Update Activity Report

The Update Activity Report is a listing of all valid updates processed against the employee master file. The report format is as follows:

   a. Use the Page Banners provided in the Copy Library.

   b. Separate the column Headings from the banner by two blank lines. Items to be included in the column headings are: Social Security Number, Name, Type of Update (Increase or Decrease Salary), Previous Salary and New Salary in the following format.

```
Social Security Number    Name     Type of Update      Salary
     111111111            Joe        Increase      From: $1000.00
                                                   To:   $1200.00
```

   c. Single-space within transactions and double-space between transactions.

   d. Valid Transaction Codes are:

> I – Increase Salary
> D – Decrease Salary

2. Transaction Error Report

The Error Report is a listing of all transactions that result in errors. The format is as follows:

   a. Use the Page Banners provided in the Copy Library.

   b. Separate the column headings from the banner with two blank lines. Items to be included in the column headings are:

> Transaction Record and Error Message

   c. Detail Lines are double-spaced and include the entire invalid transaction record and an error message. The transaction should be written as it was read. If a transaction has more than one error, only the subsequent error messages should be written. The transaction record should only be written once.

   d. Transaction errors that can occur are:

- Employee not on File (for this error, no others need be checked for).
- Invalid Transaction Code.
- Transaction salary increase/decrease is invalid.

3. Updated Employee Master File

An Updated Employee Master File should be created in conjunction with the update process. This file should contain all the records on the original Master File.

After the update is complete, print the contents of the file. The format is as follows:

   a. Page Banner as in 1a.

   b. The column Heading should be two rows of column numbers from 1 to 61 over the corresponding data column.

   c. Double-space the detail lines.

4. In each of the reports, there should be 20 detail records per full page.

5. The DATA FILES are:

> MASTER – EMPLOYEE
> TRANSACTION – TRANS

6. You will need the following COPYLBRY Elements:

```
PAGEBAN1
PAGEBAN2
PAGEBAN3
FDEMPL
WSEMPREC
FDTRANS
TRANSREC
```

7. REQUIREMENTS

 a. Turn in:

 - Cover sheet
 - Hierarchy chart
 - IPO chart
 - Detailed program flowchart
 - Source listing
 - Results

### EMPLOYEE SYSTEM—VSAM Files Assignment

**Problem Statement.** As you know, we use sequential update techniques to update a file because a high percentage of the records are updated each time the program is executed (this is known as a high activity ratio). However, when we accomplish maintenance of a file, we expect a relatively low percentage of the records to be affected during program execution. In this assignment, you are responsible for accomplishing the master file maintenance using indexed accessing techniques.

You are responsible for:

(1) Building a VSAM-organized Employee File on your account, using the sequentially organized master file, EMPLOYEE located in the class account. You may use the IDCAMS shown in the Chapter on Indexed File Processing or your professor will provide you with the appropriate information.

(2) Accomplishing the maintenance processing producing both an EMPLOYEE MASTER FILE MAINTENANCE LOG and an EMPLOYEE MASTER FILE MAINTENANCE ERROR REPORT, as well as a former employees FILE.

(3) Producing a sequential dump of the Employee Master and Former Employees FILES after the maintenance process has been completed. As always, COBOL programming and documentation standards are applicable.

1. The Employee Master File Maintenance Error Report

 This report is to be produced during the maintenance process. The format of the report is as follows:

 a. The page banner will use the standard format.
 b. Column headings will be underlined. Specific items included in the headings are the DATA RECORD and the ERROR DESCRIPTION with the data record heading including column numbers: 12345678901234.....
 c. Detail lines will be double-spaced, and will consist of the transaction record and the error description.

    d. Transaction errors that can occur include:

      1) Attempt to add a record that already exists
      2) Attempt to delete a record that doesn't exist
      3) Attempt to change a record that doesn't exist
      4) Invalid transaction code

2. The Employee Master File Maintenance Log

The log is also produced during the maintenance process. Its format is as follows:

    a. Page banners are standard.
    b. Specific items included in the headings are SOCIAL SECURITY NUMBER, TYPE OF MAINTENANCE, and MAINTENANCE DATA.
    c. A detail entry will consist of one or two lines.

When adding an employee, a single line consisting of the social security number, type of transaction, and the new employee's data will be printed.

For a deletion, a single line consisting of the social security number, type of transaction and the data being deleted will be printed.

Whenever a change is made, two detail lines will be generated:

    ■ The first line will consist of the social security number, type of transaction, "FROM:" and the original data in the field that is going to be changed.

    ■ The second line in a change transaction will include "TO: " and the new data.

    d. Double-space between detail entries.

3. In each of the above reports, the standard page length of no more than 50 lines and no less than 47 lines between the first page banner line and the last detail line will be expected.

4. The Employee Master FILE and Former Employee FILE dumps printed upon completion of the maintenance process will be produced by a SEPARATE program. This second program will sequentially access the VSAM-organized Employee Master file and the sequential Former Employee file produced during the update.

5. Your input data files are:

    a. The VSAM-organized file that you create in your account.
    b. The maintenance file, MAINT.

6. You will need the following COPYLBRY elements:

```
PAGEBAN1      FDEMPVSM      WSMAINTR
PAGEBAN2      FDMAINT       WSEMPREC
PAGEBAN3
```

## 7. REQUIREMENTS

a. Turn in:

- Cover sheet
- Hierarchy chart
- IPO chart
- Detailed program flowchart
- Source listing
- Results

A. THE DEAN FILE
B. THE PERSONNEL FILE
C. THE INVENTORY FILE

# DATA FILES

# DATA FILES

## DATA FILE A

### FORMAT ONE

```
File Name:          DEAN FILE
Data Set Name:      DEANFILE (GPRDEAN)
Source:             Your Professor's Account
Organization:       Sequential
Blocking Factor:    100


Item    Characters    Type    Description

1        1-30        30 AN    NAME

2        31-39        9 AN    ID

3         40          1 N     MAJOR CODE

4         41          1 N     CLASSIFICATION CODE

5         42          1 N     SEX CODE

6        43-47        5 N     GPR(GRADE  POINT  RATIO)
                                 FOUR DECIMAL PLACES
```

## DEAN FILE
## DATA SET

```
THOMAS WILKINSON          12345678944137619
DON VILLANOSKI            98765432111127500
MICHAEL FOWLER            55555555522138966
TIA FOWLER                88888888833234943
CLINT SMITH               33333333323119839
HOWARD PORTER             45454545411123158
APRIL JONES               77777777723228025
APRIL JACKS               78787877844225649
BRYAN MANN                23232323231126667
ZEKE MORGAN               43435656922128947
BILL ADAM                 10230222044128092
JILL MATSON               01010120621228947
TINA MARIO                00000022243223380
CLYDE FELD JR.            12983476542129057
GEORGE MARINAKIES         10001005551127083
JAMES PAPPAS              34253789153123253
STEVE PARKS               90876510111238000
LYNDA MATHER              20304050633227538
KEVIN MCKENN              44445555523134933
IRENE SMITH               00112233441220000
EMILY LYLE                99988877711222667
PEG PORTERHOUSE           12332112334229703
DAN ROBESON               65676567943122400
DANA MILLS                90807060044227500
GEORGE RYAN               56473100912124000
BILLY BOB BARRETT         11100022214122500
MARY JO MARTINEZ          10293847524223077
POLLY ANN FLOWERS         50111223444225773
MATHEW ALTMEN             98098098053132258
DIANE LAWERNCE            26371881852225714
SARA WALKER               82834756153235375
MARIA SANTIAGO            77734577752224444
ANTONIO MARTINEZ          77333066653130000
ROBERTO SMITH             31123009944129000
ANDY BUENZA               00000111112127429
MARIA SANCHEZ             50115500343232000
STACY PHARR               44434434424235263
MICHAEL RYAN              71727374721132727
MARY LITTLE               39495869024231579
ANNIE MARINOS             01020304021222727
C. H. FLOWER              40404040424126887
ROY JOICE                 10245055514135045
DAVID LETTER              97867564331120000
JANE CATES                13243546731227600
KEN MARTINEZ              00290399234127704
GEORGE COMONOS            51697242041132400
SESSIE PARSONS            80818880842225106
PEGGY MARTTA              22228888554220635
THOMAS THOMPSON           84483993151122857
WAYNE HEDDER              24680864254139694
```

## FORMAT TWO

```
File Name:           DEAN FILE
Data Set Name:       DEANFILE (HOURDEAN)
Source:              Your Professor's Account
Organization:        Sequential
Blocking Factor:     100
```

| Item | Characters | Type | Description |
|------|-----------|------|-------------|
| 1 | 1-30 | 30 AN | NAME |
| 2 | 31-39 | 9 AN | ID |
| 3 | 40 | 1 N | MAJOR CODE |
| 4 | 41 | 1 N | CLASSIFICATION CODE |
| 5 | 42 | 1 N | SEX CODE |
| 6 | 43-45 | 3 N | TOTAL HOURS TAKEN |
| 7 | 46-48 | 3 N | TOTAL GRADE POINTS |

```
NOTE: THIS FORMAT CONTAINS THE TOTAL HOURS TAKEN
      AND TOTAL GRADE POINTS NEEDED TO CALCULATE GPR.
```

## DEAN FILE
## DATA SET

```
THOMAS WILKINSON          123456789441105395
DON VILLANOSKI            987654321111012033
MICHAEL FOWLER            555555555221058226
TIA FOWLER                888888888332087304
CLINT SMITH               333333333231062123
HOWARD PORTER             454545454111019044
APRIL JONES               777777777232081227
APRIL JACKS               787878778442131336
BRYAN MANN                232323232311003008
ZEKE MORGAN               434356569221038110
BILL ADAM                 102302220441131368
JILL MATSON               010101206212019055
TINA MARIO                000000022432071166
CLYDE FELD JR.            129834765421053154
GEORGE MARINAKIES         100010055511024065
JAMES PAPPAS              342537891531083193
STEVE PARKS               908765101112015057
LYNDA MATHER              203040506332065179
KEVIN MCKENN              444455555231075262
IRENE SMITH               001122334412024048
EMILY LYLE                999888777112015034
PEG PORTERHOUSE           123321123342101300
DAN ROBESON               656765679431075168
DANA MILLS                908070600442100275
GEORGE RYAN               564731009121050120
BILLY BOB BARRETT         111000222141120270
MARY JO MARTINEZ          102938475242130300
POLLY ANN FLOWERS         501112234442097250
```

*(continued)*

```
MATHEW ALTMEN              980980980531062200
DIANE LAWERNCE             263718818522035090
SARA WALKER               828347561532080283
MARIA SANTIAGO            777345777522045110
ANTONIO MARTINEZ          773330666531080240
ROBERTO SMITH             311230099441100290
ANDY BUENZA              000001111121035096
MARIA SANCHEZ            501155003432075240
STACY PHARR             444344344242095335
MICHAEL RYAN            717273747211022072
MARY LITTLE            394958690242095300
ANNIE MARINOS        010203040212011025
C. H. FLOWER         404040404241106285
ROY JOICE            102450555141111389
DAVID LETTER         978675643311020040
JANE CATES          132435467312025069
KEN MARTINEZ        002903992341135374
GEORGE COMONOS      516972420411025081
SESSIE PARSONS      808188808422047118
PEGGY MARTTA        222288885542126260
THOMAS THOMPSON     844839931511014032
WAYNE HEDDER        246808642541098389
```

## FORMAT THREE

```
File Name:          DEAN FILE
Data Set Name:      DEANFILE (ALPHDEAN)
Source:             Your Professor's Account
Organization:       Sequential
Blocking Factor:    100
```

| Item | Characters | Type | Description |
|------|-----------|------|-------------|
| 1 | 1-30 | 30 AN | NAME |
| 2 | 31-39 | 9 AN | ID |
| 3 | 40 | 1 AN | MAJOR CODE |
| 4 | 41 | 1 N | CLASSIFICATION CODE |
| 5 | 42 | 1 N | SEX CODE |
| 6 | 43-47 | 5 N | GPR(GRADE POINT RATIO) FOUR DECIMAL PLACES |

```
NOTE: THIS FORMAT CONTAINS A NONNUMERIC MAJOR CODE
      TO DEMONSTRATE THE USE OF THE SEARCH VERB.
```

## DEAN FILE
## DATA SET

```
THOMAS WILKINSON          123456789G41105395
DON VILLANOSKI            987654321A11012033
MICHAEL FOWLER            555555555I21058226
TIA FOWLER               888888888F32087304
CLINT SMITH              333333333I31062123
HOWARD PORTER            454545454A11019044
APRIL JONES              777777777I32081227
APRIL JACKS              787878778G42131336
BRYAN MANN               232323232F11003008
ZEKE MORGAN              434356569I21038110
BILL ADAM                102302220G41131368
JILL MATSON              010101206I12019055
TINA MARIO               000000222G32071166
CLYDE FELD JR.           129834765G21053154
GEORGE MARINAKIES        100010055K11024065
JAMES PAPPAS             342537891K31083193
STEVE PARKS              908765101A12015057
LYNDA MATHER             203040506F32065179
KEVIN MCKENN             444455555I31075262
IRENE SMITH              001122334G12024048
EMILY LYLE               999888777A12015034
PEG PORTERHOUSE          123321123F42101300
DAN ROBESON              656765679G31075168
DANA MILLS               908070600G42100275
GEORGE RYAN              564731009A21050120
BILLY BOB BARRETT        111000222A41120270
MARY JO MARTINEZ         102938475I42130300
POLLY ANN FLOWERS        501112234G42097250
MATHEW ALTMEN            980980980K31062200
DIANE LAWERNCE           263718818K22035090
SARA WALKER              828347561K32080283
MARIA SANTIAGO           777345777K22045110
ANTONIO MARTINEZ         773330666K31080240
ROBERTO SMITH            311230099G41100290
ANDY BUENZA              000001111A21035096
MARIA SANCHEZ            501155003G32075240
STACY PHARR              444344344I42095335
MICHAEL RYAN             717273747I11022072
MARY LITTLE              394958690I42095300
ANNIE MARINOS            010203040I12011025
C. H. FLOWER             404040404I41106285
ROY JOICE                102450555A41111389
DAVID LETTER             978675643F11020040
JANE CATES               132435467F12025069
KEN MARTINEZ             002903992F41135374
GEORGE COMONOS           516972420G11025081
SESSIE PARSONS           808188808G22047118
PEGGY MARTTA             222288885K42126260
THOMAS THOMPSON          844839931K11014032
WAYNE HEDDER             246808642K41098389
```

## DATA FILE B

```
File Name:        PERSONNEL FILE
Data Set Name:    PERSON
Location:         Professor's Account
Organization:     Sequential
Blocking Factor:  100
```

| Item | Characters | Type | Description |
|------|-----------|------|-------------|
| 1 | 1-30 | 30 AN | NAME |
| 2 | 31-39 | 9 AN | SOCIAL SECURITY NUMBER |
| 3 | 40 | 1 N | STORE NUMBER (1-3) |
| 4 | 41 | 1 N | DEPARTMENT NUMBER (1-4) |
| 5 | 42-50 | 9 N | YEAR TO DATE EARNINGS (YTDE) TWO DECIMAL PLACES |

## PERSONNEL FILE
## DATA SET

```
ROY DEJOIE              56473233711000098750
RICHARD LONG            22222222211001500000
MARY JONES              91827364512000000900
IRENE HIGGS             00011001112000350000
HOWARD PORTER           32902004512000250000
JILL BOTTOMS            67809809813000007550
DONNA FRASER            52535455513000300000
JOHN PEARSON            34213433314080000000
DEAN DECENSA            10293847614006950050
JOANN ALTMEN            30405060721150000000
KEVIN MCKENSIE          34512332222000098750
LICA HOEKSTRA           38912098723000098750
TOM DEATS               81112290024000700000
MICHAEL FOWLER          58493456624900000000
TIA FOWLER              65432123424030000000
JOE SMITH               11111111131000100000
ROD ALTMEN              54682098831300065000
POLLY ANN FOWLER        98120933431000000500
ANN THOMAS              54678233431000000500
NANCY PORTS             98767898732000007550
BILL OWENS              77977977933000097500
TOMMY JONES             09809878833000590050
JAMES MARTIN            09098080034000055000
CLYDE PORTERFIELD       12309912334007500075
MICHAEL FOWLER          23450987434500000000
```

## DATA FILE C

```
File Name:          INVENTORY FILE
Data Set Name:      Used in Examples in Text
Source:             Your Professor
Organization:       Used Sequentially and Randomly in
Examples
Blocking Factor:    100  (where appropriate)


Item      Characters       Type      Description

1            1-5            5 N       ITEM NUMBER

2            6-30           25 AN     ITEM DESCRIPTION

3            31-34          4 N       QUANTITY ON HAND (QOH)

4            35-42          8 N       COST PER UNIT

5            43-46          4 N       REORDER POINT (ROP)

6            47-48          2 N       SUPPLIER CODE (1-3)

7            49-50          2 N       BUYER CODE (1-4)
```

### INVENTORY FILE
### DATA SET

```
02222ANTI-GLARE SCREEN       0010000400000005 0102
03001TURTLENECK SWEATER      0025000080000015 0101
08234SPARK PLUGS 1 DOZ       0040000012000050 0103
11653LEATHER JACKET          0007000150000005 0104
12345BROWN LEATHER BELT      0020000015000015 0201
12355BLACK LEATHER BELT      0022000015000015 0201
21100PRINT SILK SCARVES      0013000018000010 0301
21133T-SHIRT DRESSES         0008000021000005 0302
21143SWEATER DRESSES         0012000032000010 0303
22165DESIGNER SWEATER        0008000050000005 0301
22298ST COTTON SHORTS        0020000019000015 0304
22324BLUE JEANS PLEATS       0030000030000020 0202
22346SOLID SWEAT SHIRTS      0023000022000015 0302
22700LG COTTON SHORTS        0019000014000010 0202
22835SWEAT PANTS             0030000010000020 0302
22988DESIGN SWEAT SHIRT      0022000045000020 0103
23334BLUE JEANS STRAIGHT LEG 0040000023000025 0203
23342DRESS BLOUSES BOWTIE    0013000050000010 0104
23444DESIGNER POLO SHIRTS    0032000050000025 0301
23453COTTON BOTTONDOWNS      0038000045000030 0202
23552DESIGNER COTTON BLOUSES 0024000055000020 0301
23664BUDGET POLO SHIRTS      0021000026000020 0201
24345ACID WASHED JEAN JR     0013000018000010 0204
24350ACID WASHED J SKIRT     0018000022000015 0204
24355ACID WASHED MINI-SKIRT  0010000024000008 0203
```

# APPENDICES

STANDARDS

# FLOWCHARTING

A flowchart is a semigraphical representation of the steps which comprise a process, depicting the logical relationships and sequence of steps involved. A good flowchart will make it possible to "see" graphically both the logical and illogical, efficient and inefficient, and desirable and undesirable features of the system.

Flowcharting techniques have general application. Flowcharts are useful both in the design and analysis of processes (either physical or abstract), such as accounting systems, inventory control systems, information systems, data processing systems, work flow systems, etc.

Our specific interest is in data processing applications, and particularly in the design and construction of workable and efficient computer programs. The task of preparing a problem for computer solution consists of at least three phases:

1. Clearly state the problem.
2. Formulate the solution as a sequence of logical steps (the program flowchart).
3. Translate the steps into a form usable on the computer (the computer program).

In the first phase, a general systems flowchart helps in outlining a clear and accurate statement of the problem. In phase two, the detailed flowchart is formulated. Once this is done, translation of the logic into a programming language from the flowchart is a much easier task and may be accomplished by a person not acquainted with the actual problem. After completion of the program, the flowchart is updated to show any revision in logic that took place during the coding and is attached to the program as illustrative material for documentation.

For a flowchart to serve as the basis for writing a computer program, it should obey two rules:

1. It must be complete, clear, and accurate, so that a working computer program may be prepared directly from it by someone who has no knowledge of the problem.
2. It must be machine and language independent.

The descriptions and programming flowcharting symbols on the following page conform to the IBM flowcharting template available in most bookstores.

In a flowchart, the exact operation to be performed is written within the appropriate symbol. The symbols are then connected by arrows showing lines of logical flow, arranged such that the flow is generally down the page. Standardly, input/output, preparation, and processing symbols will have exactly one entry arrow and one exit arrow; decision symbols will have one entry arrow and more than one exit arrow; the terminal and connector symbols will have only one arrow, either entry or exit as appropriate.

## FLOWCHART SYMBOLS

 termination; used to show the beginning and ending of a module

 input/output block; used to show the reading or writing of a record of data

 process block; used to show a process, one equation per block

 decision block; used to show a decision point and the alternates available

 predefined process; names a routine that is a module itself that is defined external to the current module

 program; used in system flowcharting to identify a program

 on-page connector; used to show continuation of logic flow on the same page

 off-page connector; used to show continuation of logic on another page

 annotation; descriptive clarification or comments with dotted lines extending to associated symbol

# RESERVED WORDS

ACCEPT
ACCESS
ADD
ADVANCING
AFTER
ALL
ALPHABET *
ALPHABETIC
ALPHABETIC-LOWER *
ALPHABETIC-UPPER *
ALPHANUMERIC *
ALPHANUMERIC-EDITED *
ALSO
ALTER
ALTERNATE
AND
ANY
ARE
AREA
AREAS
ASCENDING
ASSIGN
AT
AUTHOR

BEFORE
BINARY *
BLANK
BLOCK
BOTTOM
BY

CALL
CANCEL

CD
CF
CH
CHARACTER
CHARACTERS
CLASS *
CLOSE
COBOL
CODE
COLLATING
COLUMN
COMMA
COMMON *
COMMUNICATION
COMP
COMPUTATIONAL
COMPUTE
CONFIGURATION
CONTAINS
CONTENT *
CONTINUE *
CONTROL
CONTROLS
CONVERTING *
COPY
CORR
CORRESPONDING
COUNT
CURRENCY

DATA
DATE
DATE-COMPILED
DATE-WRITTEN

DAY
DAY-OF-WEEK *
DEBUG-CONTENT
DEBUG-ITEM
DEBUG-LINE
DEBUG-NAME
DEBUG-SUB-1
DEBUG-SUB-2
DEBUG-SUB-3
DEBUGGING
DECIMAL-POINT
DECLARATIVES
DELETE
DELIMITED
DELIMITER
DEPENDING
DESCENDING
DESTINATION
DETAIL
DISABLE
DISPLAY
DIVIDE
DIVISION
DOWN
DUPLICATES
DYNAMIC

ELSE
ENABLE
END
END-ADD *
END-CALL *
END-COMPUTE *
END-DELETE *

END-DIVIDE *
END-EVALUATE *
END-IF *
END-MULTIPLY *
END-OF-PAGE
END-PERFORM *
END-READ *
END-RECEIVE *
END-RETURN *
END-REWRITE *
END-SEARCH *
END-START *
END-STRING *
END-SUBTRACT *
END-UNSTRING *
END-WRITE *
ENTER
ENVIRONMENT
EOP
EQUAL
ERROR
ESI
EVALUATE *
EVERY
EXCEPTION
EXIT
EXTEND
EXTERNAL *

FALSE *
FD
FILE
FILE-CONTROL
FILLER
FINAL
FIRST
FOOTING
FOR
FROM

GENERATE
GIVING
GLOBAL *
GO
GREATER
GROUP

HEADING
HIGH-VALUE
HIGH-VALUES

I-O
I-O-CONTROL

IDENTIFICATION
IF
IN
INDEX
INDEXED
INDICATE
INITIAL
INITIALIZE *
INITIATE
INPUT
INPUT-OUTPUT
INSPECT
INSTALLATION
INTO
INVALID
IS

JUST
JUSTIFIED

KEY

LABEL
LAST
LEADING
LEFT
LENGTH
LESS
LIMIT
LIMITS
LINAGE
LINAGE-COUNTER
LINE
LINE-COUNTER
LINES
LINKAGE
LOCK
LOW-VALUE
LOW-VALUES

MEMORY
MERGE
MESSAGE
MODE
MODULES
MOVE
MULTIPLE
MULTIPLY

NEGATIVE
NEXT
NO
NOT

NUMBER
NUMERIC
NUMERIC-EDITED *

OBJECT-COMPUTER
OCCURS
OF
OFF
OMITTED
ON
OPEN
OPTIONAL
OR
ORDER *
ORGANIZATION
OTHER *
OUTPUT
OVERFLOW

PACKED-DECIMAL *
PADDING *
PAGE
PAGE-COUNTER
PERFORM
PIC
PICTURE
PLUS
POINTER
POSITION
POSITIVE
PRINTING
PROCEDURE
PROCEDURES
PROCEED
PROGRAM
PROGRAM-ID
PURGE *

QUEUE
QUOTE
QUOTES

RANDOM
RD
READ
RECEIVE
RECORD
RECORDS
REDEFINES
REEL
REFERENCE *
REFERENCES
RELATIVE

| | | |
|---|---|---|
| RELEASE | SORT | TRUE * |
| REMAINDER | SORT-MERGE | TYPE |
| REMOVAL | SOURCE | |
| RENAMES | SOURCE-COMPUTER | UNIT |
| REPLACE * | SPACE | UNSTRING |
| REPLACING | SPACES | UNTIL |
| REPORT | SPECIAL-NAMES | UP |
| REPORTING | STANDARD | UPON |
| REPORTS | START | USAGE |
| RERUN | STATUS | USE |
| RESERVE | STOP | USING |
| RESET | STRING | |
| RETURN | SUBTRACT | VALUE |
| REWIND | SUM | VALUES |
| REWRITE | SUPPRESS | VARYING |
| RIGHT | SYMBOLIC | |
| ROUNDED | SYNC | WHEN |
| RUN | SYNCHRONIZED | WITH |
| | | WORDS |
| SAME | TABLE | WORKING-STORAGE |
| SD | TALLYING | WRITE |
| SEARCH | TAPE | |
| SECTION | TERMINAL | ZERO |
| SECURITY | TERMINATE | ZEROES |
| SEGMENT | TEST * | ZEROS |
| SEGMENT-LIMIT | TEXT | |
| SELECT | THAN | + |
| SEND | THEN * | − |
| SENTENCE | THROUGH | * |
| SEPARATE | THRU | / |
| SEQUENCE | TIME | ** |
| SEQUENTIAL | TIMES | > |
| SET | TO | < |
| SIGN | TOP | = |
| SIZE | TRAILING | |

The maroon asterisk denotes reserved words included in the COBOL '85 compiler that are not part of the '74 compiler reserved word list.

# SAMPLE DOCUMENTATION PACKAGE—CIRCLE CLUB PROGRAM

## INTRODUCTION

The following pages constitute an appropriate documentation package for the Circle Club example program. The package contains the following elements:

- Title page
- Problem statement in outline format
- IPO chart
- Input file design
- Output design
- Hierarchy chart
- Detailed flowchart
  [You may use other logic design tools.]

Every documentation package you hand in should contain all of the above elements. Your documentation packages do not have to be typed, however they must have a professional appearance. This means they should be neat, legible and correct.

The Circle Club demonstration program is in the Class Control account under the file name CIRCLPR. You should run a copy of the program and examine it in reference to this sample documentation package. The JCL file that runs the Circle Club program is also in the Class control account under the file name CIRCLJCL.

```
                    George C. Fowler

                   Circle Club Program

                   January 25, 1988

                 COBOL Programming Class

                      Section 503
```

### *Circle Club Program Problem Statement*

1. Develop a COBOL Program that processes the Circle Club master file and generates an accounts receivable report consisting of:

   a. Report heading

      1) Date and page number line
      2) Company name line
      3) Column heading line

   b. Detail lines containing member number, member name, member address and amount due

      1) Amount due includes current restaurant bill, past due amount and any discounts.

   c. Summary line

      1) Indicates the total amount due from all customers in the CIRCLE CLUB master file.

## IPO CHART

**IPO CHART**

| PROGRAM: | PROGRAMMER: | | DATE: |
|---|---|---|---|
| **MODULE NAME:** | **REF:** | **FUNCTION:** | |

| INPUT | PROCESS | OUTPUT |
|---|---|---|
| **Customer File**<br><br>membership number<br>member name<br>member address<br>restaurant bill<br>bar bill<br>other charges<br>amt outstanding | Write headings<br>Total amount due = 0<br>Read customer file<br>Do while more records<br>  If restaurant bill > 200<br>    Restaurant bill = 0.95*<br>      Restaurant bill<br>  If bar bill > 400<br>    Bar bill = bar bill * 0.95<br>  Total bill (current) =<br>    Restaurant bill + bar bill<br>    + other charges<br>  If total bill > 1000<br>    Total bill = total bill * 0.97<br>  Add amt outstanding to total bill<br>  Add total bill to total amount due<br>  Write customer record<br>  Read customer file<br>End do while<br><br>Write summary line | **Report One:**<br><br>membership number<br>member name<br>address<br>amount due<br><br>**Report Two: Summary**<br><br>"total amount due<br>from all customers is"<br>Total amount due |

# INPUT DESIGN

## Circle Club Program

```
                    INPUT DESIGN
                  Circle Club Program


        File Name:        CIRCLDAT
        Location:         A018.XX
        Organization:     Sequential
        Blocking Factor:  79



        Item        Characters      Type      Description

        1           1-3             3 AN      MEMBER NUMBER

        2           5-29            25 AN     MEMBER NAME

        3           31-48           18 AN     MEMBER ADDRESS

        4           49-53           5 N       RESTAURANT BILL
                                                 9(3)V9(2)
        5           55-59           5 N       BAR BILL
                                                 9(3)V9(2)
        6           61-65           5 N       OTHER CHARGES
                                                 9(3)V(2)
        7           67-72           6 N       PAST DUE AMOUNT
                                                 9(4)V9(2)
```

## Circle Club Data Set

```
                              CIRCLE CLUB
                               DATA SET


        586 LANZA, MARIO          101 CARUSO WAY      35790 42883 15222 005288
        355 BEASLEY, REGGIE R     2035 HARVEY         09523 05737 04277 014570
        004 RASKOLNIKOV, FYODOR   4321 GULAG MANOR    00099 00120 00000 013400
        996 IVANOVNA, ALYONA      401 HAY MARKET      62599 00000 32500 002500
        829 SMITHE, BYRON L.      90 DEVONSHIRE       95000 99930 03456 000050
        193 RANCHER, TEX A.       740 GURENSEY        12088 04746 09510 000000
        811 CORTEZ, SIGNIO H.     1818 CHEVERALLA     01045 00000 04721 000399
        045 MUDD, HARCORT FENTON  2111 NAGGA WAY      08298 40256 53049 820042
        355 RICH, RICHY           1 PROFLIGATE PL.    00022 00048 06028 000000
        492 MOON, WARREN          50 ZENITH RD.       50000 00000 02558 000000
        933 MCHALE, KEVIN         5 SECOND LANE       00378 94021 02485 470099
        810 KELLY, GENE           53 RAINDANCE DR.    00825 00640 00523 000000
        500 KIRKPATRICK, GENE     1300 PENN AVE.      21200 00000 00000 177600
        287 DROVELL, ROBERT H.    77 SUNSET STRIP     05075 04026 12518 003800
        001 MONT BENI, DONATELLO  100 GRANS TOWER     50000 25000 03499 050000
        900 KIPLING, KIMBAL       25 INDIA AVE        00500 00000 00400 000000
        503 KAFKA, FRANZ          75 PARADISE CT.     02500 01500 00500 000000
        984 BLAIR, ERIC           15 BUTTER DR.       10000 05000 02350 001573
        345 TWAIN, MARK           39 RIVER ROAD       02800 25000 00450 000000
        489 ORWELL, GEORGE        51 FLY STREET       90000 05100 00500 090000
        543 CLEMENS, SAMUEL       93 BOAT AVE.        08200 52000 00540 000000
```

## OUTPUT DESIGN

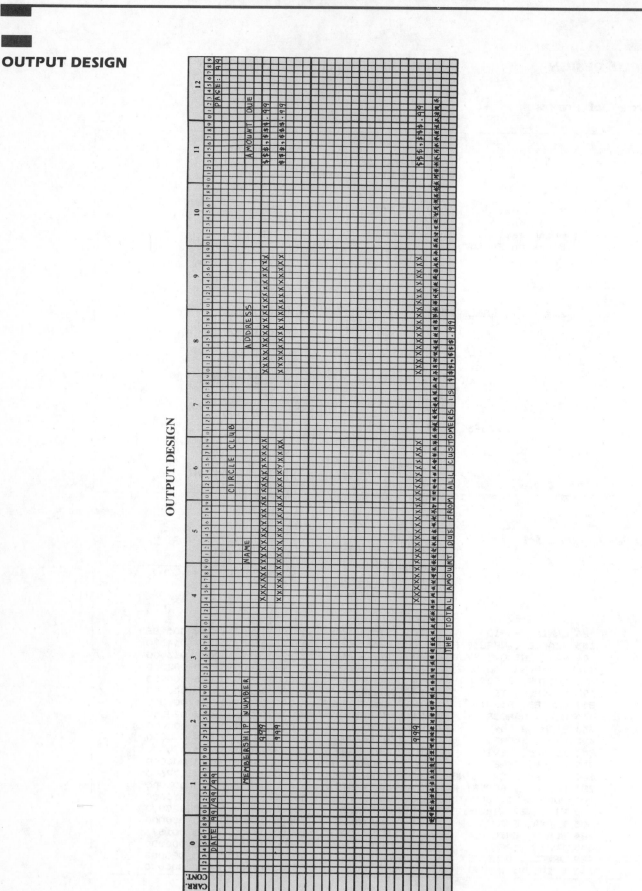

## CIRCLE CLUB HIERARCHY CHART

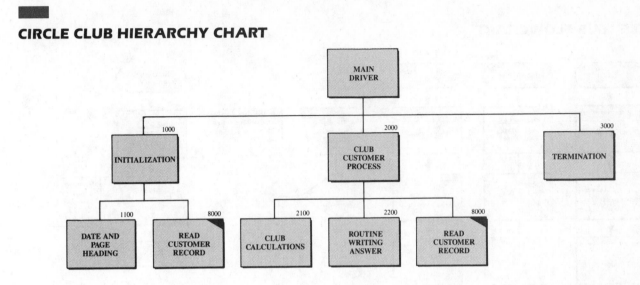

## CIRCLE CLUB FLOWCHART

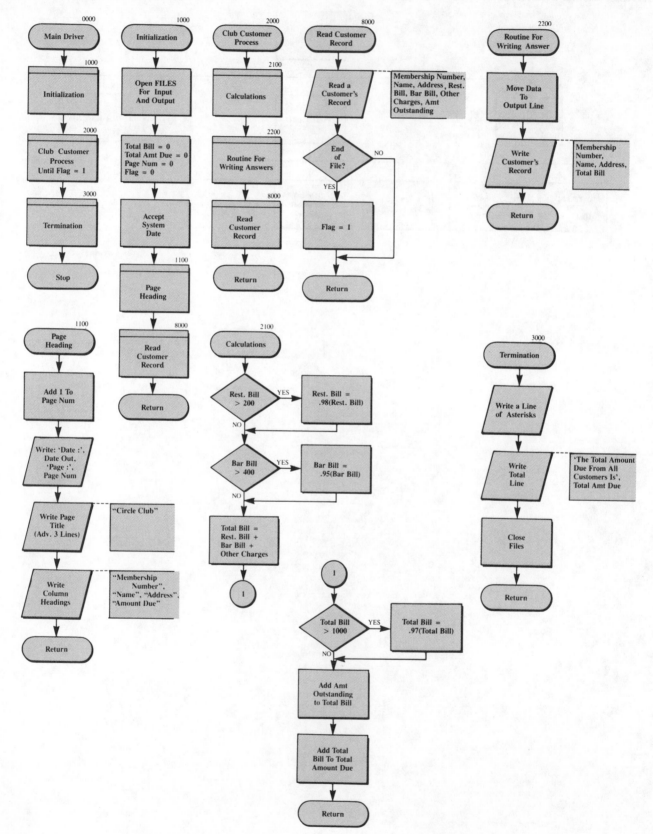

## SAMPLE PROGRAM

```
PP 5740-CB1 RELEASE 2.4                    IBM OS/VS COBOL  JULY  1, 1982

     1                        9.14.38      FEB 10,1988

00001   ...................................................................
00002   .                                                                 .
00003   .   WHEN KEYING A COBOL PROGRAM, THERE ARE TWO MARGINS THAT       .
00004   .   REQUIRE CONSIDERATION.  THE 'A' MARGIN (COLUMNS 8 TO 11) AND  .
00005   .   THE 'B' MARGIN (COLUMNS 12 TO 72). ALL  DIVISION  NAMES,      .
00006   .   SECTION NAMES, PARAGRAPH NAMES, FD'S, AND 01 AND 77 LEVELS    .
00007   .   MUST BEGIN IN THE 'A' MARGIN, WHILE THE REST OF THE COBOL     .
00008   .   STATEMENTS MUST BEGIN IN THE 'B' MARGIN. (IMPORTANT - DO NOT  .
00009   .   KEY PAST COLUMN 72 IN COBOL, BECAUSE THIS AREA IS RESERVED    .
00010   .   FOR IDENTIFICATION OR SEQUENCING AND IS IGNORED BY THE        .
00011   .   COMPILER.  THE BLANK LINES SEEN AT APPROPRIATE PLACES IN      .
00012   .   THE  PROGRAM  ARE  INSERTED  BY  THE  PROGRAMMER TO  GREATLY  .
00013   .   IMPROVE PROGRAM READIBILITY. THEY  ARE  IGNORED BY THE        .
00014   .   COMPILER, AND SHOULD BE USED IN ALL COBOL PROGRAMS FOR        .
00015   .   READABILITY.                                                  .
00016   .                                                                 .
00017   ...................................................................
00018   IDENTIFICATION DIVISION.
00019   ...................................................................
00020   .                                                                 .
00021   .   IN THE IDENTIFICATION DIVISION,  THE ONLY REQUIRED STATEMENT  .
00022   .   IS PROGRAM-ID.  THE OTHERS  GIVE  PERTINANT INFORMATION       .
00023   .   ABOUT THE PROGRAM.  THE REMARKS PARAGRAPH USUALLY CONTAINS A  .
00024   .   BRIEF DESCRIPTION OF THE PROGRAM, CARD INPUT, ETC.  THIS      .
00025   .   PROVIDES A SIMPLE WAY TO FURTHER  DOCUMENT YOUR PROGRAM AND   .
00026   .   WILL BE EXPECTED ON ALL ASSIGNMENTS.                          .
00027   .                                                                 .
00028   ...................................................................
00029
00030   PROGRAM-ID.
00031                   BILLING.
00032   AUTHOR.
00033                   GEORGE FOWLER.
00034   INSTALLATION.
00035                   TEXAS A & M UNIVERSITY.
00036   DATE-WRITTEN.
00037                   SEPTEMBER 8, 1985.
00038   DATE-COMPILED. FEB 10,1988.
```

```
     2      BILLING      9.14.38      FEB 10,1988

00040   ...................................................................
00041   .                                                                 .
00042   .   ASSIGNMENT NUMBER                                             .
00043   .   DATE ASSIGNED                                                 .
00044   .   DATE DUE                                                      .
00045   .   PURPOSE:           THIS IS A BILLING PROGRAM FOR  THE  CIRCLE .
00046   .   CLUB RESTAURANT AND BAR. IT CALCULATES THE TOTAL AMOUNT DUE   .
00047   .   FROM EACH CUSTOMER AND A GRAND TOTAL DUE FROM ALL ACCOUNTS.   .
00048   .   THERE ARE DISCOUNTS ALLOWED UNDER CERTAIN CONDITIONS.  THEY   .
00049   .   ARE:                                                          .
00050   .      2 PERCENT FOR A RESTRAURANT BILL OVER $200.00             .
00051   .      5 PERCENT FOR A BAR BILL OVER $400.00                     .
00052   .      3 PERCENT FOR A TOTAL BILL OVER $1,000.00 AFTER           .
00053   .        OTHER DISCOUNTS HAVE BEEN SUBTRACTED.                    .
00054   .                                                                 .
00055   .   INPUT FILE SPECIFICATIONS:                                    .
00056   .      CARD COLUMNS                     DESCRIPTION               .
00057   .         1- 3                          MEMBERSHIP NUMBER         .
00058   .         5-29                          MEMBER NAME               .
00059   .        31-48                          MEMBER ADDRESS            .
00060   .        49-53                          RESTAURANT BILL           .
00061   .        55-59                          BAR BILL                  .
00062   .        61-65                          ANY OTHER CHARGES         .
00063   .        67-72                          PAST DUE AMOUNT           .
00064   .                                                                 .
00065   .   THE OUTPUT CONTAINS MEMBERSHIP NUMBER,  NAME,  ADDRESS,  AND  .
00066   .   AMOUNT DUE.   THE SUMMARY CONTAINS THE TOTAL AMOUNT DUE FROM  .
00067   .   ALL CUSTOMERS.                                                .
00068   .                                                                 .
        ...................................................................
```

*(continued)*

```
   3        BILLING          9.14.38      FEB 10,1988

00071          ..............................................................
00072          .                                                            .
00073          .                     ENVIRONMENT DIVISION                   .
00074          .                                                            .
00075          ..............................................................
00076          ENVIRONMENT DIVISION.
00077
00078          ..............................................................
00079          .                                                            .
00080          .  IN COBOL, ALL ASPECTS OF THE DATA  PROCESSING  PROBLEM  THAT .
00081          .  DEPEND ON THE PHYSICAL CHARACTERISTICS OF A SPECIAL COMPUTER .
00082          .  ARE WITHIN THE  ENVIRONMENT DIVISION OF THE SOURCE  PROGRAM .
00083          .  THUS A CHANGE IN  COMPUTERS  ENTAILS  MAJOR CHANGES  IN ONLY .
00084          .  THE ENVIRONMENT DIVISION.          THE  ENVIRONMENT DIVISION IS .
00085          .  DIVIDED INTO TWO SECTIONS: THE CONFIGURATION SECTION AND THE .
00086          .  INPUT-OUTPUT SECTION.  THE CONFIGURATION SECTION HAS  THREE .
00087          .  PARAGRAPHS WHICH WE WILL USE:   SOURCE-COMPUTER, OBJECT-COM- .
00088          .  PUTER, AND SPECIAL-NAMES. THE INPUT-OUTPUT SECTION TELLS THE .
00089          .  COMPUTER WHICH HARDWARE DEVICES ARE REQUIRED FOR I/O.       .
00090          .                                                            .
00091          ..............................................................
00092
00093          CONFIGURATION SECTION.
00094
00095          SOURCE-COMPUTER.
00096                          IBM-370.
00097          OBJECT-COMPUTER.
00098                          IBM-370.
00099          SPECIAL-NAMES.
00100                          C01 IS TOP-OF-NEXT-PAGE.
00101
00102          INPUT-OUTPUT SECTION.
00103
00104          FILE-CONTROL.
00105
00106              SELECT CUSTOMER-FILE
00107                ASSIGN TO DA-S-INFILE.
00108
00109              SELECT REPORT-FILE
00110                ASSIGN TO UT-S-OUTFILE.
00111
```

```
   4        BILLING          9.14.38      FEB 10,1988

00113          ..............................................................
00114          .                                                            .
00115          .                        DATA DIVISION                       .
00116          .                                                            .
00117          ..............................................................
00118          DATA DIVISION.
00119
00120          ..............................................................
00121          .                                                            .
00122          .  THE   DATA  DIVISION   OF  A  COBOL  PROGRAM  CONTAINS   THE .
00123          .  DESCRIPTION OF ALL INFORMATION  TO BE PROCESSED BY  THE PRO- .
00124          .  GRAM.     FIRST IS THE SECTION THAT CONTAINS A DESCRIPTION OF .
00125          .  ALL EXTERNALLY STORED DATA.      THERE IS ALWAYS ONE FD (FILE .
00126          .  DESCRIPTION) FOR EACH SELECT  CLAUSE  IN THE INPUT-OUTPUT .
00127          .  SECTION OF THE ENVIRONMENT DIVISION.     THE NEXT PART IS THE .
00128          .  WORKING-STORAGE SECTION WHICH CONTAINS DESCRIPTIONS  OF  ALL .
00129          .  RECORDS THAT ARE NOT PART OF EXTERNAL FILES,  BUT ARE DEVEL- .
00130          .  OPED AND PROCESSED INTERNALLY.    EXAMPLES OF WORKING-STORAGE .
00131          .  AREAS ARE  TOTALS  COUNTERS,  DESCRIPTIONS OF HEADINGS   AND .
00132          .  DETAILED DESCRIPTIONS OF INPUT-OUTPUT RECORDS.             .
00133          .                                                            .
00134          ..............................................................
```

```
   5        BILLING          9.14.38      FEB 10,1988

00136          FILE SECTION.
00137
00138          FD  CUSTOMER-FILE
00139              RECORD CONTAINS 72 CHARACTERS
00140              BLOCK CONTAINS 88 RECORDS
00141              LABEL RECORDS ARE OMITTED
00142              DATA RECORD IS CUSTOMER-RECORD.
00143
00144          01  CUSTOMER-RECORD          PIC X(72).
00145
00146          FD  REPORT-FILE
00147              LABEL RECORDS ARE OMITTED
00148              DATA RECORD IS REPORT-LINE.
00149
00150          01  REPORT-LINE      PIC X(133).
00151
```

*(continued)*

```
    6        BILLING          9.14.38      FEB 10,1988

00153    ••••••••••••••••••••••••••••••••••••••••••••••••••••••••••••••••••••
00154    •                                                                  •
00155    •                    WORKING STORAGE SECTION                       •
00156    •                                                                  •
00157    ••••••••••••••••••••••••••••••••••••••••••••••••••••••••••••••••••••
00158    WORKING-STORAGE SECTION.
00159
00160        77   TOTAL-BILL              PIC 9(6)V99   VALUE ZERO.
00161        77   TOTAL-AMT-DUE           PIC 9(6)V99   VALUE ZERO.
00162        77   PAGE-NUM                PIC 9(8)      VALUE ZERO.
00163
00164        01   INDICATORS-GROUP.
00165             03   ARE-THERE-MORE-RECORDS-  PIC X(3)    VALUE 'YES'.
00166                  88   MORE-RECORDS                    VALUE 'YES'.
00167                  88   NO-MORE-RECORDS                 VALUE 'NO '.
00168
00169        01   CUSTOMER-RECORD-IN.
00170             03   MEMBER-NUMBER-IN        PIC 9(3).
00171             03   FILLER                  PIC X(1).
00172             03   NAME-IN                 PIC X(25).
00173             03   FILLER                  PIC X(1).
00174             03   MEMBER-ADDRESS-IN       PIC X(18).
00175             03   REST-BILL               PIC 9(3)V99.
00176             03   FILLER                  PIC X(1).
00177             03   BAR-BILL                PIC 9(3)V99.
00178             03   FILLER                  PIC X(1).
00179             03   OTHER-CHARGES           PIC 9(3)V99.
00180             03   FILLER                  PIC X(1).
00181             03   AMT-OUTSTANDING         PIC 9(4)V99.
00182             03   FILLER                  PIC X(8).
```

```
    7        BILLING          9.14.38      FEB 10,1988

00184        01   DETAIL-LINE.
00185             03   FILLER                  PIC X(22)  VALUE SPACES.
00186             03   MEMBER-NUMBER-OUT       PIC 9(3).
00187             03   FILLER                  PIC X(19)  VALUE SPACES.
00188             03   NAME-OUT                PIC X(26).
00189             03   FILLER                  PIC X(10)  VALUE SPACES.
00190             03   MEMBER-ADDRESS-OUT      PIC X(19).
00191             03   FILLER                  PIC X(13)  VALUE SPACES.
00192             03   AMT-DUE                 PIC $$$,$$$.99.
00193             03   FILLER                  PIC X(11)  VALUE SPACES.
00194
00195        01   TITLE.
00196             03   FILLER                  PIC X(61)  VALUE SPACES.
00197             03   FILLER                  PIC X(11)  VALUE
00198                  'CIRCLE CLUB'.
00199             03   FILLER                  PIC X(61)  VALUE SPACES.
00200
00201        01   COLUMN-HEADINGS.
00202             03   FILLER                  PIC X(15)  VALUE SPACES.
00203             03   FILLER                  PIC X(17)  VALUE
00204                  'MEMBERSHIP NUMBER'.
00205             03   FILLER                  PIC X(18)  VALUE SPACES.
00206             03   FILLER                  PIC X(4)   VALUE 'NAME'.
00207             03   FILLER                  PIC X(30)  VALUE SPACES.
00208             03   FILLER                  PIC X(7)   VALUE 'ADDRESS'.
00209             03   FILLER                  PIC X(22)  VALUE SPACES.
00210             03   FILLER                  PIC X(10)  VALUE 'AMOUNT DUE'.
00211             03   FILLER                  PIC X(10)  VALUE SPACES.
00212
00213        01   TOTAL-LINE.
00214             03   FILLER                  PIC X(36)  VALUE SPACES.
00215             03   FILLER                  PIC X(43)  VALUE
00216                  'THE TOTAL AMOUNT DUE FROM ALL CUSTOMERS IS'.
00217             03   AMOUNT                  PIC $$$$,$$9.99.
00218             03   FILLER                  PIC X(43)  VALUE SPACES.
00219
00220        01   BLANK-LINE                   PIC X(133) VALUE SPACES.
```

*(continued)*

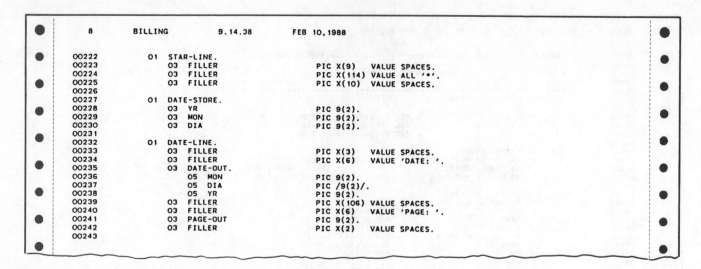

```
    8         BILLING        9.14.38      FEB 10,1988

00222        01  STAR-LINE.
00223            03  FILLER              PIC X(9)   VALUE SPACES.
00224            03  FILLER              PIC X(114) VALUE ALL '*'.
00225            03  FILLER              PIC X(10)  VALUE SPACES.
00226
00227        01  DATE-STORE.
00228            03  YR                  PIC 9(2).
00229            03  MON                 PIC 9(2).
00230            03  DIA                 PIC 9(2).
00231
00232        01  DATE-LINE.
00233            03  FILLER              PIC X(3)   VALUE SPACES.
00234            03  FILLER              PIC X(6)   VALUE 'DATE: '.
00235            03  DATE-OUT.
00236                05  MON             PIC 9(2).
00237                05  DIA             PIC /9(2)/.
00238                05  YR              PIC 9(2).
00239            03  FILLER              PIC X(106) VALUE SPACES.
00240            03  FILLER              PIC X(6)   VALUE 'PAGE: '.
00241            03  PAGE-OUT            PIC 9(2).
00242            03  FILLER              PIC X(2)   VALUE SPACES.
00243
```

```
    9         BILLING        9.14.38      FEB 10,1988

00245        ••••••••••••••••••••••••••••••••••••••••••••••••••••••••
00246        •                                                      •
00247        •                    PROCEDURE DIVISION                •
00248        •                                                      •
00249        ••••••••••••••••••••••••••••••••••••••••••••••••••••••••
00250
00251        PROCEDURE DIVISION.
00252
00253        ••••••••••••••••••••••••••••••••••••••••••••••••••••••••
00254        •                                                      •
00255        • THE PROCEDURE DIVISION OF A COBOL PROGRAM CONTAINS THE ACTUAL •
00256        • INSTRUCTIONS FOR SOLVING A PROBLEM  WHICH MAY INCLUDE •
00257        • SENTENCES, STATEMENTS, CONDITIONAL STATEMENTS, PARAGRAPHS, •
00258        • PROCEDURES AND SECTIONS.                              •
00259        •                                                      •
00260        ••••••••••••••••••••••••••••••••••••••••••••••••••••••••
00261
00262
00263        0000-MAIN-DRIVER.
00264            PERFORM 1000-INITIALIZATION.
00265            PERFORM 2000-CLUB-CUSTOMER-PROCESS
00266                UNTIL NO-MORE-RECORDS.
00267            PERFORM 3000-TERMINATION.
00268            STOP RUN.
```

*(continued)*

```
    10        BILLING        9.14.38      FEB 10,1988

00270      ..........................................................
00271      .                                                        .
00272      .   1000 INITIALIZATION                                  .
00273      .                                                        .
00274      .     - OPENS THE INPUT AND OUTPUT FILES                 .
00275      .     - WRITES THE FIRST PAGE COLUMN-HEADINGS            .
00276      .     - READS FIRST RECORD                               .
00277      .                                                        .
00278      ..........................................................
00279
00280       1000-INITIALIZATION.
00281           OPEN   INPUT CUSTOMER-FILE
00282                  OUTPUT REPORT-FILE.
00283           ACCEPT DATE-STORE FROM DATE.
00284           PERFORM 1100-PAGE-HEADING.
00285           PERFORM 8000-READ-RECORD.
00286
00287       1100-PAGE-HEADING.
00288           WRITE REPORT-LINE FROM BLANK-LINE
00289               AFTER TOP-OF-NEXT-PAGE.
00290           MOVE CORRESPONDING DATE-STORE TO DATE-OUT.
00291           ADD 1 TO PAGE-NUM.
00292           MOVE PAGE-NUM TO PAGE-OUT.
00293           WRITE REPORT-LINE FROM DATE-LINE
00294               AFTER ADVANCING 1 LINES.
00295           WRITE REPORT-LINE FROM TITLE
00296               AFTER ADVANCING 3 LINES.
00297           WRITE REPORT-LINE FROM COLUMN-HEADINGS
00298               AFTER ADVANCING 3 LINES.
00299      ..........................................................
00300      .                                                        .
00301      .   2000 CLUB CUSTOMER PROCESS                           .
00302      .                                                        .
00303      .   THIS PARAGRAPH IS PERFORMED UNTIL THERE ARE NO MORE MASTER .
00304      .   RECORDS.  IT:                                        .
00305      .                                                        .
00306      .     - PERFORMS THE CALCULATION PARAGRAPH               .
00307      .     - PERFORMS THE DETAIL WRITING PARAGRAPH            .
00308      .     - PERFORMS THE READ PARAGRAPH                      .
00309      .                                                        .
00310      ..........................................................
00311
00312       2000-CLUB-CUSTOMER-PROCESS.
00313           PERFORM 2100-CALCULATION-PARA.
00314           PERFORM 2200-ROUTINE-WRITING-ANSWER.
00315           PERFORM 8000-READ-RECORD.
00316
```

```
    11        BILLING        9.14.38      FEB 10,1988

00318      ..........................................................
00319      .                                                        .
00320      .   2100 CALCULATION PARA                                .
00321      .                                                        .
00322      .     - CALCULATES THE BAR BILL DISCOUNTS                .
00323      .     - CALCULATES THE CUSTOMER'S TOTAL BILL AMOUNT      .
00324      .     - ACCUMULATES THE GRAND TOTAL BILL AMOUNT          .
00325      .                                                        .
00326      ..........................................................
00327
00328       2100-CALCULATION-PARA.
00329           IF REST-BILL IS GREATER THAN 200
00330               MULTIPLY 0.98 BY REST-BILL.
00331           IF BAR-BILL > 400
00332               MULTIPLY .95 BY BAR-BILL.
00333           ADD REST-BILL, BAR-BILL, OTHER-CHARGES GIVING TOTAL-BILL.
00334           IF TOTAL-BILL GREATER THAN 1000
00335               MULTIPLY TOTAL-BILL BY 0.97 GIVING TOTAL-BILL.
00336           ADD AMT-OUTSTANDING TO TOTAL-BILL.
00337           ADD TOTAL-BILL TO TOTAL-AMT-DUE.
```

*(continued)*

```
   12        BILLING        9.14.38      FEB 10, 1988

00339        ................................................................
00340        .                                                              .
00341        .   2200 ROUTINE WRITING ANSWER                                 .
00342        .                                                              .
00343        .     - MOVES INPUT FIELDS TO OUTPUT LINE                       .
00344        .     - MOVES CUSTOMER'S TOTAL BILL AMOUNT TO OUTPUT LINE       .
00345        .     - WRITES DETAIL LINE                                      .
00346        .                                                              .
00347        ................................................................
00348
00349        2200-ROUTINE-WRITING-ANSWER.
00350            MOVE TOTAL-BILL TO AMT-DUE.
00351
00352        ................................................................
00353        .                                                              .
00354        . NOTE:    WHEN TOTAL-BILL IS MOVED TO AMT-DUE, A  PROBLEM COULD .
00355        . OCCUR  BECAUSE  THE  PICTURE  FOR  TOTAL-BILL  IS ONE CHARACTER .
00356        . LARGER THAN THE PICTURE  FOR  AMT-DUE  AND  YOU COULD LOSE THE .
00357        . HIGH ORDER DIGIT OF THE LARGER PICTURE.                       .
00358        .                                                              .
00359        ................................................................
00360
00361            MOVE MEMBER-NUMBER-IN TO MEMBER-NUMBER-OUT.
00362            MOVE NAME-IN TO NAME-OUT.
00363            MOVE MEMBER-ADDRESS-IN TO MEMBER-ADDRESS-OUT.
00364            WRITE REPORT-LINE FROM DETAIL-LINE
00365                AFTER ADVANCING 2 LINES.
```

```
   13        BILLING        9.14.38      FEB 10, 1988

00367        8000-READ-RECORD.
00368            READ CUSTOMER-FILE INTO CUSTOMER-RECORD-IN
00369                AT END
00370                    MOVE 'NO ' TO ARE-THERE-MORE-RECORDS.
00371
```

```
   14        BILLING        9.14.38      FEB 10, 1988

00373        ................................................................
00374        .                                                              .
00375        .   3000 TERMINATION                                            .
00376        .                                                              .
00377        .     - MOVES GRAND TOTAL BILLING AMOUNT TO SUMMARY LINE        .
00378        .     - WRITES GRAND TOTAL LINES                                .
00379        .     - CLOSES FILES                                           .
00380        .                                                              .
00381        ................................................................
00382
00383        3000-TERMINATION.
00384            WRITE REPORT-LINE FROM STAR-LINE
00385                AFTER ADVANCING 3 LINES.
00386            MOVE TOTAL-AMT-DUE TO AMOUNT IN TOTAL-LINE.
00387
00388        ................................................................
00389        .                                                              .
00390        . NOTE: THE ABOVE MOVE STATEMENT IS A SIMPLE MOVE, WE ARE MOVING .
00391        . DATA FROM  ONE  LOCATION  TO  ANOTHER  WITH  BOTH  DATA  NAMES .
00392        . (TOTAL-AMT-DUE AMOUNT) BEING UNIQUE; THAT IS, THEY APPEAR ONLY .
00393        . ONCE IN THE DATA DIVISION.                                    .
00394        .                                                              .
00395        ................................................................
00396
00397            WRITE REPORT-LINE FROM TOTAL-LINE
00398                AFTER ADVANCING 3 LINES.
00399            CLOSE CUSTOMER-FILE, REPORT-FILE.
```

```
DATE: 02/10/88                                                          PAGE: 01

                                   CIRCLE CLUB

    MEMBERSHIP NUMBER              NAME                    ADDRESS         AMOUNT DUE
         586                 LANZA, MARIO             101 CARUSO WAY         $963.22
         355                 BEASLEY, REGGIE R.       2035 HARVEY           $341.07
         004                 RASKOLNIKOV, FYODOR      4321 GULAG MANOR      $136.19
         996                 IVANOVNA, ALYONA         401 HAY MARKET        $963.47
         829                 SMITHE, BYRON L.         90 DEVONSHIRE       $1,857.94
         193                 RANCHER, TEX A.          740 GUERNSEY          $263.44
         811                 CORTEZ, SIGNIO H.        1818 CHEVERALLA        $61.65
         045                 MUDD, HARCORT FENTON     2111 NAGGA WAY      $9,196.32
         355                 RICH, RICHY              1 PROFLIGATE PL.       $60.98
         492                 MOON, WARREN             50 ZENITH RD.         $515.58
         933                 MCHALE, KEVIN            5 SECOND LANE       $5,622.81
         810                 KELLY, GENE              53 RAINDANCE DR.       $19.88
         500                 KIRKPATRICK, JEAN        1300 PENN AVE.      $1,983.76
         287                 DROVELL, ROBERT H.       77 SUNSET STRIP       $254.19
         001                 MONT BENI, DONATELLO     100 GRAND TOWER     $1,274.99
         900                 KIPLING, KIMBALL         25 INDIA AVE.           $9.00
         503                 KAFKA, FRANZ             75 PARADISE COURT      $45.00
         984                 BLAIR, ERIC              15 BUTTER DR.         $189.23
         345                 TWAIN, MARK              39 RIVER ROAD         $282.50
         489                 ORWELL, GEORGE           51 FLY STREET       $1,838.00
         543                 CLEMENS, SAMUEL          93 BOAT AVE.          $581.40

.........................................................................................

          THE TOTAL AMOUNT DUE FROM ALL CUSTOMERS IS  $26,460.62
```

# CODING AND DOCUMENTATION STANDARDS

## DOCUMENTATION

Program coding and documentation standards are used extensively in business. Each company has their own set of standards. In fact, part of a new programmer/analyst's training is to learn the corporation's documentation and coding standards.

While each company has their own somewhat unique set of standards, they all have common elements and a common purpose. The documentation helps with several aspects of a program's life. It is primarily useful in development and in maintenance but is also helpful in problem solving and with personnel turnover.

The components of a complete documentation package are also different from company to company. However, we will use the following in our text:

- Input and output file design
- Logic design
    - Hierarchy chart
    - IPO chart(s)
    - Detail flowcharts or pseudocode
- Compiler listing of source code
- Sample output/test run(s)

## CODING STANDARDS

As we discussed in Chapter 1, COBOL was designed to allow the programmer to document coding. If the programmer utilizes the self-documenting features of COBOL (easy to read, sentence structure similar to English, meaningful data names), then the code becomes a "good" part of the documentation package. With this purpose in mind, and remembering that, like documentation standards, coding standards vary from company to company, let's look first at some general guidelines.

## GENERAL GUIDELINES

There are coding guidelines that are global to the COBOL program. That is, they apply to all divisions of the program.

All division names, section names, and paragraph names must begin in the A-margin and must be on a line by themselves. This also applies to all FDs, 01s, and 77s. All other level numbers and statements are placed in the B-margin.

Each division should start on a page and sections and paragraphs should not be continued from one page to the next. In fact, paragraphs should also start a page. Since a paragraph is a module, this makes working with the logic easier. You would have the flowchart on a page and the corresponding code on a page.

I should mention that for class assignments, many modules are rather short, and therefore, more than one is allowed per page ... I don't like to waste trees!

This paging can be accomplished with the compiler directing command **EJECT**. Place this command in your code in column 12 at the point you want the compiler to skip to the next page. Depending on your system environment a slash (/) in column 7 may also cause the same page skipping.

In-line documentation should be used to aid the reader in understanding the program. However, it should not be so extensive that it hampers the readability of the code or the understandability of the code. Documentation within the program is accomplished by placing an asterisk (*) in column 7. This tells the compiler that what follows is not code and should only be printed on the program listing. In most cases the documentation should immediately precede the code it is describing and it should be easy to distinguish from the code itself. With this in mind all in-line documentation should be bordered by asterisks.

Lastly you will notice that blank lines are used throughout the examples and programs in the text. This again is done to enhance readability. However, don't get carried away (remember our trees).

## IDENTIFICATION DIVISION

The IDENTIFICATION DIVISION is primarily used to provide information about the program and programmer. It is essentially just documentation. Our standard is illustrated below:

```
IDENTIFICATION DIVISION.

PROGRAM-ID.            UPDATE.
AUTHOR.                MARY PORTERFIELD.
INSTALLATION.          A&M COMPUTER CENTER.
DATE-WRITTEN.          NOVEMBER 21, 1987.
DATE-COMPILED.
SECURITY.              NORMAL FILE PROTECTION.
```

```
**********************************************************************
*       This program updates the inventory master file using the trans-  *
*       action file.                                                 *
*                                                                    *
*       Initialization                                               *
*           Open files                                               *
*           Write report headings                                    *
*       Process transactions                                         *
*           Read master and transaction records                      *
*           Receipts of merchandise                                  *
*           Sale of merchandise                                      *
*           Write error lists                                        *
*           Write transaction log                                    *
*       Print updated master file listing                            *
**********************************************************************
```

The entries shown above should all be included in your COBOL programs, with the possible exception of security. I'll leave that up to your professor. However, all the information supplied by you should be aligned vertically as shown. This enhances readability.

Notice that the comments in the IDENTIFICATION DIVISION are in outline form and state the program's general purpose. The comments should not be extensive, but should tell the reader what to expect in the program.

## ENVIRONMENT DIVISION

The ENVIRONMENT DIVISION contains two sections — the CONFIGURATION SECTION and the INPUT-OUTPUT SECTION. Both sections should be set apart from the rest of the code by preceding and following each with a blank line.

Entries in the CONFIGURATION SECTION should include the SOURCE-COMPUTER, OBJECT-COMPUTER, and SPECIAL-NAMES. The information supplied with these entries should be vertically aligned as in the IDENTIFICATION DIVISION.

In the INPUT-OUTPUT SECTION, the FILE-CONTROL paragraph is the only requirement for our programs. The entry (or entries) in this paragraph is the SELECT statement. As you can see in the example, the SELECT starts in column 12 (B-margin) with each subsequent statement indented on a separate line. Critical to our standards are the file names (data names used to describe a file). The file name should be descriptive of the file and should include the suffix FILE. These rules are illustrated below:

```
EJECT

ENVIRONMENT DIVISION.

CONFIGURATION SECTION.

SOURCE-COMPUTER.            IBM-370.
OBJECT-COMPUTER.            IBM-370.
SPECIAL-NAMES.             C01 IS PAGE-TOP.
```

```
INPUT-OUTPUT SECTION.

FILE-CONTROL.
    SELECT  INVENTORY-MASTER-FILE
            ASSIGN TO DA-S-MASTER
            ORGANIZATION IS SEQUENTIAL
            ACCESS MODE IS SEQUENTIAL.
    SELECT  TRANSACTION-FILE
            ASSIGN TO DA-S-TRANS
            ORGANIZATION IS SEQUENTIAL
            ACCESS MODE IS SEQUENTIAL.
    SELECT  ERROR-REPORT-FILE
            ASSIGN TO UT-S-ERROR.
    SELECT  TRANSACTION-LOG-REPORT-FILE
            ASSIGN TO UT-S-LOG.
```

## DATA DIVISION

The data division always starts a new page (EJECT or /) and all sections will again be preceded by and followed by a blank line. For a lengthy program, or for all programs if desired, the WORKING-STORAGE SECTION should start a new page. This also applies to the SCREEN SECTION and REPORT SECTION.

In the FILE SECTION, the FDs, SDs (for sorting), and RDs (for report writer) will be coded so that the FD, SD, or RD entry is on a line by itself. All other clauses will be one per line, indented, and vertically aligned.

The WORKING-STORAGE SECTION can be very lengthy, and format and organization becomes very important. All 77 level items, if used, will appear first and may be ordered if desired (by you or by your professor!). Seriously, if there are a large number of 77s then placing them in alphabetic order or functional order helps readability.

Some professionals do not like 77 items and code all 77 items as 01s or functionally group them under an appropriate group heading. If this is done, these 01s should also be listed first in WORKING-STORAGE.

Immediately following the 77s will be all detail record descriptions — 01s. All 01s should be preceded by a blank line. The 01s must be in the A-margin and successive levels should be indented at least four spaces from the previous entry, and the data names should be separated from the level number by two spaces. An 01 should not be split between pages.

**Level Numbers.** Numbering of the successive entries may be done in several ways. I suggest two ways. First, 01, 03, 05, etc., and second, 01, 05, 10, 15, etc. In each case, "room" is left between levels. In *no case* should you use 01, 02, 03, 04, 05 .... All elementary level items within a group item should be aligned, and the programmer should be consistent in the use of PICTURE or PIC.

**Data Names.** A word about data names is needed here. Data names should describe the function or purpose of the data item. Generally input and output records should have a suffix of record or record-in or record-out. Appropriate abbreviations are acceptable but should only be used to keep the length of the data-name within the limit of 30 characters.

Following are some examples of these rules:

Following are some examples of these rules:

```
FILE SECTION.

DATA DIVISION.

FD  STUDENT-FILE
    LABEL RECORDS ARE OMITTED
    RECORD CONTAINS 100 CHARACTERS
    BLOCK CONTAINS 50 RECORDS
    DATA RECORD IS STUDENT-REPORT-RECORD.

01  STUDENT-RECORD                      PIC X(100).

FD  HONORS-STUDENT-REPORT-FILE
    LABEL RECORDS ARE OMITTED
    RECORD CONTAINS 133 CHARACTERS
    DATA RECORD IS  STUDENT-REPORT-RECORD.

01  STUDENT-REPORT-RECORD               PIC X(133).

WORKING-STORAGE SECTION.

77  STUDENT-COUNT                       PIC 9(3)        VALUE 0.
77  TOTAL-GPR                           PIC 9(3)V9(4)   VALUE 0.
77  END-OF-FILE-FLAG                    PIC X(3)        VALUE 'NO '

01  STUDENT-RECORD-IN.
    03  STUDENT-NAME                    PIC X(30).
    03  SOCIAL-SECURITY-NUMBER.
        05  FIRST-PART                  PIC X(3).
        05  MIDDLE-PART                 PIC X(2).
        05  LAST-PART                   PIC X(4).
    03  MAJOR-CODE                      PIC X(1).
    03  GPR                             PIC 9(1)V9(4).
```

**PICTURE Clause.**     A few more rules are needed. Rules on the PIC clause entries and value clauses are needed, as well as other items such as clauses like the OCCURS and entries like condition names, 88s.

While X(3) and XXX are both acceptable to the compiler and "say" the same thing, the X(3) form is the preferred form. In general if more than two places are being defined then the parentheses form must be used. However, let me suggest that in a record description the parentheses form always be used. Using both forms can be confusing when doing program testing and/or maintenance.

**VALUE Clause.**     As you would expect, the value clauses within a group should also be aligned. If the value specified is too long to fit on the same line then it should be placed on the next line with the left apostrophe beginning so that it is aligned with the last character in the data-name or the "R" in FILLER.

This is an example of the value clause rules:

```
01  REPORT-HEADING.
    03  FILLER                    PIC X(56)   VALUE SPACES.
    03  FILLER                    PIC X(22)   VALUE
                'EXAMPLE REPORT HEADING'.
    03  FILLER                    PIC X(55)   VALUE SPACES.
```

While I use the OCCURS clause to illustrate the next rule, generally any clause used to define data should be on a separate line and should be vertically aligned as shown below.

```
01   COUNT-TABLE.
     03   KOUNT              PIC 9(5)
                             OCCURS  50  TIMES
                             INDEXED BY  COUNT-INDEX
                                         STUDENT-INDEX.
```

**Condition Names.**     Condition names, or 88 levels, should be used whenever appropriate. The condition names should be descriptive of their associated value or value's function. The data-name containing the 88s should be in question form where possible. For example:

```
01   END-OF-FILE-INDICATOR.
     03   ARE-THERE-MORE-RECORDS     PIC X(3).
          88   MORE-RECORDS                         VALUE 'YES'.
          88   NO-MORE-RECORDS                      VALUE 'NO '.
```

## PROCEDURE DIVISION

The PROCEDURE DIVISION should start on a new page. All modules and paragraphs will also start a new page and will be numbered. The first module, module 0000, will be on the same page as the PROCEDURE DIVISION statement.

The paragraph names, like data names, should be descriptive of the module's function. They should also be "close" in name to what was used in the hierarchy chart and flowchart. Furthermore, a numbering system should be used that helps show relationship between paragraphs and helps identify the corresponding paragraphs, hierarchy modules, and flowchart modules.

All modules will be preceded by comments enclosed in asterisks. They will also be preceded by a blank line and will be coded on a line by themselves.

Generally every COBOL statement should be coded on a line by itself. In other words, only one statement per line is permitted. Conditional statements should also adhere to this rule. The statements that are executed as the result of a condition statement being evaluated as true or false should be coded one per line and also indented from the conditional statement. For example:

```
IF   STUDENT-MAJOR IS EQUAL TO 'ACCOUNTING'
     ADD 1 TO ACCT-STUDENT-COUNT.
```

and

```
READ STUDENT-FILE INTO STUDENT RECORD-IN
     AT END
          MOVE 'NO ' TO ARE-THERE-MORE-RECORDS.
```

and

```
PERFORM 5010-CALCULATIONS-PARA
     VARYING SUB FROM 1 BY 1
     UNTIL SUB > 50.
```

**IF Statement.** The IF statement in COBOL requires a further look. If more than two conditions are checked within an IF, each condition is placed on a separate line. You may also put each on a line when only two conditions are included if it helps readability. In either case, each subsequent line should start with the "AND" or "OR" and, again, should be indented.

Let's turn our attention to the ELSE option of the IF. With the IF-THEN-ELSE structure, the ELSE and the IF, it is "else-ing," that is, its corresponding IF must be vertically aligned. The ELSE itself is on a separate line and all statements within the IF should be indented. For example:

```
IF   STUDENT-MAJOR = 'ACCOUNTING'
     ADD 1 TO ACCT-STUDENT-COUNT
ELSE
     IF   STUDENT-MAJOR = 'INFORMATION SYSTEMS'
          ADD 1 TO INFO-SYS-STUDENT-COUNT
     ELSE
          :
          :
```

and

```
IF   STUDENT-COLLEGE = 'BUSINESS'
     AND GPR > 3.25
          ADD 1 TO OUTSTANDING-STUDENT-COUNT.
```

**GO TO Statement.** The GO TO statement should only be used within the COBOL sort sections and only to branch forward to the EXIT paragraph. The GO TO ... DEPENDING ON statement should not be used. Use nested IF statements to handle the case structure. If you are using a COBOL '85 compiler then you should use the EVALUATE command.

**PERFORM ... THRU.** You also should *not* use the PERFORM THRU. This causes implicit execution of paragraphs which may cause serious problems during maintenance.

**Scope Terminators.** A word about the COBOL '85 scope terminators (END-IF, END-PERFORM, END-READ, etc). If you use scope terminations, say within nested IFs, then be consistent with their use. For example:

**Correct**

```
IF   condition₁
     statement
     statement
     IF   condition₂
          statement
          statement
     ELSE
          statement
          statement
     END-IF
     IF   condition₃
          statement
     ELSE
          statement
     END-IF
END-IF.
```

**Incorrect**

```
IF   condition₁
     statement
     statement
     IF   condition₂
          statement
     ELSE
          IF   condition₃
               statement
          END-IF.
```

Notice that in the correct example each IF was matched with an END-IF. In the second example, only the last IF has a corresponding END-IF. While this inconsistent use of the END-IF did not cause a logic problem, it is not acceptable coding practice.

# REPORT WRITER

## INTRODUCTION

In this text, we have looked at several techniques for writing ordered reports in COBOL. In fact, one of COBOL's great pluses is that it allows for handling the reporting of large volumes of data easily. We saw where even adding multiple control breaks was relatively easy to handle procedurally in COBOL. Well, believe it or not, COBOL has a special built-in feature designed specifically for handling the writing of reports. It is called, appropriately, the REPORT WRITER feature.

Before we look at REPORT WRITER, it will help us to understand the features if we first look at the make up of a report. Let's examine a couple: a simple listing and a control break.

Figure E.1 shows a sample listing report. Notice the elements. We start with a report heading. This is followed by the column headings that will appear on each page. The detail lines are then printed. The report may or may not have totals, but if it did, the report totals would follow the detail lines on the last page.

The report also indicates desired spacing. That is, the report heading is to be printed on line 1, while the column/page headings are to start on line 5. The detail lines are to be double-spaced and be separated from the column heading by two blank lines. Furthermore, we do not want to print detail lines beyond line 55, because we want to leave room for report totals to print on line 58.

If we added a control break, what could we generalize about our report? Well, remember that we looked at two formats in the Control Break Chapter. One used the group description as a heading, while the other included the description as a column but printed it only once for each group (group indicated). The two formats shown in Figures E.2 and E.3 are those shown in Chapter 9, Figures 9.17 and 9.18, respectively.

On examination of the first format, Figure E.2, we see a familiar report format. We may start out with a report heading and then have a control heading followed by page/column headings. Notice the similarity to our previous design, where the control-break field was also used more as a title printed before the column headings.

**Figure E.1**
*Sample Listing*
*Report*

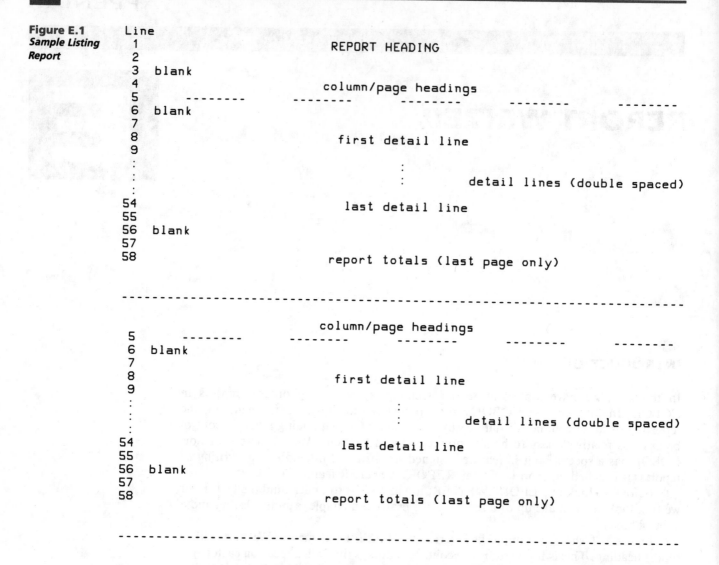

```
Line
 1                            REPORT HEADING
 2
 3   blank
 4                        column/page headings
 5       --------       --------      --------      --------      --------
 6   blank
 7
 8                         first detail line
 9
 :                                    :
 :                                    :          detail lines (double spaced)
 :
54                        last detail line
55
56   blank
57
58                  report totals (last page only)


 5       --------       column/page headings
 6   blank --------      --------      --------      --------      --------
 7
 8                         first detail line
 9
 :                                    :
 :                                    :          detail lines (double spaced)
 :
54                        last detail line
55
56   blank
57
58                  report totals (last page only)
```

The group-indicated report using the columns format, Figure E.3, is also easily handled by REPORT WRITER. In fact, it also matches what we did before using REPORT WRITER. For each control group, the control field is printed only the first time for each group, and as we can see from Figure E.3, a report heading, page/column heading, control totals and spacing are all defined.

**Figure E.2**
*Group Indication as a Heading*

```
REPORT HEADING
    control heading
  column/page headings
- - - - - - - -    - - - - - - - -    - - - - - - - -    - - - - - - - -    - - - - - - - -

             :
             :              detail lines (double spaced)
             :
        control total
      control heading
             :
             :              detail lines (double spaced)
             :
        control total
      control heading
             :
             :              detail lines (double spaced)
             :
        control total
- - - - - - - - - - - - - - - - - - - - - - - - - - - - - - - - - - - - - - - - - - - - - -

      control heading
    column/page headings
- - - - - - - -    - - - - - - - -    - - - - - - - -    - - - - - - - -    - - - - - - - -

             :
             :              detail lines (double spaced)
             :
        control total
      control heading
             :
             :              detail lines (double spaced)
             :
        control total
      control heading
             :
             :              detail lines (double spaced)
             :
        report total
- - - - - - - - - - - - - - - - - - - - - - - - - - - - - - - - - - - - - - - - - - - - - -
```

**Figure E.3**
*Group Indication as Column Entries*

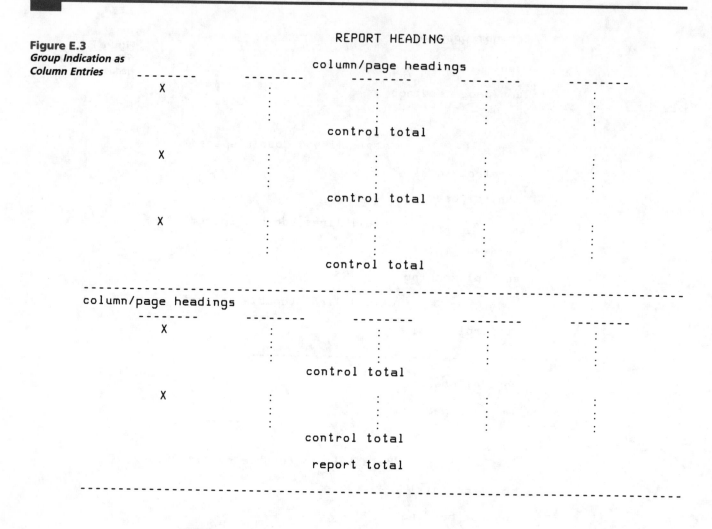

## REPORT WRITER FEATURES

Using the REPORT WRITER feature requires that we study several new items. These will involve entries in the DATA DIVISION and PROCEDURE DIVISION. We will describe the report in the DATA DIVISION—line spacing, data movement, headings, line skipping and so on. That's correct, we do these things in the DATA DIVISION. Different, isn't it? Guess what we do in the PROCEDURE DIVISION? We simply tell the system to generate the report. In a very sketchy pseudocode, take a look at the logic:

```
Initialize
Initiate the report
Read 1st record
Do while more records
   Generate report
   Read 2nd-Nth record
End Do
Terminate the report
```

You're right, it's still our lead read technique and our sequential file model, but notice what is different. Procedurally, all we say is initiate (start) the report, and, while we still have records, write (generate) the report's detail lines. Isn't that what we have been doing during detail time anyway? How does the data get moved? How do totals get summed? How about line spacing? Headings? All that is done automatically for us by REPORT WRITER. Magic, right? Not by a long shot! All the features of the report and what, when, and where to print them are specified by us in the DATA DIVISION, REPORT SECTION.

## DATA DIVISION

The big change here involves the new section—REPORT SECTION. Remember that we are defining a report or reports. To do this we use a printer file. Therefore, we still need a SELECT and corresponding FD. However, there is a difference. If the file is to be generated with the report writer, then we need to say so in the FD. The SELECT and FD would look like:

> SELECT REPORT-FILE ASSIGN TO UT-S-REPORT.
>
> FD REPORT-FILE
>     RECORD CONTAINS 133 CHARACTERS
>     LABEL RECORDS ARE OMITTED

$$\left\{ \begin{array}{l} \underline{\text{REPORT}} \text{ } \underline{\text{IS}} \\ \underline{\text{REPORTS}} \text{ } \underline{\text{ARE}} \end{array} \right\} \text{ report-name.}$$

The new clause, REPORT IS or REPORTS ARE, will specify the name or names of the reports associated with this file. Notice that an 01 is not included. All the record descriptions associated with this report will be described in this section. The REPORT SECTION physically follows the WORKING-STORAGE SECTION of the DATA DIVISION. Each report specified by a REPORT IS clause is fully described in this section using an RD (report description). It is within the RD, using various options, that all the report features are defined.

### Report Description

The format of the report description, RD, is shown below:

> $\underline{\text{RD}}$ report-name
>
> $$\left\{ \begin{array}{l} \underline{\text{CONTROL IS}} \\ \underline{\text{CONTROLS ARE}} \end{array} \right\} \text{ data-name}_1 \text{ [data-name}_2 \text{ ..._____]}$$
>
> $$\underline{\text{PAGE}} \left\{ \begin{array}{l} \underline{\text{LIMIT}} \text{ } \underline{\text{IS}} \text{ numeric-value } \underline{\text{LINE}} \\ \underline{\text{LIMITS}} \text{ } \underline{\text{ARE}} \text{ numeric-value } \underline{\text{LINES}} \end{array} \right\}$$
>
> [$\underline{\text{HEADING}}$ numeric-value]
> [$\underline{\text{FIRST\_DETAIL}}$ numeric-value]
> [$\underline{\text{LAST\_DETAIL}}$ numeric-value]
> [$\underline{\text{FOOTING}}$ numeric-value]

**CONTROLS Clause.**    As the name of the clause indicates, this specifies what field or fields on which control breaks will occur. For example, with our DEAN-FILE causing control breaks on class within major, we would write:

```
CONTROLS ARE MAJOR CLASS
```

Notice that the order of the control fields is from highest to lowest. If you want just a grand total at the end of the report, you say FINAL.

## THE PHYSICAL REPORT SPECIFICATIONS

With the PAGE clause, we specify the number of lines on a report page. Then with the HEADING clause, we specify the first line of the page heading. As you would expect, the FIRST DETAIL and LAST DETAIL clauses specify where the first and last lines are to print. Finally, the FOOTING clause specifies that a control footing or report footing will print.

There are some relationships that need to be considered. Most follow common sense, but for instance don't say:

```
PAGE 50 LINES
    :
FOOTING 55.
```

Or don't say the FIRST DETAIL comes before HEADING:

```
HEADING 5
FIRST DETAIL 3
```

and of course LAST DETAIL must be larger than FIRST DETAIL.

However, some relationships are not so obvious. If the HEADING is more than one line, then the FIRST DETAIL must allow for all HEADING lines. The same is true for FOOTING. That is, the number of lines in the FOOTING must be allowed for in the PAGE clause.

So, do you see all that? It's not that complicated. Just lay out your report and then code the report description (RD). For instance, does this RD make sense?

```
PAGE LIMIT     60
HEADING         8
FIRST DETAIL   11
LAST DETAIL    47
FOOTING        55
```

Sure it does! All specifications are mutually compatible. They don't conflict. Or do they? Well, you can't fully tell. You still have to consider the line spacing, which is specified in the record descriptions called report groups.

## REPORT GROUPS

Remember that a report is usually made up of one or more different lines. Normally these lines are each described by an 01 level entry. That relationship changes in report groups (01s) because in each we have the ability to describe multiple report lines. Furthermore, we may also specify spacing of lines and pages in the report groups (01s). Each report group 01 must specify the line **TYPE**. Just as with any report we have worked with before report writer, we have different types of lines:

- Headings
  - report
  - page
  - control group
- Detail
- Footings
  - control
  - page
  - report

Guess what type of lines we can describe with report groups? You're right! All of the above.

The form of the record description report group 01 with the various TYPE clauses is:

01 [record-name] **TYPE IS**

$$\left\{ \begin{array}{l} \underline{\text{REPORT HEADING}} \\ \underline{\text{PAGE HEADING}} \\ \underline{\text{CONTROL HEADING}} \text{ data-name}_1 \ldots \underline{\text{FINAL}} \\ \underline{\text{DETAIL}} \\ \underline{\text{CONTROL FOOTING}} \text{ data-name}_2 \ldots \underline{\text{FINAL}} \\ \underline{\text{PAGE FOOTING}} \\ \underline{\text{REPORT FOOTING}} \end{array} \right\}$$

For each report group, you must specify one **TYPE**. And for each **RD** you must have at least one report group. Except, of course, for top-secret reports where nothing is printed.... Just joking; you must have at least one report group.

### Heading Types

The REPORT WRITER feature supports several types of headings. These include REPORT HEADING, PAGE HEADING and CONTROL HEADING.

**REPORT HEADING.**   The **REPORT HEADING** clause describes a line or lines that will be printed just once for a report. You have already told it on what line to print with the HEADING clause in the RD.

**PAGE HEADING.**   Following the printing of the report heading is the page heading. The **PAGE HEADING** type does just what it says. It will cause a page heading to print at the top (HEADING LINE) of each page.

If both report and page heading types are used, then both will print on the first page. By using a PAGE option, you can print the report heading by itself on the first page. However, be careful. If both are printed on the first page, make sure that the HEADING line and FIRST DETAIL lines are compatible. If the total lines described in report and page headings is, say line 6, and heading started on line 5, then the detail had better start no earlier than line 11.

**CONTROL HEADING.** The last type of heading is directly associated with control-break reporting. By using the **CONTROL HEADING** type, we can print a line or lines before each control group. As you would expect, we must include in the type description the data field being used for the control-break logic. Look back at the RD. See the CONTROL clause? Well, whatever data-name you specified here, you must now specify with the **CONTROL HEADING** type.

That makes sense, doesn't it? If I'm breaking on class, then doesn't it follow that I want to write control headings that correspond?

### Footing Types

Well, so much for headings. What about footings? I know I skipped detail types. But I'll get back to them in a while. I think discussing footings at this time makes sense. You'll see why in just a moment.

**CONTROL FOOTING.** Notice how FOOTINGs sort of match HEADINGs in a way. The **CONTROL FOOTING**, for instance, will cause information to be printed when a control break occurs. Just like **CONTROL HEADING**, the data-name being used to break on may be specified with this REPORT GROUP.

**PAGE FOOTING.** Like its cousin PAGE HEADING, **PAGE FOOTING** will print at the bottom of every page. **REPORT FOOTING** prints just once, at the end of the report. For both of these footings the **PAGE LIMIT**, **LAST DETAIL**, and **FOOTING** clauses must be specified. It seems reasonable that these specifications be known to print the footings. If the page footing and/or report footing takes six lines, where will we print it/them? If we don't know how long the page is, how do we know it will fit?

### Detail Type

The **DETAIL** clause is what it says. It is the REPORT GROUP that describes our detail lines for the report. Since it is the only one that we reference in the PROCEDURE DIVISION, it must have a record name. Let me suggest that for documentation and maintenance reasons we should always use record names for all report group types.

One other thing may not jump out at you later on. All headings and footings, including control headings and control footings, are done automatically for you at appropriate times: page headings on top of a new page; control footing at a control break and so on. The only thing for which you get to dictate the print is the detail lines. You simply say GENERATE and specify which detail line to generate. Since you may have more than one detail line (different format), you need the control afforded by the GENERATE detail line.

The fun part of what we used to call the detail record description and now call the detail type, is how we set it up. I think the best way to start this discussion is to jump in feet first. Let's look at a detail report group:

```
01   STUDENT-LINE     TYPE IS DETAIL.
     05  LINE NUMBER       PLUS 2.
         10  COLUMN NUMBER IS 5          PIC X(30)
             SOURCE IS NAME-IN.
         10  COLUMN NUMBER IS 40         PIC X(9)
             SOURCE IS ID-IN.
         10  COLUMN NUMBER IS 55         PIC 9(1)
             SOURCE IS MAJOR-IN.
         10  COLUMN NUMBER IS 65         PIC 9(1)
             SOURCE IS CLASS-IN.
         10  COLUMN NUMBER IS 75         PIC 9(1)
             SOURCE IS SEX-IN.
         10  COLUMN NUMBER IS 85         PIC 9.9(4)
             SOURCE IS GPR-IN.
```

I told it to double-space with the LINE **NUMBER** clause. While that's neat, look at the other entries (level 10). I've simply said where to start the field, the picture and where the data comes from. No, it's not the MOVE verb, but its DATA DIVISION cousin the **SOURCE IS** clause. Furthermore, I didn't even need data names for all those output fields.

What does all that do for us? Well, with the **TYPE** clause for the STUDENT-LINE shown above, we specify:

- Spacing
- All output fields and sizes
- All sources for the fields
- Space on the line

Yes, all that with a record description.

## REPORT GROUP ENTRIES

Just as with other record descriptions, level 01 is used for the record and levels 02–49 for all other entries. We also use the PICTURE (PIC) clause as before. But then things change.

You probably noticed three new items in the record description:

- 
- 
- 

Let's take one at a time.

**LINE NUMBER.**   The **LINE NUMBER** is used for spacing. That is, "LINE NUM-BER PLUS 2" says the same as "WRITE ... AFTER 2". And, there are other forms:

$$\underline{\text{LINE}} \text{ NUMBER IS} \quad \left\{ \begin{array}{l} \text{number on } \underline{\textbf{NEXT}} \text{ PAGE} \\ \underline{\textbf{PLUS}} \text{ number} \end{array} \right\}$$

so that we could say:

```
LINE NUMBER IS 10
```

to specify that the line starts on line 10, while

LINE NUMBER IS 10 ON NEXT PAGE

says that the line is to be printed on the 10th line of the next page. There is another clause that may be used for spacing. It is the NEXT GROUP clause. This specifies the spacing to take place between groups, the group it is used in and the next group. Its format is:

$$\underline{\text{NEXT GROUP}} \quad \left\{ \begin{array}{l} \text{number} \\ \underline{\text{PLUS}} \text{ number} \\ \underline{\text{NEXT PAGE}} \end{array} \right\}$$

**COLUMN NUMBER.**   The **COLUMN NUMBER** clause simply says that this is an entry on the line and the first position is specified by the number:

$$\underline{\text{COLUMN}} \text{ NUMBER IS number} \ldots$$

**SOURCE.**   Finally, in our example you see the **SOURCE** clause. This specifies that at the time we GENERATE a detail line, the data for this item comes from the data-name specified. In this sense SOURCE acts like a move.

$$\underline{\text{SOURCE}} \text{ IS data-name}$$

## PROCEDURAL STATEMENT

Using REPORT WRITER causes us to shift many of the procedural statements and controls from the PROCEDURE DIVISION to the DATA DIVISION. Things like spacing with the AFTER clause now are done with the LINE NUMBER clause. Checking for the end of a page and reprinting headings that require IF logic have also been moved to the DATA DIVISION.

All the checks for control breaks and summing data fields for these control breaks are now all done automatically for us using the report writer and the SUM clause.

So what's left for the PROCEDURE DIVISION? Well, not much. We are required to dictate when to start a report, when to generate the detail lines and when to stop a report. We do this with the **INITIATE**, **GENERATE** and **TERMINATE**. But you probably already suspected the need for these particular verbs from our discussions so far. Remember our sketchy pseudocode look at the logic? Well, look back at it. Notice the three verbs? Good! But look closely. Even though we are using these new verbs, they are used with our sequential file model again. Let's look at the verbs and then put together a little program to see how they work.

### The INITIATE Verb

You must start a REPORT WRITER specified report by using the **INITIATE** verb. Its format is:

$$\underline{\text{INITIATE}} \text{ report-name}$$

Notice that we must name the report that we want to start. The report name must be the name specified in the RD.

The **INITIATE** verb causes:

- All data names referenced by the SUM clause to be set to 0
- LINE-COUNTER to be set to 0
- PAGE-COUNTER to be set to 1

Note that **INITIATE** does not open files, and you may not execute a second **INITIATE** for a report without first issuing a **TERMINATE**.

### The GENERATE Verb

**GENERATE** is the workhorse for us. It causes most of the automatic features and associated control-break tests, summations, page breaks and the like to be done.

There are two forms of **GENERATE**. I will discuss the one that generates detail lines first. (The use of it to generate summary reports I'll leave for later.)

**GENERATE** record-name FOR TYPE DETAIL

**GENERATE** has two phases:

1. The actions it causes the 1st time it executes.
2. The action it causes the 2nd through nth times.

Actions during 1st execution:

- Report headings.
- Page headings.
- Control headings, in the order specified (final, major to minor).
- Data is moved as specified by the SOURCE clauses.
- Print detail line.

Actions during 2nd through nth execution:

- Increments and tests LINE CONTROL against the page limit specified.
- Produces page breaks and rewrites page headings after incrementing PAGE-COUNTER.
- Tests for all required control breaks.
- If break(s) occur, produces all CONTROL FOOTINGS and CONTROL HEADINGS (if we specified these types).
- Handles all sums to include the control field that broke and all subordinate control-break fields (recognize the hierarchical relationship we discussed pre-report writer).
- Reinitializes the appropriate sum fields.
- Data is moved as specified by the SOURCE clauses.
- Print detail line.

I told you it was the workhorse. Don't get frustrated. It just does all those things you would do for a control-break report.

### The TERMINATE Verb

As the verb implies it causes the termination of a report that has been initiated. It goes without saying that you cannot **TERMINATE** a report without first initiating it, and you cannot (well, you can, but the system will get you) re**TERMINATE** a report.

The format of **TERMINATE** is:

**TERMINATE** report-name ...

What happens when TERMINATE is executed? Well, here's a list of actions:

- It produces all control footings as if a control break had occurred. Remember my saying that EOF was like a control break? Well, here it is again.
- It produces the page and report footing if we defined them.

You should note that TERMINATE does not close files. We must do that ourselves as we had to open them ourselves.

## THE PROBLEM

Let's put all this knowledge together in a simple program. I'm not going to use the DEAN-FILE (yet). I'll save the DEAN-FILE for one of the sample programs. Let's use the PERSONNEL-FILE shown in Data File B for a change.

Our manager has just asked us to prepare a report listing all employees. The report should group all employees by department within each store location. The manager wants the total year-to-date earnings (YTDE) for each department and each store. He also wants the report format to be as shown in Figure E.4:

Several new features will be used for this report: the NEXT GROUP, the SUM CLAUSE and the GROUP INDICATE clause. As I mentioned earlier, the NEXT GROUP helps spacing between groups. When used with the NEXT PAGE option, we can start the next group on a new page.

**Figure E.4**
*Sample Personnel Report*

| Store # | Department # | Name | S.S. # | YTDE |
|---|---|---|---|---|
| X | X | : | : | : |
| | X | : | : | : |
| | X | : | : | : |
| | | Department Total | | XXXXX |
| X | X | : | : | : |
| | X | : | : | : |
| | X | : | : | : |
| | | Department Total | | XXXXX |
| X | X | : | : | : |
| | X | : | : | : |
| | X | : | : | : |
| | | Department Total | | XXXXX |
| | | Store Total | | XXXXX |

## THE SUM CLAUSE

The SUM clause is very nice for generating control totals of data fields automatically. We use the SUM clause on control groups only. It takes the following form:

> SUM IS data-name ...
>  [UPON data-name]
>  [RESET ON FINAL data-name]

The most-used form of the **SUM** for control breaks is the simple **SUM IS** data-name. However, if a total of some field other than a field in the detail group being printed is wanted then the **UPON** clause may be used. The **RESET** allows us to **RESET** the sum(s). Since the **SUM**(s) are automatically reset for us on a control break we only need **RESET** if we want to initialize other than at a control break.

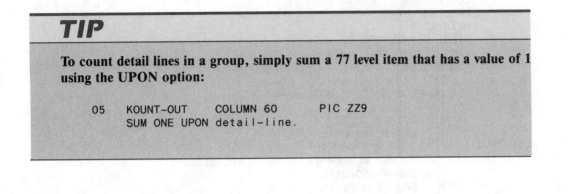

---

**TIP**

To count detail lines in a group, simply sum a 77 level item that has a value of 1 using the UPON option:

```
05    KOUNT-OUT    COLUMN 60        PIC ZZ9
      SUM ONE UPON detail-line.
```

---

## THE GROUP INDICATE CLAUSE

For our particular problems and report format, the **GROUP INDICATE** is a very useful clause. It allows us to specify a field in the detail group that should print only on the first line for the group. For multiple control breaks, the printing will be associated with the fields and their relative order as specified in the RD CONTROL ARE clause. For example:

```
RD ...
    :
    CONTROLS ARE STORE-IN DEPT-IN
```

says we have two control breaks—department within store. Then we can use **GROUP INDICATE** in the detail type as shown:

```
01   PERSONNEL-LINE    TYPE DETAIL
     10   COLUMN NUMBER 4              PIC 9(1)
          GROUP INDICATE    SOURCE STORE-IN.
     10   COLUMN NUMBER 12             PIC 9(1)
          GROUP INDICATE    SOURCE DEPT-IN.
            .
            .
```

The segment shown will cause the DEPT-IN value to print on the first line within a department and STORE-IN and DEPT-IN values to print for each new store. (I've included example programs for both the DEAN-FILE and PERSONNEL-FILE at the end of the chapter.)

Well, so much for talking about it. Let's look at the code for the personnel problem.

```
FD   REPORT-FILE
     LABEL RECORDS ARE OMITTED
     RECORD CONTAINS 133 CHARACTERS
     REPORT IS PERSONNEL-REPORT.
     :

RD   PERSONNEL-REPORT
     CONTROL IS STORE-IN DEPT-IN
     PAGE 60 LINES
     HEADING 5
     FIRST DETAIL 8
     LAST DETAIL 50
     FOOTING 55.

01   PERSONNEL-LINE TYPE DETAIL.
     05   LINE PLUS 2.
          10   COLUMN NUMBER 4          PIC 9(1)
               GROUP INDICATE
               SOURCE STORE-IN.
          10   COLUMN NUMBER 12         PIC 9(1)
               GROUP INDICATE
               SOURCE DEPT-IN.
          10   COLUMN NUMBER 20         PIC X(30)
               SOURCE NAME-IN.
          10   COLUMN NUMBER 60         PIC X(9)
               SOURCE SOCIAL-SECURITY-NUMBER-IN.
          10   COLUMN NUMBER 80         PIC $$,$$$,$$9.99
               SOURCE YTDE-IN.

01   DEPT-TOTAL-LINE TYPE CONTROL FOOTING DEPT-IN.
     05   LINE PLUS 3.
          10   COLUMN NUMBER 10         PIC X(16)
               VALUE 'DEPARTMENT TOTAL'.
          10   COLUMN NUMBER 30         PIC X(40)
               VALUE ALL '*'.
          10   DEPT-TOTAL COLUMN NUMBER 80
                                        PIC $$$,$$$,$$9.99
               SUM YTDE-IN.

01   STORE-TOTAL-LINE TYPE CONTROL FOOTING STORE-IN.
     05   LINE PLUS 2.
          10   COLUMN NUMBER 10         PIC X(16)
               VALUE 'STORE TOTAL      '.
          10   COLUMN NUMBER 30         PIC X(40)
               VALUE ALL '*'.
          10   STORE-TOTAL COLUMN NUMBER 80
                                        PIC $$$,$$$,$$9.99
               SUM DEPT-TOTAL.
```

```
01   GROUP-HEADING TYPE CONTROL HEADING STORE-IN
          NEXT GROUP NEXT PAGE.
          05  LINE NUMBER' PLUS 1.
              10   COLUMN NUMBER 3           PIC X(5)
                   VALUE 'STORE'.
              10   COLUMN NUMBER 8           PIC X(5)
                   VALUE 'DEPT.'.
              10   COLUMN NUMBER 20          PIC X(4)
                   VALUE 'NAME'.
              10   COLUMN NUMBER 53          PIC X(14
                   VALUE 'SOCIAL SECURITY'.
              10   COLUMN NUMBER 80          PIC X(12)
                   VALUE 'YTD EARNINGS'.
```

Obviously these are only the main parts of the DATA DIVISION that we need to look at for the particular REPORT WRITER features we need for the personnel listing.

Notice in the RD I specified two controls: STORE-IN and DEPT-IN within STORE-IN. I then group-indicate for both in my **TYPE DETAIL** line, PERSONNEL-LINE.

In the control footing lines I set up my control totals. DEPT-TOTAL-LINE has a field that is the sum of the YTDE-IN field from the detail line. It is also controlled by DEPT-IN. STORE-TOTAL-LINE then has a field that is the sum of no, not YTDE-IN, but the sum of the department total, DEPT-TOTAL. The control on this footing is specified as STORE-IN.

Do you see how all that ties together? We told REPORT WRITER that the report has two controls. Then we GROUP INDICATE on the control fields, and finally we accumulate and write totals based on these same control fields.

One other thing I've done is ask REPORT WRITER to start a new page for each store. This is specified in TYPE CONTROL HEADING.

What does the PROCEDURE DIVISION look like?

```
0000-MAIN-PARA.
     PERFORM 1000-INITIALIZATION.
     PERFORM 2000-READ-PARA.
     PERFORM 3000-PROCESS PARA
          UNTIL NO-MORE-RECORDS.
     PERFORM 4000-TERMINATE-PARA.
     STOP RUN.

1000-INITIALIZATION.
     OPEN INPUT PERSONNEL-FILE.
     OPEN OUTPUT REPORT-FILE.
     INITIATE PERSONNEL-REPORT.

2000-READ-PARA.
     READ PERSONNEL-FILE INTO PERSONNEL-RECORD-IN
          AT END
               MOVE 'NO ' TO ARE-THERE-MORE-RECORDS.

3000-PROCESS-PARA.
     GENERATE PERSONNEL-LINE.
     PERFORM 2000-READ-PARA.

4000-TERMINATE-PARA.
     TERMINATE PERSONNEL-REPORT.
     CLOSE PERSONNEL-FILE.
     CLOSE REPORT-FILE.
```

## SOME LOOSE ENDS

We have covered a lot of material. It takes a while to digest. The material is complex and full of implied interactions between and among features. Don't let these discourage you. It's just new, and you will get used to it in time. In fact the technique of doing more in the DATA DIVISION and less procedurally is what we see in database languages and 4GLs.

I have included complete sample programs at the end of this appendix for reference. In them you will probably notice some things I haven't fully discussed, things like PAGE-COUNTER and LINE-COUNTER. You may also remember that GENERATE may be used to produce summary reports. I haven't fully discussed that either. Well, let's look at the obvious things first.

### Page and Line Control

The **PAGE** and **LINE COUNTERS** are automatic features of REPORT WRITER. They are incremented and reinitialized for us. We don't have to worry about doing it ourselves. Nice!

### Summary Reporting

Producing a summary report without the detail may be done via the GENERATE. Instead of specifying the TYPE DETAIL, we specify the report name. That is, instead of GENERATE PERSONNEL-LINE, we would say GENERATE PERSONNEL-REPORT. Doing this will suppress any detail line printing but all sum(s) will still be done and all control groups will be printed. Nice again, right?

## SUMMARY

In this Appendix we studied COBOL's report writer feature. This was a big change in coding from what we had been used to in COBOL. We did procedure things in the DATA DIVISION. COBOL automatically did things for us. This was nice, and gave us a look at what some 4GLs do.

We looked at the features like REPORT SECTION that contained the REPORT DESCRIPTION (RD) and all REPORT GROUP (01s) descriptions. These groups were for heading (report, page, and control), footings (report, page, and control), and detail lines making up the report. All spacing and the report's physical description was laid out in this SECTION.

Group indication was discussed. We saw how this feature is handled so nicely for us in REPORT WRITER. In fact, totaling and counting using the SUM was also very nice.

When we looked at the PROCEDURE DIVISION, we saw something very familiar—our sequential file model. There it was again, and this time it was probably good to see an old friend. Once we discussed the new features of INITIATE, GENERATE and TERMINATE, we realized that what REPORT WRITER had done was make the PROCEDURE DIVISION simple for us.

## SAMPLE PROGRAMS

The following are complete running COBOL programs using many of the features and techniques discussed in this Appendix. These two programs use the Dean File Data Set.

### *One-Level Control Break with Counters*

```
PP 5740-CB1 RELEASE 2.4                    IBM OS/VS COBOL   JULY 1, 1982        14.29.51  DATE SEP  2,1988


    1                      14.29.51       SEP  2,1988


00001        IDENTIFICATION DIVISION.
00002        PROGRAM-ID. SUMCOUNT.
00003        AUTHOR. FOWLER.
00004        DATE-WRITTEN.  JULY 1988
00005        DATE-COMPILED. SEP  2,1988.
00006        REMARKS.
00007
00008   ************************************************************
00009   *  ASSIGNMENT NUMBER                                      *
00010   *  DATE ASSIGNED                                          *
00011   *  DATE DUE                                               *
00012   *  PURPOSE: THIS PROGRAM USES THE REPORT WRITER FEATURE OF COBOL*
00013   *           TO PRODUCE A ONE LEVEL CONTROL BREAK REPORT.  THE   *
00014   *           STUDENT RECORDS WILL BE PRINTED BY MAJOR.  THE      *
00015   *           TOTAL COUNT OF STUDENTS WITHIN EACH MAJOR WILL BE   *
00016   *           PRINTED AFTER EACH BREAK.                           *
00017   *                                                        *
00018   *                                                        *
00019   *     INPUT FILE SPECIFICATIONS:                         *
00020   *          CARD COLUMNS                    DESCRIPTION    *
00021   *     ------------------------             -----------    *
00022   *            1-30                     STUDENT'S NAME      *
00023   *           31-39                     STUDENT'S ID NUMBER *
00024   *           40-40                     MAJOR CODE          *
00025   *           41-41                     CLASS CODE          *
00026   *           42-42                     SEX CODE            *
00027   *           43-47                     GPR (TO 4 DEC. PLACES)*
00028   *                                                        *
00029   ************************************************************
00030
```

```
    2        SUMCOUNT       14.29.51        SEP  2,1988


00032        ENVIRONMENT DIVISION.
00033
00034        CONFIGURATION SECTION.
00035
00036        SOURCE-COMPUTER. IBM.
00037        OBJECT-COMPUTER. IBM.
00038        SPECIAL-NAMES.   CO1 IS PAGE-TOP.
00039
00040        INPUT-OUTPUT SECTION.
00041
00042        FILE-CONTROL.
00043
00044            SELECT DEAN-FILE
00045                ASSIGN TO DA-S-NEW.
00046
00047            SELECT REPORT-FILE
00048                ASSIGN TO UT-S-REPORT.
00049
```

(continued)

```
     3          SUMCOUNT        14.29.51       SEP  2,1988

   00051            DATA DIVISION.
   00052
   00053            FILE SECTION.
   00054
   00055            FD  DEAN-FILE
   00056                LABEL RECORDS ARE OMITTED
   00057                RECORD CONTAINS 47 CHARACTERS
   00058                BLOCK CONTAINS 100 RECORDS
   00059                DATA RECORD IS STUDENT-RECORD.
   00060            01  STUDENT-RECORD PIC X(47).
   00061
   00062
   00063            FD  REPORT-FILE
   00064                LABEL RECORDS ARE OMITTED
   00065                REPORT IS STUDENT-LISTING.
   00066
```

```
     4          SUMCOUNT        14.29.51       SEP  2,1988

   00068            WORKING-STORAGE SECTION.
   00069
   00070            ************************************************************
   00071            *  BOTH 77'S ARE USED WITH THE "SUM UPON" CLAUSE OF REPORT  *
   00072            *  WRITER                                                   *
   00073            *                                                          *
   00074            ************************************************************
   00075
   00076            77  STUDENT-COUNT PIC 9(4) VALUE O.
   00077            77  ONE          PIC 9(1) VALUE 1.
   00078
   00079            01  STUDENT-RECORD-IN.
   00080                03 NAME-IN    PIC X(30).
   00081                03 ID-IN      PIC X(9).
   00082                03 MAJOR-IN   PIC 9(1).
   00083                03 CLASS-IN   PIC 9(1).
   00084                03 SEX-IN     PIC 9(1).
   00085                03 GPR-IN     PIC 9(1)V9(4).
   00086
   00087
   00088            01  ARE-THERE-MORE-RECORDS PIC X(3) VALUE 'YES'.
   00089                88 MORE-RECORDS    VALUE 'YES'.
   00090                88 NO-MORE-RECORDS VALUE 'NO'.
   00091
   00092            01  MAJOR-VALUES.
   00093                03 FILLER PIC X(13) VALUE 'ACCOUNTING'.
   00094                03 FILLER PIC X(13) VALUE 'INFO. SYSTEMS'.
   00095                03 FILLER PIC X(13) VALUE 'FINANCE'.
   00096                03 FILLER PIC X(13) VALUE 'MANAGEMENT'.
   00097                03 FILLER PIC X(13) VALUE 'MARKETING'.
   00098
   00099            01  MAJOR-TABLE REDEFINES MAJOR-VALUES.
   00100                03 MAJOR-DESCRIPTION PIC X(13) OCCURS 5 TIMES.
   00101
```

*(continued)*

```
     5      SUMCOUNT        14.29.51       SEP  2,1988

00103           REPORT SECTION.
00104
00105           RD  STUDENT-LISTING
00106               CONTROL IS FINAL MAJOR-IN
00107               PAGE LIMIT 60 LINES
00108               HEADING      1
00109               FIRST DETAIL    10
00110               LAST DETAIL   52
00111               FOOTING       55.
00112
00113           01  TYPE IS PAGE HEADING.
00114               05  LINE NUMBER IS 5.
00115                   10  COLUMN NUMBER IS 15   PIC X(12) VALUE
00116                           'DEAN LISTING'.
00117               05  LINE NUMBER PLUS 3.
00118                   10  COLUMN NUMBER IS 1    PIC X(2) VALUE
00119                           ' 2'.
00120                   10  COLUMN NUMBER IS 3    PIC X(2) VALUE
00121                           '10'.
00122                   10  COLUMN NUMBER IS 5    PIC X(2) VALUE
00123                           '88'.
00124                   10  COLUMN NUMBER IS 125  PIC Z(5)
00125                           SOURCE PAGE-COUNTER.
00126
00127               05  LINE NUMBER PLUS 2.
00128                   10  COLUMN NUMBER IS 10   PIC X(5) VALUE
00129                           'CLASS'.
00130                   10  COLUMN NUMBER IS 25   PIC X(2) VALUE
00131                           'ID'.
00132                   10  COLUMN NUMBER IS 35   PIC X(4) VALUE
00133                           'NAME'.
00134                   10  COLUMN NUMBER IS 70   PIC X(3) VALUE
00135                           'SEX'.
00136                   10  COLUMN NUMBER IS 80   PIC X(3) VALUE
00137                           'GPR'.
00138                   10  LINE NUMBER PLUS 1.
00139
00140           01  STUDENT-LINE-OUT TYPE IS DETAIL.
00141               05  LINE NUMBER PLUS 2.
00142                   10  COLUMN NUMBER IS  7   PIC 9(1)
00143                           SOURCE CLASS-IN.
00144                   10  COLUMN NUMBER IS 20   PIC 9(9)
00145                           SOURCE ID-IN.
00146                   10  COLUMN NUMBER IS 35   PIC X(30)
00147                           SOURCE NAME-IN.
00148                   10  COLUMN NUMBER IS 70   PIC 9(1)
00149                           SOURCE SEX-IN.
00150                   10  COLUMN NUMBER IS 78   PIC 9(1).9(4)
00151                           SOURCE GPR-IN.
00152
```

*(continued)*

```
      6         SUMCOUNT        ,14.29.51      SEP  2,1988

00154          01  MAJOR-HEADING TYPE IS CONTROL HEADING MAJOR-IN.
00155              05  LINE NUMBER PLUS 2.
00156                  10  COLUMN NUMBER IS 50    PIC X(25)
00157                          SOURCE MAJOR-DESCRIPTION (MAJOR-IN).
00158                  10  LINE NUMBER PLUS 2.
00159
00160          **************************************************************
00161          *   THE SUM FEATURE IS USED TO COUNT THE NUMBER OF DETAIL LINES *
00162          *   AND THUS THE NUMBER OF STUDENTS                             *
00163          *                                                              *
00164          **************************************************************
00165
00166          01  MAJOR-COUNT-LINE TYPE IS CONTROL FOOTING MAJOR-IN.
00167              05  LINE NUMBER PLUS 3.
00168                  10  COLUMN NUMBER IS 10    PIC X(5) VALUE
00169                          'TOTAL'.
00170                  10  COLUMN NUMBER IS 20    PIC X(30) VALUE
00171                          ALL '*'.
00172                  10  STUDENT-COUNT COLUMN NUMBER IS 55 PIC ZZZ9
00173                          SUM ONE UPON STUDENT-LINE-OUT.
00174              05  LINE NUMBER PLUS 5.
00175
```

```
      7         SUMCOUNT         14.29.51      SEP  2,1988

00177          PROCEDURE DIVISION.
00178
00179          0000-MAIN-PARA.
00180              PERFORM 1000-INIT-PARA.
00181              PERFORM 2000-READ-PARA.
00182              PERFORM 3000-INITIATE-PARA.
00183              PERFORM 4000-PROCESS-PARA
00184                      UNTIL NO-MORE-RECORDS.
00185              PERFORM 5000-TERMINATE-PARA.
00186              STOP RUN.
00187
00188          1000-INIT-PARA.
00189              OPEN INPUT DEAN-FILE.
00190              OPEN OUTPUT REPORT-FILE.
00191
00192          2000-READ-PARA.
00193              READ DEAN-FILE INTO STUDENT-RECORD-IN
00194                  AT END
00195                      MOVE 'NO' TO ARE-THERE-MORE-RECORDS.
00196
00197          3000-INITIATE-PARA.
00198              INITIATE STUDENT-LISTING.
00199
00200          4000-PROCESS-PARA.
00201              GENERATE STUDENT-LINE-OUT.
00202              PERFORM 2000-READ-PARA.
00203
00204          5000-TERMINATE-PARA.
00205              TERMINATE STUDENT-LISTING.
00206              CLOSE DEAN-FILE.
00207              CLOSE REPORT-FILE.
```

*(continued)*

```
        DEAN LISTING

21088
        CLASS       ID      NAME                        SEX     GPR
                                    ACCOUNTING

          1       987654321   DON VILLANOSKI               1     2.7500

          1       454545454   HOWARD PORTER                1     2.3158

          1       908765101   STEVE PARKS                  2     3.8000

          1       999888777   EMILY LYLE                   2     2.2667

          2       564731009   GEORGE RYAN                  1     2.4000

          2       000001111   ANDY BUENZA                  1     2.7429

          4       111000222   BILLY BOB BARRETT            1     2.2500

          4       102450555   ROY JOICE                    1     3.5045


        TOTAL   *****************************        8



                                    INFO. SYSTEMS


          1       717273747   MICHAEL RYAN                 1     3.2727

          1       010101206   JILL MATSON                  2     2.8947

          1       010203040   ANNIE MARINOS                2     2.2727

          2       555555555   MICHAEL FOWLER               1     3.8966

          2       434356569   ZEKE MORGAN                  1     2.8947
```

```
            DEAN LISTING

21088

        CLASS        ID      NAME                    SEX     GPR
         3       333333333   CLINT SMITH              1     1.9839
         3       444455555   KEVIN MCKENN             1     3.4933
         3       777777777   APRIL JONES              2     2.8025
         4       404040404   C. H. FLOWER             1     2.6887
         4       102938475   MARY JO MARTINEZ         2     2.3077
         4       444344344   STACY PHARR              2     3.5263
         4       394958690   MARY LITTLE              2     3.1579

        TOTAL    *****************************    12



                            FINANCE

         1       232323232   BRYAN MANN               1     2.6667
         1       978675643   DAVID LETTER             1     2.0000
         1       132435467   JANE CATES               2     2.7600
         3       888888888   TIA FOWLER               2     3.4943
         3       203040506   LYNDA MATHER             2     2.7538
         4       002903992   KEN MARTINEZ             1     2.7704
         4       123321123   PEG PORTERHOUSE          2     2.9703
```

```
            DEAN LISTING

21088
            CLASS       ID        NAME                      SEX      GPR
            TOTAL     *****************************    7



                                    MANAGEMENT

      1           516972420     GEORGE COMONOS              1      3.2400
      1           001122334     IRENE SMITH                 2      2.0000
      2           129834765     CLYDE FELD JR.              1      2.9057
      2           808188808     SESSIE PARSONS              2      2.5106
      3           656765679     DAN ROBESON                 1      2.2400
      3           000000222     TINA MARIO                  2      2.3380
      3           501155003     MARIA SANCHEZ               2      3.2000
      4           123456789     THOMAS WILKINSON            1      3.7619
      4           102302220     BILL ADAM                   1      2.8092
      4           311230099     ROBERTO SMITH               1      2.9000
      4           787878778     APRIL JACKS                 2      2.5649
      4           908070600     DANA MILLS                  2      2.7500
      4           501112234     POLLY ANN FLOWERS           2      2.5773

            TOTAL     *****************************   13
```

```
          DEAN LISTING

21088

     CLASS        ID      NAME                          SEX      GPR
                                    MARKETING

       1       100010055    GEORGE MARINAKIES            1      2.7083

       1       844839931    THOMAS THOMPSON              1      2.2857

       2       263718818    DIANE LAWERNCE               2      2.5714

       2       777345777    MARIA SANTIAGO               2      2.4444

       3       342537891    JAMES PAPPAS                 1      2.3253

       3       980980980    MATHEW ALTMEN                1      3.2258

       3       773330666    ANTONIO MARTINEZ             1      3.0000

       3       828347561    SARA WALKER                  2      3.5375

       4       246808642    WAYNE HEDDER                 1      3.9694

       4       222288885    PEGGY MARTTA                 2      2.0635


     TOTAL    *****************************       10
```

## Two-Level Control Break with SUMs

```
PP 5740-CB1 RELEASE 2.4                  IBM OS/VS COBOL   JULY 1, 1982      21.45.38  DATE NOV 10,1988


      1                      21.45.38        NOV 10,1988


  00001           IDENTIFICATION DIVISION.
  00002           PROGRAM-ID. RPTBRK.
  00003           AUTHOR. FOWLER.
  00004           DATE-WRITTEN.  JULY 1988
  00005           DATE-COMPILED. NOV 10,1988.
  00006           REMARKS.
  00007
  00008     ***********************************************************
  00009     *  ASSIGNMENT NUMBER                                      *
  00010     *  DATE ASSIGNED                                          *
  00011     *  DATE DUE                                               *
  00012     *  PURPOSE: THIS PROGRAM USES THE REPORT WRITER FEATURE OF COBOL*
  00013     *           TO PRODUCE A TWO LEVEL CONTROL BREAK REPORT.  THE   *
  00014     *           PERSONNEL RECORDS WILL BE PRINTED BY DEPARTMENT     *
  00015     *           WITHIN STORE.  THE YTD EARNINGS WILL BE ACCUMULATED *
  00016     *           FOR EACH DEPARTMENT (WITHIN STORE) AND EACH STORE.  *
  00017     *                                                         *
  00018     *                                                         *
  00019     *  INPUT FILE SPECIFICATIONS:                             *
  00020     *           CARD COLUMNS                 DESCRIPTION       *
  00021     *  ------------------------              -----------       *
  00022     *           1-30                   EMPLOYEE'S NAME         *
  00023     *           31-39                  EMPLOYEE'S SOC SEC NUM  *
  00024     *           40-40                  STORE CODE              *
  00025     *           41-41                  DEPARTMENT CODE         *
  00026     *           42-50                  YTD EARNINGS            *
  00027     *                                                         *
  00028     ***********************************************************
  00029
```

```
      2        RPTBRK        21.45.38        NOV 10,1988


  00031           ENVIRONMENT DIVISION.
  00032
  00033           CONFIGURATION SECTION.
  00034
  00035           SOURCE-COMPUTER. IBM.
  00036           OBJECT-COMPUTER. IBM.
  00037           SPECIAL-NAMES.   C01 IS PAGE-TOP.
  00038
  00039           INPUT-OUTPUT SECTION.
  00040
  00041           FILE-CONTROL.
  00042
  00043               SELECT PERSONNEL-FILE
  00044                    ASSIGN TO DA-S-PERSON.
  00045
  00046               SELECT REPORT-FILE
  00047                    ASSIGN TO UT-S-REPORT.
  00048
  00049
  00050           DATA DIVISION.
  00051
  00052           FILE SECTION.
  00053
  00054           FD  PERSONNEL-FILE
  00055               LABEL RECORDS ARE OMITTED
  00056               RECORD CONTAINS 50 CHARACTERS
  00057               BLOCK CONTAINS 100 RECORDS
  00058               DATA RECORD IS PERSONNEL-RECORD.
  00059           01  PERSONNEL-RECORD PIC X(50).
  00060
  00061
  00062           FD  REPORT-FILE
  00063               LABEL RECORDS ARE OMITTED
  00064               REPORT IS PERSONNEL-REPORT.
  00065
```

*(continued)*

```
      3        RPTBRK         21.45.38        NOV 10,1988

   00067        WORKING-STORAGE SECTION.
   00068
   00069        01   PERSONNEL-RECORD-IN.
   00070             03 NAME-IN                      PIC X(30).
   00071             03 SOCIAL-SECURITY-NUMBER-IN     PIC X(9).
   00072             03 STORE-IN                      PIC 9(1).
   00073             03 DEPT-IN                       PIC 9(1).
   00074             03 YTDE-IN                       PIC 9(7)V9(2).
   00075
   00076
   00077        01   ARE-THERE-MORE-RECORDS PIC X(3) VALUE 'YES'.
   00078             88 MORE-RECORDS      VALUE 'YES'.
   00079             88 NO-MORE-RECORDS VALUE 'NO'.
   00080
```

```
      4        RPTBRK         21.45.38        NOV 10,1988

   00082        REPORT SECTION.
   00083
   00084        RD   PERSONNEL-REPORT
   00085             CONTROL IS FINAL STORE-IN DEPT-IN
   00086             PAGE LIMIT 60 LINES
   00087             HEADING        5
   00088             FIRST DETAIL    8
   00089             LAST DETAIL    50
   00090             FOOTING        55.
   00091
   00092        01   GROUP-HEADING TYPE IS CONTROL HEADING STORE-IN.
   00093
   00094             05  LINE NUMBER NEXT PAGE.
   00095                 10   COLUMN NUMBER IS  2   PIC X(5) VALUE
   00096                          'STORE'.
   00097                 10   COLUMN NUMBER IS  10 PIC X(5) VALUE
   00098                          'DEPT.'.
   00099                 10   COLUMN NUMBER IS 20   PIC X(4) VALUE
   00100                          'NAME'.
   00101                 10   COLUMN NUMBER IS 53   PIC X(15) VALUE
   00102                          'SOCIAL SECURITY'.
   00103                 10   COLUMN NUMBER IS 80   PIC X(12) VALUE
   00104                          'YTD EARNINGS'.
   00105                 10   LINE NUMBER PLUS 1.
   00106
   00107        *************************************************************
   00108        *  NOTE THE TWO GROUP INDICATORS FOR THE DEPARTMENT AND THE  *
   00109        *  STORE                                                     *
   00110        *                                                            *
   00111        *************************************************************
   00112
   00113        01   PERSONNEL-LINE TYPE IS DETAIL
   00114             LINE NUMBER PLUS 2.
   00115                 10   COLUMN NUMBER IS  4   PIC 9(1)
   00116                          GROUP INDICATE
   00117                              SOURCE STORE-IN.
   00118                 10   COLUMN NUMBER IS 12   PIC 9(1)
   00119                          GROUP INDICATE
   00120                              SOURCE DEPT-IN.
   00121                 10   COLUMN NUMBER IS 20   PIC X(30)
   00122                          SOURCE NAME-IN.
   00123                 10   COLUMN NUMBER IS 60   PIC X(9)
   00124                          SOURCE SOCIAL-SECURITY-NUMBER-IN.
   00125                 10   COLUMN NUMBER IS 80   PIC $$,$$$,$$9.99
   00126                          SOURCE YTDE-IN.
   00127
```

*(continued)*

```
    5       RPTBRK          21.45.38        NOV 10,1988

00129        ****************************************************************
00130        *    THE SUM FEATURE IS USED TO ACCUMULATE THE CONTROL BREAK   *
00131        *    DEPARTMENT TOTAL.   THIS IS ACCOMPLISHED AS EACH DETAIL    *
00132        *    LINE IS PROCESSED.                                         *
00133        *                                                              *
00134        ****************************************************************
00135
00136        01   DEPT-TOTAL-LINE TYPE IS CONTROL FOOTING DEPT-IN
00137                 LINE NUMBER PLUS 3.
00138                     10   COLUMN NUMBER IS 10          PIC X(16) VALUE
00139                             'DEPARTMENT TOTAL'.
00140                     10   COLUMN NUMBER IS 30          PIC X(63) VALUE
00141                             ALL '*'.
00142                     10   DEPT-TOTAL COLUMN NUMBER IS 99 PIC $$$,$$$,$$9.99
00143                             SUM YTDE-IN.
00144                 05   LINE NUMBER PLUS 2.
00145
00146        ****************************************************************
00147        *    THE SUM FEATURE IS USED TO ACCUMULATE THE CONTROL BREAK   *
00148        *    STORE TOTAL.   THIS IS ACCOMPLISHED AS DEPARTMENT BREAK    *
00149        *    IS ENCOUNTERED.                                           *
00150        *                                                              *
00151        ****************************************************************
00152
00153        01   STORE-TOTAL-LINE TYPE IS CONTROL FOOTING STORE-IN
00154                 LINE NUMBER PLUS 2.
00155                     10   COLUMN NUMBER IS 10          PIC X(16) VALUE
00156                             'STORE TOTAL'.
00157                     10   COLUMN NUMBER IS 30          PIC X(63) VALUE
00158                             ALL '*'.
00159                     10   STORE-TOTAL COLUMN NUMBER IS 96 PIC $$,$$$,$$$,$$9.99
00160                             SUM DEPT-TOTAL.
00161                 05   LINE NUMBER PLUS 2.
00162
```

```
    6       RPTBRK          21.45.38        NOV 10,1988

00164            PROCEDURE DIVISION.
00165
00166            0000-MAIN-PARA.
00167                PERFORM 1000-INIT-PARA.
00168                PERFORM 2000-READ-PARA.
00169                PERFORM 3000-INITIATE-PARA.
00170                PERFORM 4000-PROCESS-PARA
00171                    UNTIL NO-MORE-RECORDS.
00172                PERFORM 5000-TERMINATE-PARA.
00173                STOP RUN.
00174
00175            1000-INIT-PARA.
00176                OPEN INPUT PERSONNEL-FILE.
00177                OPEN OUTPUT REPORT-FILE.
00178
00179            2000-READ-PARA.
00180                READ PERSONNEL-FILE INTO PERSONNEL-RECORD-IN
00181                    AT END
00182                        MOVE 'NO' TO ARE-THERE-MORE-RECORDS.
00183
00184            3000-INITIATE-PARA.
00185                INITIATE PERSONNEL-REPORT.
00186
00187            4000-PROCESS-PARA.
00188                GENERATE PERSONNEL-LINE.
00189                PERFORM 2000-READ-PARA.
00190
00191            5000-TERMINATE-PARA.
00192                TERMINATE PERSONNEL-REPORT.
00193                CLOSE PERSONNEL-FILE.
00194                CLOSE REPORT-FILE.
```

| STORE | DEPT. | NAME | SOCIAL SECURITY | YTD EARNINGS | |
|-------|-------|------|-----------------|--------------|--|
| 1 | 1 | ROY DEJOIE | 564732337 | $987.50 | |
| | | RICHARD LONG | 222222222 | $15,000.00 | |
| | | DEPARTMENT TOTAL ********************************************************** | | | $15,987.50 |
| 1 | 2 | MARY JONES | 918273645 | $9.00 | |
| | | IRENE HIGGS | 000110011 | $3,500.00 | |
| | | HOWARD PORTER | 329020045 | $2,500.00 | |
| | | DEPARTMENT TOTAL ********************************************************** | | | $6,009.00 |
| 1 | 3 | JILL BOTTOMS | 678098098 | $75.50 | |
| | | DONNA FRASER | 525354555 | $3,000.00 | |
| | | DEPARTMENT TOTAL ********************************************************** | | | $3,075.50 |
| 1 | 4 | JOHN PEARSON | 342134333 | $800,000.00 | |
| | | DEAN DECENSA | 102938476 | $69,500.50 | |
| | | DEPARTMENT TOTAL ********************************************************** | | | $869,500.50 |
| | | STORE TOTAL ********************************************************** | | | $894,572.50 |

```
STORE   DEPT.   NAME                    SOCIAL SECURITY      YTD EARNINGS

  2       1     JOANN ALTMEN              304050607          $1,500,000.00

          DEPARTMENT TOTAL  ***************************************************      $1,500,000.00


  2       2     KEVIN MCKENSIE            345123322              $987.50

          DEPARTMENT TOTAL  ***************************************************          $987.50


  2       3     LICA HOEKSTRA             389120987              $987.50

          DEPARTMENT TOTAL  ***************************************************          $987.50


  2       4     TOM DEATS                 811122900            $7,000.00
                MICHAEL FOWLER            584934566        $9,000,000.00
                TIA FOWLER                654321234          $300,000.00

          DEPARTMENT TOTAL  ***************************************************      $9,307,000.00


          STORE TOTAL       ***************************************************     $10,808,975.00
```

| STORE | DEPT. | NAME | SOCIAL SECURITY | YTD EARNINGS |
|-------|-------|------|-----------------|--------------|
| 3 | 1 | JOE SMITH | 111111111 | $1,000.00 |
|   |   | ROD ALTMEN | 546820988 | $3,000,650.00 |
|   |   | POLLY ANN FOWLER | 981209334 | $5.00 |
|   |   | ANN THOMAS | 546782334 | $5.00 |
|   |   | DEPARTMENT TOTAL ************************************************************** | | $3,001,660.00 |
| 3 | 2 | NANCY PORTS | 987678987 | $75.50 |
|   |   | DEPARTMENT TOTAL ************************************************************** | | $75.50 |
| 3 | 3 | BILL OWENS | 779779779 | $975.00 |
|   |   | TOMMY JONES | 098098788 | $5,900.50 |
|   |   | DEPARTMENT TOTAL ************************************************************** | | $6,875.50 |
| 3 | 4 | JAMES MARTIN | 090980800 | $550.00 |
|   |   | CLYDE PORTERFIELD | 123099123 | $75,000.75 |
|   |   | MICHAEL FOWLER | 234509874 | $5,000,000.00 |
|   |   | DEPARTMENT TOTAL ************************************************************** | | $5,075,550.75 |
|   |   | STORE TOTAL ************************************************************** | | $8,084,161.75 |

## EXERCISES

*Review Questions*

1. The REPORT WRITER feature:

   a. Requires less procedural code
   b. Requires more procedural code
   c. Applies only applies to control-break logic
   d. Requires less code in the data division
   e. None of the above

2. The statement to cause REPORT WRITER to use Field-A and Field-B for control breaks; B within A, would be:

   a. CONTROLS ARE Field-A Field-B
   b. CONTROLS ARE Field-B Field-A
   c. CONTROLS ARE Major Field-A, Minor Field-B
   d. CONTROLS ARE Minor Field-B, Major Field-A
   e. None of the above

3. The physical format for a report is found in the:

   a. FD
   b. RD
   c. 01 in WORKING-STORAGE
   d. REPORT SECTION
   e. None of the above

4. Which of the following is not a report group TYPE?

   a. REPORT HEADING
   b. REPORT FOOTING
   c. DETAIL
   d. SUMMARY
   e. CONTROL FOOTING

5. Specifying a REPORT FOOTING requires that we also specify:

   a. PAGE LIMIT
   b. LAST DETAIL
   c. FOOTING clause
   d. All of the above
   e. None are required

6. In order to write a report with REPORT WRITER the data:

   a. Must be sorted
   b. May be unsorted
   c. Must have a field to be group indicated
   d. Both a and c
   e. None of the above

7. To cause detail lines to print on a report using REPORT WRITER we must use the:

    a. INITIATE Verb
    b. WRITE verb
    c. GENERATE verb
    d. TERMINATE verb
    e. None of the above

8. The SUM verb may only be used to sum a field within the detail record.

    a. True
    b. False

9. To print a summary report using REPORT WRITER we would:

    a. Need to GENERATE a detail report first
    b. Simply say GENERATE report-name (RD name)
    c. Simply say GENERATE ... SUMMARY
    d. Not need to produce a detail report
    e. Both b and d are true

10. In order to group-indicate a report using a particular data field we would use:

    a. GENERATE verb
    b. CONTROL verb
    c. GROUP INDICATE verb
    d. GROUP verb
    e. None of the above

11. The sequential file model is still evident with report writer.

    a. True
    b. False

12. The TERMINATE verb:

    a. Is only needed for detail reports
    b. Is only needed for summary reports
    c. Closes all files
    d. Produces all requested control headings
    e. None of the above

## Discussion Questions

1. Contrast the use of REPORT WRITER with our nested PERFORM code for doing control-break logic.
2. Explain how the PROCEDURE DIVISION for a program using REPORT WRITER is still our sequential file model.
3. Explain the relationship of the FD and RD.
4. Contrast the TYPE DETAIL record description with our normal D-R-D.

## Programming Assignments

1. Write the COBOL program to produce a report of all employees in the Personnel File, Data File B. Group-indicate the report on store and department within store.
2. For the Program at the end of the appendix, PROGRAM-ID. REPORT2, generate a summary report also.

# INTERACTIVE PROGRAMMING

## INTRODUCTION

Interactive programming is the area of a user communicating with a running program. Put another way, during execution the user may give and receive data/information from and to a program. Interactive programming is accomplished by using the DISPLAY and ACCEPT verbs, with some special features. Depending on whether or not the compiler allows a screen section, the code is found predominantly either in the DATA DIVISION or the PROCEDURE DIVISION.

Since SCREEN SECTION is not standard, I will discuss two compilers, one with SCREEN SECTION, Microsoft (MS) COBOL, and one without SCREEN SECTION, Ryan McFarland (RM) COBOL. You will see how the two compilers handle the interactive features of the ACCEPT and DISPLAY. You will also see the same application program written using each compiler.

## CHARACTERISTICS OF INTERACTIVE PROGRAMMING

Interactive programs share certain characteristics. The programs must allow for two-way communications, and they must have mechanisms to paint the monitor screen. The PROCEDURE DIVISION will also reflect interactive programming techniques.

### Communicating

Both compilers use the ACCEPT verb to allow the user to enter information. Both also use the DISPLAY verb to communicate with the user. The link between both situations is that the screen is the medium for communications. When programmers want to tell the user something and/or solicit a response, they want to do it with a meaningful screen, one that is easy to read and understand.

So how do we design and use screens? With Microsoft COBOL we use SCREEN SECTION, while with Ryan McFarland COBOL we design and show the screens as part of the DISPLAY verb.

**The Problem.**   Let's design an interactive program to allow for building an inventory file. The program should solicit the data for each inventory item from a user. The user will then enter the appropriate data. Once the data is correct, the record is written to a sequential file. This process is repeated until no more data is entered. A screen that could be used is shown in Figure F.1.

**Figure F.1**
*Example Screen for Entering Data*

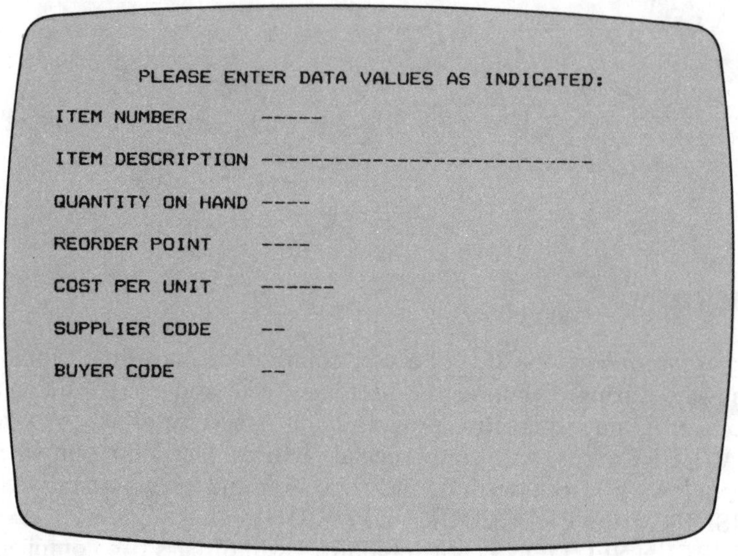

```
          PLEASE ENTER DATA VALUES AS INDICATED:

ITEM NUMBER         -----

ITEM DESCRIPTION    ---------------------------------

QUANTITY ON HAND    -----

REORDER POINT       -----

COST PER UNIT       ------

SUPPLIER CODE       --

BUYER CODE          --
```

The logic to do this problem interactively is given below.

```
SET CONTINUE TO 'YES'
DO WHILE CONTINUE = 'YES'
    DISPLAY SCREEN                  <----- displays screen
    ACCEPT DATA                            in Figure F.1
    WRITE RECORD TO FILE
    DISPLAY 'ENTER NO TO STOP'
    ACCEPT CONTINUE
END DO
```

Did you recognize the general form? It's the sequential file model (almost). Instead of accepting the first YES, we just initialize CONTINUE to YES. Then the last thing we do is accept from the user a YES or NO to continue the process or not.

### The Screen

Let's take a look at the screen now that we have seen the processing logic, and we know what we want the screen to look like.

Using RM COBOL, the DISPLAY screen in the pseudocode would convert to the following.

```
DISPLAY-PARA.
    DISPLAY
        "PLEASE ENTER DATA VALUES AS INDICATED" LINE 2 POSITION 21
        "ITEM NUMBER"        LINE  4 POSITION 1
        "ITEM DESCRIPTION"   LINE  6 POSITION 1
        "QUANTITY ON HAND"   LINE  8 POSITION 1
        "REORDER POINT"      LINE 10 POSITION 1
        "COST PER UNIT"      LINE 12 POSITION 1
        "SUPPLIER-CODE"      LINE 14 POSITION 1
        "BUYER-CODE"         LINE 16 POSITION 1.
```

Notice a few things. Each literal displayed must be located on the screen. We used an RM COBOL feature, LINE and POSITION, with each literal displayed. Therefore, "ITEM NUMBER" is shown on the screen starting in column 1 of line 4. Pretty straightforward, isn't it?

Well, we have other options that we can use with DISPLAY to make the screen pretty. We can beep the user; we can reverse video; we can use a prompt; we can display video high or low intensity. And there are more options, but before we look at them, let's first look at the screen with MS COBOL.

Remember that I said earlier that with MS COBOL we have a screen section that we use for designing the screen. Consequently, the equivalent screen to the RM COBOL screen is done in the DATA DIVISION instead of the PROCEDURE DIVISION. In RM COBOL you display literals, while in MS COBOL you display a record that contains the literals. Let's look at what I'm saying.

```
SCREEN SECTION.
01   INVENTORY-SCREEN.
     03   LINE  2 COLUMN 21  VALUE
              'PLEASE ENTER DATA VALUES AS INDICATED'.
     03   LINE  4 COLUMN 1    VALUE 'ITEM NUMBER'.
     03   LINE  6 COLUMN 1    VALUE 'ITEM DESCRIPTION'.
     03   LINE  8 COLUMN 1    VALUE 'QUANTITY ON HAND'.
     03   LINE 10 COLUMN 1    VALUE 'REORDER POINT'.
     03   LINE 12 COLUMN 1    VALUE 'COST PER UNIT'.
     03   LINE 14 COLUMN 1    VALUE 'SUPPLIER CODE'.
     03   LINE 16 COLUMN 1    VALUE 'BUYER CODE'.
```

Do you see the similarities? In both cases we have to locate each literal. In RM COBOL we use line number and position number, while in MS COBOL we use line number and column number. What does the display paragraph look like now?

```
DISPLAY INVENTORY-SCREEN.
```

See what I mean about MS COBOL being less procedure-oriented? It's one short DISPLAY. All the work is done in the DATA DIVISION. As with RM COBOL, MS COBOL allows us to make the screen pretty with several options.

Now that we have displayed the screen and asked the user to respond, we must accept the response. How? With the ACCEPT verb. The relationship between RM COBOL and MS COBOL that was evident with the DISPLAY is also evident with the ACCEPT.

It stands to reason that we would like to accept the individual fields that are included on the displayed screen. Therefore, we would like to build the ACCEPT statement to allow for this with each compiler.

RM COBOL's ACCEPT that corresponds to the screen we designed follows.

```
ACCEPT-PARA.
    ACCEPT
        ITEM-NUMBER        LINE 4 POSITION 20
        ITEM-DESCRIPTION   LINE 6 POSITION 20.
```

See what I'm doing? I'm accepting the value for the data item by locating the cursor beside the data-name on the screen—line 4, line 6. I'm also placing the cursor on position 20 for each field for continuity. Well, let's go on.

```
QUANTITY-ON-HAND    LINE  8 POSITION 20
REORDER-POINT       LINE 10 POSITION 20
COST-PER-UNIT       LINE 12 POSITION 20
SUPPLIER-CODE       LINE 14 POSITION 20
BUYER-CODE          LINE 16 POSITION 20.
```

Look back at the DISPLAY and compare it to the ACCEPT. See how they go together? There is a one-for-one relationship.

How about MS COBOL? Well, believe it or not, the ACCEPT would be:

```
ACCEPT INVENTORY-RECORD.
```

You're right. For that ACCEPT to work we need the record INVENTORY-RECORD defined in the SCREEN SECTION. Guess what it looks like? The INVENTORY-SCREEN! It is also very similar to RM COBOL's ACCEPT. Following is the companion record description.

```
SCREEN SECTION.
    .
    .
    .
01   INVENTORY-RECORD.
     03  LINE  4 COLUMN 20 TO ITEM-NUMBER.
     03  LINE  6 COLUMN 20 TO ITEM-DESCRIPTION.
     03  LINE  8 COLUMN 20 TO QUANTITY-ON-HAND.
     03  LINE 10 COLUMN 20 TO REORDER-POINT.
     03  LINE 12 COLUMN 20 TO COST-PER-UNIT.
     03  LINE 14 COLUMN 20 TO SUPPLIER-CODE.
     03  LINE 16 COLUMN 20 TO BUYER-CODE.
```

With this record description and inventory screen record description, we could now say procedurally DISPLAY INVENTORY-SCREEN and then ACCEPT INVENTORY-RECORD.

## MAKING THE SCREEN PRETTY

Now that you understand how the DISPLAY and ACCEPT may be used for interactive programming, let's look at how to make the conversation a little nicer: HIGHLIGHT, REVERSE VIDEO, UNDERLINE, BEEP, and so on. Both compilers allow for basically the same controls. However, there are some differences. Figure F.2 shows the various options and their functions.

OPTIONS

| RM | MS | FUNCTION |
|---|---|---|
| LINE # | LINE # | positions cursor to a line |
| POSITION # | COLUMN # | positions cursor on a line |
| ERASE | BLANK SCREEN | clears the screen |
| BEEP/NO BEEP | BEEP | causes a beep when input is expected |
| OFF | SECURE | will not show keystrokes on screen |
| REVERSE | REVERSE VIDEO | will show the field in reverse video: black on white and so on |
| HIGH | HIGHLIGHT | displays field in bright intensity |
| LOW | – | displays field in lower intensity |
| BLINK | BLINK | causes the field to alternately be displayed and blanked |
| TAB | default is TAB | requires return key to be depressed before going to next field |
| default is AUTO | AUTO | allows cursor to go to the next field automatically when current field is filled |
| PROMPT | – | will display an underline showing the number of positions in the field |
| UPDATE | default is AUTO | leaves current value unchanged if new value is not entered |
| – | FULL | requires every position to contain data |
| – | REQUIRED | requires at least one character in field |

**Note: For other features refer to respective manuals**

How do you use these features to make the screen nicer to read and use? Well, let's say that our screen design in Figure F.1 also includes the following specifications.

1. The title should be highlighted.
2. The field names should be low intensity.
3. A beep should indicate a field is to be entered. (Some of my colleagues don't like the beep. I'm just trying to demo some features, not drive them up a wall!)
4. The screen should be cleared before beginning.
5. The return should be required to end a field.
6. The user should be prompted for the current field size.

Looking at RM COBOL to demonstrate this would result in some changes to the DISPLAY and ACCEPT. Some of the specs affect the DISPLAY and others impact the ACCEPT. Let's examine DISPLAY first.

```
DISPLAY
"PLEASE ENTER DATA VALUES AS INDICATED" LINE 2 POSITION 21
                                        ERASE HIGH
"ITEM NUMBER"       LINE  4 POSITION 1 LOW
"ITEM DESCRIPTION"  LINE  6 POSITION 1 LOW
"QUANTITY ON HAND"  LINE  8 POSITION 1 LOW
"REORDER POINT"     LINE 10 POSITION 1 LOW
"COST PER UNIT"     LINE 12 POSITION 1 LOW
"SUPPLIER CODE"     LINE 14 POSITION 1 LOW
"BUYER CODE"        LINE 16 POSITION 1 LOW.
```

Notice how the screen title contains two features, ERASE to clear the screen and HIGH to display the title brighter. All the other items have the low intensity specification as required.

Let's look at the modified ACCEPT that would meet the specifications.

```
ACCEPT
    ITEM-NUMBER       LINE  4 POSITION 20 BEEP TAB PROMPT
    ITEM-DESCRIPTION  LINE  6 POSITION 20 BEEP TAB PROMPT
    QUANTITY-ON-HAND  LINE  8 POSITION 20 BEEP TAB PROMPT
    REORDER-POINT     LINE 10 POSITION 20 BEEP TAB PROMPT
    COST-PER-UNIT     LINE 12 POSITION 20 BEEP TAB PROMPT
    SUPPLIER-CODE     LINE 14 POSITION 20 BEEP TAB PROMPT
    BUYER-CODE        LINE 16 POSITION 20 BEEP TAB PROMPT.
```

All data fields have the same specifications—BEEP, TAB and PROMPT. If ITEM-NUMBER has a picture of 9(5), then on the screen we would see:

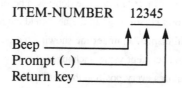

I hope you see that with the features shown in Figure F.2 you could make the screen really something special. You could make things blank, reverse video, beep and so on. However, don't overdo it. Imagine yourself sitting and looking at the blinking, high intensity, beeping screen all day. You would be ready for a new career in no time.

---

### TIP

**Making the field name low intensity and the data itself high, improves screen readability.**

---

## A PROBLEM

Let's assume that we want to build a sequential inventory file interactively using RM COBOL features. The data is to be entered from the keyboard.

Notice that up to the PROCEDURE DIVISION only minor changes can be seen. The SELECT clause contains the file name using DOS operating standards. There is no SELECT needed for the keyboard.

```
IDENTIFICATION DIVISION.

PROGRAM-ID.    INVBUILD.
AUTHOR.        TIA FOWLER.

ENVIRONMENT DIVISION.
```

```
CONFIGURATION SECTION.
SOURCE-COMPUTER.      IBM-PC-CLONE.
OBJECT-COMPUTER.      IBM-PC-CLONE.

INPUT-OUTPUT SECTION.                         ┌── PC file name
FILE-CONTROL.                              ┌──────┴──────┐
    SELECT INVENTORY-FILE  ASSIGN TO DISK, "INVFILE.DAT"
    ORGANIZATION IS LINE SEQUENTIAL.
                       └──────┬──────┘
                              └───────── equivalent to sequential


DATA DIVISION.

FILE SECTION.
FD  INVENTORY-FILE
    LABEL RECORDS ARE STANDARD
    RECORD CONTAINS 50 CHARACTERS
    DATA RECORD IS INVENTORY-RECORD.
01  INVENTORY-RECORD              PIC X(50).

WORKING-STORAGE SECTION.

01  IS-FILE-COMPLETED-INDICATOR   PIC X(3)   VALUE 'NO'.
    88  FILE-COMPLETED        VALUE 'YES'.
    88  FILE-NOT-COMPLETED    VALUE 'NO'.

01  IS-RECORD-CORRECT-INDICATOR   PIC X(3)   VALUE 'NO'.
    88  RECORD-CORRECT       VALUE 'YES'.
    88  RECORD-WRONG         VALUE 'NO'.

01  INVENTORY-RECORD-IN.
    03  ITEM-NUMBER               PIC 9(5).
    03  ITEM-DESCRIPTION          PIC X(25).
    03  QUANTITY-ON-HAND          PIC 9(4).
    03  REORDER-POINT             PIC 9(4).
    03  COST-PER-UNIT             PIC 9(6)V9(2).
    03  SUPPLIER-CODE             PIC 9(2).
    03  BUYER-CODE                PIC 9(2).
```

The PROCEDURE DIVISION that follows will reflect the logic shown in the pseudocode given below.

```
OPEN FILE
DO WHILE MORE DATA
SET IS-RECORD-CORRECT-INDICATOR TO 'NO'
    DO WHILE RECORD-WRONG
        DISPLAY INVENTORY-SCREEN
        ACCEPT INVENTORY-SCREEN
        DISPLAY MESSAGE-SCREEN              <--- allows user to
        ACCEPT IS-RECORD-CORRECT-INDICATOR       correct data
        IF RECORD-CORRECT                        entered
            WRITE INVENTORY-RECORD
    END DO
    ACCEPT IS-FILE-COMPLETED-INDICATOR
```

The inner DO WHILE is a technique that allows the user to go back and correct mistakes that might have been made before the record is written to the file. Let's look at the PROCEDURE DIVISION.

```
PROCEDURE DIVISION.
0000-MAIN-PARA.
    PERFORM 1000-INIT-PARA.
    PERFORM 2000-PROCESS-PARA
        UNTIL FILE-COMPLETED.
    PERFORM 3000-TERMINATION-PARA.
    STOP RUN.

1000-INIT-PARA.
    OPEN OUTPUT INVENTORY-FILE.

2000-PROCESS-PARA.
    MOVE SPACES TO INVENTORY-RECORD-IN.  <----- needed to blank
                                                out record using
                                                update feature

    PERFORM 2100-GET-DATA-PARA
        UNTIL RECORD-CURRENT.

    DISPLAY
        "ENTER YES TO ENTER ANOTHER RECORD"  LINE 22 POSITION 10 LOW
        "ENTER NO IF FINISHED"               LINE 23 POSITION 10 LOW.

    ACCEPT IS-FILE-COMPLETED-INDICATOR      BEEP PROMPT REVERSE.

    MOVE 'NO' TO IS-RECORD-CORRECT-INDICATOR.  <--- resets inner
                                                    loop for next
                                                    data record

2100-GET-DATA-PARA.
    PERFORM 2110-DISPLAY-SCREEN-PARA.
    PERFORM 2120-ACCEPT-DATA-PARA.
    PERFORM 2130-CHECK-CORRECTNESS-PARA.
    IF RECORD-CORRECT
        WRITE INVENTORY-RECORD FROM INVENTORY-RECORD-IN.

2110-DISPLAY-SCREEN-PARA.
    DISPLAY
    "PLEASE ENTER DATA VALUES AS INDICATED" LINE 2   POSITION 21
                                            ERASE HIGH
    "ITEM NUMBER"                           LINE 4   POSITION 1  LOW
    "ITEM DESCRIPTION"                      LINE 6   POSITION 1  LOW
    "QUANTITY ON HAND"                      LINE 8   POSITION 1  LOW
    "REORDER POINT"                         LINE 10  POSITION 1  LOW
    "COST PER UNIT"                         LINE 12  POSITION 1  LOW
    "SUPPLIER CODE"                         LINE 14  POSITION 1  LOW
    "BUYER CODE"                            LINE 16  POSITION 1  LOW.

2120-ACCEPT-DATA-PARA.
    ACCEPT
        ITEM-NUMBER       LINE 4  POSITION 20 TAB PROMPT UPDATE
        ITEM-DESCRIPTION  LINE 6  POSITION 20 TAB PROMPT UPDATE
        QUANTITY-ON-HAND  LINE 8  POSITION 20 TAB PROMPT UPDATE
        REORDER POINT     LINE 10 POSITION 20 TAB PROMPT UPDATE
        COST-PER-UNIT     LINE 12 POSITION 20 TAB PROMPT UPDATE
        SUPPLIER-CODE     LINE 14 POSITION 20 TAB PROMPT UPDATE
        BUYER-CODE        LINE 16 POSITION 20 TAB PROMPT UPDATE.
```

```
2130-CHECK-CORRECTNESS-PARA.
    DISPLAY
        "INDICATE YOUR DATA STATUS"    LINE 20 POSITION 1 LOW
        "YES - DATA IS CORRECT"        LINE 21 POSITION 5  LOW
        "NO - DATA IS NOT CORRECT"     LINE 22 POSITION 5  LOW.
    ACCEPT IS-RECORD-CORRECT-INDICATOR  POSITION 0 BEEP REVERSE.
```

While reading the procedure division you probably recognized many of the features we have been discussing. The DISPLAY in 2110 paragraph is our earlier example as is the ACCEPT in 2120 paragraph. Well, OK, I did change the ACCEPT a little; I left off the BEEP (to keep my friends from going mad), I kept the TAB and PROMPT options and added the UPDATE option.

The overall structure of the PROCEDURE DIVISION is an outer loop; PERFORM 2000...., that allows the users to enter data until they say they are finished. The inner loop; PERFORM 2100.... actually handles the screen interaction (display and accept paragraphs). It also allows the user to check the data just entered and make needed changes. That's why I used the UPDATE option on the accept. If a field is wrong, it can be re-entered. If it is correct a simple return keeps the correct value eliminating the need to re-enter values that are correct which could end up causing more errors.

The Microsoft program would be very similar. Following the WORKING-STORAGE SECTION would be the SCREEN SECTION. The SCREEN SECTION would contain the 01 INVENTORY-SCREEN and 01 INVENTORY RECORD we designed earlier. The PROCEDURE DIVISION would also change some. 2100 paragraph would simply contain DISPLAY INVENTORY-SCREEN and 2120 paragraph would contain ACCEPT INVENTORY-RECORD. That's as you expected from our earlier discussions comparing RM and MS COBOL.

One other change that I should point out is that the format of the other accepts and displays would have to be changed to MS format.

## SUMMARY

This was a brief look at interactive programming on PCs. We looked at Ryan McFarland and Microsoft COBOL Compilers in order to compare interactive programming concepts and techniques with a compiler that has the screen section available and one that doesn't.

You were shown how the main communications tools are the ACCEPT and DISPLAY VERBS. You also saw that in each compiler options are available with each verb to help make communications easier.

Finally we examined a complete RM COBOL program to illustrate the features and techniques. We also identified the changes that would be needed for the same program done in MS COBOL.

# ANSWERS TO EVEN–NUMBERED CHAPTER REVIEW QUESTIONS

| Chapter | Question Number | | | | | | | | | | | |
|---|---|---|---|---|---|---|---|---|---|---|---|---|
| | 2 | 4 | 6 | 8 | 10 | 12 | 14 | 16 | 18 | 20 | 22 | 24 |
| 1 | b | b | c | b | e | d | b | | | | | |
| 2 | c | b | a | c | b | a | d | c | e | e | | |
| 3 | e | b | b | a | b | d | c | | | | | |
| 4 | b | e | d | d | c | e | d | | | | | |
| 5 | b | d | e | c | e | b | b | c | a | b | | |
| 6 | a | a | d | e | e | e | c | c | b | | | |
| 7 | b | e | b | e | c | b | d | | | | | |
| 8 | e | d | b | b | c | b | e | d | | | | |
| 9 | e | b | a | a | e | a | a | | | | | |
| 10 | e | c | c | a | b | e | b | | | | | |
| 11 | b | e | e | e | b | b | b | b | c | e | d | b |
| 12 | b | a | a | a | d | b | a | c | | | | |
| 13 | a | c | b | d | a | c | e | | | | | |
| 14 | b | a | b | e | d | b | c | | | | | |
| 15 | b | e | b | b | a | c | b | b | e | e | a | b |
| 16 | e | a | e | a | b | b | c | | | | | |

# INDEX